Lecture Notes in Computer Science 8521

Commenced Publication in 1973
Founding and Former Series Editors:
Gerhard Goos, Juris Hartmanis, and Jan van Leeuwen

Lecture Notes in Computer Science 8521

Sakae Yamamoto (Ed.)

Human Interface and the Management of Information

Information and Knowledge Design and Evaluation

16th International Conference, HCI International 2014
Heraklion, Crete, Greece, June 22-27, 2014
Proceedings, Part I

 Springer

Volume Editor

Sakae Yamamoto
Tokyo University of Science
Department of Management Science
Kagurazaka Shinjuku-ku
Tokyo, 162-8601, Japan
E-mail: sakaeyam@jcom.home.ne.jp

ISSN 0302-9743   e-ISSN 1611-3349
ISBN 978-3-319-07730-7   e-ISBN 978-3-319-07731-4
DOI 10.1007/978-3-319-07731-4
Springer Cham Heidelberg New York Dordrecht London

Library of Congress Control Number: 2014940076

LNCS Sublibrary: SL 3 – Information Systems and Application,
incl. Internet/Web and HCI

Typesetting: Camera-ready by author, data conversion by Scientific Publishing Services, Chennai, India

Printed on acid-free paper

Springer is part of Springer Science+Business Media (www.springer.com)

Organization

Human–Computer Interaction

Program Chair: Masaaki Kurosu, Japan

Jose Abdelnour-Nocera, UK
Sebastiano Bagnara, Italy
Simone Barbosa, Brazil
Adriana Betiol, Brazil
Simone Borsci, UK
Henry Duh, Australia
Xiaowen Fang, USA
Vicki Hanson, UK
Wonil Hwang, Korea
Minna Isomursu, Finland
Yong Gu Ji, Korea
Anirudha Joshi, India
Esther Jun, USA
Kyungdoh Kim, Korea

Heidi Krömker, Germany
Chen Ling, USA
Chang S. Nam, USA
Naoko Okuizumi, Japan
Philippe Palanque, France
Ling Rothrock, USA
Naoki Sakakibara, Japan
Dominique Scapin, France
Guangfeng Song, USA
Sanjay Tripathi, India
Chui Yin Wong, Malaysia
Toshiki Yamaoka, Japan
Kazuhiko Yamazaki, Japan
Ryoji Yoshitake, Japan

Human Interface and the Management of Information

Program Chair: Sakae Yamamoto, Japan

Alan Chan, Hong Kong
Denis A. Coelho, Portugal
Linda Elliott, USA
Shin'ichi Fukuzumi, Japan
Michitaka Hirose, Japan
Makoto Itoh, Japan
Yen-Yu Kang, Taiwan
Koji Kimita, Japan
Daiji Kobayashi, Japan

Hiroyuki Miki, Japan
Hirohiko Mori, Japan
Shogo Nishida, Japan
Robert Proctor, USA
Youngho Rhee, Korea
Ryosuke Saga, Japan
Katsunori Shimohara, Japan
Kim-Phuong Vu, USA
Tomio Watanabe, Japan

Engineering Psychology and Cognitive Ergonomics

Program Chair: Don Harris, UK

Guy Andre Boy, USA
Shan Fu, P.R. China
Hung-Sying Jing, Taiwan
Wen-Chin Li, Taiwan
Mark Neerincx, The Netherlands
Jan Noyes, UK
Paul Salmon, Australia

Axel Schulte, Germany
Siraj Shaikh, UK
Sarah Sharples, UK
Anthony Smoker, UK
Neville Stanton, UK
Alex Stedmon, UK
Andrew Thatcher, South Africa

Universal Access in Human–Computer Interaction

**Program Chairs: Constantine Stephanidis, Greece,
and Margherita Antona, Greece**

Julio Abascal, Spain
Gisela Susanne Bahr, USA
João Barroso, Portugal
Margrit Betke, USA
Anthony Brooks, Denmark
Christian Bühler, Germany
Stefan Carmien, Spain
Hua Dong, P.R. China
Carlos Duarte, Portugal
Pier Luigi Emiliani, Italy
Qin Gao, P.R. China
Andrina Granić, Croatia
Andreas Holzinger, Austria
Josette Jones, USA
Simeon Keates, UK

Georgios Kouroupetroglou, Greece
Patrick Langdon, UK
Barbara Leporini, Italy
Eugene Loos, The Netherlands
Ana Isabel Paraguay, Brazil
Helen Petrie, UK
Michael Pieper, Germany
Enrico Pontelli, USA
Jaime Sanchez, Chile
Alberto Sanna, Italy
Anthony Savidis, Greece
Christian Stary, Austria
Hirotada Ueda, Japan
Gerhard Weber, Germany
Harald Weber, Germany

Virtual, Augmented and Mixed Reality

**Program Chairs: Randall Shumaker, USA,
and Stephanie Lackey, USA**

Roland Blach, Germany
Sheryl Brahnam, USA
Juan Cendan, USA
Jessie Chen, USA
Panagiotis D. Kaklis, UK

Hirokazu Kato, Japan
Denis Laurendeau, Canada
Fotis Liarokapis, UK
Michael Macedonia, USA
Gordon Mair, UK

Jose San Martin, Spain
Tabitha Peck, USA
Christian Sandor, Australia

Christopher Stapleton, USA
Gregory Welch, USA

Cross-Cultural Design

Program Chair: P.L. Patrick Rau, P.R. China

Yee-Yin Choong, USA
Paul Fu, USA
Zhiyong Fu, P.R. China
Pin-Chao Liao, P.R. China
Dyi-Yih Michael Lin, Taiwan
Rungtai Lin, Taiwan
Ta-Ping (Robert) Lu, Taiwan
Liang Ma, P.R. China
Alexander Mädche, Germany

Sheau-Farn Max Liang, Taiwan
Katsuhiko Ogawa, Japan
Tom Plocher, USA
Huatong Sun, USA
Emil Tso, P.R. China
Hsiu-Ping Yueh, Taiwan
Liang (Leon) Zeng, USA
Jia Zhou, P.R. China

Online Communities and Social Media

Program Chair: Gabriele Meiselwitz, USA

Leonelo Almeida, Brazil
Chee Siang Ang, UK
Aneesha Bakharia, Australia
Ania Bobrowicz, UK
James Braman, USA
Farzin Deravi, UK
Carsten Kleiner, Germany
Niki Lambropoulos, Greece
Soo Ling Lim, UK

Anthony Norcio, USA
Portia Pusey, USA
Panote Siriaraya, UK
Stefan Stieglitz, Germany
Giovanni Vincenti, USA
Yuanqiong (Kathy) Wang, USA
June Wei, USA
Brian Wentz, USA

Augmented Cognition

**Program Chairs: Dylan D. Schmorrow, USA,
and Cali M. Fidopiastis, USA**

Ahmed Abdelkhalek, USA
Robert Atkinson, USA
Monique Beaudoin, USA
John Blitch, USA
Alenka Brown, USA

Rosario Cannavò, Italy
Joseph Cohn, USA
Andrew J. Cowell, USA
Martha Crosby, USA
Wai-Tat Fu, USA

Rodolphe Gentili, USA
Frederick Gregory, USA
Michael W. Hail, USA
Monte Hancock, USA
Fei Hu, USA
Ion Juvina, USA
Joe Keebler, USA
Philip Mangos, USA
Rao Mannepalli, USA
David Martinez, USA
Yvonne R. Masakowski, USA
Santosh Mathan, USA
Ranjeev Mittu, USA

Keith Niall, USA
Tatana Olson, USA
Debra Patton, USA
June Pilcher, USA
Robinson Pino, USA
Tiffany Poeppelman, USA
Victoria Romero, USA
Amela Sadagic, USA
Anna Skinner, USA
Ann Speed, USA
Robert Sottilare, USA
Peter Walker, USA

Digital Human Modeling and Applications in Health, Safety, Ergonomics and Risk Management

Program Chair: Vincent G. Duffy, USA

Giuseppe Andreoni, Italy
Daniel Carruth, USA
Elsbeth De Korte, The Netherlands
Afzal A. Godil, USA
Ravindra Goonetilleke, Hong Kong
Noriaki Kuwahara, Japan
Kang Li, USA
Zhizhong Li, P.R. China

Tim Marler, USA
Jianwei Niu, P.R. China
Michelle Robertson, USA
Matthias Rötting, Germany
Mao-Jiun Wang, Taiwan
Xuguang Wang, France
James Yang, USA

Design, User Experience, and Usability

Program Chair: Aaron Marcus, USA

Sisira Adikari, Australia
Claire Ancient, USA
Arne Berger, Germany
Jamie Blustein, Canada
Ana Boa-Ventura, USA
Jan Brejcha, Czech Republic
Lorenzo Cantoni, Switzerland
Marc Fabri, UK
Luciane Maria Fadel, Brazil
Tricia Flanagan, Hong Kong
Jorge Frascara, Mexico

Federico Gobbo, Italy
Emilie Gould, USA
Rüdiger Heimgärtner, Germany
Brigitte Herrmann, Germany
Steffen Hess, Germany
Nouf Khashman, Canada
Fabiola Guillermina Noël, Mexico
Francisco Rebelo, Portugal
Kerem Rızvanoğlu, Turkey
Marcelo Soares, Brazil
Carla Spinillo, Brazil

Distributed, Ambient and Pervasive Interactions

Program Chairs: Norbert Streitz, Germany, and Panos Markopoulos, The Netherlands

Juan Carlos Augusto, UK
Jose Bravo, Spain
Adrian Cheok, UK
Boris de Ruyter, The Netherlands
Anind Dey, USA
Dimitris Grammenos, Greece
Nuno Guimaraes, Portugal
Achilles Kameas, Greece
Javed Vassilis Khan, The Netherlands
Shin'ichi Konomi, Japan
Carsten Magerkurth, Switzerland

Ingrid Mulder, The Netherlands
Anton Nijholt, The Netherlands
Fabio Paternó, Italy
Carsten Röcker, Germany
Teresa Romao, Portugal
Albert Ali Salah, Turkey
Manfred Tscheligi, Austria
Reiner Wichert, Germany
Woontack Woo, Korea
Xenophon Zabulis, Greece

Human Aspects of Information Security, Privacy and Trust

Program Chairs: Theo Tryfonas, UK, and Ioannis Askoxylakis, Greece

Claudio Agostino Ardagna, Italy
Zinaida Benenson, Germany
Daniele Catteddu, Italy
Raoul Chiesa, Italy
Bryan Cline, USA
Sadie Creese, UK
Jorge Cuellar, Germany
Marc Dacier, USA
Dieter Gollmann, Germany
Kirstie Hawkey, Canada
Jaap-Henk Hoepman, The Netherlands
Cagatay Karabat, Turkey
Angelos Keromytis, USA
Ayako Komatsu, Japan
Ronald Leenes, The Netherlands
Javier Lopez, Spain
Steve Marsh, Canada

Gregorio Martinez, Spain
Emilio Mordini, Italy
Yuko Murayama, Japan
Masakatsu Nishigaki, Japan
Aljosa Pasic, Spain
Milan Petković, The Netherlands
Joachim Posegga, Germany
Jean-Jacques Quisquater, Belgium
Damien Sauveron, France
George Spanoudakis, UK
Kerry-Lynn Thomson, South Africa
Julien Touzeau, France
Theo Tryfonas, UK
João Vilela, Portugal
Claire Vishik, UK
Melanie Volkamer, Germany

HCI in Business

Program Chair: Fiona Fui-Hoon Nah, USA

Andreas Auinger, Austria
Michel Avital, Denmark
Traci Carte, USA
Hock Chuan Chan, Singapore
Constantinos Coursaris, USA
Soussan Djamasbi, USA
Brenda Eschenbrenner, USA
Nobuyuki Fukawa, USA
Khaled Hassanein, Canada
Milena Head, Canada
Susanna (Shuk Ying) Ho, Australia
Jack Zhenhui Jiang, Singapore
Jinwoo Kim, Korea
Zoonky Lee, Korea
Honglei Li, UK
Nicholas Lockwood, USA
Eleanor T. Loiacono, USA
Mei Lu, USA

Scott McCoy, USA
Brian Mennecke, USA
Robin Poston, USA
Lingyun Qiu, P.R. China
Rene Riedl, Austria
Matti Rossi, Finland
April Savoy, USA
Shu Schiller, USA
Hong Sheng, USA
Choon Ling Sia, Hong Kong
Chee-Wee Tan, Denmark
Chuan Hoo Tan, Hong Kong
Noam Tractinsky, Israel
Horst Treiblmaier, Austria
Virpi Tuunainen, Finland
Dezhi Wu, USA
I-Chin Wu, Taiwan

Learning and Collaboration Technologies

Program Chairs: Panayiotis Zaphiris, Cyprus, and Andri Ioannou, Cyprus

Ruthi Aladjem, Israel
Abdulaziz Aldaej, UK
John M. Carroll, USA
Maka Eradze, Estonia
Mikhail Fominykh, Norway
Denis Gillet, Switzerland
Mustafa Murat Inceoglu, Turkey
Pernilla Josefsson, Sweden
Marie Joubert, UK
Sauli Kiviranta, Finland
Tomaž Klobučar, Slovenia
Elena Kyza, Cyprus
Maarten de Laat, The Netherlands
David Lamas, Estonia

Edmund Laugasson, Estonia
Ana Loureiro, Portugal
Katherine Maillet, France
Nadia Pantidi, UK
Antigoni Parmaxi, Cyprus
Borzoo Pourabdollahian, Italy
Janet C. Read, UK
Christophe Reffay, France
Nicos Souleles, Cyprus
Ana Luísa Torres, Portugal
Stefan Trausan-Matu, Romania
Aimilia Tzanavari, Cyprus
Johnny Yuen, Hong Kong
Carmen Zahn, Switzerland

External Reviewers

Ilia Adami, Greece
Iosif Klironomos, Greece
Maria Korozi, Greece
Vassilis Kouroumalis, Greece

Asterios Leonidis, Greece
George Margetis, Greece
Stavroula Ntoa, Greece
Nikolaos Partarakis, Greece

HCI International 2015

The 15th International Conference on Human–Computer Interaction, HCI International 2015, will be held jointly with the affiliated conferences in Los Angeles, CA, USA, in the Westin Bonaventure Hotel, August 2–7, 2015. It will cover a broad spectrum of themes related to HCI, including theoretical issues, methods, tools, processes, and case studies in HCI design, as well as novel interaction techniques, interfaces, and applications. The proceedings will be published by Springer. More information will be available on the conference website: http://www.hcii2015.org/

General Chair
Professor Constantine Stephanidis
University of Crete and ICS-FORTH
Heraklion, Crete, Greece
E-mail: cs@ics.forth.gr

Table of Contents – Part I

Visualisation Methods and Techniques

Multimodal Interaction

Knowledge Management

Information Search and Retrieval

Supporting Collaboration

Design and Evaluation Methods and Studies

Table of Contents – Part II

E-learning and E-education

Decision Support

Information and Interaction in Aviation and Transport

Safety, Security and Reliability

Communication, Expression and Emotions

Art, Culture and Creativity

Information and Knowledge in Business and Society

Visualisation Methods and Techniques

Visualization Tool for Finding
of Researcher Relations

Takafumi Aoki[1], Yoshikazu Sasamoto[1], Keisuke Makita[2], and Shingo Otsuka[2]

[1] Kanagawa Institute of Technology, Atsugi-shi Kanagawa 243-0292, Japan
{s1121033,s1021076}@ccy.kanagawa-it.ac.jp
[2] Graduate School of Kanagawa Institute of Technology,
Atsugi-shi Kanagawa 243-0292, Japan
s1385022@cce.kanagawa-it.ac.jp, otsuka@ic.kanagawa-it.ac.jp

Abstract. It is possible to collect knowledge of interest research field effectively if we can look for the key person of the field. In addition, when the people who belong to administrations and companies want to undertake information gathering to the person of a particular field, it is convenient if the key person of the field is found easily. In this paper, we propose the visualization tool for finding of researcher relations using the conference programs.

1   Introduction

It is possible to collect the information about the field effectively if we understand the human relations in the field. Hence, we visualize the human relations in the specific field using conference programs, and we build the tool which can identify people with a strong relations. In general, conference programs are comprised of the session that put together the study of the same field. Each session is comprised of one chairperson and several presentations, and one or plural authors are listed in a presented paper. The papers are more likely to be collaborative research if the authors consist of several varying in affiliation. Therefore we can suppose that strong human relations are built. Moreover, there is some kind of relations between authors who presented in the same session because each session compiles the presentations of the same research field. And about chairperson, it is similar. We might extract human relations by using many conference programs. We extract the information of chairpersons and authors using the held program in the holding schedule of the IEICE and conference information that we obtained originally. Furthermore, we visualized human relations using the Graphviz[1] that AT&T Research provided and the JAVA.

2   Related Works

SPYSEE [2] is famous for a tool@checking human relations on webpages in Japan. Figure 1 shows an example of human relations in SPYSEE. This person is famous in Japanese companies. This person is investigated using information

S. Yamamoto (Ed.): HIMI 2014, Part I, LNCS 8521, pp. 3–9, 2014.

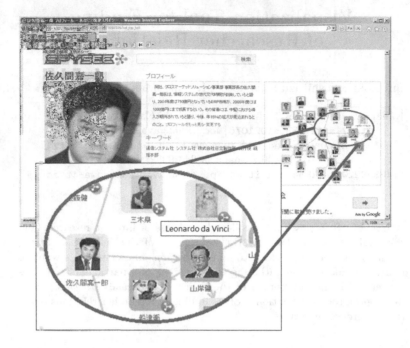

Fig. 1. Example of "SPYSEE"

of webpages and the relation graph is displayed by SPYSEE. However, this graph is wrong because there is Leonardo da Vinci to the friend of the friend of this person. There is doubt the authenticity of search results because this systems use information drawn from the webpages. On the other hand, there are many challenge of the extraction of researchers' relationships and the creation of the overhead view of research field using the bibliography information of the article [3,4,5,6,7,8]. In these studies, it extract the related information by using references and the author information of the articles. It is a subjective judgment because the references are recognized by authors to be the related studies. Our method is an objective judgment because we use the conference programs that the program chair compiles related study and divided into every session.

3   Acquisition of Research Group Data

We describe the authors list of that we acquired from the conference programs placed in the society pages. We also describe the Graphviz and the method of build process of "dot files".

3.1   Build Process of Authors' List Using Conference Programs

We extract the information of the session chair and the authors in the webpages of the conference programs for extracting researcher relations. We use two

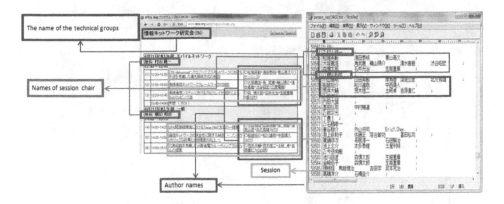

Fig. 2. Example of creating data set

dataset in our experiment. One is authors' list which we made hand-operated using the conference programs in conjunction with the database community in Japan, and the other is authors' list which we made one by manual operation using the conference programs of "the Institute of Electronics, Information and Communication Engineers (IEICE)"[9]. The website of IEICE has Technical Committee Submission System page[10]. Each information of conference schedule is made automatically as the left side of Figure 2. We extract authors and session chairs automatically using web scraping technology. We show a part of the list of authors on the right side of Figure 2. The list of persons in the right-side of Figure 2 shows following information.

- "S:" means a study group name.
- "Z:" means session chair(s).
- The line after "Z:" means authors. We express the multi-author using tab delimited.

3.2   Conversion from Authors' List to DOT Notation

We made a program to convert from the authors' list to DOT notation. The DOT notation is an expressing a graph with a text and describes it like Figure 3. It is easy to understand the human being while being the form that it is easy to computerize. We show the example which painted pictures using the Graphviz in Figure 4. We understand that "6" is connected from "1", "1" is connected from "4" and "2" is connected from "5". We use non-directed graph in our examination however it is possible to use directed graph in changing a parameter. And it is possible to change a color and size by appointing the attribute of the node and the edge.

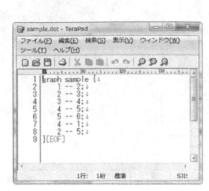
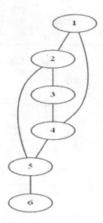

Fig. 3. Example of dot notation   **Fig. 4.** Example of graphviz

3.3   Image Transformation Using Graphviz

The dot files convert picture files using the Graphviz. We express the associated person with "one to one" and express the strength of ties in "len" as follows in our experiments. The value of "len" grows big if the number of times of co-author, same session and relation with chairperson and presenter. It becomes the layout that is placed near if a value of "len" is big. And we expressed the strong relation in a red line because there are many displayed number of nodes (researchers).

graph "g" "Takafumi Aoki" – "Keisuke Makita" [len = 42.00]; "Keisuke Makita" – "Yoshikazu Sasamoto" [len = 41.00];

4   Experimental Result

4.1   Details of Dataset

We use the conference programs written in Japanese in ours experiments. Dataset A is conference program data of the workshop and the forum for 41 times related to the databases community in Japan. Dataset B added data set A to the conference program data for 2,306 times which we are able to acquire from 2,457 links in "the technical Committee Submission System pages" in the IEICE website. And we succeed in collecting the 60,000 researchers' names. We visualize human relations of two dataset using the Graphviz and the graph tool which we made by JAVA.

4.2   Visualization Examples

We show the example of the Graphviz visualization using dataset A in the Figure 5. We confirm that a researcher tied to a great many people in the center

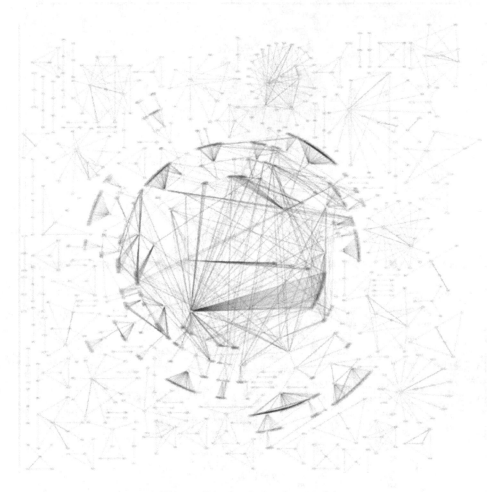

Fig. 5. Result of visualization(1)

of Figure 5. In fact, this researcher is one of the key person in the database community and the many pupils of this researcher play an active part. There are many sectors in a Figure 5. The sectors express master and pupil relations and a sector tends to be big as laboratory of the large family.

Next, we show the example of our original tool using dataset A in the Figure 6. There is a slide bar changing the number of the nodes (researchers) under the center in the Figure 6. The edges are displayed if the degree of relation between nodes (researchers) is high. And the edges are short as the degree between nodes relation is high. The position of each node does not have the meaning. Each node is placed at random first. When time passes, the nodes that are high in a degree of relation become near. It is possible to fix the node if the users click the left button of a certain node and the color of the nodes related to the node changes if the users click the right button. The example in the Figure 6, we understand

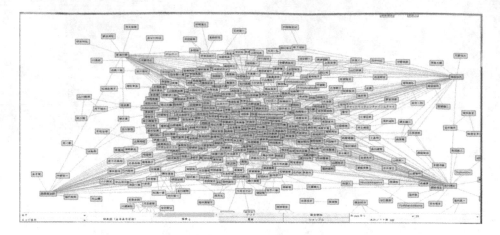

Fig. 6. Result of visualization(2)

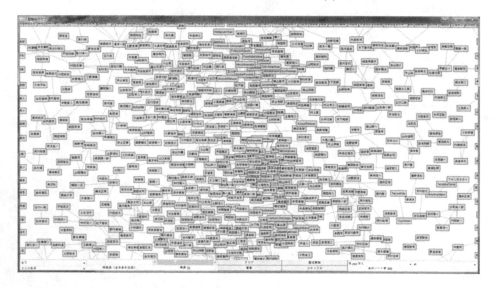

Fig. 7. Result of visualization(3)

that the nodes are many and gathered in a circular pattern as this node is the well-known researcher of the database community.

Finally, we show the example which we visualize with our tool using dataset B in Figure 7. We understand that it becomes the form that scattered in whole although there is the place where the nodes interval becomes dense. The dataset B includes approximately 60,000 researchers. With 27 inches of display which we used by the experiments, indication of about 1,000 nodes is a limit. So we make frequency a considerably high value. Therefore, the most of the nodes displayed here seem to be the well-known researchers.

Figure 5 and Figure 6 shows an example about a particular technical group. The color of the nodes in conjunction with the selected node changes. It is possible to understand the relation between researchers in detail. However, the number of nodes that the user with our tool can grasp depends on the screen size.

4.3 Discussion

The relations of the researchers are captured for overlooking using the Graphviz in experimental results. And our tool can grasp the relations between researchers in greater detail. As problems of the present, we must thin out the number of the nodes to display beforehand because the node number that the Graphviz can express has a limit. Moreover, the correspondence to the dynamic demand of the users is difficult because the Graphviz makes a conversion to an image. In our original tool, the improvement of the point that the number of nodes that the users can grasp depends on display size for is necessary.

5   Conclusion

We try to visualize human relations using the conference programs. We also extract researchers' information using the society webpages and visualize human relations about a particular field. We will perform the visualization and the comparison in other research fields in future.

References

1. Graphviz, http://www.graphviz.org/Home.php
2. SPYSEE, http://spysee.jp/
3. Kondo, T., Nanba, H., Takezawa, T., Okumura, M.: Technical trend analysis by analyzing research papers' titles. In: Vetulani, Z. (ed.) LTC 2009. LNCS, vol. 6562, pp. 512–521. Springer, Heidelberg (2011)
4. Nanba, H., Kondo, T., Takezawa, T.: Automatic creation of a technical trend map from research papers and patents. In: Proc. the 3rd International CIKM Workshop on Patent Information Retrieval (PaIR 2010), pp. 11–15 (2010)
5. Fukuda, S., Nanba, H., Takezawa, T.: Extraction and visualization of technical trend information from research papers and patents. In: Proc. the 1st International Workshop on Mining. Scientific Publications (2012)
6. Karamon, J., Matsuo, Y., Yamamoto, H., Ishizuka, M.: Generating social network features for link-based classification. In: Kok, J.N., Koronacki, J., Lopez de Mantaras, R., Matwin, S., Mladenič, D., Skowron, A. (eds.) PKDD 2007. LNCS (LNAI), vol. 4702, pp. 127–139. Springer, Heidelberg (2007)
7. Nguyen, M., Kato, D., Hashimoto, T., Yokota, H.: Research history generation from metainformation of research papers using maximum margin clustering. International Journal of Business Intelligence and Data Mining 7, 217–231 (2012)
8. Jin, Y., Matsuo, Y., Ishizuka, M.: Extracting social networks among various entities on the web. In: Franconi, E., Kifer, M., May, W. (eds.) ESWC 2007. LNCS, vol. 4519, pp. 251–266. Springer, Heidelberg (2007)
9. The Institute of Electronics, Information and Communication Engineers, http://www.ieice.org/eng/index.html
10. IEICE Technical Committee Submission System, http://www.ieice.org/ken/program/index.php?lang=eng

Selection Classification for Interaction with Immersive Volumetric Visualizations

Amy Banic

University of Wyoming, USA
abanic@cs.uwyo.edu

Abstract. Visualization enables scientists to transform data in its raw form to a visual form that will facilitate discoveries and insights. Although there are advantages for displaying inherently 3-dimensional (3D) data in immersive environments, those advantages are hampered by the challenges involved in selecting volumes of that data for exploration or analysis. Selection involves the user identifying a set of points for a specific task. This paper preliminary data collection on natural user actions for volume selection. This paper also presents a research agenda outlining an extension for volume selection classification, as well as challenges, for designing components for a direct selection of volumes of data points.

Keywords: HCI methods and theories, Human Centered Design and User Centered Design, Interaction design, Visualization methods and techniques.

1   Introduction and Motivation

Visualization enables scientists to transform data in its raw form to a visual form that will facilitate discoveries and insights. It has also been shown that there are advantages for analysis to displaying inherently 3-dimensional (3D) data, such as LiDAR data, geo-spatial data, and volumetric data, in 3D rather more difficult to see in 2D [16,17,28] Furthermore, displaying these 3D visualizations in immersive environments has additional advantages, such as additional depth information and spatial relationships. Researchers have demonstrated this in a number of applications, such as 3D seismic data [7], oil and gas exploration [6], and geoscience [16,17]. It has been also shown that understanding, discovery and scientific workflows can be also enhanced through immersion [10,17]. However, static visual information is not enough. Data selection and exploration is identified as a critical aspect of making discoveries from visualizations. Previous research has shown that interaction fosters analysis and discovery [21,22]. Yet, interaction is still identified as one of the areas that is in need of focused study. The 2006 NIH/NSF Visualization Research Challenges Report identifies interaction fosters analysis and discovery, yet is it one of the challenges needing more research in the context of visualization [14]. In immersive visualizations, volumes of data that the user may select are likely not to be pre-determined individual colored objects or point clouds may be displayed representing each data point, where

S. Yamamoto (Ed.): HIMI 2014, Part I, LNCS 8521, pp. 10–21, 2014.

a user may wish to select many of these points. Although there are some effective ways to interact with such visualizations, these techniques may require additional training. As a result, advantages provided by immersion may be hampered by the lack of suitable interaction for immersive visualizations. We have now reached the stage in which user interaction tools need to be designed, evaluated, and established specifically for immersive visualizations.

One type of interaction that we will focus on is called selection, where a user identifies an area for analysis. Many selection methods have been designed with the assumption that the areas, which the user may select, are volumes predetermined by underlying model. For example, if selecting an object with a predefined volume, such as a table, one can select at least one point on the surface mesh of that model and as a result the rest of the points defining that mesh can be associated with that selection. An example of this is 'Ray-Casting', a selection technique in which a ray is cast from the users input device out into 3D space in order to make the selection [4]. The first point that the ray intersects is the selected point. However, the selected point is usually a part of a defined surface mesh. Therefore, the entire surface mesh and associated object is selected. These types of selection techniques work well for these types of volumes in order to reduce effort needed to select each individual point of the volume. The mesh may make up a volume, but the individual points of that volume are not individually selected. 3D data points visualized in an environment may not have a predefined mesh that consists of a set of points. These data points may have a variety of related or not related features, but may not make up a volumetric mesh. How those points connect or relate to each other as a volume of data may not be predetermined. Therefore, there is a need for the user to be able to define the volume of data the user wishes to select. Individual colored objects or point clouds may be displayed representing each data point, where a user may wish to select a subset of these points, whether within a particular range of parameters or not. Furthermore, interacting with a visualization 3D data point clouds, consisting of thousands or millions of data points can be particularly difficult due to the density of the data, occlusion, opacity variations, and limited color scheme of features.

Although there are a few selection methods that allow users to interact with multiple points or filtering techniques, they do not necessarily allow the user to directly define the volume which users visually want to select. Picking enables users to choose individual points, but can be time consuming and tedious if the user wishes to select larger sets of points [35]. Filtering techniques, such as brushing, enables users to select larger sets of points, but the problem with these techniques is that the user needs to be searching for points that fit within a particular range of parameters [2,13]. At times, scientific workflow is best supported through exploration and direct selection. As a result, advantages provided by immersion may be hampered by the lack of suitable interaction techniques for immersive visualizations. There is the need for accurate, efficient, low fatigue, volumetric selection techniques for immersive visualizations, or other similar types of selection in an immersive environment. This paper focuses on detailing a classification of selection interaction for volumetric data. Additionally this paper discusses the current and future research challenges in human-computer interaction for immersive visualizations. Through a preliminary study, we found that users often intend to reach for or point to particular data of initial interest. Also in an initial preliminary study we found that users tend to bring the data closer to view and orient the data prior to performing other tasks. Other deductions are revolves around strategic choices based on type of user.

For volumetric selection, preliminary work identified several components to for bimanual interaction: a) defining the volume for selection b) manipulating the volume c) task assignment d) mapping function and e) manipulation function. This work was designed with the assumption that the volume for selecting is concrete. A limitation of this work are that one of two situations occur: either the user is not able to select all of the areas that is desired or that areas not desired are selected because there is only one way to select all of the desired areas. We extend this classification further to apply to more generalizable volumetric selection and address the limitations of previous work. This paper presents this extended, more detailed, classification of actions for selection interaction of volumetric data. This work can assist with the design and development of volumetric selection techniques for visualizations of 3D scientific data. Additionally, this paper demonstrates use this classification for techniques which extend across multiple platforms. And finally, the paper outlines research challenges in the context of defining selection techniques for volumetric data.

2   Background and Related Work

2.1   Volumetric Data

Volume data consist of 3D (possibly time-varying) spatially-located positions which contain information about that point. Information can consist of one to many measurable features associated with this 3D position, such as velocity, temperature, pressure, etc. They may not consist of tangible surfaces and edges. Information is obtained through sampling real world information or through computer generated simulations. The visual complexity increases with increase of number, density, coloring, occlusion and other properties of data points. Data points within the volume often are defined as a voxel, having x, y, z position and other attributes per which the data point is colored, and other visual aspects are defined , such as opacity, etc. Volume data is typically is inherently 3D spatial, however in some cases other types of data may be scaled down or scaled up to a 3D spatial context. An example of a visualization of volumetric data is shown in Figure 1.

2.2   Volumetric Visualizations

Volume visualizations are developed as a means of gaining perspective or meaningful information from these types of data using graphics and rendering for representation, interaction and manipulation [11]. Volume rendering or direct volume rendering is the process of creating an image from the extracted information derived from 3D volumetric data [11]. Usually visual representation, or coloring of, each data point is generated based on one of those features. In visualizations that display 3D volumetric data, the objects are rendered with splat-based, illustrative, or other rendering techniques such that the volumetric areas are defined by clouds of color with varying opacity, or by some other representation [1,12,15]. Using these rendering techniques an underlying mesh may not always define the relationships between each point sample. 3D volumetric visualizations can be difficult to interact with due to these properties of volumetric data and the various rendering types used in the visualizations [15].

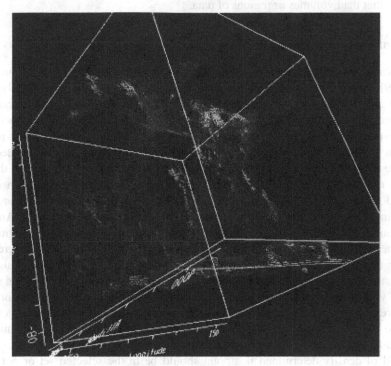

Fig. 1. Example of Visualization of Volumetric Data

2.3 Interaction with Volumetric Visualizations

The visual complexity and complex relationships of 3D volumetric data makes the development of effective 3D interaction techniques particularly challenging. Interaction classifications and guidelines have been developed for 3D polygonal data, or data which consists of points that define a polygonal mesh [4,32]. These papers outline taxonomies for the interaction and evaluation frameworks for testing the performance of the techniques. Designers can use the performance results of these studies to help guide them on decisions in designing interaction techniques for optimal performance. However, these guidelines and techniques for selection have been typically based on the assumption that the mesh defines the relationship between the points [27]. Scientific workflow, exploration, and analysis can be enhanced through appropriate design and evaluation of interaction and user interfaces. Although this has been completed some in previous work [4], there has been little work completed to develop guidelines specifically for volumetric visualizations. The following outlines initial design of selection techniques for volumetric data. Ray-casting methods adapted for volumetric displays were found to provide better selection than a 3D-point cursor when tasked with selecting multiple individual targets [8]. Lasso techniques have been developed for multiple object selection [15,9,25,26]. A few of these have integrated refinement capabilities. However these bodies of work only evaluated selection of individual targets rather than volumes or regions of data.

2.4   Interaction with Immersive Volumetric Visualizations

Recently interaction techniques have been developed and evaluated for 3D volumetric data [8,9]. Conic selection techniques were designed for interaction with polygonal data but can be used for volume selection [23]. In these techniques a ray is cast out into space where the ray defines a central spline where the radius of a cone increases out from that spline as the ray continues into space. Rectangular volume or region selection techniques have been developed specifically for volumetric data selection, but more thoroughly evaluated for bimanual control [29]. The results revealed that an asymmetric-synchronous selection technique is best for potentially long periods of time and for cognitively demanding tasks. However when optimum accuracy is needed, a bimanual symmetric-synchronous technique was best for selection. Another study found that asynchronous actions increased cognitive demand in asymmetric techniques [30].The limitations of these previous works are that they lack the creation of other types of volumes, such as convex volumes, or more organic. Initial techniques have been developed that are more focused on more dynamic or organic selection for volumetric data. A technique, CloudLasso, was developed to select organic shaped regions through use of 2-degrees of freedom gestures. Using the 2D gestures to define the outline of a region overlaid the visual display of data, the remaining of the volume was selected using a systematic algorithm of Marching Cubes, where threshold of density determined if a point should be in the selected set or not [34]. Additionally, another technique, called the Volume Cracker, was developed to use hand gestures to slice open volumes of data and found it to be better for exploration tasks than a standard desktop technique [3] Some work has been completed to help improve selection for immersive volumetric data, there is a need for guidelines and classification of techniques from the human-computer interaction community to better allow visualization experts and scientists to benefit from the appropriate interaction. The potential is for improved scientific workflow, exploration and analysis leading to improved discoveries.

3   Classification

3.1   Preliminary Work

Some have classified types of interaction in other types of visualizations such as "select: marking something of interest, explore: showing me something else, reconfigure:

show me a different arrangement, encode: show me a different representation, abstract/ elaborate: show me more or less detail, filter: show me something conditionally, and connect: show me related items" [33]. Little work has been conducted to actually classify and evaluate interaction guidelines for 3D volumetric data. This paper specifically focuses on selection. An initial taxonomy of volumetric selection has been defined [31] as means to classify interaction components for volumetric selection. The taxonomy outlines the basic components of volumetric selection as: a) defining the volume for selection b) manipulating the volume c) task assignment d) mapping function and e) manipulation function. Defining the volume was limited to identifying a particular base shape, such as a sphere, a cube, a lasso, or other. Manipulating the volume include translation, rotation, and scaling of the selection volume. Task assignment and functions for manipulation and mapping refer to how each of the definition and manipulation components are assigned to the input.

3.2   Data Collection

We set out to expand on the preliminary classification work, and wanted to learn more about what users were inclined or innately felt how they would identify volumes of data. The purpose of this work was to determine what were the more natural actions that a user would perform as a way to expand the classification with an emphasis on user intuitiveness and user-centric design.

Study Design. We designed an initial study to collect data on how individuals would want to explore and select regions of interest based on real world actions. To simulate a set of volumetric data, physical cotton balls and stretched cotton were used as target regions for selection. Target areas were colored and other regions were not. The participants' task was to use any way possible to let the system know which regions they wanted to select (which were the colored target regions). The means of completing this task was intentionally left open-ended so that participants could describe any imaginable tool, perform any action, or tell the facilitator how they would like to complete their task. Position and orientation data was collected on physical actions through tracked hand movements. Observational notes were made by one facilitator. Audio was recorded and additional notes were taken by another observer in order to record the comments by the participants. Video recorded how the target data and other data were manipulated. The main goal was to take a user-centric approach in collecting information about designing interaction for this type of task. Instead of limiting the user to a specific set of methodology, a more open-ended approach allowed for exploration of the users wanted. It was set up this way so that we could study more about users' intentions for selection and how their actions were spatially related to the volume of data.

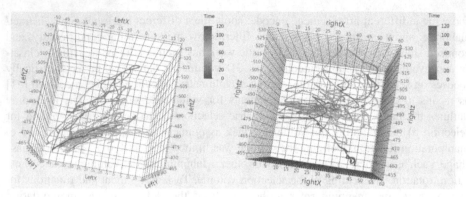

Fig. 2. Top-down view of 3D Scatterplot of left and right hand movements of participants, colored by time

Results. Data was collected on 10 participants. These participants were a mix of novice (N=4) and expert (N=6) users. Quantitative and qualitative data was collected. We limit the data presented to those which support our classification scheme presented in this particular paper.

Quantitative Data. Quantitative data included the position of the left and right hands as the participants performed their task. This data revealed that participants strategized their actions for volume definition over time (Figure 2). Any portions of the volume close to the user, were defined first. Defining volumes which were further from reach and out of sight, or occluded, were defined in the later portion of the time sequence. Using this data, we can classify actions of volume definition into portions actually defined by the properties of the volume itself, such as occlusion and proximity to user. Quantitative data was also used to break down larger groups of actions into subsets of actions. Actions can be broken down into initial volume definition and then later a refinement step to that volume. Actions can also be broken down into defining the volume, adjusting the view or manipulating the data to have a better advantage for selection tasks, and strategizing. Strategizing involves users studying the volume for features about what to select and alternatively about how to select it.

Qualitative Data. Observational data revealed that users often intend to physically reach for or point to particular data of initial interest, but then bring it closer for more actions to that task. We can classify these actions as change in context, anything which users will to do change their view or to bring data closer to them for more detailed interaction. Users also tended to bring the data closer to view and change the orientation of the data prior to indication of selection. Quantitative data collected supports these observational action sequences. This can also be interpreted that, before any selection, there is an observational or exploration step. Users are strategizing the best way to identify their region of interest. Strategizing can be based on time (ie. what is seen first, may be selected), or overall volumetric region of data (all data is seen, but what is the most efficient way to identify that volume).

Data Based on User Type. Differences between expert and novice users were as follows. Quantitative data indicated that expert users were quicker (M= 70 sec, SD=1.34) in their decision-making or strategizing processes. Novice users had more delay between actions, with total time being longer (M=120 sec, SD=2.45) indicating they were thinking for longer periods of time in order to determine their course of actions to select the volume. Qualitative data revealed that expert users were more interested in how to explore the data. Often expert users move other data away from the target data to have more space around the target data to be able to see, explore, and select it. Novice users were more interested in completing the task as accurately as possible. This could attribute to why it took them longer as well.

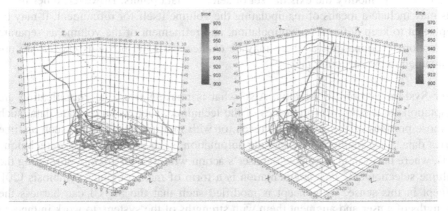

Fig. 3. 3D scatterplot showing reach actions to bring data within closer proxmmitity to the user

3.3   Discussion of Classification Extension and Challenges

We present extensions of the current classification for volumetric selection: a) selection volume definition b) selection volume manipulation c) task assignment d) mapping function and e) manipulation function [31], discussed in section 3.1. These guidelines as described in this classification, may be extended across spatial dimensionality, display type, and platforms. This classification can be used as a means for designing new selection techniques for volumetric data to ensure appropriate functionality and components are present for the user.

Defining Volume Selection Sets. There are two ways to classify definition of the volume: additive or subtractive. In an additive technique, users can identify data points or volumes of data points to add to the selection set. To remove them, they identify them again to switch them from being in the set to out of the set. In a subtractive technique, a user identifies all of the data which they do not want selected. Any data that is not identified will be included in the selection set. To remove data from the selected set, users will then identify those data, and as a result, remove them from the selected set. The challenges coupled with definition are occlusion, blending issues, data too densely populated, etc. To help with this challenge, implementing techniques which account for user-system symbiotic actions (Section 3.3.3) or data manipulation (Section 3.3.4) of the extended classification. Furthermore, methods which can provide more organic or specific spine patterns to encompass the data may be useful.

Refining the Volume Selection Sets. From previously designed techniques and our presented data, what is missing in the two sections, of defining and manipulating the volume, are methods to refine the volume, such as adding or removing data from the selected volume. Volumetric selection techniques should have a means by which to edit the volume of the selected data points. Additive and subtractive methods may also be used to modify the existing set of selected data points. However, other methods may include a means of manipulating the volume itself for refinement. It may be important to keep definition, manipulation, and refinement of the volume as separate interaction functionalities as there may be challenges if the methods chosen are not best-suited to the particular task.

User-System Symbiotic Actions. Also what is missing from the classification are adaptations to account for properties of the technique, such as large-scale data, such as those portions of the data out of reach, or with multiple dimensions, such as time series data. Such methods may include automation, such as in Yu's Lasso technique [34], where the system augments the user's action with its own attempt at refining the volume selection set. This augmentation is a form of man-computer symbiosis [20]. Except in this sense, we concept is modified such that the 3D UI can harness the strengths of a user and augment them with strengths of the system, to work in tandem to select and explore the data. A challenge with this aspect of the classification is that there is not a well-defined line when to engage the system and when to harness the user's capabilities. Some of this may be domain-specific, however it is important when designing to consider the trade-offs between the two. Also one may confuse this with system tools. The main idea to keep in mind is to maintain this idea of a partnership, where the system picks up where the user left off and the user picks up where the system left it.

Data Manipulation: Extension of Self or Retraction of Data. Another adaptation to this would allow for extension of selection techniques to move beyond reach of the user, or provide functionality to bring the data closer to them, as we concluded from our collected data. The data itself can be manipulated, such as decoupled as in [3], scaled, deformed, etc. This may allow for a perspective on the data that can permit a better selection. An important aspect to remember for visualizations is that when designing interaction techniques, the data itself needs to maintain its relative scale and relationships. Manipulation of the data will permit the user to bring data closer, but techniques need to either retain the relationships or allow the user to revert back to them once completed with interacting with the data in its modified form. The challenge with this aspect is determining or providing the flexibility to decide when to manipulate the view as compared with when to manipulate the data. There are advantages and disadvantages to either that are particularly domain-specific.

Strategy Driven. Techniques that either adapt to the user or learn from time intervals between actions can be used to enhance the user's completion of selection. For example, if a user is delayed, it might mean that they are either a novice user, and are unsure what to do, or are an expert user, so suggesting elements of selection might be of use. Implementing in the system a way to learn the users strategies can be helpful to providing more insight and detracting from the user interface itself. The challenge here is how to determine what the users' intention really was or ultimately learning from those strategies. Other input mechanisms and data collected can assist to help determine users strategies as other ways to help determine intent and augment the discovery process.

4   Conclusion and Future Work

This paper presented some initial research work on more what users are more inclined to or innately felt how they would identify volumes of data. Through quantities and qualitative analysis, an extension to an existing classification was provided to serve as a way to design future volumetric interaction techniques. In conclusion the extensions to the classification include: more dynamic and organic ways to define the volume selection set, methods for refining the volume selection set, user-system symbiotic actions and functionality, data manipulation, and strategy driven. The purpose of this work was to determine what were the more natural actions that a user would perform as a way to expand the classification with an emphasis on user intuitiveness and user-centric design. Each were based on previous and preliminary work of data collected of users actions. Each section provided description, examples, and challenges to consider. In the future, we will implement these concepts into design and provide benchmarks for evaluations of volumetric interaction techniques.

Acknowledgements. Neera Pradhan and Anh Nguyen were instrumental for writing code for the software to collect the data. Neera Pradhan and Zhibo Sun helped to perform initial collection of the data for this work. A special thanks is extended to them for their efforts.

References

1. Ayala, D., Pla, N., Vigo, M.: Splat representation of parametric surfaces. Computing 79, 101–108 (2007)
2. Becker, R.A., Cleveland, W.S.: Brushing scatterplots. Technometrics 29(2), 127–142 (1987)
3. Laha, B., Bowman, D.A.: Volume cracker: a bimanual 3D interaction technique for analysis of raw volumetric data. In: Proceedings of the 1st Symposium on Spatial User Interaction (SUI 2013), pp. 61–68. ACM, New York (2013)

4. Bowman, D., Kruijff, E., LaViola, J., Poupyrev, I.: 3D User Interfaces: Theory and Practice. Addison-Wesley, Boston (2004)
5. Elmqvist, N., Dragicevic, P., Fekete, J.: Rolling the Dice: Multidimensional Visual Exploration using Scatterplot Matrix Navigation. IEEE Transactions on Visualization and Computer Graphics 14(6), 1141–1148 (2008)
6. Evans, F., Volz, W., Dorn, G., Frohlich, B., Roberts, D.M.: Future trends in oil and gas visualization. In: VIS 2002: Proceedings of the Conference on Visualization 2002, pp. 55–62. IEEE Computer Society, Washington, DC (2002)
7. Frohlich, B., Barrass, S., Zehner, B., Plate, J., Gobel, M.: Exploring geo-scientific data in virtual environments. In: Proceedings of IEEE Visualization, pp. 169–173 (1999)
8. Grossman, T., Balakrishnan, R.: The design and evaluation of selection techniques for 3D volumetric displays. In: UIST 2006, pp. 3–12. ACM Press (2006)
9. Grossman, T., Wigdor, D., Balakrishnan, R.: Multi-finger gestural interaction with 3d volumetric displays. In: UIST 2004, pp. 61–70. ACM Press (2004)
10. Gruchalla, K.: Immersive well-path editing: investigating the added value of immersion. IEEE Virtual Reality, 157–164 (2004)
11. Hansen, C.D., Johnson, C.R. (eds.): The Visualization Handbook, p. 120. Elsevier (2005)
12. Jang, J., Ribarsky, W., Shaw, C.D., Faust, N.: View-Dependent Multiresolution Splatting of Non-Uniform Data. In: Proceedings of the Symposium on Data Visualization. ACM International Conference Proceeding Series, vol. 22, pp. 125–ff (2002)
13. Janicke, H., Bottinger, M., Scheuermann, G.: Brushing of attribute clouds for the visualization of multivariate data. IEEE Transactions on Visualization and Computer Graphics 14(6), 1459–1466 (2008)
14. Johnson, C., Moorhead, R., Munzner, T., Pfister, H., Rheingans, P., Yoo, T.S.: NIH/NSF Visualization Research Challenges Report. IEEE Press (2006)
15. Kalaiah, A., Varshney, A.: Modeling and Rendering of Points with Local Geometry. IEEE Transactions on Visualization and Computer Graphics 9(1), 30–42 (2003)
16. Kreylos, O., Bawden, G., Bernardin, T., Billen, M., Cowgill, E., Gold, R., Hamann, B., Jadamec, M., Kellogg, L., Staadt, O., Sumner, D.: Enabling scientific workflows in virtual reality. In: Proceedings of the 2006 ACM International Conference on Virtual Reality Continuum and its Applications, VRCIA 2006, pp. 155–162. ACM, New York (2006)
17. Kreylos, O.: Environment-Independent VR Development. In: Bebis, G., et al. (eds.) ISVC 2008, Part I. LNCS, vol. 5358, pp. 901–912. Springer, Heidelberg (2008)
18. Kreylos, O., Bawden, G.W., Kellogg, L.H.: Immersive visualization and analysis of LiDAR data. In: Bebis, G., et al. (eds.) ISVC 2008, Part I. LNCS, vol. 5358, pp. 846–855. Springer, Heidelberg (2008)
19. Kopper, R., Bacim, F., Bowman, D.A.: Rapid and Accurate 3D Selection by Progressive Refinement. In: Proc. 3DUI, pp. 67–74. IEEE Computer Society, Los Alamitos (2011)
20. Licklider, J.C.R.: Man-computer symbiosis. IRE Transactions on Human Factors in Electronics (1), 4–11 (1960)
21. Lin, C., Loftin, R., Stark, T.: Virtual reality for geosciences visualization. In: Proceedings of 3rd Asia Pacific Computer Human Interaction Conference, pp. 196–201 (1998)
22. Lin, C., Loftin, R., Nelson, J.: Interaction with geoscience data in an immersive environment. In: Proceedings of IEEE Virtual Reality, pp. 55–62 (2000)
23. Liang, J., Green, M.: JDCAD: A Highly Interactive 3D Modeling System. Computers & Graphics 18(4), 499–506 (1994)
24. Yu, L., Efstathiou, K., Isenberg, P., Isenberg, T.: Efficient Structure-Aware Selection Techniques for 3D Point Cloud Visualizations with 2DOF Input. IEEE Transactions on Visualization and Computer Graphics 18(12), 2245–2254 (2012)

25. Lucas, J.F., Bowman, D.A.: Design and Evaluation of 3D Multiple Object Selection Techniques. Report, Virginia Polytechnic Institute and State University, USA (2005)
26. Olwal, A., Feiner, S.: The flexible pointer- An interaction technique for selection in augmented and virtual reality. In: UIST 2003, pp. 81–82 (2003)
27. Sherman, W.R., Craig, A.B.: Understanding Virtual Reality: Interface, Application, and Design. Morgan Kaufmann Publishers Inc. (2002)
28. Tory, M., Kirkpatrick, A., Atkins, M.S., Moller, T.: Visualization Task Performance with 2D, 3D, and Combination Displays. IEEE Transactions on Visualization and Computer Graphics 12(1), 2–13 (2006)
29. Ulinski, A., Wartell, Z., Hodges, L.F.: Bimanual Task Division Preferences for Volume Selection. In: Spencer, S.N. (ed.) Proceedings of the 2007 ACM Symposium on Virtual Reality Software and Technology, VRST 2007, pp. 217–218. ACM, New York (2007)
30. Ulinski, A., Zanbaka, C., Wartell, Z., Goolkasian, P., Hodges, L.F.: Two Handed Selection Techniques for Volumetric Data. In: Proceedings of the 3D User Interfaces, 3DUI 2007, pp. 107–114. IEEE Computer Society (2007)
31. Ulinski, A.: Ph.D. Dissertation, UNC-Charlotte (2008)
32. Ware, C., Rose, J.: Rotating virtual objects with real handles. ACM Trans. Comput.-Hum. Interact. 6, 162–180 (1999)
33. Yi, J.S., Kang, Y., Stasko, J.T., Jacko, J.A.: Toward a Deeper Understanding of the Role of Interaction in Information Visualization. In: Proceedings of InfoVis 2007, vol. 13, pp. 1224–1231 (2007)
34. Yu, L., Efstathiou, K., Isenberg, P., Isenberg, T.: Efficient Structure-Aware Selection Techniques for 3D Point Cloud Visualizations with 2DOF Input. IEEE Transactions on Visualization and Computer Graphics 18(12), 2245–2254 (2012)
35. Zhang, J.H., Liang, C., Li, G.Q.: 3D Primitive Picking on GPU. Journal of Engineering Graphics 1, 10 (2009)

Analyzing HCI Issues in Data Clustering Tools

Clodis Boscarioli[1], José Viterbo[2], Mateus Felipe Teixeira[1],
and Victor Hugo Röhsig[2]

[1] Western Paraná State University (UNIOESTE), Cascavel, Paraná, Brazil
{clodis.boscarioli,mateus.teixeira}@unioeste.br
[2] Federal Fluminense University (UFF), Niterói, Rio de Janeiro, Brazil
{viterbo,vrohsig}@ic.uff.br

Abstract. Due to the rapid growth in the volume of data stored in organizational databases and the human limitations in analyzing and interpreting data, appropriate technics are necessary to allow the identification of a large amount of information and knowledge in such databases. In this context, several techniques and tools have been proposed for enabling the end user to interpret his dataset. In this work we discuss the ways of interacting with cluster analysis tools, taking into account both the clustering and the interpretation stages. We investigate how usability and user experience aspects of such tools can improve the understanding of the discovered knowledge. Moreover, we evaluate the role of visualization methods in the comprehension of groups formed in cluster analysis using Knime, Orange Canvas, RapidMiner Studio and Weka data mining tools.

Keywords: Data Mining Tools, HCI, User Evaluation.

1 Introduction

Due to the rapid growth in the volume of data stored in organizational databases and the human limitations in analyzing and interpreting data, appropriate technics are necessary to allow the identification of a large amount of information and knowledge in such databases. The emerging analytical process called Knowledge Discovery in Databases (KDD), and for [1], is a non-trivial process for discovering valid, new, useful and accessible patterns in databases. KDD comprises three main steps: pre-processing for data preparation, data mining and post-processing, which includes the debugging and/or synthesis of the discovered patterns.

Data Mining is the core of the KDD process. It relies on a set of different algorithms to extract hidden patterns in databases. Such algorithms vary according with the purpose of the analysis, which may be identifying association rules or defining models for data regression, data classification or data clustering. Data clustering, in particular, may be defined as the identification of groups, i.e., subsets of data, in which there is a high internal cohesion among the objects that belong to a group, but also a large external insulation among groups.

S. Yamamoto (Ed.): HIMI 2014, Part I, LNCS 8521, pp. 22–33, 2014.

The cluster analysis process comprises two different stages. In the first stage, one or several algorithms, each using different ways for the identification and representation of its results, may be applied to identify the data clusters. The second stage consists in performing the interpretation of the results, what can be done applying methods based on data visualization. The main purpose of data visualization is to integrate the end user in the knowledge discovery process, providing a graphical representation of the database or the data clustering result. The end user will be able to interpret the results, for example, by identifying characteristics of a particular group, the relationship between patterns and distinctions between groups, spatial distribution of patterns, among others characteristics.

Human-Computer Interaction (HCI) and Data Mining researchers have long been working to develop methods to help end users to identify, extract, visualize and understand useful information extracted from huge masses of high dimensional databases. In this work we discuss the ways of interacting with cluster analysis tools, taking into account both the clustering and the interpretation stages. We investigate how usability and user experience aspects of such tools can improve the understanding of the discovered knowledge. Moreover, we evaluate the role of visualization methods in the comprehension of groups formed in cluster analysis. For this purpose, we selected a set of free and widely used tools: KNIME, Orange Canvas, RapidMiner and Weka.

This paper is organized as follows. Section 2 and Section 3 present some basic concepts about data clustering and data visualization, respectively. Section 4 describes the tools that were selected for our study. Section 5 discusses the HCI evaluations. Finally, in Section 6 we present our conclusions.

2   Data Clustering

The goal of data clustering, also known as cluster analysis, is to discover the natural grouping of a set of patterns, points, or objects [2]. At the end of the process, patterns belonging to the same group are more similar to each other and dissimilar to those patterns in other groups, based on a given measure of similarity. The basic idea of grouping data can be defined as the internal cohesion and external isolation of objects between groups [3].

To [4], data clustering is a general name for computational methods that analyze data regarding the discovery of sets of homogeneous observations. Given a database with n patterns, each measured by p variables, the goal of cluster analysis is to find a relationship that separates those patterns in g groups. The final purpose is to find out implicit relationships among data instances that were previously unknown.

There are several data clustering algorithms, each applying different techniques to identify and represent their results. The choice of which algorithm to use depends on the type of data to be analyzed and the purpose of the analysis.

In this work, we chose to use only the k-means algorithm, which was available in all analyzed tools. Even though it was first proposed over 50 years ago [5][6][7], k-means is one of the simplest and still one of the most widely used algorithms for clustering. Ease of implementation, simplicity, efficiency, and empirical success are the main reasons for its popularity [2].

Algorithm 1. - *K-means* algorithm

```
Step 1: Select K initial centroids
Step 2: Repeat
Step 3:    Assign each standard to the closest centroid
Step 4:    Recalculate centroids
Step 5: Until the groups remain stable
```

Algorithm 1 illustrates the process. Initially, we define the number k of groups to be formed. After that, we determine the initial k centroids, which can be calculated based on the available patterns, applying one of several different cluster initialization heuristics. For the next step each pattern in the database is associated to the closest centroid, based on a distance measure. After that, the k centroids are recalculated by finding the point that minimizes the average distance for each pattern in the group. This process is repeated until there is no more change in the formed groups.

Typically, k-means is run independently for different values of k and the partition that appears the most meaningful to the domain expert is selected. Different initializations can lead to different final clustering because k-means only converges to local minima. One way to overcome the local minima is to run the k-means algorithm, for a given k, with multiple different initial partitions and choose the partition with the smallest squared error [2].

3   Data Visualization

In a scenario where large amounts of data have to analyzed, the availability of data visualization techniques is particularly important to allow the end user to efficiently interpret the results of a clustering method, for example, by identifying common characteristics in a particular group, the relationship between patterns and the distinction between groups, the spatial distribution of patterns, among others.

The main idea of data visualization is to integrate the end user into the data analysis process, by providing a graphical representation of the database and the resulting data clusters. Besides that, the user can interact with the graphical representation and thus interpret the data clustering results in a more effective way [8].

Visualization is the process of representing data and information in a graphical way, based on visual representations and an interactive mechanism. The purpose of visualization is to give to the user some perception of what is being represented, not only creating a figure. In data clustering operations, the main interest is the visualization of clusters, so that their quality may be assessed, or the spatial distribution of patterns in a cluster can be understood.

There are different techniques of data visualization, but most are limited by the dimensionality of the database to be explored, along with the dimensionality that can be represented by computational methods. Over time, various techniques have been developed for different types of data and also for different dimensionalities.

According to [9], the techniques of data visualization can be divided into:

- Two dimensions (2D) and three dimensions (3D) visualization techniques, such as pie charts, scatter and line charts, bar charts and cityscapes charts;
- Visualization techniques based on geometric projections such as parallel coordinates and star graph;
- Visualization techniques based on icons or iconographic, such as Chernoff faces;
- Pixel-oriented visualization techniques, such as Circle Segments;
- Hierarchical techniques, such as dendrogram, cone trees and cam trees.

4   Data Mining Tools Analyzed

The tools selected for evaluation in this study are briefly described ahead. For each one, we first identified the available clustering techniques and cluster visualization methods. Knime [10] is a tool proposed for use in data mining, statistics and other areas. It has several methods that enable full knowledge extraction of a particular database. All the operation of Knime is based on the idea of adding method nodes to an execution workflow. Figure 1 shows Knime screen. In the upper left corner, the user can see the available methods. In the center, there is a window where the execution workflow is defined. In the bottom, the results are shown in textual format in a window. Some features are not explicitly presented, which can hinder their use. For k-means, Knime presents only the description of the centroids as textual output, with values that each feature and how many standards this centroid comprises.

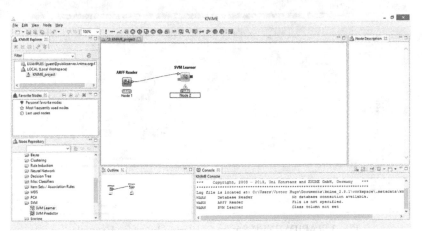

Fig. 1. KNIME Clustering Interface Example

Orange Canvas [11] is an open source tool for data mining with a focus on data classification, data regression and visual data mining. It also has data evaluation and data binding methods. The execution workflow of the tool is simple. Figure 2 shows Orange Canvas screen. As knime, it presents the structure of nodes, where each node added to the workflow canvas will perform a certain task. It also features a feedback system for each method, showing the input and output of each method.

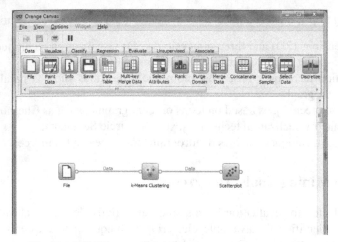

Fig. 2. ORANGE CANVAS Clustering Interface Example

RapidMiner Studio [12] is a data mining tool also focused on statistical, database and data analysis processes. It is a proprietary tool but there is also a trial version. Its main purpose is to provide a fully graphical desktop environment, with graphic elements that represent an operation of interest, for example, a data mining method. Figure 3 shows RapidMiner screen. The tool has a very intuitive execution workflow, where nodes represent a particular process. The output is textual, showing the number of groups formed and how these patterns are formed, and also a data table.

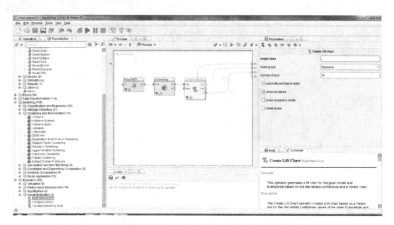

Fig. 3. RAPIDMINER Studio Clustering Interface Example

Weka [13] is an open source collection of machine learning algorithms for data mining tasks that contains tools for data pre-processing, classification, regression, clustering, association rules, and visualization. As a result of the execution of the k-means method, Weka shows the number of the iteration, the sum of the squared error within groups and the centroids formed. Weka technique of dispersion chart of does not show the data dispersion of a particular group, but the data dispersion according to one of its features depending on the group it belongs. Figure 4 shows Weka screen.

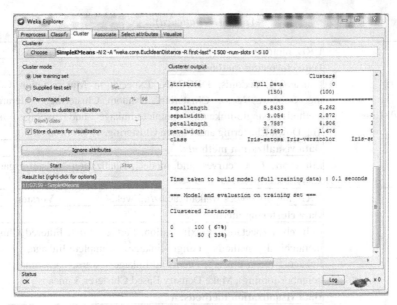

Fig. 4. WEKA Clustering Interface Example

Table 1 shows the clustering methods and data visualization available in the evaluated tools. It is noteworthy that in the evaluation and accounting of the number of methods available, only basic methods were considered. For example, k-means variants present in some tools, such as fast k-means, were not counted as another data clustering method. For the hierarchical methods, each connection was not considered as a method, but the presence of the function was, since the hierarchical links were regarded as execution parameters in all tools.

Table 1. Data mining tools and methods of data clustering and data mining

Tool	Characteristics	
Knime	**URL**: http://www.knime.org/	**Version**: 2.7.2
	Data clustering methods: 5	
	Fuzzy c-Means, hierarchical methods (single-linkage, complete-linkage and average-linkage), SOTA – (Self Organizing Tree Algorithm), Learner e Predictor and k-means.	
	Data visualization methods: 8	
	Box plot, histogram, lift chart, line plot, parallel coordinates, pie chart, scatter plot matrix and dispersion chart.	
Orange Canvas	**URL**: http://orange.biolab.si/	**Version** : 2.6.1
	Data clustering methods: 2	
	k-means, hierarchical methods (single-linkage, complete-linkage, average-linkage and ward) .	
	Data visualization methods: 12	
	frequencies distribution, box plot, general dispersion, linear projection, radviz, polyviz, parallel coordinates , survey plot, correlation analysis, mosaic display, sieve diagram, sieve multigram.	

Table 1. (*continued*)

RapidMiner	**URL**: rapidminer.com/products/rapidminer-studio/ **Version** : 5.3.015
	Data clustering methods: 9
	k-means, k-medoids, DBSCAN, Expectation Maximization Clustering, Support Vector Clustering, Random Clustering, hierarchical methods (single-linkage, complete-linkage and average-linkage), Top Down Clustering and Flatten Clustering.
	Data visualization methods: 3
	Lift chart, ROC curves and model visualization by self-organizing maps.
Weka	**URL**: http://www.cs.waikato.ac.nz/ml/weka/ **Version** : 3.7.8
	Data clustering methods: 7
	Cobweb, Expectation Maximization, Farthest First, Filtered Clusterer, hierarchical methods (single-linkage, complete-linkage, average-linkage, mean-linkage, centroid-linkage, ward, adjcomplete and neighbor-joining), Make Density Based Clusterer, k-means.
	Data visualization methods: 4
	Histogram, dispersion chart, scatter matrix and tree visualization.

5   HCI Evaluations

In order to evaluate how easy a user can learn to use each of these tools, we performed an evaluation by inspection using the cognitive walkthrough method [14], an IHC evaluation method whose primary purpose is to evaluate the ease of learning of an interactive system through the usage of its interface. As such, we developed a real use scenario, based on which usability tests were performed by a group of users.

The users' profile we defined for this inspection comprised IT professionals or students, who have interest in performing data mining tasks and already have at least a minimal prior contact with such area. Two different types of users performed the usability tests: (i) six graduate and undergraduate computer science students that attended data mining classes; (ii) five lecturers in the area of artificial intelligence, data mining or, statistics. For each tool, each user should execute the following steps:

1. Load a test file ("Iris.arff", obtained from [15])
2. Select, as the task to be performed, data clustering using k-means with $k = 3$;
3. Execute the data clustering operation;
4. Visualize the results.

After executing these tasks, the users answered questionnaires, providing data on their experience about using these tools. The questions, enumerated as follows, were formulated to assess the user profile (1 and 2), the organization of the tool's interfaces (3 to 6) and the usability and user's interaction with the tool (7 to 10).

1. How do you rate your knowledge on data mining?
2. How long have you used these systems?
3. The information available in the system's interface is well distributed, so as to contribute to the user's learning and memorizing?
4. The icons and control commands are well detached from other interface items?
5. Does the system's interface describes the task options offered, i.e., given a particular icon or menu, is there a brief specification of its functionality?
6. In the error messages, the help button is available?
7. This system is easy to use ?
8. Did you have some sort of difficulty in finding the information necessary to perform the requested tasks?
9. How do you evaluate the presentation of the data clustering results?
10. Did the available data visualization techniques help in the interpretation of the generated clusters?

5.1   General Overview

In order to execute the tasks included in the usability test, the user must identify the buttons or menu options for (a) specifying the path and name of the input file and loading the data; (b) selecting the k-means method, setting the necessary parameters and executing it; (c) selecting visualization methods and creating charts.

Although the pathways to accomplish the actions are different in each tool, we can conclude that the user will try to achieve the right outcome, since he knows the theoretical aspects of the implemented methods in order to perform the parameter settings. He must as well know the contents of the database to be analyzed, to be able to perform a semantic verification of the results obtained.

Moreover, among the tools there are particularities of interaction. In Knime or RapidMiner Studio, for example, the user needs to know in which category is classified each item he needs to perform the desired task. Each item/node (such as, loading database, clustering method and visualization method) is divided into subcategories, which should be known by the user. In such cases, the experience with any other tool or even some data mining theoretical knowledge will help the user to make an association between the interface elements and his objective.

In Weka, for action to open/load the database may get errors in identifying the tool component. For example, in some places, the component is called "ARFF Reader" and in others, it is available as "FILE". The idea that this component can also open/load a file with extension "ARFF" is implicit. Also on Weka, for choosing a data clustering or data visualization method, the user must know which methods to use and in which part of the tool interface he can find the desired items.

If the user does not know a priori the workflow necessary for carrying out his data mining tasks, he must learn while performing his activities. In Knime, RapidMiner Studio and Orange Canvas, the user is allowed to interact with the tool to build a workflow even when a node is being wrongly defined. These tools issue a warning to the user about the error only at the end, when he tries to execute the data mining process workflow. This behavior causes the user to lose time in his interaction with the tool, probably forcing the user to rebuild his workflow, entirely or in part, for not knowing exactly where the error occurred. A possible solution for this problem would be having the tool verifying the workflow node by node, while the user is building it, in order to identify possible errors and show alerts to the user as soon as possible.

5.2   Results Analysis

The usability test aims to assess how easily the user understands the usage of each selected interacting with its interface. The objectives of the usability test were defined and presented to the users, who, using the tools, should try to reach them. The users were divided in a group of lecturers, with a better understanding of data mining and greater experience with the tools, and a group of students with only basic knowledge, as depicted on Figure 5. The charts show that most users are well acquainted to Weka, while many never used Knime or Orange Canvas.

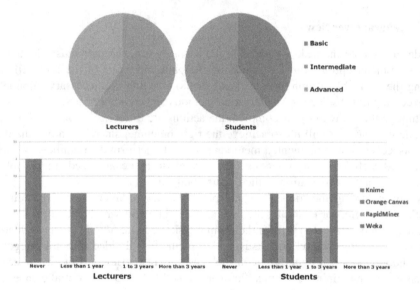

Fig. 5. Charts representing the level of expertise (top) and familiarity with the tools (bottom) of the two different user groups

Regarding the interface, both groups of users thought that the tools have the information well distributed, with the icons are well detached, what contributes to an easy understanding of the interaction process, as depicted in Figure 6 (a). Except for RapidMiner Studio, that has not been positively evaluated by the group of students with regard to this aspect. The reason may be that the set of objects needed to perform a task is large and complexly organized, requiring prior knowledge about these features, which was only found in the group of lecturers.

Orange Canvas and RapidMiner were poorly evaluated by the lecturer with regard to the description of the tasks offered by the interface, i.e., such users considered that the interface of those tools tools did not provide enough explanation on the functionalities provided, as depicted in Figure 6 (c). The tools also had poor rating with respect to the descriptions of the elements contained in the interface and help options, as depicted in Figure 6 (d).

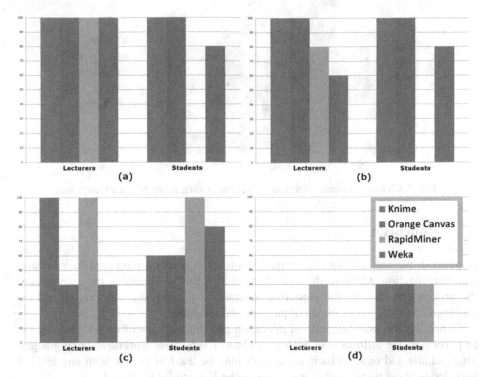

Fig. 6. Charts representing the proportion of users that evaluate positively the distribution of information in the interface (a), the emphasis in icons and commands in the interface (b), the description of the tasks offered by the interface (c), the availability of error messages (d)

According to the students, the Knime is the tool that presents the interface in which is easier to find information and the desired elements, while RapidMiner was the most negatively evaluated by this group, as depicted in Figure 7 (a). Among the group of lecturers, Weka was considered the best one, probably because in general all those users had great familiarity with the tool, as indicated in Figure 5.

As to the presentation of the data clustering results, Knime got the worst evaluation reported by the group of lecturers, but a good result among the students, as depicted in Figure 7. Using colors and providing the confusion matrix for presentation, were some of the improvement suggestions cited by the evaluators. On the other hand, Orange got a great result according to the students, while the lecturers found the per-formance the performance of the tool for visualizing the results is satisfactory. This is probably due to ease of visualization of the results provided by the tool, but that are somehow superficial. The other tools had a regular a performance.

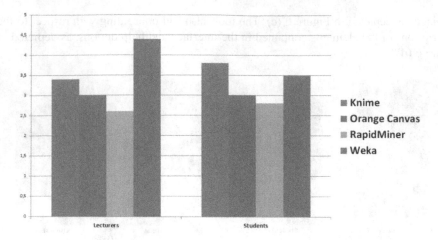

Fig. 7. Charts representing the user's average evaluation on how easy each tool

6   Conclusion

In general, we noticed that the analyzed tools have a very strong approach towards data visualization. Many of the tools discussed in this work enable the user to view the groups generated by the clustering methods, understanding, interpreting and extracting knowledge about the set of patterns and clusters.

Generally, the usability, ease of operation and the methods of each tool are good. In particular, the utilization of each tool, show a very clear workflow, having beginning, middle and end. As such, these tools may be used by people with any level of knowledge about them, or even about the methods provided by these tools.

We believe that the interdisciplinary integration of KDD and HCI may bring some significant contributions, such as improving the user's ability to gain useful knowledge from organizational databases and helping the end users to gain added values by making date useable and useful. However, the tools analyzed show that still several other HCI aspects need to be thoroughly approached.

References

1. Fayyad, U.M., Piatetsky-Shapiro, G., Smyth, P., Uthrusamy, R.: Advances in knowledge Discovery & Data Mining, California (1996)
2. Jain, A.K.: Data clustering: 50 years beyond K-means. Pattern Recognition Letters 31(8), 651–666 (2010)
3. Cormack, R.M.: A Review of Classifications. JRSS, A 134, 321–367 (1971)
4. Everitt, B.S., Landau, S., Morven, L.: Cluster Analysis, 4th edn. Hodder Arnold Publishers, Londres (2001)
5. Macqueen, J.B.: Some Methods for classification and Analysis of Multivariate Observations. In: Proceedings of 5th Berkeley Symposium on Mathematical Statistics and Probability, California (1967)

6. Wong, P.C.: Visual Data Mining. In: IEEE Computer Graphics and Applications, Los Alamitos (1999)
7. Ball, G., Hall, D.: ISODATA, a novel method of data anlysis and pattern classification. Technical report NTIS AD 699616. Stanford Research Institute, Stanford, CA (1965)
8. Steinhaus, H.: Sur la division des corp materiels en parties. Bull. Acad. Polon. Sci. IV(C1.III), 801–804 (1956)
9. Keim, D., Ward, M.: Visual Data Mining Techniques. Intelligent Data Analysis: An Introduction. University of Konstanz, Worcester Polytechnic Institute, USA (2002)
10. KNIME, Site Oficial da Ferramenta KNIME (2013), http://www.knime.org/ (Acesso September 25, 2013)
11. CANVAS, Site Oficial da Ferramenta ORANGE CANVAS (September 09, 2013), http://orange.biolab.si/ (acesso September 25, 2013)
12. RAPIDMINER, Site Oficial da Ferramenta RAPIDMINER STUDIO (2013), http://rapidminer.com/products/rapidminer-studio/ (acesso November 17, 2013)
13. WEKA, Waikato Environment for Knowledge Analysis (2013), http://www.cs.waikato.ac.nz/ml/weka/ (acesso September 25, 2013)
14. Whartonm, C., Rieman, J., Lewis, C., Poison, P.: The Cognitive Walkthrough Method: A Practitioner's Guide. Usability Inspection Methods, New York (1994)
15. Bache, K., Lichman, M.: UCI Machine Learning Repository. University of California, School of Information and Computer Science, Irvine (2013)
16. Keim, D.A., Kriegel, H.: Visualization Techniques for Mining Large Databases: A Comparison. IEEE Trans. Knowledge & Data Engineering, 923–936 (1996)
17. Keim, D.A., Kriegel, H.P.: VisDB: Database Exploration using Multidimensional Visualization. IEEE Computer Graphics and Applications (1994)
18. Keim, D.A.: Information Visualization and Visual Data Mining. IEEE Transactions on Visualization and Computers Graphics 8, 1–8 (2002)

A Post-simulation Assessment Tool for Training of Air Traffic Controllers

Aslak Wegner Eide, Stian Støer Ødegård, and Amela Karahasanović

SINTEF, Oslo, Norway
{aslak.eide,amela.karahasanovic}@sintef.no,
stiancid@outlook.com

Abstract. This paper proposes a post-simulation assessment tool that aims to improve the training of air traffic controllers (ATCOs) by visualizing their performance. The tool helps the controllers to identify bottlenecks in flight traffic and find alternative solutions that might improve traffic throughput. The usefulness of the tool was evaluated in a study involving benchmark tests and interviews with five experienced ATCOs. The results from the study indicate that the tool can help ATCO students to (1) identify irregularities in their work, (2) find possible underlying causes of these irregularities, and (3) find alternative solutions preventing these irregularities. Visual feedback consisting of workflow graphs and radar replays might generate valuable insights that enable self and peer assessment during ATCO training. Our results might be interesting both for the practitioners working with ATCO training and for researcher investigating the effects of visualization in education.

Keywords: visualization, air traffic control, training, real-time simulation.

1   Introduction

The continuously growing demand in air transport has heightened the need to improve productivity in air traffic control. Coping with this challenge requires not only new automation tools and enhanced procedures, but also a rethinking of air traffic controllers (ATCOs) training [1-2]. In order to achieve the required learning effects, existing training programs need to integrate hands-on training with knowledge acquisition and skill development [3]. Training should not only teach users how new tools should be used, but also help overcome resistance to change.

In today's practice, real-time simulation (RTS) of work scenarios is regularly used as a cost-effective way of training new and experienced ATCOs. One of the great advantages of RTS, compared with other learning aids, is the ability to freeze and replay scenarios directly, enabling instructors to provide timely feedback on a given traffic situation and on the quality of the decisions made by the trainee [4]. However, the delivery of such feedback requires the full attention of an instructor, and may also cause disruptions in the internal planning process of the trainees, making it difficult for them to progress and positively reinforce their learned skills [5]. Furthermore, shortage of time, inadequacy of the feedback, fear of failure, and negative environments might also cause problems during the ATCOs training [5].

S. Yamamoto (Ed.): HIMI 2014, Part I, LNCS 8521, pp. 34–43, 2014.

In light of the abovementioned challenges, this paper proposes a post-simulation assessment tool that aims to improve the training of ATCOs by allowing them to review their own work, and the work of others, without the need for an instructor to be present. The tool achieves this by providing visual feedback that help ATCOs identify bottlenecks in their work and alternative solutions that could result in higher traffic throughput. Our study positions the tool as a useful supplement to RTS, which can help mitigate the challenge of obtrusive feedback during ATCO training.

The training tool is described in Section 2, followed in Section 3 by a description of the study conducted to evaluate the tool. The results from the study are presented in Section 4. A discussion of the results in the context of current research is given in Section 5. The final conclusions of the paper are given in Section 6.

2   Post-simulation Training Tool

To improve ATCO training, we developed a post-simulation assessment tool that help ATCOs review their workflow and performance immediately following an RTS. The tool was developed through an iterative and user-centered design process involving requirements engineering, prototyping, and end-user evaluations. Throughout this process, the tool evolved from paper-based prototypes, into the functional software application presented here. The final version of the tool consists of 3 components: (i) a workflow graph, (ii) a radar image, and (iii) a set of timeline controls (see Fig. 1). The workflow graph shows the flights that the ATCOs handled during the simulation, distributed along a global timeline. Each flight is visualized by a bar in the graph.

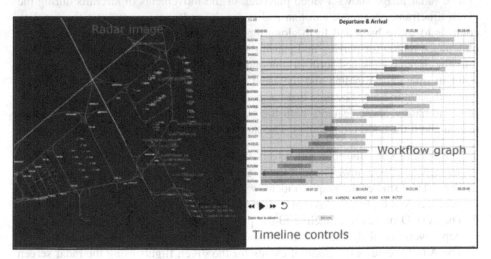

Fig. 1. Overview of the training tool

For departing flights, the bar runs from the point in time when the flight first requested departure clearance, to the point in time when the flight is no longer touching the runway (see Fig. 2). The end of the black horizontal line shows the calculated take-off time (CTOT) of departing flights, which is the point in time when the flight should (according to the flight plan) leave the runway. For arriving flights, the bar runs from the point in time when the flight was given clearance to land, to the point in time when the flight has arrived at gate (see Fig. 3). The bar is divided into blocks with different coloring, depending on which controller managed the flight at the time. In a control tower, responsibilities are often divided among the following roles: Clearance Delivery (CDC), Apron (APRON1 and APRON2 in our case), Ground, and Tower.

Fig. 2. Visualization of a departing flight in the workflow graph: The bar should be read from left to right. The colored blocks in the bar show which controller that managed the flight at the given time periods. The first (leftmost) block represents the timespan when the flight was managed by the CDC controller. Block two, three and four represents the timespans when the flight was managed by the APRON2 controller, the GROUND controller and the TOWER controller.

Fig. 3. Visualization of an arriving flight: The bar should be read from left to right. The colored blocks in the bar show which controller that managed the flight at the given time periods. The first (leftmost) block represents the timespan when the flight was managed by the TOWER controller. Respectively, block two and three represents the timespans when the flight was managed by the GROUND controller and the APRON1 controller.

The radar image shows a video playback of the movements of aircrafts during the given timeframe. A trainee can pan and zoom the radar image, and use the timeline controls to move back and forth along the timeline. The timeline controls include a play/pause button for playing and pausing the time, fast forward and fast rewind buttons for moving back and forth in time, and a numeric field for jumping to an exact point in time. The timeline and the radar screen are synchronized according to the selected point in time. The time that has passed is colored gray in the workflow graph. In combination, these features help the trainee to identify non-optimal flights, and reason about the underlying causes. The standard use-case of the tool is given below:

1. The ATCO starts the tool and selects the training simulation or the work period he/she wants to review. The tool shows the corresponding graph and radar image.
2. The ATCO studies the graph to identify bottlenecks and potential for improvement (e.g., delayed flights, flights that waited too long to get departure clearance).
3. The ATCO moves the timeline to the point in time when the flights identified in step 2 were handled. The radar image shows the airport state at the time.
4. The ATCO reviews the chain of events for the given flights using the radar screen image and the graph, and tries to understand the causes of the irregularities.
5. The ATCO identifies the causes of the irregularities, and tries to come up with an alternative solution for how the irregularity could have been avoided.

3   Research Method

The usefulness of the training tool was assessed in a study at Gardermoen airport tower. The study made use of individual benchmark testing [6] where participants used the training tool to review a flight traffic scenario from Hamburg airport, and open-ended interviews. A sample of five experienced ATCOs took part in the study, selected by means of convenience sampling [7]. The participants differed somewhat in their level of experience. Three participants were certified ATCOs at Gardermoen tower and two participants were currently undergoing training to achieve such certification. All participants were experienced ATCOs, with working experience ranging from 7 to 14 years (median 10). The study lasted approximately 35 minutes per participant and consisted of three parts that were conducted individually for each participant. In the first part we introduced the participant to the training tool, explaining its purpose and functionality. The participant was also given an introduction to the airport layout in the scenario that was to be used during the benchmark testing, and was given an explanation of which position is responsible for which area at this airport.

In the second part, the participant was seated in front of a computer running the high fidelity prototype of the training tool, loaded with the predefined scenario from an earlier RTS training session involving Hamburg airport. As soon as the participant was ready, he/she was then asked to solve a set of predefined benchmark tasks by using the training tool (see Table 1 for an overview of the tasks). The benchmark tasks were designed to assess the tool's ability to generate insight, enabling ATCOs to identify non-optimal flights and reason about them. Due to the complexity of the scenario, there were several correct answers for the second and third task. For data collection we used the think-aloud protocol [8]. The participants were encouraged to say what they were looking at, thinking, doing, and feeling. This was audio recorded. In addition, we collected screen captures and observer notes.

Table 1. Overview of benchmark tasks

#	Benchmark task	Expected solution
1	Find the flight with the largest delay.	The flight with the largest delay was flight DLH8UV (we refer to a flight by using its unique flight identifier number). This task had only one correct answer.
2	Find a possible cause for the delay of this flight.	One main cause of the delay was that flight DLH4WA was given departure clearance before flight DLH8UV (even though DLH4WA had a later CTOT than DLH8UV), causing DLH8UV to have to wait in line behind DLH4WA.
3	Find an alternative solution where this delay could have been avoided.	One main alternative solution was to prioritize flight DLH8UV before flight DLH4WA, and thus allow DLH8UV to take off before DLH4WA.

The last part of the study consisted of individual interviews with each participant. During the interviews, the participant was asked open-ended questions designed to trigger subjective reflection on the usefulness of the tool, particularly in terms of its ability to facilitate learning in tower control rooms. The participant was also encouraged to come up with suggestions for tool improvement, and was asked about his/her experience with similar tools. The interviews were also recorded by audio.

To assess whether the training tool was capable of generating valuable insight, we analyzed the correctness of the solutions that the participants gave to each of the three benchmark tasks. We transcribed the audio recordings from the think-aloud protocol and registered the participants' interactions with the training tool by replaying the screen capture recordings. The transcriptions and interactions of each participant were then sorted chronologically in a spreadsheet, allowing the researchers to take both the thoughts and the interactions of the participants into account when assessing their solutions to benchmark tasks. For the first task, which only had one correct solution, the participants' solutions were compared with the correct solution. For the second and third task, which had several possible solutions, the researchers judged the correctness of the solution.

The spreadsheet containing transcriptions and interactions was also used to determine which strategies the users made use of to solve the various benchmark tasks. This was achieved by comparing the participants' interactions with the tool during each of the benchmark tasks, while looking for patterns in their style of interactions.

The audio recordings from the interviews were transcribed. The researchers then summarized the answers from the participants for each interview question.

4   Results

The results from the study indicates that the proposed training tool helped the participating ATCOs to identify non-optimal flights, to reason about possible underlying causes, and to find alternative solutions. The detailed results from the benchmark tests and the interviews are described in the sections below.

4.1   Benchmark Tests

Figure 4 gives a summary of the benchmark results, showing the number of plausible solutions identified by each single participant for each of the three benchmark tasks. Due to a corrupted screen-capture recording for participant 3 that could not be replayed, we were unable to adequately interpret his proposed solutions to tasks 2 and 3, forcing us to omit these data from the results, and from the overview in Figure 4.

As shown in Figure 4, all five participants managed to find the correct answer to the first benchmark task (identification of the flight with the largest delay). The participants seemed certain in their assessment during this task, and did not come up with more than one solution each. The users' approach for solving the task was to use the workflow graph to identify the flight with the longest visual distance between the actual take-off time (ATOT) and the CTOT. The users did not use the radar image or timeline controls for solving this task.

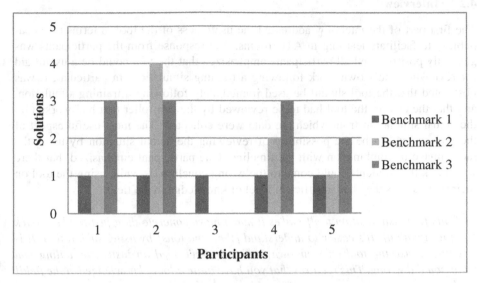

Fig. 4. Frequency of identified solutions per participant

In the second benchmark task, the participants were to find a possible cause for the delay identified in the first task. Excluding participant 3, whose dataset was omitted from the results, all participants managed to come up with a plausible solution for this task. Two of the participants identified more than one possible solution (see Fig. 4). The typical approach for solving the task was to fast forward the radar image to the point in time where the delayed flight was handled and then review the flight's progression from gate to runway. During this process, the participants often used the workflow graph in combination with the radar image to keep track of which controller was handling the flight at any given point in time. Although the participants managed to come up with plausible explanations, they emphasized that there were several possible causes of the delay, and that they were uncertain with respect to the validity of their answers. One participant postulated that he could not establish a solid explanation for the delay based solely on the information in the tool.

In the third benchmark task, the participants were to find an alternative solution for the situation causing the delay of the flight in the first task. Again excluding participant 3, all participants managed to find more than one plausible solution. The participants' approach for solving the task was to replay the flight's progression from gate to runway using the timeline controls, and to identify flights in the graph that were given departure clearance before the delayed flight, despite having a later CTOT. The participants also studied the route taken by the delayed flight, looking for points where it could sneak in before other flights. In similarity with the second task, the participants emphasized that there were several possible solutions, and that their suggestions were only speculations.

4.2   Interviews

The first part of the interview addressed the usefulness of the tool in terms of its capability to facilitate learning in ATC rooms. The response from the participants was generally positive, and all participants emphasized that the tool could be a useful aid for reviewing one's own work following a training simulation. In particular, it was postulated that the tool should be used immediately following a training simulation, and that the data in the tool had to be reviewed by the controller that had worked on the actual simulation from which the data were collected. The most useful aspect of the tool seemed to be the possibility of reviewing the actual situation by using the radar image in combination with the timeline. One participant emphasized that there was a risk that students could come to the wrong conclusions while using the tool on their own, unless they had a sufficient level of knowledge in the field:

"This [the visualization tool] makes it much more concrete than just thinking back [on the situation]. It's easier to understand [the situations] by using such a tool. It is possible to use the tool on your own, and you don't need an instructor telling you what you did wrong. This requires that you have quite a lot of knowledge [in the field] so that you don't create a source of error in yourself..."

During the interview the participants were also asked if there was any additional information and/or functionality that should be available in the tool in order to enhance learning. Several participants suggested that the radar image should be supplemented with audio playback of the communication between ATCOs, and between ATCOs and pilots. This would give the users a better understanding of how the controllers were reasoning, and an opportunity for the users to assess the clarity of their own commands. Furthermore, the participants also suggested that the radar image should display other traffic in the airport (e.g. ground vehicles, fire trucks, luggage trains), as well as more detailed information about the flights. Another highlighted issue was that the general quality of the radar image needed to be improved so that users can make out fine details, such as airplane codes and statuses. The icons on the radar screen should be color coded according to the graph so that they are easier to locate in order to see which ATCO responsibility area they are in.

When asked to reflect upon how well they managed to solve the given tasks, several participants made it clear that the tool was completely new for them, and that this affected their ability to make efficient use of it. They would need more time to get to know the tool before they could use it in an efficient manner. Several participants also emphasized that they had not seen any system similar to the visualization tool in their line of work, and that the tool would mostly be useful for students. A quote exemplifying this is included below.

"Not of this type. We do runs in a simulator where we can freeze the situation, but we cannot rewind. I think it can be used, but I don't know how actively. When you have worked for a while you have accumulated routines so that you know what you have done wrong independently of this tool. The tool will be most useful for students."

5   Discussion

All the participants in our study managed to find possible solutions to the three given benchmark tasks although they had no earlier knowledge of the traffic patterns and layout of the airport in the given scenario. In general, these findings suggest that the tool is capable of generating insight that can enable ATCO students to identify bottlenecks and potential for improvement in their work. However, due to the limited size of the study, both in terms of the number of participants and the time they spent using the tool, the results should be treated cautiously. Further research is needed to investigate the effects of this tool. An accurate measure of the tool's impact on learning quality would require longitudinal, continuous, and comparable studies, as suggested by earlier studies [9-11]. More studies are needed to explore the effects of different visualizations and to fine-tune the tool.

Although the participants were positive towards using this tool in training, they also mentioned the possibility of misuse. To reduce the possibility that users would come to the wrong conclusions while using this type of tool, they would need to have a certain level of knowledge in the field of ATC. Other studies, such as [12], have indeed shown that students with domain knowledge gained more from certain visualizations than students lacking that knowledge. This might seem obvious, but it also highlights the point that users must know what they are looking for in order to understand and make sense of the information that is presented in visualizations [13]. With regards to this, it is clear that the tool should not be used as a replacement for normal classroom lectures, but rather as a supplemental learning aid.

Several RTS facilities have the ability to freeze and replay simulation scenarios [4]. The training tool proposed in this paper extends this functionality by providing a workflow graph that helps students assess where errors have been made, as well as a timeline for navigating back and forth in the simulated scenario. The tool is also different from a regular simulator by not being restricted to a classroom setting. Students could use the tool to review simulations individually, and an instructor could give training tasks that the students could solve on their own time. The individual solutions could then be presented and compared in group discussions, allowing the instructor to provide feedback in a less obtrusive manner. As a result, one could avoid the disruptions of the internal cognitive processes of the trainees which are often observed during traditional RTS training [5]. Further, as the tool does not require the presence of an instructor or access to RTS facilities, it could also save resources in terms of cost and time.

Another suggestion is to use the tool in a collaborative way by allowing students to compare and discuss the performance of their individual solutions. By introducing such game-like elements in a student environment, one could increase the students' interest in using the tool [14-15] and in turn increase the time they spend on learning.

6   Conclusion

In this paper we have proposed and evaluated a post-simulation assessment tool that aims to improve the training of ATCOs. The results from the study indicate that visual feedback consisting of interactive workflow graphs and radar replays can be a useful means to support self and peer assessment during ATCO training. By adopting such assessment techniques in the training process, one could expect significant enhancements in the learning quality [16-17], and also help mitigate the known challenge of obtrusive instructor feedback during RTS training. Such enhancements will be increasingly important during the forthcoming modernization of the ATM industry introduced by the SESAR and NextGen programs [18-19]. The findings may also be relevant for other domains where RTS is used for training purposes, such as the fields of emergency and crisis management, defense, and health care.

Acknowledgments. This work is co-financed by EUROCONTROL acting on behalf of the SESAR Joint Undertaking (the SJU) and the EUROPEAN UNION as part of Work Package E in the SESAR Programme. Opinions expressed in this work reflect the authors' views only, and EUROCONTROL and/or the SJU shall not be considered liable for them or for any use that may be made of the information contained herein. The authors are particularly grateful to the controllers that participated in the study, for their valuable input and great effort. We also thank Prof. Carl-Herbert Rokitansky and Thomas Gräupl from the University of Salzburg for providing us with realistic simulation data.

References

1. Battiste, H., Choi, W., Mirchi, T., Sanchez, K., Vu, K.-P.L., Chiappe, D., Strybel, T.Z.: The effects of early training with automation tools on the air traffic management strategies of student ATCOs. In: Yamamoto, S. (ed.) HIMI/HCII 2013, Part II. LNCS, vol. 8017, pp. 13–21. Springer, Heidelberg (2013)
2. Higham, T.M., Vu, K.-P.L., Miles, J., Strybel, T.Z., Battiste, V.: Training air traffic controller trust in automation within a nextgen environment. In: Yamamoto, S. (ed.) HIMI/HCII 2013, Part II. LNCS, vol. 8017, pp. 76–84. Springer, Heidelberg (2013)
3. Fisher, S.G., Kulick, I.: Air traffic controller training: A new model. In: Smolensky, M.W., Stein, E.S. (eds.) Human Factors in Air Traffic Control, 1st edn., pp. 273–298. Academic Press, United States of America (1998)
4. Hitchcock, L.: Air traffic control simulation: Capabilities. In: Smolensky, M.W., Stein, E.S. (eds.) Human Factors in Air Traffic Control, 1st edn., pp. 327–340. Academic Press, United States of America (1998)
5. Voller, L., Fowler, A.: Human Factors Longitudinal Study to Support the Improvement of Air Traffic Controller Training. In: Kirwan, B., Rodgers, M., Schäfer, D. (eds.) Human Factors Impacts in Air Traffic Management. Ashgate Publishing Limited, England (2005)
6. North, C.: Toward measuring visualization insight. IEEE Comput. Graph. Appl. 26(3), 6–9 (2006)
7. Weiss, R.S.: Learning from Strangers, 1st paperback edn. The Free Press (1995)

8. Lewis, C.: Using the "thinking-aloud" method in cognitive interface design. IBM TJ Watson Research Center (1982)
9. Saraiya, P., North, C., Lam, V., Duca, K.A.: An insight-based longitudinal study of visual analytics. IEEE Transactions on Visualization and Computer Graphics 12(6), 1511–1522 (2006)
10. Shneiderman, B., Plaisant, C.: Strategies for evaluating information visualization tools: multi-dimensional in-depth long-term case studies. In: Proceedings of the 2006 AVI Workshop on Beyond Time and Errors: Novel Evaluation Methods for Information Visualization, pp. 1–7. ACM (2006)
11. Isenberg, P., Zuk, T., Collins, C., Carpendale, S.: Grounded evaluation of information visualizations. In: Proceedings of the 2008 Workshop on Beyond Time and Errors: Novel Evaluation Methods for Information Visualization, p. 6. ACM (2008)
12. Sarayia, P., North, C., Duca, K.: An insight-based methodology for evaluating bioinformatics visualizations. IEEE Transactions on Visualization and Computer Graphics 11, 443–456 (2005)
13. Wills, G.: Visualizing time. Springer (2012)
14. Groh, F.: Gamification: State of the Art Definition and Utilization. In: Proceedings of the 4th Seminar on Research Trends in Media Informatics (RCMI 2012), pp. 39–46 (2012)
15. Zichermann, G., Cunningham, C.: Gamification by Design: Implementing Game Mechanics in Web and Mobile Apps. O'Reilly, Sebastopol (2011)
16. Race, P.: A briefing on self, peer & group assessment, vol. 9. Learning and Teaching Support Network, York (2001)
17. Boud, D., Falchikov, N.: Rethinking Assessment in Higher Education Learning for the Longer Term. Routledge (2007)
18. Sesar Joint Undertaking, http://www.sesarju.eu/about/background
19. NextGen, http://www.faa.gov/news/fact_sheets/news_story.cfm?newsid=8145

Label Embedded Treemapping: A Label Overlap Prevention Technique for Zoomable Treemaps and a User Interaction Technique

KwangHyuk Kim[1,2] and JungHyun Han[2]

[1] Samsung Electronics Co Ltd, Korea
[2] Dept. of Computer and Radio Communications Engineering, Korea University, Seoul, Korea
kwanghyuk.a.kim@gmail.com

Abstract. Data navigation of a treemap—a widely used tool for visualizing tree data—becomes more difficult as the amount of data increases. To solve this problem, treemap techniques using zoomable user interface (ZUI) methods—the most typical of which is the zoomable treemap (ZTM)—have been proposed. However, ZTMs can incur face text overlapping issues between examined nodes. In order to increase ZTM readability, we propose a label embedded tree map technique that prevents label overlapping and a direct node selection method for the highlighting of focused parent nodes. The proposed tree map technique resolves the ZTM label conflict and the direct node selection method can efficiently improve data navigation.

Keywords: Visualization, Treemap, Zoomable, ZUI, Label, Overlapping.

1 Introduction

Two visualization techniques are commonly used to present tree data: node linking [1] and treemapping [2]. In node linking, hierarchical structures of data are represented as sets of nodes interconnected by lines, while treemapping is a space-partitioning method in which the screen space is divided into adjacent rectangles that represent data [3,4]. Whereas node linking does not fully use the screen space, treemapping can maximize space efficiency because the method displays nodes as a geological map-like structure. However, treemaps begin to incur perception problems [5] with increasing data size (Fig. 1), which makes navigation through larger treemaps more difficult. Various techniques have been proposed to solve the navigation problem, including the treemap partitioning algorithm, a technique that has produced exciting results and which has been the most popular area of research. However, the most typical partitioning method, known as slice-and-dice layout [1], can essentially only divide the screen vertically or horizontally, which results in rectangles (tiles) with aspect ratios that differ significantly from one, i.e., from a square shape. A proposed squarified layout technique [6] can produce tiles with more suitable aspect ratios but does not consider the ordering of the tiles; to do this, strip treemapping using a partitioning algorithm [7,8] has been suggested, but this method does not produce improved data navigation as the data size increases.

S. Yamamoto (Ed.): HIMI 2014, Part I, LNCS 8521, pp. 44–53, 2014.
© Springer International Publishing Switzerland 2014

Other approaches for improving data navigation involve the use of visualization effects. Cushion treemapping [9] uses a shading effect to improve the hierarchical perception of tree data and a color lens [10] to assign a unique color to the focused area, but again, this technique does not appear to provide a suitable navigation solution for large data sets.

Approaches utilizing the distortion effect have also been proposed. K. Shi et al. [11] suggested a distortion treemap in which the focused node is enlarged while surrounding nodes are reduced, and the balloon focus technique [12] extends the distortion effect to multiple focus nodes. Fish eye treemapping [13] involves the use of a lens effect in order to enlarge the focused area. Nevertheless, as these methods do not use the full screen area for the focused node, none of them can produce the most space efficient solutions.

Zoomable user interfaces (ZUIs) [14] can provide information progressively depending on the zoom level (tree level). A ZUI integrated treemap is a photo mesa [15] that extends specific regions of interest but cannot represent the hierarchical relationships between parents and children. The University of Maryland (UMD) treemap [16] represents hierarchical relationships by allocating separate spaces to label parent (or container) nodes and also extends the focal node to the full screen. However, because the layout changes when the zoom interaction ends, the UMD treemap does not produce smooth transition animation during zooming, making it necessary to use a separate layout algorithm to allocate the parent's label information. Although the zoomable treemap (ZTM) [17] overcomes the layout and transition animation problems of the UMD treemap, many of its labels will overlap owing to conflicts between leaf and upper side parent nodes (Fig. 2). In this paper, we present a novel treemapping technique that avoids overlapping between nodes as well as a user interaction technique that assures the direct node selection and smooth continuous treemap transition animation.

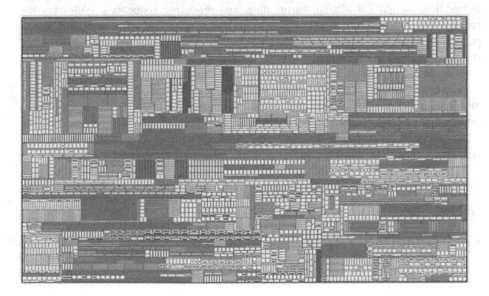

Fig. 1. Example of the treemap perception problem

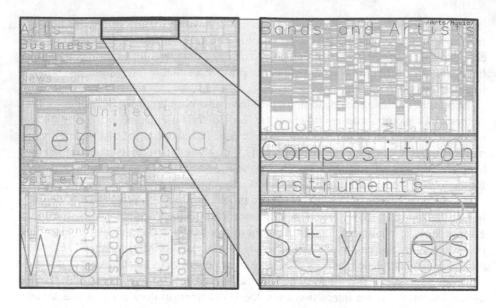

Fig. 2. Label overlapping problem using ZTM

2   Label Embedded Treemap

An initial concept and a prototype implementation of the label embedded technique were presented at a domestic conference [18]; a more accurate explanation of the proposed visualization process is shown in Fig. 3, which describes the parsing, label embedding, weight calculating, partitioning, and rendering sequences. Following the parsing stage, tree data are used to construct the tree structure, which is translated from a general structure into a label embedded tree in the label embedding stage. After a tree structure is constructed, weight value for the newly inserted node is calculated. The position of each rectangle in the treemap is set in the partitioning stage, and the nodes are rendered based on their hierarchical relationship by individually visiting the rectangles in the rendering stage. To construct the label embedded treemap, the treemap partitioning and rendering algorithm is used without modification. Through this mechanism, a label embedded tree can be automatically translated without modification into a label embedded treemap by using the partitioning mechanism of the treemap.

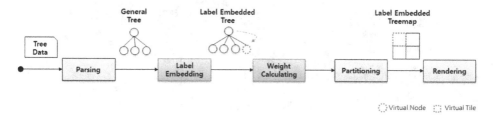

Fig. 3. Construction of a label embedded treemap

2.1   Tree Reconstruction

As parent nodes are placed into the treemap as leaf nodes without allocating specific spaces, a given parent node can neighbor its own child leaf nodes (Fig. 4). Each parent label node can be assigned to a treemap space without the use of an additional space allocation algorithm.

Because the parent nodes are inserted starting from the bottom of the tree structure, the label embedded tree is newly reconstructed from the general tree after each parent node insertion; however, this reconstruction causes no partitioning or rendering delay.

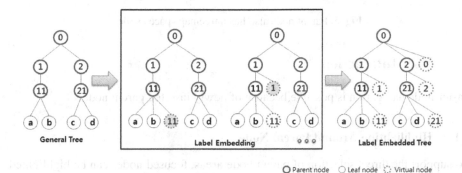

Fig. 4. Parent node insertion process

2.2   Calculating Weight Value of Parent's Label Node

As a newly inserted parent label node has no weight value, one must be generated following the label embedding process.

For a specific parent node has s children, let W_c represent the weight value of the k-th child, which can be formulated as the product of n, the number of leaf nodes contained by W_c, and α, a constant relating to the weight valence (formula (2)). The weight value for the parent node, W_p, is then the sum of all children nodes, which is calculated recursively using formula (1):

$$Wp = \sum_{c=1}^{s} Wc \qquad\qquad (1)$$

$$Wc = \alpha * n \qquad\qquad (2)$$

2.3   Partitioning Using Label Embedded Tree

After the label embedding, re-constructed tree structure is just used for partitioning process. As a result newly added label node is also get a separate treemap space. (Fig 5)

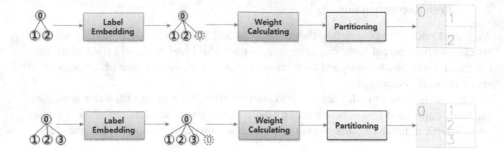

Fig. 5. Parent node also has a treemap space as tile

3   User Interaction

Faster node navigation is possible because of newly inserted parent node.

3.1   Highlighting Around Parent Node

To support the direct selection of parent node areas, focused nodes can be highlighted (Fig. 6). If a selected node is a label node corresponding to a parent, a focus line is formed around the area including the parent node, which helps the user to better understand the area being navigated.

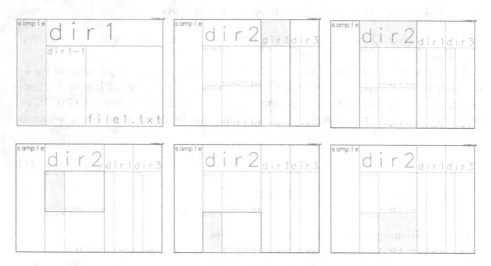

Fig. 6. Focused area is sized according to the focused node's children tree

3.2   Direct Node Selection and Smooth Animation Transition

After a node is selected, the selected area is expanded to full screen, as shown in Fig. 7. The zooming operation used to implement this process is completely consistent, causes no layout changes, and supports move rover animated transitions; essentially, this operation supports the same level of user interactivity as ZTM.

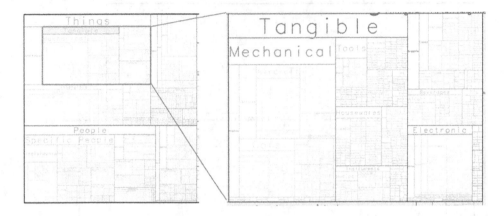

Fig. 7. Zoomed view corresponding to highlighted area

4   Evaluation

To confirm that our technique works correctly, we developed and tested an implementation of the proposed label embedded treemapping method using ZTM. We determined that we could generate label embedded trees that, following partitioning, could successfully function as label embedded treemaps for which rendered results could be generated. The transition animation process used for zooming was, of course, nearly identical to that used in ZTM, as it employed the same zooming operation based on the treemap structure. Finally, we confirmed that the focused node highlighting process functioned smoothly, making the process of direct node selection using highlighted focused label nodes quite useful for smooth treemap navigation.

A simple dataset containing three hierarchical nodes was rendered to produce a single leaf node, as shown in Fig. 9. It is seen that, although overlapped text labels occur at the top and bottom of the ZTM treemap space, there is no overlapping text between nodes on the label embedded treemap.

The rendering results generated by ZTM for a larger data set (Animalia [19], which has around 155,000 data items) are shown in Fig. 9, in which it is seen that many labels overlap. The rendering results produced by applying the label embedded treemap technique are shown in Fig. 11, in which no overlapping labels can be seen.

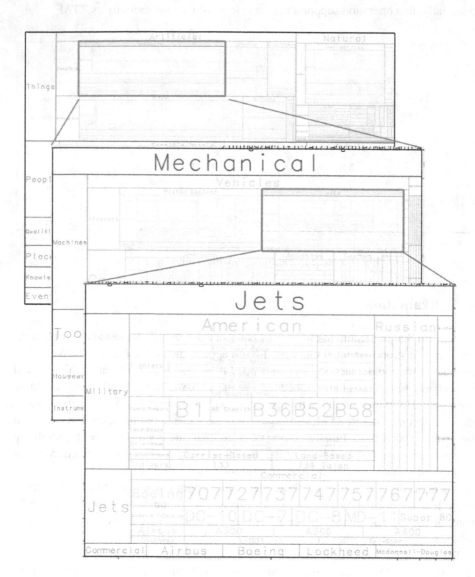

Fig. 8. Working example of direct node selection

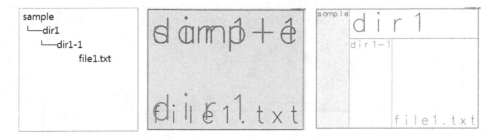

Fig. 9. (left) Simple dataset consisting of one file with three layers of folders. (middle) Rendering results using ZTM. (right) Rendering results using label embedded treemap.

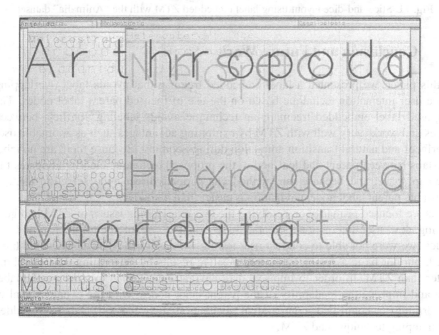

Fig. 10. Slice-and-dice layout using ZTM with the "Animalia" dataset

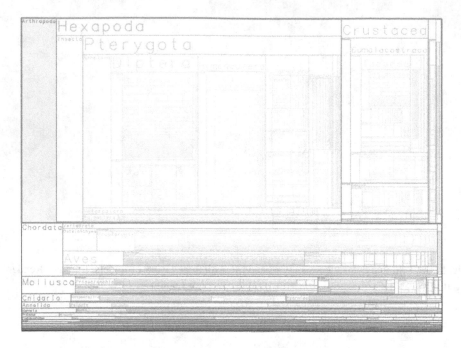

Fig. 11. Slice-and-dice layout using label embedded ZTM with the "Animalia" dataset

5   Conclusion and Future Work

In this paper, we presented a label embedded treemap that avoids label overlapping and a user interaction technique based on the use of focused parent label nodes. The proposed label embedded treemapping technique avoids labeling conflicts between nodes and works very well with ZTM by exploiting advantages such as zoomable user interfaces and natural transition animation during zooming. Because there are no label overlaps between parent and leaf nodes, the proposed technique clearly navigates the treemap space, and because our method can support direct node selection using a focusable parent label node, navigation is easier than with ZTM.

As we focused primarily on resolving the text overlapping issues of ZTM and generating new user interaction potential based on the use of focusable parent label nodes, we were not able to conduct user testing with as much rigor as we would have liked, but our basic assessment showed positive results by performing data searching faster than ZTM. In order to improve data navigation, we plan to increase the label size and improve the readability of the parent label nodes, with the eventual goal of performing a controlled comparative evaluation between our label embedded treemapping technique and ZTM.

Acknowledgements. This research is supported by the Ministry of Culture, Sports and Tourism (MCST) and the Korea Creative Content Agency (KOCCA) in the Culture Technology (CT) Research & Development Program 2013.

References

1. Reingold, E.M., Tilford, J.S.: Tidier Drawings of Trees. IEEE Trans. Software Engineering SE-7(2), 223–228 (1981)
2. Johnson, B., Shneiderman, B.: Tree-Maps: A Space-Filling Approach to the Visualization of Hierarchical Information Structures. In: Proc. IEEE Conference on Visualization 1991, pp. 284–291 (1991)
3. McGuffin, M.J., Robert, J.M.: Quantifying the Space-Efficiency of 2D Graphical Representations of Trees. Information Visualization 9(2), 115–140 (2010)
4. Baudel, T., Broeskema, B.: Capturing the Design Space of Sequential Space-Filling Layouts. IEEE Trans. Visualization and Computer Graphics 18(12), 2593–2602 (2012)
5. Fekete, J.D., Plaisant, C.: Interactive Information Visualization of a Million Items. In: Proc. IEEE Symposium on Information Visualization, pp. 117–124 (2002)
6. Bruls, M., Huizing, K., van Wijk, J.J.: Squarifiedtreemaps. In: Proceedings of Joint Eurographics and IEEE TCVG Symposium on Visualization (TCVG 2000), pp. 33–42 (2000)
7. Shneiderman, B., Wattenberg, M.: Ordered Treemap Layouts. In: Proceedings of the IEEE Symposium on Information Visualization (INFOVIS 2001), p. 73 (2001)
8. Bederson, B.B., Shneiderman, B., Wattenberg, M.: Ordered and quantum treemaps: Making effective use of 2D space to display hierarchies. ACM Transactions on Graphics (TOG) 21(4), 833–854 (2002)
9. van Wijk, J.J., van de Wetering, H.: Cushion treemaps: Visualization of hierarchical information. In: Proceedings of the IEEE Symposium on Information Visualization (INFOVIS 1999), pp. 73–78 (1999)
10. Elmqvist, N., Dragicevic, P., Fekete, J.: Color Lens: Adaptive Color Scale Optimization for Visual Exploration. IEEE Transactions on Visualization and Computer Graphics 17(6), 795–807 (2010)
11. Shi, K., Irani, P., Li, B.: An evaluation of content browsing techniques for hierarchical space-filling visualizations. In: Proceedings of IEEE Information Visualization (INFOVIS 2005), pp. 81–88 (2005)
12. Tu, Y., Shen, H.: Balloon Focus: a Seamless Multi-Focus+Context Method for Treemaps. IEEE Transactions on Visualization and Computer Graphics 14(6), 1157–1164 (2008)
13. Keahey, T.A.: Getting along: Composition of visualization paradigms. In: Proceedings of IEEE Information Visualization, INFOVIS 2001 (2001)
14. Perlin, K., Fox, D.: Pad: An Alternative Approach to the Computer Interface. In: Proc. ACM SIGGRAPH 1993, pp. 57–64 (1993)
15. Bederson, B.B.: PhotoMesa: A Zoomable Image Browser Using Quantum Treemaps and Bubblemaps. In: Proc. ACM Symposium on User Interface Software and Technology 2001, pp. 71–80 (2001)
16. Plaisant, C., Shneiderman, B.: Treemap 4.1.1 (2004),
    http://www.cs.umd.edu/hcil/treemap/
17. Blanch, R., Lecolinet, E.: Browsing ZoomableTreemaps: Structure-Aware Multi-Scale Navigation Techniques. IEEE Trans. Visualization and Computer Graphics 13(6), 1248–1253 (2007)
18. Kim, K.H., Han, J.H.: Label-embedded treemap. In: Proc. Korea Computer Congress 2013, pp. 1064–1066 (2013)
19. Blanch, R.: ZTM 1.0.2 (2012),
    http://iihm.imag.fr/blanch/projects/ztm/src/

An Interactive Approach to Constraint-Based Visualizations

Wendy Lucas

Bentley University, Waltham, MA, USA
wlucas@bentley.edu

Abstract. This paper describes an approach that puts even inexperienced users in charge of force-directed layouts. The visual interface to a powerful but relatively easy to use visualization grammar has been augmented with sliders for controlling the strength of constraints applied to visual objects. Users can change the balance of power between constraints while an animated visualization is running, turn off the constraints affecting the layout, or return a layout to its pre-constraint-solving specification. An initial empirical evaluation supported the usefulness of this interactive design intervention for providing user control over force-directed layouts. This approach is a step towards addressing the lack of tools with which less sophisticated users can design customized visualizations that best meet their needs.

Keywords: Visualization language, force-directed layout, constraint specification, information visualization.

1   Introduction

The built-in charting tools available in consumer software products, such as Microsoft Excel and Google Spreadsheets, are very popular because they are easy to use for generating graphic displays of data. Chart types are limited, however, to a standard set of options. Higher-level visualization tools, such as Tableau [1], QlikView [2], and Spotfire [3], provide greater flexibility and support for data exploration and analytics, but outputs are still constrained by predefined templates. While designers with programming expertise can make use of graphic libraries for developing customized visualizations, those without such expertise have been largely ignored [4].

The information visualization language described in [5] was developed to address the need for tools with which non-experts can design their own novel visualizations of data. It is based on the concept of providing direct access to "first principles," i.e., the basic building blocks from which informational graphics are built. Visualizations are constructed with a powerful but relatively easy to use grammar that ties the graphical properties of generic objects, such as points, lines, polygons, text, etc., to data values. The relationship between data values and graphical values is mediated by a function called a scale, which may be depicted graphically by a legend, such as an axis or a color bar. The actual placement of objects is governed by constraints that enable the

S. Yamamoto (Ed.): HIMI 2014, Part I, LNCS 8521, pp. 54–63, 2014.

use of positional information in a more flexible way than directly tying property values to specific locations. Constraints are solved by reduction to mass-spring systems and iterative relaxation in conjunction with user manipulations of the positions of objects, as in [6].

This paper demonstrates how all users, including non-experts, can gain greater control over rendered visualizations by providing them with visual mechanisms for manipulating the strength of constraints embedded in layout specifications. In addition to the constraints of *equality*, *approximate equality* (henceforth referred to as *near*), and *non-overlap* previously defined in [5], *horizontal* and *vertical alignment* constraints have been added to the language. The graphical front-end has been augmented with sliders that permit the precise specification of the strength of each of these constraints. As users interact with the sliders, the force-directed layout changes dynamically. To prevent constraint-driven changes to the layout, users can simply set the strength of each constraint to zero. Users can manually adjust the layout by dragging any object whose location has been specified by a *near*, as opposed to *equality*, constraint while the animation is running as well as when it has been stopped. To reset the layout to its initial specification (i.e., pre-constraint-solving), the user can set the *near* constraint slider to its maximum value and all other constraint sliders to zero. The ability to precisely control the strength of constraints governing a force-directed layout while it is actively running, including turning those constraints on and off, is the unique contribution of this work.

The next section of this paper discusses related work. This is followed by a more detailed description of the constraints that have been implemented and examples of how user control over their strengths affects visual layouts. The results of an initial empirical evaluation of this approach are then presented. The paper concludes with directions for future research.

2   Related Work

The numerous tools available for information visualization support varying amounts of user interaction for controlling presentation properties. The previously mentioned charting tools that are often built into spreadsheet packages are among the least interactive, with users selecting a chart type from a predefined set and associating data with it. Customization of the output is limited to the selection of presentation properties such as colors and labels. More control is possible if the application also supports the embedding of code. Experienced users of Microsoft Excel, for example, can create more advanced visualizations by writing macros in Visual Basic for Applications (VBA). Interactive features such as selecting parameters from lists and displaying graph properties via mouse clicks can be added in this way.

Visual analytics tools provide additional features for interactive data analysis and exploration. Users of Tableau, the commercialized version of Polaris [7], construct a visual specification by dragging fields from a database schema onto shelves that correspond to visual encodings [8]. Show Me [9], an integrated set of user interface commands and defaults based on the algebraic specification language VizQL [10], allows the user to choose among alternative views of the data. Supported user interactions include sorting and filtering of visualized data, creating interactive dashboards, and clicking on a mark to display user-specified field values. Spotfire also allows users to create dashboards from combinations of different chart types and provides several controls for filtering the visualized data [8]. None of these tools, however, allows users to define their own visualizations.

For greater control over layouts and representations, users may turn to general purpose diagramming tools, but these can be laborious and inexact for depicting data visualizations. There are, however, specialized drawing tools that can be very effective for particular types of layouts. Two examples are the GLIDE [6] and Dunnart [11] constraint-based authoring tools, in which the graph layout engines run continuously while the author applies placement constraints to guide the layout of network diagrams. Both support a range of constraint types, including non-overlap of nodes, horizontal alignment, and vertical alignment. In addition, the minimum distance between nodes can be adjusted via a slider in Dunnart. While these systems bear the most similarity to the approach described in this paper, they are limited to a particular type of layout and do not permit user control of constraint strengths.

Graphics libraries and toolkits provide far more flexibility and expressiveness for enabling the design of advanced, interactive visualizations, but they are intended for designers with considerable programming expertise. The InfoVis Toolkit [12] uses interactive components, or "widgets," for constructing visualizations. Widgets represent lower-level elements as well as higher order visualizations. New visualizations can be added through subclassing of existing ones or programmed from scratch.

With the Prefuse [13] toolkit and its successor, Flare [14], abstract data is mapped to visual object representations. Visual parameters, such as location, color, and shape, are set by designers using a series of configurable operators, and customized visualizations are rendered from the configured objects. Controls provide interactive operations such as drag, hover, pan and zoom, and selection. There are several layout options that the user can specify programmatically, including node-link trees, icicle trees, and force-directed. New operators and objects can also be added by expert users.

Protovis [15], an extensible graphical toolkit, defines a domain-specific language for visualization design. As in [5], visualizations are constructed from graphical primitives, or marks, such as bars, lines, and labels. These marks serve as building blocks for creating visualizations, with their visual properties defined as functions of data. Event handlers can be registered with marks to enable interactivity in response to mouse and keyboard events. Protovis has been succeeded by the Data-Driven Documents (D3) JavaScript visualization library [16]. The main difference between the two is that in D3, the visual elements are defined by the web's document object model (DOM) rather than by graphical marks. A number of layouts have been defined in both Protovis and D3 to support the reuse of useful techniques, including force-directed. While it is possible to change the strength of applied forces and constraints programmatically, there are no built-in means for interacting with those constraints while a force-directed animation is running.

3   Manipulating Visual Constraints

The key difference between the approach presented here and those described above is that it provides two ways in which users can manipulate the placement of graphical objects in a visualization: (1) by the standard means of dragging objects to different locations, and (2) by manipulating the strength of the constraints controlling the force-directed positioning of those objects. The latter way makes it possible for users to stop an animation, reset it to its pre-animated state, and change the balance of power between conflicting forces.

In the declarative visualization language described in [5], each graphical object in a user-specified layout has at least one positional attribute for defining its initial placement. If an *equality* constraint (=) defines the relationship between that attribute and a location, then that position is fixed. If, however, it is defined by a *near* constraint (~), then the position can change in response to direct user manipulation or the enforcement of other constraints specified in the layout. A positional property can also be set equal or near to a property of another graphical object. To simplify this type of association, a find function has been added to the language that makes it possible to select graphical objects based on an attribute value.

Three types of constraints between two or more objects have been defined within the language. A *non-overlap* (*NO*) constraint specifies that no parts of the graphical representations of the constrained objects can overlap. *Horizontal alignment* (*HAlign*) signifies that the graphical representations of the constrained objects must be aligned along the x-dimension, while *vertical alignment* (*VAlign*) indicates alignment along the y-dimension.

The visual interface to the language has been augmented with sliders that allow the user to control the strengths of the *near*, *non-overlap*, and *alignment* constraints. Setting any of the sliders to zero nullifies the associated constraint, while setting a slider to its upper limit maximizes its strength. Because there is interplay between the constraints, adjusting the strength of one constraint may impact the influence of others. For example, say a point is subject to two constraints, one that says it must be near a particular location and another that says it cannot overlap with any other points. Strengthening the *non-overlap* constraint while leaving the *near* constraint unchanged will cause the point to move farther away from the specified location if that location overlaps with another point. Weakening the *non-overlap* constraint and strengthening the *near* constraint will move the point closer to its initial placement.

Figure 1 displays a screenshot of the interface, with the (partial) code for generating a visualization shown in the left side panel, the results of running that code shown in the center panel, and sliders for controlling the strengths of the constraints in the right side panel. In this case, the mathematical expression $b * a * d * c$ from the data shown in Table 1 is being visualized as a scatterplot of scatterplots. Two of the sliders have been adjusted from their default positions: the strength of the *near* constraint has been increased, while the strength of the *non-overlap* constraint has been decreased. The strengths of the *horizontal* and *vertical alignment* constraints have been left at their default values, as they have no role in this visualization. The result is that the visual data points in the lower right quadrant have moved slightly so that each is distinguishable from the other but not as far apart as they would be if the *non-overlap* constraint were more strictly enforced. The user could also turn off both the *near* and *non-overlap* constraints by setting their sliders to zero and could then freely move the visual points through direct manipulation to any desired location.

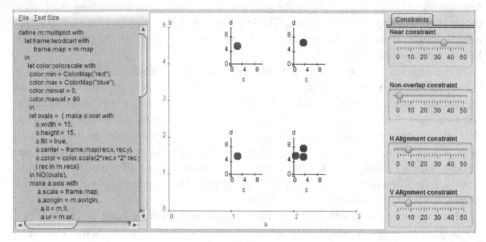

Fig. 1. Scatterplot of scatterplots

Table 1. Data to be visualized

a	b	c	d
1	1	2	5
1	4	2	5
2	1	2	5
2	1	3	5
2	1	3	6
2	4	3	6

Having the ability to interact with both the strengths of the constraints being applied and the visual objects being affected by them lets the user take advantage of the power of force-directed layouts while still maintaining ultimate control over the resulting visualization. It also allows for the effective resolution of constraints that may be overspecified. For example, if an object is dithering between two locations as a result of conflicting constraints, the user can decide which constraints should take precedence and which can be relaxed. The placement of the object can then be adjusted in accordance with the user's preferences, which may differ from the coordinates determined by the constraint-solving process. These types of user interactions are illustrated by the following example.

3.1   Illustrative Example

Let us consider again the data shown in Table 1, but this time, the mathematical expression $b * a * d * c$ will be depicted by a tree-type visualization, as in [17]. Figure 2a shows the results of running a program written in the language of [5] for specifying a vertical tree layout in which the initial placements of the nodes are in conflict with the constraints being applied. *Near* constraints have been used to set all of the nodes of the same color to the exact same location and all of the different colored nodes to positions that are aligned vertically. *Non-overlap* constraints have been specified to prevent nodes from overlapping, while *horizontal alignment* constraints have been applied to nodes of the same color. Since the *near* constraints are in conflict with the *non-overlap* and *horizontal alignment* constraints and all have been left at their default strengths, the nodes in this layout are dithering between locations.

In Figure 2b, the user has interacted with the constraints to increase the strengths of the *non-overlap* and *horizontal* constraints while decreasing the strength of the *near* constraint. In addition, she has dragged nodes to adjust the vertical distances between each row, with all of the nodes of a particular color moving in lock step due to enforcement of the *horizontal alignment* constraint.

To generate the layout shown in Figure 2c, the *horizontal alignment* constraint specified in the initial program was changed to a *vertical alignment* constraint. Once again, the user has interacted with the constraints, this time increasing the *non-overlap* and *vertical alignment* constraint strengths while decreasing the near constraint strength. All nodes of the same color have moved together as the user dragged any one of them in a horizontal direction.

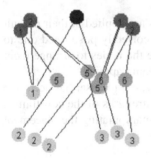 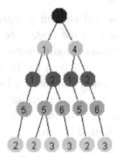 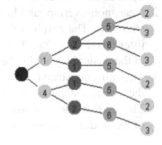

Fig. 2a. Tree layout with default constraint settings   **Fig. 2b.** Horizontally aligned tree layout   **Fig. 2c.** Vertically aligned tree layout

As illustrated by this example, being able to adjust the strengths of constraints in force-directed layouts and directly manipulate the placement of graphical objects puts the user in control of the visual outcome. At the same time, the enforcement of constraints saves time for the user, who does not have to manually adjust every node. This approach leverages the ability of the visualization application to render complex visualizations with the user's more nuanced understanding of the most suitable way to present the underlying data.

4   Empirical Evaluation

An initial empirical evaluation of the approach described in this paper was conducted to (1) determine if users could successfully construct a specified visualization using the interventions provided in the interface, and (2) provide qualitative assessments of the usefulness of the constraint strength sliders as a means for controlling force-directed layouts. Eleven participants, ranging from non- to expert-users of visualization tools, participated in this evaluation. Of the eleven, two had little to no experience with any charting, graphics drawing, or visualization tool. Five had at least some experience with a charting or graph drawing tool, and four had considerable experience. Two of those last four also had used higher-level visualization tools, with one of those two qualifying as an expert, based on her experience developing visualization applications in Java.

4.1   Procedure

The graphical tree layout described in Section 3.1 was used in this study. The 11 participants were instructed to create the graphical tree representation shown in Figure 2b under three different conditions:

1. No constraint forces are applied to the node-edge layout beyond the equality constraints attaching edges to nodes. All of the nodes of the same color are initially rendered to the same location and all of the different colored nodes are aligned vertically (see Figure 3). The user must manually manipulate the nodes to arrange them in the desired layout.
2. Near, non-overlap, and horizontal alignment constraints are applied at their default strengths. The result is that some of the nodes are not correctly positioned due to jitter (see Figure 2a). The user can manually manipulate the nodes to arrange them in the desired layout but has no control over the forces being applied.
3. The same constraints as in Condition 2 above are in play, but the user has access to the visual sliders shown in Figure 1 for controlling the strengths of the constraints. The user can now adjust those strengths in addition to manipulating the placement of the nodes for achieving the desired layout.

Fig. 3. Tree layout with overlapping nodes at each level

Each of the above conditions was demonstrated to the user prior to her having to perform the visualization task. Instead of the tree layout, a different network visualization was used for the three demonstrations, and the participant was invited to ask questions before beginning on the assigned task.

4.2   Results

All eleven participants were able to successfully render the tree visualization under all three conditions, thus answering the first question concerning if the user could make successful use of the sliders. In addition, all found the third condition with the sliders to be the most useful. Ten participants had highly positive experiences with this treatment and preferred it over the other two, while one claimed it was only marginally better than the first condition. Table 2 summarizes the most frequently heard positive (+) and negative (-) comments about constructing the tree layout under each of the three conditions:

Table 2. Summarized findings on three interaction conditions

Condition	+/-	Summarized Comments
1 - unconstrained	+	Very flexible
	+	Easy to use for simple layouts
	-	Unhelpful, have to do same thing over and over
	-	Inefficient, particularly for complex visualizations
2 - constrained	+	Very effective, saves time
	+	Gives initial idea - very important, particularly when just getting started
	+	Fun, more pleasant, nicer output
	-	Much less flexibility
	-	Much harder to control - don't know what to expect, frustrating
3 - sliders	+	A lot easier to control than (2), and less time-consuming
	+	Just as flexibile as (1), but now computer helps you with adjusting the layout
	+	Nice to have computer figure things out first and then respond to your guidance
	+	Removes the feeling of being constrained
	-	Bit of a learning curve - need coaching on how to use sliders
	-	Need to develop a strategy for using sliders

As these comments suggest, preliminary findings concerning the usefulness of providing users with interactive control over constraint strengths in force-directed layouts are encouraging. Users ranging from the least experienced to the most appreciated the flexibility provided by the sliders. Increasing the strength of the constraints helped them develop the initial structure for the layout, which was much more efficient than having to move each component to its desired position. Lowering constraints gave much greater control to the user than the force-directed layout without sliders, and all took advantage of the ability to turn off the constraints at some point in their interactions. Keeping the horizontal constraint at its highest level allowed users to take advantage of what some referred to as a "snap-to" experience, which simplified node placement as the aligned nodes moved together. While more thorough testing is needed, the results from this initial empirical evaluation support the premise that the approach described in this paper provides users with more control for rendering visualizations that meet their individual requirements.

5   Conclusions

Today's visualization toolkits are geared toward designers with considerable programming expertise, while less savvy users must typically make do with predefined layout templates [4]. The approach presented in this paper is a step toward bringing the ability to create customized visualizations to a broader range of users. Coupling an interactive mechanism for adjusting the strengths of constraints with a declarative grammar that is flexible and expressive enables the specification of force-directed layouts that can be precisely controlled, as was demonstrated by example. The usefulness of this approach was supported by a preliminary empirical evaluation, which also confirmed that users of all experience levels could make effective use of the sliders provided for setting constraint strengths.

More thorough testing with a wider range of visualizations and a greater number of participants is needed to confirm the initial findings presented here. Methods for making the setting of constraint strengths more intuitive will also be explored and tested. Other directions for future work include implementing additional layout constraints within the language, such as bounding boxes, symmetry, and even spacing, and enabling user-control over their strengths. Providing users with the ability to add and remove constraints visually while a force-directed layout is running will also be a focus of future design efforts.

References

1. Tableau, http://www.tableausoftware.com/
2. QlikView, http://www.qlikview.com/
3. Spotfire, http://spotfire.tibco.com/
4. Pantazos, P., Lauesen, S.: Constructing Visualizations with InfoVis Tools – An Evaluation from a User Perspective. In: Proceedings of the International Conference on Information Visualization Theory and Applications (IVAPP 2012), pp. 731–736 (2012)
5. Lucas, W., Shieber, S.M.: A Simple Language for Novel Visualizations of Information. In: Filipe, J., Shishkov, B., Helfert, M., Maciaszek, L.A. (eds.) ICSOFT/ENASE. CCIS, vol. 22, pp. 33–45. Springer, Heidelberg (2008)
6. Ryall, K., Marks, J., Shieber, S.M.: An interactive constraint-based system for drawing graphs. In: Proceedings of the 10th Annual Symposium on User Interface Software and Technology (1997)
7. Stolte, C., Tang, D., Hanrahan, P.: Polaris: a System for Query, Analysis, and Visualization of Multidimensional Relational Databases. Communications of the ACM 11, 75–84 (2008)
8. Heer, J., Shneiderman, B.: Interactive Dynamics for Visual Analysis. ACM Queue 10(2), 30–35 (2012)

9. Mackinlay, J., Hanrahan, P., Stolte, C.: Show Me: Automatic Presentation for Visual Analysis. IEEE Transactions on Visualization and Computer Graphics 13(6), 1137–1144 (2007)
10. Hanarahan, P.: VizQL: A Language for Query, Analysis and Visualization. In: Proceedings of the 2006 ACM SIGMOD International Conference on Management of Data (SIGMOD 2006), p. 721. ACM, New York (2006)
11. Dwyer, T., Marriott, K., Wybrow, M.: Dunnart: A constraint-based network diagram authoring tool. In: Tollis, I.G., Patrignani, M. (eds.) GD 2008. LNCS, vol. 5417, pp. 420–431. Springer, Heidelberg (2009)
12. Fekete, J.: The InfoVis Toolkit. In: Proceedings of the IEEE Symposium on Information Visualization (INFOVIS 2004), pp. 167–174 (2004)
13. Heer, J., Card, S.K., Landay, J.A.: Prefuse: a Toolkit for Interactive Information Visualization. In: Proceedings of the SIGCHI Conference on Human Factors in Computing Systems (CHI 2005), pp. 421–430. ACM, New York (2005)
14. Flare, http://flare.prefuse.org
15. Bostock, M., Heer, J.: Protovis: A Graphical Toolkit for Visualization. IEEE Transactions on Visualization and Computer Graphics 15(6), 1121–1128 (2009)
16. Bostock, M., Ogievetsky, V., Heer, J.: D^3 Data-Driven Documents. IEEE Transactions on Visualization and Computer Graphics 17(12), 2301–2309 (2011)
17. Wilkinson, L.: The Grammar of Graphics (Statistics and Computing). Springer-Verlag New York, Inc., Secaucus (2005)

User Similarity and Deviation Analysis for Adaptive Visualizations

Kawa Nazemi[1,2], Wilhelm Retz[1], Jörn Kohlhammer[1,2], and Arjan Kuijper[1,2]

[1] Fraunhofer IGD, Fraunhoferstr. 5, 64283 Darmstadt, Germany
[2] Technische Universität Darmstadt, Fraunhoferstr. 5, 64283 Darmstadt, Germany
{kawa.nazemi,wilhelm.retz,joern.kohlhammer,
arjan.kuijper}@igd.fraunhofer.de

Abstract. Adaptive visualizations support users in information acquisition and exploration and therewith in human access of data. Their adaptation effect is often based on approaches that require the training by an expert. Further the effects often aims to support just the individual aptitudes. This paper introduces an approach for modeling a canonical user that makes the predefined training-files dispensable and enables an adaptation of visualizations for the majority of users. With the introduced user deviation algorithm, the behavior of individuals can be compared to the average user behavior represented in the canonical user model to identify behavioral anomalies. The further introduced similarity measurements allow to cluster similar deviated behavioral patterns as groups and provide them effective visual adaptations.

1 Introduction

The increasing amount of data in data bases and on Web poses a great challenge for the human access to relevant information. Various disciplines face the problem of human information access with different and complementary approaches. To face this problem, the area of user-adaptive visualization proposes different approaches that adapt information visualization to users' behavior. Most of these adaptive visualization approaches adapt the visual interface based on individual's user models, whereas clustering, grouping and identifying usage anomalies are commonly not investigated.

This paper proposes an approach for measuring usage similarities and deviations based on a canonical user model. We will first introduce the state-of-the-art in adaptive visualizations to outline the gap that will be filled by our approach. Thereafter we define the basic element of our approach, the canonical user model. This user model is the baseline for measuring the distance between common users and anomalies. Further it provides the ability to measure the similarity of users and create user groups. Therewith we introduce a conceptual model that measures both, deviations between the canonical user and individual users and similarities between users for user-grouping.

The main contribution of our paper is the generation of a canonical user model from implicit user interactions with visual environments to inference relevant visualization types for common users. Further these common users are applied

S. Yamamoto (Ed.): HIMI 2014, Part I, LNCS 8521, pp. 64–75, 2014.

as baseline for identifying groups and in particular deviations. Such deviations can be used to infer anomalies in usage behavior and identify experts and novices.

2   Related Work

The term *adaptive visualization* is used for different levels of adapting the visual representation, filtering and recommending data to be visualized. GOLEMATI et al. [1, 2] introduced a context-based adaptive visualization that concerns user profiles, system configuration and the document collection (data set) to provide an adequate visualization. They state that the choice of 'one' adequate visualization from a pool of visualizations leads to a better performance. The adaptation of the visualization is based on the "context" which has to be generated manually [1]. An implicit interaction analysis is not performed; further the use user similarity or deviations is not is not investigated. A similar approach is proposed by Gotz et al. with the HARVEST tool [3]. HARVEST makes use of three main components: a reusable set of visualization widgets, a context-driven visualization recommendation and semantic-based approach for modeling user's analytical process. Here the limitation is the need of experts who have to define an initial design for the interaction patterns and the resulting visualization recommendation [3]. With the *APT tool* [4] and the consecutive *Show Me* system [5], Mackinlay et al. differ from the previously described works in a metaphor of small multiple displays and an enhanced aspect of user experience in visual analytics. Although they propose an adaptive visual system, the used algebra is defined for data to provide a better mapping of data-tables to visual representations. Another approach for data-adaptive visual presentation is HiMap [6]. The system reduces the graph-layout complexity (visual density) by an adaptive data-loading algorithm. Similarly, DA SILVA et al. investigated the reduction of complexity by adapting the data [7]. The adaptation of a spatial visual presentation layer based on user preferences is proposed in the *Adaptive VIBE* system by AHN and BRUSILOVSKY ([8], [9]). Their approach uses algorithms for identifying data similarities [8]. The introduced examples demonstrate the upcoming popularity of adaptive visualization concepts. However, the majority of the systems require the involvement of either experts to model an initial visualization design or the active involvement of users'. The use of canonical user model with similarity and deviation analysis are not considered for training the adaptive behavior.

3   User Modeling by Interaction Analysis

The measurement of users' similarities or deviation can be performed through a consistent representation of users' behavior. Our approach targets at modeling users through their interaction behavior with a visualization. This section introduces some concepts of our interaction analysis algorithm introduced in [10] and [11] to enable a comprehensible picture of the entire user analysis procedure.

3.1 Formal Representation of Users' Interactions

The adaptation of information visualization requires the acquisition of users' informational context. To provide such a context, we introduced in [10–12] an interaction analysis algorithm that allows the analysis of users' interaction to model a behavioral pattern and provide interaction predictions. This paper will use parts of the algorithm to model users and measure similarities and deviations between users. According to [13] we first define an interaction event I as a relation instantiated with leaf values of the domains equivalent to *Relational Markov Models* as $I = r(k_1, ..., k_n)$, $k_i \in leaves(D_i)$ *with* $1 \le i \le n$. Thereby $leaves(D_i)$ are the leaf nodes of the domain D_i and r is a relation over the domains $D_1, ..., D_n$ [10]. This formal representation of users' interaction enables to model each interaction in a unique way and analyze them to model the behavior or measure predictions and probabilities.

3.2 Deriving Users' Interaction Behavior

Users' interaction behavior is the way hoe users interact with a system to achieve theirs goals. This behavior can give us information about preferences in system use or even indicates the expertise level of users. The users' interaction behavior can be described as the probability distribution of users' interactions in contrast to the entire possible interactions with the system. To compute the probability distribution of users' interactions, we first determine the Steady State Vector (SSV) as a relative measurement for the occurrence of interaction events. The SSV is a normalized probability distribution with $\sum_{i=1}^{n} p_i = 1$ and therewith a probability distribution over the entire possible interactions. We use the frequency distribution of the interactions. The frequency distributions is computed based on the quantitative occurrence of an interaction i in contrast to the entire interactions. Therewith the probability for occurrence of an interaction i is defined as $p_i = \frac{v_i}{|A|}$, where v_i is the amount of all occurrences of the interaction i and $|A|$ is the amount of interactions the user performed previously. We use for the set of all previous interactions A either the set of interactions of the individual or canonical user [14].

The formal representation of the interactions provides context information of the interaction events. Abstractions of interaction events are defined as sets of interaction events by instantiating the relation r with the inner nodes of the domains [10, 13]. There a frequency distribution and therewith a probability of all domains can be computed on each degree of the domain abstraction [13]. Based on the defined quantitative occurrence measurement, we define the function $quant(depth_{D_1}, ..., depth_{D_k})$, where $depth_{Di}$ is the level of abstraction for every domain D_i as the hierarchical level of the domain, starting with 0 for the highest level. With each occurrence of the function $quant(depth_{D_1}, ..., depth_{D_k}))$ a set L of the abstraction levels is generated illustrated according to the abstraction levels of ANDERSON et al. [13, p. 3] $L = \{r(\delta_1, ..., \delta_k)\}$, with $\delta_i \in nodes_i(depth_{D_i})$ and $0 \le depth_{D_i} \le maxDepth(D_i)$, and $1 \le i \le k$.

Thereby $nodes_i(depth_{Di})$ are the nodes of the domain D_i with the depth $depth_{Di}$, and the maximum abstraction level of the domain D_i is defined as $maxDepth(D_i)$. In our case we instantiate this function with $k = 3$ thus, we have the three domains of *Device*, *Visual Layout* (SemaVis), and *Data*. Therewith the function is used as $quant(depth_{D_1}, depth_{D_2}, depth_{D_3})$. The type of users' interaction is based on the *Device* and the targets to be achieved, here a predefined taxonomy is given. The second domain of *SemaVis* is representing the different visual layouts. The visualization environment contains an enhanceable set of visual layouts with a predefined taxonomy. The third domain of *Data* contains the semantic hierarchy of the data entities. The semantic hierarchy of the data is gathered by an iterative querying approach [15] and used as taxonomy for this particular domain. With the automatic inclusion of the semantic hierarchy and the generated taxonomy on inheritance-level any changes of the database can be performed without restrictions, thus the underlying semantics provides appropriate structure for the formal representation of the user interactions.

The probability p_α for each abstraction $\alpha \in L$ is calculated with the probabilities from the SSV s [10] as $p_\alpha = \sum_{q_i \in \alpha} ssv(q_i)$, thereby $ssv(q_i)$ is the probability of the interaction q_i from the SSV. Hence the result is a probability distribution over sets of interaction events.

The probabilistic distribution of users' interactions over the different levels of abstraction enable us to measure various values for preferences and knowledge of the users. Modeling users' can be performed on a detailed level by investigating all abstraction levels of the three identified domains.

3.3 Modeling Users

The main goal of analyzing users' interaction behavior with data and visualizations is to represent these for generating an abstract model of the behavior and provide sufficient visual adaptations. SLEEMAN proposed that the main aspects in modeling users are the *nature* and the *structure* [16]. Thus nature refers to user characteristics or feature that are in our approach gathered just implicitly from users' interaction, we constrain these features to users' interest and tasks [16–18]. The structure of the user model should be transferable to other domains of knowledge (data-sets) and should therewith enable the use of the model in various data domains.

With the introduced SSV and the various levels of abstraction, we already defined an abstract model of the user. The SSV represents the probability distribution of users' interaction in different level of abstraction. Further it refers to three dimensions: the used device and type of interaction, the visual layout, and the data [12].

For a more comprehensible illustration for modeling users and to enable in the next steps measuring users' similarities and deviations with the canonical user model, we introduce some general definitions, that are used throughout this paper. We define the set $U = \{u_1, u_2, ..., u_n\}$, where each u is a user. Additionally, we define the set $V = \{v_1, v_2, ..., v_k\}$ with each v being a visual layout of all visual layouts from the first abstraction level of the visual layout domain D_2. Further we define d being a data element from the set of all data elements D of all abstraction levels from the data domain D_3. For considering the users' behavior on individual user level, we extend the equation described in Section 3.2 by allowing the look-up from the SSV ssv_u of each individual user $u \in U$ as follows:

$$p_{u,\alpha} = \sum_{q_i \in \alpha} ssv_u(q_i) \tag{1}$$

Furthermore we introduce $p_{u,v,d}$ as a short form to extract the probability of an individual user for the correlation of a visual layout v and a data element d.

$$p_{u,v,d} = p_{u,r(device,v,d)} \tag{2}$$

Although the interaction type $Device\ D_1$ is gathered in each users' interaction, we dismiss this information in this context and use the abstraction level 0. This lets us extract the relevance value of the data element d in combination with the visual layout v for a specific user u. In the next step, we introduce two relevance vectors for each user in the user model. The *visual layout usage- vector* $\boldsymbol{vl}$ contain the relevance values of visual layouts according to their usage of each user and provides us information about users' "visual layout preferences" that is again a probability distribution of the interaction behavior with the visual layouts. The *data interests- vector* $\boldsymbol{di}$ contain the relevance values of the data elements according to the interest and previous knowledge of the individual users. Each entry $p_V(u,v)$ in the $\boldsymbol{vl}$ of an individual user contains the normalized relevance values of each visual layout $v \in V$ and is calculated as follows:

$$p_V(u,v) = \frac{\sum\limits_{d \in D} p_{u,v,d}}{\sum\limits_{d \in D} \sum\limits_{v_i \in V} p_{u,v_i,d}} \tag{3}$$

The creation of $\boldsymbol{di}$ for each user uses the semantic inheritance relations in addition to the relevance values between visual layouts and data elements. Let, as previously stated, $p_{u,d,v}$ be the relevance value of an individual user $u \in U$ for a data element d in combination with a visual layout v and let $S_d \subseteq D$ be a set of all data elements, which have a semantic relation with data element d. The relevance value $p_D(u,d)$ of a individual user $u \in U$ for a data element d is calculated as follows:

$$p_D(u,d) = \max_{v \in V} p_{u,v,d} + \sum_{d_i \in S_d} \frac{\max\limits_{v \in V} p_{u,v,d_i}}{|S_{d_i}|} \tag{4}$$

These relevance values of the individual data elements form $\boldsymbol{vl}$. In contrast to $\boldsymbol{vl}$, the individual relevance values between data elements and visual layout are not added up while creating the vector. Instead, the visual layout relevance values is being used, which has the highest value for the corresponding data element.

With the introduced definition so far, the users' interest and preferences are modeled. For determining the tasks, we use as described in [10] the occurrences of similar interaction sequences O as behavioral patterns. To model a "training file" that is continuously updated by users' behavior and leads to a more efficient way of identifying the occurrence of similar and frequent sequences, we use the *canonical user model* [14]. Our algorithm make use of the interactions as relations between data and visual layout, whereas the interaction type *Device* is investigated too as the first domain of the SSV D_1. This domain can be used to determine different dependencies on transition level. The users' interactions with data and visualization may have different relevance. To gather the information the first domain $D1$ of the SSV is used that provides information about the type of users' interaction, e.g. as *Device.Mouse.selectVis*. The procedure allows to weight successful interactions that leads to achieving the goal or explicit selecting visual layout higher than those interactions that lead to removing visual layouts. This procedure is coupled to the activity or task recognition of the algorithm proposed in [10] and modeled through the general and frequent behavior of the canonical user. Therewith the formal description can be derived from the users' interaction behavior and the prediction of users' action as described in [10] and [11]. Figure 1 illustrates schematically the described procedure.

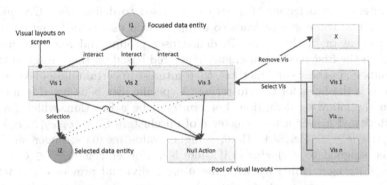

Fig. 1. Schematic illustration of the interaction relevancies

The Canonical User

The canonical user model represents the average users' behavior with the visualization system. This user model is the baseline for adapting the visual layout and data for all users and improves therewith the general usage of the visualization system. Thus it is used on the one hand for the general adaptation and on the other hand for measuring certain behavioral deviations and anomalies for individual user, it is one of the core components of our approach. Every user that interacts with the visualization environment pulls one's weight to the canonical user model. The interaction of each user, even if the adaptivity of the system is disabled, contributes to this model.

To describe the interaction behavior and therewith the probability distribution for the canonical user in context of visual layouts, we use the probability values $p_{u,v,d}$. Based on these probabilities the interaction behavior of a canonical user can be computed as illustrated in equation 5. Where the sum of interaction probabilities of each user $u \in U$ with a certain visual layout v is divided by the amount of all users $|U|$.

$$can_V(v) = \frac{1}{|U|} \sum_{u \in U} p_V(u, v) \tag{5}$$

A similar correlation can be built between users and data. The main difference is that the leaf nodes are investigated in different levels of abstraction. Thereby either a data or information entity can be a leaf node or an intermediate node of the entire taxonomic structure. We previously defined $d \in D$ as a data element from a set of all data elements in all abstraction levels from the data domain D_3. Additionally, for the canonical user, only users who interacted with the specific data are considered. Therefor we do by the amount of users, who interacted with this data entities.

$$can_D(d) = \frac{1}{|\{u | u \in U, p_D(u,d) > 0\}|} \sum_{u \in U} p_D(u, d) \tag{6}$$

User Group and Role Definition
Similar interaction behavior of users can be used to define *User Groups*. The identification of these groups leads to define certain user roles based on the interaction behavior of the users. To define user groups and roles, we use two methods: In the first method, users are clustered based on their usage of the visual layouts V, in the second method, their interest in certain data or knowledge dimensions is the basis for the clustering. A specific user is assigned to a cluster based on the following definition. Let $sim(c, u)$ be a function, which provides the similarity of a user u to a cluster c of all clusters $C = \{c_1, c_2, ..., c_n\}, c_i \subseteq U, \forall c_i, c_j : i \neq j, c_i \cap c_j = \emptyset$. Here, a higher value means stronger similarity. A user is assigned to a cluster c, if there is no other cluster $c_i \in C, c \neq c_i$, that has a stronger similarity with the users individual previous interactions: $\forall c_i \in C, c_i \neq c : sim(c_i, u) < sim(c, u) \rightarrow u \in c$. The average value of each cluster c of all visual layout cluster C_V is calculated in the same way as for the canonical user. With the main difference that only users in their respective clusters are considered. The normalized value $p_V(c, v)$ of a visual layout v of a cluster c is calculated as $p_V(c, v) = \frac{1}{|c|} \sum_{u \in c} p_V(u, v)$. The average value of each individual cluster c of all data domain clusters C_D is also calculated similar to the calculation of the canonical user. Additionally, the normalization only considers users, who contributed to the calculated value. The measurement of this normalized average value $p_D(c, d)$ of a data entity d of a cluster c is calculated as $p_D(c, d) = \frac{1}{|\{u | u \in c, p_D(u,d) > 0\}|} \sum_{u \in c} p_D(u, d)$.

Figure 2 illustrates the previously presented abstract depiction of the user model with additional clustering. The "+"-signs represent the center of each cluster. The individual clusters are aligned in the form of rays radial around the canonical user in the center of the figure. With this procedure different user clusters can be determined automatically, even if the clusters are not labeled. Figure 3 illustrates the user grouping in a more hierarchical way to outline the relationship to the canonical user model. Every user, regardless, if he or she belongs to a group, provides interaction information to the canonical user model and their models inherit from the canonical user model. Grouped users inherits further from the average group user model and provides interaction information to the average group user models too.

4 User Similarity Analysis

User similarity measurements allow the comparison of individual users through a numerical quantity value [19, 20]. This value can be used to measure how similar users are according to their behavior. These measurements are used for the calculation of the similarity between a user and a user group in addition to the similarity of two different users. Figure 2 illustrates abstractly the similarity between users and user groups. The angle between two objects represents their similarity to each other. A smaller angle means more similar objects. The green gradient illustrates regions of high to low similarity of the selected user (blue icon) to other users in these regions.

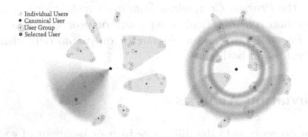

○ Individual Users
● Canonical User
◁ User Group
● Selected User

Fig. 2. User similarity and deviation analysis based on the canonical user

The basis for the calculation of the similarity are the two previously described vectors (**vl** and **di**). Their composition differ, **vl** is normalized and not very sparse after a short usage of the visual system by a specific user, because commonly new visual layouts are only added in large time intervals. In contrast to that, **di** is very sparse, even after a very thorough usage of the visual system by the specific user. Because many and new data elements can be added or removed continuously. This is the main reasons, why different similarity measurements are used to determine the similarity between users and other users or user groups.

For the calculation of the similarity between users on the basis of their data interests relevance values, the *Pearson Correlation Similarity* [19–21] metric is used. Let $u_a \in U$ and $u_b \in U$ be two users and $p_D(u_a, d)$, $p_D(u_b, d)$ their respective relevance values for the data element $d \in D$. The similarity between these two users $sim_D(u_a, u_b)$ is calculated as follows:

$$sim_D(u_a,u_b)=\frac{\sum\limits_{d\in D_{ab}}(p_D(u_a,d)-\overline{p_D(u_a)})(p_D(u_b,d)-\overline{p_D(u_b)})}{\sqrt{\sum\limits_{d\in D_{ab}}(p_D(u_a,d)-\overline{p_D(u_a)})^2}\sqrt{\sum\limits_{d\in D_{ab}}(p_D(u_b,d)-\overline{p_D(u_b)})^2}} \quad | \; D_{ab}=D_{u_a}\cap D_{u_b} \quad (7)$$

Here, $\overline{p_D(u)} = \frac{1}{|D|}\sum\limits_{d\in D} p_D(u,d)$ is the mean value of all values in $\boldsymbol{di}$ for a user $u \in U$.

The calculation of the similarity between users on the basis of their visual layout relevance values also uses the *Pearson Correlation Similarity* metric. But here, no normalization with the mean value of the respective vector occurs, because these vectors are already normalized. The value for the similarity of two users $u_a \in U$ and $u_b \in U$ and their respective relevance values $p_V(u_a,v)$ and $p_V(u_b,v)$ for the visual layout v is calculated as illustrated in Equation 8.

$$sim_V(u_a, u_b) = \frac{\sum\limits_{v\in V_{ab}} p_V(u_a,v)p_V(u_b,v)}{\sqrt{\sum\limits_{v\in V_{ab}} p_V(u_a,v)^2}\sqrt{\sum\limits_{v\in V_{ab}} p_V(u_b,v)^2}} \quad | \; V_{ab} = V_{u_a} \cap V_{u_b} \quad (8)$$

The choice of the *Pearson Correlation Similarity* metric for the determination of the similarity between users and other users or user groups is based on the fact, that the *Pearson Correlation Similarity* only considers elements, which have relevance values on both sides.

5   User Deviation Analysis

The user deviation represents the difference in user behavior of each individual user to the average behavior of the canonical user. It is assumed, that users can also be similar to each other, if they differ similarly in their interaction behavior from the average behavior. Thereby their direct similarity to each other is not measurable. This can happen, if e.g. the adaptive system could not yet determine the overlapping interests for the particular users.

Figure 2 illustrates an abstract depiction of the deviation of users' behavior from the average behavior of the canonical user in addition to the previously calculated user groups from the similarity analysis. The distance of the user to the canonical user and accordingly the radius represent the aforementioned behavioral deviation. For a selected user, the gradient of the ring symbolizes the region with very similar deviation in behavior.

The calculation of this behavioral deviation is also based on the two previously described vectors ($\boldsymbol{vl}$ and $\boldsymbol{di}$), which were also used for the modeling of the canonical user and for the creation of the user groups.

Unlike the calculation of the similarity between the users, we used the *Cosine Similarity* metric [20–23] for calculating the behavioral deviation. This is because the consideration of the relevance values that are not common for both users are relevant for the measurement of the deviation. Since the *Cosine Similarity* metric does not perform a normalization, the calculation of $\boldsymbol{vl}$ and $\boldsymbol{di}$ are identical.

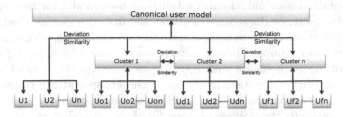

Fig. 3. Deviation and similarity relations to the canonical user model

Let $p_D(u, d)$ be the relevance value of a data element d of the data element set D for a user $u \in U$ and $can_D(d)$ the relevance value of the canonical user for the data element d. The information deviation (interest-deviation) $dev_D(u)$ of a user u can be calculated as follows:

$$dev_D(u) = \frac{\sum\limits_{d \in D} p_D(u,d)can_D(d)}{\sqrt{\sum\limits_{d \in D} p_D(u,d)^2}\sqrt{\sum\limits_{d \in D} can_D(d)^2}} \tag{9}$$

This leads to the definition of a similarity between two users based on their interest-deviation from the canonical user $sim\_dev_D(u_a, u_b)$, which can be expressed as follows:

$$sim\_dev_D(u_a, u_b) = 1 - |dev_D(u_a) - dev_D(u_b)| \tag{10}$$

Equivalently, the similarity between two users based on the deviation in the usage of visual layouts to the canonical user can be calculated as follows:

$$dev_V(u) = \frac{\sum\limits_{v \in V} p_V(u,v)can_V(v)}{\sqrt{\sum\limits_{v \in V} p_V(u,v)^2}\sqrt{\sum\limits_{v \in V} can_V(v)^2}} \tag{11}$$

$$sim\_dev_V(u_a, u_b) = 1 - |dev_V(u_a) - dev_V(u_b)| \tag{12}$$

The returned value is in the range between one (identical distance) and zero (completely different distance). The analysis of deviations is performed between the canonical user and either one individual user or the average user of a certain identified group.

6   Conclusion

This paper introduced an approach for modeling the average users' behavior within visual environments to improve the general adaptation effects. Therefore, the canonical user model and its formal representation was introduced. Based on this the deviance measurement was illustrated. We showed that the measured distance between the canonical user and individual users can be used to detect anomalies in user behavior, which may lead to "screw down" the adaptation effect. If the distance between the user behavior is similar to that of the canonical user, the canonical user model can be taken as user model for new situations, visual layouts, users, or data-bases. Further the distance can be used to determine the application of the canonical user to new situations, visual layouts, or data bases for user groups. These groups are determined by applying similarity algorithms on users' behavior and provide an "average user model" that can be used for measuring the distance between the group and the canonical user. Based on this measurement further aspects can be determined: In this case of similar user behaviors the average user model of the group inherits the canonical behavior or in case of large distance the adaptation effects are reduced until enough information of the users' in that particular group are gathered. Further the measured similarities between same distanced users (Figure 2) are used to detect similarities as described in the Section 4. If the distance of two users or average user groups are similar according to the canonical user model, the similarity algorithm is applied to measure certain similarities between the groups or users. If similar behavioral patterns are detected and one of the user groups contains certain information that is missing in the other group, these information are applied to extend the average user model of that group (Figure 3).

Acknowledgments. This work has been carried in the FUPOL project, partially funded by the European Commission under the grant agreement no. 287119 of the 7th Framework Programme. This work is part of the SemaVis technology, developed by the Fraunhofer IGD (http://www.semavis.net).

References

1. Golemati, M., Halatsis, C., Vassilakis, C., Katifori, A., Lepouras, G.: A context-based adaptive visualization environment. In: Proceedings of the Conference on Information Visualization, IV 2006, pp. 62–67. IEEE Computer Society, Washington, DC (2006)
2. Golemati, M., Vassilakis, C., Katifori, A., Lepouras, G., Halatsis, C.: Context and adaptivity-driven visualization method selection. In: Mourlas, C., Germanakos, P. (eds.) Intelligent User Interfaces: Adaptation and Personalization Systems and Technologies, pp. 188–204. IGI Global (2009)
3. Gotz, D., When, Z., Lu, J., Kissa, P., Cao, N., Qian, W.H., Liu, S.X., Zhou, M.X.: Harvest: An intelligent visual analytic tool for the masses. In: Proceedings of the First International Workshop on Intelligent Visual Interfaces for Text Analysis, IVITA 2010, pp. 1–4. ACM, New York (2010)
4. Mackinlay, J.: Automating the design of graphical presentations of relational information. ACM Trans. Graph. 5, 110–141 (1986)
5. Mackinlay, J., Hanrahan, P., Stolte, C.: Show me: Automatic presentation for visual analysis. IEEE Transactions on Visualization and Computer Graphics 13, 1137–1144 (2007)
6. Shi, L., Cao, N., Liu, S., Qian, W., Tan, L., Wang, G., Sun, J., Lin, C.Y.: Himap: Adaptive visualization of large-scale online social networks. In: Visualization Symposium, PacificVis 2009, pp. 41–48. IEEE Pacific (2009)
7. da Silva, I., Santucci, G., del Sasso Freitas, C.: Ontology Visualization: One Size Does Not Fit All. In: EuroVA 2012: International Workshop on Visual Analytics, pp. 91–95. Eurographics Association (2012)

8. Ahn, J.W., Brusilovsky, P.: Adaptive visualization of search results: Bringing user models to visual analytics. Information Visualization 8, 180–196 (2009)

9. Ahn, J.W.: Adaptive Visualization for Focused Personalized Information Retrieval. PhD thesis, School of Information Sciences, University of Pittsburgh (2010)

10. Nazemi, K., Stab, C., Fellner, D.W.: Interaction analysis for adaptive user interfaces. In: Huang, D.-S., Zhao, Z., Bevilacqua, V., Figueroa, J.C. (eds.) ICIC 2010. LNCS, vol. 6215, pp. 362–371. Springer, Heidelberg (2010)

11. Nazemi, K., Stab, C., Fellner, D.W.: Interaction analysis: An algorithm for interaction prediction and activity recognition in adaptive systems. In: Proc. of IEEE ICIS, pp. 607–612. IEEE Press, New York (2010)

12. Nazemi, K., Stab, C., Kuijper, A.: A reference model for adaptive visualization systems. In: Jacko, J.A. (ed.) Human-Computer Interaction, Part I, HCII 2011. LNCS, vol. 6761, pp. 480–489. Springer, Heidelberg (2011)

13. Anderson, C.R., Domingos, P., Weld, D.S.: Relational markov models and their application to adaptive web navigation. In: KDD 2002: Proceedings of the Eighth ACM SIGKDD International Conference on Knowledge Discovery and Data Mining, pp. 143–152. ACM, New York (2002)

14. Nazemi, K., Retz, R., Bernard, J., Kohlhammer, J., Fellner, D.: Adaptive semantic visualization for bibliographic entries. In: Bebis, G., et al. (eds.) ISVC 2013, Part II. LNCS, vol. 8034, pp. 13–24. Springer, Heidelberg (2013)

15. Nazemi, K., Breyer, M., Forster, J., Burkhardt, D., Kuijper, A.: Interacting with semantics: A user-centered visualization adaptation based on semantics data. In: Smith, M.J., Salvendy, G. (eds.) Human Interface, HCII 2011, Part I. LNCS, vol. 6771, pp. 239–248. Springer, Heidelberg (2011)

16. Sleeman, D.: Umfe: a user modelling front-end subsystem. Int. J. Man-Mach. Stud., 71–88 (1985)

17. Brusilovsky, P., Millán, E.: User models for adaptive hypermedia and adaptive educational systems. In: Brusilovsky, P., Kobsa, A., Nejdl, W. (eds.) Adaptive Web 2007. LNCS, vol. 4321, pp. 3–53. Springer, Heidelberg (2007)

18. Nazemi, K., Burkhardt, D., Breyer, M., Kuijper, A.: Modeling users for adaptive semantics visualizations. In: Stephanidis, C. (ed.) Universal Access in HCI, Part II, HCII 2011. LNCS, vol. 6766, pp. 88–97. Springer, Heidelberg (2011)

19. Luo, H., Niu, C., Shen, R., Ullrich, C.: A collaborative filtering framework based on both local user similarity and global user similarity. Mach. Learn., 231–245 (2008)

20. Gong, S.: A collaborative filtering recommendation algorithm based on user clustering and item clustering. Journal of Software 5, 745–752 (2010)

21. Guo, L., Peng, Q.: A combinative similarity computing measure for collaborative filtering. In: Proceedings of ICCSEE 2013. Advances in Intelligent Systems Research, pp. 1921–1924. Atlantis Press (2013)

22. Brusilovsky, P., wook Ahn, J., Dumitriu, T., Yudelson, M.: Adaptive knowledge-based visualization for accessing educational examples. In: Tenth International Conference on Information Visualization, IV 2006, pp. 142–150 (2006)

23. Symeonidis, P., Nanopoulos, A., Manolopoulos, Y.: Feature-weighted user model for recommender systems. In: Conati, C., McCoy, K., Paliouras, G. (eds.) UM 2007. LNCS (LNAI), vol. 4511, pp. 97–106. Springer, Heidelberg (2007)

Evaluating the Dot-Based Contingency Wheel: Results from a Usability and Utility Study

Margit Pohl[1], Florian Scholz[1], Simone Kriglstein[1],
Bilal Alsallakh[2], and Silvia Miksch[2]

[1] Institute for Design and Assessment of Technology,
Vienna University of Technology, Austria
{margit,florian,simone.kriglstein}@igw.tuwien.ac.at
[2] Institute of Software Technology & Interactive Systems,
Vienna University of Technology, Austria
{alsallakh,miksch}@ifs.tuwien.ac.at

Abstract. The Dot-Based Contingency Wheel is an interactive visual-analytics method designed to discover and analyze positive associations in an asymmetrically large $n \times m$ contingency table. Such tables summarize the relation between two categorical variables and arise in both scientific and business domains. This paper presents the results of a pilot evaluation study based on interviews conducted with ten users to assess both the conceptual design as well as the usability and utility of the Dot-Based Contingency Wheel. The results illustrate that the Wheel as a metaphor has some advantages, especially its interactive features and ability to provide an overview of large tables. On the other hand, we found major issues with this metaphor, especially how it represents the relations between the variables. Based on these results, the metaphor was redesigned as Contingency Wheel++, which uses simplified and more familiar visual representations to tackle the major issues we identified.

Keywords: Visual Analytics, Evaluation, User Interface, Interview, Contingency Tables.

1 Introduction

Categorical data appear in many data tables both in scientific and in business domains. In contrast to numerical variables, the values of a categorical variable have no inherent order. Therefore, common analysis techniques that handle numerical variables are usually inapplicable to analyze categorical data. The analysis of categorical data is usually based on contingency tables. A two-way contingency table is a matrix that records how often each combination of categories from two categorical variables appears in the database. An example would be the combination of color of hair and color of the eyes. A contingency table would, in this example, contain the frequency of the co-occurrence of blue eyes and blond hair, brown eyes and brown hair etc. An example for a contingency table in the context of medical applications would be types of diseases vs. groups

S. Yamamoto (Ed.): HIMI 2014, Part I, LNCS 8521, pp. 76–86, 2014.

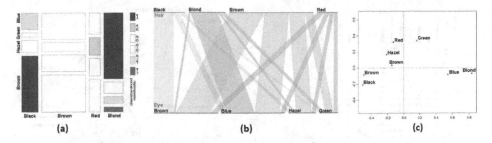

Fig. 1. Three visualizations of for contingency tables: (a) Mosaic Displays [1], (b) Parallel Sets [2], (c) Correspondence Analysis [3] (Screenshot by Alsallakh et al. [4])

of patients (e.g., female or male). In medical or business domains, the amount of data which has to be handled can get very large. It is difficult for users to find patterns or relationships in contingency tables in tabular form.

Beside several statistical techniques to extract information from such tables, several methods have been developed to visualize these tables such as mosaic displays [1], Parallel Sets [2], and correspondence analysis (CA) [3]. These visualization methods offer insights into the table such as an overview of the distribution of the data or how categories are associated with each other (see Figure 1). For example, a blue tile in mosaic displays, a thick arc in Parallel Sets, and close points in a CA plot mean that the corresponding categories are highly positively associated. Such categories appear more often together than on average in the database.

While the above-mentioned methods offer relatively intuitive representations to visualize contingency tables, they suffer from limited scalability. Only a small number of categories from both variables can be depicted in the visualization. The Contingency Wheel [4] has been proposed as a visual-analytics method designed to discover and analyze positive associations in contingency tables that have a few number of columns but a large number of rows. It uses dots to visually map these associations on a ring chart, as we explain in Section 2.

The following paper presents the results of an evaluation study of the Contingency Wheel which is based on interview data. The motivation of our evaluation study was to find out how users interact with a complex visualization like the Contingency Wheel. The findings of the evaluation help us to identify which functionalities need further improvements. Therefore, we chose a qualitative approach for the evaluation, described in Section 3. Carpendale [5] argues that such methods yield a rich understanding of the various factors influencing the interaction with information visualizations. Qualitative analysis also enables investigators to obtain contextual information about the usage of information visualization or visual analytics methodologies. In Section 4 an overview of the investigation is presented. The prototype we evaluated is described in detail in Section 5. The results we got from the analysis of the interviews are discussed in Section 6, whereas a discussion and a short overview about the improvements

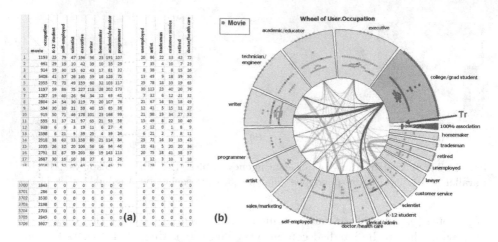

Fig. 2. (a) A large contingency table and (b) the corresponding Dot-Based Contingency Wheel present how the movies are associated with the user groups. Only cells that exhibit positive association larger than $T_r = 25\%$ between the rows and the columns are mapped to dots (on a scale between -100% and $+100\%$).

based on these findings is presented in Section 7. Section 8 concludes the paper and gives an outlook on future work.

2   The Dot-Based Contingency Wheel

The Contingency Wheel [4] is a visualization technique for large contingency tables. To cope with such tables, it adopts a visual-analytics paradigm by first computing associations in the table using statistical residuals. These associations along with the table data are then mapped to the following visual elements:

- **Sectors** represent the table columns and form a ring chart. The size of a sector is proportional to the marginal frequency of the corresponding column, which is equal to the sum of the cell frequencies in this column.
- **Dots** represent a subset of the table cells. A dot is created for a cell in the sector of its column, if its rows and column are positively associated. Such cells contain values that are larger than would be if the row and column variables were independent. The radial position of a dot is proportional to the value of this positive association. The higher the association, the closer is the dot to the outer boundary (the same information is encoded using color in mosaic displays, thickness in Parallel Sets, and proximity in a CA plot). The dots are spread along the angular dimension to reduce overlapping.
- **Lines** represent the existence of shared data between the sectors. A line is drawn between two sectors if at least two cells from the same row result in dots in both sectors. The line is thicker if the two sectors contain more such dots and the higher the associations these dots represent.

– In addition, a purple **slider** shows the value of the threshold T_r that can be adjusted to filter the dots. Only dots that represent associations higher than T_r are retained in the visualization.

Figure 2 shows an example wheel visualization for a large 3706×21 contingency table. The rows represent movies, while the columns represent user groups and are mapped to sectors. The cells represent how many times each movie was rated by users from each user group, and are mapped to dots. One user group is selected to highlight all dots that represent movies positively associated with it. Such movies were more often watched by users from this group than the average of all users. Some of these movies are also positively associated with other user groups, as indicated by the highlighted lines and dots in other sectors.

3   Goal of the Investigation

The motivation of our evaluation study was to find out how users interact with visual-analytics methods, especially with complex visualizations like the Contingency Wheel. The evaluation of the fundamental idea served as an initial test instrument to find out the advantages and drawbacks of the representation. The findings of the evaluation help us to identify which functionalities need further improvements and to check if users missed important features which should be considered for the redesign of the methodology. For this purpose, the main questions which we wanted to investigate are:

1. What are the main advantages of the Contingency Wheel?
2. What are its main disadvantages?
3. Are the concepts underlying the Contingency Wheel clear?
4. How useful are the interactions provided by the methodology?

4   Description of the Investigation

We tested the prototype with ten persons who studied computer science. The reason for this choice of participants was that they were familiar with computers as well as statistical methods. In this way, the focus was on the visualization itself and not on how users get acquainted with basic principles of the tested software. Five participants were additionally visualization experts who worked with visualizations very often. Testing sessions for each participant took about 90 minutes.

The dataset used for the evaluation concerned the answers to standardized psychological tests of 300 young patients, their parents and their teachers. These answers were collected in the course of testing the patient for ADHD ("attention deficit hyperactivity disorder") and mostly diagnosing them with it. The motivation to use this dataset was to ensure that our test persons had no ties to this domain and had the same previous knowledge about the dataset.

From this dataset we extracted an 94 × 9 contingency table. The rows of this table represent the 94 questions that constitute the psychological test. The 9 columns represent the 3 × 3 possible combinations of two answers to a question, one from the parent and one from the teacher (answers to a question can be Not True, Often True, or Very True). A cell in the extracted 94 × 9 contingency table counts for the corresponding question how many times the corresponding parent/teacher answers combination occurred among the 300 the young patients. The aim of the analysis is to find out to which questions there was a higher degree of agreement, partial agreement or disagreement on the answers between the parents and the teachers.

For the evaluation, we conducted semi-structured interviews [6,7,8]. This is a research method which is often used in evaluation studies of information visualizations. It gives a more detailed overview of participants' attitudes to the tested software than more formal methods [9]. The design of our evaluation study was divided into four parts:

- **Introduction:** At the beginning, the structure of the datasets and the basic functions of the prototype were introduced.
- **Tutorial:** The goal of the second subpart was that the participants gained a first impression of the visualization and interacted with the visualization, so that they got familiar with it. Participants had to solve small tasks with the aim to support them to learn the basic functions. For example, one task was to change the value of the slider. After they finished the tutorial part, there was a little break with the goal to clear up misunderstandings about the basic functions.
- **Main Study:** This part included tasks which were designed to assess if the fundamental idea of the visualization was clear. Participants were asked: to merge all sectors representing answer-combinations where the parents checked "Very True or Often True"; to split them up again; to observe how the lines changed when they moved the slider; to find out, if the row-sums were all identical (they were not, differing in this from the tutorial-dataset); to select all answers where the frequency of the parent/teacher combination "Not True"/"Very True or Often True" was above the expected value; to tell us how many of these there were; and to tell us the absolute frequency of the questionnaire-item from the most outlying of the aforementioned set. The tasks were developed in cooperation with domain experts.
- **Interview:** After the subjects had finished the tasks, we asked them about the impressions that they gained during their work with the visualization. The questions used in the interview reflect the research questions described above in Section 3.

The interviews were recorded. Based on these recordings, the analysis of the data was conducted. We looked for significant statements concerning the research questions. Then we compared the subjects' answers and tried to interpret them, following the methods of Bortz and Döring [10].

5   The Evaluated System

The system used for the evaluation differs in some points from the one introduced in Section 2. We removed the interfaces for creating different Wheel configurations and presented our participants only pre-defined Wheel visualizations. Figure 3 shows a screenshot of the evaluation system. Many other features and interfaces where removed with the intent to focus on the evaluation of the basic functionalities, without distracting our participants by the multitude of configuration options.

Moreover, we adapted the existing interfaces for showing the current selection (see F in Figure 3) and the underlying contingency table (see G in Figure 3) to provide multiple views. By that we show these views side-by-side together with the Wheel visualization, and provide new functionality to facilitate the interplay between these views, e.g. to highlight the current selection in the tabular view showing the underlying contingency table.

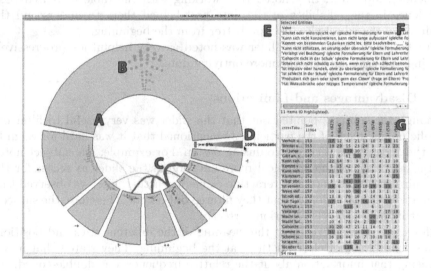

Fig. 3. The system used for the evaluation. A) sectors represent the answer-combinations from parents vs. teachers (the table columns), B) dots represent the psychological test questions and are positioned in different sectors depending on how often the sector's answer-combination appear in the database, C) lines between sectors indicate if shared questions exist in both of them, and D) is slider to filter the dots depending on an association strength. The area indicated by E) contains the Wheel visualization, F) the selection list, and G) the corresponding contingency table.

6   Interview Results

In this section we present the results of the interviews according to the research questions described in Section 3.

6.1   Advantages

Users mentioned that, compared to the tabular presentation, the wheel visualization can present large amounts of data without scrolling. They saw this as a considerable advantage. Most of the participants stated that the wheel visualization gave them a good first overview about the datasets, so they could analyze the points in the sectors more easily. They pointed out, for example, that it was easier for them to see the extreme values and outliers in the wheel visualization than in the table.

Moreover, it was mentioned that the merging and splitting functionality of sectors is useful (e.g., it was mentioned as "quick, simple and uncomplicated"). The participants also appreciated the performance of this functionality, e.g., that merging and splitting happened immediately without noticeable delay.

The interplay between the wheel visualization and the table was noted as very useful. Participants also stated that the table gave them the possibility to deal with the values in more detail (e.g., to see the information about absolute frequency). Moreover, they noted that working with the table increased their confidence in the reliability of the data and helped them to understand the meaining of the wheel visualization better from the beginning.

Furthermore, the usage of slider was noted as very helpful for progressively filtering and showing only the more outlying dots.

6.2   Disadvantages and Limitations

Although the subjects pointed out that the slider was very useful to filter out specific points, most of the participants mentioned that it was hard for them to find the slider, because of its confusing design. For example, one subject noted that s/he identified the graphical representation of the slider as sector for the remaining values and not as interaction element. Furthermore, we observed that the participants often forgot that they filtered out points. Therefore, the subjects did not interpret the visualization correctly.

Moreover, it was noted that the meaning of the different sizes and positions of the points was not clear for them at the beginning. They stated that it was confusing that information about the relative frequency was double-coded. Although the subjects found it generally difficult to understand the meaning of the connecting lines at the beginning, the double-coding of the line thickness was one reason that the participants had problems to interpret the connecting line between sectors correctly. For example, one participant noted that s/he was confused that a line was thicker although the connected sectors had fewer shared points than two other connected sectors.

Several usability issues were mentioned. For example, they missed the possibility to deselect items and it was for the participants unusual not to click on the selected item to open the context menu. Another design problem was that the points were too small if they were in small sectors or too close together so that the subjects had problems to select a point or that they were not sure if they selected the desired point. Furthermore we could observe that participants often did not notice that sectors had been merged.

6.3   Comprehension of the Concepts

Participants felt that the visualization was very complex and sometimes felt confused, especially in the beginning. Some expressed confusion due to the fact that size and (radial) position of the dots convey the same meaning and also that their angular position does not have any inherent meaning as such (it is determined by the decluttering algorithm). It was stated that after overcoming these obstacles the dots were generally understandable. In a similar way, some users understood the meaning of sectors only after a certain period of interaction with the system.

The way how the selected dots and sectors were represented in the table was often found to be confusing. For example, when selecting a single sector, sometimes table cells in a column of a different sector would be marked as selected, too. The meaning of differently colored cells in the table was rather difficult to understand.

Doubts mentioned about understanding the slider concerned the value that it was set to and its meaning. For illustration, during the experiment we observed a participant setting the slider to a value of "5%" with the intention of showing only significant dots (in a statistical sense).

Lines seemed to have been a challenging concept for our participants. They initially were not able to tell what the line connecting two sectors means. If the lines were understood they were perceived as useful. Nevertheless, the meaning of the strength/thickness of a line was not always clear. One participant expressed being confused by a situation where one line would be stronger than another, even though the pair of sectors connected by it actually showed fewer common dots. This happens because the thickness does not only depict the count of common dots, but also how highly these dots are associated with the sectors.

6.4   Usefulness of Interactions

Our participants appreciated the slider and its filter functionality. They found the feedback of the dotted line that indicated the cutoff when one moved the slider as useful. Being able to select both dots and sectors and having the related data highlighted in the contingency table was mentioned as very helpful.

7   Reinventing the Contingency Wheel

Some of the limitations we found, like the problems with deselecting the dots, are usability problems, and are very specific to the prototype we tested. But other problems we found are more interesting and seem to relate to the metaphor of the Dot-Based Contingency Wheel itself.

Based on our results, Alsallakh et al. [11] introduced a redesign of the Dot-Based Contingency Wheel to cope with the issues we found. The new design, called Contingency Wheel++ simplifies the visualization by replacing the dots with histograms along the radial dimension (Figure 4). By analyzing the limitations reported in Section 6, they found that dots are not suitable as a metaphor

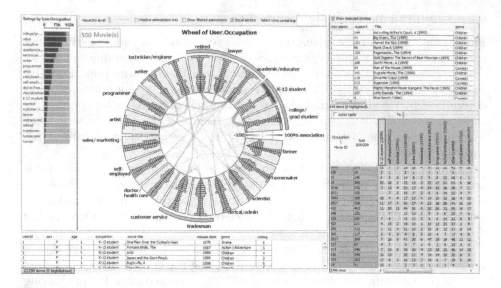

Fig. 4. The Contingency Wheel++ showing the same data as in Fig. 2 (screenshot by Alsallakh et al. [11])

to represent the table cells. They encode the deviations from the expectancy values, while the users expected to see the absolute values when they look at the dots.

Histograms are better suited to show the distribution of entities along a dimension than item-based representations. This solves the issue of what a dot represents and/or "means", and also both the problem with the double-coding of the association value (as dot radial position and size) and with the implied meaning of the angular position of the dot (which encodes no information). The angular dimension encodes the bar lengths of the histograms instead. Furthermore, when using histograms, the lines have clearer semantics than when using dots. The line thickness encodes the similarity between two distributions rather than high associations of shared dots.

The redesign of the Wheel metaphor does not associate information with sector sizes or with cell colors in the contingency-table-view by default. Other visual aids were introduced and made more salient, to address cases like forgotten slider-settings.

Finally, Contingency Wheel++ adopts the multiple views we introduced in our evaluation prototype (Section 5). Our participants found the multiple views connected by brushing-and-linking mechanisms very useful. This could confer benefits not only to users relatively new to the system but also to experts [11].

8   Conclusions

According to our evaluation study, we found that the users appreciated the utility of the Contingency Wheel to gain an overview of large contingency tables and to quickly find extreme values in them. Despite some usability issues, the users also appreciated the abilities to filter and interact with the data, and the combination of the Wheel visualization and the contingency table side-by-side.

The more critical issues we found with the Dot-Based Contingency Wheel are related to the design of its visual metaphor, in particular the dot metaphor to represent table cells. The dots were not straightforward to understand, and sometimes caused the users to draw wrong conclusions about the data. The lines between the sectors were also difficult to understand, mainly because their interpretation was related to the dots.

Subsequently, the presented system was redesigned by replacing the dots with histograms [11]. Histograms serve as abstraction of the dots, and can hence resolve the major issues with the original design. We also recommend such aggregations to deal with large amount of data in similar systems. Histograms are familiar representations that offer an effective alternative to simplify cluttered item-based representations.

Our work demonstrates the value of qualitative evaluation methods, especially for evaluating the first design of a new visual-analytics technique. They help not only in finding usability issues, but also in quickly assessing the clarity of the conceptual design of this technique. This enables spotting major issues with this design, and provides valuable guidance to iteratively refine the design, before conducting a thorough quantitative evaluation.

The interview study is part of a larger evaluation study. We also asked the users to think aloud during their interaction with the prototype. Moreover, we captured the activities of the users on the screen and recorded log files for a detailed analysis. One of our next steps is to substantiate the findings from the interview study with this data and carry out additional investigations on cognitive strategies adopted by the users.

Acknowledgments. This work is conducted in the context of the Centre of Visual Analytics Science and Technology (CVAST). It is funded by the Austrian Federal Ministry of Economy, Family and Youth in the exceptional Laura Bassi Centres of Excellence initiative. We thank Susanne Ohmann and Christian Popov for providing the medical data set and for the assistance in formulating the tasks.

References

1. Hartigan, J., Kleiner, B.: Mosaics for contingency tables. In: Computer Science and Statistics: Proceedings of the 13th Symposium on the Interface, New York, vol. 22, pp. 286–273 (1981)
2. Bendix, F., Kosara, R., Hauser, H.: Parallel sets: visual analysis of categorical data. In: Proc. of the IEEE Symposium on Information Visualization, pp. 133–140 (2005)
3. Benzécri, J.P.: Correspondence Analysis Handbook. Marcel Dekker, New York (1990)
4. Alsallakh, B., Gröller, E., Miksch, S., Suntinger, M.: Contingency wheel: Visual analysis of large contingency tables. In: Proceedings of the International Workshop on Visual Analytics, EuroVA (2011)

5. Carpendale, S.: Evaluating information visualizations. In: Kerren, A., Stasko, J.T., Fekete, J.-D., North, C. (eds.) Information Visualization. LNCS, vol. 4950, pp. 19–45. Springer, Heidelberg (2008)
6. Courage, C., Baxter, K.: Understanding Your Users: A Practical Guide to User Requirements Methods, Tools, and Techniques. Morgan Kaufmann (2005)
7. Wilson, C.: User Experience Re-Mastered: Your Guide to Getting the Right Design. Morgan Kaufmann (2009)
8. Stone, D., Jarrett, C., Woodroffe, M., Minocha, S.: User Interface Design and Evaluation User Interface Design and Evaluation. Morgan Kaufman (2009)
9. Adams, A., Cox, A.: Questionnaires, in-depth interviews and focus groups. In: Cairns, P., Cox, A. (eds.) Research Methods for Human-Computer Interaction, pp. 17–34. Cambridge University Press, Cambridge (2008)
10. Bortz, J., Döring, N.: Forschungsmethoden und Evaluation für Human- und Sozialwissenschaftler, 4th edn. Springer, Heidelberg (2006)
11. Alsallakh, B., Aigner, W., Miksch, S., Gröller, E.: Reinventing the contingency wheel: Scalable visual analytics of large categorical data. IEEE Transactions on Visualization and Computer Graphics, Proceedings of IEEE VAST 2012 18(12), 2849–2858 (2012)

Prediction or Guess? Decide by Looking at Two Images Generated by a "MATLAB MySQL" Algorithm

Carlos Rodríguez

University of Central Florida,
Institute for Simulation and Training,
3100 Technology Pkwy, Orlando, FL 32826
calirodriguez@knights.ucf.edu

Abstract. In the field of data mining, predictive modeling refers to the usage of a statistical model built on a training data set in order to make predictions about new prospects contained in the scoring data set. A model should not be used to predict when it encounters unseen data in the scoring set because such predictions would be a guess or a speculation. This paper proposes an algorithm that will produce two simple images and a "level of guessing" (LOG) pie chart. These images will tell the analyst whether or not it is appropriate to use a statistical predictive model to make predictions on a particular scoring set. The proposed algorithm will offer a solution to the scoring adequacy problem based on subsets of the original data. The algorithm will be implemented with a user interface built with MATLAB code, which acts on MySQL databases that contain the data.

Keywords: predictive modeling, data mining, scoring set, supervised learning, MATLAB, MATLAB GUI, MySQL.

1 Introduction

To my knowledge, there is no automated process or algorithm available that uses images to determine the adequacy of a statistical model to predict given new data. Even if a model shows very strong performance in the training data, this does not guarantee its applicability towards scoring new data since the scoring data might have values absent in the training data. The process presented here seeks to find differences between training and scoring data because such differences will impact the ability to make accurate predictions. The outcome of the process will send a message to the analyst highlighting these differences in the form of two simple images and a LOG pie chart.

It is often found in real world applications that a model built on a training data fails to produce accurate predictions in the scoring data. There are two reasons for that outcome:

    i.   The training set observations present different characteristics than those in the scoring set, hence a predictive model "speculates" when it classifies based on unseen data (for example, imagine that one of the important

S. Yamamoto (Ed.): HIMI 2014, Part I, LNCS 8521, pp. 87–97, 2014.

explanatory variables of the training set is OCCUPATION and its distinct values are A,B,C,D but in the scoring set OCCUPATION has the following values A,B,C,D,E,F,G,H,I,J; classifications based on F,G,H,I, J will be speculative and the analyst must know this caveat before making predictions in the scoring set).

ii.   The training set observations look like those in the scoring set, but prospects with similar characteristics behave differently in the scoring set (for example, imagine that one of the important explanatory variables of the training set is OCCUPATION and its distinct values are A,B,C,D and in the scoring data OCCUPATION also has the values A,B,C,D but in the training set A and B responded to a marketing mailing campaign at a 30% rate, yet in the scoring set, once the outcome is known, A and B only respond to a mailing campaign at a 3% rate).

For situation (i) above, scoring should not be performed if the degree of "speculation" is considerable. The magnitude of "considerable" depends on the application or in the risk preference of the analyst given the implications of the decision. For situation (ii) scoring should occur because it is meant to predict a "similar" universe of prospects. There is no way around situation (ii) simply because patterns in old data did not hold in new data; given past information it is unrealistic to avoid this error.

Analysts cannot control the outcome of the target in the scoring set, but they can decide on the adequacy of a statistical predictive model to score new data. The proposed algorithm will produce two simple images plus a LOG pie chart that will inform the analyst about differences between the training set and the scoring set.

When predictions do not conform to the actual outcomes analysts are often not sure what caused the model to underperform. In order to reach an explanation, analysts may spend considerable amount of time trying to determine why their predictions were off. The images produced by this algorithm will answer that question quickly, indicating if the problem was different data between training and scoring universes (like situation (i)) or different individuals with similar data (like situation (ii)). Ideally the images produced by the proposed algorithm should be used before scoring in order to avoid speculation in the scoring process.

2   Proposed Algorithm for Determining Differences between Training Set and Scoring Set

The algorithm that follows will produce two images and a LOG pie chart that will provide information about the applicability of a statistical model M, built on a training set T, and used to make predictions on a scoring set S. The adequacy between training T and scoring S will be analyzed only for those variables found in T that are also found in S. In other words, if there is a missing explanatory variable in S, the algorithm will still find the adequacy of the remaining variables. Any model created in T will not work on S due to the missing variables required in S; any data modeling software will make you aware of this issue right away.

Let T be a $n \times (k+1)$ array representing a training dataset for which a statistical model M has been built. T can be broken as a dependent variable array Y_{nx1} and an array of k final explanatory variables X_{nxk}. Array X_{nxk} can have numeric, date and class variables. M explains Y_{nx1} as a function of X_{nxk}. M will be used to predict $\hat{Y}_{rx1}$ given a new array of explanatory variables $\hat{X}_{rxk}$, where r is the number of records or rows in the scoring set. The algorithm treats class variables differently than it treats numeric and date variables.

2.1   Class Explanatory Variables

Let v be the number of class variables out of the k explanatory variables. X_{nxv} is a $n \times v$ non numerical array of class variables with each class explanatory variable represented by a nx1 non numerical array called x_{Tci}, i=1 ... v. Each non numerical array x_{Tci} will have L_i number of levels or distinct values, so $L_i \leq n$. Let τ_i={all levels of class variable i in the training set T}, i=1 ... v, so the set τ_i has L_i elements.

If v class variables were used in the creation of the final statistical model in T, then the same v class variables must be present in the scoring set S represented by $\hat{X}_{rxk}$; otherwise the scoring process will fail. Then the set $\hat{X}_{rxv}$ is the subset from the scoring set $\hat{X}_{rxk}$ that contains the class variables from $\hat{X}_{rxk}$ and $k \geq v$. Let x_{Sci} be a rx1 non numerical array, i=1 ... v, so all the x_{Sci} arranged together next to each other make up array $\hat{X}_{rxv}$. Each non numerical array x_{Sci} will have P_i number of levels or distinct values, so $P_i \leq r$. Let ρ_i={all levels of class variable i in the scoring set S}, i=1 ... v, so the set ρ_i has P_i elements.

For the scoring process to be completely valid the condition {$\rho_i \in \tau_i$ for all i, i=1 ... v } must hold because otherwise the prediction will not be completely based on prior knowledge leading to guessing or speculation. This is condition 1.

In real world applications there might be small violations to condition 1. An analyst might consider that the violations are not significant and score using model M. By using the proposed algorithm, the decision of whether to score using model M will be well informed and based on calculated risks. For instance, the analyst might conclude that it is better to remove the unseen levels from the scoring set before scoring or add more records to the training data to account for the unseen levels from S.

If condition 1 does not hold, that is, if there are elements in ρ_i not found τ_i, which is the same as saying that there are elements in the scoring set S not found in the training set T, then it is important to quantify the magnitude of the violation of condition 1. Such magnitude will help the analyst decide if the differences between training and scoring set are significant or if they are negligible for practical purposes.

For example, if we go back to the first situation why a predictive model performs poorly, recall that in the example it was argued that classifications based on F,G,H,I and J would be speculative, because levels F,G,H,I and J were not found in the training data (i.e. {F,G,H,I,J} $\in \rho_i$ and {F,G,H,I,J} NOT $\in \tau_i$). Let q_i be the number of rows out of the r rows of class array x_{Sci} for which condition 1 is violated, i=1...v. In other words, q_i represents the number of rows from the scoring set S with a level not found in the training set T for class variable i, i=1 ... v. Then we can define

$$\alpha = \frac{\sum_{i=1}^{v} q_i}{vr} \tag{1}$$

$0 \leq \alpha \leq 1$. α is the overall percentage of violation of condition 1 for all class explanatory variables. The number α provides information on the severity of violation of condition 1. Large values of α indicate that there is considerable difference between training set T and scoring set S. The larger α, the more evidence against using a statistical model built on training set T to predict data found in scoring set S.

2.2   Numeric Explanatory Variables and Date Explanatory Variables Converted to Numbers

Let d be the number of numerical variables out of the k explanatory variables (date variables can be converted to numbers using the YYYYMMDD format so they are considered here). X_{nxd} is a $n \times d$ matrix with each variable represented by a nx1 vector called $x_{T\eta i}$, i=1...d. X_{nxd} is a matrix composed by the numerical variables from array X_{nxk} and arranged as vectors $x_{T\eta i}$. Each $x_{T\eta i}$ vector will have a maximum and minimum value labeled $MINT_i$ and $MAXT_i$. Let $\theta_i = \{MINT_i, MAXT_i\}$, i=1...d, so each set θ_i has 2 elements.

Each numeric variable from the scoring array $\hat{X}_{rxk}$ is represented by a rx1 vector called $x_{S\eta i}$ i=1...d. Each vector $x_{S\eta i}$ will have a maximum and minimum value labeled $MINS_i$ and $MAXS_i$. Let $\lambda_i = \{MINS_i, MAXS_i\}$, i=1...d, so each set λ_i has 2 elements.

For the scoring process to be valid the condition $\{$ $MINT_i \leq MINS_i \leq MAXT_i$ and $MINT_i \leq MAXS_i \leq MAXT_i$ $\}$ must hold because otherwise the predictions will be based on extrapolation at least one time. Equivalently $MINS_i \in [MINT_i, MAXT_i]$ and $MAXS_i \in [MINT_i, MAXT_i]$, i=1...d. This is condition 2.

Let b_i be the number of rows out of the r rows of vector $x_{S\eta i}$ for which a value of is not in the interval $[MINT_i, MAXT_i]$, i=1...d. In other words b_i represents the number of rows where extrapolation will be needed. Then we can define

$$\beta = \frac{\sum_{i=1}^{d} b_i}{dr} \tag{2}$$

$0 \leq \beta \leq 1$. β is the percentage of violation of condition 2 for all numerical (and date converted to numerical) explanatory variables. Large values of β indicate that there is considerable difference between training set T and scoring set S. The larger β, the more evidence against using the statistical model built on training set T to predict data from the scoring set S.

Initially, the proposed algorithm will indicate the violation of either condition in the form of two images. The images will be a reflection of the capacity of the model to predict new data. Before defining the rationale for the generation of the images, at this point there is already enough information on α and β to reach an answer to the main question: should I use this model? If α and β are close to 0 then the model built on T is adequate to make predictions in the scoring set S. Large values of α or β is a signal that making predictions using model M involves a considerable degree of speculation or guessing.

3   Generation of the First Two Images to Determine the Adequacy of a Statistical Model

In this section I will detail how to produce the first two images that will determine the adequacy of a statistical model M to make predictions on a scoring set S. The first image will cover the information detailed by α and β. This first image is called $\alpha\beta$ **Binary Spectrum** and represents the first visual representation of adequacy. If this image indicates adequacy, then no further visual inspections are needed and scoring should be applied to the scoring set S. If the $\alpha\beta$ Binary Spectrum indicates a problem coming from α or from β or both, then a second image can be used as reference to find out where the problems are. The second image is called **Detailed Metadata Chart (DMC)**. DMC needs to be generated because the information provided by the $\alpha\beta$ Binary Spectrum is not enough to indicate the percentage of data found in S that was not found in T. $\alpha\beta$ Binary Spectrum indicates that there is a problem but does not tell where the problem is. The DMC shows the variables with problems and the magnitude of the problem. After reviewing the DMC the analyst can make a more informed decision on whether to score with model M or modify training set T in order to make it more consistent with the values found in scoring set S. The LOG pie chart is an overall summary of the findings of the process and it will be discussed later.

3.1 $\alpha\beta$ Binary Spectrum

It is a simple image of the vector $\phi = \begin{bmatrix} K\alpha \\ K\beta \end{bmatrix}$ where the entries of the vector represent the colors of the image and K is a constant that determines sensitivity to unseen data (higher K means more sensitive to unseen data; here K=150). Digital images can be created directly from a matrix, as images are numerical arrays. The farther ϕ_{11} and ϕ_{21} are from 0, the less adequate the statistical model will be. Because ϕ has two entries, the $\alpha\beta$ binary spectrum will have two bands. The left band of the $\alpha\beta$ binary spectrum is the class variables' adequacy and the right band is the numerical variables adequacy. Our imaging technique must define what color 0 takes and the farther from that color, the adequacy worsens. In this write up, 0 is represented by color black. Fig.1 shows the visual scale to determine adequacy for α and β, where leftmost is better and rightmost is worst in terms of adequacy:

Fig. 1. Visual scale for the $\alpha\beta$ binary spectrum

The ideal $\alpha\beta$ binary spectrum is shown in Fig.2 and it indicates that α=0 and β=0

Fig. 2. Ideal αβ binary spectrum representing full scoring adequacy

Fig.3 shows other examples of αβ binary spectrums

Fig. 3. Different examples of αβ binary spectrum

From left to right in Fig.3, the first αβ binary spectrum indicates a perfect adequacy in the class explanatory variables (black) and full non adequacy in the numerical variables (white). This means that numerical explanatory variables in the scoring set S are outside the range found in the training set T; if predictions are made in the scoring set S, there will be a high degree of extrapolation or speculation. In the second αβ binary spectrum from Fig.3 the numerical variables are adequate to make predictions but the class variables are not adequate. The first two αβ binary spectrums shown in Fig.3 are the extremes as they involve black and white and making a decision under these conditions is not difficult. If the αβ binary spectrum looked more like the two rightmost αβ binary spectrum from Fig.3, then the decision would not be as straight forward. In order to help the analyst make a decision, the proposed algorithm will produce a second image called Detailed Metadata Chart (DMC).

3.2   Detailed Metadata Chart (DMC)

The detailed metadata chart is a bar chart that indicates the percentage of records in the scoring set S with levels not found in the training set T for each explanatory variable. Depending on whether the variable i is numerical or class, the height of the bar that represents variable i in the DMC will be $\frac{b_i}{r}$ or $\frac{q_i}{r}$ respectively. Only positive values of $\frac{b_i}{r}$ and $\frac{q_i}{r}$ will be in the chart.

DMC helps identify where the adequacy problem is coming from. Based on the information of DMC the analyst should be able to make a better decision on how to score the new data or even a decision of not scoring at all. A hypothetical example of a DMC is shown in Fig.4.

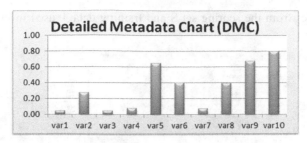

Fig. 4. Detailed Metadata Chart (DMC)

The way to read the sample DMC presented in Fig.4 is the following (for 2 of the 10 variables):

- 40% of the records in the scoring set S had a *level* for **var6** not found in the training set T.
- 80% of the records in the scoring set S had a *value* for **var10** outside the range analyzed in the training set T.

… where var6 is a class variable and var10 is numeric. The sample DMC shown above indicates that hypothetical explanatory variables var2, var5, var6, var9 and var10 would cause serious problems if used to make predictions on a scoring set S using a model M created on a training set T. DMC will only display variables with problems, so variables with all levels contained in the training data will not be displayed.

4   Illustration of the Algorithm with an Application

In order to illustrate the algorithm described in this paper I have applied it to real world training and scoring data sets. In order to perform this illustration I have used MySQL and code programmed using MATLAB, including the user interface. MATLAB connects to MySQL using the MATLAB Database Toolbox. The training and scoring data are kept in MySQL and the algorithm can be run against them with the MATLAB code. The MATLAB user interface is shown in Fig.5 and requires the analyst to input the name of the training and scoring sets (carlos.training and carlos.scoring in this example) plus the level of sensitivity to differences between the two (150). The user then presses COMPARE in order to start the process:

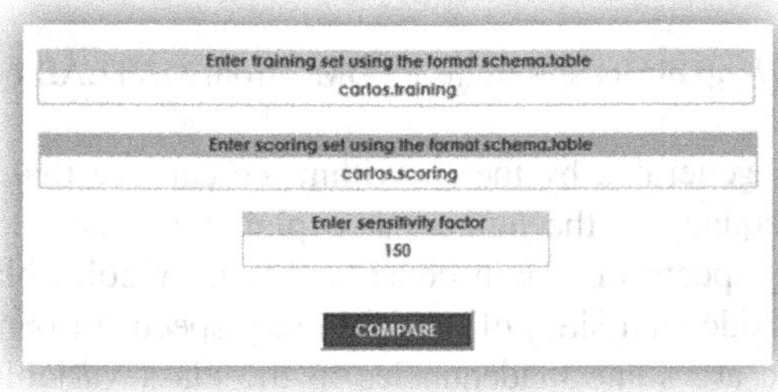

Enter training set using the format schema.table
carlos.training

Enter scoring set using the format schema.table
carlos.scoring

Enter sensitivity factor
150

COMPARE

Fig. 5. User interface that requires three inputs

The variables from the scoring set S and training data T used in this example are given in Fig.6.

Fig. 6. Variables from sample training and scoring sets

As can be seen, the training data T contains the known target variable labeled as RESPONDER. The scoring set S does not have RESPONDER as we will try to predict it using a model M. There are 6 numerical explanatory variables and 6 class explanatory variables (so $d=6$ and $v=6$). A statistical model M was used to fit the data using all the "important" explanatory variables detailed in the training set T. M can be a regression, neural network, decision tree, etc.; the selection of the optimal modeling approach is a common functionality of data mining software such as SAS Enterprise Miner or SPSS Modeler based on statistical coefficients (i.e. AIC, BSC, ROC Area, etc.). But no matter what modeling approach is selected as the optimal, it will not work well if there are unseen values and/or levels in the scoring set S. In other words, how will a model classify or predict on something it has not seen?

The proposed algorithm will analyze all variables in the scoring set present in the training set (i.e. the intersection). After running the MATLAB code the resulting 2 images are shown in Fig.7.

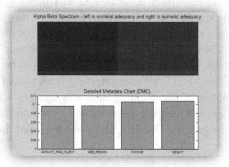

Fig. 7. αβ binary spectrum and DMC from MATLAB output

From the images generated by the algorithm we can see that the αβ binary spectrum suggests inadequacy in the numerical explanatory variables because the right side of the αβ binary spectrum departs considerably from color black (reddish appearance). The nominal side (left side) of the αβ binary spectrum is not completely black (brownish), so there are some inadequacies in the class variables as well. Because there is inadequacy we can revise the details in the DMC. The DMC confirms the information from the αβ binary spectrum and gives us the details of the inadequacy. We can see that extrapolation will be needed in the fields AMOUNT_PAID_ IN_ENT, INCOME and WEIGHT. Also, there are levels of GEO_REGION found in the scoring set S that were not found in the training set T. On each of the inadequate variables, the level of inadequacy is about 11%; another way to explain this is:

- For GEO_REGION, 11% of the records found in set S had levels not found in set T.
- For WEIGHT, 11% of the records found in set S had values outside the range used in set T.
- For INCOME, 11% of the records found in set S had values outside the range used in set T.
- For AMOUNT_PAID_IN_ENT, 10% of the records found in set S had values outside the range used in set T.

The decision about what do after this information is up to the analyst. Options include removing unseen data from the scoring set or add more data into the training set that includes the current missing levels and numeric values.

5   Sample MATLAB Output and MATLAB Code

The only inputs required by the algorithm are the training and scoring sets loaded into MySQL and defined in the user interface with the desired sensitivity. The algorithm "loops" thru each variable performing all the necessary computations. Variable identification from training and scoring sets plus the overlap between the two as shown in Fig.8.

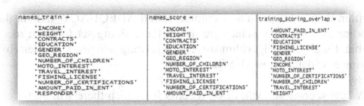

Fig. 8. MATLAB Output of the variables found in training and scoring

Fig.9 shows other key results of the MATLAB processing, including SQL queries.

The algorithm loops identifying variable type and processing them accordingly. For processing speed, it is better to keep in the training set only those variables used in the model M before running the code.

In addition to αβ binary spectrum and DMC, the algorithm also produces the LOG pie chart shown in Fig.10. This is a pie chart with the proportion of records out of the scoring set S with at least one variable having a value or level not found in the training data.

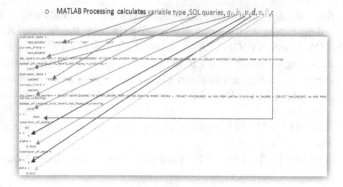

Fig. 9. MATLAB calculation of different coefficients and SQL queries

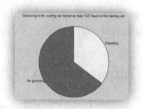

Fig. 10. LOG Pie Chart

6   Proposed Solution to the Scoring Adequacy Problem

The algorithm then computes a new column called ADEQUACY_IND in the scoring set that indicates how many values are not in the training set for each record of the scoring table. Finally, the algorithm solves the scoring adequacy problem by creating the following new data sets in MySQL:

i.   A new scoring set with those records for which there will be no guessing in the original scoring set. This is called scoring set "OK" because it contains the rows from the original data that were completely found in the training data. In other words, "OK" contains records where ADEQUACY_IND=0.

ii.   A new training set that will be used to produce a new model to score the problematic records. This training set is called training set "ALT" because it is an alternative training set where new models will be built. "ALT" does not contain variables found in the DMC.

iii. A new scoring set with the problematic records, which can be scored with the model built on training "ALT". This scoring set is called scoring set "ALT" because it will be scored, without any guessing, using models built in training set "ALT". Adequacy between scoring set "ALT" and training set "ALT" is perfect by construction. Scoring "ALT" contains records from original scoring set S where ADEQUACY_IND>0.

7   Conclusion

This paper presents a algorithm to determine, by using two images and a "level of guessing" (LOG) pie chart, the adequacy of a statistical predictive model M created on a training set T to predict new data from a scoring set S. Often in practice we observe that predictive models do not perform as expected and this can happen because of two reasons: the first one, we train on certain characteristics in T and the individuals to be predicted in S have different set of characteristics; the second one, individuals with same characteristics behaved differently in T than they do in S. In the second reason we just have to accept the errors as previous patterns in the data did not hold true in new data. The proposed algorithm addresses situations where data in T does not contain values and levels found in S. Making predictions when scoring data S has values not found in training data T is a guess or a speculation because model M has never seen such values, hence does not really know how to classify or predict based on them.

The first image is the $\alpha\beta$ binary spectrum and it presents two rectangles, the left one represents the inadequacy coming from class data and the right one represents the inadequacy coming from numerical and date data. The more these rectangles approach the color black, the better, meaning that levels found in the scoring set S were also found in the training set T. The further away these rectangles are from black, the worst the adequacy of models built on T to score S. The second image is called Detailed Metadata Chart (DMC) and it shows the percentage of inadequacy for each explanatory variable. DMC summarizes the percentage of records with levels or values found in the scoring set S that were not found in the training set T. If both rectangles of the $\alpha\beta$ binary spectrum are black, there is no need to focus on DMC but if any of the rectangles depart from color black, the DMC will detail where the inadequacy is coming from. Finally, the LOG pie chart summarizes the findings.

The user interface and sample MATLAB output were provided. The only inputs required by the algorithm are the training and scoring sets plus the sensitivity factor. The algorithm offers a solution to the scoring adequacy problem by breaking the original scoring set S in two subsets, "OK" and "ALT", where "OK" will be scored with the original models built in the original training set T and "ALT" will be scored with new models built in new training set "ALT", that contains only those variables that guarantee full scoring adequacy in the problematic records.

References

1. Kutner, M., Nachtsheim, C., Neter, J.: Applied linear statistical models. Irwin, Chicago (2004)
2. Kuhn, M., Johnson, K.: Applied predictive modeling. Springer, New York (2013)
3. Attaway, S.: MATLAB: A practical introduction to programming and problem solving. Butterworth-Heinemann, Waltham (2011)
4. MySQL, A., MySQL Administrator's Guide and Language Reference. MySQL, Indianapolis (2006)
5. Coulson, L.: MATLAB Programming (e-book). Global Media, Chandni Chowk (2009), Available from: eBook Collection (EBSCOhost), Ipswich, MA (accessed October 29, 2013)
6. Cerrito, P.: SAS I. Introduction to Data Mining Using SAS Enterprise Miner (e-book). SAS Institute, Cary (2006); Available from: eBook Collection (EBSCOhost), Ipswich, MA (accessed October 30, 2013)

A Step Beyond Visualization: Applying User Interface Techniques to Improve Satellite Data Interaction

Tatiana A. Tavares[1] and Humberto A. Barbosa[2]

[1] Federal University of Paraiba, Informatics Institute, Campus Castelo Branco, s/n,
58059-900 João Pessoa-PB, Brazil
[2] Federal University of Alagoas, Campus A.C. Simões, BR 104 Norte - Tabuleiro do Martins,
Maceio-AL, Brazil
`tatiana@lavid.ufpb.br`, `barbosa33@gmail.com`

Abstract. In this paper, we discuss the potential of applying interaction techniques to manipulate GEO satellite data. The proposed study shows the potential of Meteosat Second Generation (MSG) data in refining the mesoscale analyses incorporating HCI techniques, as natural interaction resources. Moreover the software tools used to develop the interaction layer,is based on open source codes. Open source codes are also used for geolocation and geographical information systems, written for the transformation of MSG data into input files. This feature have demonstrated a great flexibility and ease of use. The study open up an avenue for successive validation and refinement of the analyses together with their improved implementation for operational nowcasting and very short range forecasting applications.

1   Introduction

The information provided by geostationary (GEO) satellites is very important for the Earth and its atmosphere. In fact, the satellite sensors receive radiation from the Earth and its atmosphere in several visible (VIS) and infrared (IR) spectral bands, from which several Earth and atmospheric parameters are retrieved such as cloud top temperature, water vapour absorption. GEO satellite data need to be properly evaluated in order for them be useful for operational use and climate change adaptation plans.

Several variational data visualization tools or systems are available nowadays but they are implemented in centres where large computational resources are available and are generally used for global analysis. These sophisticated technologies for visualization are essential for bridging the gap between such systems and users. For Kerher [3] typical visualization tasks cover visual exploration, visual analysis and presentation. In other words, visualization is concern to generate static images that can represent GEO satellite data. Furthermore, going beyond the visualization analysis, complex data manipulation requires solutions "out-of-core" including hardware and software techniques [2].

For Jennifer Ouellette [1], today's big data is noisy, unstructured, and dynamic. The idea is to reduce large, raw data sets of many dimensions to a compressed

S. Yamamoto (Ed.): HIMI 2014, Part I, LNCS 8521, pp. 98–107, 2014.

representation in lower dimensions without sacrificing the most relevant topological properties. So, it is necessary to combine many things and create something greater that is new and different. During the last few years, new advanced methods of data manipulation provided by Human Computer Interaction (HCI) techniques, have been developed and applied in entertainment, health and military fields. So, it is possible to manipulate data with interactivity features as pointers for navigation, immersive resources or remote control. To what extent such new methodologies can be successfully applied to GEO satellite data, such as the cloud cover analysis and humidity analysis packages.

The evolution of HCI techniques enables us to go further than graphical user interfaces or pixels on bit-mapped displays. Immersive environments, natural interaction user interfaces and interactive surfaces are example of approaches to supporting collaborative design and simulation to support a variety of spatial applications [4]. For example, e-Health systems can offer to physicians complex models visualization (as human body 3D models) and also makes easier the data manipulation without touchable controls, using natural interaction resources. At this way, physicians can interact with patient data as exams or clinical reports, during a medical procedure [5].

Going back in time we can observe that visualization tools based just in one dimension (text) gave space to GUI (Graphical User Interface). The use of GUIs opened space to think about hierarchical visualization and manipulation of complex data. Today a great variety of HCI techniques can be used to enrich the interaction with complex data. Visualization issues can be addressed and we can also have other tools for data analysis using new approaches for user interfaces.

In this paper, we discuss the potential of applying interaction techniques to manipulate GEO satellite data. The proposed study shows the potential of Meteosat Second Generation (MSG) data in refining the mesoscale analyses incorporating HCI techniques, as natural interaction resources. Moreover the software tools used to develop the interaction layer,is based on open source codes. Open source codes are also used for geolocation and geographical information systems, written for the transformation of MSG data into input files. This feature have demonstrated a great flexibility and ease of use. The study open up an avenue for successive validation and refinement of the analyses together with their improved implementation for operational nowcasting and very short range forecasting applications.

2   Visualization versus Interaction

Scientific visualization is a research area that integrates images, diagrams, or animations for representation with specific areas of scientific application. Visualization through images has been an effective way to relate the scientific questions that the methods and tools are designed to explore [16]. These methods and tools are used to depict some information that is beyond direct or everyday experience. For instance, the complex meteorological interactions that occur in a developing thunderstorm, hurricane, or tornado.

If some decades ago user interfaces were all about how to visualize things, today the concern of any user interface is the better way to interact with these. Graphics, images, videos, 3D objects, animations are used to share any kind of digital information. Also, the Internet is not open to only computers anymore. Internet access is a feature of modern cell phones, domestic equipment, cars, and many other devices. This is changing the way that society deals with digital content. It is transforming user's needs, actions and reactions [17]. If sometime ago users were used to navigate between tons of text data, today users want to go further and inside data in any format of representation.

This trend is also improved by the diversity of formats to represent data in the digital world. The evolution of the user interfaces brought news ways to visualize and interact with computer based applications in several areas. Ishhi et al. illustrates this evolution using an iceberg metaphor as we can see in Fig.01.

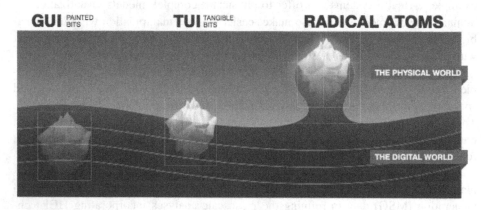

Fig. 1. Iceberg metaphor [4]

The iceberg metaphor puts the GUIs (Graphical User Interface) through the surface of the water.GUIs are typically based in screens and users can interact with them through remote controls such as a mouse, a keyboard, or a touch screen. The main functions of a GUI includes the visualization of digital information. A step forward a TUI (Tangible User Interface) is like an iceberg. It means that there is a portion of the digital world that emerges beyond the surface of the "water" into the physical world. Tangible interfaces can be seen as a complement to GUIs, working embodied in the physical world. This feature allows the use of physical manifestations, making easier and natural the direct user interaction (the "tip of the iceberg"). The last level – radical atoms – represents the vision of Ishii for the future of user interfaces, in which all digital information has physical manifestation so that we can interact directly with its.

In fact the current user interfaces technologies enable us to go further than graphical user interfaces or pixels on bit-mapped displays. Immersive environments, natural interaction user interfaces and interactive surfaces are example of approaches to supporting collaborative design and simulation to support a variety of spatial applications [4].

For example, e-health systems can offer to physicians' complex models visualization and also makes easier the data manipulation. At this way, physicians can visualiaze patient data as exams or clinical reports in real-time. More than that, they want to see the data moving into realistic models which are touchable and interactive. Sometimes, the "realistic" feature is not enough, they want to see a hair size structure in a wall size with more details that our eye could notice in the real environment.

Let's check the scenario shown in Fig.02 that illustrates the adoption of innovative user interfaces for enriching the user experience using a telemedicine tool [05].The tool provides the possibility to manipulate 3D objects, especially human anatomical structures, while viewing other streams, such as video. We analyzed this work into three levels: the plan mode, the switchable mode and the touchable mode. The plan mode is the pixels-based one, the visualization is the main goal (see Fig.02 (a)). As we can see in Fig.02 (b) the next step was the addition of several streams at the same time. Also, higher quality for projection area and a switchable structure was addopt. In this case, the user interface is more versatile and engaging even pixels-based. The "touchable" mode denotes theintegration of 3D models, live video and natural interaction controls. In this example the use of natural interaction controls (using Kinect to manipulate 3D objects) makes easier the manipulation of human body models by the professor. So, the professor can use his own hands to go inside the models, interacting with them and their detailed structures as tissues and cells, for instance. (see Fig.2 (c)).

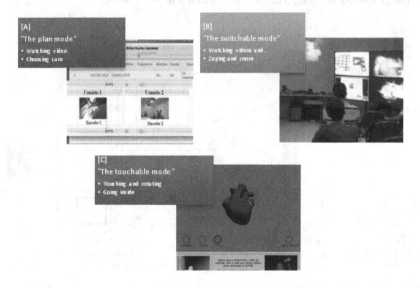

Fig. 2. Telemedicine Scenario

Interaction instead just visualization is something common in the presented cases. The innovative ideas from Ishii [4] or the real examples from e-health systems [5] showed to us that taking part in user interfaces is more than a user desire, is a user need. In complex data, as GEO satellite data, it is a challenge and also an opportunity to go further and understand the behavioral aspect of data.

3   GEO Satellite Data

GEO imagery data portray a variety of data types, including visible, infrared and water vapor. The image products, especially from the SEVIRI data is distributed to the
user mainly through the EUMETCast system [18], provide the forecaster with a great
deal of information, including winds, precipitation, and so on. The EUMETCast
system is destined to the retransmission to users in various points on the planet, of
codified data and products originating from meteorological, oceanographic, and environmental satellites, via telecommunication commercial geostationary satellites in
different frequencies. The concept of this dissemination service is based on the standard technology of Digital Video Broadcasting (DVB).

The antennas of the EUMETCast system users are basically divided into two types,
which are destined to the Ku band reception via the Hotbird-6 satellite, and the antennas destined to the C band reception via the AtlanticBird 3 and SES-6 satellites. The
C band transmits in the cover areas of Africa and South America. While the transmission in Ku band is for Europe. The minimum diameter of the antennas is in the 2.4
m order for the South American continent and 80 cm for the European continent, in
Ku band. The basic antenna components are a parabolic reflector of 2.6 meters, supply with LHC polarization, and a universal LNB amplifier to amplify the signals of
low-level potential, and cables for connections. To receive the signal, the antenna is
pointed to NSS-806 satellite. The SES-6 is located at 40.5° west.

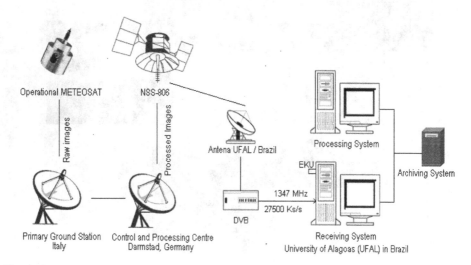

Fig. 3. Overview of the broadcasting ground reception and processing system at the University
of Alagoas (UFAL) in Brazil

The antenna of the user receives the PC signal and plaque (Technisat SkyStar2 TV
PCI or other DVT plaque) identifies the packages (Packed ID-PID) which are trans-
mitted in the MPEG-2 format for the EUMETSAT application, called T-System
Tellicast. The PIDs are defined in the application of the DVT plaque, called

Setup4PC. And the transmission of the packages is achieved via the TCP/IP protocol (Transmission Control Protocol/Internet Protocol). After the transfer, the TelliCast verifies if the eToken key (EUMETCast Key Unit-EKU) is suitable for the recuperation of the archive [19].

The system-configuration, exhibits in Fig., provides a low cost alternative to the "non-traditional meteorological" user community in Brazil applying the MSG data to a multitude of important environmental science related applications. The MSG capabilities and current favorable data distribution policy-license agreement of EUMETSAT, for Research and Education Institutes like the Federal University of Alagoas (UFAL), have recently opened the way for new initiatives [20].

4   Representing Satellite and Climate Data

How should MSG data be displayed on a computer screen? The processing of a full set of data of all 12 images: (i) Data acquisition stage (via EUMETCast system), (ii) Data decoding stage (calibration) and (iii) Data scientific processing stage (rectification, normalization), plus extraction of nowcasting products, is performed within a few minutes so that the data are available to the weather forecasters in near real-time. Nowadays computer capacities and processing time are no longer an issue and storage capacity for large volumes of satellite data is also no problem, not even so much from a financial point of view.

New applicative tools allow the forecaster to combine data types into single displays. For instance, Nocke et al. [2] highlights that designing intuitive and meaningful visual representations in climate context faces a variety of challenges. The first thing to consider is the heterogeneity and diversity of climate related data. The most common view of climate data uses the gridded format. Grids are used to group data and can aggregate information just using columns and lines or adding colors. But this is not the best way to make spatial and temporal information understandable. So, using 2D-maps or 3D objects is a way to represent multivariate and region-based information.

The interpretation of MSG images can be strongly supported and facilitated when multispectral image data are presented in appropriate combinations of the colors red, green and blue (RGB). Fig. 4 shows the RGB image that is composed from MSG channels as follows: red: 12.0 - 10.8 μm, green: 10.8 - 8.7 μm, blue: 10.8 μm. For more details as regards RGB images, please refer to www.lapismet.com. This product detects deep convection (dark red color).

In meteorology, the best kind of external representation might be one that emphasizes the qualitative aspects of the data. One good example of this is the winds, shown in Fig. 4. Winds are often referred to according to their strength, and the direction from which the wind is blowing. A wind barb shows both wind speed (by the number and length of the barbs) and direction (by the direction of the major line). Thinking about general users, vector fields do not speak for themselves. After all there is a lot of simultaneous information going on: speed, direction, and temporal and spatial data. A new design for presenting this data is introduced in [10]. A resource calledreal-time wind animation provided by HINT.FM [11] uses computer models to compile data and then overlays the wind flow on a map.

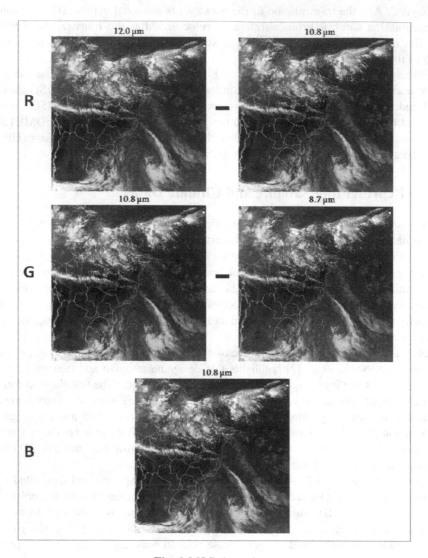

Fig. 4. MSG channels

Even using animation techniques, in the user point of view, it is still a passive visualization. Let's check some interactive examples. By using ChronoZoom [14], was developed a solution to illustrate changes in climate from the beginning of the planet through today. This solution includes images, diagrams, graphs, and time-lapse movies that illustrate changes in the environment. Using timeline users can do their own virtual tours at any speed and level of detail they want. This timeline is an interactive resource to manipulate the data.

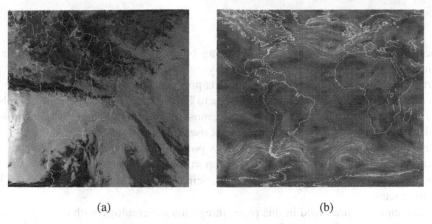

(a)   (b)

Fig. 5. In (a) MSG RGB composite image and (b) wind data representation

Another possible interactive feature is the integration. Fig. 5 (a) and (b) shows integration of SEVIRI IR10.8μm image with both the Low Cloud Cover and Total Column Water Vapor fields (derived from the Numerical Weather Prediction (NWP) data), respectively. In particular, the two NWP fields reproduce the structure generated in SEVIRI RGB composite (Fig.5 (b)). However, it is uncertain if the two NWP fields are sensitive enough to discriminate between low *stratiform* water clouds and fog cover.

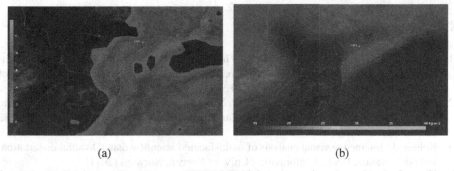

(a)   (b)

Fig. 6. In (a) Brightness Temperature SEVIRI IR10.8μm in conjunction with the Low Cloud Cover map (ECMWF parameter). GRU (Guarulhos' international airport). In (b) Brightness Temperature SEVIRI IR10.8μm in conjunction with Total Column Water Vapor map (ECMWF parameter). GRU (Guarulhos' international airport).

Erlebache G. et al. (2001) states that the future of visualization includesa multidisciplinary approach involving many fields. Visualization ubiquity collaboration and visualization displays are highlighted fields. Also, exchange of visual data becomes as ubiquitous as exchange of text documents and graphics [12].

5   Discussion

The next generation of applications is going beyond user interfaces based in pixels. Science fiction is becoming even more day-by-day things. Movies as "Minority Report", "Matrix", "The 6th Day" presented us products that we can also buy today. As we discussed above GUIs are giving space to 3D images, sensitive surfaces, embedded interaction resources. Using our hands, muscles or brain to control application is a reality that can favor the creation process of user interfaces.

New formats and technologies bring new possibilities. The design of effective user interfaces is a challenge and also a great opportunity to promote multidisciplinary and innovative solutions what stimulate the participation of several skills integrated in a creative team.

The approach presented in this paper integrates metereology with computing techniques. We are exploring the brand new possibilities of user interfaces to offer innovative solutions for climate data. It's clear that there is a huge gap between take care of a ton of data and interacting with them. So, interaction techniques to facilitate the exploration of climate data is a multidisciplinary opportunity. We believe that today we are a step beyond visualization and satellite data interaction is a key point to the development of user interfaces for big data applications.

Acknowledgments. Thanks to the Brazilian Program - Science without Borders - and the Global Lab Project for contributing for this research.

References

1. Ouellette, J.: The Mathematical Shape of Things to Come - Scientific data sets are becoming more dynamic, requiring new mathematical techniques on par with the invention of calculus. Quanta Magazine (October 4, 2013)
2. Nocke, T., Sterzel, T., Böttinger, M., Wrobel, M.: Visualization of climate and climate change data: An overview. In: Digital Earth Summit on Geoinformatics, pp. 226–232 (2008)
3. Kehrer, J.: Interactive visual analysis of multi-faceted scientific data (Doctoral dissertation. PhD dissertation, Dept. of Informatics, Univ. of Bergen, Norway) (2011)
4. Ishii, H., Lakatos, D., Bonanni, L., Labrune, J.B.: Radical atoms: beyond tangible bits, toward transformable materials. Interactions 19(1), 38–51 (2012)
5. Tavares, T.A., Medeiros, A., de Castro, R., dos Anjos, E.: The use of natural interaction to enrich the user experience in telemedicine systems. In: Stephanidis, C. (ed.) Posters, HCII 2013, Part II. CCIS, vol. 374, pp. 220–224. Springer, Heidelberg (2013)
6. Tavares, T.A., Motta, G.H.M.B., Souza Filho, G., Mello, E.: Experiences with Arthron for Live Surgery Transmission in Brazilian Telemedicine University Network. In: Kurosu, M. (ed.) Human-Computer Interaction, HCII 2013, Part II. LNCS, vol. 8005, pp. 197–206. Springer, Heidelberg (2013)
7. Post, F.H., van Wijk, J.J.: Visual representation of vector fields. In: Rosenblum, L., et al. (eds.) Scientific Visualization: Advances and Challenges, pp. 367–390 (1994)

8. Ota, S., Tamura, M., Fujimoto, T., Muraoka, K., Chiba, N.: A hybrid method for real-time animation of trees swaying in wind fields. The Visual Computer 20(10), 613–623 (2004)
9. Buckley, A.: Guidelines for the Effective Design of Spatio-Temporal Maps. In: 26th International Cartographic Conference, ICC 2013 (2013),
http://icaci.org/files/documents/ICC_proceedings/ICC2013/_
extendedAbstract/443_proceeding.pdf
10. Viégas, F., Wattenberg, M., Hebert, J., Borggaard, G., Cichowlas, A., Feinberg, J., ... Wren, C.: Google+ Ripples: a native visualization of information flow. In: Proceedings of the 22nd International Conference on World Wide Web, pp. 1389–1398. International World Wide Web Conferences Steering Committee (2013)
11. HINT.FM
12. Erlebacher, G., Yuen, D.A., Dubuffet, F.: Current trends and demands in visualization in the geosciences. Visual Geosciences formerly Electronic Geosciences 6(3), 1–59 (2001)
13. Heinrich, M., Thomas, B., Mueller, S.: ARWeather - An Augmented Reality Weather System. In: IEEE International Symposium on Mixed and Augmented Reality 2008, Cambridge, UK, pp. 15–18 (2008)
14. chronozoom,
http://blogs.msdn.com/b/msr_er/archive/2013/11/20/warming-
up-to-a-new-tool-for-teaching-climate-change.aspx
15. http://www.ufunk.net/en/techno/augmented-reality-sandbox/
16. Doswell, C.A., Maddox, R.A.: The role of diagnosis in weather forecasting. In: Proceedings of the 11th Conference on Weather Forecasting and Analysis, pp. 177–182. American Meteorological Society, Boston (1986)
17. Tavares, T.A., Schofield, D.: Interaction Design for Convergence Medias and Devices: a Multisensory Challenge. In: Lugmayr, A., Zotto, C.D., Lowe, G.F. (eds.) Convergent Divergence? – Cross-Disciplinary Viewpointon Media Convergence, 1st edn. Springer-Verlag Handbook (2013)
18. EUMETCast—EUMETSAT's broadcastsystem for environmental data. EUM TD 15, Darmstadt, Germany, 34 p. EUMETSAT (2004)
19. Meteosat second generation—system overview. EUM TD07, Darmstadt, Germany, 44 p. EUMETSAT (2001)
20. Barbosa, H.A.: Sistema EUMETCast: Uma abordagem aplicada dos Meteosat Segunda Geração, 1st edn., vol. 2, 186, p. EDUFAL, Maceió (2013)

An Intuitive Way to Describe Our World:
A Microblog LBS Visualization System

Jian-Min Wang[1,2], Lai Gan[2], Ri-Peng Zhang[2], and Fang You[1,2]

[1] School of Arts and Media, Tongji University, Shanghai, China
wangjianmin@tongji.edu.cn
[2] School of Information Science and Technology, Sun Yat-sen University, Guangzhou, China
{503187646,pk_mati}@qq.com, youfang@tongji.edu.cn

Abstract. With the help of LBS provided by some social network service provider, people can obtain knowledge and perceive the world around them more conveniently. However, since the contradiction of a large number of POI nodes and the limited displaying space, finding a better layout algorithm to visualize the POI nodes is important for better user experience. This paper presents a new layout algorithm called Virtual Layout algorithm, which can solve the problem of the uneven POI nodes distribution and make a better presentation of the geospatial information. We also deployed a microblog LBS visualization system which consists of Virtual Layout algorithm, stylized map and location reference frame to verify the performance of the proposed algorithm.

Keywords: LBS visualization, Microblog, Layout algorithm, POI.

1   Introduction

Weibo.com, the main microblog service provider in China, with its convenient and social characteristics, is widely used by large amount of users. However, just publishing the common information (text/image) could not satisfy the users' demand, so the LBS (Location Based Service) was applied as a value-added service of Weibo.com. LBS is combination of different location-acquisition technologies, like Global Positioning System (GPS) and Geographic Information System (GIS). In detail, LBS obtains precise locating data (e.g., longitude & latitude) from mobile terminals, and combines them with the location profiles stored in the GIS database, providing users a more intuitive way to organize the geographic and social information of our real world [1].

With development of LBS and social network, people make much extra information for each GPS coordinates, which we called POI (Point Of Interest) [2]. Through POI data and LBS visualization, people can acquire and understand the contextual information around them more conveniently. For instance, we can present relationships between user and location, location and location, etc. Such kinds of information are bridges connecting the virtual world and the real world which can be inferred of some useful patterns.

S. Yamamoto (Ed.): HIMI 2014, Part I, LNCS 8521, pp. 108–119, 2014.

However, microblog LBS visualization is not just a way for demonstrating information [3]. In the process of creating an effective visualization, we should consider many factors such as scene, perception and cognition. An effective visualization should have a clear purpose and convey information directly. Unfortunately, there are still some problems on the visualization of microblog LBS.

- Most of the visualization systems are over dependent on the real map and weaken the relationship between different POI nodes. For instance, when we visualize dense or sparse POI nodes, it will lead to the result that some nodes are overlapped or some isolated nodes are too far away from the major region, which will make visualization illegible and waste of displaying space.
- As the displaying problem described above, owing to the limited displaying space of the overlapped POI nodes, we are not able to display enough valuable information on each POI node, so in some cases, it will lead to useless visualization.

In summary, developing an efficient model and a better visualization method for geospatial data to achieve more satisfactory visualization is worth detailed study [2]. Thus, in this paper, a geospatial model Weigeo and a layout algorithm Virtual Layout algorithm are developed for microblog LBS visualization. At the last of our research, we developed a microblog LBS visualization system based on the dataset obtained from Weibo.com to illustrate the Weigeo model and Virtual Layout algorithm. The microblog LBS visualization system, differing from the previous map visualization system, it provides a more even distribution of nodes for visualization, which can offer users a more clear way to understand the structural relationships between different POI nodes.

The paper is organized as follows: First, we describe some previous work on geospatial visualization; second, we describe the Weigeo model based on the POI data obtained from Weibo.com; third, we propose a new layout algorithm called Virtual Layout algorithm to rearrange the distribution of the POI nodes; fourth, we illustrate the performance of our visualization system; fifth, we present the implementation of our system; and last, we draw our conclusions and propose the future work we attempt to conduct.

2 Relative Work

Currently, the researchers mainly focus on the domains about LBS modeling and geospatial data modeling. For example, Xiaoyan Chen et al. [4] built an effective system for geospatial information publication and subscription, but this is a theoretical model and not directly manifest the relationship between different locations. Moreover, Christian S. Jensen et al. [5] proposed a multidimensional data model which well matching the geospatial data in order to reveal multidimensional information. Nevertheless, the data model is difficult to be applied in current geospatial data system. Thus, this model is not being implemented in practical use. Joao

Mourinho et al. [6] utilized the geographical draft of the spider map to upgrade the LBS experience. The spider map puts the contextual information related to users such as central location of the user, related stay points and end points on the geographical draft which could help users eliminate the mass of irrelevant information to improve the user experience. Through these significant researches, we figure out that it is important to develop an appropriate model and a more intuitive method for LBS based on the features of the POI data.

3   Modeling

According to the POI data we obtained from Weibo.com, we construct a geospatial model called Weigeo. This model consists of four components, POI node, POI zone, POI links and POI virtual distance. Following we will describe notation of each component.

3.1   POI Node

POI node is the basic data obtained from Weibo.com, each POI node contains 27 attributes, such as title, longitude, latitude, check-in number, check-in user number, category, address, etc. So our goal is to rearrange the distribution of these POI nodes for presenting maximum of the attributes.

3.2   POI Zone

POI zone consists of POI nodes. We define a POI node is a part of a POI zone if this POI node is in the distance of zoneRange (analogous to radius of a circle). Moreover, if a POI node belongs to other POI zone in the distance of zoneRange to current POI zone, we can merge these two POI zones into a larger POI zone. In Section 4, we will detailed introduce the Divide Zone algorithm.

3.3   POI Link

POI link is depicted by connecting line, which represent the transformational distance between each POI nodes or POI zones.

3.4   POI Virtual Distance

POI virtual distance is proposed to solve the uneven distributing problem of the POI nodes. Virtual distance represents the final transformational position of a POI node, as shown in Fig. 1. The process of Virtual Layout algorithm will be detailed described in Section 4.

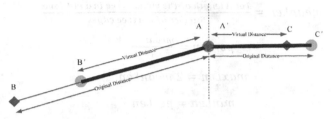

Fig. 1. Original Distance and Virtual Distance

4   Method

Currently, there're several main visualization layout algorithms, such as force-directed algorithm [7], multidimensional scaling algorithm [8] and relaxation algorithm [9], etc. Although these algorithms can ensure the information distributed evenly by moving the positions of points, but they have a serious deficiency that the original direction between point and point would be neglected, so these algorithms can not meet our requirements.

In this section, we proposed a novel graphic layout algorithm called Virtual Layout algorithm. The Virtual Layout algorithm mainly consists of three sub algorithms—Divide Zone algorithm, POI nodes virtual tree algorithm and POI zones virtual tree algorithm. These three sub algorithms cannot be separated from each other, the input of later sub algorithm depends on the output of previous sub algorithm. Following we will detailed describe these three sub algorithms.

4.1   Divide Zone Algorithm

Divide Zone is an algorithm which mainly applies DBSCAN [10] to cluster the POI nodes into a POI zone in accordance with the size of zoneRange (zoneRange is a parameter determining the size of clustering range). We cluster two POI nodes into one POI zone if their distance is less than the zoneRange, and if two POI zones are overlapped, we also cluster them together until all the nodes are divided into POI zones. In practical use, we use the ratio of the screen width as the zoneRange (e.g., a 1366×768 resolution screen, 0.01 zoneRange means 13.66 pixel units. And we transform pixel value to definitive GPS degree to cluster the POI nodes). The value of zoneRange can be customized by users for their convenient.

4.2   POI Nodes Virtual Tree Algorithm

In Section 3, we have presented the concept of POI virtual distance. POI virtual distance is the output of Virtual Layout algorithm, which is substitute of original distance. It can refine the distance of every two POI nodes, avoiding some nodes located too close or too loose. First of all, we will present some parameter of this algorithm:

$$meanLen = \frac{Total\ length\ of\ the\ virtual\ tree\ in\ a\ POI\ zone}{Number\ of\ the\ tree\ edges} \tag{1}$$

$$perLen = \frac{meanLen}{5} \tag{2}$$

$$maxLen = 2\ meanLen \tag{3}$$

$$minLen = perLen \tag{4}$$

MeanLen represents the average length of the virtual tree in a POI zone and different POI zone will come to different meanLen, so as the maxLen and minLen. This results a dynamic adaptation of different POI zones. The procedure of POI nodes virtual tree algorithm is described as follows:

1. If a POI node is in stable state, select another POI node which is closest to this node but not in the stable state, then connect these two nodes.
2. After obtaining the original distance of these two nodes, we can calculate the virtual distance according to Table 1.

Table 1. Output of Virtual Distance

Original Distance	Virtual Distance
0<Original Distance<minLen	minLen
minLen<Original Distance<maxLen	Original Distance/perLen
maxLen<Original Distance<zoneRange	maxLen

So we can see the schematic diagram shown in Fig. 2. The POI nodes virtual tree algorithm actually makes a centralized tendency of the edges of which distances are too short or too long. After this process, we can obtain an even distribution of nodes in each POI zone.

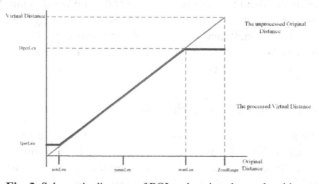

Fig. 2. Schematic diagram of POI nodes virtual tree algorithm

For example, as shown in Fig. 1, the three diamonds represent the original positions of three POI nodes (A, B and C), the three circulars represent the final positions
(A', B' and C'). First, we can set A as a stable node (So A' and A is the same), and
then we choose node C which is closest to A, calculate their virtual distance. As edge
<A', C> is too short, we should stretch this edge to minLen as shown in Table 1. Fi-
nally, we can figure out the new position of C'. Similarly, edge <A', B> is too long
and we should shrink it to maxLen, and we can figure out the new position of B'.

4.3   POI Zones Virtual Tree Algorithm

Once all the POI nodes are all well rearranged in the POI zones, we can obtain the
scope and central point of each POI zone. Then we adjust each POI zone to ensure the
distance among all the POI zones is reasonable. The process is familiar with POI
nodes virtual tree algorithm, finding the connection between every two POI zones is
actually to find the minimum connection of two POI nodes respectively belong to
different POI zones. In the process of moving the POI zones, all the POI nodes of this
POI zone should also be moved.

As a whole, we can summarize the Virtual Layout algorithm into four states shown
in Fig. 3. Figure (a) shows state of the original POI nodes. Figure (b) shows state of
different POI zones clustered by Divide Zone algorithm. Figure (c) shows state of
generating virtual tree among POI nodes in each POI zone and we can also see the
status of POI zone such as scope and central point changing during this process.
Figure (d) shows state of the final status of generating stable virtual tree among POI
zones. It is obvious to see that the Virtual Layout algorithm is effective to make an
even distribution and provide more displaying space for POI attribute information.

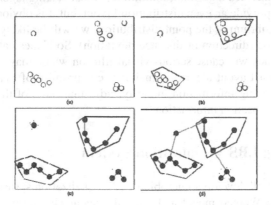

Fig. 3. Four States of the Virtual Layout Algorithm

4.4   The Features of VIRTUAL Layout Algorithm

Virtual Layout is a graph layout algorithm based on the graphic point distribution. It
aims to distribute nodes on a plane more rational, and ensure the distance between

each node is not too close nor too loose which lead to the result of losing some valid information or wasting some displaying space. Compare to other graphic layout algorithms, Virtual Layout algorithm has following features.

1. No iteration, only one time can reach equilibrium state

Force-directed algorithm, multidimensional scaling algorithm and relaxation algorithm are algorithms simulating physical models, so they need a series of iteration to reach the equilibrium state and obtain the location coordinates. Due to repeated iteration, if the number of points is large, it will be bound to cause a long time to reach equilibrium state. However, Virtual Layout algorithm can reduce time complexity and we do not need constant iteration to keep the equilibrium state. To sum up, firstly, we use a clustering algorithm (Divide Zone algorithm) to generate POI zones, of which time complexity is O(NlogN); second, we generate virtual trees for the POI nodes, of which time complexity is O(N*N*M) and M is the number of clustering number. Finally, we generate virtual trees among POI zones, of which time complexity is O(N*N). The final location of each node will be obtained by only one process, thus it is a more efficient algorithm compared to others.

2. Clear view of distribution

Virtual Layout algorithm adopted virtual distance to transform continuous distance to discrete length, which can do good effort to avoid visual illusion and provide a clear view of all the POI nodes.

3. Strong direction information

Although force-directed algorithm, multidimensional scaling algorithm and relaxation algorithm can provide an even distribution layout, but it is obvious that if we over emphasize the equilibrium of the point distribution, we will be likely to cause significant information loss (direction or distance deviation). So if these algorithms are applied on the map, they will cause serious visual illusion which may mislead the users. Accordingly, Virtual Layout algorithm makes a compromise of making distribution equilibrium and keeping information integrity, adjusting parts of the POI nodes and keeping most of the location information.

5   Microblog LBS Visualization System

In this section, we will develop a microblog LBS visualization system to illustrate the performance of the Weigeo model and Virtual Layout algorithm. Fig. 4 shows the framework of microblog LBS visualization system. The system can be divided into two modules, data collection module and visualization module. Data collection module takes charge of crawling data from Weibo.com and OpenStreetMap, processing the raw data and storing the processed data in database. These data includes POI information and stylized map data, which compose the foundation of the whole system. The second module is visualization module, including stylized map, Virtual Layout algorithm and location reference frame. In Section 4, we have detailed introduced the Virtual Layout algorithm, following we will introduce the stylized map and location reference frame.

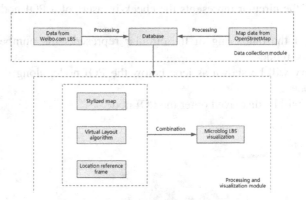

Fig. 4. Microblog LBS visualization system framework

5.1   Stylized Map

The general map contains various kinds of geographic information, in some cases, it will puzzle users to get a clear view of their concerning POI nodes. So in order to show the most valuable information on a limited map and eliminate the redundant factors, we apply stylized map. We utilize OpenStreetMap geographic data as our basic geographic data and use TileMill to edit the OpenStreetMap data. The OpenStreetMap data includes attributes of map such as background, labels, roads and rivers, etc. We use Carto Css to program the stylization files. Fig. 5 shows the final output of our stylized map, we can see that this customized map eliminates much of the redundant labels, but keeps the key geographic information.

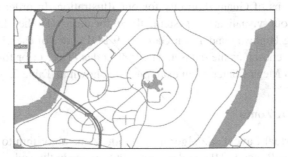

Fig. 5. Output of stylized map

5.2   Location Reference Frame

Location reference frame is a measurement of the POI nodes of a region. Since a POI node contains up to 27 attributes, too much information would be difficult for displaying in limited displaying space, so we design a location reference frame for our visualization system. We will describe our POI node designed for microblog LBS visualization system as follows:

1. The size of the circular represents the check-in users of a POI node, more will be bigger.
2. The color of the outer ring of the circular represents the number of check-ins, hotter will be redder.
3. The category will be shown as icon below the POI node, along with the name of this POI node.
4. Timestamp will be displayed outer the POI node.

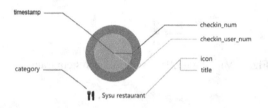

Fig. 6. Design of the location reference frame

6   Implementation

6.1   Data Preparation

Microblog LBS visualization system stored two kinds of data, one is geospatial data, and the other is stylized map data, both of which are obtained by a specific web crawler. Finally, we obtained 147 POI categories, 8437 POI nodes, 519,687 users and 1,007,702 check-ins of Guangzhou city for our illustration. In order to illustrate the performance of our visualization system, three locations (Higher Education Mega Center, Xinguang Highway and Taian Garden), 9 POI nodes of each location, 27 POI nodes in total are chosen as the dataset. The POI nodes (Take prior four POI nodes of Higher Education Mega Center as an example) are shown in Table 2.

6.2   Divide POI Zones

First we used Virtual Layout sub algorithm Divide Zone algorithm to cluster the POI nodes. We set zoneRange = 0.03, and we get 3 POI zones in the end.

Table 2. POI nodes of Higher Education Mega Center

Poiid	Title	Longitude, Latitude	Check-ins	Users	Category
B2094752D46A A2FE429E	Agricultural bank of China Panyu city branch	(23.047653, 113.378603)	1	1	Bank
B2094757D06A AAFA4399	GOGO new plaza	(23.062707, 113.391915)	6073	4412	Shopping Mall
B2094757D06F A6FE439A	Higher Education Mega Center North	(23.058074, 113.385632)	1811	1575	Subway Station
B2094757D06E AAFE429A	Sun Yat-sen University (East Campus)	(23.066774, 113.391935)	3821	2414	University
......	......	......	......	......	......

6.3   Generate Virtual Tree Among POI Nodes

By using POI nodes virtual tree algorithm presented in Section 4, we can acquire new position of each POI node. Take the POI nodes around Higher Education Mega Center as an example, we build a virtual tree in this POI zone, some POI links of the virtual tree are shown in Table 3.

Table 3. POI links around Higher Education Mega Center

POI link	From	To	Original distance (perLen)	Virtual distance (perLen)
(B2094752D46AA2FE429E, B2094757D06FA6FE439)	(23.048, 113.379)	(23.058, 113.386)	11.622881	10.0
(B2094757D06AAAFA4399, B2094654D468A0FB459)	(23.063, 113.392)	(23.063, 113.390)	2.0022447	2.0022447
(B2094757D06FA6FE439A, B2094757D065A4F8429)	(23.058, 113.386)	(23.056, 113.392)	5.697238	5.697238
(B2094757D06EAAFE429A, B2094654D468A0FB459)	(23.063, 113.390)	(23.067, 113.392)	3.6607623	3.6607623
......	......	......	......	

Once all the virtual trees are established, we can draw the virtual trees on the map. As Fig. 7 shows, Figure (a) is the result of virtual tree, Figure (b) is the comparison of original POI nodes and processed POI nodes. The virtual distance is set the range from minLen = 1perLen to maxLen = 10perLen. According to the transformation shown in Table 1, most of the links are within the limits of the range except for the first link, which is too long and need to be shrunk. On the whole, the POI nodes are mostly parallel to the original nodes. Although the algorithm makes some excursion and shrink, it keeps the relative direction between each node.

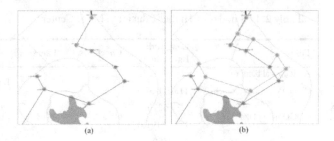

Fig. 7. Generate virtual tree among POI nodes

6.4   Generate Virtual Tree Among POI Zones

To find out the connection of POI zones is actually to find the shortest distance of POI nodes belong to different POI zones. As POI nodes have been divided into three POI zones, so we just need two POI links to connect the three POI zones as Table 4 shown.

Table 4. POI links of three POI zones

POI link	From	To	Original distance (perLen)	Virtual distance (perLen)
(B2094752D46AA2FE429E, B2094654D46FA0FD4998)	(23.048, 113.379)	(23.065, 113.345)	1.2626879	0.8
(B2094757D06EAAFE429A, B2094654D46CA6F9469B)	(23.063, 113.392)	(23.122, 113.386)	1.8961813	0.8

In Fig. 8, we can see that the new positions of POI nodes which keep the original directions but offer a more even distribution. And by using stylized map, we can reduce useless geographic redundancy and provide a more aesthetic visualization. We can infer that Virtual Layout algorithm is able to make an improvement for the LBS visualization and it can become an extra pattern of map information presentation.

Fig. 8. Generate virtual tree among POI zones

7   Conclusion

With the development of location technology, the combination of LBS and social network is enriching our lives. Microblog LBS visualization system, presented by this paper, is not only a kind of visualization, but also an important bridge connecting the virtual world and real world, offering a more convenient way for people to explore places they are interested in. Weibo.com as a primary social network service provider in China, it has a variety of geospatial and social information. How to effectively use these information to construct a better model to describe our world and detect valuable pattern is a promising direction for the future researching. In the end, we hope that in the future, we can improve the performance of Virtual Layout algorithm for three-dimensional visualization and apply it in other domains. And for our microblog LBS visualization system, we want to find a better interaction method to present more POI information in the limited displaying space.

Acknowledgements. This work was supported by the National Natural Science Foundation of China under Grant No.61073132 and 60776796; the Fundamental Research Funds for the Central Universities (101gpy33); Project 985 of Innovation Base for Journalism & Communication in the All-media Era, Sun Yat-sen University.

References

1. Chen, X., et al.: System architecture of LBS based on spatial information integration. In: Geoscience and Remote Sensing Symposium. IEEE (2004)
2. Contributors, W.: Point of interest, in Wikipedia, The Free Encyclopedia (2013)
3. Iliinsky, N.: On beauty. Beautiful Visualization: Looking at Data through the Eyes of Experts, 1–14 (2010)
4. Chen, X., Chen, Y., Rao, F.: An efficient spatial publish/subscribe system for intelligent location-based services. In: Proceedings of the 2nd International Workshop on Distributed Event-Based Systems 2003, pp. 1–6. ACM, San Diego (2003)
5. Jensen, C.S., et al.: Multidimensional data modeling for location-based services. In: Proceedings of the 10th ACM International Symposium on Advances in Geographic Information Systems 2002, pp. 55–61. ACM, McLean (2002)
6. Mourinho, J., Galvao, T., Falcão e Cunha, J.: Spider Maps for Location-Based Services Improvement. In: Snene, M., Ralyté, J., Morin, J.-H. (eds.) IESS 2011. LNBIP, vol. 82, pp. 16–29. Springer, Heidelberg (2011)
7. Chernobelskiy, R., Cunningham, K.I., Goodrich, M.T., Kobourov, S.G., Trott, L.: Force-Directed Lombardi-Style Graph Drawing. In: Speckmann, B., et al. (eds.) GD 2011. LNCS, vol. 7034, pp. 320–331. Springer, Heidelberg (2011)
8. Davison, M.L.: Multidimensional scaling. Wiley, New York (1983)
9. Fry, B.: Visualizing data: exploring and explaining data with the Processing environment. O'Reilly Media (2008)
10. Ester, M., et al.: A density-based algorithm for discovering clusters in large spatial databases with noise. In: KDD (1996)

Google Analytics Spatial Data Visualization: Thinking Outside of the Box

Wanli Xing[1], Rui Guo[2], Ben Richardson[1], and Thomas Kochtanek[1]

[1] School of Information Science and Learning Technologies,
University of Missouri, Columbia, MO 65211, USA
{wxdg5,benjaminrichardson}@mail.missouri.edu,
KochtanekT@missouri.edu
[2] Department of Civil and Environmental Engineering,
University of South Florida, Tampa, Columbia, FL 33620, USA
rui@mail.usf.edu

Abstract. This paper showcases a methodology to assist website managers in determining the influence of their websites in regard to a particular location. This is achieved through enhancing Google Analytics by supplementing it with outside data sources. Though GIS software namely ArcGIS, the approach allows for more comprehendible geospatial analysis while also presenting maps overlays that are easier to grasp than the tools currently offered by Google Analytics. The Truman Presidential Library website serves as a case study to explore the potentiality of this approach.

Keywords: GIS, Google Analytics, Visualization, decision making, library.

1   Introduction

Google Analytics (GA) is the most commonly used web traffic analysis tool with over 80% of websites that track and monitor traffic data utilizing GA services. GA provides a variety of analytic tools to describe web traffic usage that are accessed through the GA dashboard. Despite its many benefits, GA is limited in its functionality especially with regard to geospatial data. The most frequently used methods to describe users' traffic data use statistics and graphs are derived from basic features in the GA dashboard. As a result, when it comes to spatial distribution associated with visitor traffic, researchers that examine the efficacy of GA geography dashboard (Figure 1) (which only provides the number of hits over a particular region (Country, State, City, etc.) are just beginning to determine how this information can assist web managers in facilitating decision-making. According to Turner (2010), broad measures of website usage such as virtual visits can be useful, but do not adequately portray the bigger picture of website statistics as these numbers provide little insight or ability to measure website performance on deeper levels of understanding. Consequently, a more sophisticated measure of the geospatial distribution of visits needs to be developed in order to assist decision makers in effectively evaluating their website.

S. Yamamoto (Ed.): HIMI 2014, Part I, LNCS 8521, pp. 120–127, 2014.

In an attempt to address the geospatial potential of GA, Clifton (2010) introduced the geomap overlay technique for adding other dimensions into the visitors' geographical distribution map to deliver information visually, and in turn, provide a more comprehensive picture of the performance of the website.

Until recently, few studies have applied these techniques or explored their potential for enhancing the visualization of geospatial data. This could be due to the fact that there has not been a mature framework developed that can extract or exhibit additional outside data to work in conjunction with GA. For instance, Clifton's map overlay method has inherent limitations in that the dimensions he suggested are limited to the data factors already contained in GA. For example, geospatial visit distribution data for the United States can be cross-referenced with data from the search engines visitors are using (data already collected by Google Analytics) and then displayed in the same graph. This technique does not add outside dimensions into the GA geographical graph which could have significant impact on website stakeholders' decision-making. For instance, academic websites may need to evaluate usage over different school districts (Xu et al, 2010) and commercial sites might want to consider a website's influence on different demographics (age, race, or income scale etc.) in different areas (Kumar et al, 2009). Therefore, Clifton's map overlay methodology is limited by not adding additional outside factors to the graph that could enhance the potential to provide a meaningful diagnosis of web traffic data.

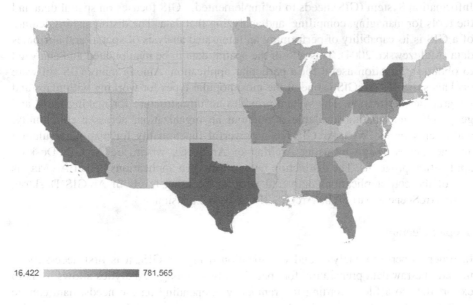

16,422 ▬▬▬▬▬▬▬ 781,565

Fig. 1. Google Analytics nation-wide spatial distribution of Truman Library website visits dashboard

From an aesthetical and cognitive perspective, using a screenshot of the GA dashboard is insufficient because it merely presents a flat, color-coded graph. Various researchers have indicated that enhanced aesthetics with different display formats can improve the perceivers' information processing dynamics from a design, psychological and practical perspective (Tractinsky, 2013 & 1997, Reber et al, 2004, Petersen et al, 2004). Moreover, the GA flat dashboard is incapable of displaying multi-measures. This makes the web managers' task of comprehending the graph more difficult as they attempt to process the overcrowded measures of information on the graph. In summary, current geospatial distribution in GA has three flaws: 1) no sophisticated metrics exist; 2) lack of empirical experience in adding other dimensions to the graph; 3) the graphical display is limited in the GA flat dashboard. Researchers using GA should explore new methods and tools for graphing measurements of visitors' spatial distribution and presentation.

To fill this gap, this study creates a new density metric to gain more insight into website usage and explores Geographic Information System (GIS) for visualization of web visitors' spatial distribution of a library website. This approach is capable of being employed with any website that utilizes GA.

2   Methodology

2.1   ArcGIS

In order to conduct spatial density analysis of a resource inventory, a Geographic Information System (GIS) needs to be implemented. GIS focuses on spatial data and the tools for managing, compiling, and analyzing that data. The distinguishing feature of a GIS is its capability of performing an integrated analysis of spatial and attributes data (Malczewski, 2004). This allows the spatial data to be manipulated and analyzed to obtain information useful for a particular application. Among many GIS software packages, ESRI's ArcGIS is one of the most popular types for working with maps and geographic information. The system provides an infrastructure for making maps and geographic information available throughout an organization, across a community, and openly on the Web. ArcGIS has a powerful functionality for map manipulation and aesthetics design by using ArcMap or ArcScene, whcih are ArcGIS Desktop application programs. The distinction between the two applications is that ArcMap is one of the core applications delivered with all licensing levels of ArcGIS Desktop, while ArcScene is part of the ArcGIS 3D Analyst extension.

Scope Selection

In order to perform analysis and visualization using ArcGIS, it is first necessary to initiate the raw data preparation for spatial analysis. Google Analytics allows users to export data to a file according to granularity. Depending on the needs, data can be exported out by country, continent, sub-continent, state, city and metropolitan etc. for further processing. Relying on the characteristic of the website, various study scopes can be defined. For instance, if the main target users of the website are located in the United States, then the United States can be chosen as the primary study scope to compare the distribution features between various states.

Supplementing Data

In undertaking any GIS-based work, the most common sources of spatial data should be collected to generate the base map. This is a significant step to introduce the outside source to Google Analytics. The source data includes data for layer generation and data for computation. In our study, we mainly supplement the TIGER/Line Shape-file data and population information for primary and secondary study scope, respectively.

Density Computation

In addition to the total visits by location directly obtained from Google Analytics, the visits density (representing the number of visits per person at one place), is computed for comparison. This outside population data is introduced to add an additional measure. While the common practice for web managers is to assess the influence of their companies or organization over a particular region this is merely based on the number of visitors from that particular place. To enhance this practice, we introduced the density measure to provide another perspective to measure such influence. Because it is natural that when a state has a larger population, it would have a much bigger possibility to have more visits. However, this alone does not necessarily mean that companies or organizations have more influence over that area. As an example, in terms of influence, 100 people heard of your organization in a city that has 1 million population does not necessarily outperform 50 people in a city which has 1000 population in total. Therefore, density for that place is calculated.

Assuming there are M representative years in the log datasets and website visits are cumulated through the total studied time period for different locations, density of website visits can be computed by the following equation.

$$Ds = \left(\sum_s \sum_{t=1}^{t=m} V_{ts}\right) / \left(\sum_s P_s\right)$$

Where, Ds denotes the density of website visits (visits/person) at location s, V_{ts} refers to website visits of the studied time period t at location s, and P_s is the population of location s. Here, s could be nation-wide, state-wide and city-wide etc.

Visualization

Using ArcGIS, multiple measures, density and visits to a particular location are displayed in the same graph.

2.2   Research Context

http://www.trumanlibrary.org

The Truman Presidential Library website as shown in Figure 2 was chosen for this research. The Truman Presidential Library website serves as a portal to online resources pertaining to the life of Harry Truman as well as providing information about visiting the Truman Museum. As such, it is a popular website that attracts many visitors from around the United States and worldwide that generates thousands of hits per day.

Fig. 2. Truman Library Website

2.3   Dataset

As an example, we experimented with this methodology to compare Truman Library's influence over different states. Since Google Analytics collects all the data for us automatically, we just simply downloaded the data by state. To compute density of visits, the 2012 population data for each state (except Alaska and Hawaii) of the United States was used. Additionally, TIGER/Line Shape-files by different layer types (e.g., block groups, census tracts and school districts) were collected from different online open sources. In order to facilitate the display of the graph and explanation, each state is assigned a number as table 1. Moreover, Figure 3 shows the visits for each state in each year.

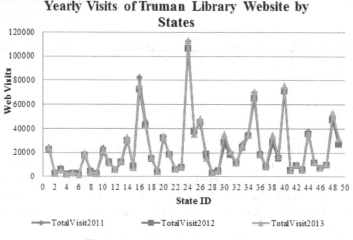

Fig. 3. State Visits in Truman Library

Table 1. State ID

StateID	1	2	3	4	5	6	7
State Name	Washington	Montana	Maine	North Dakota	South Dakota	Wyoming	Wisconsin
StateID	8	9	10	11	12	13	14
State Name	Idaho	Vermont	Minnesota	Oregon	New Hampshire	Iowa	Massachusetts
StateID	15	16	17	18	19	20	21
State Name	Nebraska	New York	Pennsylvania	Connecticut	Rhode Island	New Jersey	Indiana
StateID	22	23	24	25	26	27	28
State Name	Nevada	Utah	California	Ohio	Illinois	District of Columbia	Delaware
StateID	29	30	31	32	33	34	35
State Name	West Virginia	Maryland	Colorado	Kentucky	Kansas	Virginia	Missouri
StateID	36	37	38	39	40	41	42
State Name	Arizona	Oklahoma	North Carolina	Tennessee	Texas	New Mexico	Alabama
StateID	43	44	45	46	47	48	49
State Name	Mississippi	Georgia	South Carolina	Arkansas	Louisiana	Florida	Michigan

3   Results

3.1   Density

By introducing various data sources, we computed the density for each state as in Figure 4 according to the formula we proposed above. From the density graph we could

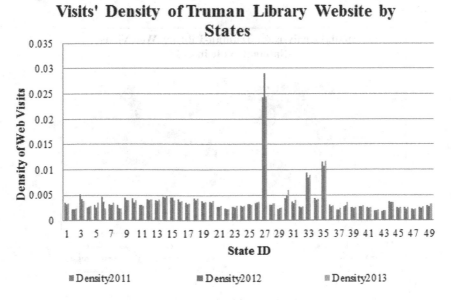

Fig. 4. Density Measurement

see which state density is the highest in combination with the State ID. In addition, in some regards, this density could also inform managers which state has the most influence.

3.2   Visualization

In order to assist mangers in their information processing, we implemented ArcGIS to visualize the information. As stated, ArcGIS is a powerful spatial data visualization tool and enables the visualization of a graph to hold multiple measures. In our context, we tried to present both the visits in each state and density measure in the same graph. As an example, we put the 2012 graph below.

As shown in the Figure 5, Texas and California had the most visitors, but in terms of density Missouri and DC have the highest value. This is understandable because Texas and California are the most populated states. However, Missouri is the location that hosts the Truman Library and DC is a location that supports many of the Truman Library activities. Therefore, Texas and California may have the most visits, but this does not necessarily mean Truman Library has the most influence over these places. In fact, it can be postulated from this data that the Truman Library has the most influence in Missouri and DC. In turn, density might be a better gauge to assess influence of the organization and company over a particular community.

In addition, compared with the Google Analytics flat graph, ArcGIS empowered maps can allow managers to process multiple-dimensional information simultaneously. While Google Analytics could only display the visits to that particular location, ArcGIS is able to present various measures and information at the same time. Another significant aspect is to introduce the outside factor and measure to Google Analytics which is unattainable by using map overlay or similar techniques residing in Google Analytics.

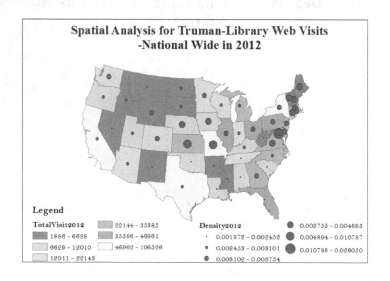

Fig. 5. ArcGIS Visualization

4   Conclusion

In sum, in this case study we utilized density metrics for measuring a website's influence over a region rather than merely depending on the numbers of visits to make conclusions. Further, we demonstrated that additional map layers and labels could be overlaid on an existing graph, and thus, present all of this information in one graph to provide a more refined analysis. It is hoped that website managers can utilize this approach to assist in their decision making process when examining the influence of their websites.

References

1. Clifton, B.: Reports Explained. In: Advanced Web Metrics with Google Analytics, pp. 97–127. Wiley. com (2012)
2. Kumar, C., Norris, J.B., Sun, Y.: Location and time do matter: A long tail study of website requests. Decision Support Systems 47(4), 500–507 (2009)
3. Malczewski, J.: GIS-based land-use suitability analysis: a critical overview. Progress in Planning 62(1), 3–65 (2004)
4. Petersen, M.G., Iversen, O.S., Krogh, P.G., Ludvigsen, M.: Aesthetic Interaction: a pragmatist's aesthetics of interactive systems. In: Proceedings of the 5th Conference on Designing Interactive Systems: Processes, Practices, Methods, and Techniques, pp. 269–276. ACM (August 2004)
5. Reber, R., Schwarz, N., Winkielman, P.: Processing fluency and aesthetic pleasure: is beauty in the perceiver's processing experience? Personality and Social Psychology Review 8(4), 364–382 (2004)
6. Tractinsky, N.: Aesthetics and apparent usability: empirically assessing cultural and methodological issues. In: Proceedings of the ACM SIGCHI Conference on Human Factors in Computing Systems, pp. 115–122. ACM (March 1997)
7. Tractinsky, N.: Visual Aesthetics. In: Soegaard, M., Dam, R.F. (eds.) The Encyclopedia of Human-Computer Interaction, 2nd edn. The Interaction Design Foundation, Aarhus (2013), http://www.interaction-design.org/encyclopedia/visual_aesthetics.html
8. Xu, B., Recker, M., Hsi, S.: The data deluge: Opportunities for research in educational digital libraries. In: Internet Issues: Blogging, the Digital Divide and Digital Libraries. Nova Science Pub Inc., New York (2010)

A Visualization Concept for Mobile Faceted Search

Bianca Zimmer, Romina Kühn, and Thomas Schlegel

TU Dresden - Junior Professorship in Software Engineering of Ubiquitous Systems, Germany
{bianca.zimmer,romina.kuehn,thomas.schlegel}@tu-dresden.de

Abstract. Nowadays, people are increasingly using their mobile devices to find different kinds of information, for example, about products, trips or latest news. Therefore, mobile devices such as smartphones and tablets have become a constant companion for many users to have access to information at any time and any place. The large amount of data and information that is provided to the user by mobile devices differs in its feature set and visual representation. To ensure the success of an app and to keep the user from an information overload by presenting too much information, a wise preparation and visualization of the data is necessary. Faceted search provides an opportunity to focus on specific information by filtering. In this paper we present a general visualization concept for faceted search on mobile devices, especially on smartphones.

Keywords: visualization, faceted search, mobile devices, design patterns.

1 Introduction

People are continuously looking for different kinds of information at any time and any place. To act location- and time-independent most people use their mobile devices such as smartphones or tablets. Since mobile devices usually have small displays, all information has to be adapted to these kinds of display. Consequently, the importance of proper search tools rises to achieve desired search results. Our approach is to adapt information by using faceted search to filter the given data. Faceted search is a technique of progressively refining search results by selecting filter criteria in any combination [1, 2].

While many mobile applications currently offer the possibility to filter results, most of them cannot be compared to desktop solutions [1]. Often there is an attempt to reduce search refinement options to a minimum for the mobile version due to the limited screen size. The developers' intent is to keep the user interface simple, which results in the limitation of functionality. To avoid this limitation we present a concept to visualize faceted search on mobile devices.

This paper is structured as follows: In section 2 some related work is presented. In section 3 we summarize a short survey that is the basis for our visualization concept. Section 4 describes our visualization concept for mobile faceted search in detail. We introduce different design patterns and facets that are extracted from various current applications. Section 5 presents a prototype that was implemented to show the feasibility of our concept. Section 6 concludes our paper and shows some future work.

S. Yamamoto (Ed.): HIMI 2014, Part I, LNCS 8521, pp. 128–136, 2014.

2   Related Work

Ben Shneiderman summarized the following fundamental principle as the "Visual Information Seeking Mantra": "Overview first, zoom and filter, then details-on-demand" [3]. This general guideline emphasizes how users can be supported in exploring data. The use of filtering techniques provides dynamic queries that can reduce large data amounts and highlight relevant items. Filters are usually organized by independent properties (facets) with several options (facet values) appearing under each facet [4]. For example, a product might be classified by using a color facet in which green is an exemplary facet value.

A few research projects such as FaThumb [5] have already covered the topic of faceted search on mobile devices. FaThumb enables query refinement displaying a 3x3 grid with filter options in the lower part of the screen, which is grouped in nine zones corresponding to the nine numeric keys on mobile phones. However, in the age of touchscreens these solutions are not appropriate anymore. The e-commerce company Amazon was among the first to establish a mobile application that enriches mobile search with faceted navigation [2]. By now several apps on mobile market places exist that provide faceted search following desktop versions.

There are general principles for designing effective faceted search experiences, for example, displaying only currently available facet values [4]. Furthermore, when designing the query refinement for mobile devices the following aspects should be taken into account:

- Refinement Page: Dedicating a separate filter layer (a dialog or even an entire screen) to faceted navigation, which can be accessed from the search result view, for presenting more than a handful of facets [4, 6]. The refinement page should not contain more than ten facets, arranged by importance, in order to avoid confusing the user [7].
- Facet Value Entry: Matching the displayed input format to the semantics of the facet values is particularly relevant to mobile devices. There are numerous data entry patterns with different intended use, e.g.:
  - Checkboxes for displaying multi-select facets,
  - Sliders for displaying quantitative data with specific ranges. Depending on the context, two types can be distinguished: single-ended and double-ended,
  - Stepper for entering a number between 0 and 5 via a Minus button and a Plus button. [4, 6]
- Navigation: Using a hierarchy as flat as possible to avoid deep drilling (more than three levels) [8]. In this way, facet values can be selected with just a few taps.

The mobile experience strategist Greg Nudelman outlines an experimental pattern in his book "Android Design Patterns": Slider with Histogram [6]. The idea behind this suggestion is to visualize the distribution of results with a histogram above the slider (cf. Fig. 1). Thus, the user gets an overview of the distribution and could select a wider range. For example, a user would normally place the slider position of a price range at $100 as the limit, not knowing that there are most of the results in the range of $103 -$105. The visual representation of the quantity of results can be a helpful tool for supporting faceted search and is part of the following visualization concept.

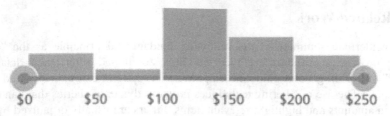

Fig. 1. Price slider with histogram pattern according to Greg Nudelman [6]

3   User Survey

To investigate filters we conducted a brief user study with thirteen participants. The participants were asked to evaluate the following three different types of filters for mobile devices:

- Vertical tabs (cf. Fig. 2 left),
- Spinner wheels (cf. Fig. 2 middle), and
- Dropdown lists (cf. Fig. 2 right) with plain text options.

The three examples given in Fig. 2 visualize these three types of filters. The first example on the left side shows a tab filter that represents a selection of a single value or a range of values. In the middle there is a spinner wheel that can be rotated by swipe gestures. On the right side, a dropdown list allows the selection of a single value for each facet.

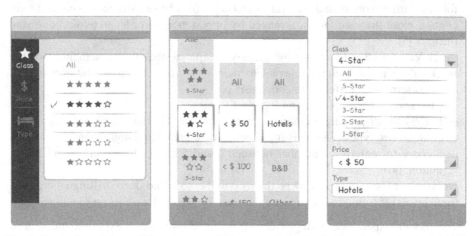

Fig. 2. Examples of three different types of filters: vertical tabs (left), spinner wheels (middle) and dropdown list (right)

The test persons were selected based on their experience with smartphone apps. In general, with a higher experience with apps we implied more experience in using different filter forms to find specific information, too.

The users were asked to evaluate the three kinds of filters by answering an online questionnaire about the visualization in general, the effort to use these filters, the suitability of the filter to specify data and the range of selection options. The test participants got Likert scales from "suits best" to "does not suit at all" (or "very good" to "not good at all") to choose the rate of the filters or to select what filter they prefer.

The main result of the survey is that tabs were rated best. Dropdown lists were considered suitable to filter data, too. Spinner wheels were evaluated as least appropriate to solve a filtering task. Some of the key characteristics of these three kinds of filter forms are summarized in Table 1. Dropdown lists have the advantage that the entire filter view can be scrolled, which therefore means that many facets can be displayed one below the next. Spinner wheels give an overview of all selected values for each facet and even the other selectable facet values are visible in the same view. Nevertheless, spinner wheels only allow single selection and the number of facets is limited by screen size. Vertical Tabs also offer a limited number of facets but the area besides the tabs provides enough space for the appropriate display format.

Table 1. Comparison of different types of filter forms

	Vertical Tabs	**Spinner Wheels**	**Dropdown Lists**
Number of facets that can be displayed	limited by screen size (mostly up to 5)	limited by screen size (mostly up to 3 or 4)	infinite
Display of facet values	all selected and selectable values for 1 facet	all selectable and selected values for each facet	all selected values for each facet
Selection of facet values	single and multiple	single	normally single

Furthermore, the participants were asked to evaluate different possibilities to visualize quantitative data according to recognizability and also appearance. Besides usual visualization methods such as bar graph and pie chart, other forms of graphical representation were taken into account. In the field of nutrition, which was taken as an application example, an illustration of a beam balance could be used as an example to demonstrate weight control.

Nearly all participants rated the bar graph the best representation of quantitative data due to the fact that this solution is generally known and permits immediate comparisons between numerical values.

The evaluation indicated that vertical tabs are appropriate to represent facets, even though they are limited by screen size. Moreover, bar graphs were identified as a suitable solution to visualize quantitative data. These results have been considered in the following visualization concept.

4   Visualization Concept

Within the scope of this work, we developed a general visualization concept for faceted search on mobile devices, especially on smartphones. This concept is based on the analysis of several existing apps and visualization methods, also taking into account current mobile design patterns. Furthermore, different mobile design solutions for filtering information were evaluated by users in the aforementioned survey. The results of this survey were taken into account in our visualization concept, too.

As already mentioned, many mobile apps represent facets in filter forms as dropdown lists or cascading lists with plain text options. This method causes difficulties in dealing with a large number of facets since users may need to scroll through a long list of values or navigate through more hierarchy levels. In order to simplify this selection, we developed a design concept for filter forms, which is shown in Fig. 3. The filter form is organized by tab controls which can be scrolled vertically and therefore contain a large number of facets.

Another advantage of this method is that the user receives an overview of multiple facets and also sees the values of the selected tab. Fig. 3 also illustrates visual aids supporting the user with information seeking:

- Facet Icons: the use of appropriate icons for each facet (e.g., a currency symbol for the *price* facet) and for a facet value subset (e.g., stars for ratings),

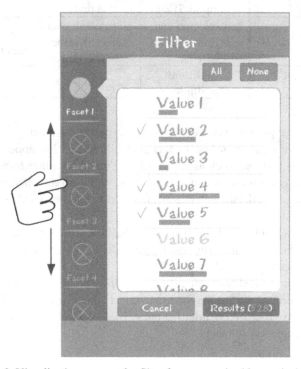

Fig. 3. Visualization concept for filter forms organized by vertical tabs

- Display Formats for Values: the selection of an appropriate display format with respect to the semantics of the facet values (e.g., checkboxes for displaying multi-select facets),
- Number of Results: the presentation of the number of results to support dynamic queries and to avoid returning empty results.

Icons have become increasingly popular due the fact that they are the most common form of images used in mobile design [9]. These simplified graphics can be memorized easily and, thus, provide users with additional visual assistance [10]. In our visualization concept icons for facets and, if appropriate, facet values are used to become memorable images for the user, too. In this way, recurrent facets can be identified quickly.

Using appropriate data entry patterns is particularly important for mobile devices. The developed visualization concept provides enough space for display formats of any kind while still allowing the user to keep an overview of the facets on the left side.

Although updating results dynamically might slightly increase the loading time, an immediate response can be guaranteed. This is important to display only the currently available facet values and, hence, to avoid empty results. A striking example is the selection of amenities values, e.g. *restaurant* or *swimming pool*, in the filter options for finding a suitable hotel. These values applied within the same facet *amenities* are combined conjunctively. A user might select *restaurant* and *swimming pool*, not knowing that there are no results that match his selection. It would be better to dynamically set the value *swimming pool* disabled after the user selected the value *restaurant*. This dynamic aspect is also part of our visualization concept.

The bars below the different values in Fig. 3 indicate the quantity of results for each value and allow immediate visual comparisons. This histogram will dynamically update as soon as facet values are selected. With the help of these visual components, the user can compare the respective number of results at a glance. In addition, the *Results* button displays the exact number of the filtered results.

In addition to the refinement page we already presented, according to Shneiderman, the following two components (or views) are also important parts of a comprehensive concept to support users in exploring data:

- Overview of results (*"Overview first..."*)
- Detail view of a result item (*"...then details-on-demand"*).

Therefore, we included these views into our visualization concept, too.

5   Prototype

In order to demonstrate and evaluate the visualization concept, we developed the Android advisory app *NutriGuide* for smartphones, which is based on the visualization concept applied to the domain of healthy nutrition. NutriGuide enables the user to receive relevant information about groceries and nutrition. In Fig. 4 two screenshots of the prototype are shown. The left view in Fig. 4 gives an initial overview of the food categories. The recognizable icons of different color provide users with additional visual assistance. By selecting a food category, the user switches to the next hierarchy level with an overview list of results (cf. Fig. 4 right).

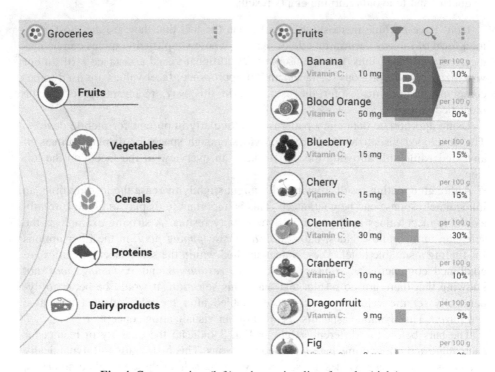

Fig. 4. Category view (left) and overview list of results (right)

The refinement page can be opened by selecting the filter symbol in the upper action bar (cf. Fig. 5). Similar to the concept in Fig. 3, facets are organized in vertical tabs and suitable domain specific icons are used to give a better overview. A histogram of the exemplary *Nutrients* facet visualizes the number of results for each facet value dynamically, retrieved from a database containing information on food and its nutrient content. In this example, the user can see quickly that the results include no low calorie items and only a few low fat items when selecting the value *Vitamin C-rich*.

This prototypical filter form currently offers only three facets with respect to healthy nutrition, but could be easily extended to include additional aspects such as special dietary needs for faceted search, too.

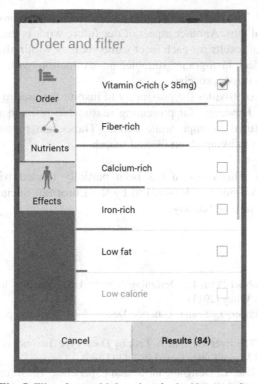

Fig. 5. Filter form with bar chart in the *Nutrients* facet

6   Conclusions and Future Work

In our paper, we presented a general visualization concept for mobile faceted search. We analyzed different applications that use filter forms to specify the amount of data. Furthermore, we conducted a brief user survey to include ideas and experience in dealing with filtering on mobile devices. As a result of our study, vertical tab filters were evaluated best for mobile usage. Due to the fact that this approach can only represent a limited number of facets, we extended this solution by enriching the tabs with scrolling. In addition we stressed visual aids supporting the user with information seeking. An important part of our filter concept is that there is no search that leads to empty results. Users only see selection values to which results are available. Our visualization concept complies with the basic principle of Shneiderman's "Visual Information Seeking Mantra". In general, it can be applied to an unlimited number of data and facets and is therefore scalable with respect to the amount of information that can be displayed. However, if possible the filter form should not contain more than ten facets. Otherwise, the user would be unable to cope with too many filter options.

Although the presented visualization concept is based on the analysis of several existing apps and takes into account current mobile design patterns, it will be necessary to evaluate this approach in a user study. To this end, the current prototype needs to be further developed. The filter form requires more facets to demonstrate and evaluate the scrollable vertical tabs. Another aspect of our future work is the visual representation of the quantity of results for each facet value via bars within the filter form. Even if Nudelman considers histograms suitable, an evaluation with potential users is necessary to confirm this approach.

Faceted search also provides the possibility to inspire the user to take advantage of new search options. However, for presenting reasonable refinement pages, the data must be well structured in appropriate facets. Thus, data preparation is also an important point when thinking about faceted search.

Acknowledgements. This research has been partially funded within the SESAM project under the grant number 100098186 by the European Social Fund (ESF) and the German Federal State of Saxony.

References

1. Nudelman, G., Gabriel-Petit, P.: Designing Search: UX Strategies for eCommerce Success, pp. 270–273. Wiley (2011)
2. Morville, P., Callender, J.: Search Patterns: Design for Discovery, p. 98. O'Reilly Media (2010)
3. Shneiderman, B.: The Eyes Have It: A Task by Data Type Taxonomy for Information Visualizations. IEEE Visual Languages, 336–343 (1996)
4. Russell-Rose, T., Tate, T.: Designing the Search Experience: The Information Architecture of Discovery, pp. 168–245. Elsevier, Inc. (2013)
5. Karlson, A.K., Robertson, G.G., Robbins, D.C., Czerwinski, M.P., Smith, G.R.: FaThumb: a facet-based interface for mobile search. In: CHI 2006: Proceedings of the SIGCHI Conference on Human Factors in Computing Systems, pp. 711–720. ACM Press (2006)
6. Nudelman, G.: Android Design Patterns: Interaction Design Solutions for Developers, pp. 153–201. Wiley (2013)
7. Magazine, S.: How to Create Selling eCommerce Websites. Smashing Magazine, 66 (2012)
8. Neil, T.: Mobile Design Pattern Gallery, p. 76. O'Reilly Media, Inc. (2012)
9. Fling, B.: Mobile Design and Development: Practical concepts and techniques for creating mobile sites and web apps, p. 134. O'Reilly Media (2009)
10. Weiss, S.: Handheld Usability, pp. 70–91. Wiley (2003)

Multimodal Interaction

Food Practice Shooter: A Serious Game with a Real-World Interface for Nutrition and Dietary Education

Yuichi Bannai[1], Takayuki Kosaka[1], and Naomi Aiba[2]

[1] Department of Information Media, Kanagawa Institute of Technology
[2] Department of Nutrition and Life Science, Kanagawa Institute of Technology
{bannai,kosaka}@ic.kanagawa-it.ac.jp,
aiba@bio.kanagawa-it.ac.jp

Abstract. Along with the recent increase in the diversity of food options especially soft foods, problems of unbalanced eaters and insufficient chewing have gained notice. Games, which many children are enthusiastic about, may provide an opportunity to encourage children to voluntarily consume disliked foods. In this paper, we describe Food Practice Shooter, a serious game with a physical interface and public gameplay that presents food consumption as a win condition. This game can be used for dietary education to induce balanced eating behavior and sufficient chewing in children.

Keywords: Serious Game, Nutrition, Dietary Education, Chewing, Public Gameplay, Smile.

1 Introduction

Along with the recent increase in the diversity of food options, the number of "unbalanced eaters"—people who eat only the foods they like—is increasing. The resultant diet, which comprises a very limited number of foods chosen solely based on personal taste, is referred to as an unbalanced diet. Extremely unbalanced diets are deficient in many necessary nutrients and are a serious public health concern.

Another modern problem that has recently gained notice is the lack of sufficient chewing, related to an increase in soft foods. In children, this reduction in chewing duration may not only cause malocclusion by hindering development of the jaw but also negatively impact digestion by decreasing secretion of saliva. Thus, proper chewing is very important for promoting growth and maintaining health in children.

Many toxic or spoiled foods taste bitter or sour, respectively. Aversion to these tastes therefore allows humans to avoid consuming substances that may endanger health. For this reason, many children naturally dislike bitter or sour vegetables such as carrots, tomatoes, and green peppers. Such children will avoid eating vegetables even when encouraged or ordered to do so. Furthermore, children find the process of being forced to eat their disliked foods extremely unpleasant and uncomfortable.

S. Yamamoto (Ed.): HIMI 2014, Part I, LNCS 8521, pp. 139–147, 2014.

Games, which many children are enthusiastic about, may provide an opportunity to encourage children to voluntarily consume disliked foods. In this paper, we describe Food Practice Shooter, a serious game with a physical interface that presents food consumption as a win condition. This game can be used for dietary education to induce balanced eating behavior in children.

2   Concepts

2.1   Serious Games with Operant Conditioning

Although the book Serious Game by Abt [1] is the origin of the term, several definitions of "serious games" were proposed in the 2000s, when home computer games spread explosively. For example, Ritter-field [2] defined serious games as "any form of interactive computer-based game software for one or multiple players to be used on any platform and that has been developed with the intention to be more than entertainment." Fujimoto [3] defined serious games from the viewpoint of intent of use and development of the game, noting that a serious game "is intended to be used in a particular context other than entertainment. The game is designed with the intention associated with playing the game."

What sort of serious game could be used to promote nutrition and dietary education? More specifically, can serious games motivate individuals to eat disliked food through gameplay? Skinner theorized that most of human behavior is formed through operant conditioning. Voluntary, active reactions (behaviors) occurring in response to a stimulus are reinforced by their subsequent outcomes, causing a change in behavior through operant conditioning [4]. The reinforcer in this case is a positive event such as a reward (i.e., positive reinforcement).

We also consider contingency management, which further reinforces certain actions using the theory that the action is enhanced by its outcome. We consider it likely that associating the act of playing a game is a strong reinforcement for eating disliked vegetables. Because the player gains a sense of accomplishment upon winning the game and therefore experiences a weaker feeling of resistance toward eating a disliked food, incorporating the eating of the food within the gameplay could be a trigger for increasing self-efficacy.

2.2   Public Games

When a game is played at home, there may be remote interaction with other players over a network, but there is not usually an audience in the player's immediate physical vicinity. On the other hand, players in public spaces are praised by onlookers when they succeed at their game, which serves as reinforcement.

A child observing other children playing a game can comprehend the possibility of success by observing the children enjoying the game and succeeding at it. This child can then easily engage in the game.

These behaviors are explained by the social cognitive theory, first proposed by Bandura [5], who states that learning can be achieved from not only one's own experience and behavior, but also from observing and mimicking the behavior of others in a process called modeling. For example, by observing that when others work harder they are praised, vicarious reinforcement strengthens the observer's own behavior. This is in contrast to Skinner's reinforcement, which is mostly direct.

An important factor in this process of observation and vicarious reinforcement learning is that the person being observed is in not far level from the observer. Because it is important for children to observe that other children are succeeding at our serious game, we therefore decided it should be set in a public space.

2.3   Smiling

Nutrition education to establish a good foundation of eating habits should be implemented between infanthood and school age. Imada [6] noted that the food preferences of children are likely to be acquired based on emotional context, such as facial expressions and family support, and that the frequency with which children spontaneously consume even non-favorite foods is increased in bright and fun eating environments.

We have focused on the hypothesis that smiling creates a sense of fun. The facial expression hypothesis, based on the James-Lange theory, states that we feel happy because we laugh, not that we laugh be-cause we are happy; therefore, facial movement can influence the emotional experience rather than simply reflecting it [7].

Strack et al. [8] tested this hypothesis by comparing groups of people with different facial positions and their assessment of the funniness of a cartoon. The group that had a smiling facial position (holding a pen in the teeth) reported the cartoon as significantly more amusing then the participants who held a pen in the lips or who held a pen in the non-dominant hand.

Taken together, we believe that the results of these previous studies, indicate that a player can come to consider food consumption as enjoyable by smiling while playing a game.

3   Food Practice Shooter

Food Practice Shooter is a serious game, which has a designed progression of eating, chewing, smiling, and defeating the enemy. After attaching the chewing sensor to the head, the player holds the gun-shaped controller and shoots various types of virtual bullets at monsters displayed onscreen.

The player has a finite number of bullets and cannot shoot when the gun is empty. To reload the gun, the player must eat real food on a table in front of them. The bullet type is determined by the type of food eaten, and the number of bullets reloaded is determined by chewing duration. The bullets are finally loaded into the gun once the player smiles.

3.1   System Configuration

Figure 1 shows the system configuration for Food Practice Shooter. The system consists of the chewing sensor, which detects user's mastication; the gun device, which serves as the game controller; the smile sensor, which reads and detects the player's smiling face; and the food sensor, which measures the weight of food.

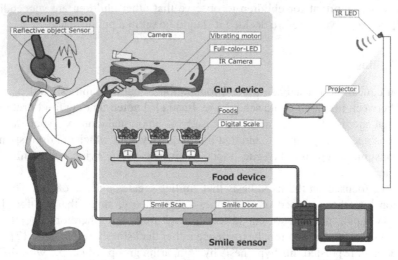

Fig. 1. System Configuration for Food Practice Shooter

3.2   Chewing Sensor

Human masticatory muscles, which are attached to the mandible, comprise the masseter, temporalis, pterygoideus internus, and pterygoideus externus (Figure 2).

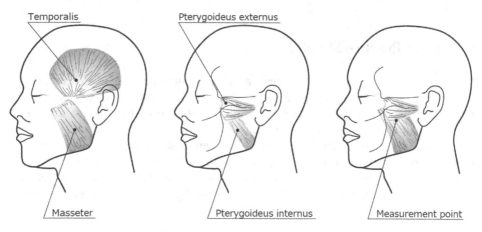

Fig. 2. Human Masticatory Muscles

The overall bite force is exerted collectively during mastication by these muscles. The muscle that noticeably tightens on the outside of the jaw when the teeth are clenched is the masseter, which moves when chewing hard food.

The temporal muscle, located at the temple, pulls the mandible and moves the chin back and forth. The pterygoideus externus, which extends the chin, is attached to the inside of the mandible and works in conjunction with the masseter and the temporalis.

We confirmed in preliminary experiments that the area that moves most dramatically during mastication is where the masseter, pterygoideus internus, and pterygoideus externus overlap. We therefore set the measurement point in this area.

Fig. 3. Chewing Sensor

Figure 3 shows the chewing sensor, which uses a reflective optical sensor attached to the microphone of a headset. The optical sensor (LBR-127HLD; Letex Technology Corp) measures in real time the distance between the measurement point on the skin and the sensor.

The waveform of the signal output by the chewing sensor indicating these changes in distance over several chews is shown in Figure 4.

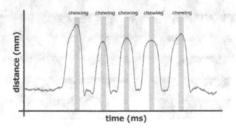

Fig. 4. Detection of Chewing

3.3   Gun Device

The gun device, shown in Figure 5, consists of an infrared camera, a vibration motor, an inverter, a trigger switch, a full-color LED, an Arduino MEGA microcontroller, and a smile-detection camera.

The infrared camera installed on the head of the gun detects infrared LEDs on the corners of the screen and calculates the player's aiming coordinates. The vibration motor, inverter, and trigger are controlled through the Arduino board.

Fig. 5. Gun Device

3.4   Smile Sensor

The smile detection camera mounted on the gun device captures the player's face, and the acquired image is sent to the smile sensor, (Smile Door and Smile Scan; both manufactured by Omron Inc.). Smile Scan is a processor that detects a person's face in an image and automatically measures the proportion of smile as a percentage. The smile data are then sent to the PC via Smile Door. Figure 6 shows some example pictures of smiling faces detected by Smile Scan.

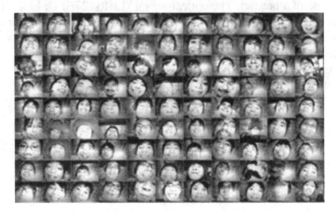

Fig. 6. Smiling Faces Detected by Smile Sensor

3.5   Food

Vegetable cookies (Vegecuit, Ito Biscuits) were used as the food in the game (Figure 7). The Vegecuit series consists of cookies with flavors that many children do not like, such as green pepper, carrot, tomato, burdock, and ginger. The vegetable cookies are made from real powdered vegetables, and therefore taste authentic despite having the consistency of cookies.

Before each player started the game, we confirmed that they had no food allergies to any of the ingredients, using an allergen table and list of ingredients. Only individuals with no allergies were allowed to play, after disinfecting their hands.

Fig. 7. Vegetable cookies (Vegecuit, Ito Biscuits)

3.6   Food Sensor

Three kinds of food the player will consume are placed into each of three cups placed on digital scales (TL-280, Tanita) as shown in Figure 8. With precision of 1 g, the digital scale outputs the weight of the food to the PC via a RS-232C port.

The food sensor detects in real time the quantity and the order in which the player eats the food by calculating the reduction in weight, and converts the amount into the number of cookies the player removed based on a threshold corresponding to the average weight of a cookie.

Fig. 8. Food Sensor

4   Post-game Questionnaire

Food Practice Shooter has been exhibited at several locations, including Tokyo and Kanazawa in Japan, and the Laval Virtual conference in France. A questionnaire survey was conducted among 179 people who played the game at the Kanazawa exhibition.

Figure 9 shows the proportion of players in different age brackets. The reason why the proportion of players under 20 years of age is high might be due to the subject of the game, which was to fight off monsters with a gun. The game was therefore able to appeal to children, which is important because it is intended to correct unbalanced diet.

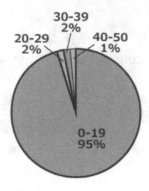

Fig. 9. Percentages of players by age

Among the players, 118 individuals reported that they did not have a dislike of carrots, green peppers, or tomatoes. Among the 61 individuals who a disliked food, the survey item "Which food do you dislike most: carrots, green peppers, or tomatoes?" revealed that 2, 48, and 13 individuals disliked carrots, green peppers, and tomatoes, respectively.

However, 90% of the players who disliked a food (55 out of 61 individuals) reported that they ate vegetable cookies during the game. This result indicates that it could be possible to correct unbalanced diet by setting food consumption as the game's win condition.

5   Conclusion and Future Work

We have developed a serious game intended to correct unbalanced diet by incorporating food consumption as the game's win condition. The results suggest that playing the game in an environment where the player had an audience, including family, encouraged the behavior of eating disliked food, and gave the player confidence.

In regard to behavioral aspects, the acquisition of food preferences through conditioning from Food Practice Shooter seems to be very effective. However, regarding the psychological aspects of preference acquisition, Imada [6] pointed out that conditioning does not necessarily reflect a change in behavior.

A preference is not acquired even if the frequency of behavior (here, food consumption) increases when the relationship between behavior and reward is extremely strong. Given that Pliner [9] stated that the food can become liked if an individual has repeated exposure, it is necessary to conduct a long-term evaluation of repeated use of Food Practice Shooter to determine whether it can induce the acquisition of food preferences in children.

Because shooting is the main action in Food Practice Shooter, we observed that the player attempted to eat, chew, and smile as fast as possible when reloading (in spite of the fact that game clock was stopped during this phase).

From the point of view of dietary education, proper chewing is an important habit because it suppresses overeating and promotes the breakdown of visceral fat. Shooting actions in the game play gave the player a sense of urgency and immersive, as a result it was ineffective for controlling the speed of eating.

We believe that Food Practice Shooter can provide a way for children to consume food they dislike by presenting it as a game, although it is not a foolproof method for correcting unbalanced diet. However, a person who dislikes a certain food may believe from past experience that they could not eat it, and this attitude can be sometimes changed given the opportunity, which our game provides.

We conclude that Food Practice Shooter has the potential to correct unbalanced diet by giving children confidence as well as providing the opportunity for consuming disliked food in a game setting.

References

1. Abt, C.C.: Serious Games. Viking, New York (1970)
2. Ritterfeld, U., Cody, M., Vorderer, P.: Serious Games: Mechanisms and Effects. Routledge, London (2009)
3. Fujimoto, T.: Serious Games Transforming Education and Society Through Digital Games. TDU Press, Tokyo (2007) (in Japanese)
4. Hata, E., Doi, Y.: Behavioral Science-Theory and Application for Health Promotion. Nankodo, Tokyo (2003) (in Japanese)
5. Bandura, A.: Social Learning Theory. Prentice Hall, Englewood Cliffs (1977)
6. Imada, S.: The Psychology of Eating: Why We Eat What We Eat. Yuhikaku, Tokyo (2005) (in Japanese)
7. McIntosh, D.N.: Facial feedback hypotheses: Evidence, implications, and directions. Motivation and Emotion 20 (1996)
8. Strack, F., Martin, L.L., Stepper, S.: Inhibiting and facilitating conditions of facial expressions: A non-obtrusive test of the facial hypothesis. Journal of Personality and Social Psychology 54 (1988)
9. Pliner, P.: The effects of mere exposure on liking for edible substances. Appetite 3(3), 283–290 (1982)
10. Anzman-Frasca, S., Savage, J.S., Marini, M.E., Fisher, J.O., Birch, L.L.: Repeated exposure and associative conditioning promote preschool children's liking of vegetables. Appetite 58, 543–553 (2012)

A New Computational Method
for Single-Trial-EEG-Based BCI
Proposal of the Number of Electrodes

Shin'ichi Fukuzumi[1], Hiromi Yamaguchi[2], Kazufumi Tanaka[2],
Toshimasa Yamazaki[2], Takahiro Yamanoi[3], and Ken-ichi Kamijo[1]

[1] NEC Corporation, Kawasaki, Japan
{s-fukuzumi,kamijo}@aj.jp.nec.com
[2] Kyushu Institute of Technology, Iizuka, Japan
{n673229h,t-ymzk}@bio.kyutech.ac.jp,
kazu@kasuke.jp
[3] Hokkai gakuen University, Sapporo, Japan
yamanoi@eli.hokkai-s-u.ac.jp

Abstract. In this paper, the categorization of single-trial EEG data recorded during the MI-related task, as another data reduction, will be attempted, because the categorical data would require less storage and computational time than continuous one. The categorization will be realized by equivalent current dipole source localization (ECDL). To analyze this, we used EEG data and visually evoked related potentials (v-ERP) led by 32 electrodes. From the result of single-trial v-ERP, only 6 electrode v-ERPs have a remarkable reaction. Therefore, from the view point of business, it is found that the minimum number of electrodes have been seven.

Keywords: EEG, Brain Computer Interface, equivalent current dipole source localization, topography.

1   Introduction

In non-invasive Brain-Computer Interfaces (BCIs), scalp-recorded-electroence-phalo gram (EEG)-based BCIs with motor imagery (MI) have extensively progressed in the past two decades [1]. Such BCIs consist of feature extraction and classification using the features. Most of the BCIs utilize the sensorimotor rhythmic (SMR) features. These features could be extracted from event-related desynchronization (ERD) and synchronization (ERS) in mu, beta and gamma rhythms over the SM cortex during MI tasks [2], [3], [4], as well as actual movement ones [4], [5], [6]. The features over these broad frequency bands require multi-channel EEGs of more than 1 s. Moreover, very high-dimensional feature vectors and continuous-valued patterns are necessary for spatiotemporally checking the features (e.g., [7], [8], hence yield an enormous amount of data and much computational time (e.g., [9]. Therefore, various data reductions such as downsampling [10], [11], [12] and optimal EEG channel configurations [13], [14].

S. Yamamoto (Ed.): HIMI 2014, Part I, LNCS 8521, pp. 148–156, 2014.

This study was motivated by another data reduction and non-rhythmic characterization of ERD and ERS in the BCIs, one of whose solutions could be multiple equivalent current dipole source localization (mECDL) with independent component analysis (ICA). There had been already a few of the former approaches to the BCIs [15], [16], [17], [18]. However, the first three studies had limited to one- or two-dipole, and the fourth one had not led to data reduction, because four hundred dipoles were estimated. The ICA methods are now widely used for separating artifacts from scalp-recorded EEG and related data [19], [20], [21], and have been already practiced in EEG-based BCIs [8], [22], [23].

In this paper, the categorization of single-trial EEG data recorded during the MI-related task, as another data reduction, will be attempted, because the categorical data would require less storage and computational time than continuous one. The categorization will be realized by equivalent current dipole source localization (ECDL). Some of the authors had already found the parietal and premotor cortices as the neural correlates for the MI from the multiple ECDL using the averaged EEGs [24]. Moreover, from our event-related functional magnetic resonance imaging (ERfMRI) study [25], it followed that the MI activated the superior and inferior frontal gyri, the pre- and post-central gyri and the superior and inferior parietal lobuli. These findings will be incorporated into Hayashi's second method of quantification which could quantify categorical data consisting of samples, items and categories (features) (hereafter, this method is abbreviated to H2MQ) mentioned below. In order to separate scalp-recorded EEGs into functionally independent sources, including neural components originating from different brain areas and artifact components attributed to eye movement, blinks, muscle, heart and line noise [23], ICA will be applied to the EEG data, then the ECDL with one dipole to reconstructed EEG from each IC corresponding to only neural activity by the deflation procedure.

2   Experiments

2.1   Subjects

Ten healthy male subjects between the ages of 22 and 35 (mean age 28.7years; SD 4.12) participated in this experiment. All the subjects were right handed according to the Edinburgh Inventory[26].

2.2   Experimental Protocol

Subjects were seated inside an electrically shielded room with sound attenuation, and gazed at a monochromatic monitor of an AV tachistscope (IS-701B, IWATSU ISEL) 0.9 m away from their eyes. They were requested to relax their both hands on a table and with their chins on a chinrest (Fig.1). In the present experiment, three kinds of line drawings of hands were presented on the monitor: (1) right-hand stimulus to imagine being shaken with the subject's right hand, (2) left-hand one for the subject's left hand imagery and (3) open-right-hand one as control (Fig.2). These stimuli were sequentially and randomly presented with probabilities of 0.20, 0.20 and 0.60, respectively. Among all the stimulus conditions, the following two kinds of trials were chosen for data analysis. That is, the subject's task is to imagine grasping the right-hand stimulus with her or his own right hand as soon as possible when the stimulus was displayed (right-hand-movement imagery: RH-MI); one to image grasping the left-hand stimulus with her or his own when the stimulus was presented (left-hand-movement imagery: LH-MI). Both hands were hidden under a black coverlet so that it is easier for the subjects to imagine the hand movement. There was a short training session during which the subjects' hands were not covered with the coverlet. One test session includes the two conditions with a five-minute break between the conditions, where each condition contains 130, 130 and 400 trials for the above (1), (2) and (3), respectively. Therefore, it took about 45 minutes to finish one session. Note that different subject had different order of the conditions.

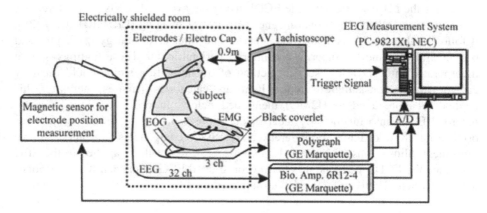

Fig. 1. Experimental system for the measurements of EEG, EOG, EMG and electrode positions and for stimulus presentation [28]

2.3   Electrophysiological Recordings

With an electro cap (ECI, Electrocap International), EEG was recorded from 32 electrodes (FP1, FPz, FP3, F7, F3, Fz, F4, F8, FC5, FC1, FC2, FC6, T3, C3, Cz, C4, T4, CP5, CP1, CPz, CP2, CP6, T5, P3, Pz, P4, T6, PO3, POz, PO4, O1, Oz, O2) at scalp positions that were defined on the basis of the International 10-20 System [27]. All the electrodes were referred to A1, the ground electrode was attached to FPz and their impedances were kept below 5kΩ. Vertical and horizontal eye movements were monitored with two electrodes placed directly above the nasion and the outer canthus of the right eye. Another two electrodes were placed at both the medial antibrachiums to record arm electromyogram (EMG) so that EEGs could be excluded from the average when mistakenly grasping during the movement imagery.

The 32 signals of the EEGs were amplified by a Biotop 6R12-4 amplifier (GE Marquette Medical Systems Japan, Ltd.), and filtered in a frequency bandwidth of 0.01-100 Hz. The amplified signals were sampled at a rate of 1 kHz during an epoch of 100 ms preceding and 700 ms following the stimulus onset. The inter-stimulus interval was 1600 ms (figure 3). The on-line A/D converted EEG signals were immediately stored on a hard disk in a PC-9821Xt personal computer (PC) (NEC Corporation). The EOG and EMG data was also amplified by a Polygraph 360 amplifier (GE Marquette Medical Systems Japan, Ltd.), and sent to the same PC.

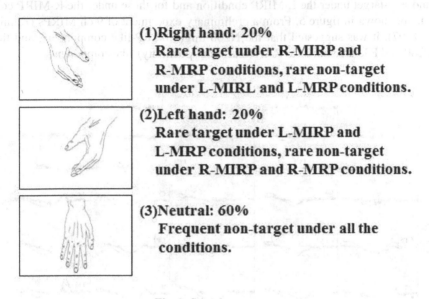

(1)**Right hand: 20%**
Rare target under R-MIRP and
R-MRP conditions, rare non-target
under L-MIRL and L-MRP conditions.

(2)**Left hand: 20%**
Rare target under L-MIRP and
L-MRP conditions, rare non-target
under R-MIRP and R-MRP conditions.

(3)**Neutral: 60%**
Frequent non-target under all the
conditions.

Fig. 2. Stimulus contents

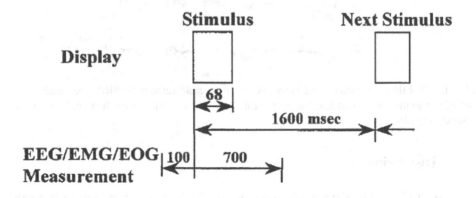

Fig. 3. Time-scheduling of the stimulus presentation and the measurements of EEG, EOG and EMG

3   Results

Figures 4a and b show the rare target and non-target 32-channel grand average ERP waveforms from all the ten subjects under the L-and R-MIRP conditions, respectively. Scalp topographic maps of 16 instantaneous timepoints, N200 at 200 ms, 200 ms, 200 ms and 200 ms, respectively, P280 at 280 ms, 271 ms, 280 ms and 271 ms, respectively, early P300 (P3e) at 333 ms, 333 ms, 338 ms and 323 ms, respectively, and late P300 (P3l) at 376 ms, 376 ms, 376 ms and 359 ms, respectively, for the rare target and non-target under the L-MIRP condition and for those under the R-MIRP condition, are shown in figure 5. From a preliminary experiment of 9 ch MIRPs (Kamijo et al. 1997), it was suggested that the N200 might be RP-like components, and that the P280 and P3e are similar to RAP (reafferent positivity)-like components.

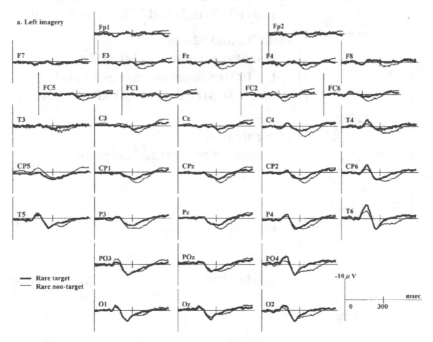

Fig. 4. a. L-MIRP condition of 32 channels of left mastoid referenced ERP, overlapping the waveform to the rare targets and that to the rare non-targets, depicted by thick and thin lines, respectively [28]

4   Discussion

Kamijo, et al. tried to show a difference of visual ERPs during movement imagery tasks between the condition of 9 scalp electrodes and 32 electrodes[28]. From this, in case of 9 electrodes, movement imagery might involve partially the same neural

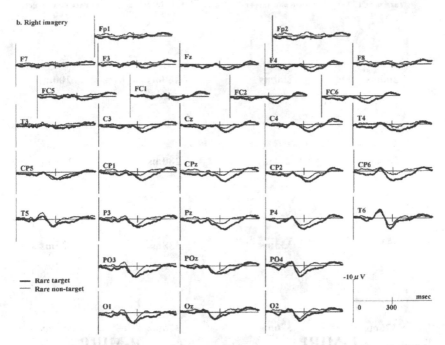

Fig. 5. b. R-MIRP condition of 32 channels of left mastoid referenced ERP, overlapping the waveform to the rare targets and that to the rare non-targets, depicted by thick and thin lines, respectively [28]

structures as during actual movement. In case of 32 electrodes, existence of early components and late components in P300s was shown. On the other hands, in the view point of silent speech, Yamamoto et al. succeeded to correspond images of "rock", "paper" and "scissors" to   silent speech of them by using single-trial EEGs of 19 electrodes[29]. In that time, ICA and ECDL were also used as analysis methods. However, considering this technology applying to business area, a brief measurement method by a few electrodes is necessary.

This time, we used 32 electrodes on scalp. From ERP data shown in Figure 4a and 4b, the response of 6 electrodes, they are "CP5", "CP6", "T5", "T6", "PO3" and "PO4", are found to be remarkable for both case. Thus, the feature change in potential data led by remaining 26 electrodes was not found. From this, 26 electrodes' data could be considered same. By giving any one electrode data on 26 to the other 25 electrodes and using responded six electrodes data, we can deal with totally 32 channel data. Therefore, this result shows the possibility to estimate movement imagery by using seven electrodes.

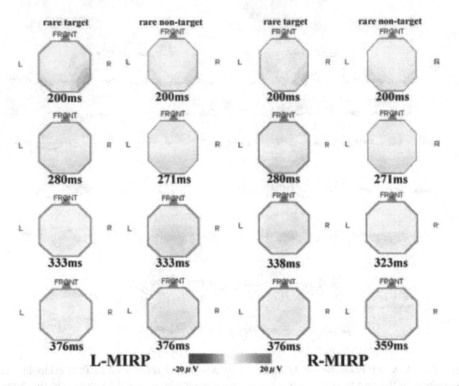

Fig. 6. Topographic maps of the N200, P280, P3e and P3l for the rare target under the L-MIRP condition (1st column); those for the rare non-target under the L-MIRP condition (2nd column); those for the rare target under the R-MIRP condition (3rd column); those for the rare non-target under the R-MIRP condition (4th column) [28]

5   Conclusion

This study was undertaken to record visual ERPs during movement imagery for right-handed subjects, and to investigate the temporal aspects of the neural structures involved in movement imagery. From this, we found that the response of seven electrodes, they are "CP5", "CP6", "T5", "T6", "PO3", "PO4", and any one of remaining 26 electrodes are found to be remarkable. Thus, we suggest that we can extract characteristics of visual ERPs using our proposal analysis method.

References

1. Wolpow, J., Birbaumer, N., McFarland, D., Pfurtscheller, G., Vaughan, T.: Brain-Computer Interfaces for communication and control. Clinical Neurophysiology 113, 767–791 (2002)

2. Townsend, G., Graimann, B., Pfurtscheller, G.: Continuous EEG classification during motor imagery-Simulation of an asynchronous BCI. IEEE Transaction of Neural System and Rehabilitation Engineering 12, 258–265 (2004)
3. Pfurtscheller, G., Lopes da Silva, F.H.: Event-related EEG/MEG synchronization and desynchronization: basic principles. Clinical Neurophysiology 110(11), 1842–1857 (1999)
4. Miller, K.J., Schalk, G., Fetz, E.E., den Nijs, M., Ojemann, J.G., Rao, R.P.N.: Cortical activity during motor execution, motor imagery, and imagery-based online feedback. PNAS 107, 4430–4435 (2010)
5. Leocani, L., Toro, C., Manganotti, P., Zhuang, P., Hallett, M.: Event-related coherence and event-related desynchronization / synchronization in the 10 Hz and 20 Hz EEG during self-paced movements. Electroencephalography and Clinical Neurophysiology / Evoked Potentials Section 104(3), 199–206 (1997)
6. Pfurtscheller, G., Neuper, C., Flotzinger, D., Pregenzer, M.: EEG-based discrimination between imagination of right and left hand movement. Electroencephalography and Clinical Neurophysiology 103(6), 642–651 (1997)
7. Zhou, J., Yao, J., Deng, J., Dewald, J.P.A.: EEG-based classification for elbow versus shoulder torque intentions involving stroke subjects. Computers in Biology and Medicine, 443–452 (2009)
8. Wang, D., Miao, D., Blohm, G.: Multi-class motor imagery EEG decoding for brain-computer interfaces. Frontier in Neuroscience 6, article 151, 1–13 (2012)
9. Hsu, W.Y.: EEG-based motor imagery classification using neuro-fuzzy prediction and wavelet fractal features. Journal of Neuroscience and Methods 189, 295–302 (2010)
10. Krusienski, D.J., Sellers, E.W., McFarland, D.J., Vaughan, T.M., Wolpaw, J.R.: Toward enhanced P300 speller performance. Journal of Neuroscience Methods 167, 15–21 (2008)
11. Sakamoto, Y., Aono, M.: Supervised Adaptive Downsampling for P300-Based Brain-Computer Interface. In: 31st Annual International Conference of the IEEE Engineering in Medicine and Biology Society, EMBC 2009 (2009)
12. Arvaneh, M., Guan, C.T., Ang, K.K., Quek, C.: Optimizing the channel selection and classification accuracy in EEG-based BCI source. IEEE Transaction of Biomedical Engineering 58, 1865–1873 (2011)
13. Kamrunnahar, M., Dias, N.S., Schiff, S.J.: Optimization of Electrode Channels in Brain Computer Interfaces. In: Conference Proceedings of IEEE Engineering and Medical Biological Society, pp. 6477–6480 (2009)
14. Sannelli, C., Dickhausa, T., Halderc, S., Hammerc, E., Mullera, K., Blankertz, B.: On optimal channel configurations for SMR based braincomputer interfaces. Brain Topography, 186–193 (2010)
15. Qin, L., Ding, L., He, B.: Motor Imagery Classification by Means of Source Analysis for Brain Computer Interface Applications. Journal of Neural Engineering, 135–141 (2004)
16. Kamousi, B., Liu, Z., He, B.: Classificationi of motor imagery tasks for brain-computer interface applications by means of two equivalent dipoles analysis. IEEE Transaction of Neural System and Rehabilitation Engineering 13(2), 166–171 (2005)
17. Congedo, M., Lotte, F., Lecuyer, A.: Classification of movement intention by spatially filtered electromagnetic inverse solution. Physics in Medicine and Biology 51, 1971–1989 (2006)
18. Noirhomme, Q., Kitney, R.L., Macq, B.: Single-trial EEG source reconstruction for brain-computer interface. IEEE Transaction of Biomedical Engineering 55, 1592–1601 (2008)
19. Makeig, S., Bell, A.J., Jung, T.P., Sejnowski, T.J.: Independent component analysis of electroencephalographic data. Advances in Neural Information Processing Systems, 145–151 (1996)

20. Delorme, A., Sejnowski, T.J., Maikeig, S.: Enhanced detection of artifacts in EEG data using higher-order statistics and independent component analysis. Neuroimage 34, 1443–1449 (2007)
21. Hoffman, S., Falkenstein, M.: The correction of eye blink artefacts in the EEG: a comparison of two prominent methods. PLoS One 3 (2008)
22. Xu, N., Gao, X., Hong, B., Miao, X., Gao, S., Yang, F.: BCI competition 2003-Data set IIb: enhancing P300 wave detection using ICA-based subspace projections for BCI applications. IEEE Transaction of Biomedical Engieeing 51, 1067–1072 (2004)
23. Wang, Y., Wang, Y.T., Jung, T.P.: Translation of EEG spatial filters from resting to motor imagery using independent component analysis. PLoS One 7, e37665 (2012)
24. Kamijo, K., Kiyuna, T., Takaki, Y., Kenmochi, A., Tanigawa, T., Yamazaki, T.: Integrated approach of an artificial neural network and numerical analysis to multiple equivalent current dipole source localization. Frontier Medical and Biological Engineering 10(4), 285–301 (2001)
25. Kamijo, K., Kawashima, R., Yamazaki, T., Kiyuna, T., Takaki, Y.: An event-related functional magnetic resonance imaging study of movement imagery. Transaction of the Japanese Society for Medical and Biological Engineering 42, 16–21 (2004)
26. Oldfield, R.C.: The assessment and analysis of handedness: the Edinburgh Inventory. Neuropsychologia 9, 97–113 (1971)
27. Soufflet, L., Toussaint, M., Luthringer, R., Gresser, J., Minot, R., Macher, J.P.: A statistical evaluation of the main interpolation methods applied to 3-dimensional EEG mapping. Electroenceph. Clin. Neurophysiol. 79, 393–402 (1991)
28. Kamijo, K., Yamazaki, T., Kiyuna, T., Takaki, Y., Kuroiwa, Y.: Brain Topgraphy 14(4), 279–292 (2002)
29. Yamamoto, K., Yamazaki, T., Kamijo, K., Yamanoi, T., Fukuzumi, S.: Ailent speech BCI: Learning and decoding algorithms using single-trial EEGs and speech signals. In: Proceedings of BPES 2011 (2011)

Menu Hierarchy Generation Based on Syntactic Dependency Structures in Item Descriptions

Yukio Horiguchi, Shinsu An, Tetsuo Sawaragi, and Hiroaki Nakanishi

Dept. of Mechanical Engineering and Science, Kyoto University, Kyoto, Japan
horiguchi@me.kyoto-u.ac.jp

Abstract. The present paper proposes a procedural design method which makes use of dependency structures underlying menu item descriptions in order to generate well-structured and easily-learned menu hierarchies. A dependency structure captures syntactic relations among conceptual units that constitute a natural language description of what function the corresponding menu item stands for. The proposed method classifies computerized system functions after dependency structure prototypes and then serializes variable elements to be specified in each function class after phrase structure analysis. Its clear and consistent policy provides generated menu systems with high communicability to users. The effectiveness of the method is empirically investigated.

Keywords: Menu, Conceptual Dependency, Phrase structure analysis, Interface design, Human-Computer-Interaction, Usability.

1 Introduction

Organization of items in a hierarchy impacts the menu system usability [1]. Menus that are not designed consistent with the user's way of thinking would cause breakdowns in user-system communication [2]. They can easily misdirect and confuse users searching for items in the hierarchy. Regarding this issue, we have been studying menu interface design techniques to generate menu hierarchies based on "dependency structures" [3]. A dependency structure captures syntactic relations among conceptual units that constitute a natural language description of what function the corresponding menu item stands for.

According to Sperber and Wilson [4], a hearer of an utterance forms anticipatory hypotheses about the overall syntactic structure of that utterance on the basis of what s/he has already heard. Such an "anticipatory syntactic hypothesis" helps the hearer resolve ambiguities and referential indeterminacies contained in the utterance allowing her/him to access some of the encoded concepts before other utterances. The same can apply to the menu-based human-computer interaction. Menus structured for users to posit anticipatory hypotheses can help them easily develop mental image on the overall structure of the menu hierarchy through interaction.

The present paper proposes a procedural design method which makes use of such a syntactic feature underlying item descriptions in order to generate well-structured and

S. Yamamoto (Ed.): HIMI 2014, Part I, LNCS 8521, pp. 157–166, 2014.

easily-learned menu hierarchies. The method classifies computerized system functions after dependency structure prototypes and then serializes variable elements to be specified in each function class after phrase structure analysis. Its clear and consistent policy is expected to provide generated menu systems with high communicability to users. The effectiveness of the proposed method is empirically investigated.

2   Dependency Structure

2.1   Conceptual Dependency

Schank has proposed the theory of Conceptual Dependency (CD) as a model of natural language understanding to be used in artificial intelligence systems [5,6]. In the theory, understanding of language is considered as the process of connecting words with certain conceptual constructions that exist in one's memory, which is named "conceptualization". There are two distinct levels of analysis in CD to represent concepts underlying utterances without relation to the language encoding them. One is the sentential level in which utterances of a given language are encoded within a syntactic structure of that language. The other is the conceptual level in which conceptualizations take place. A conceptualization consists of concepts and formal relations between the concepts. This level of analysis is conducted using formal representations of the conceptual base by which two sentences identical in their meaning have a single representation. A conceptual dependency network is the result of the analysis which is given by a linked network of concepts with dependencies between the concepts.

The proposed method extracts dependency structures from menu item descriptions and then visualizes them in diagrams like a CD network. According to CD, a large number of verbs can be rewritten into a small number of "primitive actions" [5,6] like MOVE. Different primitive actions give different structures of dependencies. Based on this idea, conceptual networks out of item descriptions will be classified into a limited number of structural patterns. The proposed method utilizes such patterns to organize menu items into a hierarchy. Bækgaard and Anderson's scheme [7] is employed to analyze typical dependency structures for computerized system functions.

2.2   Interaction Primitives

Bækgaard and Anderson [7] have proposed a description scheme to analyze and diagrammatically represent various human-related activities dealing with information systems. An interaction primitive is defined as a prototypical action which gives basic forms of interaction and combines other activity elements/participants in a specific way to represent a certain type of activity.

Table 1 presents a partial list of semantic roles of elements involving interaction primitives to be used in the present study. Bækgaard and Anderson have elaborated the following four primitives as the most basic set of actions:

- **SENSE** is the action that comes with three interaction roles of *Experiencer*, *Source*, and *Phenomenon*. It represents a situation in which the *Experiencer* senses the *Phenomenon* as an aspect(s) of the *Source*.
- **MOVE** is the action that comes with roles of *Agent*, *Object*, *Source*, and *Destination*. It represents a situation in which the *Agent* moves the *Object* from the *Source* to the *Destination*.
- **MODIFY** is the action that comes with roles of *Agent* and *Object*, representing a situation in which the *Agent* modifies the state of the *Object*.
- **CONTROL** is the action that comes with two interaction roles of *Agent* and *Object* or *Experiencer*, representing a situation in which the *Agent* requests the *Experiencer* to do something or the *Agent* physically controls the *Object*.

Bækgaard and Anderson [7] have also defined "mediation" in their scheme to represent activities which consists of two or more different interaction primitives. Primitives in a mediated activity share at least one element that is named a mediator. Mediated SENSE, Mediated MOVE, Mediated CONTROL, and Mediated MODIFY are instances of those mediated activities.

Table 1. Definition of roles of interaction elements (extracted from [7])

Role	Definition
Agent	The active participant that initiates and controls the event
Object	The passive participant that is most affected by the event
Experiencer	The participant affected by information about a Phenomenon
Phenomenon	That which is thought, felt, or sensed by the Experiencer
Instrument	The passive participant that enables the event
Location	The spatial boundary of the event
Source	The location from which an object is transported
Destination	The location to which an object is transported

2.3   Dependency Structure Prototypes

Prototypical dependency structures to classify computerized system functions have been acquired from our former study analyzing hundreds of electric appliances functions [3]. Table 2 presents linguistic and graphical expressions of typical dependency structures commonly found in the analyzed function set. Each structure represents a unique interaction pattern in which a certain type of action takes place involving associated roles of elements in order to run a particular type of functions within the device. For example, Structure #1 represents functions that the system moves an object from somewhere (i.e., the source) to another place (i.e., the destination). The proposed method utilizes these function patterns.

3   Menu Hierarchy Generation Method

3.1   Item Classification After Dependency Structure

The proposed method assumes that individual items in a menu hierarchy are given together with natural language descriptions of what functions they stand for. Processing these descriptions, they are classified into either one of the dependency structure prototypes defined in the previous section. After the classification, elements constituent of each structure separate into two types. One is the type of element that has a common value within that structure class while the other has variable values depending on instances. To designate a unique item in the function set, it is required to specify all variables in addition to its dependency structure type.

Table 2. Linguistic and graphical expressions of dependency structure prototypes

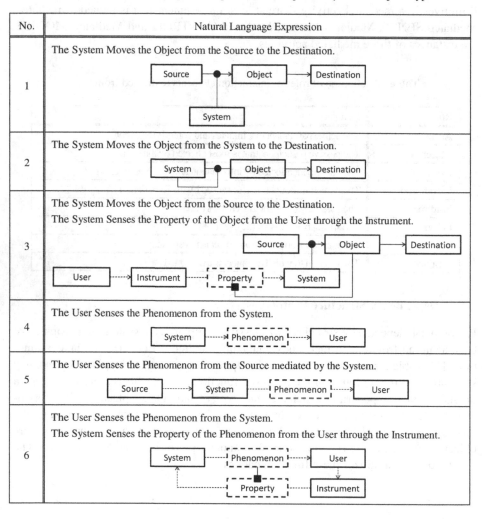

No.	Natural Language Expression
1	The System Moves the Object from the Source to the Destination.
2	The System Moves the Object from the System to the Destination.
3	The System Moves the Object from the Source to the Destination. The System Senses the Property of the Object from the User through the Instrument.
4	The User Senses the Phenomenon from the System.
5	The User Senses the Phenomenon from the Source mediated by the System.
6	The User Senses the Phenomenon from the System. The System Senses the Property of the Phenomenon from the User through the Instrument.

Table 2. (*continued*)

No.	Natural Language Expression
7	The System Modifies the Object from one state to another. 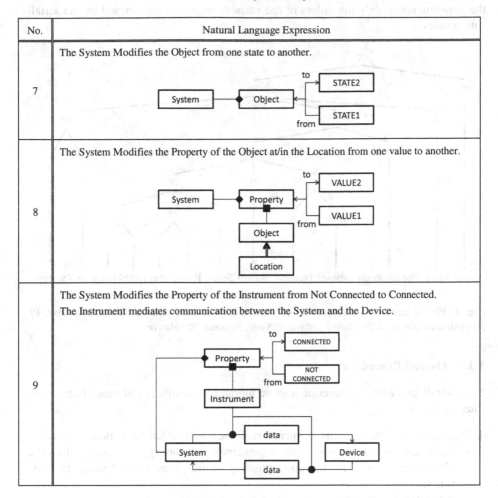
8	The System Modifies the Property of the Object at/in the Location from one value to another.
9	The System Modifies the Property of the Instrument from Not Connected to Connected. The Instrument mediates communication between the System and the Device.

3.2   Serialization of Variable Elements in Dependencies

A set of rules will be referred to for serializing variable elements in a dependency structure after phrase structure analysis. For an instance of the rules, verbs ought to come first before any other elements. This rule was defined because the choice of verb decides the dependency structure to be focused and what elements to be specified afterward. The choice of dependency structure type followed by a series of selections for its subordinate variables shapes the basic structure of the generated menu hierarchy.

Figure 1 shows a tree diagram representing the phrase structure, i.e., phrase maker, of Structure #6. Alphabets in the diagram denote constituent parts of the sentence (S), i.e., verb (V), noun (N), relative (R), verb phrase (VP), noun phrase (NP), prepositional phrase (PP), and relative phrase (RP). Numbers in parentheses besides the constituents specify the orders of the variable elements determined by the serialization rules.

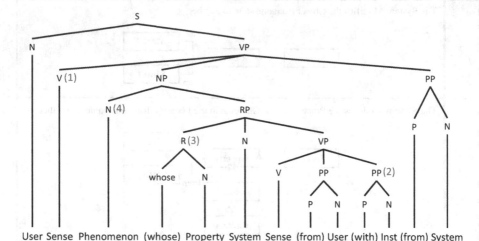

User Sense Phenomenon (whose) Property System Sense (from) User (with) Inst (from) System

Fig. 1. Phrase marker of Structure #6 (S: sentence, VP: verb phrase, NP: noun phrase, PP: prepositional phrase, RP: relative phrase, V: verb, N: noun, R: relative)

3.3   Overall Procedure

The overall procedure to generate a menu hierarchy out of a set of menu items is defined as below:

1. Prepare a list of menu items of interest with their natural language descriptions.
2. Classify items into either one of the dependency structure types, filling in the structure's element slots with the corresponding words/phrases constituting their descriptions.
3. Sort out items in each structure to identify variable elements.
4. Arrange variables of each structure in sequence after the serialization rules.
5. Generate a menu hierarchy as follows.
   (a) Determine one concrete verb per dependency structure to represent the set of items in each structure class. The resultant verbs will be used for item labels at the top level of the menu hierarchy.
   (b) Items at each level below the top menu give options for a variable element of the corresponding structure class. The selection sequence conforms to the order of variables determined by Step 4.

Menu hierarchies resulting from the above procedure ask users to choose a verb first to specify a certain dependency type of functions. The users are then to fill in "blanks" in turn that correspond to variable elements in those functions. This principle gives consistency in the order of choices within the same type of functions.

In addition, interactions to be developed between user and menu system share the higher-level context even across different interaction types. The selection of action precedes selections of objects as well as modifiers. These characteristics are expected to facilitate users' development and application of their mental models on the usage of the menu system.

4   Experiment

An experiment was conducted to validate the effectiveness of the proposed method.

4.1   Setup and Procedure

A DVD recorder was employed as the target of operation whose menu interface was emulated on a personal computer (Figure 2). Participants in the experiment explored a menu hierarchy searching for particular items that could give solutions to their assigned tasks.

In the experiment, a menu hierarchy generated by the proposed method was compared to that resulting from alterations of its structure. The latter hierarchy was created by altering the orders of variable elements in the dependency structures in a random manner. Figure 3 shows a part of the menu hierarchy generated by the proposed method.

Fig. 2. Experimental setup

The following eight search tasks were given to participants:

- **Task 1:** Play back an audio file stored in the SD card.
- **Task 2:** Change the broadcast category for a programed recording onto the HDD to the Terrestrial Digital Broadcasting.
- **Task 3:** Search TV programs in which actor A will show up.
- **Task 4:** Import pictures stored in the SD card onto the HDD.
- **Task 5:** Program a timer recording of program A onto the HDD using the Electronic Program Guide.

- **Task 6:** Connect the recorder to the video intercom.
- **Task 7:** Dub a video stored on the HDD to the DVD.
- **Task 8:** Change the classification tag of a video stored in the DVD to "Drama".

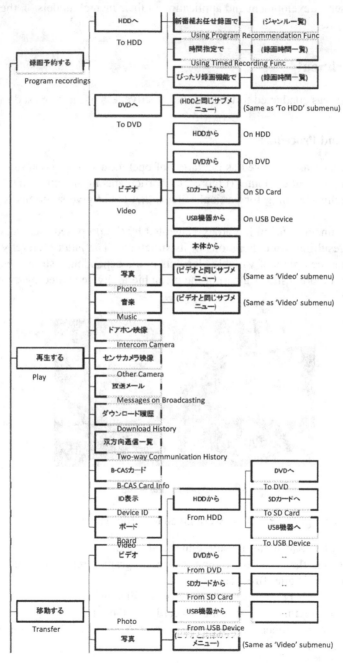

Fig. 3. Menu hierarchy generated by the proposed method

This task set was designed consisting of two blocks, one of which is from Task 1 to 4, and the other of which is from Task 5 to 8. These two blocks share same types of functions for solutions to their individual tasks. For instance, items that give solutions to Task 4 and 7 and those to Task 2 and 8, belong to Structure #1 and #8, respectively. Comparing these pairs in task performance gives data to look at effects of the previous search experiences onto the next search opportunities for menu items unsearched.

Twenty participants were recruited from a pool of faculty members, undergraduates, and graduate students at the department of mechanical engineering in Kyoto University. All of them gave informed consent to participation in this study. The study was designed as a between-subjects experiment. The participants separated into two groups of ten for the two different menu hierarchy conditions. In addition, in order to balance the difficulty between the two task blocks, the ten for each condition divided into two groups of five. Five participants performed Task 1 through 4 for the first half of the experiment and then went on Task 5 to 8 for the second half, while the other five did in the reverse order.

4.2   Result

Figure 4 presents (a) task time and (b) number of "back" button uses per task, comparing the first and the second half of the experiment as well as the two different menu hierarchy conditions. Whiskers represent standard deviations. Student's t-test confirmed significant differences between the two menu hierarchies in both of the two performance metrics in the second half ($p < 0.05$). It was also observed that the proposed method group's variations in them became much smaller in the second half, different from the other menu hierarchy group.

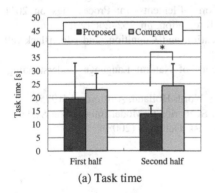

(a) Task time

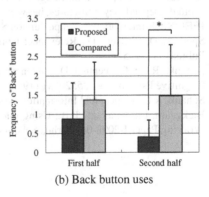

(b) Back button uses

Fig. 4. Experimental result (*$p < 0.05$)

These results indicate that the participants in the proposed method group completed search tasks in the second half more quickly and accurately based on what they had learnt from their experience with tasks in the first half. The proposed method proves to generate menu hierarchies that can benefit users as it allows them to develop solid mental images for navigating in the hierarchies. The structural regularity embedded in the menu hierarchies enable users to learn paths to items they have never experienced with.

5   Conclusion

This paper has proposed a procedural design method to generate a menu hierarchy based on dependency structures shared among menu item descriptions. A dependency structure captures syntactic relations among elements involving a set of interactions to realize a particular system function. This property gives generated menu hierarchies structural consistency so that, through interaction with them, users can easily develop solid mental images for navigating in the hierarchies.

A comparative experiment was conducted to validate the effectiveness of the proposed method. The method proved to generate menu hierarchies that enable the users to learn paths to items they have never experienced with from past experiences in search for "functionally" similar items.

References

1. Norman, K.L.: Better Design of Menu Selection Systems Through Cognitive Psychology and Human Factors. Human Factors 50(3), 556–559 (2008)
2. Horiguchi, Y., Nakanishi, H., Sawaragi, T., Kuroda, Y.: Analysis of Breakdowns in Menu-Based Interaction Based on Information Scent Model. In: Jacko, J.A. (ed.) Human-Computer Interaction, HCII 2009, Part I. LNCS, vol. 5610, pp. 438–445. Springer, Heidelberg (2009)
3. Horiguchi, Y., Gejo, W., Sawaragi, T., Nakanishi, H.: Menu System Design Based on Conceptual Dependency Structures between Functional Elements. In: Proceedings on 2011 IEEE/SICE International Symposium on System Integration, pp. 262–266 (2011)
4. Sperber, D., Wilson, D.: Relevance: Communication and Cognition, 2nd edn. Blackwell Publishers (1995)
5. Schank, R.C.: Conceptual Dependency: A Theory of Natural Language Understanding. Cognitive Psychology 3, 552–631 (1972)
6. Schank, R.C.: Conceptual Information Processing. North-Holland, Amsterdam (1975)
7. Bækgaard, L., Anderson, P.B.: Using Interaction Scenarios to Model Information Systems. Working Paper I-2008-04, Aarhus School of Business, Denmark (2008)

Liquid Tangible User Interface: Using Liquid in TUI

Masahiro Hotta[1], Makoto Oka[2], and Hirohiko Mori[2]

[1] System Information Engineering,
Tokyo City University,
Tokyo, Japan
[2] Department of Industrial and Management Systems Engineering,
Tokyo City University,
Tokyo, Japan
{g1381813,moka,hmori}@tcu.ac.jp

Abstract. In recent years, tangible user interface (TUI) has been paid attention on as a next generation user interface. In most TUI researches, solid body is mainly used as manipulators to assist interaction and they do not focus on "liquid". So, I focused on liquid as real world object, and I proposed the interaction using liquid in TUI and confirmed advantages of the interaction. As the result, there are some advantages in the adjustment of a sensuous amount comparing solid TUI.

Keywords: Tangible User Interface, Liquid, Education.

1   Introduction

Tangible user interface (TUI) is one of the active research fields in Human-Computer Interaction. In TUI, physical affordance of real world objects is utilized to assist the interaction. In most of TUI researches, solid bodies, such as blocks and panels, are used, as real world object to assist interaction [3, 4, 5, 6, 7] and only few researches have not paid attention to "liquid" which is one of real world object as the physical objects though there must be some specific advantages to using liquid in TUI as real object.

One of studies about using liquid in TUI is Mann's study[1]. In this study, water is used instead of piano keys and the users can listen to a song as if they play the piano when they press down their fingers into the continuous water flow. However, they just replace the piano key to the water and don't utilize the features of liquid.

In this paper, therefore, we propose an interaction used liquid in TUI, named Liquid Tangible, and discover the advantages in Liquid Tangible.

While solid is a discrete substance, liquid is a continuous substance. So, using liquid as a manipulator in TUI must have two merits. First, we can use much information by using liquid. Liquid can represent decimal point number, while it is hard to represent it by solid. For example, if we want use blocks to represent decimal numbers, we need many types of block (for example, brocks for the one's place, the ten's place, the tenth's place and etc of block) and many blocks. Second, we can more easily adjust

S. Yamamoto (Ed.): HIMI 2014, Part I, LNCS 8521, pp. 167–176, 2014.

volume continuously with liquid than with solid, because liquid is a continuous substance.

To utilize these advantages, we focused on the virtual "chemistry experiment" because they require the subtle adjustment of chemical reagents. By adopting the Liquid Tangible to the chemical experiments, the system allows users to observe various stage of chemical reaction by the difference in the amount of multiple chemical reagents according to the users' sensible adjustments of their amounts.

Song[2] was developed a virtual chemical experiment system using used empty beakers and table-top interface . However, in this system, there is no movement of the actual content, because of using empty beaker. Consequently, they don't discuss advantages of using liquid in this study.

2   Liquid Tangible System

In this study, I focused on neutralization experiments and salt crystallization experiments as chemical experiments. In this system, we use water instead of chemical reagents.

We also designed some actions for the Liquid Tangible chemical experiments by mimicking the actions which are used in actual chemical experiments. There are three types of actions. First action is the one to mix multiple types of liquid. To mix multiple types of chemical reagents, user can actually pours each liquid into a beaker. By this action, the system visualizes the process of chemical reaction according to the poured amount (Fig.1). The process of changing the molecular structure is displayed just beside the beaker and the colors of liquid also change according to the pH value as same as in using bromothymol blue.

The second action is stirring liquid by a stick. This action is used to mix the liquid well. By this action, the chemical reaction proceeds more when the molecules are separated from each other (Fig.2).

The final action is adding hot water. This action represents boiling liquid (Fig.3). The temperature of the poured hot water means the heating power. Only this action is different from the actual operation. I prepare this action because I confirm whether the actions different from actual actions are accepted by users.

In this way, Liquid Tangible can easily represent more information than using solid. The table 1 shows the information that is considered to be represented.

Table 1. The information that is considered to be represented

	using solid	Liquid Tangible
type of color	yellow,green,blue	from yellow to blue
pictures of numerator structure	2 type	9 types

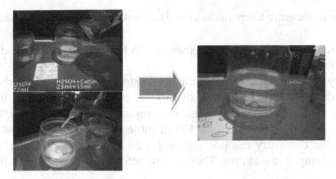

Fig. 1. The reaction by mixing multiple types of chemical

Fig. 2. The reaction by stirring by stick

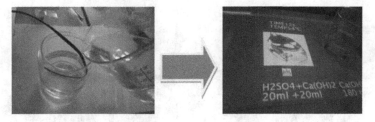

Fig. 3. The reaction by adding hot water

3   System Architecture and Implementation

This system consists of electronic weight scales, stirring sticks, thermometers, projector, WEB camera and PC. The electronic weight scales, the stirring stick and the thermometer are connected with the microcomputer board and WEB camera and microcomputer board are connected with PC by USB cables (Fig.4)

The electronic scales are used to measure how much liquid are poured into the beaker (Fig. 5). This device is made by disassembling a commercial electronic scale, and sends the weight to the PC via a microcomputer board. We implemented two of this device in order to measure the two types of chemical reagents. Accordingly, it is possible to mix two types of chemical reagents in this prototype.

We also implemented the electronic stirring stick (Fig.6). The stirring stick recognizes a stirring motion by triaxial acceleration sensor. The thermometer was used thermal sensor to measure temperature (Fig.7). The thermal sensor can measure from 0℃ to 100℃.

To recognize what kinds of chemical reagents, WEB camera and QR code attached on each beaker are utilized (Fig.8).

In this study, hydrochloric acid, sulfuric acid, nitric acid as the acidic chemical reagents and sodium hydroxide, calcium hydroxide, potassium hydroxide, barium hydroxide as the alkaline chemical reagents are prepared as virtual chemical reagents. The color of chemical reagents and the CG of molecular structure to show the information about the chemistry reaction are projected from the projector (Fig.9). The information is changed in real time. They are projected as so to overlap on the beakers (Fig.10).

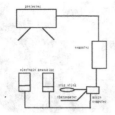

Fig. 4. Overall system architecture   **Fig. 5.** electronic scales

   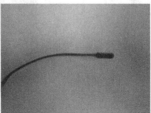   

Fig. 6. stir stick   **Fig. 7.** Thermometer   **Fig. 8.** Recognition of chemical

   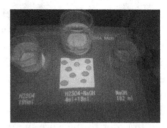

Fig. 9. The screen   **Fig. 10.** Overlapped on the beakers

4   How to Use Liquid Tangible

In this section, we explain how to use the system in neutralization and salt crystallization experiment.

4.1   Neutralization Experiment

Here, we will show one usage of this system for the neutralization experiment. In preparation, user chooses the beaker of one acidic chemical reagent and one of alkaline one attached the QR code which has information of each chemical on the electronic scales.

First, user adds the acidic reagent to beaker on the center. At this time, only the molecular structures of the acidic reagents are displayed. The color of the beaker is, of course, yellow.

Then, user pours the alkaline reagent to beaker on the center. If the user stops adding when the quantity of acidity is more than alkalinity, many figures of molecular structures of acidic reagent and a little of molecular structure of alkaline agent molecular structure are displayed. The color of the liquid is yellow-green. The state of the molecular structure changes to the salt when user stirs the liquid by the stirring sticks.

When the user adds alkaline reagent until the same amount of acidic reagent into the beaker on the center, only the figure of the salt comes out. The color becomes green.

If the user continues to add alkaline reagent, the figures of the salt and the alkaline molecular structures are displayed.

4.2   Salt Crystallization Experiment

Here, we will explain one example of the salt crystallization experiment. To extract the crystallized salt, generally, the neutralized reagent is boiled until the water is disappeared. In this system, this process is done by adding hot water into the neutralized reagent. The reason we adopted a different operation from the actual one is to investigate whether user accept the virtual behavior for a computational function.

In this system, after the neutralization experiment, boiling the reagent begins when the user pours hot water into it. The speed of the reaction changes by the temperature of hot water.

Fig. 11. Information in salt formation experiment

Here, the user can observe the process of forming the solid salt from first step to the end. The chemical formula of a salt, the quantity of salt crystal and the picture of the salt crystal was displayed (Fig11).

5   Acceptance Evaluation

5.1   Experiment Procedure

We conducted an experiment to investigate the users' acceptance for the Liquid Tangible. In this experiment, 4 participants, who are undergraduate students from 21 to 23 years old were participated.

The experiment are consists of four steps as follows: 1) Explain how to use the system, 2) Use the solid tangible object in the neutralization experiment (Fig.12), 3) Use Liquid Tangible in the neutralization experiment 4) Use Liquid Tangible in salt crystallization experiment. After the experiment, we conducted the interview about the Liquid Tangible's usability and advantage.

In neutralization experiment with the solid tangible objects, user uses the blocks instead of beakers filled with water. In this experiment, user can't adjust amount by using solid. Instead of stirring the liquid by the stirring stick in the Liquid Tangible, the participants asked to hit the block to each other to mix the reagent.

5.2   Result and Consideration

The participants' responses for Liquid Tangible were very positive. All participants mentioned that Liquid Tangible allows us to be more understandable about the chemical reaction than using solid objects. Such opinions means the mutual relation between adjusting the mount of the liquid and observing the change of the status according to the operation can enhance the understanding of the chemical reactions.

Furthermore, all participants claimed that our interaction is intuitive because it is close to actual chemical experiment. Many participants also claimed that the interaction can use for the education in the elementary school. One participant mentioned about the reason as follows: "This interaction is very fun because I felt to do a real chemical experiment. So, I think curious children must enjoy leaning more secure than an actual experiment". As the results, it can be said that Liquid Tangible was accepted by participants because they mentioned the very positive feedback.

On the other hands, there were some negative opinions to be improved. Some participants claimed that it was little bit hard to understand the molecular structures because their figures were too small. So, we improved the size of the displayed figures. Some participants also claimed that it is hard to understand the process of chemical reaction because the CG animation changes too fast. So, we also improve the speed of the CG animations. The improved system was used in the next experiment (Fig. 13)

6   Comparison with Solid TUI

We have been described adjusting amount by using solid is difficult because solid is discrete substances so far. However, there are some ways to adjust amount with solid

Fig. 12. Use solid in neutralization experiment

Fig. 13. after Improvement of a system

Fig. 14. using solid with the slide bar

TUI, for example, using dials or sliders, combining the TUI and GUI, and so on. To comparing the Liquid Tangible and traditional solid TUI, adjustment of the amount must be able to be controlled in both conditions. In this experiment, we adopted the way of combining the TUI and GUI to adjust the amount in solid TUI (Fig. 14). In this way, though the users can acquire the same information, only the operations of adjusting amount and the speed of molecular bond are different in both conditions.

6.1   Experiment Procedure

10 participants who are undergraduate students ages ranging from 21 to 23 years old involved in this experiment. This experiment consists of following four steps: 1) Explain how to use the system 2) Try Solid Tangible in neutralization experiment (Fig.15) 3) Try Liquid Tangible in neutralization experiment (Fig.16) 3) Try Liquid Tangible in salt crystallization experiment (Fig.17). 4) Answer the questionnaire.

We asked the participants to answer five questions in the questionnaires: (i) Do you feel the chemical reaction is more understandable with Liquid Tangible than solid TUI? (ii) Do you feel adjusting amount is easier with Liquid Tangible than solid TUI? (iii) How do you feel using hot water to start boiling? and (iv) Do you feel using liquid in the system make sense? The question (i) and (ii) are the ones to investigate the advantages of Liquid Tangible against solid TUI, the question (iii) and (iv) are the one to investigate the effectiveness of the Liquid Tangible

Fig. 15. use Solid Tangible in neutralization experiment

Fig. 16. Use Liquid Tangible in neutralization experiment

Fig. 17. Use Liquid Tangible in salt formation experiment

7   Results and Considerations

The table 2 shows the result and its reason of questions. For the question (i), 8 participants answered positively and they claimed "it is easy to understand the chemical
reaction because the system is close to the real environment and allows us to control
the amount with my feelings". For the question (ii), on the other hands, only the half
of the participants answered positively. They claimed that "I can adjust the amount

Table 2. The feedbacks of questionnaire

questions	positeve	negative
(i)	8 participants	2 participants
	it is easy to understand in order to perate it by my hands.	it cares about adjustment of amount.
	the system is close to the real environment and allows us to control the amount with my feelings	
	it is easy to imagine a direction with a liquid.	
(ii)	5 participants	5 participants
	I can adjust the amount easily because the state of decreasing water works as the target of controlling amounts	I can't adjust the amount because there was a time lag.
(ii)	6 pariticipants	4 pariticipants
	because I imagined sensusouly.	I tought that how to go up temperaturer was insufrficient with hot water.
	it was easy to imagine boiling by adding hot water.	I think that doing hot water and using fire have a difference.
	I was actually abele to feel heat.	
(iv)	9 pariticipants	1 pariticipant
	it is easy to understand by actually working.	it seldom seemed to be about a meaning
	because the image in which it is experiment in solid from is not made.	
	I think that change may be seen when adjusting amount.	

easily because the state of decreasing water works as the target of controlling amounts." Though, on the other hands, five participants responded the negative answer, two of them claimed that the time delay between pouring water and changing displayed information make the adjustments difficult. Their comments means the difficulty does not due to the nature of Liquid Tangible but the implemented way of the system. From the results of question (i) and (ii), therefore, it can be said that Liquid Tangible is useful for the tasks which require controlling the amount.

Looking at the results of the question (iii), some people can come the boiling the reagent to mind by the pouring hot water and some cannot. This means if the behavior which is different from the real operation is assigned to a computer function carefully, it could work well.

Finally, to the question (iv), most of participants answered positively. The results indicate that Liquid Tangible is acceptable to the user and is useful in for the task of amount control and the education.

8   Conclusion

In this paper, we propose Liquid Tangible and implemented the prototype system in virtual chemical experiment. As a result from acceptance evaluation, users accept Liquid Tangible and it provide fun to the users. And, in the tasks which require adjusting amount, Liquid Tangible allows the users to control amount instinctively and is, therefore, effective in comparison with the solid TUI.

9   This Study Is an Initial Effort toward the Developing Interactions Using Liquid

In the future, I confirm that using liquid is used in other environments based on environments that can be taken advantage of Liquid Tangible in this study. Use by paint software can be considered as the environment. First, paint software has much information, including a color etc. Second, it is necessity to adjust instinctively amount when making color. Third, users imagine paints by using a viscous liquid. I think that it is necessity to make it adapted for various environments including paint software because it isn't the field fully studied

References

1. Mann, S., Janzen, R., Post, M.: Hydraulophone Design Considerations: Absement, Displacement, and Velocity-Sensitive Music Keyboard in which each key is a Water Jet. In: MM 2006, Santa Barbara, California, USA, October 23-27 (2006)
2. Song, K., Lee, J., Kim, G.: CheMO: Mixed Object Instruments and Interactions for Tangible Chemistry Experiments. In: CHI 2011, Vancouver, BC, Canada, May 7-12. ACM (2011) 978-1-4503-0268-5/11/05

3. Ishii, H.: Tangible Bits: Beyond Pixels. In: TEI 2008, Bonn, Germany, February 18-20 (2008)
4. Girouard, A., Treacy Solovey, E., Hirshfield, L.M., Ecott, S., Shaer, O., Jacob, R.J.K.: Smart Blocks: A Tangible Mathematical Manipulative. In: TEI 2007, Baton Rouge, Louisiana, USA, February 15-17 (2007)
5. Horn, M.S., Jacob, R.J.K.: Designing Tangible Programming Languages for Classroom Use. In: TEI 2007, Baton Rouge, Louisiana, USA, February 15-17 (2007)
6. Zigelbaum, J., Horn, M.S., Shaer, O., Jacob, R.J.K.: The Tangible Video Editor: Collaborative Video Editing with Active Tokens. In: TEI 2007, Baton Rouge, Louisiana, USA, February 15-17 (2007)
7. Xie, L., Antle, A.N., Motamedi, N.: Are Tangibles More Fun? Comparing Children's Enjoyment and Engagement Using Physical, Graphical and Tangible User Interfaces. In: TEI 2008, Bonn, Germany, February 18-20 (2008)

Three Key Challenges in ARM-COMS for Entrainment Effect Acceleration in Remote Communication

Teruaki Ito[1] and Tomio Watanabe[2]

[1] The University of Tokushima, 2-1 Minami-Josanjima, Tokushima 770-8506, Japan
`tito@tokushima-u.ac.jp`
[2] Okayama Prefectural University, 111 Tsuboki, Souja, Okayama 719-1197, Japan
`watanabe@cse.oka-pu.ac.jp`

Abstract. Remote communication systems, which are getting popular these days, allow us to enjoy the benefit of audio/video communication over the network. However, communication based on these systems is still not identical to face-to-face meetings. For example, open issues include lack of tele-presence, lack of entrainment in communication, etc. In order to tackle these issues, this study proposes an idea of remote individuals' connection through augmented tele-presence systems called ARM-COMS: ARm-supported eMbodied COmmunication Monitor System. ARM-COMS is composed of a tablet PC as an ICT (Information and Communication Technology) device and a desktop robotic arm which manipulates the tablet. Two types of modes, or intelligent tablet mode (IT-mode) and intelligent avatar mode (IA-mode), play a key role in ARM-COMS to implement the three functions; namely, autonomous positioning (AP), autonomous entrainment movement (AEM), and autonomous entrainment positioning (AEP). This paper proposes the basic concept of ARM-COMS to accelerate the entrainment effect in remote communication.

Keywords: Embodied communication, augmented tele-presence robotic arm manipulation, human interface, remote communication.

1 Introduction

Thanks to the development of ICT (Information and Communication Technology) technologies and the expanding internet connection services, remote communication systems are now one of the popular applications today. Apart from the high quality commercial systems at the top, many of the application software for remote communication are freely downloadable. [Abowdm et al. 2000]. Even though remote communication is getting popular over the network, several drawbacks are still unsolved, such as lack of tele-presence and lack of relationship in communication [Greenberg et al. 1996].

As for tele-presense issues, an idea of mobile robot-based remote communication proposes one solution. Using a mobile robot for remote communication, the experimental results in several studies show the effectiveness of these remote controlled robots in communication [Tariq et al. 2011; Kashiwabara et al. 2012]. Embodiment of

S. Yamamoto (Ed.): HIMI 2014, Part I, LNCS 8521, pp. 177–186, 2014.

an agent using anthropomorphization of an Object [Osawa, et al. 2012] is also an interesting idea to show the presence [Sirkin et al 2012].

These robots could provide tele-presence of the operator in the remote site and even enables some kinds of tele-operating tasks from distance. These robots provide basic function to support distance communication using several critical functions such as face image display of the operator [Otsuka et al. 2008], drivability to move around, tele-manipulation on remote objects as well as basic communication functions including talk/listen/see [Kim et al. 2012]. However, there are still a gap between robot-based video conferences/meetings and face-to-face ones.

A new challenge was undertaken by a robotic arm type system with mobile function [Wongphati et al. 2012]. For an example of non-mobile arm type system, Kubi [Revolve Robotics] allows the remote user to "look around" during their video call by commanding Kubi where to aim the tablet using intuitive remote controls over the web. An idea of enhanced motion display [Otsuka et al. 2011] has been reported. The effectiveness of dynamic motion of display to represent the physical object has been reported [Yakuyama et al, 2011]. However, it has not been applied to the movement of human body. Therefore, non-verbal movement of the remote person is still an open issue.

This study focuses on the critical aspect of entrainment in communication [Watanabe 2011]. This paper proposed an idea for connecting remote individuals through augmented tele-presence systems called ARM-COMS(ARm-supported eMbodied COmmunication Monitor System), focusing on the two issues; lack of tele-presence and lack of relationship in communication [Ito et al. 2013]. However, considering the advantages of tablet PC as one of the mobile ICT devices, the idea of ARM-COMS has been upgraded by integrating IT-mode in addition to IA-mode. Therefore, this paper proposes an updated idea of ARM-COMS to cover the whole idea.

2   A Proposal of an Idea of Active Monitor Arm for Augmented Tele-presence – ARM-COMS

This study proposes an idea of augmented tele-presence systems, which is called ARM-COMS. ARM-COMS is designed to integrate the two components (a tablet PC and a robotic arm) with two manipulation modes: intelligent tablet mode (IT-mode) and intelligent avatar mode (IA-mode). The tablet PC is integrated into ARM-COMS for video communication manipulated by an active monitor arm as well as for information retrieval by using it as a general information device. IT-mode and IA-mode are interchangeable based on the situation of the user. This section covers the two basic modes of ARM-COMS.

2.1   IT-Mode in ARM-COMS

The tablet PC is one of the very popular mobile ICT devices today. As a typical situation in using a tablet PC, a user holds the devise in left hand and manipulates it on the touch screen with right fingers. However, if both hands are not free, it is not suitable to use it this way. If a user is in bed, for example, it would not be comfortable to use it this way, either. Considering the characteristic feature of tablet PC as a mobile device, it would lose this feature if a tablet PC is placed on a desktop holder, which is often seen these days. Since the tablet PC is a convenient mobile tool, it would be an ideal situation that our own tablet autonomously and automatically approaches to us when we need it and where we need it even if we do not do anything. This is what IT-mode of ARM-COMS is aiming at.

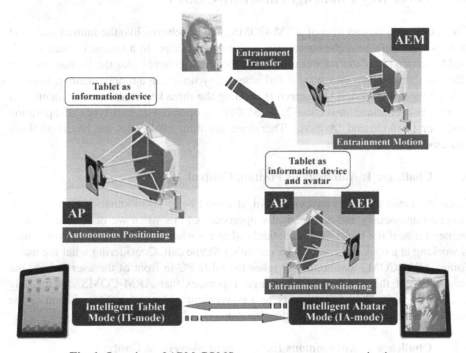

Fig. 1. Overview of ARM-COMS to support remote communication

2.2   IA-Mode in ARM-COMS

As mentioned above, the tablet PC is one of the very popular mobile ICT devices, it allows us not only to retrieve information, but also to communicate with others over the network. As a typical situation in using a tablet PC for communicating with others, the user holds the devise in left hand and manipulates the touch screen with right fingers, which is quite similar to that of IT-mode operation mentioned above. However, when we compare video communication with face-to-face communication, there is a significant difference from the two points of view. When we talk with somebody in a face-to-face meeting, what we share is not merely the same physical space, but also an invisible communication space or atmosphere. As a result, entrainment will occur between the participants of the conversation. However, when we talk with somebody over the network, we can only see the face on the screen and cannot share the same physical space. As a result, this kind of entrainment is different from that of a face-to-face meeting. Since the entrainment is associated with physical movement of a person, a dynamic movement of a tablet PC during remote communication will make some effect on entrainment acceleration. In addition to the physical movement of a person, the physical distance between things or people implicitly expresses a relationship of people. This is what IA-mode of ARM-COMS is aiming at.

3   Three Key Challenges in ARM-COMS

This study proposes an idea of ARM-COMS, which behaves like the human neck and mimics a person's movements to play a role as an avatar. In addition to that, ARM-COMS understands the intention of users so that it behaves like the human hand to offer something when they want it and where they want it in a timely manner. In order to implement this idea, this research is tackling the three key challenges as mentioned below. As mentioned in section 2, ARM-COMS operates on two types of operation mode, or IT-mode and IA-mode. Therefore, the three challenges are based on these two modes.

3.1   Challenge 1: Autonomous Position Control

Since the tablet PC is a convenient tool, it would be an ideal situation that our own tablet autonomously and automatically approaches to us when we need it and where we need it as if the tablet PC understands what we want. For example, suppose a user is working at a desk and receives an incoming Skype call. Considering what the use is doing, ARM-COMS autonomously takes the table PC in front of the user to urge the acceptance of the connection. Challenge 1 pursues that ARM-COMS dynamically locates the tablet PC autonomously at a convenient and comfortable position to the user when they need it and where they need it.

3.2   Challenge 2: Autonomous Entrainment Movement Control

Challenge 1 does not directly relate to video communication. However, Challenge 2 and 3 are directly related to video communication usage. It has been reported that entrainment among participants emerges during conversation if the participating subjects share the same physical space and engage in the conversation [Okada et al. 1994; Watanabe et al. 2004]. However, this kind of entrainment in a face-to-face meeting is different from that of remote communication. Tracking the head movement of a speaking person in a remote site, ARM-COMS manipulates the tablet PC [Tomotoshi et al. 2012; Wongphati et al. 2012] as an avatar to mimic the head movement of the remote person so that entrainment emerges as if the local person interacts with the remote person locally.

3.3   Challenge 3: Autonomous Entrainment Position Control

In a face-to-face meeting, each person takes a meaningful physical position to represent the relationship with the others, or to send non-verbal messages to others.

A closer position would be taken for friends, showing close relationship, whereas a non-closer position would be taken for strangers, showing unfriendly relationship [Osawa 2012]. ARM-COMS controls a tablet PC to dynamically locate an appropriate position in space and to explicitly represent the relationship with other participants, by sending non-verbal messages. For example, the tablet PC would be approaching to the speaking person to show that the remote person is interested in the talk.

4   Design of AEM in ARM-COMS

4.1   Basic Motion Control for ARM-COMS AEM

During conversation, various types of body/head movements can be observed. In order to mimic some of these movements, this study focuses on three types of head movements, namely, nodding, head-tilting, and head shaking movements. All of these are very typical non-verbal expression in Japan during conversation. Nodding means affirmative, agree, listening, etc. Head-titling means ambiguous, not sure, impossible to answer, etc. Head shaking means negative, disagree, no way, etc. Fig.3 shows the corresponding physical motions implemented by the robotic arm control. If the monitor behaves like these in conversation, it is assumed that the physical movements could send a non-verbal message. Technically speaking, these three types of movements can be regarded as the rotation around each axis as shown in Fig. 3. Therefore, the rotation angles of these three motions can be calculated as in Scheme (1), (2) and (3).

For nodding movement, roll angle can be calculated by scheme (1), where α is the rotation angle around y-axis, and X,Z are the acceleration value for each direction.

$$\alpha = \sin^{-1}\left(\frac{-X}{\sqrt{X^2 + Z^2}}\right) \cdots \cdots \qquad (1)$$

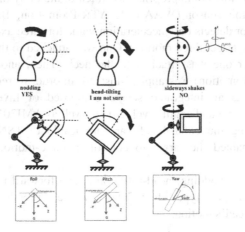

Fig. 2. Three types of target head motion

For "I am not sure" movement, pitch angleβcan be calculated by scheme (2), whereβis the rotation angle around x-axis, and Y,Z are the acceleration value for each direction.

$$\beta = \sin^{-1}\left(\frac{-Y}{\sqrt{Y^2 + Z^2}}\right) \cdot \cdot \cdot \cdot \cdot \cdot \cdot \tag{2}$$

For sideway shaking movement, yaw angle ξcan be calculated by scheme (3), whereξis the rotation angle around z-axis, ω is the angle subtracted from the horizontal angle andΔt is the sampling interval, which was 100[ms] here.

$$\xi = \sum \omega \Delta t \quad \cdot \cdot \cdot \tag{3}$$

4.2   Prototype System for ARM-COMS AEM

A prototype robotic arm system for AEM in ARM-COMS was configured as shown in Fig.3. The robotic arm system is composed of a table top robotic arm (Lynxmotion) with motor controller board (SSC-32 Ver.2.0) which is connected to PC (Windows 7) by a serial cable.

First, this robotic arm was controlled by a PC using a remote controller (Wii Remote + Wii Motion Plus) through Bluetooth connection. The combination of Wii Remote and Wii Motion plus made it possible to trace the acceleration of the neck at the three axis and three rotation angle around these three axis. Control software for the arm was developed by Visual C++ with library Wiimotelib v.1.8. As a result, the robotic arm was wirelessly controllable by Wii Remote manipulation.

According to the feasibility test of the first prototype, it was recognized that the prototype could mimic the head motion if the Wii remote was attached to the head. However, Wii remote was not appropriate to attach to the body of human. Therefore, a wireless acceleration sensor (WAA-001, ATR-Promotion, Bluetooth type) was used. Since this sensor detects only acceleration value for three axes, a pair of sensors was used to cover the target three motions. One was attached to the ear portion of the head, while the other one was attached to the neck. Then, another type of sensor (TSND-121, ATR Promotion) was applied instead, in order to reduce the number of sensors. TSND-121 is an integrated sensor composed of InvenSence MPU6050 which covers acceleration and angular velocity, as well as AMI306 which covers gyro motion. By modifying the control software applicable to TSND-121, the ARM-COMS prototype enabled the target to control in three-motion only by a single TSND-121.

Fig.3 also shows the nodding, head-tilting and lean forward motion, all of which were mimicked by the prototype ARM-COMS, where a pseudo-display attached to the arm follows the head's motion.

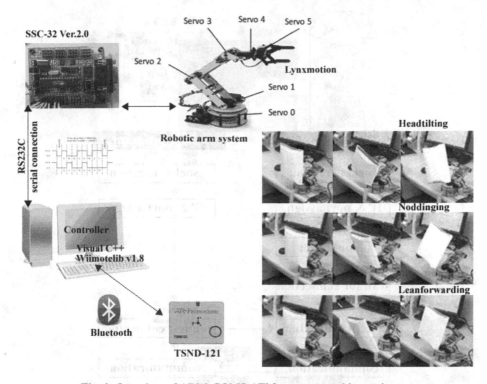

Fig. 3. Overview of ARM-COMS AEM prototype and its motion

Fig. 4 shows the flow diagram of server-client control software which was developed to control the robotic arm for ARM-COMS AEM.

A server process is started on a PC as a detached process of socket at remote site where ARM-COM AEM is connected. When the client PC starts the client program, it sends a request to the socket for connection. When the server program receives the request signal, it will accept the connection. Once the connection is established between the server and the client, the controlling command is sent to the remote PC. The command is generated based on Scheme (1) – (3) using the sensing data obtained from the integrated sensor, TSND-121. The remote PC controls the ARM-COMS based on the command received from the local PC. Three types of head movement were shown in Fig.3.

4.3   Feasibility Study of ARM-COMS AEM

Feasibility tests of ARM-COM AEM were conducted to compare the video communication with and without ARM-COMS to make clear the effectiveness of the idea of ARM-COMS between the two different places, or Site-A and Site-B.

Site-A was regarded as a local site where ARM-COMS was installed equipped with a smart phone as a pseudo-active display. Subject-A communicates with Subject-B via Skype on the smart phone. A magnetic sensor (Fastrak, POLHEMUS) was

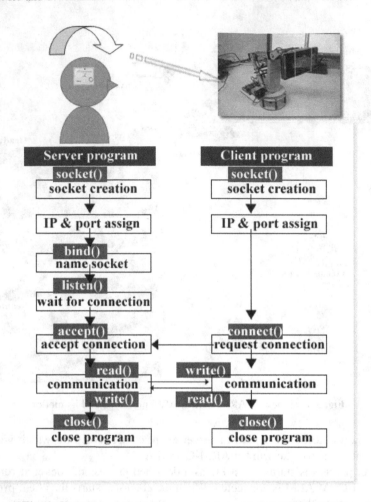

Fig. 4. Overview of client-server program to control ARM-COMS

attached to the head of Subject-A during conversation to detect the head motion of subject-A. Site-B was regarded as a remote site where Subject-B communicates with Subject-A in Site-A via Skype on a laptop PC. A multi-sensor TSND-121 was attached to the head of Subject B to trace the head movement during conversation, which was also used to control ARM-COMS in Site-A. The sensing data from the multi-sensor was transmitted to the client program in the laptop through Bluetooth. The socket program communicates with the server program in desktop PC on Site-A, and controls the ARM-COMS via Wi-Fi network. In this way, a remote communication environment was set up to conduct the feasibility tests.

Feasibility experiments in remote communication with/without ARM-COM AEM were conducted. Based on the video recording data for the movement of subjects, head movement data during the conversation, synchronization data between the subjects, etc, feasibility of ARM-COMS AEM was recognized as generally positive.

5   Concluding Remarks

The paper proposed an idea of active monitor arm named ARM-COMS with the two types of modes in ARM-COM system and described the three challenges based on these modes. Namely, autonomous position control, autonomous entrainment movement control, and autonomous entrainment movement control. Active display presents the tele-existence of a remote object shown in the display by physical movement. However, ARM-COMS not only presents the tele-presence of a remote person, but also explicitly shows the relationship between the remote person and the local participants by way of the entrainmental behavior of a table PC.

ARM-COMS employs only a general tablet PC attached to the sub-system of robotic arm, which will be specifically designed and built for this purpose. ARM-COMS not only presents a new idea for remote communication system, but also opens a potential new market for non-industrial robotic arm design and products.

The future works include the design and manufacturing of sub-system for ARM-COMS robotic arm, development of the entrainment movement/positioning algorithm and its feasibility study.

References

1. Abowdm, D.G., Mynatt, D.E.: Charting past, present, and future research in ubiquitous computing. ACM Transactions on Computer-Human Interaction (TOCHI) 7(1), 29–58 (2000)
2. Greenberg, S.: Peepholes: low cost awareness of one's community. In: Conference Companion on Human Factors in Computing Systems: Common Ground, Vancouver, British Columbia, Canada, pp. 206–207 (1996)
3. Ito, T., Watanabe, T.: ARM-COMS: Arm-supported embodied communication monitor system. In: Yamamoto, S. (ed.) HIMI/HCII 2013, Part III. LNCS, vol. 8018, pp. 307–316. Springer, Heidelberg (2013)
4. Kashiwabara, T., Osawa, H., Shinozawa, K., Imai, M.: TEROOS: a wearable avatar to enhance joint activities. In: Annual conference on Human Factors in Computing Systems, pp. 2001–2004 (May 2012)
5. Kim, K., Bolton, J., Girouard, A., Cooperstock, J., Vertegaal, R.: TeleHuman: Effects of 3D Perspective on Gaze and Pose Estimation with a Life-size Cylindrical Telepresence Pod. In: Proc. of CHI 2012, pp. 2531–2540 (2012)
6. Kubi, http://revolverobotics.com/meet-kubi/
7. Okada, K., Maeda, F., Ichikawa, Y., Matsushita, Y.: Multiparty videoconferencing at virtual social distance: MAJIC design. In: SCW 1994 Proceedings of the 1994 ACM Conference on Computer Supported Cooperative Work (CSCW 1994), pp. 385–393 (1994)
8. Osawa, T., Matsuda, Y., Ohmura, R., Imai, M.: Embodiment of an agent by anthropo morphization of a common object. Web Intelligence and Agent Systems: An International Journal 10, 345–358 (2012)
9. Ohtsuka, S., Oka, S., Kihara, K., Tsuruda, T., Seki, M.: Human-body swing affects visibility of scrolled characters with direction dependency. In: 2011 Symposium Digest of Technical Papers, Society for Information Display (SID), pp. 309–312 (2011)

10. Otsuka, T., Araki, S., Ishizuka, K., Fujimoto, M., Heinrich, M., Yamato, J.: A Realtime Multimodal System for Analyzing Group Meetings by Combining Face Pose Tracking and Speaker Diarization. In: Proc. of the 10th International Conference on Multimodal Interfaces (ICMI 2008), Chania, Crete, Greece, pp. 257–264 (2008)
11. Sirkin, D., Ju, W.: Consistency in physical and on-screen action improves perceptions of telepresence robots. In: HRI 2012, Proceedings of the Seventh Annual ACM/IEEE International Conference on Human-Robot Interaction, pp. 57–64 (2012)
12. Tariq, A.M., Ito, T.: Master-slave robotic arm manipulation for communication robot. Japan Society of Mechanical Engineer, Proceedings of 2011 Annual Meeting 11(1), S12013 (2011)
13. Tomotoshi, M., Ito, T.: A study on awareness support method to improve engagement in remote communication. In: First International Symposium on Socially and Technically Symbiotic System (STSS 2012), Okayama, vol. 39, pp. 1–6 (August 2012)
14. Watanabe, T.: Human-entrained Embodied Interaction and Communication Technology. In: Emotional Engineering, pp. 161–177. Springer (2011)
15. Watanabe, T., Okubo, M., Nakashige, M., Danbara, R.: InterActor: Speech-Driven Embodied Interactive Actor. International Journal of Human-Computer Interaction 17(1), 43–60 (2004)
16. Wongphati, M., Matsuda, Y., Osawa, H., Imai, M.: Where do you want to use a robotic arm? And what do you want from the robot? In: International Symposium on Robot and Human Interactive Communication, pp. 322–327 (September 2012)
17. Yakuyama, H., Tsunami, Y., Tadakuma, R.: Evaluation of an enhanced-motion display. In: SICE Tohoku, ch. 267-17, pp. 1–5 (2011) (in Japanese)

Two-Handed Interactive Menu: An Application of Asymmetric Bimanual Gestures and Depth Based Selection Techniques

Hani Karam and Jiro Tanaka

Department of Computer Science, University of Tsukuba,
Tennodai, Tsukuba, 305-8577 Ibaraki, Japan
{hani,jiro}@iplab.cs.tsukuba.ac.jp

Abstract. In this paper, we propose a Two Handed Interactive Menu as an evaluation of asymmetric bimanual gestures. The menu is split into two parts, one for each hand. The actions are started with the non-dominant hand and continued with the dominant one. Handedness is taken into consideration, and a different interface is generated depending on the handedness. The results of our experiments show that two hands are more efficient than one; however the handedness itself did not affect the results in a significant way. We also introduce the Three Fingers Click, a selection mechanism that explores the possibility of using a depth-sensing camera to create a reliable clicking mechanism. Though difficult to maintain, our Three Fingers Clicking gesture is shown in the experiments to be reliable and efficient.

Keywords: bimanual gestures, depth-based click.

1 Introduction

Hand gestures have been investigated in Human Computer Interface, and bimanual gestures have been gaining popularity [1], [2], [6], [7]. Lévesque et al. have summed up in their research that two hands can perform better than one on a given task [13]. According to Guiard [3], bimanual gestures are classified into two parts: symmetric, where both hands are playing the same role (e.g. rope skipping) and asymmetric, where each hand is playing a different role (e.g. playing the violin).

In traditional desktop User Interface, menus are often used. Menus represent a structured way for displaying several options to the user. The advantage of menus is that, even though they can hold numerous options, they do so in a way that does not clutter the visualization surface. Several menu arrangements exist (dropdown menu, pie-menu, marked menu ...), each with its own idiosyncrasies.

To the best of our knowledge, creating a menu system that is optimized not only for hand gestures, but for bimanual gestures as well, has not been attempted before. Therefore, we present our interactive menu as an approach of applying asymmetrical bimanual gestures in User Interface design.

S. Yamamoto (Ed.): HIMI 2014, Part I, LNCS 8521, pp. 187–198, 2014.
© Springer International Publishing Switzerland 2014

Gesture data fetching has been classified into 2 main categories: glove-based and vision-based [9]. Yang et al. state that because the glove-based method uses gloves and extra sensors, those extra sensors make it easy and accurate to collect gestures data, when compared with vision-based techniques [9]. However, using a vision-based technique allows the gestures to be recognized in an untethered way, thus freeing the user from donning any special hardware or apparatus to enable him to interact with the system which gives rise to a more natural interaction [10]. For this reason, we have opted for the vision-based approach.

In our study, we first try to find the best bimanual interaction method, which can convey instructions to the menu system. Then we propose a depth-based clicking method, as a way of allowing the user to select a given command. Finally, we put together a prototype, and we conduct a series of experiments to determine the feasibility and the performance of the proposed system.

2   Related Work

Among the earliest contributions to asymmetric bimanual gestures research is Guiard's work [3], which states that human bimanual interaction is asymmetrical; while both hands work together, the dominant and the non-dominant hands are doing different gestures. Guiard created a model for bimanual interaction, known as the "Kinematic Chain Model". Hinckley et al. have argued that, with appropriate design, two hands are not only faster than one hand, but they can also provide the user with additional information that a single hand alone cannot [1]. It has also been shown that users were able to perform complex commands in a natural way using mixed hands gestures [9]. Wagner et al. have also shown that bimanual interaction outperforms unimanual interactions [7].

However, not all bimanual interfaces are better than unimanual ones; in given situations, one-handed manipulation proved better than its bimanual counterpart [8], [11]. Chen et al. [14] have also shown that under certain circumstances, one-handed techniques were faster than two-handed techniques.

Applying bimanual interactions on menus has already been approached from different perspectives. In the bimanual marking menu [15], the marking is performed by the non-dominant hand. This has been confirmed as a very efficient bimanual technique [14]. In Guimbretière et al.'s study, to activate the menu system, the user performs a pinch gesture with his non-dominant hand, moves his hand, and finally releases the pinch to finish marking [16]. This design leaves the non-dominant hand free to participate in other gesture-based activities.

Typically, issuing a command (or choosing a menu item) should be performed with some kind of selection mechanism. One way is to release a previously executed pinch to perform a marking [16]; another approach would be to use the primary hand to point out to an item, and using a selection gesture performed by the non-dominant hand to select that item [13]. A touchscreen click simulating gesture can also be implemented with a depth camera as shown by Wilson [17].

3   Design Principles for Menu Interactions

In this section, we describe the interactions that we have designed for the Two Handed Menu. Guiard states that the non-dominant hand performs the coarse movements, whereas the dominant hand performs the fine and precise movements [3]; this formed the basis of our approach to creating interaction techniques.

Bimanual tasks give rise to a better performance if the action of the dominant hand depends on the action of the non-dominant hand [11]; the non-dominant hand executes the commands that require less precision, while the more precise actions are performed by the dominant hand. Applying this to a menu system, in a general way, stipulates that the non-dominant hand selects a sub-menu from the main menu; the dominant hand then selects the desired command from a sub-menu.

To make the system more complete, the following gestures will be used: "Show menu" which displays the menu on screen, "Go up" which allows the user to go to the previous submenu, and "Hide menu" which exits the menu without issuing any command. A selection gesture will also be used to allow the user to select a menu item. "Show menu", "Go up" and "Hide menu" do not require precision, and thus can be assigned to the non-dominant hand.

This gives rise to a conflicting set of commands, such as "Show menu" and selecting a submenu, both being performed by the non-dominant hand. While it was shown that bimanual interfaces perform better than unimanual interfaces [2], [5], [6], [7] bimanual interfaces can induce a decreased performance if the interaction techniques are poorly designed [8], [11], [14].

As a first step, we have decided to find out which is the better interaction technique for commands that involve repeated use of the same hand.

3.1   Experiment 1 – Determining the Sequence of Interactions

As highlighted previously, some interactions cannot be separated into a sequence of "non-dominant hand, dominant hand" actions, rather some repetition with the same hand needs to be used at a given point. In this experiment, we aim at finding the better sequence when repetition is required.

The experiment consists of displaying a circular target at random positions. A small, hand-shaped cursor designates the current position of the user's hand. The participant has 30 seconds to hit as many targets as possible. When a target is hit, a new target appears in a different position. Three variations of this experiment have been conducted:

1. One hand: the user uses only his dominant hand to hit the target.
2. Two hands – sequential: the target position is random, but it appears alternately on either side of the screen. The user has to hit the target with the hand corresponding to its relative side (left hand for the left side, right hand for the right side).
3. Two hands – random: the targets appear in a total random way. In this case too, the user uses the corresponding hand to hit the target.

To implement the experiment, we used a SoftKinetic DS325 depth sensing camera, which uses Time-of-Flight technology [18]. The camera was placed on top of a 23" monitor with Full HD resolution, facing the user, tilted down approximately 10 degrees. A prototype has been implemented on a computer equipped with an Intel Core i5 3.2 GHz CPU. The SDK of SoftKinetic has been used to detect hand tip positions. Onscreen rendering has been implemented in OpenGL. The entire prototype was written in C++. To evaluate our system, 9 participants (5 males, 4 females) aged between 23 and 30 were recruited; 6 among them are computer scientists/engineers. 8 of them are highly familiar with computers. 2 of them are left-handed.

3.2   Results

The results show a significant increase in performance when using two-hand gestures compared against using one hand only. In their study, Chen et al. found that, in given cases, using two hands sequentially was slower than using just one hand [14]. In our experiment, the results came contrary to that, showing that using two hands sequentially was the faster interaction: Fig 1.a. shows that the number of hits in 30 seconds is greatest for "Two-handed sequential" (42.67 with a standard deviation of 5.07 for n=9). Another result that was generated by this experiment is that the interaction slows down when consecutive actions had to be repeated by the non-dominant hand: Fig 1.b indicates that the average difference of time between each hit, as well as the maximum time difference between hits, are smallest for "Two-handed sequential" (0.74 and 2.46, with a standard deviation of 0.39 for n=9)

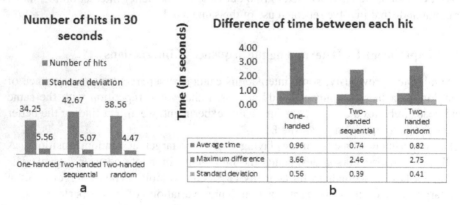

Fig. 1. Results of the experiment showing the number of hits in 30 seconds (a) and the difference of time between hits (b), for each of the three experiments variations

3.3   Interaction Design

Taking the results of the previous experiments into consideration, we have thus created the following rules for interacting with the system:

- The non-dominant hand interacts with the main menu, while the dominant hand interacts with all the submenus (a given submenu can lead to another submenu).
- "Go up" and "Hide menu" gestures do not require any precision, so they can be assigned to the non-dominant hand.
- While the "Show menu" gesture does not need any precision, it has been assigned to the dominant hand to avoid the scenario of showing the main menu and interacting with it using the non-dominant hand, conforming with the results of our experiment.

4   Three Fingers Clicking Gesture

To be able to instruct the system about a command (that is, selecting a menu item), some kind of interaction is required. In this section, we introduce the "Three fingers clicking gesture", a novel selection mechanism approach.

Some previous work consists of using the non-dominant hand to initiate this command, such as "index pointing, thumb up" gesture [13], or releasing a previously executed pinch [16]. The disadvantage of these models is that they do not rely on an intuitive way to perform the operation. An intuitive approach is to imitate the finger clicking gesture, widely used on touch displays. In some situations, a calibration of the environment is needed; Wilson calibrated the system by using a depth threshold determined from a histogram over several hundred frames of a motionless scene [17]. An ad-hoc approach that does not use calibration exploits a flood filling technique to detect whether a finger has clicked a surface [20]. These two techniques detect a physical contact with a surface. A mid-air clicking gesture is proposed in OpenNI [19]: an "L" shape is created by extending the index and thumb fingers to signal the start of the clicking gesture; then the gesture itself is performed by pushing the entire hand away from the user's body.

In our approach, we assume that a finger clicking event occurs when the index finger passes beyond a given threshold. To define this threshold, we detected the X, Y and Z coordinates of the thumb, index, and middle fingers (noted T, I and M respectively). We also detected the same information about the hand palm's center (noted P). We have defined the plane created by the points [P, T, M]. The angle θ between this plane and the vector [PI] is then computed (Fig. 2). A threshold of 12 degrees was selected empirically. The test is performed within one frame.

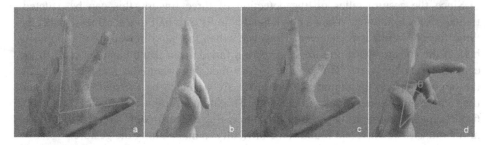

Fig. 2. 1-a and 1-b depict an unclicked state. 1-c and 1-d depict a clicked state

To perform the gesture, we assume that only the thumb, index and middle fingers are held open; the index is then bent forward to initiate a click. The advantage of this model is that no calibration is required. Another advantage is that the reference against which the threshold is tested is always moving along with the index finger; this gives the user the freedom of moving his hand in mid-air prior to performing the gesture. And since our approach does not rely on analyzing previous frames and comparing the position of the index against them, the result of the gesture is instantaneous. Because of how our prototype was designed, we were not able to accurately measure the detection speed. We plan on conducting a deeper evaluation in future work.

4.1   Experiment 2 – Determining the Accuracy of the Three Fingers Click

For this experiment, we have used the same setup as Experiment 1; the only exception being that rendering was done using the Allegro library. The same 9 participants that took part in Experiment 1 were also recruited. Handedness was not taken into consideration in this experiment, and the participants were instructed to hold open the thumb, index and middle fingers of their preferred hand, and perform 20 clicks with their index finger. A human observer counted the total number of clicks performed, in order to spot false detections.

4.2   Results

The average number of click attempts performed by the users to complete 20 clicks was 22.33. This indicates a success rate of 89.56%. 3 participants had a 100% success rate.

Using 3D coordinates allowed the gesture to be detected regardless of the hand's position or rotation. The gestures were detected even if the wrist was slightly rotated inwards, the palm was slightly pointing downward, or even if the hand was moving. This is due to the fact that the index finger and the reference all move as a single group. While in this experiment, the camera is facing the user, this technique is also applicable even if the camera is behind the user's palm and facing away from the user; the clicks were also being detected in the latter position. We suppose that our design can also be applied to tabletop setup, with a depth sensing camera pointing downwards.

Since the gesture relies on the detection of three fingers, this can be a detection/accuracy limitation. When a given hand is in its own half of the camera space, the three fingers were easily detected. However, when the hand moved into its opposite half of the camera space, the finger detection failed, even if the hand was still in the camera's field of view. This is due to the fact that when the hand crosses into the opposite space, the thumb and the index are occluded by the middle finger, and the camera fails to keep track of them (Fig. 3). Another limitation is the gesture itself: 6 participants reported that keeping the three fingers held open stressed their forearm's muscles quickly, and found some difficulty in maintaining the gesture.

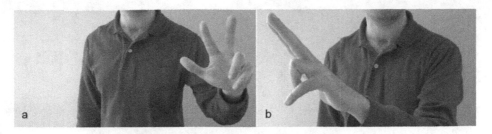

Fig. 3. The fingers of the left hand in the left half of the camera space are easily detected (a), however, detection fails when the left hand moves to the right half of the camera space (b)

5   Two Handed Menu

In this section, we present a prototype for a "Two Handed Menu". For this intent, we would like to create a new menu system that is optimized, not only for hand gestures, but for two hands as well.

Since in real-world human interaction, asymmetric bimanual motions start with the non-dominant hand, and are then followed by the dominant hand [3], we will create a menu system that is split into two parts, thus allowing the user to interact with it using both his hands. The menu system will be handedness-free, meaning that it will take into consideration whether the user is right or left-handed, and dynamically generate the appropriate user interface depending on the hand preference. We believe that having data from a group of mixed handedness participants will allow us to better evaluate the system.

Basing our menu on the traditional desktop toolbar menu, we have created a "Main Menu" containing the following items: "File", "Edit", "View", and "Help". Any menu spawning from the selection of one of those 4 items is designated as "Submenu". A submenu can spawn its own submenu. A hand-shaped cursor indicates the user's current hand tip position. The user interacts with the main menu using his non-dominant hand, while he uses his dominant hand to interact with all of the submenus. For this reason, the main menu is displayed on the non-dominant hand's side, whereas the submenus are displayed on the dominant hand's side. The user moves his arms up and down to be able to hover above the menu items, and then selects an item using the Three Fingers Click described in Section 4.

Figure 4 depicts a right-handed layout of the menu. In figure 4.a, the main menu (File, Edit, View, Help) is rendered. When the user selects "Edit" with his left hand, the Edit sub menu (Undo, Redo, Find and Replace, Select All) is then rendered on the right side of the display as shown in Figure 4.b. Upon clicking "Find and Replace" with the right hand, a new sub menu is then rendered in Figure 3.c (Quick Find, Quick Replace). In this last case, if the user performs a "Go up" gesture, he will go back to 4.b, and from there another "Go up" gesture will take him back to 4.a.

Fig. 4. Right-handed menu

Figure 5 shows a similar example, but rendered for a left handed user. In this case, the user interacts with the main menu using his right hand (Figure 5.a), then interacts with any other submenu using his left hand (Figure 5.b).

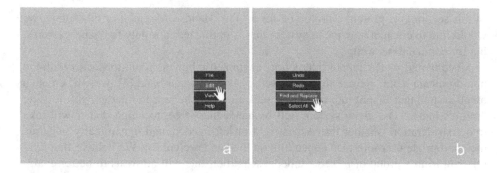

Fig. 5. Left-handed menu

Drawing conclusions from section 3, we have created a set of gestures to interact with the menu system. Table 1 shows the gestures that have been used in this prototype.

Table 1. Hand gestures used in the prototype

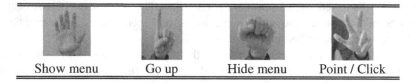

| Show menu | Go up | Hide menu | Point / Click |

An open palm is used to display the menu. Pointing up with the index instructs the system to go up one level in the menu. A clenched fist hides the menu, in case the user wants to exit the menu without issuing a command. The above mentioned "Show menu", "Go up" and "Hide menu" gestures are static gestures. As described in Section 3 as well, "Show menu" will be assigned to the dominant hand, whereas "Go up" and "Hide menu" will be assigned to the non-dominant hand. "Point/Click" will be used by both hands.

5.1   Experiment 3 – Testing the Two Handed Menu Prototype

For this experiment, we have used the same setup as Experiment 2. The same 9 participants that were involved in Experiments 1 and 2 were also recruited. They were
asked to perform the scenario described in Table 2:

Table 2. Gestures to be performed by either hand. A blank space indicates that the hand in the
same row does not perform any action.

Dominant	Show		Close	Show		Find and Replace		Undo		Exit
Non dominant		File			Edit		Go up		Show	

First, the participants were asked to perform the above scenario using their usual
handedness. Next, we switched the layout of the menu, and asked them to perform the
same scenario; all the commands now have switched handedness as well.

The participants were also asked to perform the same scenario using their preferred
hand only.

A final test was performed to evaluate the ergonomics of the hand motions. Tomita
et al. have proposed a slanted menu as a more ergonomic approach [4]. In our system,
the menu "morphed" with the hand and positioned itself around the participants' hand
tip. Instead of using an up/down motion to interact with the menu, the participants
were able to use a waving motion from top left (or top right) to the bottom center of
the display (Figure 6).

Fig. 6. Morphing menu that follows the user's hand

5.2   Results

Before presenting the results of this experiment, we duly note that no participant was
able to complete the last scenario, which uses one hand only; this is mainly due to the
limitation described in section 4.2. Even though the users attempted to circumvent
the limitation by twisting their wrists in a way so that the fingers can be detected, the
unease resulting from the strain put on the wrist and shoulder made it impossible for

them to continue the scenario. Thus, no comparison between one and two handed operations was possible.

We measured the time it took the participants to complete the given scenario. When the participants used their usual handedness, the average time to complete the scenario was 31.16 seconds (standard deviation: 6.58), whereas the average time to complete the reversed handedness scenario was 35.47 seconds (standard deviation: 15.77. The numbers were close due to the fact that the participants were moving their hands in similar fashion for either case, as well as the fact that the menu input did not require extreme precision (thus conforming to the "easy task" in [12]).

6   Evaluation

After completing the experiments, the participants were handed out the following questionnaire, to which they could respond on a five point Likert scale (-2 = Strongly Disagree, 2 = Strongly Agree):

1. Is using two hands easier than using one hand?
2. Is it easy to maintain the Three Fingers gesture?
3. Does the Clicking Gesture simulate a mouse click?
4. Is using an interface tailored to handedness easier?
5. Does using only one hand strain the shoulder/wrist?
6. Is using a Morphing Menu more natural than a traditional layout?

Most participants agreed that using two hands was easier than one hand with an average of 1.22 (standard deviation: 1.09), and most found that the Three Fingers Gesture was difficult to maintain (-0.88, 1.05). Everyone agreed that the clicking gesture simulates a mouse click (1.44, 0.52). There were mixed results regarding tailoring the interface to the handedness (0.44, 0.88). One of the left-handed participants, who uses the mouse with her right hand, gave a negative answer regarding that question. Everyone agreed that using only one hand was uncomfortable (1.77, 0.44). There were mixed results for the morphing menu as well (0.55, 1.01); the users who liked this variation stated that it felt more natural to wave the hand rather than go up and down, and it was less tiring because they were able to rest their elbows on the desk or on their lap.

7   Conclusion and Future Work

In this paper, we have presented a menu designed with a bimanual interface. The goal was to create a new approach on User Interfaces, by using the hands asymmetrically to control a menu. Our experiments showed that two hands were faster than one, but handedness itself did not affect the performance in a significant way in this specific prototype.

We have also introduced the Three Fingers Click, a novel and reliable clicking mechanism that does not need calibration.

Some design considerations were found as well, which could serve as a reference for future interface designs, especially when using a setup like ours: if fingers are to be used in an interface, the hand should move in its own half of the camera space, due to the limitations of the wrist and shoulder anatomy; thus, an interface using fingers should be designed for either one hand / one half of the camera space, or two hands across the entire camera space.

In our future work, we would like to explore in more details the depth selection mechanism that we have introduced, especially that our current prototype was not designed in a way to allow a proper quantitative assessment of its performance. We feel that our approach could serve as a base for some interesting depth based selection mechanisms. To make the mechanism easier to use, we would also like to extend it to 5 fingers in future designs.

References

1. Hinckley, K., Pausch, R., Proffitt, D., Kassell, N.: Two-handed virtual manipulation. ACM Transactions on Computer-Human Interaction 5, 260–302 (1998)
2. Veit, M., Capobianco, A., Bechmann, D.: Consequence of two-handed manipulation on speed, precision and perception on spatial input task in 3D modelling applications. Universal Comp. Science 14, 3174–3187 (2008)
3. Guiard, Y.: Asymmetric division of labor in human skilled bimanual action: The kinematic chain as a model. Motor Behavior 19, 486–517 (1987)
4. Tomita, A., Kambara, K., Siio, I.: Slant menu: novel GUI widget with ergonomic design. In: Proceedings of CHI 2012 Extended Abstracts on Human Factors in Computing Systems, pp. 2051–2056 (2012)
5. Song, P., Boon Goh, W., Hutama, W., Fu, C., Liu, X.: A Handle Bar Metaphor for Virtual Object Manipulation with Mid-Air Interaction. In: Proceedings of the SIGCHI Conference on Human Factors in Computing Systems, pp. 1297–1306 (2012)
6. Yang, R., Strozzi, A., Lau, A., Lutteroth, C., Chan, Y., Delmas, P.: Bimanual natural user interaction for 3D modelling application using stereo computer vision. In: Proceedings of the 13th International Conference of the NZ Chapter of the ACM's Special Interest Group on Human-Computer Interaction, pp. 44–51 (2012)
7. Wagner, J., Huot, S., Mackay, W.: BiTouch and BiPad: designing bimanual interaction for hand-held tablets. In: Proceedings of the SIGCHI Conference on Human Factors in Computing Systems, pp. 2317–2326 (2012)
8. Guimbretière, F., Martin, A., Winograd, T.: Benefits of merging command selection and direct manipulation. ACM Transactions on Computer-Human Interaction 12, 460–476 (2005)
9. Yang, Z., Li, Y., Zheng, Y., Chen, W., Zheng, X.: An Interaction System Using Mixed Hand Gestures. In: Proceedings of the 10th Asia Pacific Conference on Computer Human Interaction, pp. 125–132 (2012)
10. Boussemart, Y., Rioux, F., Rudzicz, F., Wozniewski, M., Cooperstock, J.: A framework for 3D visualisation and manipulation in an immersive space using an untethered bimanual gestural interface. In: Proceedings of the ACM Symposium on Virtual Reality Software and Technology, pp. 162–165 (2004)
11. Kabbash, P., Buxton, W., Sellen, A.: Two-Handed Input in a Compound Task. In: Proceedings of ACM CHI Conference, pp. 417–423 (1994)

12. Hinckley, K., Pausch, R., Proffitt, D., Patten, J., Kassell, N.: Cooperative Bimanual Action. In: Proceedings of the ACM SIGCHI Conference on Human Factors in Computing Systems, pp. 27–34 (1997)

13. Lévesque, J.C., Laurendeau, D., Mokhtari, M.: Bimanual Gestural Interface for Immersive Virtual Environments. In: Proceedings of the IEEE Virtual Reality Conference, pp. 223–224 (2011)

14. Chen, N., Guimbretière, F., Löckenhoff, C.: Relative role of merging and two-handed operation on command selection speed. International Journal of Human-Computer Studies 66(10), 729–740 (2008)

15. Odell, D., Davis, R., Smith, A., Wright, P.: Toolglasses, marking menus, and hotkeys: a comparison of one and two-handed command selection techniques. In: Proceedings of Graphics Interface, pp. 17–24 (2004)

16. Guimbretière, F., Nguyen, C.: Bimanual marking menu for near surface interactions. In: Proceedings of the SIGCHI Conference on Human Factors in Computing Systems, pp. 825–828 (2012)

17. Wilson, A.: Using a depth camera as a touch sensor. In: ACM International Conference on Interactive Tabletops and Surfaces, pp. 69–72 (2010)

18. DepthSense 325, http://www.softkinetic.com/Store/tabid/579/ProductID/6/language/en-US/Default.aspx

19. OpenNI gestures, http://www.openni.org/files/igesture3d/

20. Harrison, C., Benko, H., Wilson, A.: Omnitouch: wearable multitouch interaction everywhere. In: Proceedings of the 24th Annual ACM Symposium on User Interface Software and Technology, pp. 441–450 (2011)

Measurement of Hand Raising Actions to Support Students' Active Participation in Class

Ryuji Kawabe[1], Michiya Yamamoto[1], Saizo Aoyagi[2], and Tomio Watanabe[3]

[1] Kwansei Gakuin University, School of Science and Technology, Sanda, Hyogo, Japan
{bqb85622,michiya.yamamoto}@kwansei.ac.jp
[2] Kobe University, Graduate School of Maritime Sciences, Kobe, Hyogo, Japan
aoyagi@maritime.kobe-u.ac.jp
[3] Okayama Prefectural University, Faculty of Computer Science and System Engineering, Soja, Okayama, Japan
watanabe@cse.oka-pu.ac.jp

Abstract. In recent years, teachers have been making an effort to improve positivity in students' participation in class. However, this can be difficult because active participation depends on both communication skills and classroom atmosphere. In this study, we focus on hand-raising motions, which play an important role in interaction. Based on this, we measured and analyzed hand-raising motions in various situations.

Keywords: embodied interaction, education support, hand raising, motion analysis.

1 Introduction

In recent years, teachers have been making an effort to improve positivity in students' participation in class. For example, rather than traditional one-way communication from teacher to students, participating classes, in which students participate more positively, are receiving attention. However, it is not easy to promote participating classes as their success depends on classroom atmosphere and the skills and abilities of teachers and students.

Fuse et al. posited that positive attitudes are expressed through gaze, attentive hearing, hand raising, utterance, preparation, and homework completion [1]. They also proposed that teachers recognize such attitudes as a measure of the positivity of students' class participation. By focusing on the importance of communicative motions and actions such as nodding, the authors have developed an embodied entrainment system with speech-driven computer graphics (CG) characters called InterActors superimposed on images, and demonstrated that such communicative motions are effective for learning support [2].

In this study, the authors focus on hand-raising motion, which plays an important role in interaction and context in class [3], as the use of hand motion is much more common than gaze or attentive hearing and may have a direct impact on class participation.

S. Yamamoto (Ed.): HIMI 2014, Part I, LNCS 8521, pp. 199–207, 2014.

From this viewpoint, Fujiu modeled the procedure on teachers' questioning and students' hand raising and attempted to clarify the psychological states involved in hand raising based on educational psychology [4]. However, aside from Fujiu's study, there is almost no systematical research on this topic. We propose a concept to promote active participation in class by activating hand raising and using a novel approach to the study it, focusing on the fact that hand raising is a means of indication of intention and activates classroom participation. Following this, we measured and analyzed hand-raising motions in various classroom situations.

2   Concept

In this study, by focusing on the motions involved in hand raising, which play important roles in indicating active intentions, we propose a new concept for supporting active participation in class (Fig. 1).Many students do not feel confident in raising a hand to answer questions because of issues such as pressure and unease, which often lead to difficulties with active participation in class. Conversely, we propose that raising context, enhancing a sense of unity, and promoting the sharing of responsibility for hand raising are the keys to solving this problem. For example, one student's positive hand raising may trigger another student's hand raising because positive hand raising may produce motivation for hand raising in everyone. In addition, we posit that embodied media can facilitate active participation in class through hand raising. For example, using physical media such as CG characters and robots initiates students' hand raising. We measured and analyzed hand raising to examine this concept.

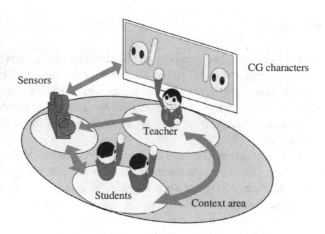

Fig. 1. Concept

3   Factors That Determine Hand Raising

3.1   Related Studies on Determinant Factors

Fujiu proposed that self-efficacy, outcome-expectancy, and outcome-value are determinant factors of hand raising. These factors determine the intention of hand raising and accompanying utterances. Specifically, when students experience self-efficacy in hand raising, they believe that they can raise their hands as often as they wish. When students experience positive outcome-expectancy, they feel that hand raising is welcomed by others in the class. When students experience high outcome-value, they feel that their actions and utterances are very important. These cognitive factors are the factors that determine hand raising.

3.2   New Framework of Determinant Factors

In this study, we defined feeling and motivation as parts of a new framework of factors to determine the assessment of hand-raising motions, in which feeling is a factor of the emotional state involved in hand raising (comfort or discomfort). Motivation is a factor of the decision-making process involved in hand raising and includes Fujiu's determinant factors. We examined the relationship between new determinant factors and hand raising in everyday life in a previous study [5].

4   Method

We conducted an experiment that participants answered questions regarding hand raising in various situations.   Here, we tried to make clear the characteristics of hand-raising motions and the factors that may affect feeling and motivation in hand raising. In the experiment, we assumed that the atmosphere in the classroom and the difficulty of the questions may have affected feeling and motivation. Therefore, we set up questions that were selected from a workbook according to difficulty level (easy or difficult) [6]. In addition, we formulated two conditions representing the experimental system's reactions to hand raising (positive or negative). For positive reactions, we played a clapping sound through a speaker and presented a positive image to promote hand raising. For negative reactions, we played booing sound through a speaker and presented a negative image to discourage hand raising. In this study, we presented a question and a classroom scene on a screen at the front of the room and asked participants to raise their hands to answer the question (Fig. 2). In addition, we directed the participants to answer all questions after raising a hand.

We show experimental procedure. (i) We instructed participants to raise a hand several times to relieve tension and embarrassment. In addition, each participant raised a hand and answered the practice question three times. (ii) We set up positive or negative reactions. (iii) We presented a question. After participants had answered the question, the system provided a positive or negative reaction. (iv) Following this, participants answered oral questionnaires about their confidence and the difficulty levels of the question. (v) we performed (iii) and (iv) at five times. (vi) Participants completed a paper questionnaire regarding seven-point bipolar ratings. We reversed the positive and negative reactions and repeated the procedure (iii) to (vi).

We projected an image on a screen located 250 cm from a projector (EPSON, EB-1735W) connected to a notebook computer, the HP Elite-Book 8730w, and the system played the sounds through a speaker (ONKYO, GX-D90(B)) placed underneath the screen. We measured the positions of participants' wrists, fingertips, elbows, and heads with a motion-capture system (VICON, VICON MX) (Fig. 3). Participants were Japanese students (16 men and 16 women) aged 18–25 years.

Fig. 2. Experimental scene

Fig. 3. Marker positions for motion capturing

5   Results

5.1   Results of Questionnaire Analysis

Fig. 4 shows the seven-point bipolar ratings. Results of a Wilcoxon signed-rank test showed that there were significant differences between all items. There were significant differences between (1), (2), (3), and (5), with significance levels of ≤ 1 %. With respect to (1) and (2), several participants replied that if a reaction was negative and they could not raise a hand comfortably, they were negative about hand raising. In (3) and (5), the positive classroom atmosphere made participants feel more comfortable about hand raising than when the atmosphere was negative.

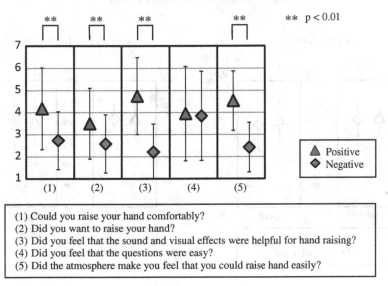

(1) Could you raise your hand comfortably?
(2) Did you want to raise your hand?
(3) Did you feel that the sound and visual effects were helpful for hand raising?
(4) Did you feel that the questions were easy?
(5) Did the atmosphere make you feel that you could raise hand easily?

Fig. 4. Results of the seven-point bipolar ratings

5.2   Analysis of Hand-Raising Imotions

We set up height, speed and angle factors (Fig. 5). Height was measured as the height of the topmost fingertip position in each trial divided by the greatest fingertip position height. Speed was measured as the maximum speed estimated from the moving distance of the fingertip per frame. Angle was measured as the angle of the elbow at the greatest height.

Fig. 6 shows the results of the motion analysis. We focused on hand-raising motions when participants were or were not confident. We also focused that the participants' replies were *correct* or *incorrect* and they reported that the question was *easy* or *difficult*. We also focused on reaction, which was either positive or negative, and difficulty level, which was either easy or difficult.

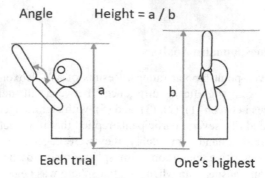

Fig. 5. Details of hand raising parameters

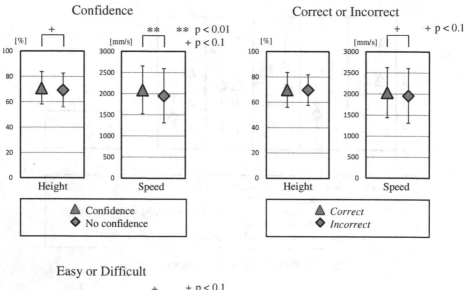

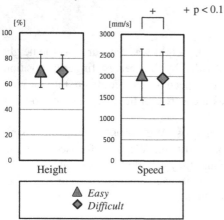

Fig. 6. Results of motion analysis

Speed in confident participants was approximately 2088.6 mm/s, and approximately 1951.6 mm/s in participants who were not confident; there was a significant difference between these two groups at a significance level of 1 %. Height in confident participants was approximately 70.8 % and in participants with no confidence, approximately 69.2 %; there was a marginally significant difference at a significance level of 10 %. Speed for *correct* responses was approximately 2043.2 mm/s and for *incorrect* responses, approximately 1959.3 mm/s; there was a marginally significant difference at a significance level of 10 %. Speed for responses of *easy* was approximately 2032.3 mm/s and for responses of *difficult*, approximately 1954.0 mm/s; there was a marginally significant difference at a significance level of 10 %. In contrast, positive and negative, and easy and difficult comparisons exhibited no significant differences in height or speed.

5.3   Analysis of Motion Characters

We analyzed hand-raising motion characteristics using video images and a motion capture system. Fig. 7 shows the results of the cluster analysis using Ward's method. Height and angle were used as variables. As a result, hand-raising forms were classified into six patterns. These were loosely grouped into straight form or bent form (Table. 1). For example, A, B, and C were straight forms, and D, E, and F were bent forms. Few participants changed form according to question difficulty level or reaction.

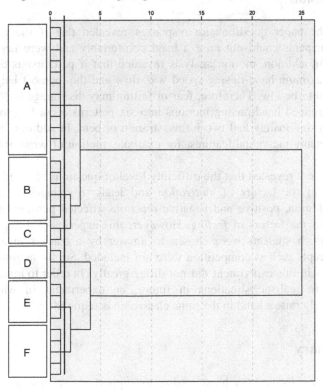

Fig. 7. Results of cluster analysis

Table 1. Patterns categorized according to cluster anasysis

Straight forms				Bent forms			
A		height	90.5 %	D		height	47.3 %
		angle	174.2 °			angle	51.6 °
B		height	81.6 %	E		height	58.5 %
		angle	134.0 °			angle	72.7 °
C		height	66.7 %	F		height	69.7 %
		angle	145.3 °			angle	109.8 °

6   Discussion

Analysis of the paper questionnaire responses revealed that if the reaction was negative, participants could not raise a hand comfortably and were negative about hand raising. In addition, motion analysis revealed that if participants did not have confidence, maximum hand-raising speed was slow and the topmost height of hand position tended to be low. Therefore, fear of failing may discourage hand raising. In contrast, we grouped hand-raising motions into six patterns according to height and angle. Hand raising mainly had two forms, straight or bent. In addition, hand-raising motions held many individual features, for example, motion of wrist and motion of hesitance.

This experiment revealed that the difficulty level of questions affected confidence, which is one of the factors of *motivation* and leads to changes in hand-raising motions. In addition, positive and negative reactions affected participants mentally, which is one of the factors of *feeling*. However, this experiment did not assume a situation in which students were chosen to answer by a teacher in a real class; therefore, concepts such as competition were not included. So, we assume that hand-raising motions in this experiment did not differ greatly. In order to investigate hand raising in more realistic situations in future, an experiment in which several participants freely raise a hand in the same classroom is required.

7   Summary

In this study, we focused on hand raising to support active student participation in class. We analyzed hand-raising motions in various situations and evaluated emotional states. Results revealed that confidence and factors regarding various situations affect hand-raising motions and emotional states.

References

1. Fuse, M., Kodaira, H., Ando, F.: Positive Class Participation by Elementary School Pupils: Motivation and Differences in Grade and Gender. The Japanese Journal of Educational Psychology 54(2), 534–545 (2006) (in Japanese)
2. Watanabe, T., Yamamoto, M.: An Embodied Entrainment System with InterActors Superimposed on Images. In: 11th International Conference on Human-Computer Interaction (HCI International 2005), vol. 4, p. 2045 (2005)
3. Yamamoto, M., Shigeno, Y., Kawabe, R., Watanabe, T.: Development of a Context-enhancing Surface based on the Entrainment of Embodied Rhythms and Actions Sharingvia Interaction. In: ACM Interactive Tabletops and Surfaces 2012 Conference, pp. 363–366 (2012)
4. Fujiu, H.: A Study on Factors that Determine Hand Raising in Classroom. Kazamashobo (1996) (in Japanese)
5. Shigeno, Y., Kawabe, R., Yamamoto, M., Watanabe, T.: Analysis of Motions of Raising Hands for Supporting Context-Enhancing Interaction. In: The 75th National Convention of IPSJ, pp. 4-329–4-320 (2012) (in Japanese)
6. Sumikura, H.: Questions and Answers on general knowledge (frequently-appearing) 1500. Takahashi Shoten (2012) (in Japanese)

Study on Perception of Vibration Rhythms

Daiji Kobayashi

Chitose Institute of Science and Technology, Hokkaido, Japan
d-kobaya@photon.chitose.ac.jp

Abstract. In this study, we researched the way of designing the accessible vibration rhythms through experiments using the mouse-type tactile interface from the vibration perception and vibration memorability. Participants were twenty young individuals and fourteen older persons. First, the threshold of vibration duration and gaps between the duration were estimated statistically. As the result, some vibration rhythms were designed and evaluated the validity of the design factors. Further, the requirements for designing memorable vibration rhythms were considered. From the results, some requirements for designing perceivable and memorable vibration rhythms for older persons were found; however, it is required to clear the effect of vibration rhythm from the cognitive aspect through further research.

Keywords: tactile interface, vibration rhythm, accessibility.

1 Introduction

Almost of mobile devices include an actuator oscillating the mobile device and informing simple message to the user such as "You got a mail". For presenting more or complex information by user interfaces, some ideas have been proposed and evaluated [1-3]. The feasibility studies successfully implemented a few rhythmical vibration patterns called "Tactons" into the proposed tactile interfaces using linear tactile actuators. Almost of the tactile interfaces proposed were used by wearing around the waist or attaching on the forearms or the wrists. On the other hand, most of the mobile devices include vibration motors with eccentric mass as the actuator oscillating the device. The wave form of the oscillation amplitudes generated by the vibration motor depends on the motor's environment such as chassis of the mobile device, then the wave form is not a sine curve but complex waveform. Regarding the factors of the vibration patterns such as roughness and frequency were experimentally considered; however, the subjects or the participants were young individuals in common. The reason for investigating the young participants could be related to the tactile sensibilities. ISO 9241-910 [4], framework for tactile and haptic interaction, mentions that it is important to consider the age of potential users of tactile/haptic devices, since there is a considerable decline in haptic sensitivity with age. From this viewpoint, we assumed that to explore the tactile device's usability for elderly persons should be required. As far as the vibration patterns are concerned, ISO 9241-910

S. Yamamoto (Ed.): HIMI 2014, Part I, LNCS 8521, pp. 208–216, 2014.

suggests that the perception of an event can be enhanced by a careful choice of patterns of oscillatory bursts. Thus, the vibration patterns should be perceptibility by a wide range of ages in order to improve the vibrating device's accessibility. Therefore, designing the vibration patterns for elderly people is considered in this study.

1.1 Vibration Perception

Vibration perception have been considered from physiological and medical viewpoints. For instance, the relation between vibration perception threshold and age, height, and etc. has been investigated using a biothesiometer [5]. The biothesiometer which is used for measuring large nerve fiber function of patients produce the varied amplitude of vibrations. As the results, the significant factor for vibration perception threshold was age rather than sex and etc.; therefore, it is assumed that the higher amplitude of vibration or the higher vibration velocity is perceptible in other parts of the older person's body such as palms. Hence the vibration velocity as described variable v in Fig. 1 should be as high as possible for the aged to perceive the vibration patterns.

On the other hand, a minimum perceptible duration of vibration (d) as well as a minimum perceptible gap (r) between vibration durations as shown in Fig.1 may change with not only the perceptive aspect of users but also the characteristics of vibration from the vibrating device. Therefore such the two thresholds (the minimums of d and r) for designing perceivable vibration patterns were measured using our custom tactile interface as described below in detail.

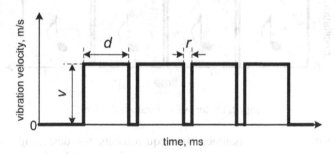

Fig. 1. Variables specifying vibration patterns

1.2 Memorability

If the elderly people are able to sense vibrations, the signal or information from the vibrations could be processed as well as young individuals. Although it is assumed that the memory ability among older adults varies with their individual, the sensed information could process at working memory. The model of working memory system is proposed by Baddeley and the system includes "visuospatial scratch-pad" and "articulatory loop" or "phonological loop" [6]. Although these systems are not for just tactile information, the tactual information could be processed based on higher-order non-tactual information [7]. In other words, the tactual information processing could be related to the characteristics of vibration patterns such as images from the tactile rhythms rather than the characteristics of the oscillation within the vibration patterns. Further, the memorability could be prompted by the skill of catching vibration patterns such as musical skill. In this case, the memorability means ease of recalling the vibration patterns correctly. Therefore, to introduce the musical rhythm patterns into vibration patterns could be appropriate because the most people are familiar with music and songs regardless of age.

1.3   Vibration Rhythm

Although the vibration patterns has been expressed using musical note in previous tactile studies, the musical rhythm or musical sound have used in mobile devices such as phone ringing. However, temporal gaps among the notes is necessary in order to express the rhythm by the vibration as shown in Fig. 2 and the duration of the gaps should be as short as possible for taking no account of the gap, and then it is possible to consider that the vibration rhythm is in order. Thus the duration of the gap should be determined according to the minimum perceptible gap so that musical rhythms are made into vibration patterns and we called the vibration patterns made from the musical rhythms is called "vibration rhythms".

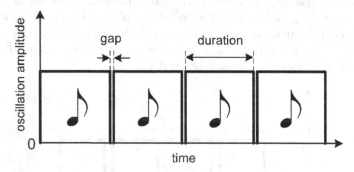

Fig. 2. Factors of a vibration rhythm

As described above, we assumed the requirements for designing the vibration rhythm in order to utilize as a way of presenting information by the vibrating device. Hence the minimum perceptible duration and the minimum perceptible gap of young individuals and older persons were measured. Further, the memorability for the young and the older persons was also investigated through the experiment.

2   Designing of the Vibration Mouse

From our previous studies, there are Japanese senior citizens who are aversion to high-tech gizmos [8]. Thus it is preferable to touch the tactile interface for the older people rather than to wear or to attach the tactile interface on their body part. Accordingly, we made a mouse-type tactile interface with a little familiar computer mouse for the Japanese senior citizens. The system of the tactile interface we made was simple and made of a vibration motor and the computer mouse (DELL USB mouse) as shown in Fig. 3. We called such mouse-type tactile interface "vibration mouse". The vibration motor in the vibration mouse rotated within a range of 0.3 - 0.7 V and oscillate the vibration mouse. The power voltage for activating the vibration motor was controlled using a high-precision analog I/O terminal (CONTEC AIO-160802AY-USB) and a personal computer (DELL Vostro 1500) running Windows 7 Professional Japanese edition. In other words, the voltage applied to the vibration motor was controlled by the I/O terminal with our custom software. The wave form of the amplitude of vibration on the top of the vibration mouse was not a sine curve but very rough. The resonant frequency of the amplitude of vibration was ranging from 74 to 116 Hz in accordance with the voltage applied to the vibration motor in the vibration mouse. In addition, the vibration mouse functioned also as the computer mouse with two buttons and a scroll wheel.

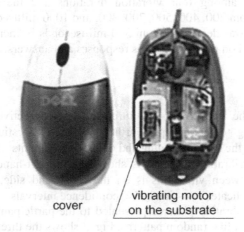

cover   vibrating motor
              on the substrate

Fig. 3. Vibration mouse presenting vibration rhythm

3   Measuring Two Thresholds for Designing Perceivable Vibration Rhythm

To measure the minimum perceptible duration and the minimum perceptible gap, we conducted an experiment using the vibration mouse.

3.1   Method

The participants were ten male and ten female young individuals and six male and eight female older persons. The young ranged from 18 to 22 years of age (mean = 20.1, SD = 1.1) and the elderly persons ranged from 65 to 85 years of age (mean = 73.8, SD = 5.7). The participants touched the vibration mouse with their palm as if they were using a computer mouse on a desk and tried to count and to answer the number of vibration durations within the presented vibration patterns. The vibration velocity was 2.3 m/s which is the producible maximum vibration velocity by the vibration mouse. The two thresholds for designing vibration rhythm was determined in the following way.

First, the vibration patterns which included three vibration durations and the respective gaps (r as described in Fig. 1) of each were presented to the participants. Each of the gaps was randomly selected from 200, 400, 500, 700, 800, and 1000 milliseconds. The duration time (d as described in Fig. 1) presenting to the participant was decreased from 300 milliseconds in increments of 5, 10, or 50 milliseconds based on the participant's responses and answers. The vibration pattern was presented repeatedly on demand until the participant answer orally the number of vibration duration included in the vibration pattern. The threshold of vibration duration was determined by whether the participant's answer was right or wrong.

Second, the threshold of gap between vibration duration was investigated in a manner similar to the first trial. However, in this trial, the each vibration pattern included three gaps among four vibration durations and the each duration was randomly selected from 200, 400, 500, 700, 800, and 1000 milliseconds. The gap (r as described in Fig. 1) was decreased from 300 milliseconds in increments of 5, 10, or 50 milliseconds based on the participant's responses and answers.

3.2   Results

As the results of the two trials, two thresholds of respective participants were determined according to age-groups. Further, we tried to estimate the thresholds statistically based on the result of young and elderly participants' threshold. The result of the threshold of vibration duration is shown on the left-hand side of Fig.4 and threshold of gap between vibrations is on the right-hand side. The error bars as described in Fig. 4 indicates two-sided 95% confidence intervals.

Although the all vibration patterns presented to the participants in the trials were not rhythmical but just like random patterns, Fig. 4 shows the thresholds by the young

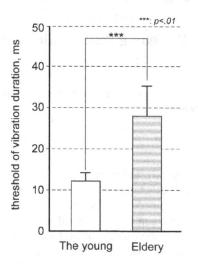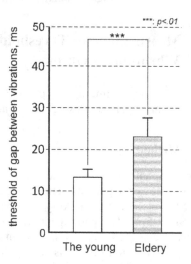

Fig. 4. Estimated thresholds of vibration rhythm by the results of two trials by the participants

and by the elderly differ significantly. Therefore, it is assumed the vibration rhythm for older persons should be slower-paced; however, two older participants said that it was difficult to count the number of vibration durations with concentrating on insensible vibration. As the two thresholds of the two older participants tended to be higher than the others' (around 50 milliseconds), the two thresholds could be affected by the cognitive characteristics of the respective participants.

Considering the distributions of the thresholds by each age-group as shown in Fig. 4, it is appropriate to determine that the minimum vibration duration included in the vibration rhythm is 50 milliseconds in round figures; therefore, the shortest musical note in the vibration rhythm such as sixteenth note in the vibration rhythm should be represented by vibration duration for 50 milliseconds and then the duration of eighth note is 100 milliseconds. However, the threshold of gap should be estimated lower for aforementioned reason and the threshold for elderly could be assumed lower if the stimuli for the participants were vibration rhythms instead of the vibration patterns. Therefore, we assumed the threshold of the gap is 20 milliseconds in round figures and tried to design the vibration rhythm as described below.

4   Memorability of Vibration Rhythm

4.1   Designing Vibration Rhythms for Older Persons

The results from previous trials suggested that the vibration duration should be over 50 milliseconds; however, it is preferable for older persons to perceive the

Table 1. Evaluated seven vibration patterns

slower-paced vibration rhythms. Therefore, we let 50 milliseconds was the length of sixteenth notes and designed the seven vibration rhythms using eighth, quarter, and half notes or rests as described in Table 1. In other words, the length of shortest vibration duration in the vibration rhythms we designed was 100 milliseconds. In addition, we let 20 milliseconds was the length of the gaps in the vibration rhythms.

4.2   Evaluation of the Vibration Rhythm from Memorability

In this experimentl evaluation, the seven vibration rhythms we made were evaluated from the memorability through experiment as described below. In the experiment, the vibration rhythms was presented in order from the pattern-A to H as shown in Table 1 and the participant perceived the vibration rhythms using the vibration mouse. The vibration velocity was 2.3 m/s as well as the former experiment. The respective vibration rhythms were presented repeatedly on demand until the participant recalled and represented the vibration rhythm or gave up the trial. The way of answering the perceived vibration rhythms was describing using a simple code. However, a few elderly participants struggled to write using the code and their performances made it more difficult to recall and to represent the vibration rhythms. Thus, the way of answering for the elderly group was to sing the recalled vibration rhythm and the same researcher judged whether the sung rhythm by elderly was right or not.

As the results of trials, the percentages of the participants who were able to recall and to answer the correct vibration rhythm were indicated in Table 2.

Table 2. Evaluated seven vibration patterns

Pattern	Vibration rhythms represented by musical note	Percentages of the participants recalling accurately	
		The young	Elderly
A		40	13
B		5	6
C		35	50
D		0	0
F		69	44
G		85	100
H		5	13

Although the percentages of participants recalling and answering the vibration rhythm accurately differed between the young and elderly participants, the percentages by pattern-A, C, F, and G were higher than by pattern-B, D, and H regardless of the participant's ages. In this regard, the vibration duration and the gap based on the previous research were valid for elderly participants; however, there were many elderly participants who were not able to recall the number of vibration duration in the rhythm accurately. Thus the vibration rhythm including many vibration duration became a vague rhythm for older persons. Meanwhile the reason of low percentages of young participants recalling accurately was because it was difficult to describe the vibration rhythm especially specifying the rests. From these results, the requirements of designing accessible vibration rhythms assume as the followings:

- Many music notes are not included;
- Varied music notes are not included;
- The same music notes are not used repeatedly.

Considering the perception of vibration rhythm, the two elderly participants whose thresholds of gap is 50 milliseconds were able to recognize the vibration rhythms including 20 milliseconds' gaps. This result indicated that the rhythm could prompt the vibration perception of elderly participants; therefore, using the vibration rhythms for tactile interface was valid.

5   Conclusion

In this study, we researched the way of designing the accessible vibration rhythms through experiments using the mouse-type tactile interface. From the results, some requirements and guidelines for designing accessible vibration rhythm for older persons were found; however, it is required to clear the effect of vibration rhythm from the cognitive aspect through further research.

Referrences

1. Brown, L.M., Brewster, S.A., Purchase, H.C.: Multidimensional tactons for non-visual information presentation in mobile devices. ACM Int. Conf. Proc. Series, vol. 159, pp. 231–238 (2006)
2. Brewster, S., King, A.: An Investigation into the Use of Tactons to Present Progress Information. In: Costabile, M.F., Paternó, F. (eds.) INTERACT 2005. LNCS, vol. 3585, pp. 6–17. Springer, Heidelberg (2005)
3. Hoggan, E., Brewster, S.: Designing Audio and Tactile Crossmodal Icons for Mobile Devices. In: ICMI 2007, pp. 12–15 (November 2007)
4. ISO 9241-910: Framework for Tactile and Haptic Interaction (2011)
5. Wiles, P.G., Pearce, S.M., Rice, P.J.S., Mitchell, J.M.O.: Vibration Perception Threshold: Influence of Age, Height, Sex, and Smoking, and Calculation of Accurate Centile Values. Diabetic Medicine 8, 157–161 (1991)

6. Baddeley, A.D., Logie, R.H.: Working Memory–The Multiple-Component Model. In: Miyake, A., Shah, P. (eds.) Models of Working Memory: Mechanisms of Active Maintenance and Executive Control, pp. 28–61. Cambridge University Press, New York (1999)

7. Kaas, A.L., Stoeckel, M.C., Gorbrl, R.: The neural bases of haptic working memory. In: Grunwald, M. (ed.) Human Haptic Perception–Basics and Applications. Birkhäuser, Basel (2008)

8. Kobayashi, D., Yamamoto, S.: Usability Research on the Older Person's Ability for Web Browsing. In: Kumashiro, M. (ed.) Prom. of W. Ability Towards Productive Aging, pp. 227–235. CRC, London (2009)

Effects of Type and Strength of Force Feedback
on the Path of Movement in a Target Selection Task

Martin T. Koltz[1], R. Conrad Rorie[2], Jose Robles[1], Kim-Phuong L. Vu[1],
Panadda Marayong[1], Thomas Z. Strybel[1], and Vernol Battiste[2]

[1] Center for Human Factors in Advanced Aeronautics Technologies,
California State University, Long Beach, Long Beach, CA 90840
{mkoltz2,jjvrobles}@gmail.com,
{kvu8,Panadda.Marayong,thomas.strybel}@csulb.edu
[2] NASA Ames Research Center, San Jose State University, San Jose, CA
{conrad.rorie,Vernol.Battiste-1}@nasa.gov

Abstract. New flight deck technologies being developed under the proposed
NextGen National Airspace System will require precise and efficient input from
flight crews. The benefits of force feedback for these types of inputs in terms
of a reduction in overall movement times have been shown in the past;
however, an important component of input efficiency is the path taken by the
cursor. The present study investigates the effects of multiple levels of two types
of force feedback (gravitational and spring forces) on the path of movement for
a target selection task. Mean square error from an ideal straight line path and
cursor speeds in terms of the distance from the target were measured. Results
suggest that increasing the gravitational force has an effect on path error at short
distances and produces higher cursor speeds as the target is approached.

Keywords: Haptic and Tactile interaction, Multimodal interaction, Force
Feedback, Input Devices.

1   Introduction

The proposed upgrades to the National Airspace System (NAS) being developed
under the Next Generation Air Transportation System include the integration of
additional automation into the flight deck which is designed to allow pilots to modify
their route and downlink to ATC for approval [1]. This type of GPS based self-routing
is intended to increase NAS efficiency by allowing for more direct, point to point,
routing. At the same time, it will help to reduce air traffic controller workload by
allowing pilots to consider traffic and weather in their modified routes thus aiding the
controller in maintaining separation assurance. In order to accomplish this goal, new
onboard technologies are needed in the modern flight deck.

Instrumentation such as the NASA Ames FDDRL Cockpit Display of Traffic
Information (CDTI which includes a Route Assessment Tool (RAT), is intended to
improve pilot traffic awareness by providing them with traffic displays, real time

S. Yamamoto (Ed.): HIMI 2014, Part I, LNCS 8521, pp. 217–225, 2014.

conflict alerting, and a graphical user interface [2]. However due to the inherent instability of the cockpit environment, the limited cockpit real estate, and the increased complexity of CDTI inputs, traditional cockpit input devices may prove to be too error prone and inefficient for flight planning. Moreover, these devices place additional demands on the pilot's visual channel and may increase the amount of head down time. Therefore, new inputs methods which are optimized for CDTI tasks are needed. In this paper, we describe work on an input device that provides force-feedback information to the pilot to improve the efficiency of CDTI inputs and relieve some of the visual demands made on the pilot.

1.1   Force Feedback

In a series of experiments, we have been developing and testing force feedback mechanisms for improving inputs to the CDTI, for example, elastic force in path stretching [3] and attractive force in target selection [4]; [5]; [6]. The targeting task is a fundamental task that is often performed on the CDTI. The operator selects a target on the screen by moving the cursor from its current position to the desired target location and then clicks on the target. This type of task resembles the movements utilized in research on Fitts' Law, where the efficiency of the movement is determined by movement time. Previous research has demonstrated that the use of certain types of force feedback, such as an attractive force, produces faster and more accurate selection of targets even when compared to traditional mouse inputs (e.g. [7]; [8]; [9]).

In an effort to better understand how force feedback affects specific portions of the target selection task, Akamatsu and MacKenzie [10] divided the task into two discrete phases, the approach phase and the selection phase. The approach phase begins as soon as the movement is initiated (i.e., a start location is clicked) and ends once the cursor breaches the target boundary. The selection phase begins at the end of the approach phase and ends when the target is clicked. Akamatsu and Mackenzie showed that a friction-based force feedback model reduced the time spent in the selection phase but had no effect on the time spend in the approach phase. They reasoned that the friction force allowed for faster stopping times because it provided the participants with multisensory feedback regarding target entry, and participants were able to more quickly stop their movement and select the target.

Hwang, Keates, Langdon, and Clarkson [11] showed that an attractive gravity based force model reduced the time spent in both the approach phase and the selection phase of movement for motion-impaired users. The authors concluded that this reduction in time spent in the approach phase of the task was due in part to an increase in cursor speed caused by the attractive force, although cursor speed was not specifically measured in their experiment.

Presently, an input device that is capable of force feedback differs significantly from an optical mouse, making it difficult to compare efficiency gains produced by force feedback to standard mouse performance. Rorie et al. [5] evaluated the impact of the input device itself and how force feedback may mitigate some input device problems. Participants performed a target selection task using a traditional mouse and a 3D force feedback input device called the Novint Falcon with and without a force modeled with a combination of gravitational and spring force. Results showed that without the force active, the Novint Falcon movement times were 40-50% slower than a traditional mouse. However, when force feedback was utilized, task selection performance met or exceeded that of a traditional mouse despite the fact that participants had much more experience using a mouse than they did the Novint Falcon [5].

Rorie et al. [6] examined the effects of different types and amounts of force feedback on CDTI target selection task by using a combination of two force feedback models. The first was an attractive force feedback model similar to that used by Hwang et al. [11], and was based on a modified version of Newton's gravity equation, where the magnitude of the force was inversely proportional to the distance between the cursor and the center of the target while the cursor was outside of the target boundary. The second was a spring-force feedback model, and was based on a standard spring equation, where the magnitude of the force was proportional to the distance between the cursor and the center of the target while the cursor was within the boundary of the target. Results showed that mean approach time was inversely related to the magnitude of the gravity force, but that the reduction in movement time decreased logarithmically with the magnitude of the force. Gravity force at high levels was most effective for small targets and at short target distances. Selection time, on the other hand, was affected only by the spring force feedback. Thus, these findings suggest that there is an ideal combination of gravity and spring force feedback levels, which would optimize device stability and overall movement time.

Although a benefit of force feedback in terms of shorter approach and selection times was found by Rorie et al. [6], an explanation of the cause of this effect requires an analysis of the path of movement [11]. Therefore, in the present study we investigated the path of movements in Rorie et al. [6], specifically the path error and path speed to determine if the benefits were due to cursor speed or deviation from the straight line path to the target.

2   Method

2.1   Participants

Seven males and five females (M = 25.83 years old) from NASA Ames Research Center participated in this experiment. All participants were right handed, over 18 years of age, and had normal or corrected-to-normal vision.

2.2   Apparatus

The experiment used two input devices, a standard Logitech optical laser mouse and the Novint Falcon. The control-display ratio (i.e., gain) of the computer mouse was reduced to approximate the C-D ratio of the Novint Falcon. The Falcon is capable of position sensing and applying force feedback in three dimensions, with an operational workspace of 4" x 4" x 4". For the purpose of this experiment, however, the device was restricted to movements in a horizontal plane parallel to the ground. The Falcon was also rotated and mounted on a stand to produce movement in the horizontal plane analogous to the mouse (*see Figure 1*).

The force feedback conditions were provided via the Novint Falcon. A modified version of Newton's gravitational law equation, shown in Equation 1 [4], was used to generate an attractive force, F_g, in the direction of the target's center, where d is the distance from the center of the target, r is the radius of the target and K_1 is the gain constant. When outside the target boundary ($\|d\| > r$), this gravitational force (expressed in Newtons/Pixel^2) pulled the user toward the center of the target, with the strength of the force increasing as the cursor approached the target's center. The unit vector of the distance (d) was used to specify the proportion of the force that was to be output along both axes (x and y).

$$F_g = \frac{K_1}{\|d\|^2}\hat{d}, for\ \|d\| \geq r \tag{1}$$

A second force model provided stability when the distance between the cursor and the target center was less than or equal to the target radius, as shown in Equation 2.

$$F_s = K_2\ \|d\|\ \hat{d}, for\ d\ < r \tag{2}$$

F_s is the spring force in Newton-Pixels, and K_2 is the gain constant. When the cursor is inside the target ($d < r$), the spring force resisted movements away from the target's center. The combination of the two models, therefore, led participants to experience an attractive force toward the target when outside its boundaries, and resistance to exiting the target once inside its boundaries. Three values of gravitational force were tested, 100, 300 and 500 Newtons/Pixel^2, and two levels of spring force were tested, 0.1 and 0.3 Newton-Pixels. These values were selected after informal pilot testing.

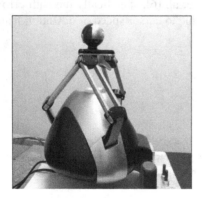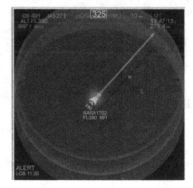

Fig. 1. Novint Falcon rotated 90 degrees (left) screen shot of the task (right)

2.3   Design and Procedure

The experimental design depended upon the input device. For experimental blocks with the Falcon, the design was a 2 (Target Size) x 2 (Target Distance) x 2

(Spring Force Level) x 3 (Gravitational Force Level) x 12 (Target Direction) repeated measures design. All five variables were manipulated and randomized within each experimental block. For experimental blocks with the mouse, a 2 (Target Size) x 2 (Target Distance) x 12 (Target Direction) repeated measures design was used since the mouse was not equipped with the spring or gravitational force models. For the mouse, all three variables were manipulated and randomized within experimental blocks. Participants completed 22 experimental blocks (20 blocks dedicated to the Falcon and 2 dedicated to the mouse), resulting in a total of 3,168 individual target selection trials.

A standard, Fitts' Law task was employed. On each trial, a green start circle (located in the center of the display) and red target circle (located at a specific direction and distance) was presented on a screen shot of the CDTI. The program had an 8" x 8" active display and was presented on a 50" x 29" computer monitor (pixel resolution: 1920 x 1080). Participants selected the green start circle to begin a trial and then moved their cursor as quickly and accurately as possible to the red target circle, clicking anywhere inside the target. After target selection, the start circle, along with the next target, appeared on the screen.

In order to determine cursor speed and path error, the cursor's position was recorded every 16 milliseconds. From the cursor position, we determined mean-squared (MS) error and average cursor speed towards the target during the approach phase. The approach phase was defined as movement of the cursor while outside the boundary of the target.

3   Results

MS error was determined by averaging the squared distance between the cursor and the straight line path to the target at each 16 millisecond interval. To determine cursor speed, the path to the target was divided into four quadrants and the average speed of the cursor in each quadrant was calculated by dividing the amount of time the cursor spent within each quadrant by the length of each quadrant (75 pixels for long distance trials and 25 pixels for short distance trials).

A 2(Target Distance) x 2(target size) x 3(Gravitational Force) x 2 (Spring Force) repeated measures ANOVA was performed for MS approach path error. Because the length of the path quadrants differed depending on the distance to the target, separate 12(direction) x 2(target distance) x 2(size) x 3(gravitational force) x 4(path quadrant) repeated measures ANOVAs were conducted on the cursor speed data for each target distance.

3.1   MS Approach Error

A significant main effect of target distance was obtained, with long target distances resulting in significantly higher MS error ($M = 96.64$, $SE=5.92$) than short target distances ($M = 26.17$, $SE = 2.21$), $F (1, 11) = 191.275$, $p < 0.001$. No significant main effects of gravitational force or spring force were found. However, a significant interaction between gravitational force and target distance was obtained, F (2, 10) = 8.89, p = 0.001. The effects of the gravitational force were only apparent for short target distances. As shown in *Figure 2*, the MS error for short target distances was significantly higher when the gravitational force was set at 100 Newtons/Pixel² (M = 121.508, SE = 4.861) than at 500 Newtons/Pixel² (M = 95.203, SE = 3.7), p = 0.001. It should also be pointed out that at long target distances the MS error for the trials in which the Falcon was used was greater than that of a traditional mouse, however for short target distances this difference in MS error was eliminated at high force values.

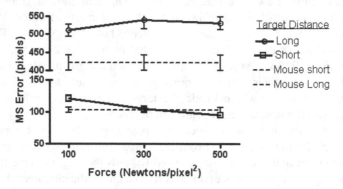

Fig. 2. MS approach error as a function of gravitational force and target distance compared to no-force mouse conditions

3.2   Cursor Speed

As mentioned earlier, the path was divided into quadrants and the average speed of the cursor was calculated for each. Separate ANOVAs were conducted for each target distance because the length in pixels of each quarter differed depending on the target distance.

For short target distances a significant main effect of gravitational force was obtained, F (2, 22) = 216.21, p <.001 as well as a significant main effect of path quadrant, F (3, 33) = 212.05, p < 0.001. As the force increased or as the cursor approached the target, cursor speeds increased significantly.

For short distances a significant interaction between gravitational force and path quadrant was found, F (6, 66) = 285.53, p < 0.001. Cursor speed was found to be equivalent through the first two path quadrants as the level of gravitation force varied. However, as shown in *Figure 3*, there was a significant difference in cursor speed at each level of force in the third and fourth quadrants. At higher levels of force participants decelerated the cursor less as they approached the target.

For long target distances, a significant main effect of force was also obtained such that higher levels of gravitational force resulted in significantly higher cursor speeds, F (2, 22) = 17.59, p < 0.001. In addition, a significant main effect of path quadrant was obtained; cursor speeds were significantly higher as the cursor neared the target, F (3, 33) = 243.09, p < 0.001.

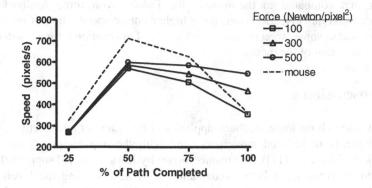

Fig. 3. Average cursor speed within each path quadrant by gravitational force at short target distances. Dotted line shows average cursor speed for mouse movements.

For long target distances a significant interaction was found between gravitational force and path quadrant, F (6, 66) = 67.34, p < 0.001. As shown in *Figure 4,* differences among cursor speeds were found only in the fourth quadrant. That is, there were no differences in cursor speed in the first three quadrants as gravity varied. In the last quadrant a significant increase in target speed was shown with increases in gravitational force levels.

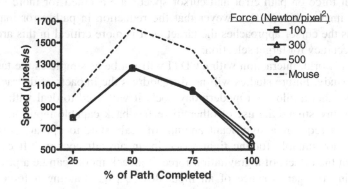

Fig. 4. Average cursor speed within each path quadrant by gravitational force for long target distances. Dotted line shows average cursor speed for mouse movements

In both Figures 3 and 4, the speed attained by the mouse movements is also shown. At both distances, it appears that movements of the mouse consisted of rapid accelerations and then decelerations, compared to the Novint Falcon. For the Falcon, the maximum speed was much lower than the mouse. At short distances, however, higher force levels produced faster speeds at the target boundary, which may account for the equivalence in movement times at these values. This is less evident in Figure 4 at long distances because the attractive force affected target speed for a smaller portion of the movement path. Looking at the results of the cursor speed it can be seen that compared to the mouse, the Falcon with force feedback initially accelerated less quickly. Moreover, these higher cursor speeds did not result in extra path error and at some target distances and levels of gravitational force, path error was comparable to that of the mouse.

4   Discussion

Previous research on force feedback applied to Fitts' Law target selection tasks have shown benefits in reduced movement time with the application of various force feedback models (e.g., [11]). The results shown by Rorie et al. [6] supported previous work and provided for a better understanding of how varying the levels of force feedback could be used to modulate performance gains. The present study showed that the performance gains due to the addition of force feedback can be explained by, increased cursor speed and in some cases decreased path error.

In both cases, however, we found that the effects of the gravitational force on approach error and speed tend to be significant only when the target distance is short. One reason for this outcome may be that when target distances are long, the cursor spends more time outside the effective range of the gravity force. That is, there is essentially no force effect while the cursor is significantly far away from the target. On short distance trials the cursor is under the effects of the gravitational force for a proportionally larger segment of the overall movement. This means the benefits of gravitational force on path error and cursor speeds are accrued for more of the total path.   It is important to note however that the reduction in path error may only be necessary as the cursor approaches the target as it is more critical in this area to have increased accuracy for target selection.

In the real world, interaction with a CDTI will not be as simple as the task used in the present study. Future studies will need to address the impacts of distractor targets and obstacles that a pilot in a modern day cockpit will need to deal with.   It is also necessary to investigate the use of other force feedback capable input devices.   The Novint Falcon requires a significant amount of real estate to operate correctly and therefore is not suitable for the tight space in an aircraft cockpit.   It can be seen however that the effects of a gravitation force feedback model can be a powerful tool for increasing the performance of an input device [5].   Finding a force feedback capable device which is suitable for use in the cockpit and has baseline (no force) performance comparable to a mouse is an important avenue for future work. The addition of force feedback models to such a device may result in performance that far exceeds that of a mouse, providing an accurate and efficient input method for tomorrow's NextGen flight decks.

Acknowledgements. This project was supported by NASA cooperative agreement NNX09AU66A, *Group 5 University Research Center: Center for Human Factors in Advanced Aeronautics Technologies* (Brenda Collins, Technical Monitor).

References

1. Federal Aviation Administration, FAA's NextGen implementation plan. Federal Aviation Administration (2013)
2. Granada, S., Dao, A.Q., Wong, D., Johnson, W.W., Battiste, V.: Development and integration of a human-centered volumetric cockpit display for distributed air-ground operations. In: Proceedings of the 12th International Symposium on Aviation Psychology (2005)
3. Park, E., et al.: Development of Haptic Assistance for Route Assessment Tool of NASA NextGen Cockpit Situation Display. In: Yamamoto, S. (ed.) HIMI/HCII 2013, Part II. LNCS, vol. 8017, pp. 163–172. Springer, Heidelberg (2013)
4. Robles, J., Sguerri, M., Rorie, C., Vu, K.-P.L., Strybel, T.Z., Marayong, P.: Integration framework for NASA NextGen volumetric cockpit situation display with haptic feedback. In: Proceedings of the IEEE International Conference on Robotics and Automation (ICRA), pp. 1033–1037 (2012)
5. Rorie, R.C., Bertolotti, H., Strybel, T., Vu, K.-P.L., Marayong, P., Robles, J.J.: Effect of force feedback on an aimed movement task. In: Landry, S. (ed.) Advances in Human Aspects of Aviation, pp. 633–642. CRC Press, Boca Raton (2012)
6. Rorie, R.C., Vu, K.-P.L., Marayong, P., Robles, J., Strybel, T.Z., Battiste, V.: Effects of Type and Strength of Force Feedback on Movement Time in a Target Selection Task. In: Proceedings of the Human Factors and Ergonomics Society 57th Annual Meeting, pp. 36–40 (2013)
7. Ahlstrom, D.: Modeling and improving selection in cascading pull-down menus using Fitts' law, the steering law and force fields. In: Proceedings of the Conference on Human Factors in Computing Systems, Portland, OR, pp. 61–70 (2005)
8. He, F., Agah, A.: Modeling and improving selection in cascading pull-down menus using Fitts' law, the steering law and force fields. Journal of Intelligent and Robotic Systems 32, 171–190 (2001)
9. Oakley, I., McGee, M.R., Brewster, S., Gray, P.: Putting the feel in "look and feel". In: Proceedings of CHI 2000 Conference on Human Factors in Computing Systems, The Hague, Netherlands (2000)
10. Akamatsu, M., MacKenzie, I.S.: Movement characteristics using a mouse with tactile and force feedback. International Journal of Human-Computer Studies 45, 483–493 (1996)
11. Hwang, F., Keates, S., Langdon, P., Clarkson, P.J.: Multiple haptic targets for motion-impaired users. In: Proceedings of the CHI 2003, Ft. Lauderdale, FL, pp. 41–48 (2003)

Effect of Haptic Perception on Remote Human-Pet Interaction

Kazuyoshi Murata, Kensuke Usui, and Yu Shibuya

Kyoto Institute of Technology, Kyoto, Japan
{kmurata,shibuya}@kit.ac.jp, usui09@sec.is.kit.ac.jp

Abstract. Even when a pet owner is away from his/her pet, he/she often wants to feel closer to the pet. The purpose of this study is to provide a means for the pet owner to feel the presence of his/her pet even when away from it; this is achieved by exchange of haptic feedback. In this paper, we describe such a remote haptic interaction system that consists of haptic devices for remote haptic communication; we also utilize tablets for video chat. A pet owner and his/her pet can feel closer to one another via haptic responses generated by corresponding haptic device. Two experimental evaluations were conducted to compare interactions between a pet owner and his/her pet using our system with another interactions achieved only via video chat. Results showed that these remote haptic interactions increased the pet owner's feeling of communicating with his/her pet. In general, pet owners reported feeling closer to their pet by using our system.

Keywords: haptic interaction, remote interaction, pet interaction.

1   Introduction

Many individuals and families have pets and often treat their pets as their family members. While pet owners are away from their pets, they still wish to interact with them. Therefore, some systems have been proposed to enable such interactions using video and audio devices [1,2]. With these systems, pet owners can enjoy watching the movements of their pets or listening to their pets' sounds. However, these systems lack an important perception, i.e., haptic perception. Haptic perception has an important role in the interaction between owners and pets.

Lee et al. introduced a haptic interaction system between a pet chicken and its owner [3]. The pet chicken wore a special jacket that reproduced the touching sensation of its owner. A pet doll that resembles the chicken was positioned in front of the pet owner. When the pet owner touched the pet doll, the touch signals were transmitted to the pet chicken through the special jacket. Further, the owner wore a special shoe that transmitted movements of the chicken as mild muscle stimulations. With this system, the owner could transmit touching sensations to his/her pet chicken. However, it seems difficult for the owner to associate the movements of the chicken with his/her touch actions.

S. Yamamoto (Ed.): HIMI 2014, Part I, LNCS 8521, pp. 226–232, 2014.
© Springer International Publishing Switzerland 2014

The purpose of our study is to give pet owners a greater ability to feel the presence of their pets while away from them by the exchange of haptic feedback. In this paper, we propose a remote haptic interaction system for owners and their pet dogs. As a typical example for using our system, we assume that owners and their dogs often pull dog treats and toys between each other. We conducted experiments to evaluate the effects of haptic perception on the interaction between the owners and spatially separated their dogs.

2   Remote Haptic Interaction System

As shown in Fig. 1, our system consists of haptic devices for transmitting force feedback between them and video/audio devices for exchanging video images and sounds. Novint Falcons [4] are used as haptic devices and Apple iPads [5] are used as video/audio devices.

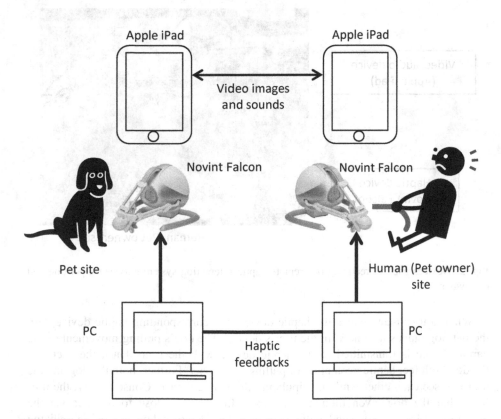

Fig. 1. Haptic devices for transmitting force feedback between a pet dog and the owner and video/audio devices for exchanging video images and sounds

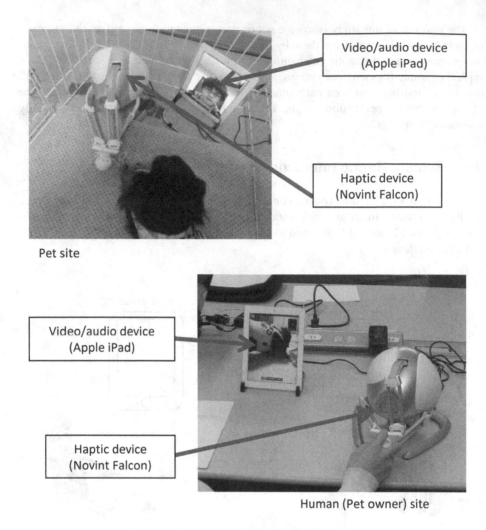

Fig. 2. Devices used in realizing our remote haptic interaction system between a pet dog and the owner

When a user manipulates the haptic device, the corresponding haptic device with the pet dog moves in sync with the user's device. The dog's pulling movement of the haptic device is transmitted to the haptic device with the user. Thus, the user and the dog both feel haptic perception of pulling each other. Further, both the dog and the user can see each other while manipulating the haptic device. Consequently, the user feels that the dog, even though away from him/her, is close to him/her via the exchange of haptic, video and audio feedbacks. Fig. 2 shows devices used in realizing our remote haptic interaction system between a pet dog and the owner.

3   Experiments

To evaluate the effectiveness of haptic perception, two types of interaction systems were used in our experiments. The first system was our proposed remote haptic interaction system, which consisted of a haptic device and a video/audio device; we denote this as "haptic system." The second system consisted only of a video/audio device, which we denote as "video/audio system."

When a participant used the haptic system, dog treats were attached to the haptic device for a dog to allow the participant and the dog to play by pulling the dog treats together, as shown in Fig. 3. In our experiments, participants were asked to interact with a pet dog.

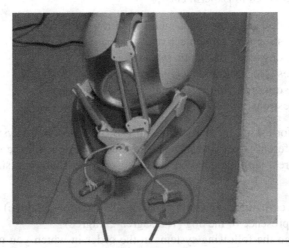

Dog treats were attached to the haptic device at the dog site.

Fig. 3. A haptic device with dog treats attached

3.1   Experiment 1: Interaction between Pet Owners and Their Pet Dog

We selected three volunteers to participate in this experiment. The participants were a pet owner, his wife and his daughter. They were asked to repeat the following task three times.

1. Play with their dog using the haptic system for 3 min
2. Answer a questionnaire for subjective evaluation
3. Play with their dog using the video/audio system for 3 min
4. Again answer a questionnaire for subjective evaluation

In the questionnaires, the participants were asked to rate the following statements using a scale of 1–5.

1. You felt like communicating with your dog (1: disagree–5: agree)
2. You felt the presence of your dog (1: disagree–5: agree)
3. Which was the more satisfying system, the video/audio system or the haptic system? (1: video/audio–5: haptic)
4. Which system would you like to use to feel the presence of your dog, the video/audio system or the haptic system? (1: video/audio–5: haptic)

3.2   Experiment 2: Interaction between Non-pet Owners and an Unknown Dog

Ten volunteers from our university were selected as participants in this experiment. Each participant was asked to perform the task below with an unknown dog. The dog was the same dog used in Experiment 1.

1. Play with the dog using the video/audio system for 3 min
2. Answer a questionnaire for subjective evaluation
3. Play with the dog using the haptic system for 3 min
4. Answer a questionnaire for subjective evaluation
5. Play with the dog using the video/audio again for 3 min
6. Answer a questionnaire for subjective evaluation

The reason for asking the participants to use the video/audio system twice was to confirm the differences between before and after experiencing the haptic system. In the questionnaires, participants were asked to rate the following statements using a scale of 1–5.

1. You felt like communicating with your dog (1: disagree–5: agree)
2. You felt the presence of the dog (1: disagree–5: agree)
3. Please arrange the following systems in the order in which you most strongly felt the presence of the dog:

- the video/audio system (1st time)
- the haptic system
- the video/audio system (2nd time)

4   Results

Fig. 4 shows the results of our questionnaires used in Experiment 1. As shown in the figure, participants felt communication with the haptic system was more effective than that with the video/audio system. The average score of questionnaire question #3 was 3.67; similarly, the average score of questionnaire question #4 was 4.11. These results indicate that participants preferred the haptic system over the video/audio system. Further, in our observations, there were few responses from the dog with the video/audio system, whereas with the haptic system, the dog and the participant actively pulled the haptic device. Participants felt that they were just looking at the dog when they used the video/audio system; conversely, with the haptic system, they felt the responses of the dog. Hence, we conclude that the evaluated values of the haptic system were higher than that of the video/audio system.

Fig. 5 shows the results of the questionnaires used in Experiment 2. As with Experiment 1, the evaluated values of the haptic system were higher than that of the video/audio system. In particular, there was a significant difference ($F_{(2,18)} = 8.870$, $p < 0.01$) in the evaluation of the statement, "You felt like communicating with your dog." Further, the evaluated value of the video/audio system on the second use was rarely different than that of the video/audio system on the first use. Results of questionnaire question #3 showed that nine participants felt the presence of the dog to be strongest when they used the haptic system.

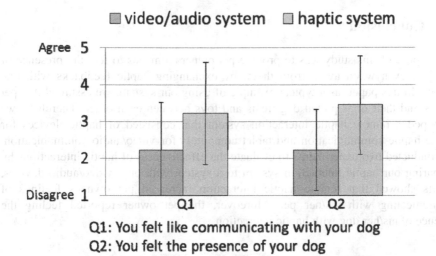

Fig. 4. Results of the questionnaires used in Experiment 1 (pet owners)

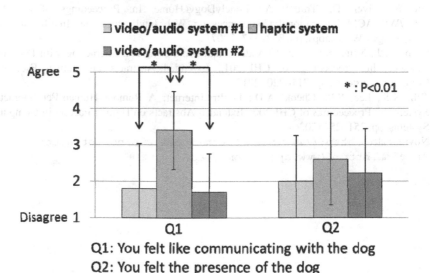

Fig. 5. Results of the questionnaires used in Experiment 2 (non-pet owners)

These results show that transmitting the force feedback of pulling the dog treats between one another enhanced the feeling of communication between the humans and the dog, even if there was no prior relationship between the human and dog.

Unlike human-to-human communication, pet owners cannot verbally communicate with their pets. Therefore, haptic interaction is an important approach that enhances communication between pet owners and their pets. From our experimental results, we believe that the haptic interaction is effective for human-pet interactions over long distances.

5   Conclusion

The purpose of this study was to provide pet owners a means to feel the presence of their pet, even when away from them, by exchanging haptic feedbacks with one another. In this paper, as a typical example of using our system, we assumed that pet owners and their dogs pulled dog treats and toys between each other. Therefore, we developed a remote haptic interaction system that consisted of haptic devices for remote haptic communication and tablet computers for video/audio communication. We conducted two experiments to evaluate the effectiveness of haptic interactions by comparing our haptic interaction system to a system with only video/audio devices. Results showed that remote haptic interaction increased pet owner's feelings of communicating with his/her pet. Moreover, the pet owner reported feeling the presence of his/her dog with haptic interaction.

References

1. Hu, F., Silver, D., Trudel, A.: LonelyDog@Home. In: Proceedings of the 2007 IEEE/WIC/ACM International Conferences on Web Intelligence and Intelligent Agent Technology - Workshops, pp. 333–337 (2007)
2. Golbeck, J., Neustaedter, C.: Pet Video Chat: Monitoring and Interacting with Dogs over Distance. In: Proceedings of CHI 2012 Extended Abstracts on Human Factors in Computing Systems, pp. 211–220 (2012)
3. Teh, K.S., Lee, S.P., Cheok, A.D.: Poultry.Internet: A Remote Human-Pet Interaction System. In: Proceedings of CHI 2006 Extended Abstracts on Human Factors in Computing Systems, pp. 251–254 (2006)
4. Novint Falcon, http://www.novint.com/index.php/novintfalcon
5. Apple iPad, http://www.apple.com/ipad/

Development of High-Speed Thermal Display Using Water Flow

Masamichi Sakaguchi, Kazuki Imai, and Kyohei Hayakawa

Nagoya Institute of Technology, Nagoya, Aichi 466-8555, Japan
saka@nitech.ac.jp
http://ral.web.nitech.ac.jp/

Abstract. A temperature sense is one kind of tactile sense. It doesn't have high spatial resolution and time resolution. But a change in the sudden temperature is also used for sense of danger. That has a high possibility that it can be applied to information display. In this study, water with the high specific heat is used as heat carrier. High-speed thermal display systems are developed by changing warm water and cold water in temperature exposition. In this paper, we explain the characteristics of the temperature measurement system and also describe thermal display system using the rectangular flow channel. Then we developed a water circulation type thermal display system.

Keywords: Thermal display, temperature control, water flow, haptic interface, virtual reality.

1 Introduction

Temperature is one of the environment parameters important for human. Many temperature controlling apparatus, such as an air-conditioner, an electric fan, a stove, and a pocket warmer, has been developed. It is the purpose to keep temperature constant and it is difficult for many of these apparatus to change temperature rapidly. Neither spatial resolution nor the time resolution of human's thermesthesia is so high. A rapid change of temperature is used also for the guess of danger, and a possibility of being applicable to various kinds of information presentation is high.

Human's thermesthesia is dependent on a difference in temperature, change speed, and presentation area. In order considering the use as a human interface to show a temperature change clearly, it is necessary to realize a high-speed temperature change. Since a temperature change is accompanied by movement of thermal energy unlike an electrical signal, a high-speed response cannot realize it easily. The temperature of a skin surface can be quickly changed by touching the object heated or cooled beforehand. However, by this method, it will be accompanied by contact sensation with an object.

When temperature change wants to present, a Peltier device is used in many cases. If the Peltier device controlled its surface temperature before it contacts with the skin surface, it can represent the rapid temperature change[1], [2].

S. Yamamoto (Ed.): HIMI 2014, Part I, LNCS 8521, pp. 233–240, 2014.

A general Peltier device has speed of response by no means as high-speed as tens of seconds from several seconds. Although research which presents a temperature change at high speed by adjusting adaptation temperature with a space division stimulus of small area [3] is done, the temperature itself is not necessarily changing at high speed. Presentation area is small although the high-speed temperature display which combined the Peltier device and the foil heater is developed[4].

In this study, the high-speed temperature display system of sufficient presentation area without contact sensation by using water for a heat medium was developed[5]

2   Development of Thermal Display System Using Water Flow

To measure the characteristic of the developed temperature display system, the thermo couple was used as a temperature sensor. In order to measure a high-speed temperature change, the response of the temperature sensor itself must also be a high speed. In this research, K type thermo couple ST-55 made from RKC Instrument Inc. was used. The diameter of the thermo couple line is 0.076 mm. Amplification amplifier used AD595GQ made from Analog Devices Inc.. It was connected to the computer through the A/D board, and temperature was measured.

The developed model figure of a temperature display part is shown in Fig.1. The acrylic board was used for material. The rectangle-like channel was dug, and the copper plate was put on the top. The section of a channel is 14 mm in width, the depth is 4.5 mm, and area is $63mm^2$. The size of a copper plate is 18 mm in width, is 72 mm in length, and is 0.5 mm in thickness. The area of the temperature display part in contact with warm or cold water is $1,267mm^2$.

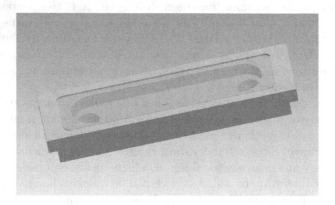

Fig. 1. Rectangle type channel temperature display part

The temperature display system which used two rectangle type channels for the temperature display part was built. The outline of a system is shown in Fig. 2. The two pumps P_1 and P_2 were installed in the tank of warm water and cold water, respectively, and water was supplied compulsorily. As shown in a figure, it has arranged combining four solenoid valves and two rectangle type channels. The solenoid valves V_1 and V_4, and V_2 and V_3 were synchronized, respectively, and it opened and closed in turns. By this method, high temperature and low temperature were shown in turns to the two temperature display parts D_1 and D_2. The photograph of a temperature display part is shown in Fig.3. The length of the water flow path was about 1,800 mm. The pump used KP-103 made from Koshin LTD., and the solenoid valve used AB41-02 made from CKD Corp.. Two tanks of warm water and cold water, four electromagnetic valves, and two temperature display part were located on the same desk. The average flow velocity of the rectangle type channel was about 1.4 m/s.

An example of an experimental result is shown in Fig. 4. The solenoid valve changed every 5 s. The blue line and light-blue line in a figure show the temperature change of the temperature display parts D_1 and D_2, respectively. It

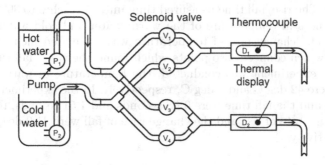

Fig. 2. Temperature display system using two rectangle type channels

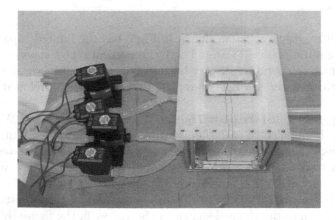

Fig. 3. Picture of electromagnetic valve and temperature display part

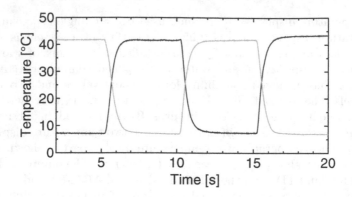

Fig. 4. Temperature change of rectangle type channel temperature display part

can check that high temperature and low temperature are shown by turns in the temperature display parts D_1 and D_2.

The rise/fall time and the change rate of temperature were found as an evaluation index. The rise/fall time measured time until it reaches to 90% from 10% of the differences in temperature of the warm water and cold water before an experiment. The change rate of temperature was calculated inclination of the straight line which connects two points which found the rise / fall time.

When this experiment was conducted, the temperature of warm water and cold water were 42 deg C and 7 deg C, respectively. In the experimental results, the rise time and the fall time were 0.68 seconds and 1.51 seconds, respectively. And the change rate of rise and the change rate of fall were 41.0 deg/s and 18.5 deg/s, respectively.

3　Development of Water Cyclical Type Thermal Display System

The temperature display system shown in Fig.2 has the limited capacity of the tank of warm water and cold water. Then, the cyclical type temperature display system in which temperature display is continuously possible was developed by circulating warm water and cold water. The model of the developed system is shown in Fig.5.

Four temperature display parts($D_1 \sim D_4$) exist in this system. Warm water or cold water is supplied to each temperature display part using pumps(P_1, P_2) from two tanks. The part of the pink in the figure shows warm water, and the light-blue part shows cold water. Four solenoid valves($V_1 \sim V_4$) are arranged at the upper stream side of a temperature display part, and another four solenoid valves($V_5 \sim V_8$) are arranged also at the lower stream side. Either warm water or cold water flows into the channel shown in the yellow in the figure by switching solenoid valves. Supplying warm water or cold water to temperature display parts by controlling the timing of opening and closing of the solenoid valves, while the

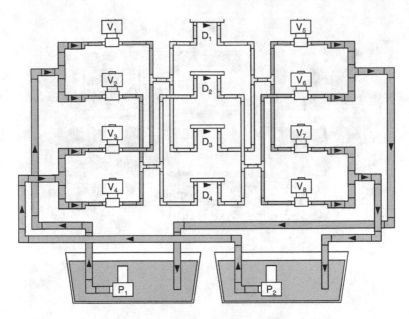

Fig. 5. Water cyclical type temperature display system

load of a pump has been constant, it can circulate through warm water on the tank of warm water, and can make the tank of cold water circulate through cold water.

The pictures of the developed cyclical type temperature display system is shown in Fig.6. Each tank of warm water and cold water with a capacity of 35 liters is located in the lower berth of a rack. Warm water and cold water were generated using the water heater and water cooler. The pump used KP-103 made from Koshin LTD., and the solenoid valve used AB41-02 made from CKD Corp.. Opening and closing of the solenoid valve were controlled using the notebook PC. The solenoid valve interlocked V_1 and V_4, V_2 and V_3, V_5 and V_8, V_6 and V_7 respectively. For example, V_1, V_4, V_5, and V_8 are opened, V_2, V_3, V_6, and V_7 are closed, display part D_1 and D_3 present high temperature, D_2 and D_4 present low temperature, The average flow velocity of the cyclical type thermal display system was about 0.4 m/s.

An example of an experimental result is shown in Fig.7. The change interval of warm water and cold water was made into 5 seconds. The blue line green line, red line, and purple line in the figure shows the temperature of display part D_1, D_2, D_3, and D_4 respectively. It turns out that the temperature display parts D_1 and D_3, and D_2 and D_4 interlocked, and it has shown high temperature and low temperature at intervals of about 5 seconds. In this experiment, the temperature of warm water was 42 deg C, the temperature of cold water was 19 deg. C, and its difference was 23 deg. C. The temperature rise time was 1.18 seconds(min.), 1.57 seconds(max.), and 1.36 seconds(ave.) respectively. The temperature increasing rate was 12.0 deg/s(min.) 15.7 deg/s(max.), and 13.9

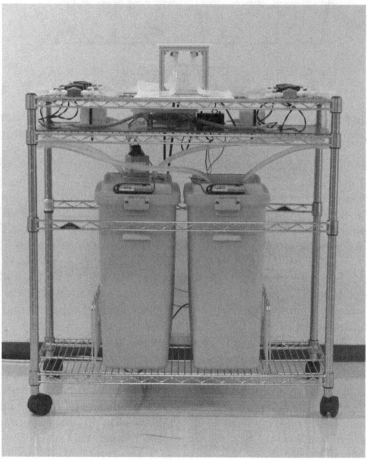

Fig. 6. Picture of water cyclical type temperature display system

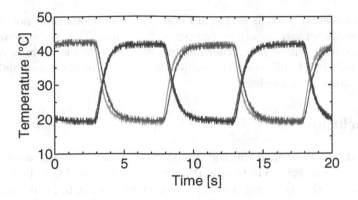

Fig. 7. Experimental result of water cyclical type temperature display system

deg/s(ave.) respectively. The temperature fall time was 1.34 seconds(min.), 1.51 seconds(max.), and 1.42 seconds(ave.) respectively. The temperature decreasing rate was 12.3 deg/s(min.) 14.4 deg/s(max.), and 13.3 deg/s(ave.) respectively.

4   Local Temperature Presentation to Fingers

The area of the temperature display part shown in Fig.1 is almost the same as the size of one finger. Since the temperature display system shown in Fig.6 has four temperature display part, it can be shown the temperature to four fingers, respectively. Local temperature distribution can be generated by touching the

Fig. 8. Local temperature distribution display system to four fingers

temperature display part, as shown in Fig.8. This thermesthesia is not accompanied by contact sensation only by temperature change. This system can change temperature distribution like a thermal grill illusion in terms of time. Although there was individual difference, the subject who feels a temperature higher than the temperature shown existed.

5   Conclusions

In this study, we developed the high-speed thermal display using water flow. In this system, the difference in temperature of 35 deg C was able to be changed in about 1 s. By using this thermal display, as shown in Fig.6, local temperature distribution is shown to a hand and fingers and it becomes possible to carry out the time variation only of the temperature information. This is applicable to control of a thermal grill illusion.

References

1. Yamamoto, A., Cros, B., Hasgimoto, H., Higuchi, T.: Control of Thermal Tactile Display Based on Prediction of Contact Temperature. In: Proc. IEEE Int. Conf. Robotics and Automation (ICRA 2004), pp. 1536–1541 (2004)
2. Ho, H.N., Jones, L.A.: Development and Evaluation of a Thermal Display for Material Identification and Discrimination. ACM Trans. Applied Perception 4, 1–24 (2007)
3. Sato, K., Maeno, T.: Presentation of Rapid Temperature Change Using Spatially Divided Hot and Cold Stimuli. J. Robotics and Mechatronics 25(3), 497–505 (2013)
4. Sakaguchi, M., Yokoi, S., et al.: Development of High Speed Controllable Thermal Display. Rep. Toyota Physic. Chem. Res. Inst. 61, 211–217 (2008) (in Japanese)
5. Sakaguchi, M., Obata, H., et al.: Construction of High-Speed Thermal Display System using Warm Water and Cold Water. In: Proc. 2012 JSME Conf. Robmec., p. 1P1-A01 (2012) (in Japanese)

Evoking Emotions in a Story Using Tactile Sensations as Pseudo-body Responses with Contextual Cues

Sho Sakurai[1], Toki Katsumura[2], Takuji Narumi[2], Tomohiro Tanikawa[2],
and Michitaka Hirose[2]

[1] Graduate School of Engineering, The University of Tokyo
[2] Graduate School of Information Science and Technology, The University of Tokyo
{sho,katsumura,narumi,tani,hirose}@cyber.t.u-tokyo.ac.jp

Abstract. In this paper, we propose a method to evoke multiple emotions by presenting a combination of some tactile sensations in the contextual situation of others' experience. Recent psychological researchers have argued that some sort of emotion evokes through recognizing not only change in real body reactions but also feedback of sensory stimuli that resemble the change in somebody reaction. On the other hand, evoked emotion varies depending on a context of their experience, even if the change in bodily response is same. Based on the knowledge, we hypothesize that providing a variety of pseudo-physiological responses with a controlled context can evoke various emotions, even when the pseudo-physiological responses are the same. In order to test this hypothesis, we made a system named "Comix: beyond," which evokes seven types of emotion using three tactile sensations as pseudo physiological responses associated with the context of the story of the comic.

Keywords: Emotion, Evoking emotion, two-factor theory of emotion, comic, context.

1 Introduction

In every museum, the information on a past event is conveyed to present through exhibiting extensive historic materials. In order to convey and promote understanding toward the past, curators have been trying to convey not only the detail of exhibited historical materials but also background information concerning the materials. The background information includes information of historical backdrop such as the reason why the materials were made, people's lives at the day and relationships between people or countries. Such background information is not easy to convey. The reason is that it is difficult to replay all backdrop since the amount of information is unduly extravagant. Besides, such information is formless. Existing ways to describe background information rely on text or visual expression such as pictures, movies and 3D models. However, there is a limit in information that can be described using only these.

S. Yamamoto (Ed.): HIMI 2014, Part I, LNCS 8521, pp. 241–250, 2014.

On the other hand, conveying the background information by reaching five senses through introduction of digital technologies has been attempted recently. This enables the visitors to experience the past event. Nevertheless, it is hard to re-create past people's subjective information, such as atmosphere of the past and past people's feeling.

We focus on human emotion, as one of the background information that is representing is not easy. The human history has been driven by human emotion. Knowing contextual the past people's emotion would enable imagining oneself in the position of the people and re-experiencing others' thinking or behavior. We think that the realization of the technology to replay contextual past people's emotion would promotes understanding of information, for example, why the past event happened and why the people took action at that time.

Then this paper discusses on methods to experience others' emotion in some context. As an experimental technique to give contextual cue and others' emotional experience, we propose a method to present the experience of a character of comics associated with the context of the comics. Comic is a medium that can present context simplistically, whether the time that is flowing depicted in the story is long or short. In this paper, we propose and make a VR system to evoke multiple emotions that is the same as emotions that the character experiences in the comic taking this advantage of the comic.

Fig. 1. Understanding the past by knowing the past others' emotion

2   Evoke Emotions Using Virtual Reality

2.1   Emotion

Emotions are the observable expressions of the movement of mind, such as pain, joy, disgust, surprise and anger. "Affect" and "feeling" are used as words with a similar connotation. In this paper, "emotion" is treated as the term referring to one's mind that includes "affect" and "feeling."

Emotion and physiological response have a close relationship. It has been discussed whether evoking emotion or change in physiological response is prior.

Some theories advocated that changing in physiological responses occurs prior to changing in emotion have been propounded during about the last hundred years. Many researchers argued the theories. The typical example of the theories is James-Lange theory [1]. Also, it is clarified that some sort of emotion evokes through recognizing not only change in real body reactions but also feedback of sensory stimuli that resemble the change in some body reactions. Valins et al. confirmed this notion through the false heart-rate feedback study [2].

On the other hands, what kind of emotions evoke is determined by not only bodily responses change but also recognition of causal attribution. Schacther et al call this for Two-factor theory of emotion [3]. The term "causal attribution" is the occasion that is earned recognition as the reason for the bodily responses changes. This theory is experimentally confirmed by Dutton et al.'s "Capilano Suspension Bridge experiment" [4]. In this study, male subjects misattributed the physiological strain resulting from going across a scary bridge to the emotional excitement of meeting an attractive woman. Causal attribution is determined by the context that the person experienced. That is to say, an evoked emotion varies depending on a context experienced even if bodily response change is the same.

2.2   Evoking Emotion Using Virtual Reality

Recently, based on above-mentioned knowledge in psychology, some HCI techniques are focused on trying to evoke and enhance a particular emotion. There are mainly two approaches for evoking and enhancing emotions.

One is an approach to evoke emotions with a feedback of specific sensory stimulus. For example, Nishimura et al. created a tactile device that attempts to control affective feelings through artificial autonomous physiological reactions [5]. Fukushima et al. proposed an interface that tries to enhance chilly feeling by raising their body-hair with static electricity during watching a scary movie [6]. Yoshida et al. showed that letting people recognize slightly deformed their face in the mirror-like system as a change in their own facial expression can evoke pleasant and unpleasant feelings [7]. "Tear Machine" is a piece of interactive artwork that can induce a powerful distressed emotional state [8]. These means control virtual bodily responses that human cannot control consciously or pay no attention normally.

Another is an approach to evoke emotions by letting users change physiological responses related to particular emotions consciously by their own. For instance Tsujita et al. propose a system that evoke pleasant mood by letting the user make smiling face intentionally by presenting a picture, which represents a face that reflects the user's facial expression [9]. Sakurai et al. created an artwork, which evokes the tense feeling by movement of a balloon in conjunction with a respiratory condition controlled actively by the user [10]. Shifting the corresponding of respiratory condition and the movements brings the situation that the user gird for what happened s/he cannot understand and the tense feeling evokes and enhances. In these ways, specific emotion evokes by replacing recognized causal attribution from the user's intention to external stimuli, such as changed face and unintended movement of the balloon.

The latter approach requires active controlling of own physiological responses. However, many of the bodily responses related to various emotions are not easy to alter, because these are automatic responses, such as heart-rate and bodily temperature. Also it is difficult to make people change any move actively in similar fashion in large space where the general public exist, like museums. Therefore, we have an approach to represent others' emotions in line with the context of the others' experience according to above the former method.

Existing ways to evoke or enhance any emotions aim to evoke a single-species emotion using a single species sensory stimulus. However, more than one bodily responses change when an emotion evokes. Also, evoked emotions vary associated with the context of the experience even if same bodily reactions change as noted before. Based on the knowledge, we hypothesis that adequately combining sensory stimuli that is recognized as change in own bodily reactions in the context of others' experience would be able to evoke the same emotions as the others' experienced.

According to the hypothesis, we propose a method to evoke multiple emotions using limited number of pseudo-bodily responses associated with the contextual other's experience.

3   Evoking Multiple Emotions Using Limited Number of Pseudo-body Responses with Contextual Cues

3.1   Evoking Multiple Emotions Using the Combination of Tactile Sensations

As previously mentioned, there are many physiological reactions that relate to emotion. Among them, we focus on heart-rate, vital warmth and chest pressure. The reason why we focus on heart-rate is that heart-rate has a close relationship with various emotions [11]. Also the reason why we take notice of vital warmth is that there is an available knowledge that the sensation is linked with pleasant-unpleasant feeling [12]. As concerns the chest pressure, although having said that it made us feel a tightening in one's chest, whether artificial chest pressure influences on both positive and negative emotion if the pressure is applied around the breast.

We developed a prototype system to present 3 sensory stimuli that resemble heartbeat, vital warmth and chest pressure. The system presents vibration as the pseudo-heartbeat with a speaker. This speaker is attached to the left side of the chest and provides tactile sensation resembling heartbeat. The configuration and the method to present the tactile sensation referes to a method proposed by Nishimura et al. [5]. The rate of pseudo-heartbeat is 96bpm.

This system also provides pseudo-vital warmth, with two Peltier devices. The Peltier devices are attached at the center of the chest and the broad on the back. Also the devices give the warm sensation / cold sensation to the body. The temperature to present each sensation is 45 / 25 degrees in Celsius. These temperatures bring pleasant / unpleasant to human [13]. The each Peltier device is covered with thin aluminum plates to spread the temperature to whole chest.

Table 1. The combination of pseudo physiological responses to evoke each emotion

Pseudo- physiological responses	heart-rate	vital warmth	chest pressure
Throb	ON	ON (warm)	OFF
Impatience	ON	OFF	ON
Tense feeling	ON	ON (warm)	ON
Fear	ON	ON (warm)	OFF
Heart ache	ON	OFF	ON
Feeling of going pale	OFF	ON (cold)	ON
Sense of security	OFF	ON (warm)	OFF

The device to present chest pressure consists of an air-bag and an air-pump. The air-bag is attached around whole chest. The air-bag inflates by taking the air in the air- bag to present the pressure. Contrarily, the air comes out from the air-bag when pressure is not required. The time from when the air begin to inflate till when the air-bag is filled up is about 10 seconds.

In this study, based on the knowledge of the relationship between body reactions and emotions, and the result of a preliminary study, we decided to evoke following 7 emotions using the devices: throb (Excitement for others or things,) tense feeling, fear, feeling of a heartache (by sadness or by affection), the feeling of going pale and sense of security. Table 1 shows parameters of tactile sensation and combinations of the sensations as pseudo-physiological responses to evoke each emotion.

To express in the change in physiological responses with a most simple combination these stimulus, this system switch pseudo heart-rate and chest pressure only on or off. Also the temperature changes to only warm condition or cold condition.

It is clarified that it is important to give the user a realization of sensory stimuli as real change in own bodily responses. In order to let the user recognize that provided sensory stimuli as own body changes and to reduce a feeling of strangeness, the devices are embedded into a cloth (a parka.) This configuration and how to attach these devices inside of a cloth are shown in Figure 2.

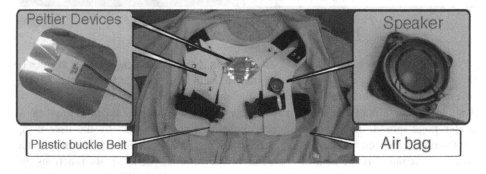

Fig. 2. The Configuration of wearable system to present tactile sensations as pseudo heart-rate, body temperature and chest pressure

3.2   Comix: Beyond: An Artwork to Evoke Emotions Depending on the Context of the Story of the Comic

As previously mentioned, a context that a user experiences influences on an evoked emotion. As the contents can provide any context, we focused on the comic. The comic is skilled at communicating formless information, such as emotion of the characters and the ambience in each scene.

How people emphasize with the characters and go into the world of the comic is depending on the expressive power of the authors. This is a limit of the paper media. Meanwhile, the knowledge about how to express the character's face and effects in order to depict any character's affects is systematized [14, 15]. Thus, anyone who has the knowledge is possible to select pseudo-body reactions for evoking and enhancing the emotion that is same as the depicted character's affect. The readers can understand the context of the content, since the comic is able to extract essence of context and express the essence briefly with highly formalized depiction.

We decided to use the comic as a tool to present the contextual cue, and made an artwork named "Comix: beyond, " which presenting the contextual cue and sensory stimuli to evoke the same emotions as the character experience in the story of the comic (Fig. 3).

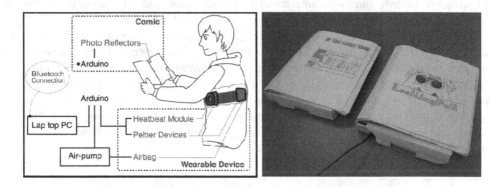

Fig. 3. System configuration of Comix: beyond

Normally various emotions or the ambience is depicted in a page of the comic. In this case, we create a comic includes a story in which a character experience 7 types of emotions above-mentioned in 3.1 as the most simplified context. The comic is designed to contain a scene that a main character has one of the 7 types of emotion in center page spread. This system detects the page, which is read by the user using photo-interrupters embedded in every page of the paper comic. By specifying the emotions as same as the central character in each scene, pseudo-body reactions are provided for evoking and enhancing the emotion associated with the context of the comic.

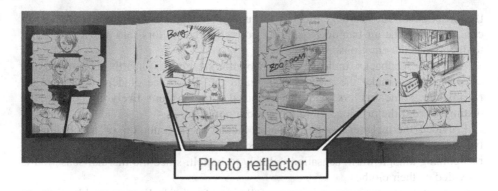

Fig. 4. The example of the pages of a comic we created

4 Case Study through Exhibiting Comix: Beyond

4.1 Exhibition

We showcased "Comix: beyond" in Siggraph Asia 2013 held at Hongkong from Nov. 19 to 22, 2013 [16]. We observed over 50 visitors who experience the work and investigated their responses. Also we obtained feedback from the visitors about this work. Figure 4 shows the scenes of the exhibition.

Fig. 5. The visitors experienced "Comix: beyond" at Siggraph Asia 2013

4.2 Feedback

Feedback about Comix: beyond from the visitor are classified into 2 broad categories. One is the comment about our proposed method for evoking emotions. Another is the comment about the use of the comic as a medium to provide contextual cue to the user.

As concerns former, we received a lot of feedbacks indicated that the chest pressure provided from the air-bag is most effective to affect emotions, especially the tense feeling. About other emotions but the tense feeling, we receive comments that the inflation of the air-bag affected for understanding what emotions evoked. In contrast, when the air-bag does not work correctly, the visitors said that it is difficult to distinguish the emotions.

Also the feedbacks indicated that vibration resembles heartbeat is relatively effectiveness to make the visitors understand the difference of depicted emotions. Meanwhile, some visitors said that depicted emotions are likely to be felt and distinguished if the provided vibration is more powerful.

Provided thermal sensation remains a matter of speculation of a relationship between temperature and emotions. Especially, cold sensation is found difficulty recognizing though warm sensation is likely to be felt, since the thermal sensation is provided on their clothes.

As for a whole our approach, we got following feedback: In contents like game or movie, the main methods for evoking multiple emotions is providing physical impact associated with the fixed context. The fresh and interesting thing about our approach is that various emotional experiences are provided by physical stimuli translated into psychological information.

As concerns latter, there were no people puzzled how to read the comic. On the other hand, people could not understand the story said the emotions aimed to evoke is incomprehensible compared with people could understand the story.

In this case, we create an original comic by ourselves. Most of half visitors experienced Comix: beyond said that they want to apply the system when they read existing or their favorite comics.

Comic requires the readers to turn the pages actively. This behavior is able to control the pace of development of the story, despite watching movie or TV programs. Some visitors remarked that the behavior or pace controlled on their own affect the emotions evoked to the readers.

4.3   Discussion

The feedbacks from the visitors indicated that they can feel and distinguish the depicted emotions if they can feel the provided stimuli as their own body reactions. In this system, we provided three kinds of stimuli; heart-rate, vital warmth, and chest pressure. According to the visitors' feedbacks, the chest pressure is the most powerful to evoke intended emotions. Using the chest pressure effectively evoked especially the tense feeling. This is thought to be due to the strength of the pressure feedback. On the other hand, according to the feedbacks, the vital warmth was not effective in this case. This is because the presented thermal sensation is too weak to feel over the clothes. Then we should reconsider the method to present this kind of pseudo-body reactions or parameters to feel the stimuli.

In this user study at the exhibition, the comic is designed to contain a scene that a main character has one of the 7 types of emotion in center page spread by ourselves. Meanwhile, normally various emotions are depicted in a page of the comic. To apply the proposed method to general comics, we should realize a method to design a timeline of emotions to depict based on the storyline in the contents. It is relatively easy when we apply the proposed method to sequential contents such as movies since temporal progress in the contents is constant.

On the other hand, when we read a comic, we can control the temporal progress. Therefore we need to a complex method to design a timeline of emotions for interactive media whose temporal progress is controlled by a user. While although the user read a comic with the intention of controlling their pace, the design of the contents sometimes strongly affects the pace unintentionally. For example, arrangement of the panels in a comic affects the reading pace and limit it within confined pace. Then the reading pace could be assumed based on the analysis of the composition of the panels.

By comparing the estimated pace based on the contents analysis and the real pace measured by the system with sensors such as a photo reflector, the system could be design the timeline of sensory stimuli to evoke emotions adaptively in response to the type of the user. By using this adaptive method, we believe that we can realize a design method to estimate an appropriate timeline to present sensory feedbacks for evoking emotions in complex story.

5   Conclusion

In this study, we proposed a method to evoke multiple emotions by presenting contextual cue and limited number of tactile sensations that resembles heart-rate, body temperature and chest pressure. Also we created an artwork named "Comix: beyond" as a trial system to realize our proposed method. This work aims to trigger the same emotions as a character experiences in the comic that the user reads.

We exhibited "Comix: beyond" in an exhibition for a user study. The feedbacks from the visitors indicated that they can feel and distinguish the depicted emotions if they can feel the provided stimuli. On the other hand, we need to explore more detail about how combinations of presented sensory stimuli affect emotions. Also we will consider about how to design a timeline of emotions to apply our approach for evoking emotion to contents has complex context.

In this paper, we discuss about the method based on the comics. The proposed method, which enables us to let a user feel an intended emotion in accordance with the contents, can be applicable for museum exhibition that provides exhibits with emotions according to the user's appreciation action. Moreover we believe the proposed method can be extended to general contents.

References

1. James, S.: The principles of psychology, vol. 2. Dover Publications, New York (1950)
2. Valins, S.: Cognitive Effects of False Heart-Rate Feedback. J. of Pers. Soc. Psychol. 4(4), 400–408 (1966)
3. Schacther, S.: The Interaction of Cognitive and Physiological Determinants of Emotional State. In: Berkowits, L. (ed.) Advances in Experimental Social Psychology, vol. 1, pp. 49–80 (1964)

4. Dutton, D., et al.: Some evidence for heightened sexual attraction under conditions of high anxiety. J. of Pers. Soc. Psychol. 30(4), 510–517 (1974)
5. Nishimura, S., Ishii, A., Sato, M., Fukushima, S., Kajimoto, H.: Facilitation of Affection by Tactile Feedback of False Heartbeat. In: Proc. of CHI EA 2012, pp. 2321–2326 (2012)
6. Fukushima, S., Kajimoto, H.: Chilly Chair: Facilitating an Emotional Feeling with Artificial Piloerection. In: Proc. of SIGGRAPH 2012, Article no. 5 (2012)
7. Yoshida, S., Sakurai, S., Narumi, T., Tanikawa, T., Hirose, M.: Manipulation of an Emotional Experience by Real- time Deformed Facial Feedback. In: Proceedings of Augmented Human, pp. 35–42 (2013)
8. Tear machine,
   http://www.weststarland.com/wp/2011/04/
   tear-machine-tearful-reflection/ (last accessed in February 12, 2014)
9. Tsujita, H., Rekimoto, J.: HappinessCounter: Smile-Encouraging Appliance to Increase Positive Mood. Extended Abstracts on CHI 2011, pp. 4285–4290. ACM Press (2011)
10. Sakurai, S., Katsumura, T., Narumi, T., Tanikawa, T., Hirose, M.: Interactonia Balloon. In: Proc. of SA 2012 E-tech, Article No.15 (2012)
11. Casioppo, J.T., Tassinary, L.G., Berntson, G.G. (eds.): Handbook of psychology, 2nd edn. Cambridge University Press, New York (2000)
12. Stolwijk, J.A.: Responses to the thermal environment. Federation Proceedings 36(5), 1655 (1977)
13. Narumi, T., Akagawa, T., Seong, Y.A., Hirose, M.: An Entertainment System using Thermal Feedback for Increasing Communication and Social Skills. In: Chang, M., Kuo, R., Kinshuk, Chen, G.-D., Hirose, M. (eds.) Edutainment 2009. LNCS, vol. 5670, pp. 184–195. Springer, Heidelberg (2009)
14. McCloud, S.: Understanding Comics. The invisible Art. Harper. Paperbacks (1990)
15. Sakurai, S., Yoshida, S., Narumi, T., Tanikawa, T., Hirose, M.: Intra-expo: Augmented Emotion By Superimposing Comic Book Images. In: Proc. of ICAT 2011, p. 139 (2011)
16. Sakurai, S., Katsumura, T., Narumi, T., Tanikawa, T., Hirose, M.: Comix: beyond: Evoking Multiple Emotions using Pseudo Body Responses Depending on the Context. In: Proc. of SA 2013 E-tech, Article 3 (2013)

Enhancement of Accuracy of Hand Shape Recognition Using Color Calibration by Clustering Scheme and Majority Voting Method

Takahiro Sugaya, Hiromitsu Nishimura, and Hiroshi Tanaka

Kanagawa Institute of Technology,
1030 Shimo-ogino, Atsugi-shi, Kanagawa, Japan
s1385015@cce.kanagawa-it.ac.jp,
{nisimura,h_tanaka}@ic.kanagawa-it.ac.jp

Abstract. This paper presents methods of enhancing the recognition accuracy of hand shapes in a scheme which is proposed by the authors as being easy to memorize and which can represent much information. To ensure suitability for practical use, the recognition performance must be maintained even when there are changes in the illumination environment. First, a color calibration process using a k-means clustering scheme is introduced as a way of ensuring high performance in color detection. In the proposed method the thresholds for hue values are decided before the recognition process, as a color calibration scheme. The second method of enhancing accuracy involves making a majority decision. Many image frames are obtained from one hand shape before the transition to the next shape. The frames in this hand shape formation time span are used for shape recognition by majority voting based on the recognition results from each frame. It has been verified by carrying out experiments under different illumination conditions that the proposed technique can raise the recognition performance.

Keywords: Color Gloves, Shape Recognition, Color Detection, Hue Value, Clustering, Majority Voting, Illumination Environment.

1 Introduction

Fingerspelling and sign language are the largest barriers to independent living for hearing impaired or speech-impaired persons. However, it is difficult to acquire the necessary deciphering skills as well as to learn the skills to express meaning. Gesture recognition systems etc. have been developed in order to solve these problems [1]. The methods which use a special sensor or devices [2, 3] involve a high cost of introduction or the need to attach sensors to the human body. In addition, since some systems have restrictions on the locations where they can be used, due to the illumination conditions, it is difficult to use these systems as universal communication tools for handicapped people.

S. Yamamoto (Ed.): HIMI 2014, Part I, LNCS 8521, pp. 251–260, 2014.

We have proposed a single vision-based hand shape recognition method, because it does not require sensors to be attached to the human body. A camera implemented in a smartphone, etc. may be applied to this method. There are two kinds of approach used in methods for vision-based recognition. One is methods using color markers, such as color gloves, and the other is methods which do not use color markers [4]. Of course, the recognition method that does not use special markers is more user-friendly. However, in the research on sign language recognition in which a color glove or markers were not used [5, 6], the complicated shape of fingers or their motion could not be accurately detected. On the other hand, although color gloves were used for hand shape recognition in another study [7], a lot of colors were used, and the evaluation test was carried out under only one illumination condition. In order to realize a hand shape recognition system which can identify each fingertip in a simpler and more robust manner, we decided to use a color glove in which a different color was assigned to each fingertip.

In general, the use of color detection techniques alone cannot maintain high detection performance in an environment of varying light conditions. Color detection is one of the most important elements in shape recognition. In our previous study [8], it was proposed to achieve high sensitivity color detection by considering thresholds for determining the hue values under different illumination conditions. However, shape recognition errors cannot be eliminated because of color detection errors which still occur in some illumination environments. It was clarified that the shape recognition performance must be improved in order to achieve satisfactory practical use.

This paper presents a means of enhancing the accuracy of hand shape recognition. First, a color calibration process using a k-means clustering scheme is introduced for color detection regardless of any difference of illumination conditions. Second, the final hand shape recognition results are determined by majority voting based on the recognition results from many image frames which are extracted from a single hand shape formation period. It is verified by experiments carried out under various illumination conditions that our proposed hand shape recognition system using these two methods can be achieved high recognition results.

2   Recognition Target and Color Detection

The authors have proposed the use of color gloves on each hand, with the fingers marked with different colors, for hand shape recognition. Color gloves have an advantage in facilitating the recognition of hand shapes in comparison with recognition by contour abstraction of hand shapes, especially when taking into account the background environment and the need for discrimination between fingers. Six colors were selected by considering their hue values, since these are used to discriminate between the colors. The portions of the glove that are colored are the tip of each finger and the wrist as shown in Fig.1. We propose a new set of finger patterns which is easy to memorize. Each finger represents a binary number, where 1 means visible from the camera, and 0 means an invisible finger, that is a finger which is folded back and not extended. The order of digits in a number follows the order of fingers, that is, the thumb represents the LSB (right-most position of 5 bits), and the little finger corresponds to the MSB, for both right and left hands. We propose that the viewing region of single camera is divided into two separate regions, namely, right hand and left hand regions. If the crossing of hands during use is not allowed, the two regions are independent and a large number of signals can be easily created.

The recognition process is performed using the scheme of "nearest neighbor", in which the result is selected on the basis of the shortest distance between template vectors of defined shapes and the feature vector of hand shape $\mathbf{f}$, shown in Fig.1, provided by the camera image. The elements are the distances from the center of the wrist to each colored finger tip region, where element value 0 is used to indicate a colored region which is invisible due to a finger being bent. The shape recognition result is obtained by selecting the hand shape which has the minimum distance between template feature vectors prepared in advance and the target feature vector which is to be recognized.

The hand shape recognition performance is governed by the color detection characteristics. Because the hand shape is recognized on the basis of the positions of each finger tip, these positions are defined as the center of gravity of each colored region. The color detection is based on the hue values for each color. These values are influenced by the illumination environment, that is, brightness and light direction. Color detection errors include the following three cases, that is, (i) color is detected in a different position to the one it should be in, (ii) color cannot be detected in the position where it should be, (iii) color is detected in a position that it should not be in (over detection).

First, the authors investigated highly accurate color detection to achieve high recognition performance. The characteristics of the color detection are strongly influenced by the illumination environment, because the hue value for each colored area depends on the illumination conditions.

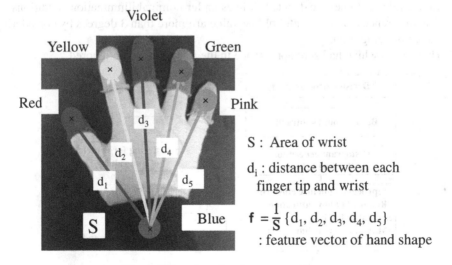

Fig. 1. Color glove for shape recognition

3   Color Threshold Calibration for Color Detection

3.1   Hue Value Decision Threshold

It is necessary to discriminate six colors correctly under any illumination conditions. The authors propose calibration of the color thresholds before the shape recognition process commences, since the hue values are altered by the illumination conditions. Therefore we propose that these values are determined by a clustering scheme. Although this clustering imposes a computing load, the k-means clustering scheme was applied in this investigation. Since the clustering operation is carried out only once, and before the recognition process, it does not result in any delay in the recognition process itself. In addition, the initial value for clustering can be easily decided by taking the nominal hue values of each color into account. This scheme can be considered as color threshold calibration for color detection, to eliminate the effect of the illumination environment and the particular camera to be used.

The proposed scheme involves the following processing, as shown in Fig.2.

1. Creating of a histogram of hue values from the image of the hand taken by the camera
2. Introduction of preprocessing before clustering from the histogram, that is, the removal of low saturation color (white), suppression of maximum values (limiting) and removal of infrequently occurring hue values as noise
3. Clustering by k-means to determine the center of the hue values for the 6 colors from the histogram data
4. Determination of hue value range for the detection of each color using the clustering result and the hue value range based on past experimental results

In addition, the following treatments are undertaken in k-means processing by taking the features of 6 colors into account.

5. Initial values of hues are decided by hues under nominal illumination conditions
6. The differences of each center of hue value are more than 3 degrees by considering the color being used.
7. Hue values which had zero appearance in the histogram were ignored.

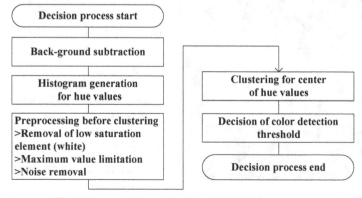

Fig. 2. Proposed hue value threshold decision process

3.2   Experimental Conditions and Results

k-means clustering processing was applied for deciding the center of the hue values of each color. Three different physical locations were selected for comparing the difference of hue values by k-means clustering. The experimental locations were, a place far from a window, a place at mid-distance from the window and a place near to the window, as shown in Fig.3. The experimental conditions such as room light, sun light from the window and background are summarized in Table 1. A Web camera (Logicool HD Pro Webcam C910, 5 million pixels, 30 frames/s) was used in this experiment. The camera was mounted on the notebook PC as shown in Fig.3 and the distance between hand and camera was set to about 50 cm.

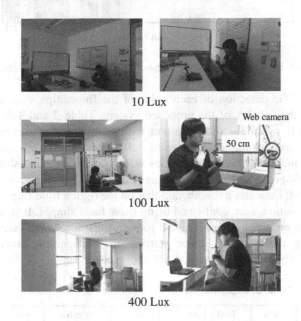

10 Lux

Web camera

50 cm

100 Lux

400 Lux

Fig. 3. Experimental environments for color clustering

Table 1. Experimental conditions for color clustering

Illumination	Position of room light	Influence of sunlight	Background
10 Lux	Only overhead light turned on. All others off	Small	White board
100 Lux	Overhead	Small	Wall
400 Lux	All lights turned off	Large	None

The hue value ranges for each color obtained is shown in Fig. 4. The centers of gravity of each color were obtained by k-means clustering. The hue value ranges for each color were investigated under several illumination conditions in advance. This method of using color calibration can lead to a decrease in color detection error.

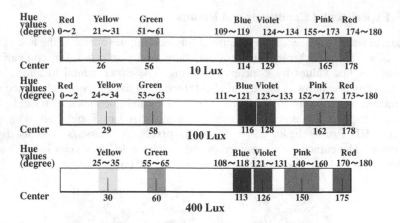

Fig. 4. Example of hue value threshold pattern for color detection

Experiments of the detection of each color of the finger tips were carried out in order to confirm the validity of the proposed system. Table 2 and Table 3 show the experimental results without calibration and with calibration, respectively. In these experiments the cases examined were with "all fingers invisible" and "all fingers visible", and the number of acquired frames was 100. In the hand shape column, 0 means a folded finger, invisible, and 1 means an extended finger, visible, and the character on the left indicates a thumb, and that on the right a little finger. The success ratios of color detection were confirmed using these hand shapes. It was verified that the color calibration we proposed gives good results for color detection. It was decided to apply this scheme before starting the recognition process, as color calibration to absorb differences in the illumination conditions.

Table 2. Experimental results without color calibration

Illumination	Hand shape	Total frames	Success frames	Error frames	Detection success ratio	Average detection success ratio
10 Lux	00000	100	41	59	41%	64.0%
	11111	100	87	13	87%	
100 Lux	00000	100	71	29	71%	85.5%
	11111	100	100	0	100%	
400 Lux	00000	100	100	0	100%	88.5%
	11111	100	77	23	77%	

Table 3. Experimental results with color calibration

Illumination	Hand shape	Total frames	Success frames	Error frames	Detection success ratio	Average detection success ratio
10 Lux	00000	100	100	0	100%	99.5%
	11111	100	99	1	99%	
100 Lux	00000	100	100	0	100%	93.5%
	11111	100	87	13	87%	
400 Lux	00000	100	100	0	100%	99.5%
	11111	100	99	1	99%	

4   Frames Used for Recognition Process and Majority Decisions

4.1   Duration of Each Hand Shape Formation

The hand shape recognition is carried out after color calibration, which involves a clustering process, as described in the previous section.   The hand shape to be recognized is a static shape, not moving.   We must separate each hand shape in time from the one before and the one after.

We use the hand shape with all fingers folded, namely "rock" (as in paper-rock-scissors) to indicate the end of each hand shape. In this shape, no finger color can be found in the camera image, except for the blue painted wrist band.   Figure 5 shows an example of movement of the center of gravity of the colored regions on the fingers. Value 0 means no movement, which means the hand shape has returned to the "rock" shape after forming a hand shape. The authors regard the time span from one 0 value, that is, "rock" shape to the next stable 0 value as the hand shape formation span.   The shaded areas indicate no color detection.   This sometimes occurs for a short period as indicated in Fig.5.   We decided to neglect such short periods, so this region is not considered as a "rock" shape indicating the end of a shape formation.   Lack of color detection for more than 5 successive frames (frame rate : 30 fps), namely about 0.17s, is interpreted as the end of a shape.

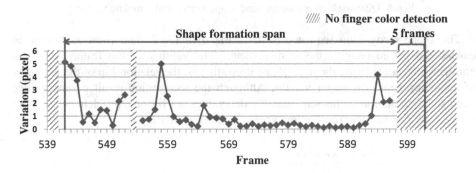

Fig. 5. Movement of center of gravity of colored regions on fingers

4.2   Shape Recognition Sequence and Majority Decisions

Figure 6 shows the distance between the target hand shape and templates vectors in the shape formation span.   The templates are prepared in advance.   The target hand shape vector to be recognized is created by a camera image, and the distance is calculated from each template, each template corresponding to a different hand shape. The number of the templates is 31 in this experiment.   The frame rate is about 30fps.

The distance is not constant as shown in this figure due to finger motion.   In this example, it is verified that the effect of finger motion and lack of color detection occurred were found in the left section. These errors affect the distances and could lead to recognition error if only one frame were used for the recognition process.

Therefore we apply a majority decision based on all the recognition results obtained using the frames for recognition, which are the frames in the second half of the shape formation span. This is expected to lead to an enhancement in recognition performance.

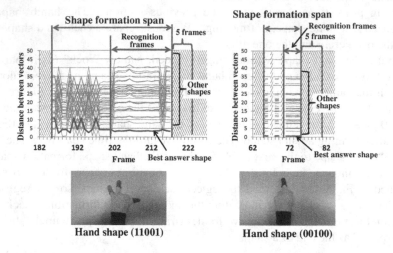

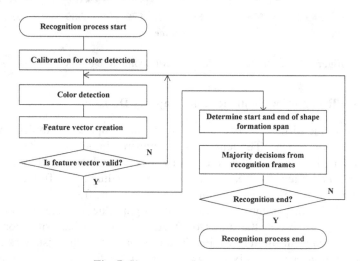

Fig. 6. Distance between target hand shape vector and template vectors

The shape recognition sequence is summarized in Fig.7. The color calibration is carried out before creating the feature vector. The validity of the feature vector is confirmed by considering the hand shape itself, that is, the relationship of the positions of each finger and the finger lengths. Although the recognition result is output after hand shape formation in this sequence, the delay does not become problem because the image capturing rate and recognition process are sufficiently rapid.

Fig. 7. Shape recognition sequence

5   Experiments and Evaluation

Five illumination environments were used in this experiment. The experimental conditions are summarized in Table 4. The camera used in this experiment was the same as in section 3.2. In this experiment, three cases are considered in a nominal illumination environment of about 100 Lux to confirm the effect of a difference in background scenery in addition to the difference in brightness. The distance between hand and camera was set to about 50 cm. Both right and left hand shapes were simultaneously evaluated to take practical usage into account. 15 typical hand shapes were formed sequentially, and this sequence was repeated 10 times, so the total number of test shapes was 150.

Table 4. Experimental conditions for evaluating recognition performance

	Illumination	Position of room light	Influence of sunlight	Background
Condition1		Overhead	Small	White board
Condition2	100 Lux	Right slanting, Left slanting	Small	Bookshelf
Condition3		All lights turned off	Medium	None
Condition4	10 Lux	Only overhead light turned on. All others off	Small	Wall
Condition5	400 Lux	All lights turned off	Large	None

Two methods were applied for this experiment and the results compared.   In one method, only the one frame in the center of the recognition span was used, and in the other a majority decision was made, based on all the recognition results for recognition frames which were the latter half of the shape formation span. Table 5 and Table 6 show the experimental recognition results. The experiment demonstrated that use of a majority decision improved the recognition accuracy under low illumination conditions.

It has been verified that the proposed method of using color calibration by a clustering scheme and a voting method, based on a majority decision of the recognition results from each frames are effective in ensuring a high performance in hand shape recognition. The cause of the small number of failures (2%) with majority voting method is due to the color detection error, that is, lack of color detection. These success ratios from 98% to 100% seem to be sufficient considering the application of intention transmission in daily life.

Table 5. Recognition experiment results without majority voting method

	Number Shapes	Right hand			Left hand		
		Success frames	Failure frames	Success ratio	Success frames	Failure frames	Success ratio
Condition1	150	135	15	90.0%	140	10	93.3%
Condition2	150	142	8	94.7%	143	7	95.3%
Condition3	150	147	3	98.0%	150	0	100.0%
Condition4	150	132	18	88.0%	137	13	91.3%
Condition5	150	147	3	98.0%	143	7	95.3%

Table 6. Recognition experiment results with majority voting method

	Number	Right hand			Left hand		
	Shapes	Success frames	Failure frames	Success ratio	Success frames	Failure frames	Success ratio
Condition1	150	147	3	98.0%	149	1	99.3%
Condition2	150	150	0	100.0%	150	0	100.0%
Condition3	150	150	0	100.0%	150	0	100.0%
Condition4	150	149	1	99.3%	147	3	98.0%
Condition5	150	150	0	100.0%	150	0	100.0%

6   Conclusion

This paper presents a hand shape recognition method using colored gloves which takes into account the surrounding environment. Two methods are proposed to realize a high recognition performance under different environmental conditions. The hue value regions are decided based on a k-means clustering result, for accurate color detection. The duration or span of each hand shape formation is introduced and the use of a majority decision based on recognition results from recognition frames, which are those in the second half of the hand formation period, is proposed as a way to raise the recognition success ratio. Evaluation tests were carried out for different five cases. It was verified that the recognition success ratio for hand shape recognition can achieve 98% to 100% and the proposed methods are viable as means to improve recognition performance.

References

1. Khan, Z.R., Ibraheem, A.N.: Comparative Study of Hand Gesture Recognition System. In: Proc. of International Conference of Advanced Computer Science & Information Technology in Computer Science & Information Technology (CS & IT), vol. 2(3), pp. 203–213 (2012)
2. Baatar, B., Tanaka, J.: Comparing Sensor Based and Vision Based Techniques for Dynamic Gesture Recognition. In: The 10th Asia Pacific Conference on Computer Human Interaction, APCHI 2012, Poster 2P-21 (2012)
3. Matsuda, Y., Sakuma, I., Jimbo, Y., Kobayashi, E., Arafune, T., Isomura, T.: Development of Finger Braille Recognition System. Journal of Biometrical Science and Engineering 5(1), 54–65 (2010)
4. Yoruk, E., Konukoglu, E., Sankur, B., Darbon, J.: Shape - Based Hand Recognition. IEEE Transactions on Image Processing 15(7), 1803–1815 (2006)
5. Suzuki, I., Nishimura, Y., Horiuchi, Y., Kuroiwa, S.: Sign Language Recognition from Video Using Particle Filter and Hidden Markov Model. IEICE Technical Report 110(384), 25–30 (2011) (Japanese)
6. Tanibata, N., Shimada, N., Shirai, Y.: Extraction of Hand Features for Recognition of Sign Language Words. In: Proc. of Int. Conference on Vision Interface, pp. 391–398 (2002)
7. Wang, Y.R., Popović, J.: Real-Time Hand-Tracking with a Color Glove. ACM Transactions on Graphics (TOG) 28(3), Article No. 63 (2009)
8. Sugaya, T., Suzuki, T., Nishimura, H., Tanaka, H.: Basic Investigation into Hand Shape Recognition Using Colored Gloves Taking Account of the Peripheral Environment. In: Yamamoto, S. (ed.) HIMI/HCII 2013, Part I. LNCS, vol. 8016, pp. 133–142. Springer, Heidelberg (2013)

Analyzing Structure of Multiparty Interaction: Group Size Effect in Story-Retelling Task

Noriko Suzuki[1], Mamiko Sakata[2], and Noriko Ito[2]

[1] Tezukayama University, Japan
[2] Doshisha University, Japan
7-1-1 Tezukayama, Nara-city, Nara, 631-8501 Japan
nsuzuki@tezukayama-u.ac.jp

Abstract. This paper examines the differences in verbal and nonverbal behaviors between different group sizes, specifically two-party and three-party interactions. An experiment was conducted using a story-retelling task. The interaction data were recorded with a video camera. Speech, gaze, and gesture data in both group sizes were analyzed. The results suggest that participants in three-party interaction change speakers more frequently by turning their gaze to each other than do those in two-party interaction.

Keywords: group size effect, multiparty interaction, verbal and non-verbal behavior, story-retelling task.

1 Introduction

In our daily life, we have many chances to collaborate face-to-face with each other in different group sizes, from two individuals to parties of ten or more individuals. The participants coordinate with each other through their behaviors during interaction. How does the difference in group size affect their verbal and nonverbal behaviors?

Conventional studies on conversational analysis have mostly focused on two-party face-to-face interaction for developing human-computer interaction system. Previous research on gesture has also analyzed conversations of a single speaker [1, 2] or two speakers [3]. However, our daily activities involve not only two participants but also larger groups. The latter type of activity is called multiparty interaction.

This paper investigates the nature of multiparty interaction in comparison with that of two-party interaction by using a quantitative approach. Few studies have compared the nature of interaction between two-party and multiparty interaction, although the work of Ishizaki [4] and Anderson [5] have indicated a difference in verbal behavior. On the other hand, there has been little focus on the effect of group size on nonverbal behaviors.

In the present task, speakers jointly retell to a listener the story from a short movie they just finished watching. We call this "the story-retelling task," and it's a kind of narrative interaction task. In this task, we prepared a short movie

S. Yamamoto (Ed.): HIMI 2014, Part I, LNCS 8521, pp. 261–270, 2014.
© Springer International Publishing Switzerland 2014

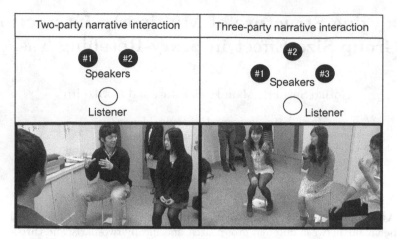

Fig. 1. Experimental settings in story-retelling task: two-party (left) and three-party interaction (right)

entitled "TSUMIKI NO IE (La maison en petits cubes)" [6] as the stimulus for speakers. This movie consists of dialog-free scenes. Neither characters nor objects in this short movie move very much.

In this experiment, we prepared two group sizes for speakers: two-party and three-party groups (Fig 1). Verbal and nonverbal behaviors of the speakers were video-recorded and analyzed. This paper presents the differences in verbal and nonverbal behaviors between the two group sizes. To this end, the contributions of speech and gaze were analyzed in the process of carrying out the story-retelling task.

2   Method

2.1   Participants

Twenty-three undergraduate students from 20 to 22 years old took part in the experiment as participants. They were divided into five groups consisting of three participants and four groups consisting of two participants. Table 1 shows the composition of each group in detail, where, in addition to a breakdown by gender, "H" means the participant felt familiar with the other or others when they talked to a teammate before the task. On the other hand, "L" means she did not feel such familiarity, since she did not previously talk to the other participant(s), or in other words, they were just on "nodding" terms with each other; "M" in this column means that the participant felt familiar with one member but not with the other.

2.2   Story-Retelling Task

The task used in this experiment was the story-retelling task. It requires just two steps: (i) two or three people together watch a short movie as stimulus for the

Table 1. Participants and groups

ID	Group size	Gender	Familiarity
		M	L
G1	3	F	L
		F	L
		M	L
G2	3	F	L
		F	L
		F	H
G3	3	F	H
		M	H
		F	L
G4	3	F	H
		F	M
		F	L
G5	3	F	L
		F	L
G6	2	F	H
		F	H
G7	2	M	L
		F	L
G8	2	F	H
		M	H
G9	2	F	L
		M	L

F: Female, M: Male; H: High, L: Low, M: H+L

story, and (ii) they jointly retell the detailed contents of the movie to a listener who has not watched it.

We chose a listener who was unfamiliar with the people retelling the story. He was asked to remain quiet while listening to the story and just nod without asking any question. Furthermore, he was called to the lab just after the other people watched the movie.

In this experiment, we used a DVD entitled "TSUMIKI NO IE (La maison en petits cubes)" [6]. Neither characters nor objects move very much in this 12-minute movie. Related studies of analyzing human behaviors in narrative interaction employed similar tasks and cartoons as stimulus [1–3].

In such studies, the storylines of cartoons are also explained through the cuts in action and the motions of the characters, without using any speech. From these stimuli, participants must express to each other spontaneous verbal and nonverbal behaviors in the course of their narration. In other words, they must narrate the storyline of the cartoon in their own words and gestures in collaboration with other participants. Accordingly, among the participants the story-retelling task has a convergent rather than a divergent tendency.

2.3   Procedure

First, two experimenters instructed the participants on the aim of the story-retelling task. This aim is to analyze the mechanism of human behavior as they narrate from memory the story of a short cartoon to a listener right after watching it. Second, participants were asked about their familiarity with the other members of their group. Then, the participants watched the movie on a 50-inch plasma display in front of them. Just after the participants watched the movie, the experimenters called a listener to the lab. The experimenters asked the participants to immediately retell the story of the stimulus from memory to the listener, in as much detail as possible according to the storyline.

During the retelling of the story, we recorded the participants' performances with a video camera. The participants finished their narration with the expression *"Korede owaridesu (That's all)"* when they agreed that they had finished explaining the entire storyline.

After the story-retelling task, speakers answered the Affective Communication Test (ACT) in Japan, which is used for measurement of nonverbal emotional expressiveness [7], as a post-experiment questionnaire.

2.4   Coding

We analyzed the speech, gaze and gesture units of each participant. All participants coded each unit using the annotation software ELAN [8].

Speech: A speech unit in cooperative work is the duration of a single participant's speech bounded by pauses. The speech units were divided into three categories: turn; speech filler, including 'um' and 'ah'; and back-channel responses, including 'yeah' and 'that's right.' However, these units do not include laughing, coughs and breathing sounds.

Gaze: The directions of the participants' gazes are estimated from the direction of the eye's dark region of the pupil and iris. The gaze units were divided into three categories by gaze direction: other group members; the listener; and other directions.

Gesture: The gestures of the participants were labeled from their motion. The gesture units were also divided into three types: representational gestures; self-adapter gestures; and nodding.

Total time: The overall duration of a narrative interaction, total time, was defined by its start and end times as follows. Start time is when one of the speakers starts to talk, i.e., the beginning of the first speech; end time is when one of the speakers finishes talking, i.e., the end of the last speech.

2.5   Predictions

The participants in the larger group size, the three-party interaction, are predicted to communicate more actively with one another, as a result of their increased behaviors of mutual concern, than those in a smaller group. Furthermore, they are expected to express the following verbal and nonverbal behaviors in the story-retelling task:

(a) The participants in three-party interaction take turns more frequently than the participants in two-party interaction.
(b) The participants in three-party interaction look at one another more often than the participants in two-party interaction.

3 Results

3.1 Verbal and Nonverbal Behaviors

Tables 2 and 3 show the results of annotation for verbal and nonverbal behaviors, including the score of the Affective Communication Test (ACT) in Japan [7].

In table 2, *SP ratio* means the ratio of speaking per minute. *NUM of turn* means the number of turns within the interaction duration. *Turn DUR* means speech duration per turn (sec). *BCR* means the duration of back channel response per minute (sec). *FIL* means the duration of speech filler per minute (sec). *SP-LTC* means the speech latency between two utterances per minute (sec). *SP-OVP* means the speech overlap duration between two utterances per minute (sec). *FRQ-SP-OVP* means the number of speech overlaps per minute.

In table 3, *GZ-OTR* means the occurrence ratio of gaze to other group members per interaction duration. *GZ-LSNR* means the occurrence ratio of gaze to the listener. *MG* means the duration of mutual gaze per minute (sec). *FRQ-MG* means the frequency of mutual gaze per minute. *R-GST* means the occurrence ratio of representational gestures per interaction duration. *S-ADP* means the occurrence ratio of self-adapter gestures per interaction duration. *NOD* means the frequency of nodding per minute. *ACT* means the score of the affective communication test (ACT) in Japan of each participant.

3.2 Group-Size Effect

Figures 2 – 4 show the results for the group size effect. Regarding the difference in the number of turns between three-party and two-party interactions, a U test shows a significant difference ($p = 0.016$) (Fig. 2). For the difference in speech duration per turn, the U test also shows a significant difference ($p = 0.047$) (Fig. 3). Again, the U test found a significant difference ($p = 0.016$) in the occurrence ratio of gaze to other group members per interaction duration (Fig. 4). These results suggest that the participants in three-party interaction change more frequently with shorter turns while giving a look to other members than do

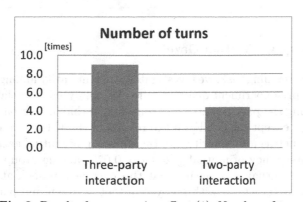

Fig. 2. Results for group size effect (1): Number of turns

Table 2. Results of verbal behaviors

ID	Gender	Seat	Total time	Familiarity	SP ratio	Num of turn	Verbal hebaviors					
							Turn DUR	BCR	FIL	SP-LTC	SP-OVP	FRQ-SP-OVP
G1	M	C1	185.4	L	0.322	4	14.937	0.000	3.660	4.164	5.115	4.207
G1	F	C2	185.4	L	0.473	11	7.979	0.971	1.294	4.164	9.449	7.443
G1	F	C3	185.4	L	0.277	6	8.558	0.324	0.324	4.164	6.328	6.149
G2	M	C1	181.0	L	0.175	15	2.113	4.310	0.663	0.163	8.275	12.267
G2	F	C2	181.0	L	0.672	11	11.064	2.321	3.647	0.163	8.574	11.604
G2	F	C3	181.0	L	0.289	12	4.358	2.652	0.332	0.163	9.311	11.272
G3	F	C1	187.0	H	0.531	9	11.036	0.642	7.059	11.309	2.695	4.813
G3	F	C2	187.0	H	0.010	5	0.380	1.604	0.000	11.309	0.887	2.246
G3	M	C3	187.0	H	0.431	16	5.035	2.888	4.171	11.309	3.088	4.813
G4	F	C1	265.0	L	0.367	4	24.310	2.717	0.679	0.634	2.780	2.491
G4	F	C2	265.0	H	0.583	5	30.894	0.906	2.038	0.634	4.181	4.755
G4	F	C3	265.0	M	0.034	2	4.509	2.038	0.000	0.634	1.761	3.396
G5	F	C1	230.0	L	0.272	10	6.260	2.089	0.552	3.022	0.357	1.304
G5	F	C2	230.0	L	0.253	19	3.063	0.048	0.004	3.022	0.321	1.565
G5	F	C3	230.0	L	0.223	6	8.558	1.828	1.567	3.022	0.162	0.783
G6	F	C1	234.0	H	0.159	4	9.325	2.500	1.500	2.436	3.088	4.615
G6	F	C2	234.0	H	0.829	4	48.500	1.250	2.500	2.436	3.088	4.615
G7	M	C1	298.0	L	0.571	5	34.029	0.201	2.215	1.100	6.220	4.631
G7	F	C2	298.0	L	0.464	4	34.533	4.228	3.423	1.100	6.220	4.631
G8	F	C1	238.7	H	0.910	2	108.646	1.006	5.530	5.110	3.610	1.257
G8	M	C2	238.7	H	0.075	7	2.558	8.296	0.000	5.110	3.610	1.257
G9	F	C1	129.9	L	0.224	4	7.285	0.000	1.385	6.963	1.649	2.771
G9	M	C2	129.9	L	0.519	5	13.488	0.000	0.924	6.963	1.649	2.771

Table 3. Results of nonverbal behaviors and ACT

ID	Gender	Seat	Total time	Familiarity	nonverbal hebaviors							ACT
					GZ-OTR	GZ-LSNR	MG	FRQ-MG	R-GST	S-ADP	NOD	
G1	M	C1	185.4	L	0.036	0.777	0.267	0.647	0.131	0.000	0.000	61
G1	F	C2	185.4	L	0.085	0.169	0.945	1.942	0.152	0.175	6.796	88
G1	F	C3	185.4	L	0.155	0.214	0.678	1.294	0.184	0.310	0.647	54
G2	M	C1	181.0	L	0.228	0.099	7.192	5.305	0.149	0.000	3.315	75
G2	F	C2	181.0	L	0.154	0.092	4.214	3.978	0.358	0.034	4.973	64
G2	F	C3	181.0	L	0.314	0.121	6.636	5.068	0.114	0.044	5.968	56
G3	F	C1	187.0	H	0.299	0.206	7.697	10.909	0.302	0.044	1.925	68
G3	F	C2	187.0	H	0.085	0.146	4.588	6.417	0.014	0.066	4.813	60
G3	M	C3	187.0	H	0.205	0.077	8.576	10.267	0.321	0.127	2.888	79
G4	F	C1	265.0	L	0.093	0.167	2.059	3.170	0.367	0.032	7.925	72
G4	F	C2	265.0	H	0.095	0.498	2.138	3.396	0.418	0.012	6.566	81
G4	F	C3	265.0	M	0.084	0.373	0.805	1.585	0.000	0.016	4.075	66
G5	F	C1	230.0	L	0.526	0.278	0.000	0.000	0.144	0.113	1.826	81
G5	F	C2	230.0	L	0.409	0.387	0.000	0.000	0.050	0.015	4.696	37
G5	F	C3	230.0	L	0.348	0.439	0.000	0.000	0.328	0.012	1.043	57
G6	F	C1	234.0	H	0.203	0.485	3.462	3.846	0.039	0.056	8.205	69
G6	F	C2	234.0	H	0.107	0.154	3.462	3.846	0.415	0.115	2.308	63
G7	M	C1	298.0	L	0.019	0.080	0.394	1.007	0.239	0.245	3.624	75
G7	F	C2	298.0	L	0.125	0.187	0.394	1.007	0.239	0.076	6.644	72
G8	F	C1	238.7	H	0.074	0.251	0.595	1.006	0.449	0.110	2.011	83
G8	M	C2	238.7	H	0.013	0.946	0.595	1.006	0.005	0.009	7.541	55
G9	F	C1	129.9	L	0.048	0.350	1.397	1.385	0.238	0.000	2.771	52
G9	M	C2	129.9	L	0.051	0.408	1.397	1.385	0.178	0.041	1.385	51

the participants in two-party interaction. Therefore, our predictions were partly supported.

3.3 Familiarity vs. Mutual Gaze

Before the story-retelling task, we investigated the familiarity among group members through a pre-experiment questionnaire. We analyzed the relation between familiarity among the participants of a group and verbal/nonverbal behaviors of the participants, except for $G4$. From the results of the U test, we found significant tendencies between familiarity and the duration of mutual gaze ($p = 0.050$) as well as the frequency of mutual gaze ($p = 0.070$) among group members. In this experiment, mutual gaze means that the participants look at one another during narrative interaction, with no eye contact between any participant and the listener. Figure 5 shows the relation between familiarity and the duration

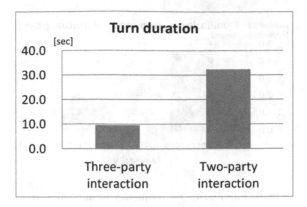

Fig. 3. Results for group size effect (2): Turn duration

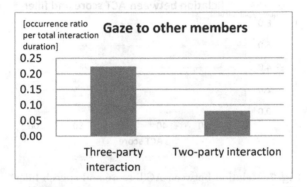

Fig. 4. Results of group size effect (3): Gaze to other group members

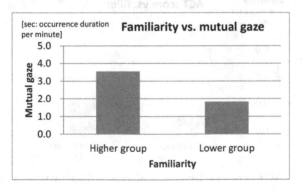

Fig. 5. Familiarity vs. mutual gaze

of mutual gaze per minute (sec), and Fig. 6 shows the relation between familiarity and the frequency of mutual gaze per minute. These results suggest that the participants with higher familiarity looked at each other much more than did the participants with lower familiarity. In other words, the participants with

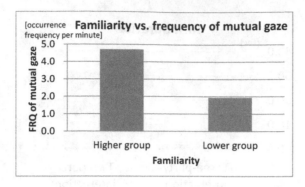

Fig. 6. Familiarity vs. frequency of mutual gaze

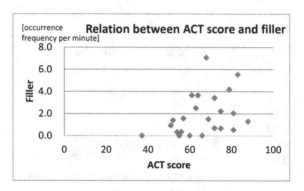

Fig. 7. Relation between ACT score and speech filler

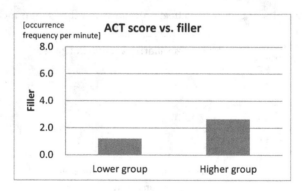

Fig. 8. ACT score vs. frequency of speech filler by score group

lower familiarity did not make nearly as much eye contact as the participants with higher familiarity.

3.4 ACT Score vs. Speech Filler

After the story-retelling task, we investigated the results of the Affective Communication Task (ACT) in Japan [7]. Originally, ACT was developed to explore nonverbal emotional expressiveness in the U.S.A [9]. It is clearly positively related to acting ability and to receiving nonverbal messages. Simply put, an ACT score is suggestive of a person's nonverbal communication skills. We use the ACT in Japan, which is an adaptation of the U.S.A version for Japanese subjects. Here, the participants used a 9-point scale to respond to 13 statements, such as "when I hear good dance music, I can hardly keep still" and "my laugh is soft and subdued." The ACT score thus highlights the nonverbal communication skills of a person.

We analyzed the relation between the ACT scores of participants and their verbal/nonverbal behaviors. We found positive correlation between the ACT score and speech filler per minute (Fig. 7). We next compared the results of two groups of participants, one scoring higher and the other lower on ACT based on the median score, for the relation between ACT score and the frequency of using speech filler per minute (Fig. 8). These results suggest that the participants with higher skills of nonverbal, emotional expressiveness tend to produce speech filler during interaction because they try to continue talking to a listener.

Unfortunately, there is no significant difference either between the ACT score and group size or between the ACT score and other verbal and nonverbal behaviors, including gaze to other participants or the listener.

4   Conclusions

This paper investigates the nature of multiparty interaction in comparison with those of two-party interaction by using a quantitative approach. Nine groups participated in the story-retelling task. Five groups consisted of three persons and the other four groups consisted of two persons. We video-recorded and analyzed their verbal and nonverbal behaviors during narrative interaction. We also investigated their familiarity among group members and the affective communication score (ACT) [7]recorded before and after the task. The results suggest that there might be a group size effect. The participants in three-party narrative interaction might change more frequently with shorter turns while giving a look to other members than do the participants in two-party interaction. In other words, the difference in group size might affect the collaborative strategy in the story-retelling task. The results also suggest that the participants with higher familiarity look at each other much more than the participants with lower familiarity. The familiarity among group members might affect their gaze interaction in the task. From the results of the affective communication test (ACT) in Japan [7], the participants with higher ACT scores might produce speech filler much more than do the participants with lower ACT scores. The higher skills of nonverbal, emotional expressiveness seemed to affect the speech interaction in the task.

As our future work, we will carry out qualitative analysis as well as quantitative analysis. Furthermore, we will conduct the same story-retelling task while using both a greater number of participants and more groups.

Acknowledgments. The authors thank all of the students in the class assigned to analyze multimodal interaction: Hisashi Fujita, Miho Harada, Ami Hattori, Naoya Hirata, Naoko Ieshiro, Mari Igei, Reia Kadono, Takayuki Kadota, Chikara Kando, Yuya Kouzuki, Hirona Kuwata, Rina Matsuura, Rina Mitsukawa, Nozomi Miyazaki, Yoshitaka Miyazaki, Kana Ogawa, Naho Oguri, Misao Shibata, Eikei Shu, Miho Takesue, Ai Tatsutomi, Hinata Uehama, and Kaori Yamagami. This work was partly supported by a fund from the Grant-in-Aid for JSPS Fellows (Grant No. 24·40261).

References

1. McNeill, D.: Hand and mind. The University of Chicago Press, Chicago (1992)
2. Kita, S., Ozyurek, A.: What does cross-linguistic variation in semantic coordination of speech and gesture reveal?: Evidence for an interface representation of spatial thinking and speaking. Journal of Memory and Language 48, 16–32 (2003)
3. Okada, S., Bono, M., Takanashi, K., Sumi, Y., Nitta, K.: Context-based conversational hand gesture classification in narrative interaction. In: Proceedings of ICMI 2013, pp. 303–310 (2013)
4. Ishizaki, M., Kato, T.: Exploring the characteristics of multi-party dialogues. In: Proceedings of the 17th International Conference on Computational Linguistics, pp. 583–589 (1998)
5. Anderson, A., Mullin, J., Katsavras, E., McEwan, R., Grattan, E., Brundell, P., O'Malley, C.: Multi-mediating multi-party interactions. In: Proceedings of INTERACT 1999, pp. 313–330 (1999)
6. Kato, K.: Tsumiki no ie (La maison en petits cubes). Robot Communications Inc. (2008)
7. Daibo, I.: Measurement of nonverbal expressivness: construction of the affective communication test (act) in japan. Bulletin of Faculty of Literature in Hokusei Gakuen University 28, 1–12 (1990) (in Japanese)
8. ELAN4.5.2 (2013), http://tla.mpi.nl/tools/tla-tools/elan/
9. Friedman, H., Prince, L., Riggio, R., DiMatteo, M.: Understanding and assessing nonverbal expressiveness: the affective communicaiton test. Journal of Personality and Social Psychology 39, 333–351 (1983)

Information Coding by Means
of Adaptive Controlling Torques

Johann Winterholler, Julian Böhle, Krzysztof Chmara, and Thomas Maier

Institute for Engineering Design and Industrial Design, Research and Teaching Department
Industrial Design Engineering, University of Stuttgart, Stuttgart, Germany
{johann.winterholler,thomas.maier}@iktd.uni-stuttgart.de

Abstract. The investigated approach shows that the currently rarely used haptic perception channel can systematically be applied for information transfer. The encoding of information by variable controlling torques and the haptic transmission of information to the user via a central control element can lead to a reduction of visual distraction and cognitive stress in difficult tasks. Furthermore, this approach allows innovative interfaces so that the usability of products can be improved and the operational safety can be increased.

Keywords: haptic, information coding, adaptive control element, adaptive controlling torque, haptic display, human-machine interaction.

1   Introduction

Due to the technical progress, an increase of functions and associated to this, a growth of control elements and audiovisual displays can be noticed [1]. This leads on the one hand to an increased complexity of usability and on the other hand to an overload of the human perception channel. Especially the visual perception channel is overloaded which might lead to operating errors.

An adaptive control element is an approach to substitute single control elements. According to Petrov an adaptive control element is characterized by its ability to vary and adapt its gestalt (structure, shape) depending on the context of the human-machine interaction [2, 3]. Combined with a haptic feedback, such a control element can be adapted to different situations, users or tasks. It can be especially used to transfer information by the haptic perception channel so that the visual channel of the user is being relieved in situations of complex information input. The aim of this research is to investigate how this haptic feedback should be designed.

2   Basics

To understand the subject the definition of some basic terms like human-machine interaction, haptic display or controlling torque is necessary.

According to standard [4] a human-machine interaction is a closed control system. In this system the user gets information from the machine by perceiving and

S. Yamamoto (Ed.): HIMI 2014, Part I, LNCS 8521, pp. 271–280, 2014.
© Springer International Publishing Switzerland 2014

recognizing the information. After the user has processed the information he interacts with the machine. This interaction which is called behaviour [5] can be a statement (verbal behaviour) or a direct operation and use (visual or kinesthetic behaviour).

But how does the user perceive the information? One way is to get the information through a visual display. But there are also other ways to perceive the information, e.g., through an auditory or a haptic display [6]. While visual and auditory displays are already well studied and well known in the practice, there are hardly any concrete findings regarding haptic displays.

According to [7] a haptic display is an element that transfers information by active touching and moving and that requires the use of muscular strength. Such an element can be a control element which adapts and varies its gestalt (structure and shape) or operating force depending on the context of the human-machine interaction. Scientific findings regarding control elements which adapt and vary its gestalt can be found in the thesis of Petrov who describes design recommendations for such control elements [2]. In contrast Hampel researched the operating forces of rotary control elements [7] with the aim to use these results for control elements which adapt and vary its operating force. For example, he researched the control torque of rotary control elements regarding to the comfort range, the positioning accuracy and the perception of differences [7].

Operating forces of rotary control elements can be classified into the type of entry. For example there are a mono-stable, a continuous and a discrete value input. The difference between them is the number of detents. In this paper the focus is on the discrete value input. As figure 1 shows this type of entry can be also classified, e.g., into a rising and falling saw tooth shape as well into a sinusoidal shape. The main parameters which can be varied are the amplitude and the rotary angle in each case.

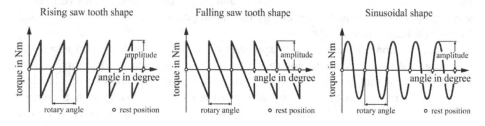

Fig. 1. Torque functions and parameters of discrete value input according to [7]

As investigations [7] and practice show [8], the falling saw tooth shape is preferred due to best comfort and precision impression which can be explained by the special characteristic of this function. The steep rising angle of the rest position ensures a high stability. In turn, this causes a high impression of comfort and operating quality. This is the reason why the following investigations were done with the falling saw tooth shape.

3   Methods

Based on the scientific findings by Hampel [7] several investigations were done to check how variable control torques must be designed for information transfer. The investigations were divided into two research studies whereby the second study was built on the first study. The number, age, and body size of the test person during the two studies are shown in Table 1.

Table 1. Number, age and body size of test person

	number [-]		age [years]		body size [cm]	
	total	relation m / f	average	standard deviation	average	standard deviation
1st study	20	10 / 10	25,7	7,0	178,1	9,2
2nd study	22	11 / 11	24,0	2,4	175,9	9,2

3.1   First Research Study

First Experiment. The first experiment of the first research study investigated the perception of linear changes of the torque amplitude and whether they can be used for haptic information transfer. Based on the falling saw tooth shape and its parameters (figure 1) different torque functions were created (figure 2).

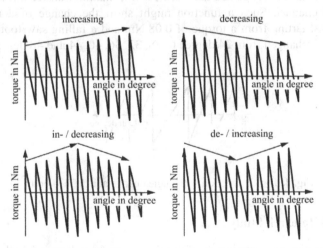

Fig. 2. Torque functions with linear increasing, decreasing and combined amplitude changes

Starting from a rotatory angle of 24 degree linear amplitude changes were installed. This resulted in functions which had an only increasing respectively decreasing or a combined (in-/decreasing respectively de-/increasing) operating character (figure 2). Related to practice these torque functions can be transferred to a passage of a menu list. A gradually increasing or decreasing torque function could be associated with the end or beginning of a list. A combined increasing and decreasing torque function might show the middle of a list through the haptic channel. Thereby, a visual control can be relieved or even omitted completely.

Second Experiment. The next experiment researched whether a single amplitude change at a defined point at the torque function can be recognized (figure 3). Such a function can be used, e.g., to display the middle of a list or a special value through the haptic perception channel. Further, it can be used during a long list to get an approximate orientation without the need of a visual control. Starting from a rotary angle of 24 degree and a torque of 0.08 Nm the torque was increased at the defined point to 0.10 Nm, 0.12 Nm and 0.15 Nm.

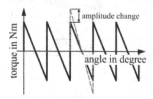

Fig. 3. Torque function with amplitude change at a defined point

Third Experiment. The last experiment investigated whether a change at the rotary angle (figure 4) can be recognized and used for information transfer through the haptic perception channel. Such a function might show the change of a menu or of grouped zones. Starting from a torque of 0.08 Nm and a falling saw tooth shape the rotary angle was changed from 24 degree to 28, 32, 36, 40, 44 and 48 degree.

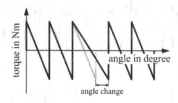

Fig. 4. Torque function with angle change at a defined point

3.2   Second Research Study

Based on the results and experiences of the first study (see chapter 4.1) the individual experiments were adjusted and detailed.

First Experiment. As the results show (see results of first experiment of the first research study) the recognition of combined amplitude changes are insufficient (figure 7). Especially the recognition of combined decreasing and increasing amplitude changes is improvable. In order to increase the recognition of such functions the gradient of the combined torque functions was adjusted and researched again.

The approach was to design the amplitude changes steplike instead of linear (compare figure 2 and figure 5).

The initial parameters were the same as in the first experiment of the first study. That means, starting from a torque of 0.08 Nm, a rotatory angle of 24 degree and a falling saw tooth shape steplike amplitude changes with a factor of 1.25 were installed. As in the first experiment of the first study functions were created which had an only increasing respectively decreasing or a combined (in-/decreasing respectively de-/increasing) operating character (figure 5).

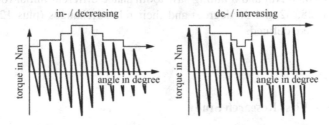

Fig. 5. Torque functions with steplike increasing, decreasing and combined amplitude changes

Second Experiment. The results of the second experiment of the first study show that users recognize – depending on the parameters – a change of the amplitude at a defined point very well (figure 8). To increase the recognition even more a detailed investigation was necessary. Therefore, based on the findings of the second experiment of the first study, further torque functions were created. The difference between them was the character of the amplitude change at the defined point (figure 6).

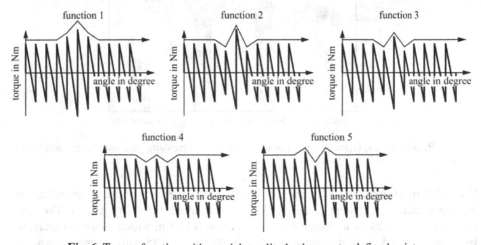

Fig. 6. Torque function with special amplitude change at a defined point

For example torque functions were installed which had at the defined point an increasing or an in-/decreasing respectively de-/increasing character. The hypothesis was that torque functions with such a special character lead to better results regarding the recognition. Starting from a rotary angle of 24 degree and a torque of 0.08 Nm the torque was increased or decreased with a factor of at most 1.5.

Third Experiment. The results of the third experiment of the first study show that changes at the rotary angle can be recognized – depending on the parameters – very well. As the results show changes from 24 degree to 36 degree or higher lead to significant recognition. Smaller changes were hardly or rarely detected. The question is whether a change of 12 degree or a change at the factor of 1.5 is deciding. Starting from a torque of 0.08 Nm and a falling saw tooth shape different initial rotary angles (12, 16, 20, 24, 28, 32 and 36 degree) and their related changes (plus 12 degree or with factor 1.5) were defined.

4   Results

4.1   Results of First Research Study

First Experiment. Figure 7 shows that an only increasing respectively decreasing amplitude change was recognized of 90 or more percent of the test persons. The recognition of combined amplitude changes is worse especially with the combined decreasing and increasing function. One reason could be the small distances during which the changes (in-/decrease) happen. That means that a haptic display for the middle of a list has to be designed by another function, e.g., by a higher torque amplitude at a defined point at the torque function.

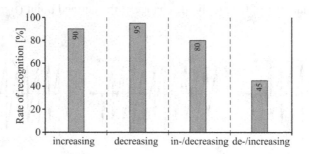

Fig. 7. Results of experiment with linear increasing, decreasing and combined amplitude changes

Second Experiment. Actually, the results show that users recognize – depending on the parameters – a change of the amplitude at a defined point (figure 8). The best results are achieved by a change from 0.08 Nm to 0.12 Nm which means an increase by a factor of 1.5. A higher increase (from 0.08 Nm to 0.15 Nm) is also recognized very well. However, such a change of the amplitude is not necessary due to the very good results of the middle change (from 0.08 Nm to 0.12 Nm). In addition, a large increase constitutes the danger that the subsequent detent will be jumped over due to the very large factor of increase.

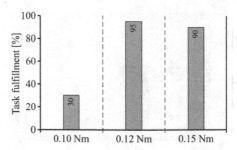

Fig. 8. Results of experiment with amplitude change at a defined point

Third Experiment. The results of the experiment with angle changes also show that such functions can be used as a haptic display (figure 9) and that they help to fulfill a task without visual control. Convincing results are achieved by changes from 24 to 36 or higher degree. The task fulfillment is 90 to 95 percent and confirmed that such functions can be used to show the change of a menu or of grouped zones. Smaller changes were hardly or rarely detected. This means that further investigations should be done with a change from 24 to 36 degree because higher changes do not achieve significant better results. The question is again whether a change of 12 degree or a change at the factor of 1.5 is deciding.

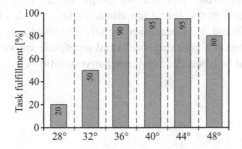

Fig. 9. Results of experiment with angle change at a defined point

Interesting is a decrease of task fulfillment at the change from 24 to 48 degree. A reason for this could be the limited slewing range of the human wrist so that the test person has to change one's grip which may lead to the lower task fulfillment.

4.2   Results of Second Research Study

First Experiment. As the results show, steplike amplitude changes do not increase the recognition of amplitude changes (compare figure 7 and figure 10). On the contrary, the results are even worse. The recognition of both, the pure increasing respectively decreasing and of the combined (in-/decreasing respectively de-/increasing) steplike functions is worse than of the linear functions.

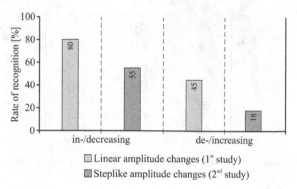

Fig. 10. Results of experiment with steplike in-/decreasing and de-/increasing amplitude changes

Second Experiment. Similar results are achieved in the second experiment of the second research study. As figure 11 shows, there are functions, e.g., number 1, 2 and 3 which the users recognize very well. But there are also functions, e.g., number 4 and 5 which can be hardly perceived by the subjects. In comparison the perception of all these functions is worse (highest value 77 percent) than the perception of the investigated function of the first study (95 percent). Interesting is the bad perception of function 4 and 5. One reason could be that the amplitude at the defined point of these functions is not higher than the initial amplitude value. And this could be the reason why the functions 1, 2 and 3 are perceived better. The amplitude at the defined point of all the three functions is higher than the initial amplitude value. This finding is very remarkable and should be researched in further investigations.

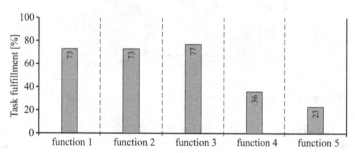

Fig. 11. Results of experiment with special amplitude change at a defined point

Third Experiment. The results of the last experiment of the second study are very interesting. The question was whether a change of 12 degree or a change at the factor of 1.5 is deciding to perceive a change in the rotary angle. As figure 12 shows, the answer depends on the initial rotary angle. For initial angles less than 24 degree the change should be 12 degree and not the factor 1.5. For initial angles bigger than 24 degree it doesn't matter whether the angle changes happen by adding 12 degree or by multiplying with the factor 1.5. The perception in both cases is nearly equal (figure 12).

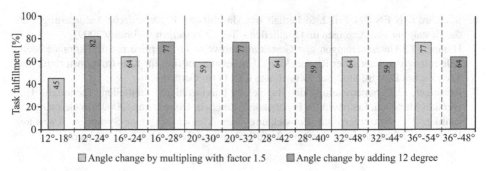

Fig. 12. Results of experiment with adjusted angle change at a defined point

5   Conclusion and Discussion

The investigated approach shows that the currently rarely used haptic perception channel [9] can systematically be applied for information transfer. For example the results show that the middle of a list or a special value can be displayed by an amplitude change at a defined point. But also other functions like linear increasing or decreasing amplitude changes or functions with angle changes at a defined point are suitable for information transfer through the haptic perception channel. The question which will be investigated next is how the functions must be in detail in order to get 100 percent recognition all the time.

Besides investigations are planned to show that the encoding of information by variable controlling torques and the haptic transmission of information to the user via a central control element lead to a reduction of visual distraction and cognitive stress in difficult tasks.

All in all, this approach allows innovative interfaces so that the usability of products can be improved and the operational safety can be increased.

References

1. Hampel, T., Maier, T.: Active rotary knobs with adaptive torque feedback - conflict of goals between positioning accuracy and difference threshold. In: 11th Stuttgart International Symposium Automotive and Engine Technology, Stuttgart, pp. 437–452 (2011)
2. Petrov, A.: Usability-Optimierung durch adaptive Bediensysteme. Universität, Institut für Konstruktionstechnik und Technisches Design, Stuttgart. Dissertation (2012) (in German)
3. Janny, B., Winterholler, J., Petrov, A., Maier, T.: Adaptive Control Elements for Navigation Systems. In: Stephanidis, C. (Hrsg.) Posters, HCII 2013, Part I. CCIS, vol. 373, pp. 473–477. Springer, Heidelberg (2013)
4. Standard DIN EN 894 Teil 1. Sicherheit von Maschinen – Ergonomische Anforderungen an die Gestaltung von Anzeigen und Stellteilen – Teil 1: Allgemeine Leitsätze für Benutzer-Interaktion mit Anzeigen und Stellteilen (January 2009)
5. Seeger, H.: Design technischer Produkte, Produktprogramme und –systeme. Industrial Design Engineering. 2. Aufl. Springer, Berlin (2005) (in German)

6. Standard DIN EN 894 Teil 2. Sicherheit von Maschinen – Ergonomische Anforderungen an die Gestaltung von Anzeigen und Stellteilen – Teil 2: Anzeigen (February 2009)
7. Hampel, T.: Untersuchungen und Gestaltungshinweise für adaptive multifunktionale Stellteile mit aktiver haptischer Rückmeldung. Universität, Institut für Konstruktionstechnik und Technisches Design, Stuttgart. Dissertation (2011) (in German)
8. Reisinger, J.: Parametrisierung der Haptik von handbetätigten Stellteilen. Technische Universität München, Lehrstuhl für Ergonomie, München. Dissertation (2009) (in German)
9. Zühlke, D.: Nutzergerechte Entwicklung von Mensch-Maschine-Systemen. Useware-Engineering für technische Systeme. 2. Aufl. Springer, Berlin (2012) (in German)

Basic Research on the Factors Influencing Perception of Texture from Images

Kimihiro Yamanaka and Kazuki Nagamura

Tokyo Metropolitan University, Tokyo, Japan
kiyamana@tmu.ac.jp, nagamura-kazuki@ed.tmu.ac.jp

Abstract. We conduct a subjective evaluation experiment by using the semantic differential method to examine the relation between the shape, color and size of an object in an image and the emergence of texture perception. The experiment consists of an evaluation survey on the perceived texture of a visual stimulus displayed on a monitor. The stimulus is a simple shape (ball, cylinder or box) created using a computer graphics application; ach shape appears in one of three colors (red, blue or green) and at one of two sizes (large or small) for a total of 18 distinct stimuli. The factors were extracted from the data by principal factor analysis, and the factor loadings were calculated by promax rotation. Furthermore, the relations between each factor and texture perception were examined through Hayashi's first quantification method, a kind of regression analysis.

The results indicated relations between each item and the sensations of smoothness, hardness and moistness, which are considered to be representative of texture perception.

Keywords: material perception "Shitsukan", semantic differential method, Hayashi's first quantification method.

1 Introduction

Research on texture perception is currently attracting considerable attention. The study of texture perception in the new academic field of brain information science incorporates the fields of engineering, psychophysics and brain physiology. This study focuses on psychophysics, with expected applications in engineering. Psychophysics explores human senses and aims to clarify the types of information perceived about objects; in texture perception research, the aim is to understand how texture perception arises from that information and to construct a stimulation system that can display simple image data to induce perception of a target texture [1].

Texture perception can be induced through various senses, such as sight (appearance), hearing (the sound produced by an object when touched) and tactile sense (the feel from touching the object). The focus on this study is sight. Taking memory color as a key concept, we focus on color perception in humans and aim to reproduce colors that match the perception characteristics of humans. According to previous research, remembered colors are recalled with increased saturation and brightness compared

S. Yamamoto (Ed.): HIMI 2014, Part I, LNCS 8521, pp. 281–288, 2014.

with the original colors [2,3]. Also, it has been suggested that remembered colors tend to remain constant over time, which alters the perception of the original color when it is encountered again. Furthermore, factors other than color, such as size and shape, are also considered to affect texture perception [4]. Although a considerable amount of research has been conducted on the influence of these factors on subjective impression, there is a lack of experimental research on the relation that these factors hold with texture perception.

In this context, we conduct a subjective evaluation experiment by using the semantic differential method to examine the relation between the shape, color and size of an object in an image and the emergence of texture perception.

2   Experimental Methods

The experimental setup is shown in Fig. 1. Participants completed a texture evaluation questionnaire about a visual stimulus displayed on a monitor or projector set up in front of a participant. The questionnaire consisted of 16 categories deemed valid for evaluating texture on the basis of research into the structure of texture evaluation [4]. Each category was ranked on a 7-point scale. The following word pairs were chosen as response categories:

(1) ugly–beautiful
(2) blunt–sharp
(3) old–new
(4) fine–coarse
(5) dull–glossy
(6) slack–tight
(7) light–heavy
(8) weak–powerful
(9) intricate–plain
(10) wet–dry
(11) moist–powdery
(12) cool–warm
(13) hard–soft
(14) airy–solid
(15) smooth–bumpy
(16) slippery–gritty.

A total of 18 different visual stimuli were prepared using a computer graphics application. The variable items for the stimuli were shape (3 categories: ball, cylinder, box) color (3 categories: red, blue, green) and size (2 categories: large, small). Fig. 2 shows the stimuli and Table 1 lists the items and categories for texture evaluation. Horizontal illuminance in front of the participant was 950 lx throughout the experiment. The 18 different stimuli were displayed in random sequence to avoid the order effect. In regard to the representation of stimulus size, stimuli were presented against a photographic background of a room, to allow for combined analysis of data obtained with different display equipment. The participants were 33 male and female university students. All participants gave consent after they were given a verbal explanation of the objectives of the experiment and the ethical issues related to the handling of data.

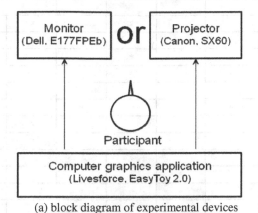

(a) block diagram of experimental devices

(b) snapshot of experimental condition

Fig. 1. Experimental setup

(a) ball-red-small   (b) box-green-large   (c) cylinder-blue-large

Fig. 2. Examples of stimuli on display

Table 1. Lists the items and categories for stimulus

stimuli	shape			color			size	
	ball	cylinder	box	red	blue	green	large	small
1	*			*			*	
2	*			*				*
3	*				*		*	
4	*				*			*
5	*					*	*	
6	*					*		*
7		*		*			*	
8		*		*				*
9		*			*		*	
10		*			*			*
11		*				*	*	
12		*				*		*
13			*	*			*	
14			*	*				*
15			*		*		*	
16			*		*			*
17			*			*	*	
18			*			*		*

3   Analysis Methods

The 18 stimulus images were evaluated on an semantic differential scale for the 16 word pairs [5]. Factor extraction by principal component analysis was performed on these evaluation data, and principal component loading was obtained by promax rotation. We used Hayashi's first quantification method [6,7] to investigate the relationship between texture and each item/category for each of the texture-related principal components found to have a high contribution ratio in the principal component loading analysis. A statistical analysis application was used.

4   Results and Discussion

Table 2 shows principal component loading and influential factors based on principal component analysis. Extraction was performed to the 5th principal component because the cumulative contribution ratio was above 60% (62.7%) up to this component. These components were given the following labels based on the characteristics of the response category included in the component:

- 1st principal component, 'light/thin' (3 items),
- 2nd principal component, 'retro' (5 items),
- 3rd principal component, 'smooth' (3 items),

Table 2. Principal component loading and influential factors

word pairs	principal component loading				
	1st principal component "light/thin"	2nd principal component "retro"	3rd principal component "smooth"	4th principal component "hard"	5th principal component "moist"
(8) weak–powerful	0.8322	0.1258	0.0917	0.0698	0.0374
(7) light–heavy	0.7977	-0.0752	-0.0291	-0.1611	-0.1021
(9) intricate–plain	-0.6374	-0.0573	-0.0120	0.0286	-0.0382
(2) blunt–sharp	-0.1565	0.5798	0.2046	-0.2423	-0.1030
(1) ugly–beautiful	-0.0207	0.5051	-0.1801	0.0314	0.1184
(6) slack–tight	0.1672	0.4901	-0.1779	0.0583	-0.0342
(5) dull–glossy	0.0469	0.4635	0.0187	0.1260	-0.0351
(3) old–new	0.0943	0.4321	-0.0122	0.2128	0.1392
(16) slippery–gritty	0.0158	-0.0663	0.6669	0.1326	0.0478
(4) fine–coarse	0.0635	-0.1985	0.6617	0.1150	0.0595
(15) smooth–bumpy	0.0254	0.1614	0.5902	-0.1965	-0.0231
(13) hard–soft	-0.0328	0.0678	0.1019	0.7852	-0.0753
(14) airy–solid	-0.0622	0.1341	0.0197	0.6958	-0.0510
(11) moist–powdery	-0.0217	0.0367	-0.0187	-0.0765	0.7120
(10) wet–dry	0.0104	-0.0015	0.1141	-0.0792	0.5544
contribution ratio (%)	19.325	14.728	11.765	9.016	7.841
cumulative contribution ratio (%)	19.325	34.053	45.819	54.835	62.676

- 4th principal component, 'hard' (2 items),
- 5th principal component, 'moist' (2 items).

We focused on the 3rd to 5th principal components, as these have the strongest association with texture.

We performed analysis by Hayashi's first quantification method to discover which items/categories could represent the feelings of smoothness, hardness, and moistness. Quantification method 1 is a method of handling qualitative data as quantitative data by converting to a dummy variable in regression analysis in cases where the independent variable is qualitative data. Tables 3 to 5 show the results of analysis for each feeling.

Table 3. Results of analysis for feeling of smoothness

item	category	quantitative data
shape	ball	**0.320**
	cylinder	**0.043**
	box	-0.362
color	red	-0.165
	blue	0.109
	green	0.057
size	large	0.072
	small	-0.072

Based on the results for 'smooth' in Table 3, the partial correlation coefficient becomes high for shape. This shows that shape makes an important contribution in embodying the feeling of smoothness. In terms of category quantities, the value was positive for ball or cylinder. This shows that balls and cylinders are appropriate for embodying the feeling of smoothness.

Table 4. Results of analysis for feeling hardness

item	category	quantitative data
shape	ball	-0.463
	cylinder	-0.057
	box	**0.520**
color	red	**0.046**
	blue	-0.294
	green	**0.248**
size	large	-9.34E-05
	small	9.34E-05

Based on the results for 'hardness' in Tables 4, the partial correlation coefficient becomes high for shape and color. It was also found that a box and the color red or green are suitable for embodying the feeling of hardness. Based on the results for 'moistness' in Tables 5, the partial correlation coefficient becomes high for color. It was also found that the color green is suitable for embodying the feeling of moistness. Size had little effect on the embodiment of any of these feelings.

Table 5. Results of analysis for feeling of moistness

item	category	quantitative data
shape	ball	-0.078
	cylinder	0.029
	box	0.049
color	red	-0.177
	blue	-0.121
	green	**0.298**
size	large	-0.089
	small	0.089

5   Conclusions

We experimentally investigated the relationship between texture components and imaging information such as color, shape and size of a visual object. The results suggested that the basic elements of image information, namely, a visual object's shape and color can influence texture components. However, this was only a preliminary study. Next we plan to investigate the precise influence of the color and shape of visual objects on the sense of texture in greater detail.

References

1. Brain and Information Science on SHITSUKAN (material perception), http://shitsukan.jp/ (access October 25, 2013)
2. Bartleson, C.J.: Memory Colors of Familiar Objects. Journal of Opticaal Society of America 50(1), 73–77 (1960)
3. Bartleson, C.J.: Color in Memory in Relation to Photographic Reproduction. Photographic Science and Engineering 5(6), 327–331 (1961)
4. Kitamura, S.: Structure of Subjective Texture. Journal of the Color Science Association of Japan 31(3), 201–205 (2007) (in Japanese)

5. Osgood, C.E.: The nature and measurement of meaning. Psychol. Bull. 49, 197–237 (1952)
6. Hayashi, C.: On the quantification of qualitative data from mathematic statistical point of view. Ann. Inst. Statistical Math. 2, 35–47 (1950)
7. Hayashi, C.: On the prediction of phenomena from qualitative data and quantification of qualitative data from the mathematic statistical point of view. Ann. Inst. Statistical Math. 3, 69–98 (1952)

Knowledge Management

KADEN Project—Towards the Construction of Model for Sharing Cognition in Manufacturing—

Takeo Ainoya

Graduate School of Art and Design, Musashino Art University, Tokyo, Japan
tacad1002@gmail.com

Abstract. One of the methods which create new ideas to secure the quality of the relationship of the product and human is to find the many participants in manufacturing and to integrate the knowledge between different fields. Therefore, in order to perform the manufacturing integrated, we aim to construct a cognitive sharing model for sharing the recognition of each other, and take advantage of the expertise of each using the shared recognition. In this paper, we propose a process that worked as project-based educational activities.

Keywords: creativity, innovation design, cognitive sharing model, design process.

1 Introduction

In order to improve the quality of home appliances in Japan, various efforts have been made currently. There is a "quality" as the part accuracy of the product. For this quality, careful consideration has been made so far in the field of quality management. Manufacturing that is hard to break, easy-to-improvement have been made by ensuring the quality. This construction-oriented manufacturing formed the basis of the manufacturing of the world. This is apparent from the fact that it was based on ISO9001. The quality of the accuracy of the performance is satisfied, products with sufficient functionality is produced. The opportunity to use in life the computer increases rapidly, rather than the traditional relationships between computer and the human being, more natural relationships are needed. Under these circumstances, it is difficult to correspond to developing a new product in the conventional idea. Therefore, manufacturing innovation through new thinking has become necessary.

IDEO is innovation consulting firm to lead the design thinking. The values of human life point of view which derive from the future are incorporated on the products and services that have been developed by IDEO. IDEO has been successful in a wide area.

Tim Brown is the president and CEO of IDEO mentions as follows: "Design thinking is a human-centered approach to innovation that draws from the designer's toolkit to integrate the needs of people, the possibilities of technology, and the requirements for business success." [1] Thus, the design of the future is essential in order to utilize the potential of the technology, to establish as a business, and to be worthwhile to

S. Yamamoto (Ed.): HIMI 2014, Part I, LNCS 8521, pp. 291–297, 2014.

human life. Therefore ideas for the innovation are required in the design process. Sugino[2] presented a model of the design process in design-driven innovation from the case analysis. This model proposed a design process for design-driven innovation that started with a finding of use of an artifact for another purpose.

The innovation thinking is required in addition the constructed type of current design process for the future of consumer electronics products in Japan. One of the methods which create new ideas to secure the quality of the relationship of the product and human is to find the many participants in manufacturing and to integrate the knowledge between different fields. Therefore, in order to perform the manufacturing integrated, we aim to construct a cognitive sharing model for sharing the recognition of each other, and take advantage of the expertise of each using the shared recognition. In this paper, we propose a process that worked as project-based educational activities.

2   KADEN Project

KADEN is an abbreviation of home appliances in Japanese. This is a so-called common name. The characteristic of this project was a project-based class of graduate school, to perform collaborative work by students of design field and engineer field, and to produce a prototype production in a short period of three months.

This project was carried out mainly in group activities, students could gain experience to come up with a good idea, and it was subjected to a membership that lets you take a niche and characteristics of people cooperating. The product was designed for the purpose rather than the design of self-expression. The education in this project was "training to learn oneself, to think, to act". This project was with the aim of fostering capacity that could be applied to own use, to create a forum to challenge the manufacturing and creative cooperative.

Students with knowledge in different fields had been taking this project. Therefore, lectures on design innovation and design thinking have been performed. The next step is to include the seeds of their own knowledge, to organize the teams. Team formation herein includes the possibility to change later. In each team, discussion about the proposed product has been made. Next chapter describes the design process to proceed in the team.

3   Design Process on KADEN Project

The seeds were conceived in early stages of the design and the process to tie the user's needs is required to achieve the products with innovation. It is possible to find the problems and use of new technologies by conceiving and conceptualizing using techniques of design thinking product ideas based on the seeds, and to achieve a product concept that links to the new value. One of the issues that arise in the design process, there is a difference in the cognitive model due to the difference in the specialized field. That is to say, problem occurs that members of another can not be recognized exactly what some members is intended because the team is composed of members with different areas of expertise. In the design process, how to express the knowledge of different disciplines, how to share the perception of each other. The method was used to prevent differences in cognitive model by visualizing at an early stage in the product image.

The main process (Fig.1) was as follows.
· Survey of proposed product
· The problem finding and analysis
· Idea, concept setting: The heavy use of scene sketches, and share images on the target product. In addition, consider the functions required for the product and users' needs.
· Prototyping: Styling sketch, consider the design requirements, dirty prototyping, real-time renderer
· Production of actual working study model

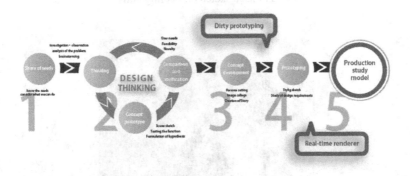

Fig. 1. KADEN Project's Design Process

4   Three Type of Cases

This report introduces the three products as a development case.

4.1   Feeling Navi

At first, "Feeling Navi" is mobile navigation with vibration. For those who get lost, there is a tendency to lose the sense of direction each time through the corner and branch point. Therefore, it is impossible to make the cognitive map, and stops in the place, it is necessary to check the map. Fig.2 shows the image sketch of "Feeling Navi". "Feeling Navi" was achieved navigation by vibration that could not rely on vision in order to always keep the sense of direction of the pedestrian. "Feeling Navi" is used around the neck. This is vibrated by bodysonic on the left, right and back side of the neck. Fig.3 shows the production study model of "Feeling Navi" and Fig.4 shows the prototype. "Feeling Navi" could be realized a navigation that do not rely on vision of seeing the map, it was considered to be useful as a navigation for people with visual impairment.

Fig. 2. Image sketch on Feeling Navi

Fig. 3. The production study model of Feeling Navi

Fig. 4. The prototype of Feeling Navi

4.2 Good Sleep Maker

The second is a "good sleep maker" pillow for a short nap in the office which is focused on the 1 / f fluctuation. This was a product that provides a nap effective environment that is proposed as a product for a comfortable break in the workplace(Fig.5).

It is known to have the effect of increasing the efficiency of work nap 15 to 30 minutes in general, and it is said that power nap.   The sense of security such as hugging organisms is obtained by the contraction and expansion in the 1 / f fluctuation on the side of the device, and it is possible to give a fragrance to give a relaxing effect.

Fig. 5. The scene of use

Fig. 6. The production study model of good sleep maker

Fig. 7. The prototype of good sleep maker

4.3   Yoriben-Narazu

The third is "Yoriben-narazu" lunch box which the contents is not biased in the slope detection.   The contents in the lunch box mess up at an angle when you carry it, the phenomenon of so-called "Yoriben" often occurs. This case paid attention to the experience which contents of lunch box got mixed and it had disappointed at eating. Fig.8 shows image sketch of "Yoriben-narazu". Then, "Yoriben-narazu" has been incorporated a mechanism to correct horizontally inside by detecting in real time the slope with an acceleration sensor. This allowed the contents of the lunch does not become messy, to realize comfortable lunch life. Fig.9 and Fig.10 show rendering and production study model.

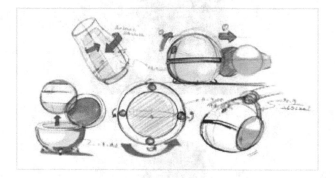

Fig. 8. Image sketch of Yoriben-narazu

Fig. 9. Real time rendering of Yoriben-narazu

Fig. 10. The production study model of Yoriben-narazu

5   Discussion

We aimed to construct a cognitive sharing model for sharing the recognition of each other, and take advantage of the expertise of each using the shared recognition in order to perform the manufacturing integrated. In this paper, we proposed a process that worked as project-based educational activities. The two characteristics of cognition in this study were the design image preceding type and Engineers thinking building type. This paper proposed the process to share the cognition of these two types. Good conflict has occurred and consciousness has been integrated by using sketch and image collage on the early stage in order to share the cognition of these two types. As a result, products with high innovation have been proposed.

Image sketch and collage are used in traditional development processes after the concept is set and design requirements are determined. However, in this development processes, image sketch and collage were used before concept was set and design requirements were determined. Therefore, it was possible to share the cognition of each other at an early stage. It was considered that concept and design requirements became apparent, then subsequent activity within the team was performed smoothly.

6   Conclusion and Future Works

In this study, it aimed to construct the shared cognitive model in order to realize the manufacturing integrated.

This report was in the education project, however, the students with different specialized fields used image sketch effectively, repeated the discussion, and were fabricated prototype to production. It was able to be a better understanding of technology and design by it, we propose the way product development collaborative.

Digital Contents EXPO is being held every year in Japan. This project was exhibited at this DC Expo and attracted the attention of the media and companies. In addition, the results of increased employment Jobs in the university were obtained.

We plan the following future issues:

- Training of entrepreneurship through business-academia collaboration project.
- Construction and use of model for sharing cognition in the design process.
- Proposal of a new idea techniques that can be continue to originate innovative products from Japan.

References

1. IDEO | A Design and Innovation Consulting Firm, http://www.ideo.com/about/
2. Sugino, M.: A Design Process for Design-Driven Innovation –Exploration of Design Process Based on the Innovation Model Proposed by Verganti. Bulletin of Japanese Society for the Science of Design 60(4), 11–20 (2013)

Enhancing Interdisciplinary Cooperation by Social Platforms

Assessing the Usefulness of Bibliometric Social Network Visualization in Large-Scale Research Clusters

André Calero Valdez[1], Anne Kathrin Schaar[1],
Martina Ziefle[1], and Andreas Holzinger[2]

[1] Human-Computer Interaction Center, Campus Boulevard 57,
RWTH Aachen University, Germany
{calero-valdez,schaar,ziefle}@comm.rwth-aachen.de
[2] Institute for Medical Informatics, Statistics and Documentation,
Medical University Graz, Austria
andreas.holzinger@medunigraz.at

Abstract. In large-scale research projects active management of the cooperation process is necessary, e.g. to ensure systematic transfer of knowledge, alignment of research goals, or appropriate dissemination of research efforts. In a large scale research-cluster at the RWTH Aachen University a cybernetic management approach is applied. As a planned measure, publishing efforts (i.e. bibliometric data) will be visualized on a social software platform accessible by researchers and the steering committee. But do researchers agree with the chosen style of visualization of their publications? As part of a user centered design, this paper presents the results of an interview study with researchers (n=22) addressing the usefulness and applicability of this approach. As central findings arguments for using the publication visualization are identified such as enabling *retrospective analysis*, acquiring *new information* about the team, improvement in dissemination *planning*, but at the same time contrasted by arguments against this approach, such as *missing information*, a possibly *negative influence on workflow* of researchers, and the *bad legibility* of the visualization. Additionally requirements and suggested improvements are presented.

Keywords: Data visualization, technology acceptance, bibliometrics, user centred-design, information systems.

1 Introduction and Motivation for Research

Large-scale research problems like health and aging or economics and production in high wage countries are no longer solvable by single disciplines or subject areas. Confronted with this, the trend to interdisciplinary research compounds gained more and more influence [1]. Interdisciplinary cooperation is perceived

S. Yamamoto (Ed.): HIMI 2014, Part I, LNCS 8521, pp. 298–309, 2014.
© Springer International Publishing Switzerland 2014

to bring along a multitude of knowhow and more innovative power than disciplinary cooperation. But mere interdisciplinarity is no guaranteed success factor. Bringing together different disciplines often brings along challenges that can burden, disturb or even scupper these actions [2]. Due to the fact that interdisciplinary research projects are promoted systematically by research funding agencies, universities, and industry, it is essential to understand the sensitive points of interdisciplinary cooperation and find adequate measures that support involved researchers, reviewers and management/supervisors to overcome theses challenges by offering guidelines, tools, and rules. The complexity and social nature of these challenges call for decentralized means of communication like a social portal.

In this paper we present an approach to use a social portal software to enhance the interdisciplinary cooperation in a research cluster (Cluster of Excellence "Integrative Production Technologies for High-Wage Countries" at the RWTH Aachen University in Germany). The presented portal is a project of the so-called Cross-Sectional Processes within this research cluster that were implemented to support "networking processes and strategic cluster developments by means of learning and knowledge management" [3]. The central goal of the portal is to support researchers in interdisciplinary large-scale research projects by addressing (among others) three aspects of interdisciplinary challenges. One of them are different uses of terminology, which are supported by using an online project specific glossary on the portal. Another part is a technology portal [4], which allows members of the cluster to exchange key parameters of developed technologies between projects. The thirds is a publication visualization tool, which can be used to understand changes in social structure indicated by publication behavior or other sociometric data. Additionally to portal offers typical social features such as member yellow pages, news feeds, topic based groups, and many more. Since all these features are interconnected (e.g. users can click on terminology entries and find the creators of the entries), it is important to evaluate each tool in context with the whole platform.

In this paper we present a study on the third feature – the publication visualization tool. Using an interview approach we tried to understand what concerns users might have regarding such a visualization and what benefits they would see with it. Additionally we wanted to find out whether the future users had ideas for improvement.

2   Related Work

In the context of the presented study general aspects from the field of bibliometrics and scientometrics must be considered. Therefore this section presents two approaches used for publication analysis (list-based and mapping-based approaches). Lastly the applied publications-visualization approach for this research is presented. This approach was developed in the context of the research cluster Integrative Production Technologies for High-wage Countries to support interdisciplinary work.

List-Based Bibliometrics. Making bibliographic efforts visible to allow researchers to understand their publication behavior has been approached by many using different approaches. Generally two types of strategies can be discerned. List-based analyses created by databases like Google Scholar, Web of Science, or Scopus give the users insight into their citation records, and how well their work is being cited. Results are presented as lists, hence the name, which can be ordered according to criteria like *most cited*, *most recent*, etc. This list-based approach has been used and constantly debated over sixty years[5]. Database approaches always bring along the problem of *database coverage* [6]. In order to track citation records accurately the database providers need to scan millions of documents, identify citations and assign them to individual papers. As a researcher interested in their own citation records must pick a database, that covers the relevant publications and that are likely to cite ones articles. Different citations indices include different types of documents or outlets and might differ in their accuracy. First technical difficulties exist. Identifying a citation correctly from PDF-data, mapping it to a unique record, and finding unique authors is computationally hard. Authors may vary their citation style, make errors in their bibliographies and many researchers have similar or equal names. All this leads to differing levels of coverage [7]. Coverage ratios also depend on the discipline of the authors [8] as disciplines vary in their publishing behavior.

Even when "correct" citation records exist, it is hard to understand what they mean, when trying to relate them to a researchers performance. Disciplines are different according to sheer size, citations per paper, citation half-life and other aspects that require a normalization process to make citations between disciplines comparable [9]. But what is a discipline? The question of *subject delineation* can either be solved by assigning certain outlets to disciplines (e.g. according to their description) or to perform citation analysis, to find coherent structures of citation networks, that are then considered disciplines. Beyond the technical difficulties manipulation (e.g. self-citations, exploiting the algorithm) of data can become a problem for some databases [10]. Even beyond these difficulties, citations can both indicate agreement or disagreement. Sometimes even honorable mentions exist, without adding to the content. Thus extracting the "meaning" of a citations is also computationally hard (i.e. sentiment analysis).

Mapping-Based Bibliometrics. Mapping-based approaches [11] try to visualize publication data in graphs in order to understand the data both visually but also mathematically from a different perspectives. Mapping can be achieved by mapping citations (i.e. who cites who), co-authorship (i.e. who writes with whom), co-citations (i.e. who gets mutually cited in a document) and many more. The relationship is assigned an edge that connected two vertices that represent the item under analysis. Using this approach allows different forms of analyses that are graph based (e.g. centrality, entropy [12], etc.). Nonetheless mapping-based approaches may also suffer from the same problems as list based approaches (i.e database coverage, sentiment analysis).

The Approach of Mixed Node Publicaion Analysis. For the reasons given above, our approach focuses on a mapping based approach and data collection is done manually by the university library (i.e. researchers are required to report their publications). We decided to not visualize citations, but focus on cooperation based measures such as co-authorship, since interpretation of citations was out of scope for our approach. The approach of our visualization tool was designed to make interdisciplinary work more visible, analyzable and steerable. To realize this, a so-called mixed-node graph visualization [13] was conceived, which allows visualizing authors, their publications, as well as their discipline (see Fig. 1) in a single graph. As Fig. 1 illustrates publications are depicted by little, authors by medium sized and the authors' disciplines by large nodes.

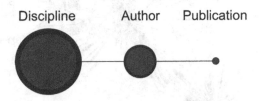

Fig. 1. Mixed node publication graph with different types of nodes. Source: [13]

When coloring the nodes that represent the authors according to their discipline, and running a force based layout algorithm (e.g. Force Atlas 2 from the Gephi Suite [14]), connectedness to other researchers and their disciplines can be analyzed visually (see Fig. 2 and see also http://vimeo.com/48446978).

Knowing that user acceptance is the essential key for the success of technological applications we have run (N=22) semi-structured interviews to find out what potential users (i.e. interdisciplinary researchers) thought about the visualization approach, continuing previous research efforts [15].

3 Methodology

We conducted twenty two interviews with researchers from two projects at the RWTH Aachen University. Interviews were divided into four main parts. Part one contained questions about the validity of the tool to accurately represent interdisciplinary team performance. Part two addressed the suitability of the approach to be used as a steering instrument for interdisciplinary research groups. Part three asked for an evaluation of the impact (positive vs. negative) of our approach on the work climate in interdisciplinary work. Part four focused on the evaluation of the approach as a tool for self-measurement for researchers, to locate themselves within their team, as well as to analyze their performance or search for cooperation partners.

The introduction of the interview was a short presentation of a prototype of the visualization tool. The presented visualization was a depiction of the publications of the sample team of the interviewee. The presented visualization showed

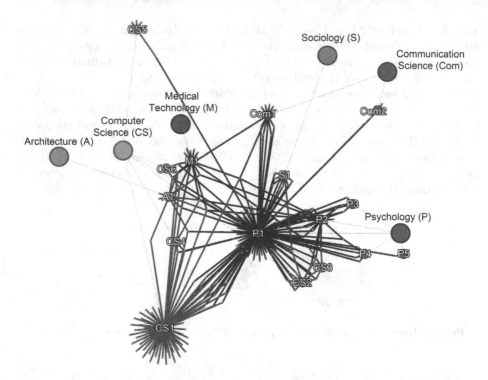

Fig. 2. Sample graph for a workgroup. Researchers are anonymized and represented as numbers according to their discipline. Source: [13]

all names of the team members as well as their disciplines and publication titles (due to privacy see an anonymized example in Fig. 2), generated according to the reduced graph described by Calero Valdez et al. [13]. After the presentation of the prototype, participants were asked to evaluate the prototype of the visualization tool.

The interviews were recorded and transcribed and then scanned for open codes. The open codes were then conceptualized and summarized into categories [16]. For each category, numbers of mentions were counted to establish relative importance. These steps were performed for both arguments for and against the tool. Additionally requirements and wishes for the tool were collected as open codes.

4   Results

The analysis of the transcript lead to the identification of 26 underlying concepts that contained arguments for and against the use of the tool (see Table 1). After identifying these concepts numbers of mentions were counted in the transcript, yielding a total of 139 mentions of the concepts. In total 76 mentions were counted for pro arguments against 63 mentions for con arguments.

Table 1. Examplary (translated) transcripts and the mapping to concepts

Concept	Transcript text
Pro 1) Retrospective analysis	*"One can say he did everything he should have done, if you look at it divided over the years."*
Pro 2) Information regarding the team	*"[...] when I see myself related to the others, it mirrors the degree of cooperation."*
Pro 3) Planning	*"It is interesting to look at for yourself and the head of the institute and to find blind spots and develop or strengthen relationships."*
Con 1) Missing information	*"There is no information about the impact factor or who the first author is."*
Con 2) Negative influence on work-flow	*"At last it might downgrade all the colleagues to little atoms which wander around the two big atoms."*
Con 3) Bad legibility	*"It's hard to see with whom you've published, because there are so many lines."*

4.1   Pro Arguments

Our results revealed that interdisciplinary working researchers have a generally positive attitude towards our visualizations approach. Main benefits are seen in the chance to analyze the group and own work retrospectively (15 mentions), in getting more information about the research group (15 mentions), as well as a positive impact on strategic publication planning (13 mentions, see Fig. 3). Fewer mentions were received by the categories performance comparison, tool for steering, and interdisciplinarity (all 6 mentions). Relatively few mentions fell on the categories quick overview (4 mentions), motivation to publish (4 mentions) and new information (3 mentions), interdisciplinary tolerance grade, bootlicking, visualization of expertise and hierarchy, and argumentation basis (1 mention each).

Retrospective analysis in this case means trying to understand how a work group has performed and cooperated over a certain period of time. Connections likes subgroups that publish together become apparent and development of work-group foci can be seen, when looking at clusters in a graph. In particular how the team has developed over time becomes visible. *Information about the team* refers to gaining insights into team make up in the current situation. It allows seeing who currently works with whom, how intensively they cooperate and who might have been left out. *Strategic publication planning* was seen as a benefit by the participants, which means that seeing your publications behavior could give you input on how to find co-authors that might benefit future publications either in regard to personal or institutional development.

Some of the participants mentioned *performance comparison*, which means the tracking of how much a person published in regard to how much publishing is expected from him. The visualization as a *tool for steering* was also mentioned by the participants, meaning that providing such a visualization to a team-leader, could allow him to actively manage publication efforts by giving him both insights into how publishing in his group works and whether requirements are met.

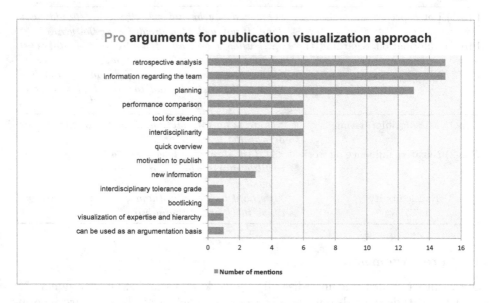

Fig. 3. Number of mentions of pro arguments for the presented visualization approach. Total number of mentions $n = 76$.

4.2   Con Arguments

The strongest concern mentioned was *missing background information* on the publications or authors (21 mentions, see Fig. 4). By simply looking at a visualization that focuses on co-authorship, personal properties such as half-time working and time at an institute are masked, as well as publication properties like an impact factor or relevance. The second strongest concern was the *negative influence on workflow* (9 mentions), which encompassed concerns like triggering competition between team-members or a general disconnect from team members. The thirst most mentioned concern was the *bad legibility* (7 mentions) of the produced graph. In particular researchers that had published multiple articles were overwhelmed by the sheer amount of lines and texts that appear in the visualization.

A general concern against the approach of visualizing publications in such a manner (i.e. not using citation data) was mentioned, that the visualization did not contain *information on quality* of the articles addressing the problem of the quality-quantity dilemma. The visualization only acknowledges quantity. A similar concern is raised by *publications are just one aspect of performance* (5 mentions), which highlights the concern, that not all useful effort researchers do is found in publications (e.g. grant applications, personal development, teaching efforts). This aspect was also mentioned by participants that saw larger graphs (i.e. members of larger work-groups), as participants found the *scope of the visualization* to large for sensible interpretation (4 mentions).

Some additional concerns were mentioned: Among them the worry, that the visualization will have *no impact on performance* (3 mentions), that distances between authors are inappropriate, and the general question, whether steering is desirable (both 2 mentions). The least concern was found for the categories *willingness for cooperation* is unclear, *publications outside the network* are not visible, *publishing and function team* are not the same thing, and *fake authorships* (1 mention each).

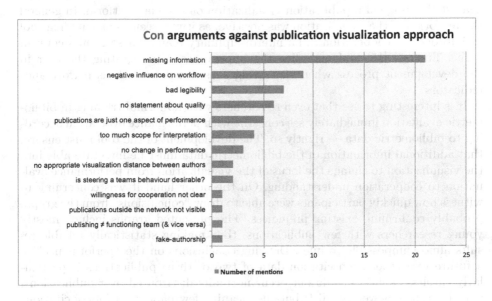

Fig. 4. Number of mentions of con arguments against the presented visualization approach. Total number of mentions $n = 63$.

4.3   Additional Requirements

Participants were also asked about wishes and added requirements for the development of the visualization tool. Among them were aspects like increasing *usability* to allow masking of nodes in order to make the text more legible. Participants also wished for a *time axis* allowing the user to move smoothly through the development of the network. Users wished that *additional information* such as impact-factors or journal names, could be attached to the nodes, to improve understanding on how and where the work group publishes. *Filter functions* such as hiding professors, other workgroups/institutes were seen as necessary, as most of the work actually happens between the individual researchers on a lower hierarchy level. One user wished to have *publishing thresholds*, that would change the color of an author if the author had not published enough according to the threshold. *Exporting the data* into a specific citation style was wished, so that it could be used at personal/institutional web pages. Allowing to visualize other *sociometric data* was also mentioned, such as proximity (who sits in the same office). A key requirement was also that clicking onto nodes should directly take the user to a *profile page* of the author.

5 Discussion

In the interview study presented in this paper we looked at arguments for and against the usage of a publication visualization on a social platform. In general the reception of the visualization was positive, as it was seen as an enabling tool to improve the cooperation in an interdisciplinary team. These results confirm earlier findings [15] and underline the importance of integrating the user in the development process when visualizing sensitive data such as performance indicators.

It is interesting to see that even researchers with no formal training in bibliometric evaluation immediately see concerns with performance evaluation according to bibliometric data — rightly so. The development of the tool must ensure, that additional information of the bibliometric data must be integrate-able into the visualization to change the focus of the visualization from performance evaluation to cooperation understanding. On the other hand it was concerning to witness how quickly participants were able to draw "conclusions" from the graph, probably confirming existing prejudices. The presented graphs include mostly young researchers with few publications, thus making statistically reliable results almost impossible to infer. Drawing conclusions on the "performance" of a future researcher from citation data of two or three publications is particularly careless as citations do not occur normally distributed over publications. Citations show power law distributions meaning few papers get lots of citations (while most get very few) and thus typical statistics like means or variances are not meaningful or even well defined [17].

From the findings we conclude, that bibliometric social network visualization can be helpful when presented in a social portal. Nonetheless it is necessary to educate future users about the interpretability of bibliometric data and stress that performance evaluations can only be executed by trained bibliometricians. In order to still reap the benefits of our visualization approach different visibility styles will be used for different purposes. On a publicly visible level only aggregated data about larger workgroups will be visible to prevent over-interpretation of individual data. Researchers will have a private view on their individual publishing track record and their co-authors so they can still reap the benefits of understanding who they work with. Furthermore we want to allow users to enable sharing of their data selectively, so they can allow other researchers to view their "private" network with their consent. This should prevent negative impacts on workflow. We also plan to give courses on bibliometric evaluation to project leaders and people in higher hierarchy positions as a requirement to access more data to leverage the visualization for steering and planning.

6 Limitations and Future Research

The limitations of this research address four main aspects. The primary aspect is sample selection, as the sample size is always a compromise of effort and validity. The other aspects are the prototypic realization of the tool, problems with bibliometric accuracy, and the social media integration.

The results presented in this study were generated by addressing twenty-two researchers from two projects at the RWTH Aachen University. And effort was made to select participants that are good representatives of the different levels of hierarchy and different structures within the projects. This selection process plus the self-selction bias (no participants were obligated to take part) might nonetheless have preferred participants that are more open to solutions like our visualization tool.

The visualization tool was presented as a prototype, not integrated into the social portal. One reason for this approach, was not to present sensitive data to an unsuspecting audience before assessing the perceived sensitivity of the data. This might have influenced the perception of applicability of the approach, because participants could not experience the context of the tool. An open questions remains, whether users will still be as positive regarding the tool, if they see it connected to their individual profile and visible to 180 colleagues. In order to ensure acceptance, a gradual introduction of visualizations accompanied by quantitative evaluation is planned for the production version of the platform.

In order to ensure comparability within an interdisciplinary setting, we will perform a study assessing the importance of individual bibliometric indicators to the communities within the research cluster. It is necessary to regard the high level of individuality to ensure, comparability is maintained or at least addressed consciously to prevent premature judgement.

Since the visualization is integrated into a social platform all aspects that matter in social media are important immediately as well. Aspects of data privacy, establishment of business process (how to deal with under- or over-performing), etiquette (how do we talk about different publishing behaviors) are important as well but were not explicitly addressed in the interview study. Prior research [18,19] has shown that user diversity factors are highly important when looking at aspects of data disclosure and establishing an etiquette for online communication. These aspects need also be addressed explicitly in a scientific context, to ensure that the second strongest concern of *negative influence on the workflow* does not occur.

Acknowledgments. We would like to thank the anonymous reviewers for their constructive comments on an earlier version of this manuscript. Furthermore we would like to thank our student assistants Tatjana Hamann and Juliana Brell for their support in conducting the interviews. The work related to the project "Integrative Production Technology in High Wage Countries" has been funded by the Excellence Initiative of the German federal and state governments.

References

1. Nissani, M.: Ten cheers for interdisciplinarity: The case for interdisciplinary knowledge and research. The Social Science Journal 34(2), 201–216 (1997)
2. Repko, A.F.: Interdisciplinary research: Process and theory. Sage (2008)
3. Jooß, C., Welter, F., Leisten, I., Richert, A., Schaar, A.K., Calero Valdez, A., Nick, E., Prahl, U., Jansen, U., Schulz, W., et al.: Scientific cooperation engineering in the cluster of excellence integrative production technology for high-wage countries at RWTH Aachen University. In: Proceedings of the ICERI 2012, pp. 3842–3846 (2012)
4. Schuh, G., Aghassi, S., Caler Valdez, A.: Supporting technology transfer via web-based platforms. In: Proceedings of PICMET 2013 Technology Management in the IT-Driven Services (PICMET), pp. 858–866. IEEE (2013)
5. Garfield, E.: Citation indexes for science. a new dimension in documentation through association of ideas. International Journal of Epidemiology 35(5), 1123–1127 (2006)
6. Harzing, A.W., Van der Wal, R.: Google scholar: the democratization of citation analysis. Ethics in Science and Environmental Politics 8(1), 61–73 (2007)
7. Nisonger, T.E.: Citation autobiography: An investigation of isi database coverage in determining author citedness. College & Research Libraries 65(2), 152–163 (2004)
8. Hicks, D.: The difficulty of achieving full coverage of international social science literature and the bibliometric consequences. Scientometrics 44(2), 193–215 (1999)
9. Leydesdorff, L., Shin, J.C.: How to evaluate universities in terms of their relative citation impacts: Fractional counting of citations and the normalization of differences among disciplines. Journal of the American Society for Information Science and Technology 62(6), 1146–1155 (2011)
10. Delgado López-Cózar, E., Robinson-García, N., Torres-Salinas, D.: Manipulating google scholar citations and google scholar metrics: simple, easy and tempting (2012)
11. Calero-Medina, C., Noyons, E.: Combining mapping and citation network analysis for a better understanding of the scientific development: The case of the absorptive capacity field. Journal of Informetrics 2(4), 272–279 (2008)
12. Holzinger, A., Ofner, B., Stocker, C., Calero Valdez, A., Schaar, A.K., Ziefle, M., Dehmer, M.: On graph entropy measures for knowledge discovery from publication network data. In: Cuzzocrea, A., Kittl, C., Simos, D.E., Weippl, E., Xu, L. (eds.) CD-ARES 2013. LNCS, vol. 8127, pp. 354–362. Springer, Heidelberg (2013)
13. Calero Valdez, A., Schaar, A.K., Ziefle, M., Holzinger, A., Jeschke, S., Brecher, C.: Using mixed node publication network graphs for analyzing success in interdisciplinary teams. In: Huang, R., Ghorbani, A.A., Pasi, G., Yamaguchi, T., Yen, N.Y., Jin, B. (eds.) AMT 2012. LNCS, vol. 7669, pp. 606–617. Springer, Heidelberg (2012)
14. Bastian, M., Heymann, S., Jacomy, M.: Gephi: An open source software for exploring and manipulating networks (2009)
15. Schaar, A.K., Calero Valdez, A., Ziefle, M.: Publication network visualization as an approach for interdisciplinary innovation management. In: 2013 IEEE International Professional Communication Conference (IPCC), pp. 1–8. IEEE (2013)
16. Glaser, B.G., Strauss, A.L.: The discovery of grounded theory: Strategies for qualitative research. Transaction Books (2009)

17. Redner, S.: How popular is your paper? an empirical study of the citation distribution. The European Physical Journal B-Condensed Matter and Complex Systems 4(2), 131–134 (1998)
18. Schaar, A.K., Calero Valdez, A., Ziefle, M.: The impact of user diversity on the willingness to disclose personal information in social network services. In: Holzinger, A., Ziefle, M., Hitz, M., Debevc, M. (eds.) SouthCHI 2013. LNCS, vol. 7946, pp. 174–193. Springer, Heidelberg (2013)
19. Calero Valdez, A., Kathrin Schaar, A., Ziefle, M.: Personality influences on etiquette requirements for social media in the work context. In: Holzinger, A., Ziefle, M., Hitz, M., Debevc, M. (eds.) SouthCHI 2013. LNCS, vol. 7946, pp. 427–446. Springer, Heidelberg (2013)

SPARQL Query Writing with Recommendations Based on Datasets

Gergő Gombos and Attila Kiss

Eötvös Loránd University, Budapest, Hungary
{ggombos,kiss}@inf.elte.hu

Abstract. When we write a SPARQL query, we need to know the structure of the dataset. In the relation databases the tables have a scheme, but the semantic data do not have. Autocompletion function exists in SQL environment, but it does not exist in SPARQL environment. We made a system that can help to write SPARQL query. The system has two features. The first is the prefix recommend. We can write shorter queries if we use prefixes because we do not need to write the long IRIs. The second feature is the predicate-based recommendation based on the type of the variable. If a variable is in the query and it has a type condition, then our system recommends further predicates of this type. Our system needs information about the dataset for the recommendation. We can get these information with simple SPARQL queries. The queries run on a federated system. It is useful because the user does not need any information about the endpoints.

Keywords: SPARQL, Semantic Web, Linked Data, LOD Cloud, Federated system.

1   Introduction

The aim of the semantic web is to make a big knowledge base from the Internet. These knowledges can be combined and we can get more information about the things. We use the SPARQL language for querying this large semantic data. The query has some conditions that decrease the result. The result need to match these conditions. This solution is similar to the SQL in the relational database environment, where the data are stored in the relational tables and we give the conditions that have to be met. If we know the syntax of the SQL, it is not a problem writing these kinds of query. We need to know just the tables and the columns of the tables. Most database clients have autocompletion feature that makes easy the creation of the query. In the semantic web world it is not so simple. We need to know the dataset and its structure in order to write a query. The advantages of the autocompletion can be used for writing SPARQL queries. When we make a query we usually use the prefix form of the entities. The prefixes give us the opportunity to use the short string instead of the long IRIs. This makes easier writing of the query for us, but the query engines need the full IRIs of the things. Therefore the prefix recommendation is an important function of the semantic recommender system. Another important thing is a predicate recommendation because the semantic data is unstructured and we do not know what kind of predicate we can use. For example even, if

S. Yamamoto (Ed.): HIMI 2014, Part I, LNCS 8521, pp. 310–319, 2014.

we know the type of a variable, we do not know the other predicates. Therefore, the rec-ommendation system queries the datasets. Because the datasets are in the LOD Cloud we need to choose the appropriate endpoint. For this we need to know the URL of the endpoint and we need to know what endpoint stores the specific data, which is usually not available for the user. Our aim is to create a general system that uses all endpoints and solves the endpoint selection problem. The federated systems select automatically the required endpoints and they summarize the results from the endpoints.

In this paper, we will describe the formal model of federated systems with Abstract State Machine (ASM). Then, we will refine the model to the current system. Then, we will present a prototype that is able to make recommendations based on a SPARQL query.

2 Related Work

The authors wrote [3] that the semantic data are difficult to access because the non-expert users cannot know the syntax of the SPARQL. They will produce the Linked Query Wizard. The hypothesis for the Linked Data Query Wizard is: the users know spreadsheet applications like Excel, and the idea is to make the semantic data into tab-ular form. Our solution provides the expert and non-expert users to make SPARQL queries easier.

The SPARQL is often given with visual tool. One of them is the SPARQL Views [5] that is an extension for Drupal. This extension helps the inexperienced users. The system queries the predicates from the given endpoint, and it recommends these to the users. The other function is the automatically prefix adding. When the user chooses a predicate, the system adds the necessary prefix to the query. Our solution uses a feder-ated system and we can use the recommendation without choose any endpoint.

Another visual SPARQL editor is the NITELIGHT [4]. The NITELIGHT tool is a web-based application in JavaScript. The application provides an ontology browser, which allows us to add predicates to our query based on ontology. The queries are made by linking the components. The completed query is syntactically correct. In contrast to our system it has not recommendations. The user of the system needs some knowledge about SPARQL.

Kramer et. all [6] wrote querying Linked Open Data with SPARQL is different from querying relational databases. Their aim is to make autocompletion function for query writing. Their solution is to build indexes to the queries from logs. If the user writes a '<' symbol then the system recommends the potential IRIs. If the user writes a '?' symbol it recommends the variables. When the user chose a variable the system recom-mends the predicates based on the previous queries. In contrast to our system provides recommendations based on the dataset.

Lehmann et all.[7] presented a technique for making SPARQL. Their solution is based on the question-answer and the positive learning techniques. The user enters a query for which the system makes recommendations. The user selects a positive ex-ample from the recommendations. That is the base of the next recommendations. This iteration runs until the user reaches the appropriate query or there are no more learnable query. This solution uses SPARQL Endpoints like our solutions.

3   Semantic Web

We mentioned the Semantic Web in our related work [12]. The Semantic Web [1] aims at creating the web of data: a large distributed knowledge base, which contains the information of the World Wide Web in a format which is directly interpretable by computers. The goal of this web of linked data is to allow better, more sensible methods for information search, and knowledge inference. To achieve this, the Semantic Web provides a data model and its query language. The data model called the Resource Description Framework (RDF) [13] uses a simple conceptual description of the information: we represent our knowledge as statements in the form of subject-predicate-object (or entity-attribute-value). This way our data can be seen as a directed graph, where a statement is an edge labeled with the predicate, pointing from the subjects node to the objects node. The query language called SPARQL [2] formulates the queries as graph patterns, thus the query results can be calculated by matching the pattern against the data graph.

4   Formal Model

We made a formal model with ASM (Abstract State Machine). ASMs represent a mathematically well founded framework for system design and analysis [10]. It is introduced by Gurevich [9]. The federated model is inspired by the ASM model of the grid systems [8]. The grid systems are distributed and parallel like the federated systems. The ASM algebra is made up of universes, functions, and rules. The universes include the entities. The functions provide the link between the universes. The rules are transaction steps and they have condition to activate. The ASM has a ground model that is a base of the system functions. This model will be refined later. The model describes the expected requirements of the system. We describe below the workflows of the federated systems with ASM and we refine for the SPARQL recommendation system.

4.1   Model for Federated System

A semantic Federated system (FEDERATED universe) operates as follows. The system receives a query (QUERY universe) which sends to several SPARQL Endpoints (ENDPOINT universe) and it summarizes the results (RESULT universe) of the endpoints and it returns with the answer. The ground model does not deal with endpoint selection method. It helps to be the model general. The endpoint selection function can be given in a refined model, but these are not discussed in this paper. The universes have the *true, false, undef* values too.

The relations between the universes can be described by functions. We describe the state of the federated system with $fstate : FEDERATED \rightarrow \{wait, start\_req, running\}$ function. This state is *wait* if the system is waiting for a request. It is *start_req* when the system prepares the requests to the endpoints. Finally, the state is *running* if the system works on a query. When a request comes into the system we can write the connection with the $fworkingOn : FEDERATED \rightarrow QUERY$ which says that the federated system works on the query. The system converts the query to requests. The exact request is not important in the ground model. It can be refined in the lower-level model because it depends on the architecture of the federated system. The query and the requests connect with *reqQuery* : *REQUEST* → *QUERY* function. A request will be executed in a given endpoint. The connection between the request and the endpoint is written with *eworkingOn* : *ENDPOINT* → *REQUEST* function. The start of the request depends on the state of the endpoint. Initially, their state are *waiting*. These endpoints are waiting for the requests. The *estate* : *ENDPOINT* → {*running, waiting, finished*} function describes the state of the given endpoint. The state of the endpoint changes when an event occurs. We describe an event with *event* : *ENDPOINT* → {*timeout, finish*}. The *timeout* occurs when the endpoint cannot answer the request and the time is out. It is necessary because the system needs minimal response time for usability. The *finish* state occurs when the result is complete on time. We get the results with *rres* : *REQUEST* → *RESULT* function. The federated system summarizes these results. The method of the summarization is not discussed in the ground model. Finally, the final result stores with *qres* : *QUERY* → *RESULT*.

The model needs an initial step. Each item of the model need to be reset. First, we set the state of the endpoints: $\forall e \in ENDPOINT : estate(e) := waiting; eworkingOn(e) := undef$ and we set the state of the system: $fstate(f) := wait$.

The system operations are described with rules.

Rule 1 (Send a Query to the Federated System). The first rule describes that the system receives a query ($q \in QUERY$). The query can run only if the system is in *waiting* state. In this time the state of the system is changed to *start_req* that means it prepares the requests and we set the query result to empty, and we set the system work on this query.

```
if  fstate(f) = wait  then
       fworkingOn(f) := q
       fstate(f) := start_req
       qres(q) := undef
endif
```

Rule 2 (Federated System Send the Request to the Endpoints). The evaluation of the query needs requests. The following rule creates a request to each endpoint that has *waiting* state. In this case, we do not deal whit what the request is. In some system this may be the whole query, in another system just the conditions of the query. When the system makes a request it is set the query and the endpoint for the request. It changes the state of the endpoint to *running* and the result of the request to empty.

```
if  fstate(f) = start_req && fworkingOn(f) = q  then
       do  forall  e ∈ ENDPOINT
           if  estate(e) = waiting  then
               EXTEND REQUEST by  req  with
                   reqQuery(req) := q
                   eworkingOn(e) := req
                   estate(e) := running
                   rres(req) := undef
```

```
            endextend
        endif
        fstate(f) = running
    enddo
endif
```

The EXTEND means that we create a new item into the universe, in this case in the REQUEST.

Rule 3 (Endpoint Finish or Timeout). A request may end in two states. One is if the query was run without any problems. The second state is if the request could not finish within a certain time. In both cases an event occurs. We take the result of the request to the result of the query with '+' operator. We do not deal what is mean the '+' operator and how is it work.

```
let  req = eworkingOn(e)
if  event(e) = finish || event(e) = timeout  then
    eworkingOn(e) = undef
    estate(e) = finished
    qres(q) := qres(q) + rres(req)
    rres(req) := undef
    REQUEST(req) = undef
endif
```

The $REQUEST(req) = undef$ means that the item (req) is removed from the universe ($REQUEST$).

Rule 4 (terminate) The last process is the termination process. This process is run when the state of each endpoint changed to $finished$. We get the result in $qres(q)$. Afterthat we need to restore the system state to the initial state for the further requests.

```
if  ∀e ∈ ENDPOINT : estate(e) = finished && fstate(f) = running  then
    do  forall  e ∈ ENDPOINT
        estate(e) := waiting
        fstate(f) := wait
        fworkingOn(f) := undef
    enddo
endif
```

4.2   Finite Model for SPARQL Recommendation

We showed in the previous model how the system gets a query and how a federated system will process this query. Now we refine this model for the current task. The aim is to make query, so the input of the system is not a QUERY, just a part of the query. For this reason, we need to introduce new universes. In this task we focus on two parts of the process. One is a prefix recommendation. For recommendation we need the SHORTPREFIX and the LONGPREFIX universes. These universes will store the short and long form of the prefixes. Another aim is the condition recommendation. For this we need introduce the CONDITION universe.

We make new expectations on the new refined model. The system is able to define the prefixes without sending a request to the endpoints. This may be because the prefixes usually are fixed, so we can use these as a constant. The REQUESTs contain CONDITION instead of QUERY. The REQUEST depends on the CONDITION and it is made if the CONDITION has a type information.

The new universes need new functions. The first is a $prefMapped$: $SHORTPREFIX \rightarrow LONGPREFIX$ which performs the mapping of the prefixes. We need to resolve the short prefix during the query writing, so this mapping is just one direction. Because the query is now divided into several parts, we need the $pbelongsTo : SHORTPREFIX \rightarrow QUERY$ and the $cbelongsTo : CONDITION \rightarrow QUERY$ functions for the connection of the three universes. We need to check that the CONDITION has a type ($rdf : type$) information, this check is made by the $hasType : CONDITION \rightarrow \{true, false\}$ function. Another checking functions are the $hasCondition : QUERY \rightarrow \{true, false\}$ and the $hasPrefix : QUERY \rightarrow true, false$. These functions check that the QUERY has PREFIX or CONDITION. In the ground model we used the $reqQuery$ function, but now we need to change this on the current model. The input of this function was QUERY, but now this will be CONDITION.

We extend the initial step with a loads process that load the short and long version of prefixes to the $prefMapped$. The exact implementation of the loading is not included the model. Another supplement is that we set the value of the $cbelongsTo, pbelongsTo$ functions based on the (sub)query.

Rule 1 (Refined). On the first rule we need just a minimal change. The ground model sent the query to the system every time, but now it sends just if the query has PREFIX or CONDITION.

```
if  fstate(f) = wait && (hasPrefix(q) || hasCondition(q))  then
     fworkingOn(f) := q
     fstate(f) := start_req
     qres(q) := undef
endif
```

Rule 2 (Refined). The second rule sends the queries to the endpoints. If the query has PREFIX it does not need to send the query because we can answer the prefix recommendation without it. If the query has CONDITION, the system works like a ground model.

```
if  fstate(f) = start_req && fworkingOn(f) = q  then
     if  hasCondition(q)  then
          do  forall  c ∈ CONDITION
               if  cbelongsTo(c) = q && hasType(c)
                    do  forall  e ∈ ENDPOINT
                         if  estate(e) = waiting
                              EXTEND REQUEST by req with
                                   reqQuery(req) := c
```

$$eworkingOn(e) := req$$
$$estate(e) := running$$
$$rres(req) := undef$$
```
                 endextend
             endif
           enddo
         endif
       enddo
       fstate(f) = running
     endif
     if  hasPrefix(q)  then
         do  forall  p ∈ PREFIX
             if  pbelongsTo(p) = q
                 qres(q) := qres(q) + prefMapped(p)
             endif
           enddo
       endif
endif
```

5 Implemented System

We built a prototype based on the previous model. The features of the prototype are the prefix recommendation and condition recommendation that were described above. On Fig. 2 we can see the Web UI of the system. It has a query box, where the user writes the query and the system send an AJAX request to the backend, where the model is working. The system uses predefined SPARQL endpoints: factbook[1], dataGov[2], dblp[3], dbpedia[4], factforge[5], openlinkSW[6], linkedMDB[7], void[8]. In addition, the system stores the short and long forms of the prefixes. The prefixes are from the prefix.cc. The federated system [11] usage is advantageous because the user does not need to know, what endpoint store the data or what is the URL of the endpoint.

The system works as follows. If there is any change in the query, then that will be sent to the backend asynchronously. We use ARQ[9] to process the SPARQL query. We get the condition from the WHERE with this tool. If the query is wrong, then the ARQ write the problem and we show them on the UI, see that on Fig. 1. If the system finds a prefix that is not defined previously, it searches them from prefixes and make a recommendation. If we want to use this recommendation, we need just click on the 'add' button. It is possible that we wrote a prefix, that the system does not recognize - this may be if we

---

[1] http://wifo5-04.informatik.uni-mannheim.de/factbook/sparql
[2] http://services.data.gov/sparql
[3] http://dblp.rkbexplorer.com/sparql
[4] http://dbpedia.org/sparql
[5] http://factforge.net/sparql
[6] http://lod.openlinksw.com/sparql
[7] http://data.linkedmdb.org/sparql
[8] http://void.rkbexplorer.com/sparql
[9] http://jena.sourceforge.net/ARQ/

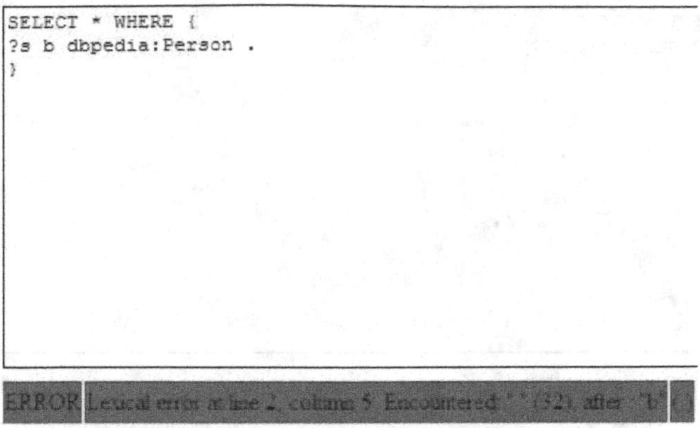

```
SELECT * WHERE {
?s b dbpedia:Person .
}
```

ERROR Lexical error at line 2, column 5. Encountered: " " (32), after " "b"

Fig. 1. Web UI of the system with error

use another short form of an IRI - then we get an error message. On Fig. 2 we can see the *dbpedia* : *Person* IRI that has the *dbpedia* as prefix. The system knows this prefix and recommends this line: 'PREFIX dbpedia: <http://dbpedia.org/resource>'.

Another function of the system is that the condition recommendation. The system makes recommendations to extend the query with new filters. The basis for that is the variable with type (*rdf* : *type* or short form *a*) information. The system collects additional information about a type with simple SPARQL queries. It sends the following query to all endpoints.

SELECT DISTINCT ?x WHERE {
    ?x rdf:type dbpedia:Person .
} LIMIT 3

We ask three items because one item may not have some predicates and another item has. Ask three items is fast enough that the system is able to respond in time. When the system gets three items that has a same type, the system asks the possible predicates of the items. We write another SPARQL query for this and the system makes the unique result.

SELECT DISTINCT ?s WHERE {
    item ?s ?p .
}

The first query returns the items that are Persons and after the second query the system makes the unique predicates.

The system completes this process on all endpoints. For fastest response time these queries run in parallel. Since some endpoint may not be available or overloaded, the answer would be a long time, so the system has a timelimit which will drop the request if it does not receive result before the limit. The limit is on our system is 5 seconds. The system is faster with limit, but we cannot get all results. In many cases this is not a problem because a lot of data are stored more endpoints.

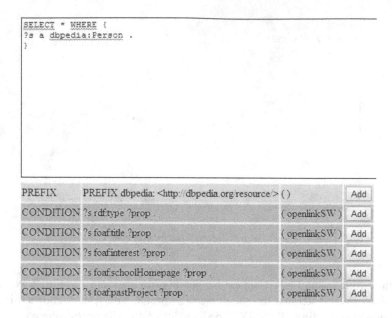

Fig. 2. Web UI of the system with recommendation

6   Conclusion and Future Work

One of the difficulties of writing a SPARQL query that we do not know the scheme of the dataset. Without the scheme we do not know what we can query about an item. Another problem is the long IRIs in the query. The SPARQL provides a solution to use prefixes, but it is often required to search them. The system, which is described in this paper, gives a solution to these problems. The system makes recommendations when we are writing the SPARQL query. It offers the necessary prefixes and the possible properties of a variable.

The system is currently used only for the preparation of SPARQL query. The final query can be used on another system. Our plan is that the query can be automatically sent to the appropriate endpoint. In addition, we would like to make the extraction of the prefixes automatically as mentioned above. Create a query usually starts with an initial item. In this system the search IRI function is not available, in turn, for example the Virtuoso has the Facet for this function. We plan to write this function to the model and implement to the system. We could make the system when we use some cache. This cache can store information about the previous requests. If some endpoint did not send any result about some type, then the system does not need to ask again.

Acknowledgments. This work was partially supported by the European Union and the European Social Fund through project FuturICT.hu (grant no.: TAMOP-4.2.2.C-11/1/KONV-2012-0013). We are grateful to Bálint Molnár for helpful discussion and comments about ASM.

References

1. Berners-Lee, T., Hendler, J., Lassila, O.: The semantic web. Scientific American 284(5), 28–37 (2001)
2. Prud Hommeaux, E., Seaborne, A.: SPARQL query language for RDF. W3C Recommendation 15 (2008)
3. Hoefler, P.: Linked Data Interfaces for Non-expert Users. In: Cimiano, P., Corcho, O., Presutti, V., Hollink, L., Rudolph, S. (eds.) ESWC 2013. LNCS, vol. 7882, pp. 702–706. Springer, Heidelberg (2013)
4. Russell, A., Smart, P.R., Braines, D., Shadbolt, N.R.: NITELIGHT: A Graphical Tool for Semantic Query Construction (2008)
5. Clark, L.: SPARQL Views: A Visual SPARQL Query Builder for Drupal. ISWC Posters & Demos (2010)
6. Kramer, K., Dividino, R., Grner, G.: SPACE: SPARQL Index for Efficient Autocompletion. In: ISWC Posters & Demonstrations Track, pp. 157–160 (2013)
7. Lehmann, J., Bühmann, L.: AutoSPARQL: Let users query your knowledge base. In: Antoniou, G., Grobelnik, M., Simperl, E., Parsia, B., Plexousakis, D., De Leenheer, P., Pan, J. (eds.) ESWC 2011, Part I. LNCS, vol. 6643, pp. 63–79. Springer, Heidelberg (2011)
8. Nmeth, Z., Sunderam, V.: A formal framework for defining grid systems. In: 2nd IEEE/ACM International Symposium on Cluster Computing and the Grid. IEEE (2002)
9. Gurevich, Y.: Evolving algebras: An attempt to discover semantics. In: Current Trends in Theoretical Computer Science, pp. 266–292 (1993)
10. Börger, E.: High level system design and analysis using abstract state machines. In: Hutter, D., Traverso, P. (eds.) FM-Trends 1998. LNCS, vol. 1641, pp. 1–43. Springer, Heidelberg (1999)
11. Rakhmawati, N.A., Umbrich, J., Karnstedt, M., Hasnain, A., Hausenblas, M.: Querying over Federated SPARQL Endpoints-A State of the Art Survey. arXiv preprint arXiv:1306.1723 (2013)
12. Matuszka, T., Gombos, G., Kiss, A.: A New Approach for Indoor Navigation Using Semantic Webtechnologies and Augmented Reality. In: Shumaker, R. (ed.) VAMR/HCII 2013, Part I. LNCS, vol. 8021, pp. 202–210. Springer, Heidelberg (2013)
13. Lassila, O., Swick, R.R.: Resource Description Framework (RDF) Schema Specification, http://www.w3.org/TR/rdf-schema

Personal Information Management Competences: A Case Study of Future College Students

Jerry Jacques and Pierre Fastrez

Center for Research in Communication, Université Catholique de Louvain, Belgium
{jerry.jacques,pierre.fastrez}@uclouvain.be

Abstract. The research project presented in this paper aims at modeling the media literacy competences required to organize and manage collections of information in the form of personal and shared digital environments. In-depth in situ interviews were conducted with future college students (N=11). During the interviews, the informants gave a guided tour of their personal space of information, and demonstrated how they used different digital tools to organize it. We identify three dimensions of personal information management (PIM) competence, based on the analysis of the way our informants describe their PIM practices by referring to and articulating (1) the constraints and affordances of the tools and devices they use, (2) the activities these tools and devices support, (3) the costs and benefits of these practices for these activities, and (4) their tastes and preferences towards them.

Keywords: personal information management, media literacy, information overload, user empowerment.

1 Introduction

Nowadays, information technology conditions access to an increasing number of aspects of the economic, political, cultural and social life of individuals, who need to develop a variety of information management skills in order to become critical citizen, productive professionals and fulfilled individuals.

Contemporary users of digital media face three types of challenges. First, there is a substantial increase in the amount of information media users have to manage on a daily basis [1]. Second, this information has never been so fragmented across multiple contexts [2]. The success of smart mobile devices, the proliferation of applications and the increasing quality of cloud computing services now offer individuals a growing number of distinct opportunities to constantly interact with information. Third, the social dimension of information has become a crucial issue of our networked society. Individuals have to deal with complex identity and relationship construction processes that span across their online and offline lives [3]. They also have to manage collective digital activities by creating shared mediated structures that support collaborative learning and work [4, 5].

In the face of these three challenges, the research project presented in this paper aims at modeling the media literacy competences required to organize and manage

S. Yamamoto (Ed.): HIMI 2014, Part I, LNCS 8521, pp. 320–331, 2014.

collections of information in the form of personal and shared digital environments. These competences involve both the ability to imagine organization schemes, and to implement them into the use of relevant digital tools. Competent individuals use digital tools (file systems, databases, hyperlinks, email, etc.) to create, modify and coordinate arrays of external representations that reify the conceptual organization of their information collections. In turn, these external representations structure their individual and collective informational activities [6]. This paper presents an ongoing research program dedicated to the profiling of these competences in college students. To do so, our study integrates a personal information management (PIM) perspective with a media literacy perspective.

2   Related Work

2.1   Personal Information Management

PIM can be defined as "the practice and the study of activities a person performs in order to acquire or create, store, organize, maintain, retrieve, use and distribute the information needed to meet life's many goals (everyday and long-term, work-related and not) and to fulfill life's many roles and responsibilities (as parent, spouse, friend, employee, member of community, etc.)" [7]. In the past decades, an increasing number of researchers have conducted studies related to PIM both in the paper world and in the digital world. These contributions can be grouped in two interwoven but different approaches [8, 9].

PIM Tool Development. The first approach is tool-oriented and focused on the development of applications designed to help individuals to manage information. These novel applications rely on an array of representational techniques that support the organization of digital information collections, e.g. dynamic document piles [10–12], combinations of folders, tags and threads for email [13, 14], hierarchical faceted categories [15], two-dimensional dynamic spatial layouts [16, 17], and time-based browsing [18].

Descriptive User Studies. The studies in second approach investigate the behavior of individuals when they interact with information. The goal of these studies is to better understand PIM practices developed by users in order to formulate recommendations for tool design. Such studies have typically focused on PIM practices related to specific types of digital resources, such as computer files [5, 19–21], emails [22–25], images [26], web bookmarks [27], or a combination thereof [28].

Most of these studies have focused either on the sorting practices developed by users within a given collection of files, emails or bookmarks, or on the extent to which users replicate folder hierarchies across collections [28, 29]. Accordingly, the fragmentation of digital collections across multiple tools and contexts of use, which has been identified as a recurring problem of PIM [2], has also been regarded as an external constraint that users struggle with [29]. Hence, little effort has been made to examine how users intentionally manage the organization (i.e. the compatibility, interoperability, and coordination) between different software tools running on the same or different devices, supporting the same activity. In the study presented in the next section of this paper, we propose to look at fragmentation both as a constraint and as an organizing process managed by users as a part of their PIM practices, in which each fragment may serve a different purpose.

Descriptive user studies of PIM have typically examined users in terms of types of organization they produce, or the types of sorting strategies they use to produce this organization.

Types of organization. In his seminal work on office workers, Malone [30] distinguished between users organizing their (brick-and-mortar) offices by piling documents or by filing them, and noted that each practice supported a different need, as files were more efficient for re-finding previously processed information, and the visibility of piles served a reminding function for their users. Malone also described unnamed piles as alternatives to named files that lowered the cognitive barrier associated with the difficulty of classifying information. The difficulties of categorizing for humans were further described by Lansdale [31] as a central issue in PIM. As categorization is a process of interpreting information in context, the ability of retrieving previously categorized information must rely on the re-instantiation of the context of interpretation in which it was categorized in the first place.

In two early studies of personal computer file management practices, Barreau and Nardi [19] described computer users as working with simple distinctions (between ephemeral, working, and archived information) to sort their personal files. In addition, subjects who filed their documents into folders archived little information, and seldom used sub-folders to do so. More recent studies have shown a greater variety across users both in terms of numbers of created folders and in terms of complexity of folder hierarchies [21, 28], which may be due to the increase in information load the average information worker has had to deal with over the years [20, 24].

Some studies have highlighted the dependence of sorting practices on the job function of the people who use them [27, 30]. More generally, the relationship between PIM practices and the requirements of the activity they support still needs to be studied in more details.

Types of sorting strategies. Other studies have contributed to describing the strategies through which users produce information organization. For example, in an early study of email use, MacKay [22] distinguished between prioritizers (who applied rules prior to reading their messages and created high priority folders) and archivers (who maintained subject-based folders). A number of studies have described sorting strategies for files, emails or bookmarks according to the frequency at which users resorted to filing, and to the proportion of their resources they filed [21, 24, 25, 28]. The types of strategies they described ranged from frequent and total filers (who essentially file every new resource as it arrives) to no-filers (who do not file anything), with different intermediary positions such as partial filers [28], or spring cleaners [25]. An important result of these studies is that most individuals adopt multiple strategies both within and between tools [28], although in different, identifiable combinations.

In contrast with most of the research works presented in this section, which focus on understanding the practices of PIM, our research is dedicated to the definition of the competences underlying these practices.

2.2   Media Literacy

Kim [9] argued that designing better tools is not the only way to tackle PIM issues, as training individuals may be an alternative, complementary solution. Indeed, behavioral studies could be a valuable source of recommendations aimed at improving the PIM skills of contemporary information technology users.

In this paper, we consider PIM competences as a part of media literacy. Media literacy is "a constellation of life skills that are necessary for full participation in our media-saturated, information-rich society" [32]. These skills allow individuals to develop creative, critical, autonomous and socialized uses of media and technologies for purposes that range from personal development to active citizenship.

In an attempt to extend and further specify the commonly accepted definition of media literacy as "the ability to access, analyze, evaluate and create messages across a variety of contexts" [33], we developed [34, 35] a theoretical framework in the form of matrix of media literacy competences. This matrix defines media literacy as the competences required to *read* (i.e. decode, understand and evaluate), *write* (i.e. create and distribute), *navigate* (i.e. search and find, or openly explore) and *organize* (i.e. categorize both conceptually and practically) media as *informational*, *technical* and *social* objects (Figure 1).

Media Literacy as the ability to...	media as...		
	informational objects	technical objects	social objects
• read			
• write			
• navigate			
• organize	Personal Information Management		

Fig. 1. A framework for the definition of media literacy

Within this theoretical framework, personal information resources (information items [7], but also PIM software tools and devices) can be regarded as media objects as they integrate the following three dimensions. They are *informational* objects in that they are designed to represent things, real or fictitious, different from themselves, through the use of different sign systems (information items represent their semantic contents, the interfaces of PIM tools represent the actions they afford). They are *technical* objects as they result from technical production processes, or are themselves designed to produce or disseminate other media objects. Finally, they are *social* objects, as they point to the individual and institutional agents who produce, diffuse and use them.

In this context, we view PIM literacy [36] as a part of the media literate user's ability to organize media as informational, technical and social objects [37]. It integrates into the larger context of contemporary media literacy, with the ability to navigate, read and write media objects. Framing PIM literacy in this way has the benefit of extending the notion of PIM beyond the practice of sorting resources and storing them in a way that affords retrieval for future use, to encompass the management and organization of collections of information items, of the software tools with which they are organized, of the devices on which these tools run, but also of mediated contacts and interactions, as well as of the different aspects of one's activity in multitasking contexts [38].

PIM literacy appears to be of special importance to higher education students [21], as a set of competences that allow them to design and manage their own personal learning environment [39]. From a constructivist perspective, the organization of school-related materials into meaningful personal spaces of information can be seen as a form of integration of new information into the student's prior knowledge [40], which is considered as an essential dimension of learning [41].

3   A Study of the PIM Competences of (Future) College Students

In this section, we present the first phase of an ongoing study aimed at modeling the development of PIM competences by college students. While the observation protocol of this study relies on the comparison of the PIM practices of a group of students before and during their freshman year, we will focus on data collected before they entered the university.

3.1   Hypotheses

We hypothesize that the PIM competences of users can be described in terms of their ability:

1. to perceive the affordances [42] and constraints of the tools and devices supporting their PIM practices;
2. to use and modify these affordances in order to optimize the cost-structure [43] of their activity;
3. to develop a reflective awareness of their own information management practices.

3.2   Method

We carried out semi-structured interviews with a sample (N = 11) of future first-year college students before the beginning of their first academic year. Follow-up interviews with the same subjects as they complete their freshman year are currently underway. Participants were recruited at the information center of our university. Each interview was conducted in the everyday context of use of their digital tools, typically at their homes.

During the interviews, the informants gave a guided tour of their personal space of information, and demonstrated how they used different digital tools to organize it. First, each informant described the digital devices (computer, tablet, phone, audio player, etc.) they used on a regular basis, and the main activities supported by these devices. Next, participants demonstrated how they typically performed each activity. Parts of the interviews also focused on the informant's capacity to reflect on their own practices. For example, they were asked to describe the pros and cons of a particular practice.

The analysis of the interviews compared practices both within subjects (between different activities) and between subjects (for the same activity). Each description of a practice involving either a different function within an application, a different application or a different device was coded separately. These coded descriptions were then used to inductively define the different dimensions of the practice they referred to. In turn, the extent to which each descriptions referred to one or more of these dimensions were used to profile each subject in terms of their PIM competences.

Two methodological principles frame our study. First, we consider our subjects' PIM practices as the performances that make their competences observable. Hence, we rely on the traces left by these practices, and the discourses that describe them to identify these competences. Second, we define our units of analysis in terms of activities supported by PIM practices, not in terms of tools (e.g. files, email, bookmarks...). As these activities cut across a variety of tools and devices, this allows us to examine the PIM practices of our subjects at three levels: (1) at the hardware level: how and why subjects organize their activity on one or several hardware configurations, and manage the coordination between them; (2) at the software level: how and why subjects use different combinations of applications and manage the coordination between them and (3) at the collection level: how and why subjects categorize information items and create organizational structures to keep them.

3.3 Preliminary Results

As the analysis of our interviews is still underway, we present preliminary results focusing on the school-related activities of our subjects, who had just completed their senior year in high school at the time of the interview.

Our informants' personal information spaces varied in terms of the complexity of the structures and arrangements they included and the array of tool affordances they took advantage of, depending not only on the nature and amount of organized information, but also on taste, style and motivation towards the activity. As far as school-related resources are concerned, our informants developed practices that range from no-filers to total filers [28]. One user claimed that she didn't have any folder, and that she was not aware of where her files were stored on the computer (with the exception of a few files stored on a USB key). She relied either on the operating system's search function or on the "recent files" function of her word processing software to retrieve them. Another user did file her school documents into folders, but deleted the whole hierarchy right after she graduated. At the other end of the filing spectrum, one user maintained a folder hierarchy within her "school folder", with a first-level folder for each school year, a second-level folder for each class (the name of which included the teacher's name, in anticipation of the fact that her little brother may re-use her files), and third-level folders for specific projects. In addition, she used two USB keys: one for documents she worked on outside her house, and another for backups.

Our analysis of the descriptions provided by our informants lead us to distinguish between four dimensions of their PIM practices: (1) the affordances and/or constraints of the device or application involved, (2) the specific activity supported by the practice, (3) the costs or benefits of the practice with respect to their activity and (4) personal preferences or tastes justifying the practice. We intend to use the way and the extent to which these dimensions are articulated in our informants' descriptions to evaluate their competence level.

Affordances and Constraints of Tools and Devices. When describing their practices, subjects may refer to the affordances and constraints of their technological environment. In those cases, behavior is explained in reference to what individuals perceived as possible or not possible in a particular context. The specificity of these descriptions is variable: from a whole platform (using Facebook to interact with classmates), to tools included in a platform (e.g. using Facebook Groups to work on collective projects), to specific functions (e.g. using live collective editing in online word processing applications). In addition to revealing the precision in the perception of what tools and devices afford or constrain, the descriptions also reveal errors or limits in these perceptions. For example, one informant claimed to use email "to send files between us, because we can't do that with Facebook". When asked why he decided to delete all but important files from his hard drive, another participant answered he did this because he feared his files may exceed the hard drive's limited capacity, which he could not estimate.

Supported Activities. Users also refer to the activities they undertake to account for the adoption of a particular practice. Again, the references to activities vary in terms of specificity, from "using Skype to work on group assignments" in general to "creating a folder for a specific French course dissertation".

Costs and Benefits of Practices. Some descriptions refer to an evaluation of benefits or costs generated by the adoption of a practice. The comparison with other (previous or hypothetical) practices is not always explicit, and the evaluation can rely on one or several of different of criteria:

- *Time evaluation:* speed is a recurring factor justifying a practice, be it from a technical standpoint ("This computer is faster, so it's easier") or a social standpoint ("People respond more quickly on Facebook than by email").

- *Physical evaluation:* the portability of devices and tools may justify their adoption ("When I need to work at someone else's house, I put my files on a USB key, it's easier than dragging my computer around").
- *Economic evaluation:* economical cost is another dimension that is mentioned by users. When asked which communication means she uses to work with other students, a subject explained that she uses phone messages after 5 p.m. because they are free.
- *Cognitive evaluation:* Some practices may be associated with different levels of perceived cognitive demands. One subject claimed she didn't want to create third-level sub-folders in her class-related folders as "I prefer when there aren't too many things that get mixed up because I get lost". This example contrasts with the discourse of another informant who found second-level sub-folders useful because "it's clear, I mean, I don't get confused between the French class stuff and the religion class stuff, which sometimes overlap. It's well separated, it's easy, it can be accessed easily".
- *Social evaluation:* some perceived benefits or costs are related to the quality or the complexity of social interaction. One subject explained that she used Skype "to be able to speak more easily than in writing". Another participant claimed that she collaborated with other students through Facebook as it allows to send messages to multiple individuals more easily.

Preferences, Tastes and Emotions. Subjects also refer to their feelings, tastes and preferences, which account both for the adoption of a particular organizational behavior, as when one informant described the old school-related files she kept as "the things that could be useful again, the things on which I worked, so I don't want to delete them either (...) I don't want to have regrets in the future", as well as for the absence of action, as when another informant explained that the fact that the computer automatically created files in her folders "doesn't bother me. (...) I like it when it's well organized, but I don't always have the courage".

4   Discussion and Future Work

The analysis of the way our informants describe their PIM practices by referring to the constraints and affordances of the tools and devices they use, the activities they support, their costs and benefits for these activities, and their tastes and preferences towards them, is the basis on which we intend to found the analysis of their PIM competences.

First, consistent with our first hypothesis, the descriptions of our informants' PIM practices revealed that they differed in their ability to perceive the affordances and constraints of the tools and devices they used. Their descriptions of these affordances and constraints differed both in terms of precision (what an application affords *vs.* what one of its functions affords) and quality (accurate perception *vs.* approximate perception *vs.* erroneous perception).

Second, consistent with our second hypothesis, subjects differed in their ability to match constraints and affordances with specific aspects of their activity.

Some descriptions of practices referred to very specific articulations between the two (e.g. using cloud word processing to be able to "see who had worked on the files" of a group assignment). Others described much looser associations (e.g. using Facebook to interact with classmates), or erroneous distinctions (e.g. thinking it is not possible to use Facebook to circulate files between classmates).

Third, consistent with our third hypothesis, subjects differed in their ability to reflect on their practices. When it came to describing them, speed, clarity and ease of use were the most cited reasons for adoption of a particular organizational behavior. However, informants differed in their reflexive ability to provide a finer, more explicit description of these reasons (e.g. what it means for an organization to be 'clearer' and how their tools of choice contribute to clarity), involving one or more of the criteria identified in our analysis (time, portability, economy, cognition, sociality).

These three dimensions of competence (affordance and constraint perception, selective affordance and constraint adoption, reflexivity on practices) define our conceptual framework for the analysis of PIM competences.

The preliminary results presented in this paper make it clear that PIM competence evaluation needs to avoid the temptation of equating a greater complexity of practices with a higher level of competence. The more competent users are not the ones who are able to create and maintain more complex structures, but to create and maintain structures that better support their activities and to reflect and explain their behavior. Indeed, our ongoing analysis of the non-school-related PIM practices of our informants reveals a variety in the complexity of their practices not only across subjects, but also within subjects. For example, one informant had a fairly simple school-related file collection, but a much more complex music file collection. This fact seems to confirm results of previous studies highlighting the ability of individuals to resort to multiple PIM strategies, even within the same activity [28]. In our model, the very ability to adapt one's strategy to the specific demands of the activity is one of the basic dimensions of PIM competence. In this context, further research is needed to understand how cost and benefit evaluations lead to strategy adaptation, especially in problematic situations where individuals decide to change their behavior.

Finally, the question of the factors of development of PIM competences still largely needs to be investigated. To conclude, we tentatively identify several such factors. On the one hand, we hypothesize that higher levels of competence may either be fostered by a higher frequency of ICT use [44], or by more diverse ICT uses, developed in more diverse social contexts [45]. As our preliminary results suggest, the individual's tastes and preferences may play the role of a mediating variable between ICT use and their level of engagement in more or less complex PIM practices, enabling them to develop their competences. On the other hand, our current observations point to the crucial role of the users' acquaintances, and specifically of family members. Informants living in families where technology-related activities are shared seem to have richer, more complex informational behavior, whereas informants living in families where technology-related activities are conducted "every man for himself" seem to have poorer interaction with digital media.

Acknowledgements. Jerry Jacques is a Research Fellow funded by the Belgian Funds for Scientific Research (F.R.S.-FNRS). Pierre Fastrez is a Research Associate funded by the Belgian Funds for Scientific Research (F.R.S.-FNRS).

References

1. Gantz, J., Reinsel, D.: Extracting Value from Chaos. State of the Universe: An executive Summary. IDC iView (2011)
2. Jones, W., Teevan, J.: Personal Information Management. University of Washington Press, Seattle and London (2007)
3. Georges, F.: Identités Virtuelles. Questions Théoriques, Paris (2010)
4. Kljun, M., Dix, A.: Collaboration Practices within Personal Information Space. In: Proceedings of the Workshop on Personal Information Management (PIM) 2012, Seattle, WA (2012)
5. Zhang, H., Twidale, M.: Mine, Yours and Ours: Using Shared Folders in Personal Information Management. Presented at the PIM 2012 Workshop, Seattle, WA (2012)
6. Kirsh, D.: Thinking with external representations. AI Soc. 25, 441–454 (2010)
7. Jones, W.: Keeping Found Things Found: The Study and Practice of Personal Information Management. Morgan Kaufmann, Burlington, MA (2008)
8. Diekema, A.R.: Unifying PIM Research: Fostering a Connection Between Descriptive PIM Studies and Prescriptive Outcomes. Presented at the Workshop on Personal Information Management (PIM) 2012 at ACM Conference for Computer Supported Collaborative Work (CSCW), Seattle, WA (2012)
9. Kim, J.: Guiding Users to Improve Personal Information Management. Presented at the Workshop on Personal Information Management (PIM) 2012 at ACM Conference for Computer Supported Collaborative Work (CSCW), Seattle, WA (2012)
10. Mander, R., Salomon, G., Wong, Y.Y.: A "pile" metaphor for supporting casual organization of information. In: Proceedings of the SIGCHI Conference on Human Factors in Computing Systems, pp. 627–634. ACM, New York (1992)
11. Bauer, D., Fastrez, P., Hollan, J.D.: Computationally-Enriched "Piles" for Managing Digital Photo Collections. In: Proceedings of the IEEE Symposium on Visual Languages and Human-Centric Computing (2004)
12. Agarawala, A., Balakrishnan, R.: Keepin' it real: pushing the desktop metaphor with physics, piles and the pen. In: Proceedings of CHI 2006, pp. 1283–1292. ACM Press, New York (2006)
13. Tang, J.C., Wilcox, E., Cerruti, J.A., Badenes, H., Nusser, S., Schoudt, J.: Tag-it, snag-it, or bag-it: combining tags, threads, and folders in e-mail. In: CHI 2008 Extended Abstracts on Human Factors in Computing Systems, pp. 2179–2194. ACM, New York (2008)
14. Rodden, K., Leggett, M.: Best of both worlds: improving gmail labels with the affordances of folders. In: CHI 2010 Extended Abstracts on Human Factors in Computing Systems, pp. 4587–4596. ACM, New York (2010)
15. Hearst, M.A.: Clustering versus faceted categories for information exploration. Commun. ACM. 49, 59–61 (2006)
16. Robertson, G., Czerwinski, M., Larson, K., Robbins, D.C., Thiel, D., van Dantzich, M.: Data mountain: using spatial memory for document management. In: Proceedings of the 11th Annual ACM Symposium on User Interface Software and Technology, pp. 153–162. ACM, New York (1998)

17. Bauer, D., Fastrez, P., Hollan, J.D.: Spatial Tools for Managing Personal Information Collections. In: Proceedings of the 38th Hawaii International Conference on System Sciences, Hawaii (2005)

18. Rekimoto, J.: Time-machine computing: a time-centric approach for the information environment. In: Proceedings of the 12th Annual ACM Symposium on User Interface Software and Technology. ACM, Asheville (1999)

19. Barreau, D., Nardi, B.A.: Finding and reminding: file organization from the desktop. SIGCHI Bulletin 27, 39–43 (1995)

20. Barreau, D.: The persistence of behavior and form in the organization of personal information. Journal of the American Society for Information Science and Technology 59, 307–317 (2008)

21. Hardof-Jaffe, S., Hershkovitz, A., Abu-Kishk, H., Bergman, O., Nachmias, R.: How do students organize personal information spaces? Educational Data Mining, 250–258 (2009)

22. Mackay, W.E.: Diversity in the use of electronic mail: a preliminary inquiry. ACM Trans. Inf. Syst. 6, 380–397 (1988)

23. Civan, A., Jones, W., Klasnja, P., Bruce, H.: Better to Organize Personal Information by Folders Or by Tags?: The Devil Is in the Details. Presented at the 68th Annual Meeting of the American Society for Information Science and Technology (ASIST 2008), Columbus, OH (2008)

24. Fisher, D., Brush, A.J., Gleave, E., Smith, M.: Revisiting Whittaker & Sidner's "email overload" ten years later. In: Proceedings of the 2006 20th Anniversary Conference on Computer Supported Cooperative Work, ACM, New York (2006)

25. Whittaker, S., Sidner, C.: Email overload: exploring personal information management of email. In: Proceedings of the SIGCHI Conference on Human Factors in Computing Systems, pp. 276–283. ACM, New York (1996)

26. Rodden, K., Wood, K.R.: How do people manage their digital photographs? In: Proceedings of the SIGCHI Conference on Human Factors in Computing Systems, pp. 409–416. ACM, New York (2003)

27. Jones, W., Dumais, S., Bruce, H.: Once Found, What Then? A Study of "Keeping" Behaviors in the Personal Use of Web Information. In: Proceedings of the ASIST Annual Meeting, vol. 39, pp. 391–402 (2002)

28. Boardman, R., Sasse, M.A.: "Stuff goes into the computer and doesn't come out": a cross-tool study of personal information management. In: Proceedings of the SIGCHI Conference on Human Factors in Computing Systems, pp. 583–590. ACM, New York (2004)

29. Bergman, O., Beyth-Marom, R., Nachmias, R.: The Project Fragmentation Problem in Personal Information Management. In: Proceedings of the SIGCHI Conference on Human Factors in Computing Systems, pp. 271–274. ACM, New York (2006)

30. Malone, T.W.: How do people organize their desks?: Implications for the design of office information systems. ACM Transactions on Information Systems 1, 99–112 (1983)

31. Lansdale, M.W.: The psychology of personal information management. Applied Ergonomics 19, 55–66 (1988)

32. Hobbs, R.: Digital and Media Literacy: A Plan of Action. The Aspen Institute, Washington D.C (2010)

33. Livingstone, S.: The changing nature and uses of media literacy. Media@LSE electronic working papers 4 (2003)

34. Fastrez, P.: Quelles compétences le concept de littératie médiatique englobe-t-il? Une proposition de définition matricielle. Recherches en Communication 33, 35–52 (2010)

35. Fastrez, P., De Smedt, T.: Une description matricielle des compétences en littératie média-tique. In: Lebrun-Brossard, M., Lacelle, N., and Boutin, J.-F. (eds.) La littératie médiatique multimodale. De nouvelles approches en lecture-écriture à l'école et hors de l'école. pp. 45–60. Presses de l'Université du Québec, Québec (2012)

36. Mioduser, D., Nachmias, R., Forkosh-Baruch, A.: New Literacies for the Knowledge Society. In: Voogt, J., Knezek, G. (eds.) International Handbook of Information Technology in Primary and Secondary Education, pp. 23–42. Springer (2008)

37. Jacques, J., Fastrez, P., De Smedt, T.: Organizing media as social objects. An exploratory assessment of a core media literacy competence. Media Education Research Journal. 4, 42–57 (2013)

38. Jenkins, H., Purushotma, R., Clinton, K., Weigel, M., Robison, A.J.: Confronting the Challenges of Participatory Culture: Media Education for the 21st Century. The John D. and Catherine T. MacArthur Foundation (2006)

39. Attwell, G.: Personal Learning Environments - the future of eLearning? eLearingPapers 2, 1–8 (2007)

40. Ausubel, D.P.: The Psychology of Meaningful Verbal Learning: An Introduction to School Learning. Grune & Stratton, New York (1963)

41. Hardof-Jaffe, S., Nachmias, R.: Students Personal Information Management. In: Herrington, J., Couros, A., Irvine, V. (eds.) Proceedings of World Conference on Educational Multimedia, Hypermedia and Telecommunications 2013, pp. 820–828. AACE, Chesapeake (2013)

42. Norman, D.A.: Cognitive artifacts. In: Carroll, J.M. (ed.) Designing Interaction: Psychology at the Human-Computer Interface, pp. 17–38. Cambridge University Press, Cambridge (1991)

43. Russell, D.M., Stefik, M.J., Pirolli, P., Card, S.K.: The cost structure of sensemaking. In: Proceedings of the INTERACT 1993 and CHI 1993 Conference on Human Factors in Computing Systems, pp. 269–276. ACM, New York (1993)

44. Schradie, J.: The digital production gap: The digital divide and Web 2.0 collide. Poetics. 39, 145–168 (2011)

45. Ito, M., Baumer, S., Bittanti, M., Boyd, D., Cody, R., Herr-Stephenson, B., Horst, H.A., Lange, P.G., Mahendran, D., Martinez, K.Z., Pascoe, C.J., Perkel, D., Robinson, L., Sims, C., Tripp, L.: Hanging Out, Messing Around, and Geeking Out: Kids Living and Learning with New Media. The MIT Press (2009)

Design Knowledge Framework
Based on Parametric Representation

A Case Study of Cockpit Form Style Design

Jing Jing, Qiang Liu, Wenyi Cai, Yang Ying, and Ting Han[*]

School of Media and Design, Shanghai Jiao Tong University, China
hanting@sjtu.edu.cn

Abstract . This paper describes a novel framework of design knowledge based on parametric representation intended for using in concept generation of cockpit form style design in civil aviation. With this parametric representation, a parametric model is built to drive a platform of cockpit form style design to enable the designer to make better-informed decisions that can offer design guidelines. And this research took cockpit form style design for example to illustrate and validate this methodology.

Keywords: Design Knowledge, Parametric Representation, Concept Generation, Cockpit Form Style Design.

1 Introduction

Design is a complex process that is omnipresent in our day-to-day life. Especially when facing the task with a large number of parts to satisfy, the designer will be under enormous pressure because the design becomes extremely complex. S.K. Chandrasegaran et al. [2] think "the design problem representation is often ill-defined", and "such factors put a substantial demand on the necessity of a wide variety of knowledge sources – heuristic, qualitative, quantitative, and so on". They also indicate that "while knowledge is viewed as structured information, it can also be considered as information in context". Y. Nomaguchi and K. Fujita [9] point out that "an advanced integrated design environment should have a representation framework for process of a designer's reflection". This research takes cockpit form style design for example to illustrate and validate this methodology.

Past research on product style can be clustered into five groups. Group one, analysis of product form and product style representation based on shape grammar. Group two, correlation study between product style and design elements based on Kansei engineering. Currently, in Japan, the United States, Taiwan and other countries and regions, some researchers work in this field, they studied the correlations between product style and design elements based on semantic differential, multidimensional scaling method. Group three, cognitive research on product style based on cognitive psychology.

---

[*] Corresponding author.

S. Yamamoto (Ed.): HIMI 2014, Part I, LNCS 8521, pp. 332–341, 2014.

Group four, research on product style based on 'five senses'. Group five, study of product style based on the integration of multi-discipline [6].

2   Methodology Description: Case-Based Reasoning

The previous research on product form style is difficult and time-consuming. The development of the novel cockpit form is also a challenging task. The platform developed in our research can assist to generate concepts automatically and rapidly, offering guidelines for designers. The study framework is as follows (Fig.1):

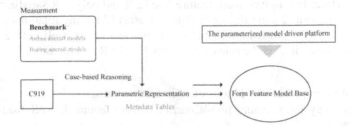

Fig. 1. Research Framework

Comparing with other fields (product reliability and usability etc.), expert knowledge and experience in product form style design are more uncertain and obscure. So the main method in this research is case-based reasoning. Case-based reasoning is an effective method to obtain the solution of the current problems by reasoning the past cases, based on the Dynamic memory theory proposed by Schank et al. [1]. The index is obtained and built by analyzing and generalizing cases, secondary cases and related cases. The index indicates the intangible relationship of design knowledge in cases.

Table 1. Description of the metadata

Metadata	Description	Property
common	Common features of product, such as dimensions features, mapping relations from the structure to the model.	Static
species	Case scenarios, such as the style intentionality, the brand attribution.	Low dynamic
special	Specific characters of the form feature line, such as the role speciality, the role behavior.	High dynamic

In CBCS (Case-base Cockpit Styling), the metadata is the best form of the index. Metadata is used to express the highly structured data of information resources, making information acquisition accurately. Since the diversity of industrial design, metadata of each case in CBCS is different from others. The case-based knowledge metadata contains three kinds of information in CBCS, which can be expressed as follows:

Metadata (i) = Metadata (common) + Metadata (species) + Metadata (special)

2.1   Role Analysis

Definition of Role: For a given form feature line E, if and only if R satisfies: (1) there is another entity (form feature line or designer or user) E' having relations with E and forming R (E,E') (2) form feature line E still exists and keeps itself before obtaining role R or after losing it, R is the role of the entity E. The Role contains six elements as follows:

- Role Definition: Formal definitions of form feature lines.
- Role Type: Key form feature lines\Connected form feature lines\Subsidiary form feature lines.
- Role Speciality: Relationships (affiliation or coordination) with other features and the correlation degree.
- Role Behavior: Specific descriptions of form feature lines.
- Role Hope: Explanations of form feature lines behaviors after deliberating.
- Role Ruler: Standards and criterions the role has to follow.

Of six elements, Role Definition and Role Type are structural. Role Hope and Role Ruler belong to functional properties. Role Speciality and Role Behavior are behavioral.

2.2   Scenario Analysis

The notion of "scenario" originally appears in cognitive psychology and related research fields. In 1896, Dewey [4] proposed the notion "scenario". He found that in fact people not only extract, but reconstruct the past when recalling [8]. Dewey's experiments also demonstrated that the result of memory depends on the scenario of extraction from the view of reconstruction memory [5]. In 1972, Tulving [3] proposed the episodic memory theory and semantic memory theory on long term memory. Episodic memory theory and semantic memory theory indicate that scenario plays an important role in memory and knowledge structure. Besides, Clancwy WJ [7], R.M.Oxman [10], Bouquet P et al. [11] point out that the knowledge is generated in the scenario of memory's production and extraction according to researches.

In our research, the scenario analysis involves Style Scenario, Brand Scenario and Type Scenario, since style, brand and type are three important factors influencing cockpit form style design.

- Style Scenario: It indicates form style features of the object having some significance on visual communication. Style Scenario is expressed by a series of adjectives.
- Brand Scenario: The clear and definite recognition is the main feature of the impressing brand. Brand Scenario focuses on the features influence on the brand.
- Type Scenario: It focuses on the characteristic of different type cockpits. In this paper, civil aviation is the only research object, so Type Scenario is out of our study.
- Four elements of Scenario are as follows:
- Scenario Description: It covers the time, the place, association objects and the arrangement. It has static or dynamic property.
- Scenario Role: It means various roles in the scenario. It can be individual or group.
- Role Relationship: It means the relationship of roles in scenario.
- Scenario Ruler: It means the standard in scenario including given behavior patterns and rules.

2.3   The Model Based on Scenario and Role

The following figure (Fig.2) presents the model based on scenario and role[12]. As an entity, the feature plays different roles in different scenarios. Features constitute the case, composed of a set of form feature lines. The knowledge of cockpit form feature can be generated with scenario and role analysis. The result of CBCS database is Metadata Tables.

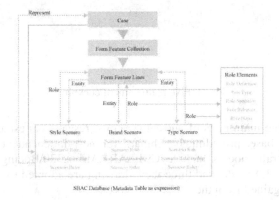

Fig. 2. The model based on scenario and role

2.4   The Framework of Cockpit form Feature Knowledge

Under different scenarios (Style Scenario, Brand Scenario and Type Scenario), the role of the form feature line varies. The framework presents the role analysis under different scenarios [13](Fig.3).

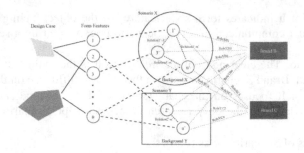

Fig. 3. The framework of cockpit form feature knowledge

3   Case Study of Cockpit Form Style Design

3.1   Measurement: Measuring Five Main Parts of Cockpit

In order to carry on the research distinct, the whole cockpit is divided into five parts: (1) Overhead panel; (2) Glareshield panel; (3) Center instrument panel; (4) Control stand and (5) Sidewall panels according to the concentration of form feature lines in cockpit form style (Fig.4).

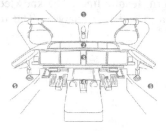

Fig. 4. Five main parts of cockpit

By measuring the main parts of current cockpits, researchers establish the cockpit form feature case-base, providing benchmark for new independent-design cockpit. Measurement aircraft models include C919\ARJ\Airbus320\Boeing737. In dealing with intricate data, 3D-model and three view drawing are adopted to present. Measuring results can be gained from the author.

3.2   Extraction of Form Feature Lines

Cockpit form feature lines are classified as the key form feature line, the connected form feature line and the subsidiary form feature line.

The Cockpit form feature lines extraction experiment aims at extracting the form feature lines, determining the range of the research. In this paper, cockpits of Boeing 777 and Airbus350 are selected as examples. Some students from Shanghai Jiao Tong University were recruited as subjects. These students were required to extract the form feature lines and classify these lines into three certain types (the main feature line, the connected form feature line or the subsidiary form feature line). Experiment results are as follows (Fig.5):

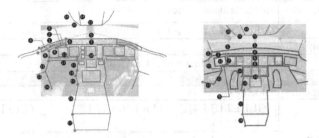

Fig. 5. The left is Form feature lines of Boeing777 (50 form feature lines are identified, including 24 key form feature lines, shown as L1-L24.) The right is Form feature lines of Airbus350 (45 form feature lines are identified, including 22 key form feature lines, shown as L1-L22.)

3.3   Metadata Tables

The cockpit can be represented from three aspects: the fundamental analysis (common), the scenario analysis (species) and the role analysis (special).

Fundamental Analysis of the Cockpit Form. The metadata contains lots of information, such as the cockpit name, the size, the cockpit start date and so on.

Table 2. Metadata of the fundamental analysis (Some subjects, A1-E1 and A2 to E2, were asked to select the influential properties with colore.)

Boeing777	A1	B1	C1	D1	E1	Example
Brand						Boeing
Model						777
Width						5.86 m
Pilot						2 persons

Scenario Analysis of the Cockpit Form. The cockpit form style is an integrated collection of features. The relationship among various roles can be obtained by scenario analysis (Style Scenario and Brand Scenario) from an overall perspective.

Scenario Description is the semantic description of current scenario. In Style Scenario, image schema is adopted to express. In Brand Scenario, it means the cockpit brand name. Scenario Role is the first five important collections of correlative form feature lines in current scenario. Scenario Standard pays close attentions on the cockpit form feature changes in different scenarios.

Role Analysis of the Cockpit Form. Vector graphs are used to represent Role Behavior. The top two roles those having close correlation are chosen to represent Role Speciality. Of six elements, Role Speciality and Role Hope are analyzed in Style Scenario and Brand Scenario respectively owing to their dynamic property.

Table 3. Metadata of the scenario analysis (Role Relationship is represented with the contribution degree, maximum 5 and minimum 1.)

Boeing777	Style Scenario
Scenario Description	Multifarious、Intricate、Curvilinear
Scenario Role	L1、$\sum$（L2 L3）、L4
Role Relationship	4、5、3
Scenario Ruler	Humanist、Modernist、Curvy organic form
Boeing777	Brand Scenario
Scenario Description	Boeing777
Scenario Role	$\sum$(L1 L2 L3 L4)、$\sum$（L8 L10 L11 L12）、$\sum$（L13 L14）、$\sum$（L20 L21）
Role Relationship	5、4、4、4、3、
Scenario Ruler	Form style features of Boeing777 cockpit

Table 4. Metadata of the role analysis (More Metadata Tables can be gained from the author.)

Elements	
Case	Boeing777
Feature Entity 1	$\sum$(L1 L3 L5 L6 L7)
Role Definition	Glareshield panel
Role Type	The main form feature line
Role Behavior	
Role Ruler	Humanist、Modernist、Curvy organic form
Style Scenario	Style Scenario
Role Hope	Multifarious、Intricate、Curvilinear
Role Speciality	
Related Entity	$\sum$(L2 L4)
Relation Degree-1	4
Relationship-1	Coordination
Brand Scenario	Brand Scenario
Role Hope	Boeing777
Role Speciality	
Related Entity	$\sum$(L2 L4)
Relation Degree -1	5
Relationship -1	Affiliation
re-entity	$\sum$(L8 L9)
re-2-1	4
Re-2-2	Coordination

3.4   Universal Model of Cockpit Form

With the achievement of Form Feature Lines and Metadata Tables of some representative aircrafts, the intermediate value is generated across the brand and aircraft model as the basis of the universal model (Fig.6).

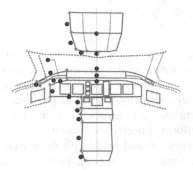

Fig. 6. Universal Model of the Cockpit

3.5   The Parameterized Model Driven Platform of Cockpit Form Style

The parameterized model driven platform of cockpit form style is established to generate concepts for cockpit design. Html5 is used to develop the platform.

Establishment. Firstly, researchers developed function expressions of form feature lines in the universal model of cockpit with Graph. Digitizer. Function expressions of straight lines can be determined immediately. While, for complex curved lines, polynomial segmentation fit is adopted to determine their function expressions. The fitting accuracy reaches 99.7% well. Then researchers developed the platform with html5 (Fig.7).

Verification. By adjusting the parameters, the platform presents form feature models of current cockpits identically. Boeing777 and Airbus380 are verified as follows (Fig.7-8).

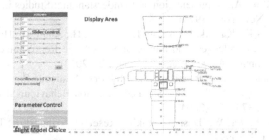

Fig. 7. Form feature model of Boeing777

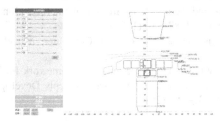

Fig. 8. Form feature model of Airbus380

4   Conclusion

The result and conclusion: (1) This paper details the framework of design knowledge based on parametric representation in the methodology, providing a new approach to acquire design knowledge. The importance of this framework is to understand and test the impact of parametric representation on the acquisition of design knowledge and products' feature. In addition, an effective computer aided tool that help designer to make better-informed decisions requires efficient knowledge representation schemes. (2) The universal model of cockpit form style is identified by summarizing all key form feature lines extracted from 11 Airbus and Boeing cockpits It can be used to describe main feature of cockpit form style effectually. (3) The parameterized model driven platform of cockpit form style is developed. This platform is applied to produce new-design concepts of cockpit form style automatically and rapidly, offering broad design guidelines. With parametric model driven platform designers can generate large alternative concepts in which main feature of cockpit form style is assessed.

Acknowledgement. This paper is sponsored by Shanghai Pujiang Program (13PJC072), Shanghai Philosopy and Social Science Program (2012BCK001), Shanghai Jiao Tong University Interdisciplinary among Hunmnity, Social Science and Natural Science Fund (13JCY02). Moreover, we thank to the students of Shanghai Jiao Tong University who contributed to this research.

References

1. Bobrow, D., Collins, A.: Representation and Understanding: Studies in Cognitive Science. Academic Press, New York (1975)
2. Chandrasegaran, S.K., Karthik, R., Sriram R.D., Imré, H., Alain, B., Harik Ramy, F., Wei, G.: The Evolution, Challenges, and Future of Knowledge Representation in Product Design Systems. Computer-Aided Design. 45, 204-228 (2013)
3. Tulving, E., Donaldson, W.: Organization of Memory. Academic Press, New York (1972)
4. Gero, J.S., Kannengiesser, U.: The Situated Function-Behaviour-Structure Framework. Design Studies 25, 373–391 (2004)
5. Goldschmidt, G., Porter, W.: Design Thinking Research Symposium: Design Representation. MIT Press, US (1999)
6. Ting, H., Qian, S.S.: Product Style Map — an Effective Tool for Product Strategy Planning. Advanced Materials Research 605–607, 472–476 (2012)
7. Clancey, W.J.: W: Situated Action: A Neurological Interpretation Rresponse to Vera and Simon. Cognitive Science 17, 87–116 (1993)
8. Kolodner, J.L.: Reconstructive Memory, a Computer Model. Cognitive Science 7, 281–328 (1983)
9. Yutaka, N., Kikuo, F.: Knowledge Representation Framework for Interactive Capture and Management of Reflection Process in Product Concepts Development. Advanced Engineering Informatics 27, 537–554 (2013)

10. Oxman, R.M.: The Library of Babel: The Representation of Technological Knowledge in Electronic Libraries, Barcelona Press, Spain (1992)
11. Bouquet, P., Srafini, L.: Comparing Formal Theories of Context in Ai. Human-Computer Interaction 16, 35–42 (2001)
12. Hao, T.: Case-Based Scenario Knowledge Model Construction and Application in Product Form Design. Hunan University (2006)
13. Danhua, Z.: Capture and Representation of the Automobile Form Feature Knowledge. Hunan University (2007)

A Map-Based Web Search Interface Using
Point of Interest Aggregation

Kwangsoon Jung[1], Sangchul Ahn[1], and Heedong Ko[1,2]

[1] Department of HCI and Robotics, University of Science and Technology
Daejeon, South Korea
[2] Imaging Media Research Center, Korea Institute of Science and Technology
Seoul, South Korea
{ksjung85,prime,ko}@imrc.kist.re.kr

Abstract. With advent of a mobile computing, the pattern of information search has been changed. Search queries through mobile devices increase; 30% of Google's organic search queries come from mobile devices, and local search, which seeks information with geospatial constraints, also increases. As of 2013 local search on mobile phones continues to grow up to 60% since 2010. However, a large number of web documents cannot be exposed to local search even though they refer to a point of interest (POI) just because they are not explicitly geo-tagged. We are interested in connecting typical web documents to spatial search based on POIs by geotagging web documents. In this paper, we present a map-based web search system that serves geospatial search queries for non-geotagged documents. The proposed system provides with fine-grained local search for typical web pages mentioning several POIs and supports semantic search in accordance with their spatial relation of inclusion.

Keywords: Point of interest, map search interface, named-entity recognition, toponym resolution, entity linking, local search.

1 Introduction

With the recent advent of mobile computing, more people seek local information near them. According to the survey [13], as of 2013 the local search, which seeks information with geospatial constraints, on mobile phones continues to grow up to 60% since 2010. The local index storing local information is needed for the users who seek local information. If the user searches the local information with the usual search engine, the usual search engine can give the information mixed local-related information and non-local-related information. For example, when the user queries "Washington" for the purpose of searching local information, the search engine will give mixed results about the person "Washington" and the location "Washington". We wish to build a map interface using the index storing local information.

However, a large amount of indexed documents in the web have no geo-tags, so they cannot be indexed in the index of geographic locations. Therefore they cannot be exposed to local search even if the web documents are talking about geographic locations.

S. Yamamoto (Ed.): HIMI 2014, Part I, LNCS 8521, pp. 342–351, 2014.

For instance, if "Eiffel Tower" is described in someone's blog, the document does not appear in the search result of Paris of geographic constraints on the map without explicit geo-tagging.

Our system is a map search interface system showing documents of no geotags for local search. Our system consists of four parts: DPOI, crawler, poi indexer and map interface. DPOI provides with the POI list to geotag. The crawler crawls the documents in the web. POI indexer takes the crawled document and detects the POIs in the document by resolving the ambiguity problem of multiple locations with the same name and constructs the POI index. Finally, the map shows the geotagged documents on the map by using the POI index. Our strong point is POI. POI is a place representation like restaurant, hotel, store, cities, etc. on a digital map. Existing works[1,2,3,4,9] in this area generally focused on building the geotagging index with cities, states, or countries that are the static geographic locations. Instead, we extend to all types of POIs including restaurant, stores, landmarks, etc. where are relatively dynamic compared to cities, states, and countries. Moreover, the existing works assume that the author writes a document in concentrating on the one geographic region[1,2,7]. Instead of representing one region to a document, we represent the focused region with hierarchical representation, we called POI level of detail (LOD). For example, we can represent the two LODs, U.S.-California-Anaheim-Disneyland and U.S.-Nevada-Las Vegas for a weblog that the author stayed the Disneyland, CA in the morning and moved to Las Vegas, NV in the afternoon.

2   Related Work

Many geo-tagging systems use a gazetteer, which is the database of geographic locations containing latitude, longitude, population, and more, to collect a set of geographic locations and its attributes. Web-a-where[1] constructs a gazetteer from the dataset of GNIS, World-gazetteer.com, UNSD, and ISO 3166-1. Geographic locations have a hierarchical structure of a world divided into continents, countries, states, and cities. STEWARD[2] extends the number of geographic locations from the number of location in Web-a-where. [3] consists the gazetteer of the several category taxonomy by using the place type, geographic containers, and the population of the place. Unfortunately, their common limitation is that they only use the source of the cities, states, countries, and continents, which do not include all types of POIs.

Geotagging involves two problems; toponym recognition and toponym resolution. Toponym recognition is the problem dealing with geo/non-geo ambiguity, which finds geospatial names in the documents. The most common way to find geospatial names is to use string-matching algorithm from a set of geospatial names in a gazetteer. However, the string-matching algorithm alone can lead to the problem. For example, "Of", a city in Turkey can be detected "of", which is a preposition in English grammar[1]. To solve this problem, many papers[1,2] use the POS(Part-of-Speech) to find noun phrase since geospatial names are always in noun form. For a fine detection, Named-Entity Recognition(NER) technique is used[2,7] as well, which classifies noun into person, organization, and location. Detected as a location are more likely to be geospatial names.

Toponym resolution is the problem coping with geo/geo ambiguity, which is the procedure that determines a specific geographic name with multiple locations of the same name. For instance, "Boston" is located in both United States and United Kingdom. When detected "Boston", we should clarify which "Boston" the author is talking about. One of popular methods is to use the assumption that the author focuses on one area theme while writing a document, so there is one geographic focus in a document. Lieberman et al. decides the one region theme by using the document specific heuristic rules such as dateline of news articles. Web-a-where assigns the scores to each region, continents, countries, states and cities and decides one geographic focus, the highest score region. NewsStand[4] uses heuristic rules depending on document type, in news, a geographic location in a title has more weights. Adelfio et al. uses a Bayesian likelihood model to determine the place category in the data set of table-based place names.

In Information Retrieval, there is a similar problem called Entity Linking. Entity Linking is a method to detect an entity in the document, and then they connect the entity to the knowledge base such as Wikipedia. Entity Linking also needs an entity resolution that, given a mention, which entity is talking about. For example, "Jordan" in the document can be a basketball player, "Michael Jordan" or a professor "Michael Jordan". One of the known methods is to use Graph-based method[8,14]. They used "random walk with restart"[10] for disambiguating entities with the same name. We can apply this method to resolve the place name.

Map-based interface is used for visualizing geographic semantics on the map by using tags in Flickr[16,17]. Hiramatsu et al. implemented the map-based interface system showing the local POIs on the map.

3   Architecture

3.1   Digital POI (DPOI)

DPOI is a gazetteer collecting the POI entities and their properties including an address, latitude, longitude, review, etc. An initial set of a POI is predefined by our POI aggregation. A POI can have various names according to different languages. We aggregated the multilingual POI titles from Korea Travel Organization(KTO) and Geonames. The credible user can add the additional POI names if necessary. One of the functions of DPOI is to assign the unique URI to a POI entity. This URI is used as the unique tagging id in the document.

3.2   Crawler

In the crawler module, the crawler crawls the documents in the web by following the URLs embedded in the crawled documents. In order to provide users with the useful information, the quality control of the documents is necessary. We crawled the

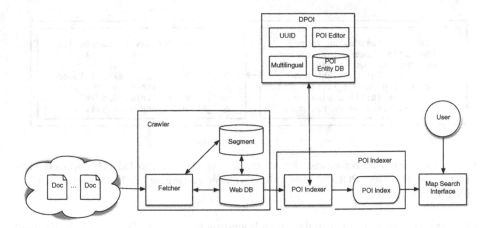

Fig. 1. System Architecture

documents of the reputed users expertising in a trip from Daum-Blog[1] and Naver-Blog[2], Korean famous blog sites. The reputed users are recommended from Daum-Blog, Naver-Blog explicitly by blog-themes for readers. After the crawler crawls the documents in the web, the crawler sends the crawled documents to POI named-entity indexer to detect POIs.

3.3   POI Indexer

When passed the crawled documents, the POI indexer geotags a POI URI to the documents. After the tagging process, the POI index is updated, which is used for search on the map. However, some POI would have a same name, but have different locations. For instance, Boston is both in United States and in United Kingdom. This requires a resolution algorithm, called POI Resolution, to determine which Boston is talking about in the document. We applied a graph-based method[8,14] that a POI mention in the document is likely to be in the same area of a country, state, or city of the other POI mentions in the document. The reason why we choose graph-based method is that if the machine learning technique is applied whenever a set of a POI changes the training should be done again.

3.4   Map Interface

The map interface consists of map, search input box, and search button. When clicks the search button with the keyword, the map interface sends the query containing the map's bounding box, which is the latitude and longitude of left-top, right-bottom of the map, and the keyword to the POI index interface. The POI index finds the POIs

---

[1] http://blog.daum.net
[2] http://blog.naver.com

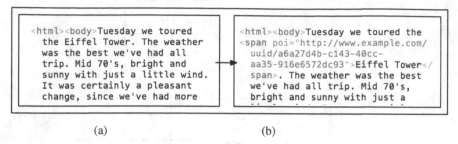

```
<html><body>Tuesday we toured
    the Eiffel Tower. The weather
    was the best we've had all
    trip. Mid 70's, bright and
    sunny with just a little wind.
    It was certainly a pleasant
    change, since we've had more
```

```
<html><body>Tuesday we toured the
<span poi="http://www.example.com/
    uuid/a6a27d4b-c143-40cc-
    aa35-916e6572dc93">Eiffel Tower</
    span>. The weather was the best
    we've had all trip. Mid 70's,
    bright and sunny with just a
```

(a)   (b)

Fig. 2. Two documents before and after geotagging. (a) shows a crawled web document mentioning "Eiffel Tower" POI. (b) shows the document geotagging "Eiffel Tower" as URI in DPOI by POI Indexer.

matched with the keywords in the given bounding box. When clicks the POI, the map interface shows the documents list related to POI. We also provide with the list of POIs on the map for a document. After using our POI Index, the documents without explicit geospatial information can be shown on the Google Map.

4   Graph-Based POI Resolution

We uses Graph-Based POI resolution algorithm[8,14] to resolve which POI the author is talking about. First, we need to construct the POI referent graph. Second, we calculate the initial evidence, which is reinforced by propagating them through the POI reference graph. Finally, the method chooses the highest evidence score, which is the highest probability.

4.1   The POI Referent Graph

The graph is the weighted graph $G(V, E)$ where the node set V comprises of all POI mentions in a document and the POI candidate entities of the mentions in a document. The edge E consists of address edge between POI candidate entity nodes and compatible edge between the POI mention node and POI candidate entity nodes.

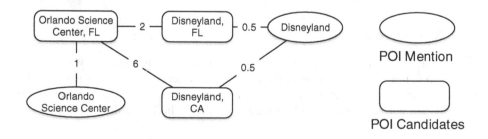

Fig. 3. Example of The Referent POI Graph

Compatible Edge: A compatible edge is an edge between the POI mention node, m, and the POI candidate entity node, e. The total number of POI candidate entities to a POI mention determines the edge weight of the POI. For example, if "Disneyland" has two POI candidate entities, where are in Florida and in California. The edge weights are both 0.5.

$$CP(m, e) = \frac{me}{|m||e|} \qquad (1)$$

Address Edge: An address edge is a edge between the POI candidate entity nodes. The weight is the address distance[15], which shows the geographical distance of POIs. In order to know the address distance, we need a LOD tree. The LOD tree has nodes that the leaf nodes represent the POI candidate entity and its parents nodes show its county, city, states, countries depending on the depths in a graph. The address distance between leaf nodes is the number of the steps between them to reach in shortest path. For example, the distance between "Orlando Science Center" in Florida and "Disneyland" in California is six. The distance between "Orlando Science Center" and "Disneyland" in Florida is two.

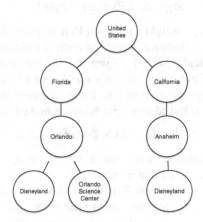

Fig. 4. Example of POI LOD

4.2 Initial Evidence and Evidence Propagation Ratio

The weight of the initial evidence is the score that will be propagating to other nodes. The initial evidence uses tf-idf term score.

$$\text{importance}(m) = \frac{tfidf(m)}{\sum_{m \in D} tfidf(m)}. \qquad (2)$$

For example, if "Disneyland" occurs 8 times and "Orlando Science Center" occurs 4 times, the importance of "Disneyland", importance("Disneyland"), is 8/12.

Given Initial evidence, the next step is to calculate the propagate ratio from the POI referent graph. The propagate ratio is the ratio propagating the initial value to other nodes. The propagating rate depends on the two edges. The propagating rate of Compatible Edge, which is an edge between a POI mention and a POI candidate entity, is below. This is the same score as a Compatible Edge score.

$$P(m \rightarrow e) = \frac{CP(m,e)}{\sum_{e \in N_m} CP(m,e)}. \tag{3}$$

The propagating rate of Address Edge, which is an edge between POI candidate entities, is below.

$$P(e_i \rightarrow e_j) = \frac{AD(e_i, e_j)}{\sum_{e \in N_{e_i}} AD(e_i, e)}. \tag{4}$$

For example, in Figure 3, the propagating rate of the address edge from "Orlando Science Center, FL" to "Disneyland, FL" is 2/6.

4.3   Collective Inference

Given a POI mention m in a document d, we decide the right POI entity as:

$$m.e = \text{argmax}_e\ CP(m, e) \times r_d(e). \tag{5}$$

where $CP(m, e)$ is the edge weight between a POI mention m and its POI candidate entity e and $r_d(e)$ is the evidence score for each document d and POI candidate entity e. We need to calculate $r_d(e)$. Given the referent graph $G(V, E)$ contains n nodes (n = the number of POI mentions + the number of POI candidate entities). Each node is assigned an integer index from 1 to $\| V \|$. We construct the referent graph G as a matrix where $G[i, j]$ is the edge weight between node i and j

$$r^0 = s;\ r^{t+1} = (1 - \lambda) \times T \times r^t + \lambda \times s. \tag{6}$$

where s is the initial evidence vector, an n × 1 where $s_i = \text{importance}(m)$ for i corresponding to m, r^t is the evidence vector at time t, an n × 1 vector where r_i is the evidence score for the node i and T is the evidence propagation matrix, an n × n matrix where T_{ij} is the evidence propagation ratio from node i to node j. We iterate $r^{t+1} = (1 - \lambda) \times T \times r^t + \lambda \times s$ until the convergence. Finally we choose the highest score entity by $\text{argmax}_e\ CP(m, e) \times r_d(e)$.

4.4   Multiple Geographic Focus Determination

After the POI resolution, we determine a geographic focus for the document. In previous papers[1,2,7], the only one geographic focus is emphasized in the document. Depending on the documents, this assumption cannot be true. For example, in a weblog, the writer can describe the trip the several area, thereby resulting in several different focuses. We find the multiple geographic focuses, and represent it by POI LOD, a tree structure of multiple geographic focuses. This is useful in that a geographic focus can be used for the geographic search term. For example, the search term Boston can result in documents, which have Boston LOD node.

5   Implementation

To show the feasibility of the proposed system, we have implemented a prototype system that provides a map-based search service for non-geotagged web documents. The user can input a set of words into the text input form and as a result, a set of POIs is shown in both map and list area. The given query is processed as a spatial search for web documents within the bounding box of map area. The system provides two search modes according to the search criteria, POI mode and document mode. The POI mode presents the search result by the media of POI as shown in Fig. 5(a). Therefore the user can browse the map showing the search result. The web documents are clustered around the selected POIs. If a POI marker is selected, the items signifying the retrieved web documents are shown around it. When the map is magnified, the POI is separated to a set of subordinate POIs. The system takes the user to the actual document by clicking the result items. The document mode intends to provide the optimal method for fine-grained browsing the web documents mentioning multiple POIs as shown in Fig. 5(b). In the right pane, the document list consisting of a teaser image and the summary of document is displayed in the right pane and each item is connected to the marker of specific POI. Because the multi-geographical focuses are supported, a web document can be associated to multiple POI connections.

(a)   (b)

Fig. 5. Two modes of map-based web search interface. (a) shows POI mediated browsing mode of web search results. (b) shows fine-grained search for multiple POIs mentioned in a single web document.

The crawler is based on Apache Nutch 2, as its typical configuration that is combined with Hadoop, HBase, and Gora. We have developed the POI indexer in Java, as a Nutch plugin. DPOI is a separated component and provides the POI entity database functions through RESTful web service. The DPOI service has been developed with Node.js and mongoDB. The map-based search user interface is executed as a web application and mainly uses OpenLayers for map presentation.

6   Conclusion

In this paper, we presented the design and implementation of a map search interface for non geo-tagged web documents. Our system detects geographic locations based on POIs including restaurants, stores, landmarks, etc. We also determine multi-geographical focuses in the document. As a future work, we need to improve the precision and recall of toponym recognition, especially the precision. Unlike the cities, states, countries names, the POI names vary in their types. Some person's names are recognized as POIs such as McDonald's, Wendy's. In order to improve the precision, we need fine-grained NER, trained by the same POI data set. Another future work is an empirical validations described in this paper.

Acknowledgments. This research is supported in part by Ministry of Culture, Sports and Tourism (MCST) and Korea Creative Content Agency (KOCCA) in the Culture Technology (CT) Research & Development Program 2013 and by the Korea Institute of Science and Technology (KIST) Institutional Program (Project No. 2E24790).

References

1. Amitay, E., Har'El, N., Sivan, R., Soffer, A.: Web-a-where: geotagging web content. In: Proceedings of the 27th Annual International ACM SIGIR Conference on Research and Development in Information Retrieval, pp. 273–280. ACM, Sheffield (2004)
2. Lieberman, M.D., Samet, H., Sankaranarayanan, J., Sperling, J.: STEWARD: architecture of a spatio-textual search engine. In: Proceedings of the 15th Annual ACM International Symposium on Advances in Geographic Information Systems, pp. 1–8. ACM, Seattle (2007)
3. Vaid, S., Jones, C.B., Joho, H., Sanderson, M.: Spatio-textual indexing for geographical search on the web. In: Medeiros, C.B., Egenhofer, M., Bertino, E. (eds.) SSTD 2005. LNCS, vol. 3633, pp. 218–235. Springer, Heidelberg (2005)
4. Teitler, B.E., Lieberman, M.D., Panozzo, D., Sankaranarayanan, J., Samet, H., Sperling, J.: NewsStand: a new view on news. In: Proceedings of the 16th ACM SIGSPATIAL International Conference on Advances in Geographic Information Systems, pp. 1–10. ACM, Irvine (2008)
5. Wood, J., Dykes, J., Slingsby, A., Clarke, K.: Interactive Visual Exploration of a Large Spatio-temporal Dataset: Reflections on a Geovisualization Mashup. IEEE Transactions on Visualization and Computer Graphics 13, 1176–1183 (2007)
6. Slingsby, A., Dykes, J., Wood, J., Clarke, K.: Interactive Tag Maps and Tag Clouds for the Multiscale Exploration of Large Spatio-temporal Datasets. In: 11th International Conference on Information Visualization, IV 2007, pp. 497–504 (2007)
7. Lieberman, M.D., Samet, H., Sankaranarayanan, J.: Geotagging with local lexicons to build indexes for textually-specified spatial data. In: 2010 IEEE 26th International Conference on Data Engineering (ICDE), pp. 201–212 (2010)
8. Han, X., Sun, L., Zhao, J.: Collective entity linking in web text: a graph-based method. In: Proceedings of the 34th International ACM SIGIR Conference on Research and Development in Information Retrieval, pp. 765–774. ACM, Beijing (2011)

9. Adelfio, M.D., Samet, H.: Structured toponym resolution using combined hierarchical place categories. In: Proceedings of the 7th Workshop on Geographic Information Retrieval, pp. 49–56. ACM, Orlando (2013)
10. Tong, H., Faloutsos, C., Pan, J.-Y.: Fast random walk with restart and its applications (2006)
11. Göbel, F., Jagers, A.: Random walks on graphs. Stochastic processes and their applications 2, 311–336 (1974)
12. M Digital Marketing Report, Q3 2013 (2013)
13. 6th Annual 15miles/Neustar Localeze Local Search Usage Study Conducted by comScore (2013)
14. Kim, K.M., Oh, H.S., Lee, K.W., Kim, E.Y., Myaeng, S.H.: A Disambiguation Method for Point of Interest Detection. Journal of KIISE (in Korean)
15. Qin, T., Xiao, R., Fang, L., Xie, X., Zhang, L.: An efficient location extraction algorithm by leveraging web contextual information. In: Proceedings of the 18th SIGSPATIAL International Conference on Advances in Geographic Information Systems, pp. 53–60. ACM, San Jose (2010)
16. Ahern, S., Naaman, M., Nair, R., Yang, J.H.-I.: World explorer: visualizing aggregate data from unstructured text in geo-referenced collections. In: Proceedings of the 7th ACM/IEEE-CS Joint Conference on Digital Libraries, pp. 1–10. ACM, Vancouver (2007)
17. Kennedy, L., Naaman, M., Ahern, S., Nair, R., Rattenbury, T.: How flickr helps us make sense of the world: context and content in community-contributed media collections. In: Proceedings of the 15th International Conference on Multimedia, pp. 631–640. ACM, Augsburg (2007)
18. Hiramatsu, K., Kobayashi, K., Benjamin, B., Ishida, T., Akahani, J.-i.: Map-based user interface for Digital City Kyoto. The Internet Global Summit, INET2000 (2000)

Quality Function Deployment Using Improved Interpretive Structural Modeling

Takeo Kato[1] and Yoshiyuki Matsuoka[2]

[1] Department of Mechanical Engineering,
Tokai University, Japan
t.kato@tokai-u.jp
[2] Department of Mechanical Engineering,
Keio University, Japan
matsuoka@mech.keio.ac.jp

Abstract. Due to the product diversification and complication, sharing the product information between the product development members has been important in the product development process. Quality Function Deployment (QFD) is one of the effective methods to share the information of the product using the quality matrices that describes the relationship between design elements needed to be considered. This paper improves QFD by applying the Interpretive structural modeling (ISM). The ISM visually expresses the complex relationship between design elements by using matrix operation. This paper also improves the ISM in order to evaluate not only the relationships between the same type of design elements but also that between in different type. The proposed QFD is applied to a disc brake design problem, and their applicability is confirmed.

Keywords: Design Methodology, QFD, ISM, Structural Modeling.

1 Introduction

The functions and mechanisms of products have diversified and have become increasingly complicated, resulting in the specialization and professionalization of design work [1]. Consequently, it is difficult for members of a product design team to share product information. This lack of information between design team members is a significant issue for manufacturing companies because it leads to design changes or quality issues in the design process.

Quality Function Deployment (QFD) [2, 3] is an effective method to resolve the above problem. Using quality charts, design elements of customer demands (considered in the early process of design) can be translated into those of the quality characteristics, product function, parts, etc. (considered in the latter process of design). Deployment charts, including allied design elements, are used to prepare quality charts, and relationship matrices depict the relationship between design elements in the different deployment charts.

S. Yamamoto (Ed.): HIMI 2014, Part I, LNCS 8521, pp. 352–363, 2014.

The conventional QFD was proposed in 1976 and contains several quality charts:

1. One expresses the relationships between demanded qualities and quality characteristics that are transformed from the demanded qualities in order to be evaluated quantitatively (Fig. 1a);
2. One depicts the relationships between quality characteristics and functions of the product extracted from the demanded qualities (Fig. 1b);
3. One depicts the relationships between quality characteristics and product parts (Fig. 1c).

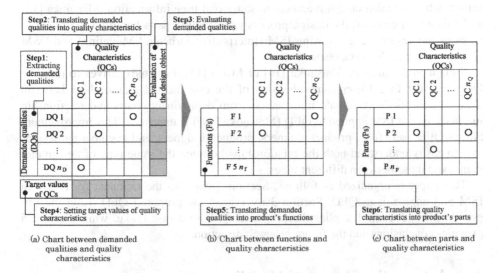

(a) Chart between demanded qualities and quality characteristics

(b) Chart between functions and quality characteristics

(c) Chart between parts and quality characteristics

Fig. 1. Conceptual diagram of quality matrices used in QFD

These quality charts enable designers to clarify the design elements of all design processes (from the demanded qualities to the product parts) and their relationships. Based on the conventional QFD, diverse QFDs have been proposed. Although most QFDs contain quality charts, their design object or objective differs. Research on QFDs can be classified as: (i) improved methods to evaluate the design elements, (ii) change in the items of the quality charts, (iii) usage assistance, and (iv) other applications of QFD.

Many groups have strived to improve the evaluation method. Kuo [4] and Chen [5] proposed a method using a fuzzy approach to reduce the vagueness and uncertainty in the decision-making with respect to the target of the demanded qualities or quality characteristics. Bode [6] calculated the product quality from the strength of the relationship between design elements shown in QFD, and suggested an optimization method to maximize QFD under a cost constraint. Hsiao [7] integrated QFD, FMEA, DFA (Design for Assembly), and AHP (Analytic Hierarchy Process) to evaluate the total quality of the product.

With respect to research to change items in the quality charts, Barad [8] proposed quality charts with the departments and tasks of the company to optimize task implementation.

Zhang [9] and Masui [10] evaluated the environment requirements using QFD. Zhang constructed GQFD (Green QFD) to conduct the LCA (Life Cycle Assessment) and LCC (Life Cycle Costing), while Masui suggested QFDE (QFD for environment) to handle the environmental and traditional product quality requirements simultaneously. Ashihara [11] applied the TSC (Technology Sensitivity Chart), which represents the relationship between new technologies and prospective demanded qualities, and proposed the inverse of QFD to clarify the objectives of product design and technology research.

With the aid in usage, Yeh [12] suggested that QFD and TRIZ be integrated to remove the bottleneck due to clarifying QFD. Huang [13] uploaded QFD onto a Web server, which enabled design members to share real-time information. Matsuoka [14] and Miwa [15] clarified the design process and modular parts based on the relationships of the design elements using ISM (Interpretive Structural Modeling) and DSM (Design Structure Matrix), respectively.

Similar to the aims of Matsuoka [14] or Miwa [15], this study strives to improve QFD in order to aid user comprehension of the complicated relationships between design elements. To calculate information from deployment charts and relationship matrices, herein ISM applied to QFD (Matsuoka [14]) is improved. This improvement allows QFD users (e.g., product planners, product designers, and engineering designers) to easily understand both the relationships between the same type of design elements and those between different types.

This paper is organized as follows. Section 2 explains the rationale for selecting ISM and applies it to QFD. Section 3 overviews the proposed QFD using the improved ISM. Section 4 applies the proposed QFD to a disc brake, while Section 5 provides conclusions and the future research direction.

2   Interpretive Structural Modeling

DSM, which is one of the most effective methods to clarify the relationship between design elements, has been applied to the QFD [14]. Additionally, DMM (Domain Mapping Matrices), which expresses the relationship of the elements in different domains (types), can be used with DSM. Similar to DMM, QFD includes multiple elements. Specifically, QFD contains three domains of design elements: functions, quality characteristics, and parts. Thus, applying DSM to QFD may be effective.

However, methods like DSM, which express relationships in matrices, have some drawbacks. 1) Compared to methods using graphical expressions (connecting the relative elements with a line), users cannot intuitively comprehend the relationship. 2) The alignment of the matrix cannot obtain more than two objectives [16]. For example, DSM cannot be simultaneously aligned for both grouping (referred to as "clustering" in the DSM) and stratifying (referred to as "partitioning").

In the field of mass customization strategies, customers can select the specifications (parts) of the merchandise. Suzić [17] employed FFA (Factory Flow Analysis) and determined the proper location of working machines in the factory line without returning flow in the production process. In FFA, parts manufactured by machines are grouped using a matrix between the working machines and parts. Then the parts are stratified by a material flow diagram (graphical expression). Because this method only considers the relationships between parts and machines, it is difficult to apply FFA to QFD, which must consider the internal and external relationships of the functions, quality characteristics, and part elements.

These conventional methods have advantages and disadvantages with respect to procedures for grouping and stratifying, graphical expressions, and inter-domain relationships evaluation. This study aims to improve the comprehension of complicated relationships and to overcome the disadvantages using ISM.

ISM is a design method to visually express complex relationships between design elements via matrix operations [18]. In ISM, direct affective matrix $\mathbf{X}$ (Fig. 2a), which expresses the relationship between design elements, is initially constructed according to the following equation:

$$\mathbf{X} = \begin{pmatrix} x_{11} & \cdots & x_{1j} & \cdots & x_{1n} \\ \vdots & & & & \vdots \\ x_{i1} & & \ddots & & \vdots \\ \vdots & & & & \vdots \\ x_{n1} & & \cdots & & x_{nn} \end{pmatrix} \tag{1}$$

where n is the number of design elements. x_{ij} values are calculated as:

$$x_{ij} = \begin{cases} 1 & \text{if } i \text{ the element relates to } j \text{ th element} \\ 0 & \text{else} \end{cases} \tag{2}$$

$$(i = 1, 2, \cdots, n \ , \ j = 1, 2, \cdots, n) \ .$$

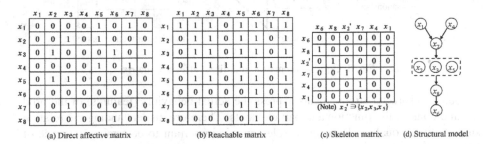

(a) Direct affective matrix   (b) Reachable matrix   (c) Skeleton matrix   (d) Structural model

Fig. 2. Conceptual diagram of ISM (x_1 - x_8 are design elements)

Secondly, reachable matrix $\mathbf{M_R}$ (Fig. 2b) is derived using matrix $\mathbf{M}$, which is calculated by adding direct affective matrix $\mathbf{X}$ and the unit matrix (i.e., $\mathbf{M} = \mathbf{X} + \mathbf{I}$), as shown in the following equation:

$$\mathbf{M_R} = \mathbf{M}^r \quad \left(\mathbf{M}^r = \mathbf{M}^{r-1} \right) \tag{3}$$

Finally, reachable matrix $\mathbf{M_R}$ is transformed into skeleton matrix $\mathbf{M_S}$ (Fig. 2c), and the structural model (Fig. 2d) is constructed based on the relationship in the matrix.

The skeleton matrix can represent the relationship of the reachable matrix using minimum relationships. This paper omits the detailed calculation of the skeleton matrix because it has already been reported [18]. This matrix has two main features: 1) elements affecting each other are grouped and 2) the higher an element is located, the more elements it can affect. Thus, ISM can simultaneously group and stratify. Additionally, ISM can provide a structural model (graphical expressing).

3   Proposed QFD Using ISM

3.1   Improvement of ISM

To apply ISM, this study introduces a correlation matrix into each of the three deployment charts in QFD. Figure 3a shows an example of a correlation matrix regarding parts. In the matrix, unidirectional relationships (i.e., element "A" relates to "B" but "B" does not relate to "A") are described by arrows, whereas bidirectional relationships (i.e., element "A" relates to "B" and "B" relates to "A") are described by circles. In Fig. 3a, design element 1 (d_1) affects both d_2 and d_n, and is affected by d_2. Figure 3b shows the direct affective matrix derived from the correlation matrix. The direct affective matrix improves the grouping and stratifying processes as well as graphical expressions in DSM, but the inter-domain relationships in FFA remain.

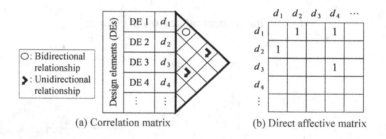

(a) Correlation matrix   (b) Direct affective matrix

Fig. 3. Correlation matrix and direct affective matrix

Quality characteristic elements express the actual behaviors (features) of the product and connect the function and part elements. Therefore, understanding the relationships between quality characteristic elements is important to determine the trade-off between functions as well as to construct modules or the design process of parts. This study improves the direct affective matrix in order to comprehend the relationships between the three domains in QFD: functions, quality characteristics, and parts. Specifically, the relationships of the quality characteristics are added to both the function and part relationships.

The procedure below clarifies the part relationships while considering the quality characteristic relationships using ISM.

Because the procedure for the function relationships is the same as that for the part relationships, its description is abbreviated. To consider the quality characteristic relationships, the following two rules are added to construct a correlation matrix. 1)

Bidirectional relationships must be derived between part elements related to a common quality characteristic element (Fig. 4a). 2) Unidirectional relationships of the part elements in the same direction must be derived as the relationship of quality characteristic elements related to the part elements (Fig. 4b).

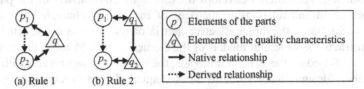

(a) Rule 1   (b) Rule 2

Legend:
p — Elements of the parts
q — Elements of the quality characteristics
→ Native relationship
⋯▸ Derived relationship

Fig. 4. Derived relationship of parts elements based on the quality characteristics relationship

The direct affective matrix of the parts based on the first rule $\mathbf{P}^{1)}$ can be expressed as:

$$\mathbf{P}^{1)} = p_{kl} = \begin{cases} 1 & \text{if } \sum_{i}^{n_q}(p_k,q_i)\cdot(p_l,q_i)=1 \\ 0 & \text{else} \end{cases} \tag{4}$$

$$\left(k=1,2,\cdots,n_p \ , l=1,2,\cdots,n_p, \ k\neq l\right)$$

where the calculation is based on Boolean operations. p_{kl} denotes the value of matrix $\mathbf{P}^{1)}$ in the k th row and l th column. q_{ij} is the value of a direct affective matrix of the quality characteristics in the i th row and j th column. (p_m, q_n) represents the value of the relation matrix between the quality characteristics and parts in the m th row and n th column. n_p and n_q denote the number of the parts and quality characteristics, respectively.

Similarly, the direct affective matrix with regard to the second rule $\mathbf{P}^{2)}$ is expressed as:

$$\mathbf{P}^{2)} = p_{kl} = \begin{cases} 1 & \text{if } (p_k,q_i)\cdot(p_l,q_j)=1 \big| q_{ij}=1 \\ 0 & \text{else} \end{cases} \tag{5}$$

$$\begin{pmatrix} i=1,2,\cdots,n_q \ , \ j=1,2,\cdots,n_q \ , i\neq j \\ k=1,2,\cdots,n_p \ , \ l=1,2,\cdots,n_p \ , k\neq l \end{pmatrix}.$$

By adding Equations 4 and 5 to the original direct affective matrix of part elements $\mathbf{P}$, the direct affective matrix that considers quality characteristic relationships $\mathbf{P}'$ can be calculated as:

$$\mathbf{P}' = \mathbf{P} + \mathbf{P}^{1)} + \mathbf{P}^{2)} \tag{6}$$

3.2   Procedure of Proposed QFD

Figure 5 shows the proposed quality matrices, which include three deployment charts (function, quality characteristics, and parts), two relationship matrices, and three correlation matrices. The procedure of the proposed quality matrices is as follows. Step 1 extracts the design elements, including quality characteristics and parts. Step 2 develops the relationship matrices between the extracted elements. Step 3 constructs the correlation matrices. Steps 1–3 are repeated until the product development members are satisfied. Then Step 4 develops the direct affective matrix of the parts based on the correlation and relationship matrices of the quality characteristics and parts using Eq. 6. Similarly, the direct affective matrix of functions is constructed. Finally, Step 5 constructs the structural models of the elements via ISM using the direct affective matrices. Based on the structural models, the designers can proceed with the parts design without design changes due to an inadequate design procedure (e.g., a later-designed part does not affect earlier-designed parts). Moreover, using the structural model of functions, product planners and designers can comprehend the trade-off between elements and their effect, allowing them to properly determine the specifications or develop a new product.

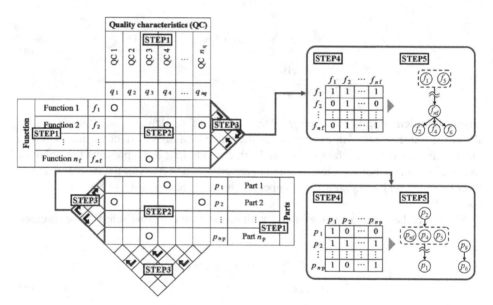

Fig. 5. Procedure of proposed QFD

4   Illustrative Example

4.1   Design Object

To confirm their effectiveness, the proposed quality matrices were applied to a design problem of a disc brake. This disc brake generates a brake torque by pushing the armature onto the disc rotor (brake pad) due to the spring force. Figure 6 shows a conceptual diagram of the disc brakes. The coil springs, which are located between the coil case and armature, push the armature onto the brake pad when braking.

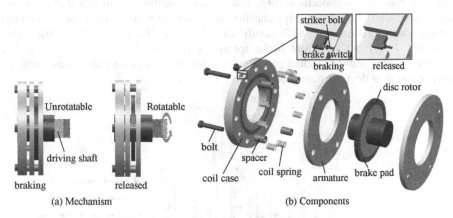

Fig. 6. Conceptual diagram of disc brake

When releasing the brake, the armature is attracted to the coil case via an electromagnetic force. To sense that the brake is braking or releasing, the brake switch, which is installed on the coil case, is set and flipped by the striker bolt set on the armature.

In a disc brake design, designers or product planners must consider a lot of design elements (e.g., the spring characteristics related to the brake torque, the coil characteristics to specify the electromagnetic force, the armature stroke, which concerns both the drive noise and brake switch characteristics) to realize the ideal brake characteristics (e.g., high brake torque, low drive noise, no brake switch glitch). Because a trade-off relationship exists between these characteristics, a design change due to an inadequate design process is likely. Additionally, inadequate specifications may delay of the product development.

4.2   Results and Discussion

Figures 7 - 10 describe the proposed quality matrices and structural models of the disc brake, respectively. Figure 9a shows a structural model of the part elements without considering the quality characteristic relationships. This type of model provides information about the geometric relationships between parts, such as mechanical interference. For example, the part elements of the coil case (p_1–p_3) relate to the part elements of the spring mounted on the coil case. Figure 9b shows a structural model that considers relationships. This type of model indicates not only the geometric relationships but also the relationship regarding engineering characteristics, such as torque or electromagnetic force. For example, the part elements of the coil case (p_1–p_3) relate to the part elements of the spacer (which assures a brake gap) via electromagnetic force and armature stroke. To summarize, the structural model constructed by the proposed QFD expresses relationships of both the geometric and engineering characteristics (generated from the product). Thus, the proposed QFD allows engineering designers to easily construct modular parts or a design procedure using the parts.

The structural model of function elements that considers quality characteristic relationships (Fig. 10b) increases bidirectional relationships compared to the model that does not consider relationships (Fig. 10a). Consequently, the model that considers quality characteristic relationships clarifies the trade-off relationships due to the engineering characteristics, such as "smooth attraction and release" (f_1) and "power consumption" (f_6) or "sufficient brake torque" (f_2) and "lower noise" (f_4). This improved clarity allows product planners or designers to appropriately determine the specifications or develop new products.

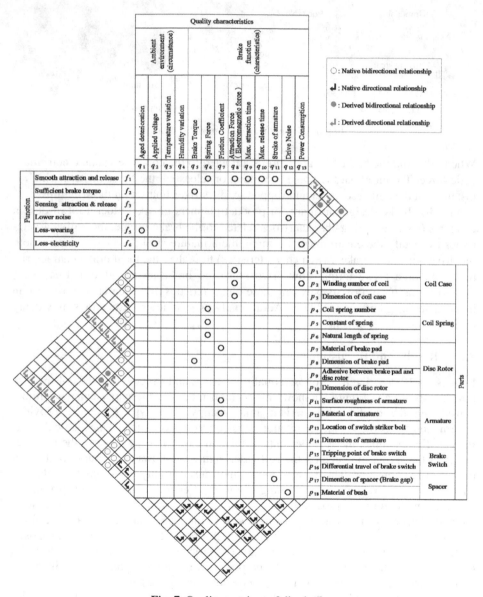

Fig. 7. Quality matrices of disc brake

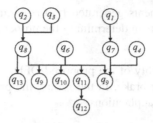

Fig. 8. Structural model of quality characteristic elements

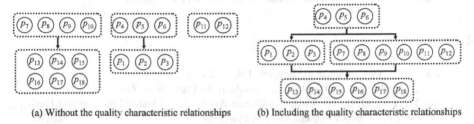

(a) Without the quality characteristic relationships   (b) Including the quality characteristic relationships

Fig. 9. Structural model of part elements

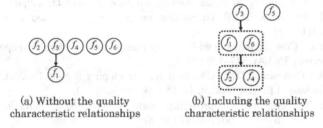

(a) Without the quality
characteristic relationships

(b) Including the quality
characteristic relationships

Fig. 10. Structural model of function elements

5   Conclusion

To clarify the complicated relationships of the design elements, this study introduces improved Interpretive Structural Modeling (ISM) into Quality Function Deployment (QFD). The following observations are made:

- The structural models of the design elements (derived by the ISM) enable users to comprehend the relationships between design elements intuitively.
- The structural model of the part elements, which consider the quality characteristic relationships (derived by the improved ISM), allows engineering designers to comprehend both the geometric relationships of the parts and the relationships based on the engineering characteristics. This improved understanding aids engineers in constructing the modular parts or design procedures for the parts.
- The structural model of the function elements, which consider relationships, enables product planners or designers to understand the trade-off relationships

between the function elements generated by the engineering characteristics. This assists planners or designers in determining the proper specifications or developing new products.

Additionally, the applicability of the proposed QFD was confirmed by applying it to a design problem of a disc brake. In the future, the proposed QFD will be implemented to many other design applications.

Acknowledgements. This work was supported by the Japan Society for the Promotion of Science, Grant-in-Aid for Scientific Research (C) (23611037).

References

1. Matsuoka, Y.: Design Science. Maruzen, Tokyo (2010)
2. Akao, Y.: Quality function deployment. Productivity Press, New York (1990)
3. Akao, Y., et al.: QFD: The Customer-Driven Approach to Quality Planning and Deployment. Asian Productivity Organization, Tokyo (1994)
4. Kuo, T.C., et al.: Integration of environmental considerations in quality function deployment by using fuzzy logic. Expert Systems with Applications 36, 7148–7156 (2009)
5. Chen, L.H., et al.: Fuzzy Nonlinear Models for New Product Development using Four-Phase QFD Processes. IEEE Transaction on Systems, Man, and Cybernetics 41(5), 927–945 (2011)
6. Bode, J., et al.: Cost Engineering with Quality Function Deployment. Computers & Industrial Engineering 35(3-4), 587–590 (1998)
7. Hsiao, S.W.: Concurrent Design Method for Developing a New Product. International Journal of Industrial Ergonomics 29, 41–55 (2002)
8. Barad, M.: Strategy maps as improvement paths of enterprises. International Journal of Production Research 46(23), 6627–6647 (2008)
9. Zhang, Y., et al.: Green QFD-2: a life cycle approach for environmentally conscious manufacturing by integrating LCA and LCC into QFD matrices. International Journal of Production Research 37(5), 1075–1091 (1999)
10. Masui, K., et al.: A Development of a DfE Methodology in Japan -Quality Function Deployment for Environment-. In: Proceedings of The First International Workshop on Sustainable Consumption Report, March 19-20 (2003)
11. Ashihara, K., et al.: Application of Quality Function Deployment for New Business R&D Strategy Deployment. In: Proceedings of 2005 ASME International Mechanical Engineering Congress and Exposition, November 5-11 (2005)
12. Yeh, C.H., et al.: Integration of four-phase QFD and TRIZ in product R&D: a notebook case study. Research in Engineering Design 22, 125–141 (2011)
13. Huang, G.O., et al.: Synchronous quality function deployment (QFD) over world wide web. Computers & Industrial Engineering 42(2/4), 425–431 (2002)
14. Matsuoka, Y.: Design Process on Product with New Structure: The Design Method of Seat (6). The Science of Design 44(2), 9–18 (1997) (in Japanese)

15. Miwa, T., et al.: Product Development Task Planning Using Worth Flow Analysis. ASME Journal of Computing and Information Science in Engineering, 9 034502-1 (2009)
16. Lindemann, U., et al.: Structural Complexity Management. Springer (2009)
17. Suzić, N., et al.: Customizing Products thorough Application of Group Technology: A case Study of Furniture Manufacturing. Strojniški vestnik – Journal of Mechanical Engineering 58(12), 724–731 (2012)
18. Warfield, J.N.: Societal Systems: Planning, Policy and Complexity. Wiley, New York (1976)

Finding Division Points for Time-Series Corpus Based on Topic Changes

Hiroshi Kobayashi and Ryosuke Saga

Osaka Prefecture University, 1-1, Gakuen-cho, Naka-ku, Sakai-shi, Osaka, Japan
kobayahi@mis.cs.osakafu-u.ac.jp, saga@cs.osakafu-u.ac.jp

Abstract. This paper describes the discovery method of finding proper points for dividing a corpus with time series information for extracting local and frequent keywords. Local and frequent keywords express a corpus with time series information and are useful for comprehending it. To extract keywords from the corpus, the previous works proposed corpus separating method. However, this method divides the corpus at equal intervals so that it cannot take into account the change of topic. To consider the change of topics and divide the corpus based on it, we utilize the idea of topic model and the topic extracted by Latent Dirichlet Allocation (LDA). In the experiment using newspaper articles during five years topics, we confirm that the topics of each document change as time passed by using the output from LDA and the point which is available on dividing the corpus by the change of topics notably is observable.

Keywords: keyword extraction, time series information, LDA.

1 Introduction

In recent years, many documents have been converted to digital form by the development of the Internet. This transition to "paperless" documentation reduces the time and effort required to manage documents and makes necessary information instantly available. The amount of digital document data is increasing enormously. Such a large amount of document data may be collectively saved as a corpus. A corpus aggregates a considerable amount of digitalized document data and is used for research such as natural-language processing [1]. To efficiently acquire information from a corpus, the features of the corpus must be known.

Keyword extraction is one way to effectively learn the features of a corpus [2]. Keywords and keyword extraction make searching and summarizing a corpus easy [3]. For example, when searching a document, the keyword expressing the document's content is useful to filter your results [4]. The keywords are first ranked by importance, and the top N keywords are extracted. The frequency of a word in the whole corpus is conventionally used as a measure of importance. Based on the frequency, there are several proposed ranking methods such as term frequency and term frequency–inverse document frequency (TF–IDF).

In contrast, several types of corpuses have time series, such as newspaper articles, magazines, papers, and blogs. Corpuses also include locally characteristic keywords,

S. Yamamoto (Ed.): HIMI 2014, Part I, LNCS 8521, pp. 364–372, 2014.

which appear locally and frequently. These keywords are important to comprehend trends and situations. For example, these keywords appear on Twitter as Trends. For extracting keywords from a corpus with time-series information, conventional methods based on word frequency are not very effective because the keywords are compared with the whole corpus. Therefore, the words which appear frequently and locally are not extracted because the weights from the methods tend to become low. But, when such a word also expresses a corpus, the word which appears frequently locally isn't extracted because the weight becomes low.

To solve this problem, Saga et al. proposed a method of dividing a corpus [5]. The words that appear locally can be extracted as keywords from the divided corpus because division narrows the period to observe documents. However, although normally the change of topic should be considered, because these keywords express the trend of topics, a corpus is divided at equal intervals in this method. Therefore, we should divide the corpus while considering changes of topics.

This paper proposes a method to find division points of a corpus with time-series information while also accounting for changes of topics. To comprehend a topic, we utilize the idea of a topic model and identify the topics using Latent Dirichlet Allocation (LDA). The paper is organized as follows. In Section 2, we introduce a conventional keyword extraction method for when a corpus includes time-series information and identify this method's problem. In Section 3, we describe a topic model and LDA. In Section 4 we perform an experiment for news articles to divide corpus by presuming the distribution of a topic in each document using LDA. Finally, Section 5 contains our conclusions and plans for future work.

2   Keyword Extraction Methods for Corpus with Time-Series Information

The keyword extraction method calculates the weight of all the words appearing in each document of a corpus. Then, words with large weights from each document are extracted as keywords for the document, and words with large weights across many documents are extracted as keywords for the corpus. The flow is shown in Fig.1. Words are generally assigned weights using TF–IDF and residual IDF [6].

However, for some corpuses, time information is important. For example, newspaper articles and blogs are published and updated daily or weekly, and conference proceedings and annual reports are published annually. These documents are organized in time series and change continuously during a certain period. This paper treats such a time-series corpus.

In a time-series corpus, some words occur frequently only during a specific period of time on account of certain occurrences and incidents. As shown in Fig. 2, when a region receives record amounts of snowfalls out of season, the phrase "heavy snow" appears in newspapers frequently and locally. In this situation, the phrase can be an important keyword (phrase). However, the frequency of the phrase is low from the viewpoint of the whole corpus because many people lose interest after the event.

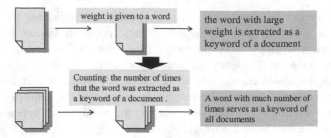

Fig. 1. The flow of keyword extraction

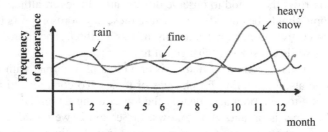

Fig. 2. The word which occurs frequently locally

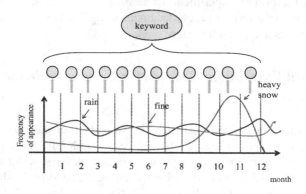

Fig. 3. The aspect of division of a corpus

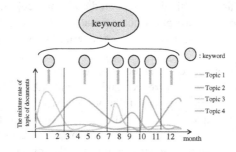

Fig. 4. The aspect of division of a corpus based on the change of topics

So the weight of the word may be lower than those of the words appearing in only a few documents during that period, but constantly, such as "fine" and "rain". As a result, words that express the features of a corpus like "heavy snow" are often not extracted as keywords.

To solve the problem of local keywords not being correctly extracted, Saga et al. proposed a method of separating a corpus according to time series. If a corpus is separated by this method, even conventional methods can be used to extract words that appear frequently but locally. This method is based on the idea that extraction of words appearing frequently and locally is attained by narrowing the period of observation for documents within a time series. Fig. 3 shows how to apply this approach to the corpus from Fig. 2. As shown in the figure, when the corpus is divided, the phrase "heavy snow," which frequently appears between October and November, can be extracted as a keyword without the interruption of other words.

This approach is useful for real data. Previous studies show how the approach can extract local keywords from newspaper articles. However, the approach divides the corpus at equal intervals. In fact, local keywords express the trends of the occurrence during certain periods, but previous studies ignore these trends.

Therefore, we must find suitable compartmental points to extract characteristic words based on changes of topics. Fig. 4 shows how to divide a corpus of documents based on changes of topics. To observe identify the changes of topics, we can utilize use the idea of topic model [7] and the topics of documents are presumed by use Latent Dirichlet Allocation (LDA) to infer the topics of documents. Using a topic model and LDA, we can try to find suitable points for compartmentalization.

3   Corpus Separation Approach Based on Topic Change.

3.1   Topic Model and LDA (Latent Dirichlet Allocation)

A topic model is the probable generation model of a document. The probability that a word will appear varies based on document topics, and then, the probabilistic of appearance of a word depends on topic and each document has multiple-topics. This A topic model is also a statistical model for discovering a certain topic from a document. Each document of a document set is classified into topics. Topics show the contents briefly and make searching and classifying documents easy. One document may have multiple topics. This image is shown in Fig. 5. In this figure, document A is categorized into Topic a and Topic b, and the mixture ratios of two topics are 0.6 and 0.4 for each.

The LDA model is a kind type of the language probabilistic model which assumes that a document consists of multiple-topics. A word can be classified into topics and a document can be classified for every topic. Prior distribution is assumed to be Dirichlet distribution. It is because multinomial distribution can be assumed to how to choose words and topics. The graphical model of LDA is shown in Fig.6. The box expresses the number of times of execution. The nodes within box D correspond to the number of times of execution in the document. N is the number of words and T is number of topics. Each topic is defined based on the distribution of words by node φ. Then, it is probability distributions. The distribution of topics in each document is generated by node θ. The topic is randomly selected from the distribution of topics by node Z. The word is randomly selected from the distribution of words by node W. When W is observed, the posterior probability of $\{\varphi, \theta, Z\}$ is calculated based on probability density approximated by sampling. Then the posterior probability is calculated based on prior probability and the likelihood of W calculated from a generation model. α, β is the parameters to assume that the prior distribution is the Dirichlet distribution and is called the hyper-parameter.

The change of topic is observable because of the distribution of topics obtained by LDA.

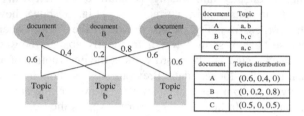

document	Topic
A	a, b
B	b, c
C	a, c

document	Topics distribution
A	(0.6, 0.4, 0)
B	(0, 0.2, 0.8)
C	(0.5, 0, 0.5)

Fig. 5. The image of a multiplex topic

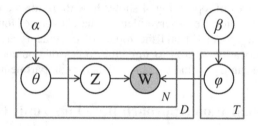

Fig. 6. Graphical model of LDA

3.2   Process of Separating a Corpus Based on Topic Change by LDA

The number of topics and hyper-parameters must be set before applying LDA to a corpus. Then, LDA learns by inputting document and outputs the topic distribution of each document. The distribution shows the mixture ratio of the topic which the document contains. Then, by illustrating the mixture ratio using time series, the rate changes of each topic in each document can be identified. These changes are easier to identify in graphs. A corpus is divided at the points where large changes of topics occur.

4   Experiments

4.1   Goal and Dataset

We performed an experiment to find the points where the topics of documents significantly changed. We used 1827 news articles from CNN.com between January 1, 2000 and December 31, 2004 as a time-series document set and the MALLET [9], a Java toolkit for machine-learning applied to natural language, to create the LDA model.

We set the number of topics (T) to 20, and optimized the hyper-parameters based on the number of topics.

4.2   Experimental Result

The word distribution outputted by LDA is shown in Table 1. We could guess some contents of topics from the LDA result. For example, Topic 6 in Table 1 is presumed to be the Iraq War because we can see words such as "iraq," "war," and "baghdad." The mixture ratio of topics in each document is shown in Table 2. We found the changes of topics of a document set, including time-series information, by observing the mixture ratio of a document for every topic. Based on Table 2, we expressed the changes of topics as the line graph shown in Fig.7.

Table 1. The word distributions of 20 topics

Topic 1	Topic 2	Topic 3	Topic 4	Topic 5	Topic 6	Topic 7	Topic 8	Topic 9	Topic 10
john	gore	police	president	male	iraq	plane	afghanistan	today	class
president	today	area	house	ph	iraqi	space	taliban	percent	width
kerry	news	case	white	great	war	flight	bin	news	style
campaign	percent	county	clinton	big	baghdad	china	laden	tax	john
senator	mccain	question	senator	thing	saddam	air	united	president	stewart
election	online	shooting	blitzer	break	forces	crew	war	press	src
vote	government	morning	george	news	military	question	president	question	table
voters	correspondent	sniper	day	commercial	hussein	chinese	states	economy	href
george	elian	investigation	united	novak	troops	today	al	market	height
state	anchor	washington	country	lin	city	aircraft	military	cut	option
debate	located	point	john	female	coalition	day	today	online	brien
tonight	fdch	scene	american	story	air	miles	terrorism	anchor	color
presidential	secure	person	republican	love	today	united	qaeda	house	today
gore	clinton	man	bill	camera	iraqis	states	york	fdch	dean
democratic	york	law	state	three	general	morning	osama	case	martha
states	states	shot	party	coming	soldiers	officials	country	kagan	border
candidate	case	enforcement	states	day	marines	point	security	bill	type
night	bill	chief	great	brien	question	course	pakistan	located	input
al	day	virginia	senate	long	army	airport	government	correspondent	align

Topic 11	Topic 12	Topic 13	Topic 14	Topic 15	Topic 16	Topic 17	Topic 18	Topic 19	Topic 20
palestinian	storm	anthrax	iraq	material	cnnbodytext	case	court	condit	iraq
israeli	hurricane	enron	war	user	class	today	florida	levy	today
israel	florida	question	weapons	news	iraq	question	police	police	kerry
arafat	hour	fbi	united	copyright	case	court	gore	news	morning
palestinians	area	government	saddam	network	media	morning	election	congressman	president
peace	winds	president	cnnbodytext	license	fdch	death	state	chandra	brien
israelis	water	news	class	cable	today	family	votes	today	costello
east	miles	today	hussein	purposes	california	trial	ballots	gary	security
middle	morning	house	president	redistribute	schwarzenegger	jury	county	question	american
yasser	power	security	inspectors	rights	brien	police	vote	case	hemmer
sharon	damage	war	nations	house	news	judge	campaign	washington	break
minister	coming	states	council	media	dean	attorney	today	online	al
jerusalem	coast	september	north	long	court	neville	recount	located	iraqi
violence	city	united	security	high	question	child	case	correspondent	live
president	beach	point	states	specific	defense	evidence	count	secure	intelligence
prime	hit	pakistan	korea	federal	cooper	man	judge	fdch	war
state	hours	fact	resolution	provide	state	defense	president	anchor	government
secretary	center	intelligence	iraqi	interests	morning	harris	law	point	day
united	live	mail	today	prepared	governor	fire	vice	family	case

From Fig. 7, we confirmed that periods existed in which the topics of documents changed notably. Topics changed significantly when events related to the topics occurred, and there are related keywords about the topics in each period. Thus, we found clues about suitable separation points for changes of topics.

However, some topics, such as topic 2 and topic 10, could not be guessed from words, whereas some topics, such as Topic 5, remained at a steady state throughout the test period, i.e., we could not find any significant changes of topic. We can guess several reasons for the appearance of such a topic. For example, the number of topics may be wrong for LDA, or LDA may not be able to extract proper topics naturally from a corpus with a time series. Regardless of the reason, some topics extracted from LDA change significantly and some slightly, so we must identify and filter useful topics to discover separation points.

Table 2. Part of the topic distribution of documents

document	topic	The mixture ratio of the topic	topic	The mixture ratio of the topic	topic	The mixture ratio of the topic
2000/1/1	4	0.428	6	0.207	1	0.178
2000/1/2	4	0.339	1	0.337	6	0.113
2000/1/3	4	0.377	1	0.367	3	0.108
2000/1/4	1	0.467	4	0.226	3	0.131
⋮						
2004/12/28	11	0.581	4	0.144	19	0.132
2004/12/29	11	0.598	4	0.110	19	0.095
2004/12/30	11	0.542	19	0.132	4	0.126
2004/12/31	11	0.365	4	0.246	19	0.137

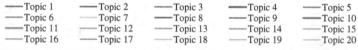

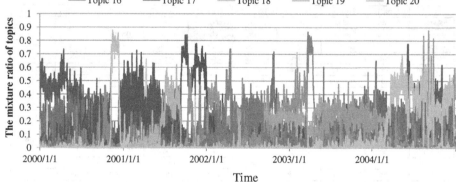

Fig. 7. The change of the mixture ratio of a document

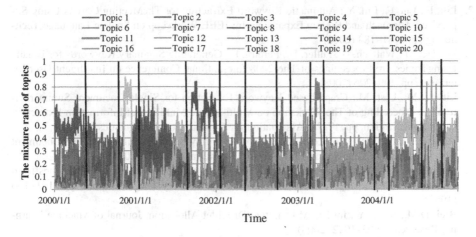

Fig. 8. The image of dividing a time series document set

5   Conclusion

In this paper, we proposed a method for finding suitable points of a corpus that includes time-series information to extract—as keywords—characteristic words appearing locally. In this case, dividing a corpus into equal time intervals is insufficient. Therefore, we needed to identify suitable compartments into which the corpus could be divided. The characteristic words appearing in a period, which is related to the topic of the document, change significantly over time. Therefore, we used LDA to examine changes of topics. As a result, we noticed that the main topics of documents changed as time passed. We can expect to extract characteristic words as keywords by dividing a document group at those points where the topic changes significantly. Fig. 8 illustrates the division of a time-series document set.

In this paper, when we performed LDA, we manually set the number of topics to 20. However, the optimal number of topics is unknown. Therefore, in future work we aim to automate the process of choosing the number of topics and evaluate the method of keyword extraction for a time-series document set

Acknowledgement. This research was supported by The Ministry of Education, Culture, Sports, Science and Technology (MEXT), Japan Society for the Promotion of Science(JSPS), Grant-in-Aid for Young Scientists (B), 23760358 and Grant-in-Aid for Scientific Research   (C), 25420448.

References

1. Liu, V., Curran, R.: Web Text Corpus for Natural Language Processing. In: Proceedings of the 11th Conference of The European Chapter of The Association for Computational Linguistics, Trento, Italy, pp. 233–240 (2006)

2. Liu, F., Liu, F., Liu, Y.: Automatic Keyword Extraction for TheMeeting Corpus Using Supervised Approach and Bigram Expansion. In: IEEE Workshop on Spoken Language Technology, pp. 181–184 (2008)
3. Dredze, M., Wallach, H., Puller, D., Pereira, F.: Generating Summary Keywords for Emails UsingTopics. In: Proceedings of The 2008 International Conference on Intelligent User Interfaces, pp. 199–206 (2008)
4. Litvak, M., Last, M.: Graph-based Keyword Extraction for Single-Document Summarization. In: Proceeding of The Workshop on Multi-source Multilingual Information Extraction and Summarization, pp. 17–24. Association for Computational Linguistics (2008)
5. Saga, R., Tsuji, H.: Improved Keyword Extraction by Separation into Multiple Document Sets According to Time Series. In: HCII, CCIS 374, pp. 450–453 (2013)
6. Church, K., Gale, W.: Inverse Document Frequency (IDF): A Measure of Deviations from Poisson. In: Proceedings of the Third Workshop on Very Large Corpora, pp. 121–130 (1995)
7. Blei, D.M., Ng, A.Y., Jordan, M.I.: Latent Dirichlet Allocation. Journal of Machine Learning Research 3, 993–1022 (2003)
8. McCallum, K.A.: MALLET, http://mallet.cs.umass.edu

Computerized Information Standards Enabling Innovation in Public Procurement of Buildings

Christian Koch and Kim Jacobsen

Chalmers University of Technology, Gothenburg, Sweden
kochch@chalmers.se
K-Jacobsen A/S, Copenhagen, Denmark
kj@k-jacobsen.dk

Abstract. Computerized and standardized information enables innovation in processes, products and services. Where early research on the impact of standards tended to focus on barriers, more recent research advocates standardisation as enabler of innovation albeit in a stakeholder-oriented, flexible manner. This paper asks whether computerized information standards enable or constrain innovation in public procurement of buildings. In architectural and engineering design of public buildings handling of information involves interoperability problems that hamper innovation. Moreover the project based product development tends be done in constellations of firms in interorganisational contracting, which do not provide stability or room for innovation. A large hospital project was investigated through interviews, documents and observations. The effects of implementing building information standards are both inter- and intraorganisational. The building client claims to have saved money, through better structured building component data that gave considerable positive effects during tendering. The IT-suppliers develop IT-tools, preparing for new markets.

Keywords: information standards, innovation, hospital building, Denmark.

1   Introduction

Interoperability of building information continues to be a major challenge for the building industry [1], [2]. As the information get incorporated in Building Information Models (BIM) and used in design, production and operations processes of buildings, a swift, efficient and smoothless transfer between partners is crucial. Moreover using BIM in an interoperable manner is a central strategy for creating innovative solutions for new sustainable housing and to enable competitive innovations for Nordic building companies, enabling their prospering both locally and globally.

Many Nordic architects, consulting engineers, contractors (AEC) and real estate firms operate across the Nordic countries rather than in just one of them [3]. This requires common tools, standards and work methods. Moreover design, production and use of state-of-the-art sustainable buildings similarly requires a set of calculation, design and monitoring tools, which today remains national in their character in

S. Yamamoto (Ed.): HIMI 2014, Part I, LNCS 8521, pp. 373–383, 2014.

contrast to the demands of the market. At present international standards such as Eurocodes and Industry Foundation Classes (IFC) [4] and defacto standards such as DWG only partially cover the Nordic building processes, even if IFC is gradually developing as a global standard.

One such new standardisation tool is the Cuneco Classification System (CCS), [5], which at present is developed in a Danish context, but designed to be used in international building sectors. The standardisation of CCS target building informations as used in design, building and operation of buildings. CCS provide automated identification and classification, and enables smoothless data transfer between software packages which today are often not interoperable, be it heating ventilation and air condition (HVAC) design- and energy calculation- software, when combining sustainable design and indoor climate design. Also CCS would, through more integrated IT infrastructures, enable virtual collaboration and coordination which gain importance in and outside the Nordic region. CCS would thereby systematically overcome obstacles for innovation in building design, production and operation.

The aim of this paper is to analyze whether computerized information standards enable or constrain innovation in public procurement of hospital buildings and investigate under what circumstances information standards would have an improved impact on innovation.

The paper focuses on a concrete set of standards (CCS) but has the broader aim of documenting their innovation-enhancing effects in the Nordic building sector. The standards are presently under development and are partly implemented in a large Danish hospital project "the new hospital west" (DNV), which acted as a test field [6]. The classification is expected be avaible for use by 2014.

Standardisation can be driven and implemented through many channels. In building, the public player has often been change agent using procurement to generate standardisation and innovation. Recently EU has pointed to the public as spearhead for energy efficient buildings mitigating climate change [7]. Public procurement of buildings involves demands of use of IT, collaboration and quality tools. This context is therefore particularly interesting for studying links between standards and innovation.

CCS has four elements [5]: Classification of building information, property data of building components and rooms in the building, information levels to control the design and further processes, and rules for measuring building components (metrics). The standards and property data will be placed on a server accessible for all users in the building industry.

A literature review is used to develop five types of impacts that standards can have on innovation. This is thus the papers primary contribution to analyse how the envisaged standardisation with CCS enables innovation in procurement of hospitals and in building in general: First it is argued that standardisation of at least parts of products and processes *indirectly* provides resources for innovation as the standardised elements require less resources. Second standardisation can nurture efficient repetition across many customoers and at a time make space for the engineering of innovation for single customers i.e. enable a mass customisation strategy of product development [8]. Third standardisation stabilises processes in the volatile project based environment of building projects. Fourth improved interoperability and interfaces between subsystems enable product innovation [9] and fifth standardisation would after the first tests create larger markets for products.

The paper is structured in the following way. After a method presentation, a selective literature review is used to develop the five types of innovation enhancing effects of standardisation. Using this framework structures the case and discussion. The paper ends with a conclusion.

2   Method

The overall approach taken here for human computer studies is critical interpretivist [10] and a sociomaterial view on innovations and standards [11]. A literature review is carried out covering human-computer interaction, innovation studies, information systems and organisational approaches, adopting a sociomaterial approach as overall paradigm [11]. The review leads to a framework of understanding of the relation between computerbased standardized information and types of innovation.

More specifically the selected domain for studying effects of standards on innovation is architectural and engineering design of public buildings. Here handling of information gives rise to substantial interoperability issues that tends to hamper innovation. Moreover the project based production of products tends be done in constellations of firms in interorganisational contracting, which do not provide stability or room for innovation. The Architecture, Engineering and Construction industry is therefore often portrayed as innovation adversive.

A large hospital project is used as test field. Interviews, document analysis and observation through presence at meetings with the design team were carried out by the authors, one closely involved, the other at a distance.

The second author acted as project manager for a test project of CCS at the hospital. The first author acts as process evaluator for "Knowledge Center for increased Productivity and Digitalization in Construction" (Cuneco) [5], together with two colleagues from 2010-2015. By February 2014, seven short half-year process evaluation reports have been elaborated. As the entire center focuses on establishing an infrastructure through classification of building information and standardization, most of the material gathered is relevant to the research questions raised here. Data collection encompasses interviews (41), participant observation of events (17), document analysis (141 documents including more basic crosscutting documents and documents for each of the projects in the centre).

The limitations of the study are that the classification studied is not a long term stabilised one, but rather a prototypes under development. Many of the more indirect innovation types relating to business models and community [12] is more of a future potential for the time being. Moreover both authors are deeply involved in the development of CCS and one author has been project management for the hospital test project central is the paper. The closeness is however seen at a time as a strength and a weakness as it provides detailed insight in the processes of the case. The other author has acted as critical external vis a vis these indepth insights.

3   Literature Review

The review develops in three steps: first some general considerations of innovations, than review of studies of the relation innovation and standardisation and third the development of the five criteria.

The understanding of innovation as crucial for development of companies, industries and societies has expanded from mostly focusing on product innovation and secondary process innovation [13] into focusing on a broad range of renewals which is often argued being far more important to company survival and prosperity [13]. This broader range of innovation encompasses financial innovation, Business model innovation, management and organisational innovation, technological and IT innovation, innovation in networks, alliances and communities [12], [14], service innovations and customer relations innovations, such as channels and brands [13], [15]. Also a lot of interest has been allocated to involving users in innovation [12], [16-17]. This development complicates defining innovation and understanding how innovation impact on business development. [15] suggests the following definition:

"An innovation is the implementation of a new or significantly improved product (good or service), or process, a new marketing method, or a new organizational method in business practices, workplace organization or external relations." [15].

We adopt this innovation definition yet embed it in an understanding of innovation processes and innovations and standards as sociomaterial [11], Timmermans and Epstein 2010)

Early work on innovation and standardisation [19-20], often pointed at the constraints and dysfunctional effects of standardisation, where later works overwhelmingly advocate standardisation [21-23]. In these works most focus is implicitly on product or process innovation whereas the broader set of possible innovation are rarely treated.

Works on mass customization and modularity in product design [8-9], thus point at first the gains involved in standardising certain repeated elements of the product structure allowing the design to focus on the specific more customer oriented elements. Such a mass customisation strategy fits well with large complex building projects like hospitals that standardised interfaces between subsystems involve. Second modularity of the product design is equally well suited. Again here most focus is on product standardisation and secondary process standardisation, even if [8] do mention some of the organisational and managerial implications of creating products through mass customisation.

It should be noted that building information and its handling in projects tends to be highly volatile and hap hazard because of the large number of players, components and processes. [24] points at the losses related to poor interoperability amongst these players.

As a perspective the possibilities of establishing markets beyond single (unique) products and even mass markets would also involve standards as enabler for such market innovation [25].

However standardisation continues to involve barriers and pitfalls also in its involvement with innovation. [26] in their empirical study of standards in use, point at the danger of finitism – attempting to create standards covering all aspects of a domain, which risks "locking" the use processes and ultimately leading to non-use of standards because they indeed become perceived as barriers.

Summarising standards impact on innovation in the following ways.

1. Standardisation of product and process elements indirectly provides resources for innovation as the standardised elements require less resources [23]
2. Standardisation can nurture efficient repetition and the engineering of innovation for single customers (i.e. a mass customisation strategy of product development, [8])
3. Standardisation stabilises processes in a volatile project based environment [27]
4. Improved interoperability and interfaces between subsystems enable product innovation [9]
5. Standardisation creates larger markets for products [25]

Adding to this list but in a more secondary manner innovation in the business model in organisation, in management, in the financing might also be relevant

4   Case A Hospital Project

DNV-Gødstrup is one of the largest hospital building projects in Denmark. 130.000 new square meters are designed, constructed and erected over a decade and from 2020 the hospital will be able to make 47.000 operations per year.

By summer 2012, the first major test project of CCS commenced in this hospital project. The first prototypes and testing activities were developed during the autumn. In this context, the building client became allied with six software suppliers. Together, their six systems cover parts of the information flow from early conceptual design of a building (one system), over detailed design (two CAD-systems and a BIM system), cost and budget calculation (one system), and space management (one system). According to the project manager, the systems are able to identify building components, classify them and sort them. This also involves data flows supported by the chain of the six systems:

"At [the hospital] we are now at classification of rooms and about to classify building components. The six participating IT companies can actually all, almost all, classify. We have made an internal demo of an information flow: [list of the six systems]. The programs are capable of doing that. With CCS we can classify, sort, identify. The programs are further than I thought" (project manager, Nov. 2012).

The classification standard was implemented in six IT systems constituting a common infrastructure and covering important parts of early conceptual design and detailed design.

The central advantage of using CCS is that it integrate the four elements of 1. Classification of building information, 2.property data of building components and rooms in the building, 3. information levels to control the design and further processes, and 4. rules for measuring building components (metrics). It is one common system for handling building information in contrast to a normally completely fragmented building design context.

4.1   Standardisation with Indirect Impact

Implementation and use of standards in the building industry such as CCS implies that a more common terminology and structures are implemented, concerning products and processes. This also enabling commencing bridging between the many different IT-solutions that are in use across the companies participating in the project teams and enables smooth communication between the IT systems. A common structuring of buildings by designers is to perceive it as composed in rooms for various purposes, which therefore is one area of classification in CCS. Moreover it is also a demand that the standards should allow new innovative solutions, giving users a tool rather than a strict and detailed coding, that might create barriers for "thinking outside" the given frames, a recurrent initiator of innovation.

To do so CCS is in principle shaped as a collection of terms and concepts that can be brought together in different ways within the code structure. Users have a large room for manoeuvre to specify products and processes at the lower levels in the classification, while CCS also maintains a precise coding structure for specification at the first three to four levels, enabling IT-interpretation of the specification and exchange of data between it-systems.

A classification system is traditionally defined as a hierarchy of classes, and thus the number of classes of components or processes is fixed in the system. E.g. the classification system OmniClass has 211 different classes for doors, and the distinction of the classes primary are based of the properties of doors [28]. By it OmniClass actually determines the number of classes of components, which may exist for the user using this classification system. It can be right a challenge find the right class among the numerous types of classes or even to find a class which is adequate for a new innovative designed door component.

In contrast to traditional hierarchical classification systems like OmniClass, CCS has only one class for all types of door components. But CCS also allows you to add CCS-properties to the class (as many as you wish or need) thus you actually defined your own class-specification for your doors. CCS classification combined with CCS properties gives the users nearly an infinite numbers of combination possibilities to specify exactly the classes of building components needed. A well-defined syntax for code structure for specifying the created classes, act as a digital syntax for digital communication and exchange of the specification of the class.

The flexibility of CCS supports the users to be able to classify new solutions and at the same time be sure of, that the CCS code structure ensures that IT systems are able to interpret the specification og the class. Thus the implementation and the use of CCS indirect release resource from digital implementation to innovate.

The consultant unit of the hospital used CCS first to program rooms and later to organise building components preparing tendering documents. The room programming became more structured because all standard and special rooms entered the same structure enabling a move towards more standard rooms. Thereby the room programming became more efficient than usual for such large and complex building, here handling about 4000 rooms, whereof 80% became classified as standard rooms. This indirectly created resources for the design of the remaining unique rooms.

Here the envisaged flexibility of CCS was used and evaluated instrumental. The combination of the classification tables and codes worked. Property data however were not readily available and the design team therefore developed their own properties to enter in the CCS structure.

The client evaluates that better structured building component data has given considerable positive effects in the tendering of contractor contracts, where the design team of engineering and architects are enabled in several ways.

4.2   Standardisation Supporting a Mass Customisation Strategy

CCS is a structure for a digital platform for the building product and supports the notion of a product master [8]. The databased embedded product master, as the CCS server, supports the generic product properties and structures as well as the specific.

The hospital project involves a large amount of repeated components, building elements up to entire blocks of beds. The engineering and architectural design group work with room programming using CCS reduced the number of special rooms and increased the standard room to 80% of the 4000 rooms. The design of the last 20%, that could not be standardardised as they were unique special rooms. This reveals using mass customisation strategies with CCS for example design, function and equipment such as doors, windows, and HVAC equipment (and for example oxygen) has become more efficient than usual for such large and complex building.

4.3   Standardisation Stabilises Processes

It is considerably easier to develop new innovative digital solution in the building industry, when your work platform is bases on a well-known and stable production environment. A production environment which not sets any technical limitation, but supports you in creating new innovative solutions, is also more or less a necessity for a creative result.

To create a stable production environment, you need to stand on a standardised digital platform, where well-defined and structured building terms are implemented and where simple data operations, like data creation, search, sorting, exchange, can be executed seamless whiteout any it-specified knowledge for the users.

The purpose of CCS is to create a standard digital platform for the building industry, on which the different parties are able to create a stable digital productions environments. An environment from which they can create new innovative solutions for their building projects, whiteout worrying about whether the solutions can enter into a digital structure or can be communicated and be interpreted digital by other parties' it-systems.

To ensure a stable digital production environment you need to implement the CCS standard platform in your working methods and IT-systems, and surely also upgrade your employees competences in how the this new platform are able to support them in producing new innovative solution based on the ever ongoing demands for new solutions and progress.

At the hospital project CCS has first supported a systematic detailed planning of the design process, digital architecture and work method. This planning created stability as it afterwards had to be followed strictly. Moreover and second CCS supported "data discipline" in all the sub activities. Also the enabled reuse of the CCS elements supported stabilisation. An important prerequisite for this was a systematic training effort of the members of the design team, especially those involved with Building Information Modelling (BIM).

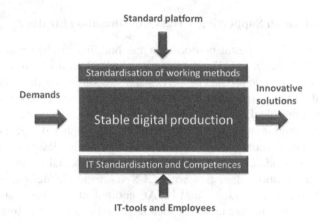

Fig. 1. Stable digital production of building [27]

4.4   Interoperability and Interfaces Enabling Product Innovation

Interoperability and interfaces within the product structure is an organised way to enable a number for players to contribute to product innovation through digital design collaboration and communication. In a somewhat similar vein as the well known apple i-phone platform, the CCS platform provides vast room for supplementary, enlarging innovations "as long" as they comply with the platform they can be taken onboard.

At the hospital project, CCS, enables handling of many types of digital objects, such as documents, BIMs, spreadsheets, data sets (in databases) and drawings. The classification codes enable automatic identification by distinguishing between the items. It is common in large complex buildings project to use considerable resources for coordination of the design activities, which is located in the many participating companies at numerous places and usually involving many different IT –systems and data structuring approaches. Here CCS supports interoperability also by standardising the interfaces between these systems.

4.5   Standardisation Creates Larger Markets for Products

Standardisation of design, production and operation processes is enabled by use of BIM. Process innovation through reuse and iterations are important new opportunities:

Reuse of parts of the sustainable design is enabled by well-structured data ordered as objects and more feasible if one encounter a (larger) Nordic market and markets beyond that.

IT suppliers participating in the hospital project have used their experiences with CCS to incorporate the classification in their IT-systems. They are currently marketing that in the Nordic and Baltic region. More in general there is a large global market for hospital design providers, where experiences of CCS can be transformed into design service offerings globally. Here it is likely however that competing standards will create future market condition [29].

5 Discussion

In the following the five innovation –standard relation types is discussed. First the standardisation is expected to indirectly provide resources for innovation. The case shows how standardisation in the tendering process prepares for cost reductions that indirectly can provide more space for innovative solutions developed in the products. The client thus claims to have saved 20 mio DKr like that [6]. The communicated tendering material is easier to access, better structured, and more homogenous, which in turn generate more comparable and cost efficient tenders. However the implementation and co-testing of the standards with the development organisation also required substantial investment in terms of hours and human resources. One issue being that the testing of the standard commenced before the standard was fully developed, i.e. a beta version was provided in the beginning and later improved. Second standardisation can promote efficient repetition and the engineering of innovation for single customers (i.e. a mass customisation). The room programming and the standardisation of it gave considerable result enabling innovation both on the standard side and the customer specific side. Third standardisation is expected to stabilises processes. In the hospital project this occurred as improved planning and also a relatively strict practice of following these plans providing stabilisation. It was carried out in a manner that demanded systematic change management, provided through training. Fourth an improved interoperability and interfaces between subsystems enable product innovation. The classification enabled handling of many types of digital objects, and supported interoperability also by standardising the interfaces between these involved systems. Fifth standardisation is expected to create larger markets for products, which in the hospital project both occurred as marketing of new solution and a still unexploited potential for offering new services. The IT-suppliers were provided with competences after having developed relevant IT-tools, which enable them diffusing the standard. More specifically the public building client evaluates that better structured data on building component give considerable positive effect in the tendering of contractor contracts, where the design team of engineering and architects are enabled i several ways by the computerized information standard. As a final note the range of possible future innovation directly and indirectly innovation involve financial, organisational and managerial innovations as well as community innovation once the hospital is build [12].

6   Conclusion

The effects of implementing building information standards for innovation is both inter- and intraorganisational and contradictory. Where the building client claims to have saved money, the IT-suppliers and design companies is provided with competences. More specifically the public building client evaluates that better structured data on building component give considerable positive effect in the tendering of contractor contracts, where the design team of engineering and architects are enabled in several ways by the computerized information standard. We have found that the standardized building information provide cost reduction and stabilised processes that indirectly opens for innovation, but also that the standardisation of rooms led to more direct innovation in the design of rooms both in the standardised and in the unique rooms, in line with a mass customisation strategy. Moreover the use of one common standard enables a far better coordination than previously. Finally we currently witness IT-suppliers using their experience with classification in providing new solutions and marketing then on a Nordic market, whereas we still have to see the event of the design companies following the same path of providing new services.

References

1. Bernstein, H.M.: The Business Value of BIM in Europe. McGraw-Hill, Bedford (2010)
2. Bernstein, H.M.: The Business Value of BIM in North America. McGraw-Hill, Bedford (2012)
3. STD: Sector Review The Consulting Engineering and Architectural Groups. A Swedish and International survey. The Swedish Federation of Consulting Engineers and Architects (STD). Stockholm (2010)
4. Laakso, M., Kiviniemi, A.: The IFC Standard - A Review of History, Development, and Standardization. Journal of Information Technology in Construction 17, 134–161 (2012)
5. Cuneco: Website in English of cuneco, the Danish center for classification and productivity in construction (accessed January 2014)
6. Andersen, U.: Digitale tilbudslister sparer Gødstrup Sygehus for mindst 20 mio. kroner. Ingeniøren 6 (September 2013)
7. EU: Directive 2012/27/EU on energyefficiency. The European Parliament and of the Council. Bruxelles (2012)
8. Piller, F.T., Tseng, M.M.: Handbook of Research in Mass Customisation and Personalization World Scientific New Jersey (2010)
9. Clark, K.B., Baldwin, C.Y.: Design Rules. The Power of Modularity, vol. 1. MIT Press, Cambridge (2000)
10. Walsham, G.: Interpreting Information Systems in Organizations. Wiley, Chichester (1993)
11. Orlikowski, W.J., Scott, S.V.: Sociomateriality: Challenging the separation of technology, work and organization. Annals of the Academy of Management 2, 433–474 (2008)
12. Botero, A., Vihavainen, S., Karhu, K.: From closed to open to what?: an exploration on community innovation principles. In: Proceedings of the 13th International MindTrek Conference: Everyday Life in the Ubiquitous Era (2009)

13. Fagerberg, J., Mowery, D.C., Nelson, R.R.: The Oxford Handbook of Innovations. Oxford University Press, Oxford (2004)
14. Koch, C.: Innovation networking between stability and political dynamics. Technovation 24(9), 729–739
15. OECD: Oslo Manual, Guidelines for collecting and interpreting innovation data, 3rd edn. OECD Publishing, Paris (2005)
16. Chang, T.-R., Kaasinen, E.: Three user-driven innovation methods for co-creating cloud services. In: Campos, P., Graham, N., Jorge, J., Nunes, N., Palanque, P., Winckler, M. (eds.) INTERACT 2011, Part IV. LNCS, vol. 6949, pp. 66–83. Springer, Heidelberg (2011)
17. Koch, C., Chan, P.: Projecting an Infrastructure - Shaping a community. In: Carrillo, P., Chinowsky, P. (eds.) Proceedings EPOC 2013 Conference. Engineering Project Organization Society, Colorado (2013)
18. Timmermans, S., Epstein, S.: A World of Standards but not a Standard World: Toward a Sociology of Standards and Standardization. Annual Review of Sociology 36, 69–89 (2010)
19. Farrell, J., Saloner, G.: Standardization, Compatibility, and Innovation. The RAND Journal of Economics 16(1), 70–83 (1985)
20. Kahan, M., Klaussner, M.: Standardization and Innovation in Corporate Contracting (Or "The Economics of Boilerplate"). Virginia Law Review 83(4), 713–770 (1997)
21. Ekholm, A., Blom, H., Eckerberg, K., Löwnertz, K., Tarandi, V.: BIM – Standardiseringsbehov. Svenska Byggbranschens Utvecklingsfond, Stockholm (2013)
22. Lillrank, P.: The Quality of Standard, Routine and NonroutineProcesses. Organization Studies 24(2), 215–233 (2003)
23. Sandholtz, K.: Making Standards Stick: A Theory of Coupled vs. Decoupled Compliance. Organization Studies 33(5-6), 655–679 (2012)
24. Gallaher, M.P., O'Connor, A.C., Jr. Dettbarn, J.L., Gilday, L.T.: Cost Analysis of Inadequate Interoperability in the U.S. Capital Facilities Industry. National Institute of Standards and Technology, Gaithersburg (2004)
25. Schilling, M.: Strategic Management of Technological Innovation. McGraw-Hill, New York (2008)
26. Bowker, G.C., Star, S.L.: Sorting Things Out: Classification and Its Consequences. MIT Press, Cambridge (1999)
27. Jacobsen, K.: Powerpoint serie om muligheder for standardisering af byggeprocesser. Balslev og Jacobsen A/S. København (2013)
28. Omniclass: Omniclass website (accessed January 2014), http://www.omniclass.org/
29. Fomin, V.V.: Standards as Hybrids: An Essay on Tensions and Juxtapositions in Contemporary Standardization. International Journal of IT Standards and Standardization Research 10(2), 59–68 (2012)

Improving Academic Listening Skills of Second Language by Building up Strategy Object Mashups

Hangyu Li[1,*] and Shinobu Hasegawa[2]

[1] School of Information Science, Japan Advanced Institue of Science and Technology,
1-1, Asahidai, Nomi, Ishikawa, 923-1292, Japan
lihangyu@jaist.ac.jp
[2] Center for Graduate Eduation Initiative, Japan Advanced Institue of Science and Technology,
1-1, Asahidai, Nomi, Ishikawa, 923-1292, Japan
hasegawa@jaist.ac.jp

Abstract. Most foreign students studying abroad lack of academic listening ability which is considered to be very important for their academic life. Among the four language activities (Reading, Listening, Speaking and Writing), the listening comprehension ability is perceived as the most difficult to improve. Therefore, the purpose of this research is to support the training of academic listening ability for the students pursuing their academic success in a foreign educational institute. Firstly, this research identifies and organizes listening strategies proved to be effective in academic listening through past researches and modulates them as sequential learning processes referred as strategy models. And then based on the various strategy models, the components of supporting functions serving as strategy objects are to be designed and developed. By putting various strategy objects together, the learners are able to build up personal learning environments (Strategy Object Mashups) based on their characteristics and conditions. At the same time, a feedback agent is to be implemented for recommending proper object mashups to the learners according to their learning situations.

Keywords: Listening Strategy, Strategy Objects, Strategy Object Mashups.

1   Introduction

Foreign students are faced with many challenges when pursuing academic success abroad, even after passing the language test required by their targeted educational institutes. Among the other language skills (Reading, Writing and Speaking), academic listening tasks pose serious challenges to F/SL (Foreign, Second Language) learners. Even for students with high level of proficiency and being comfortable with everyday listening and conversation, listening tasks encountered in academia still seem formidable [1]. Academic listening is complex, multi-faceted process which places enormous skill demands on the listener [2]. Since researches have shown that effective academic listening comprehension skills are essential for the students to achieve academic success [3-5], studies focusing on this subject are actively

S. Yamamoto (Ed.): HIMI 2014, Part I, LNCS 8521, pp. 384–395, 2014.

conducted worldwide. Among those, listening strategy is an important subject, which is playing an important part in improving academic listening skills [10]. However, students studying abroad often are faced with the difficulty of applying appropriate listening strategies for practicing their listening skills, for they study alone and lack necessary guidance from the experts. In order to address this problem, we intend to develop a learning environment which enables learners to practice their listening ability under the adaptive supporting functions according to their characteristics and learning situations. Moreover, by attaching semantic meanings (listening strategies) to the different functions used by each individual, we expect not only the awareness of strategy application to be strengthened but also the perceivable comparisons of different function use among the learners to take place, which leads to the possibility for improvement on learning skills. Therefore, unlike previous researches which provide fixed identical functions to the learners, we entitle the learners with the flexibility to build up their distinctive learning environment by putting together functional units provided, along with the self-adjustment supported by peer-reviews and system recommendation. To discuss this approach in details, the following sections are arranged like this: we firstly talk about the concept of listening strategy and the difficulties existing among F/SL learners trying to apply proper listening strategies into their practices, and then identify the limitations in recent CALL systems and the detailed purposes of this research, and finally we introduce our research method called strategy object mashups approach and describe our expectations in the end.

2   Listening Strategy

In cognitive psychology, the term 'strategy' is linked to the conceptual framework of human learning and memory and refers to mental steps or operations carried out to accomplish cognitive tasks. As a result, listening strategies are mental mechanisms carried out by second language learners to achieve reasonable comprehension when processing information contained in a large input of utterance, because they have to work under the constraints of an overloaded working memory, and a lack of linguistic, sociolinguistic and content knowledge [6-8]. O'Mally and Charmot (1985) categorized listening strategy into three classifications as shown in Figure 1: Metacognitive strategy, Cognitive strategy and Social strategy [9]. Generally speaking, cognitive strategies are fundamental operations taken by the learners directly on their learning subject to obtain knowledge. A learner who successfully inferred the meaning of an unfamiliar word during listening would be putting a cognitive strategy into operation. Metacognitive strategies are concerned with how to learn or with learning to learn, involving with planning, monitoring and self-evaluation combined with the learning process. The learners who take note to track their level of comprehension during listening, for example, are adopting a metacognitive strategy. Social strategies are social behaviors learners conduct when communicating with others, and examples include asking skilled ones for advises, to compare notes and etc.

Listening Strategies

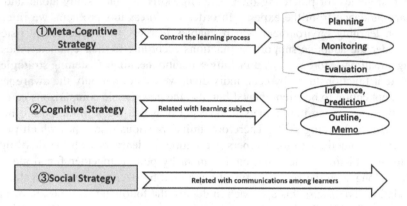

O`Malley et al.(1989) Categorized listening strategies into three classifications:

Fig. 1. Listening Strategy

Evidence from various studies revealed that L2 learners, regardless of skilled or unskilled, were all applying some listening strategies, consciously or unconsciously. The only difference lies in what they are using and the way of using them. Learners with higher listening ability tend to choose listening strategies more adaptive to their learning situations and put the chosen strategies into practice more effectively than the unskilled ones. Moreover, since what learners know about their learning can directly influence the process and even the outcome of it [10], it has been proved more than once the importance of improving learners' awareness of listening strategy through various experiments of related researches [11-12]. Goh (2008) stressed in her findings that learners need to be aware of how their listening comprehension is affected by their choice of listening strategies to develop flexibility in the use of listening strategies as well as find suitable ways for systematic practice, ultimately be able to obtain listening skills required by a successful academic life.

3   Difficulties in Applying Listening Strategies in Academia

Although researchers in the field of linguistics have repeatedly proven the effectiveness of consciously adopting adaptive strategies in listening practice through various methodologies, there are several difficulties for foreign students to successfully utilize proper listening strategies in most of the cases. Firstly, it is difficult to consciously put listening strategies into operation. Indeed, there are efforts having been put into teaching the techniques to insinuate the application of listening strategies [13], and the results of which were mostly positive. However, in academic life where foreign students often are pressed by hard schedule and mostly failed to attend such classes, self-directed learning is the main approach for practicing academic listening ability. As a result, they tend to resort to their inefficient accustomed way of practicing without being aware of what strategies they are using and how these strategies affect their learning. Secondly, it is difficult to flexibly adopt adaptive listening strategies. Factors including personal traits, motivational level and cognitive style may influence the strategy choice [14]. Because of their lacking of strategy knowledge and guidance of strategy application, it is difficult to come up with an adaptive combination of listening strategies which suits the learners' characteristics and their learning goals. Thirdly, it is difficult to put social strategies into practice. As for self-directed learning is the mainstream among foreign students to build up the necessary skills of the targeted language, it is considered inconvenient for them to get involved actively in communication or cooperation with like-minded people to ask help, exchange ideas and get advices. This leads to the missing of learning chances and sharing of knowledge.

4   Limitations in Current CALLs and Research Purposes

While researchers of the educational linguistics are focusing on the pedagogy for improving language skills, there are also attentions being drawn in the development of CALL system. The original definition of CALL are covering a wide range of computer systems as long as involved with the keywords 'computer' and 'language learning'. Since the focus of this research is to help learners cultivate necessary academic listening skills through self-directed learning. We narrowed the definition of CALL to mean self-guided learning support system which the learners work through at their own pace in a self-directed way. Back in the late 80's, and early 90's, with the fast development of information technologies and the prevailing use of computer, CALL was breaking ground in the new technology frontier and began to draw attentions. Up to now, numerous CALL systems have been developed to meet different requirements, most of those are working as an additional supplementary to actual teaching courses known as blended learning [15]. Therefore, most of these systems are not designed for self-directed learning and proved performing better only combined with the involvement of the instructors. Among those CALLs appropriate to be used in a self-directed way, though only a few of which are for training listening skills [16], there are some limitations. First of all, they failed to improve learners' metacognitive awareness of learning strategies. The current CALLs mainly focus on providing the users with a set of pre-designed functions without making the users aware of the according strategy applications which are meant to help them perform better. Secondly, they failed to offer adaptive supporting functions for different learners. Recently, there are some adaptations being considered in terms of providing diverse training materials [17], however, learners are not in the position of choosing or adjusting system functions to meet their learning goals. Thirdly, they are not providing enough support to integrate social strategies, which causes the lack of communication among learners. Although there are CALLs enabling limited sharing and peer-reviews on learning outcomes [18], the learning skills of each learner and the strategy application are difficult to represent in a recognizable way. Considering these limitations existing in current CALL systems, and in order to address the difficulties encountered by foreign students in an attempt to improve their academic listening ability, this research aims to design and develop a self-directed and community-based learning environment with the main purposes of: making learners aware of strategy application, helping them build up adaptive learning environments, and enabling them to communicate on not only leaning resources and knowledge but also learning strategies and techniques. We expect the learners to learn and improve their learning skills through: the strengthened awareness of their strategy application; the process of building up their adaptive learning environments which are constantly adjusted by themselves from peer-reviews and system recommendation; and the awareness of the connections between their learning activities and the according listening strategy.

5   Strategy Object Mashups Approach

Before getting into details of this approach, we need to understand the concept of comprehension tactics (which is referred as tactics in this paper) brought up by Goh (1998) [10]. She defined tactics as individual mental techniques through which a general strategy is operationalized. Goh also identified that the tactics used for the same strategies vary from learner to learner, and skilled learners demonstrated better on strategy choices and the combination of appropriate tactics. For example, a learner successfully inferred the meaning of an unfamiliar word by the hints received from earlier utterance; on the contrary, another learner inferred by referring to his own world knowledge combined with the current context. The fact is that they are adopting the same cognitive strategy called inference but through different tactics. The reasons for this difference, Goh indicated, may exist in the learners' differences in listening ability or whether being aware of strategy use, which we think could open up the possibility for interactions and communications on learning skills among learners of different level by comparing tactics use with each other. Since one of the purpose of this research is to improve the awareness of strategy application, the tactics through which strategies are being conducted by the learners indirectly, become a very important issue. As the tactics are in fact metal techniques taken by the learners when trying to extract meaning from an utterance, the learners are considered to be under great cognitive overload. In order to address this problem, this research will externalize the common tactics in the form of computer-assisted functions while building connections with the corresponding listening strategies, expecting not only the cognitive overload to be alleviated but also, the awareness of strategy adoption to be strengthened. In addition, we also expect the tactics adopted by each learner will be recognizable so that the communications on learning techniques can also take place.

This research firstly organizes related strategies revealed in the past researches positively applicable for cultivating academic listening ability and then, based on which, design and develop a learning environment providing adaptive supporting functions to different learners based on their features and learning situations. Figure 2 describes the concept of this approach. After identifying the related listening strategies, the tactics commonly adopted to operate those strategies will also be sought and organized to systematize respective learning strategy models. And then, the identified models will be visualized in term of various functional units as strategy objects in the system, from which the learners can choose to construct their personal assembly of the functional units as strategy object mashups. Finally, we will also construct a communication platform to not only support the communication activities on learning knowledge and resources, but also on strategy object mashups which we would like to consider as a sort of communication on learning techniques. At the same time, an agent collecting and analyzing all mashups created by everyone will be developed to recommend the learners with more appropriate strategy objects for adjustment according to their features and learning situations. The following sections will explain this approach in details.

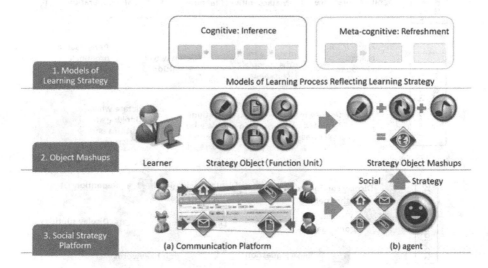

Fig. 2. The Concept of Strategy Object Mashups Approach

5.1   Learning Strategy Model and Strategy Object

The existing listening strategies are too abstract to be represented on a computer screen. However, the comprehension tactics serving as media to the according strategies, on the other hand, are understandable mental behaviors possible to be visualized as operable computer functions. For this reason, we firstly will identify and organize comprehension tactics proved to be effective in academic listening, and then modulate these tactics as sequential learning processes. Meanwhile, these tactics are corresponded to the according listening strategies in an ontological manner under the classifications of meta-cognitive, cognitive and social strategies defined by O'Mally (1985) [9]. The strategy models are expected not only to be able to represent the learning processes of different learners using distinctive tactics under the same learning strategy, but also to be presented as the model of the intellectual activities with the applicable description for designing purpose. Secondly, based on various strategy models, the components of supporting functions serving as strategy objects will be designed and developed. Figure 3 depicts the concept of strategy object and how it relates to the strategy models. In this figure, there is a typical cognitive strategy called inference.

Three comprehension tactics, for example are identified to operate this strategy: inference from related background knowledge, inference from other people's comments (this tactic also relates to the social strategy of cooperation), and inference from the related pictures. When trying to functionalize these tactics, it is possible to develop functional units such as: display comments of others, display background knowledge, display pictures and input keywords. These functional units are referred as the strategy objects from this research point of view.

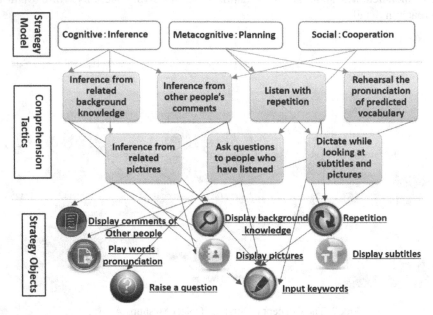

Fig. 3. Concept of Strategy Object

5.2 Construction for Adaptive Learning Environment through Building up Strategy Object Mashups

Unlike the existing CALL system providing only determined supporting functions, this system is expected to provide the learners with different listening ability and personal traits with adaptive training environment by enabling them to select and assembly strategy objects to compose their personal supporting functions as the process of building up strategy object mashups. As described in Figure 4, the strategy objects illustrated in Figure 3 are for choosing by self-directed learners. Supposedly one of the learners in the graph picked the objects of display comments of other people, display background knowledge and input keywords, the chosen three objects are working together as object mashups to support his learning activity. In this way, by tracing the comprehension tactics related with the chosen objects, a new tactic (inference from related background knowledge and comments of others and input keywords) is generated and so does its relationship with the corresponding strategies, which combined with the learner's features and learning situation will be analysed and stored by the system as a latest addition to strategy models, aiming to recommend proper strategy objects to learners for adjustment of their strategy mashups. During the process of building up personal strategy mashup, we expect them to improve their listening skills by practicing with adaptive supporting functions, while reminding them of what strategies and tactics are being used to improve their awareness of strategy application.

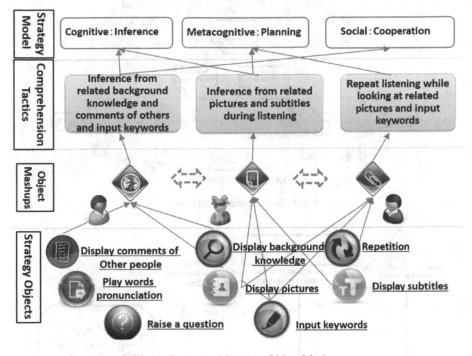

Fig. 4. Concept of Strategy Object Mashups

5.3   Social Strategy Platform and Feedback Agent

Since social strategy is playing an important role in improving academic listening ability, it is necessary for this research to combine a communication platform properly with the self-directed learning environment we intend to develop. On this platform, not only the knowledge and learning resources will be shared, but also the strategy object mashups created by each individual. Along with the comparison with the mashups of other learners, the self-adjustment of one's mashups becomes possible and the awareness of using related tactics and listening strategies is expected to be strengthened.

In order to support one's self-directed learning, providing feedbacks on one's learning process also seems to be desired. A feedback agent, as another aspect of this research, will be used to recommend proper object mashups to learners based on the analysis of their choice of the strategy objects combined with their learning situation.

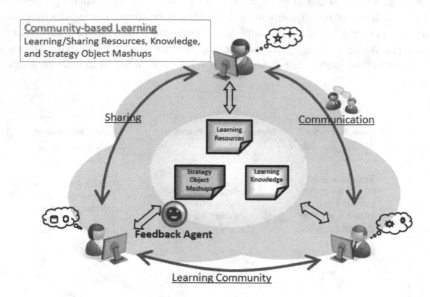

Fig. 5. Social Strategy Platform

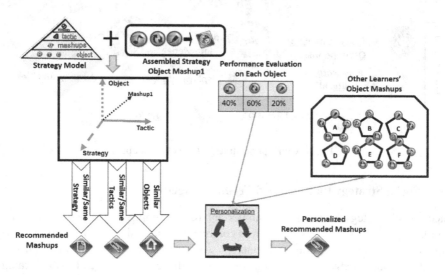

Fig. 6. Mechanism of the Feedback Agent

The Figure 6 describes the mechanism of the feedback agent. Firstly, it analyzes the current object mashup by referring to the corresponding strategy model and then maps the mashup to a proper position in the axis of object, tactic and strategy. After this, the agent provides several candidates of strategy mashups by following the roles of similar/same strategy, similar/same tactics, and similar objects compared with the current mashup. The next stage is to filter the candidates of recommended mashups for personalization by evaluating learner's performance on each selected object (such as counting the number of written keywords) to decide which object suits the learner better and which not, along with the comparison with the mashups adopted by the other learners of similar level and their performance on the chosen object. Finally the feedback agent will provide the learners with the best choices of mashups for their self-adjustment. In this way, we believe that, on the system, the learners will be able to adjust their object mashups through system recommendation and comparison with the others, as a result gradually build up their learning skills in the process

5.4   Multi-layer Model

Figure 7 summarizes what has been discussed so far as the model of this research. It shows a multi-layer model which possesses of four layers. The object layer is where the system presents all the strategy objects for the learners to choose and assemble. Also, the detailed description of each object will also be provided to the learners to help them make reasonable choices. The learners choose their wanted objects and the system assembles the selected ones into strategy object mashups on the upper layer where, basically, the learners conduct their listening practice supported by their object mashups while referring to the mashups of others if necessary. The tactic layer is where to generate new tactics based on the learners' object mashups, by putting together the tactics originated from the selected objects. And accordingly, the listening strategy related to the newly created tactics can be found on the strategy layer. The upper two layers are meant to attach semantic meanings to the functional units (object mashups) being used by the learners, with the purpose of improving their awareness of what listening strategies and tactics are being used and how they affect their learning in order to improve their listening skills. The connections between layers are to be stored and analyzed by the feedback agent for the proper recommendation of the object mashups for the learner. Therefore, by using the proposed system, the learners

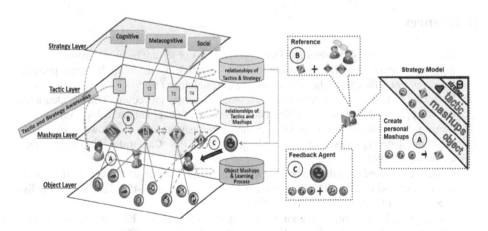

Fig. 7. Multi-layer Model

would be able to assemble their personal object mashups by putting together proper objects, to refer to others' object mashups for possible adjustment of their own, and to take into account of system's recommendation of new object mashups which could be more effective. We hope during the process of building up their personal object mashups while being made aware of the corresponding strategy and tactic use, the learners could learn and improve effective learning skills along the way.

6   Conclusion and Future Work

This paper has proposed a learning environment where the learners not only are able to construct adaptive supporting functions by putting together wanted strategy objects, but also to be aware of the corresponding comprehension tactics and listening strategies they are adopting and how are they affecting their learning with the purpose of improving their listening skills. Moreover, on the proposed platform, the learners are expected to learn through building up object mashups which can be flexibly adjusted by the comparisons with that of others' and the recommendation from the system. We believe this research might open the possibility of providing an adaptive learning environment to diverse learners and a more recognizable format for reference and communication on learning skills in a virtual place.

In the near future, we firstly will identify several useful listening comprehension tactics from related researches and start constructing a few strategy models. Based on these models, the according strategy objects will be designed and developed, so as the mashups environment as web services using Microsoft ASP.NET MVC. After finishing the pilot system, an evaluation will be conducted to firstly make sure whether the learning effectiveness can be improved through building up object mashups, and secondly whether the adjustment of mashups useful from peer comparisons and system recommendation.

References

1. Mason, A.: By dint of: Student and lecture perceptions of lecture comprehension strategies in first term graduate study. In: Flowerdew, J. (ed.) Academic listening: Research perspectives, pp. 199–218. Cambridge University Press, Cambridge (1995)
2. Richards, J.: Listening comprehension: Approach, design, procedure. TESOL Quarterly, vol. 17, pp. 219–239. Teachers of English to Speakers of Other language, Inc. (1983)
3. Benson, M.J.: Lecture listening in an ethnographic perspective. In: Flowerdew, J. (ed.) Academic listening: Research perspectives, pp. 181–198. Cambridge University Press, Cambridge (1994)
4. Dunkel, P.: Listening in the Native and Second/Foreign Language: Toward an Integration of Research and Practice. TESOL Quarterly, vol. 25(3), pp. 431–457. Teachers of English to Speakers of Other Language, Inc. (1991)
5. Vandergrifft, L.: Listening to learn or learning to listen. Annual Review of Applied Linguistics, vol. 24(3-25). Cambridge University Press, Cambridge (2004)

6. Call, E.: Auditory short term memory, listening comprehension and the Input Hypothesis. TESOL Quarterly, vol. 19(4), pp. 765–781. Teachers of English to Speakers of Other Language, Inc. (1985)
7. Farch, C., Kasper, G.: The role of comprehension in second language learning. Applied Linguistics 7, 257–274 (1986)
8. Goh, C.C.M.: A cognitive perspective on language learners' listening comprehension problems. System 28(1), 55–75 (2000)
9. O'Mally, J.A.: Listening Comprehension Strategies in Second Language Acquisition. Applied Linguistics 10(4), 418–437 (1989)
10. Goh, C.C.M.: How ESL learners with different listening abilities use comprehension strategies and tactics. Language Teaching Research 2(2), 124–147 (1998)
11. Goh, C.C.M.: Metacognitive Instruction for Second Language Listening Development: Theory, Practice and Research Implications. RECL Journal 39(2), 188–213 (2008), SAGE Publications, Los Angeles, London, New Deli and Singapore (2008)
12. Holden, R.: Facilitating Listening Comprehension: Acquiring Successful Strategies, vol. 28, pp. 257–266. Bulletin of Hokuriku University, Japan (2004)
13. Hossein, B.: Enhancing foreign language learning through listening strategies delivered in L1: An Experiment Study. International Journal of Instruction 5(1) (2013)
14. Oxford, R., Nyikos, M.: Variables Affecting Choice of Language learning Strategies by University Students. The Modern Language Journal 73(3), 291–300 (1989)
15. Wikipedia: Blended Learning,
   http://en.wikipedia.org/wiki/Blended_learning
16. Smidt, E., Hegelheimer, V.: Effects of online academic lectures on ESL listening comprehension, incidental vocabulary, and strategy use. Computer Assisted Language Learning 17, 517–556 (2004)
17. Wang, J., Mendori, T.: An Evaluation of a Customizable Ontology-driven Language Learning Support System. In: 21st International Conference on Computers in Education, pp. 11–19. Asia-Pacific Society for Computer in Education, Indonesia (2012)
18. Ogata, H., Yano, Y.: Knowledge awareness for a computer-assisted language learning using handhelds. International Journal of Continuing Engineering Education and Life Long Learning 14, 435–449 (2004)

Digital Document Network System
for Organizing Individual Knowledge

Kenji Matsunaga and Kyoko Yoshida

School of Network and Information, Senshu University, Kanagawa, Japan
{matunaga,k-yoshida}@isc.senshu-u.ac.jp

Abstract. eBooks and many other documents are being kept in recent years in personal storage in a variety of digital formatted documents with the amount of digitized documents expected to increase further. Intellectual tasks to organize this knowledge and add new meaning based on mass digital documents that will replace paper ones is needed. Thus a system that utilizes and supports the benefits of digital based on traditional work methods is required. This paper describes and evaluates the system we developed for building and searching multiple digital document networks with marks, links and memos, while reviewing useful methods to organize knowledge and add new insights.

Keywords: eBooks, Digital Document, Knowledge Management.

1   Introduction

Individuals have become able to possess many books in recent years as digital documents due to the spread of eBooks. Many documents are already maintained in an individual's storage as digital documents in a variety of formats, with the volume of digitized literature expected to jump dramatically in the future. Paper media books and documents have traditionally been a useful knowledge base for organizing an individual's knowledge, while societies have tackled larger intellectual endeavors using paper-based books and documents. Intellectual pursuits that organize knowledge and add new meaning can be obtained based on massive digital documents instead of paper books. Thus a system may be needed to utilize and support digital benefits based on traditional work methods.

iBook and Kindle are typical readers for reading eBooks. These have useful functions for bookmarks, markers and other intellectual organizing, yet they are primarily for reading one (1) book, not assuming the work to create knowledge based on multiple books. Software such as Evernote can also search keywords across the documents and list notes where the same tags are kept for tagged documents. But one cannot jump to the location where it is written in the document using a direct link because the link is not added. There is a lot of value in adding a link to eBooks, documents and other information with many pages compared to the Web where the volume of a single piece of information is comparatively small.

S. Yamamoto (Ed.): HIMI 2014, Part I, LNCS 8521, pp. 396–403, 2014.
© Springer International Publishing Switzerland 2014

We proposed a system to link multiple eBooks and switch between them while reading [1]. We also proposed a system for evaluating methods of organizing knowledge and those useful for adding new knowledge based on interviews with researchers who handle many books and documents to build a digital document network [2]. This paper describes the results of the development and evaluation of this system.

2   Analysis of Target Users

We conducted a survey of literary research methods specifically for studies where many books and documents are handled from among a wide range of research fields. We interviewed two (2) master's level students who are researching Japanese literature and ancient Japanese history on research methods and the utilization method of books.   We questioned the information collection and management methods, specifics on their work using documents, and methods they would like to use with digitized documents and obtained responses in the interviews.

The results of the interviews, suggested that the ability to choose what is needed from books, documents and other information collected, focusing on the relationships between them, thereby adding new interpretations and knowledge is needed in literary research. Researchers require a system to support work such as when they write memos to digitized books and documents, create a new network relating these memos and gaining new knowledge on network formats already obtained.

3   System Overview

This paper proposes a digital document network architecture system supporting work to organize an individual's knowledge.   A network can be created by adding a memo to a sentence (hereafter marks & notations) extracted from a digital document using this system. Memos can also be added to a link.   They can be searched using marked or linked memos with the generated network (Fig. 1).

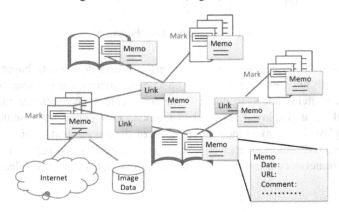

Fig. 1. Digital Document Network

3.1   System Functions

This system has "Create Network" and "Search Network" functions.

You can "Add Mark" and "Connect Links between Marks" when creating networks. Extract the marked digital document using a search keyword, etc. from an eBook or document, choose a sentence from a page to be marked from among them and place the mark there. You can add a memo to this mark. You can input these with a date, relevant items, people, comments and other "Key: Value" formats adding a memo. Choose two (2) or more items to link from among the marks, and set the links between them in order to relate links between marks. You can also add a memo to the link (Fig. 2).

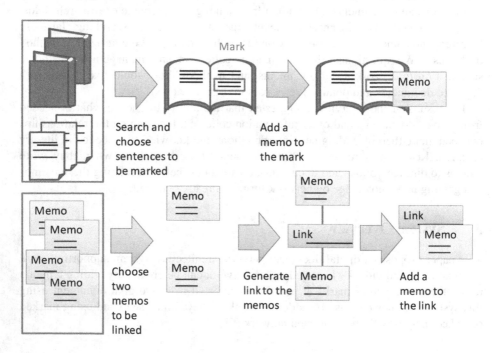

Fig. 2. Create Network Function

You can search the network created for eBooks and documents based on memo information with network search. First, choose the memo using a search keyword, etc. from the contents added to multiple memos created. The sentence marked with the memo added is displayed for marked memos. Two (2) or more sentences with links are displayed for linked memos. In terms of displayed items, you can view the location of marked sentences, as well as adjoining sentences and pages. You can also view the entire network image for all books and documents linked to selected memos (Fig. 3).

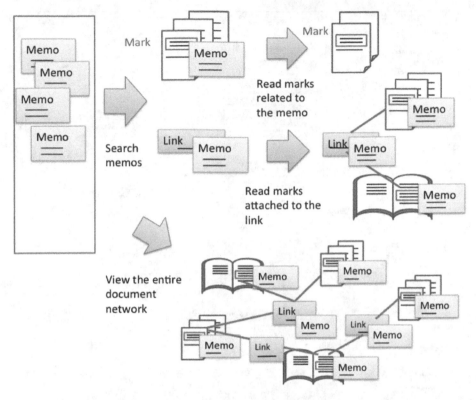

Fig. 3. Search Network Function

3.2 System Screen

Screen configurations were designed so that users could easily use system functions (Fig. 4).

A window where documents, pages and marks are arranged hierarchically is located at the left where pages can be followed while checking the marks. The document with marks embedded is shown in the center. Created, selected and searched marks and link memo contents are shown on the right. There is also a form included for searching memos. Information can be accessed from the route where the document is the origin and from the route where the mark and link are the origin via these interfaces.

Figure 4(a) shows the utility screen for choosing and reading a document, selecting the range to be marked and noting a memo for them. Figure 4(b) shows a utility screen for choosing two (2) marks, creating a link for them and noting a memo for them while a number of marks already exist.

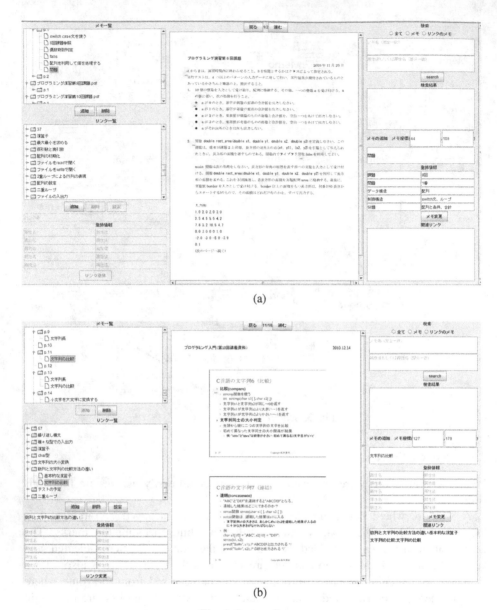

Fig. 4. System Screen

3.3 System Configuration

Figure 5 shows the system configuration. The system input files handle eBook and PDF formats here, and are intended for paper media documents to be used by converting them to PDF via scanning, etc. The internal system uses unified PDFs. Marks, links, memos and other data users created with the system edit function are stored in the database. The search function searches information saved to the database.

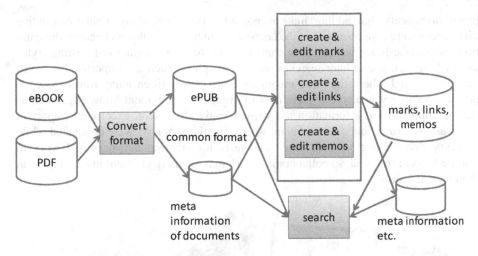

Fig. 5. The system configuration

4   System Evaluation

We conducted tests whereby we created a network for files saved to the system and searched information using the created network to evaluate it. The tests to create the network and to search information using the created network were not continuous, but conducted on separate days. Five (5) undergraduate seniors created one (1) network in 5 hours. Five (5) other undergraduate seniors conducted tests on searching information in 2 hours. A total of 11 files, five (5) being programming reference materials and six (6) being related practice problems, were the documents used. We observed and evaluated the behavior of subjects in the work process of this test (Fig. 6).

The task for the test to create the network is creating links between the 11 files for reference materials and practice problems as examples for these. Reference materials and practice problems were read, and marks and links were added to locations containing relevant items and other items to be referred. The result of this task was that around 150 marks and 70 links were created, and memos were created for each mark and link. Marks were drawn and memos were written smoothly here. However, only 20 links for these marks were drawn at first. Thus a specific example to adding links was instructing to search locations of references and examples deemed to be useful with practice problems. The tasks for tests on searching information was searching reference materials and practice problems to solve four(4) programming test problems with the created network. The knowledge required to solve these problems, not merely solving them, was extracted from reference materials and practice problems, and their locations were noted. Tests were conducted with groupware due to the long pre-trial time requirements for one (1) person to create a network for this system.

In the tests on creating the network, linking process was promoted by indicating tasks assigned. This may be because many marks and memos are often created with paper documents, but adding links is not an action done daily. Other qualitative differences were also observed in the contents of memos by subjects because there are no clear standards for writing their contents. There were instances of writing styles used where their use in later searches was not insightful such as "Important" or "Will be on test", and where the same memo contents were written many times over. A perfect example was also the usefulness in organizing document knowledge such as adding supplemental information not written in the document, excerpting important items and recording important relevant words. In addition, tests were conducted while students were talking to each other, and tests for creating networks had work to outline links in the head, so collaborative work may be more efficient in creating them than working alone.

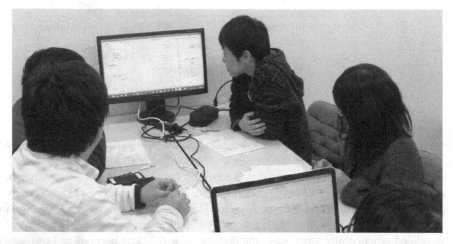

Fig. 6. User Test

Looking for the initial starting point to search was difficult in the tests for searching information. It was easy to search important information in the documents because they looked unconsciously for which documents had something written as there was a link added from the initial starting point. They located information by searching with memo contents used as tags when there was no link. For creating networks with faster searches, differences appeared based on networks being created assuming what searches would come later when creating links and memos. One may be able to learn how to add higher value links by accumulating experience in searching.

Comments on the system made by the subjects were, for example, "Links and memos were effective in searching relevant information between multiple documents together" and "It was convenient for arriving at relevant information using memo contents".

5   Conclusion

This paper described results in the development and evaluation of a system for creating a digital document network.

We will add functions for viewing the entire network structure for all books and documents relevant to selected memos and effective functions for group working. Some support may also be needed to create effective networks. The issues for this will be support for outlining links to various knowledge and preparing standards for creating networks.

References

1. Yoshikoshi, M., Matsunaga, K., Yoshida, K.: A Personal Document Network Building System for Digital Document Searches. In: Stephanidis, C. (ed.) Posters, HCII 2013, Part II. CCIS, vol. 374, pp. 458–461. Springer, Heidelberg (2013)
2. Matsunaga, K., Yoshida, K.: A Personal Document Network Building System for Organizing Knowledge. IPSJ SIG Technical Report 2013-IS-125(10), 1–5 (2013) (in Japanese)

Information Search and Retrieval

Towards Semantic Image Retrieval Using Multimodal Fusion with Association Rules Mining

Raniah A. Alghamdi and Mounira Taileb

Faculty of Computing and Information Technology,
King Abdulaziz University,
Saudi Arabia, Jeddah
{ragalghamdi,mtaileb}@kau.edu.sa

Abstract. This paper proposes a semantic retrieving method for an image retrieval system that employs the fusion of the textual and visual information of the image dataset which is a recent trend in image retrieval researches. It combines two different data mining techniques to retrieve semantically related images: clustering and association rule mining algorithm. At the offline phase of the method, the association rules are discovered between the text semantic clusters and the visual clusters to use it later in the online phase. To evaluate the proposed system, the experiment was conducted on more than 54,500 images of ImageCLEF 2011 Wikipedia collection. The proposed retrieval system was compared to an online system called MMRetrieval and to the proposed system but without using association rules. The obtained results show that our proposed method achieved the best precision and mean average precision.

Keywords: Image Retrieval, Multimodal Fusion, Association Rules Mining, Clustering.

1   Introduction

Today, a huge amount of images exists in electronic formats on the Web and in different information repositories; and their size is exponentially growing day after another. Thus, we need for an efficient Image Retrieval system (IR) to get access to these images. IR could rely purely on textual metadata which may produce a lot of garbage in the results since users usually enter that metadata manually which is inefficient, expensive and may not capture every keyword that describes the image. On the other hand, the Content-Based Image Retrieval (CBIR) could be used to filter images based on their visual contents such as colors, shapes, textures or any other information that can be derived from the image itself which may provide better indexing and return more accurate results. At the same time, these visual features contents extracted by the computer may be different from the image contents that people understand. It requires the translation of high-level user views into low-level image features and this is the so-called "semantic gap" problem. This problem is the reason behind why the current CBIR systems are difficult to be widely used for

S. Yamamoto (Ed.): HIMI 2014, Part I, LNCS 8521, pp. 407–418, 2014.

retrieving Web images. A lot of efforts have been made to bridge this gap by using different techniques. In [1], the authors identified the major categories of the state-of-the-art techniques in narrowing down the 'semantic gap' one of them is to fuse the evidences from the text and the visual content of the images. Fusion in IR is considered as a novel area, with very little achievements in the early days of research [2]. Truly, we live in a multimodal world, and there is no reason why advantage should not be taken of all available media to build a useful semantic IR system. This paper tries to narrow down this gap and enhance the retrieval performance by fusing the two basic modalities: text and visual features. To determine the appropriate fusion method, it is important to answer the following basic questions: what is the suitable level to implement the fusion strategy? And how to fuse the multimodal information?

The proposed method is a Multimodal Fusion method based on Association Rules mining (MFAR). It is considered as a late fusion. This method combines two different data mining techniques: clustering and Association Rules Mining (ARM) algorithm. It uses ARM to explore the relations between text semantic clusters and image visual features clusters by applying *Apriori* algorithm. The method consists of two main phases: offline and online. The offline phase identifies the relations among the clusters from different modalities to construct the semantic Association Rules (ARs). On the other hand, the online phase is the retrieval phase. It uses the generated ARM to retrieve the related images to the query.

The rest of the paper is categorized as following. The next section will review the current information fusion approaches and how they fused different modalities. Section three gives the required background about ARM algorithm. Then section four describes the proposed method in detail. The experiment and the conclusion are presented at sections five and six respectively.

2   Related Work

Information retrieval community found the power of fusing various information sources on the retrieving performance [3]. Information fusion has the potential of improving retrieval performance by relying on the assumption that the heterogeneity of multiple information sources allows cross-correction of some of the errors, leading to better results [4]. In literature, the fusion of the visual and the textual features was performed in different levels of the retrieval process which are early fusion, late fusion, trans-media fusion and at re-ranking level.

2.1   Early Fusion

This method first extracts the low level features of the modalities using the suitable feature extractor. Then, the extracted vectors are concatenated into one vector to form one unique feature space. The advantage of this strategy is that it enables a true multimedia representation for all the fused modalities where one decision rule is applied on all information sources. Early fusion could be used without feature weighting such in [5]; they concatenated the normalized feature spaces of the visual and the textual features. On the other hand, feature weighting was used in different works in order to provide more weight for specific features. In [6] and [7] as part of ImageCLEF 2006 and 2007 respectively, they presented a novel approach to weight features using support vector machines. The main drawback of early fusion is the dimensionality of the resulting feature space which is equal to the sum of all the fused subspaces which leads to the well-known problem the "curse of dimensionality" [8]. Also, increasing in the number of modalities and the high dimensionality make them difficult to learn the cross-correlation among the heterogeneous features [9].

2.2   Late Fusion

Late fusion (or decision level) strategies do not act at the level of one representation for all the modalities features but rather at the level of the similarities among each modality. The extracted features of each modality are classified using the appropriate classifier; then, each classifier provides a decision. Unlike early fusion, where the features of each modality may have different representation, the decisions usually have the same representation. As a result, the fusion of the decisions becomes easier. The main disadvantage of this strategy is that it fails to utilize the feature level correlation among modalities. Also, using different classifiers and different learning process is expensive in term of time and learning for each modality.

Late fusion is used widely in image retrieval systems, and there is a diversity in the proposed methods. The most widely used technique is a rule-based method [10-16]. In [16], web application called MMRetrieval is proposed which has an online graphical user interface that brings image and text search together to compose a multimodal and multilingual query. The modalities are searched in parallel, and then the results can be fused via several selectable methods. Fusion process consists of two components: score normalization and combination. It provides a combination of scores across modalities with summation, multiplication, and maximum.

2.3   Trans-media Fusion

In this method, the main idea is to use first one of the modalities (say image) to gather relevant documents (nearest neighbors from a visual point of view) and then to use the dual modalities (text representations of the visually nearest neighbors) to perform the final retrieval. Most proposed methods under this category are based on adopted relevance feedback or pseudo-relevance feedback techniques as in [17]. The authors in [17] used the pseudo-relevance feedback to gather the N most relevant documents from the dataset using some visual similarity measures with respect to the visual features of the query or, reciprocally, using a purely textual similarity with respect to the textual features of the query, then aggregate these mono-modal similarities.

2.4   Image Re-ranking

In image re-ranking level, we need first to perform the search based on the text query. Then, the returned list of images is reordered according to the visual features similarity.

In [18], the cross-reference re-ranking strategy is proposed for the refinement of the initial search results of text-based video search engines. While [18] method deals with clusters of the modalities, [19] proposed a method that construct a semantic relation between text (words) and visual clusters using the ARM algorithm. They proposed Multi-Modal Semantic Association Rules (MMSAR) algorithm to fuse key-words and visual features automatically for Web image retrieval.

MFAR in this paper is considered as a late fusion method. There are three main differences between the method of [19] and MFAR proposed method: (1) MFAR uses ARM algorithm to explore the relations between text semantic clusters and image visual feature clusters; (2) the fusion method in MFAR is used at the retrieval phase not for re-ranking the results; (3) it is possible in MFAR to make a query by example image. In literature, there are several attempts to couple image retrieval and association rules mining algorithm. First, it is used as a preprocessing strategy for a preliminary reduction of the dimensionality of the pattern space to improve the global search time for CBIR system as in [20]. Second, as mentioned earlier, ARM has been used in image re-ranking process [19].

The next section will present the required background about ARM algorithm, which helps to understand the proposed method.

3   Basics of Association Rules Mining Algorithm

ARM is a data mining technique useful for discovering interesting relationships hidden in large databases. The classical example is the rules extracted from the content of the market baskets. Items are things we can buy in a market, and transactions are market baskets containing several items. The collection of all transactions called the transactions database. Besides the market basket data, association rules mining are applicable for different applications of other domains such as bioinformatics, medical diagnosis and Web mining.

The problem of mining association rules is stated as following: $I=\{i_1, i_2, \ldots, i_m\}$ is a set of items, $T=\{t_1, t_2, \ldots, t_n\}$ is a transaction database or a set of transactions, each of which contains items of the itemset I. Thus, each transaction t_i is a set of items such that $t_i \subseteq I$. An association rule is an implication of the form: $X \rightarrow Y$, where $X \subset I$, $Y \subset I$ and $X \cap Y = \emptyset$. X (or Y) is a set of items, called itemset. If an itemset contains k items, it is called k-itemset. It is obvious that the value of the antecedent implies the value of the consequent. The process of mining association rules consists of two main steps. The first step is to identify all the itemsets contained in the data that are adequate for mining association rules. To determine that the itemset is frequent, it should satisfy at least the predefined minimum support count. To measure the support for an itemset, the following formal definition is used:

$$Supp(X) = \frac{count\ (X)}{N} \tag{1}$$

Where N is the total number of transactions in the transaction database T i.e. $N = count(T)$. The second step is to generate rules out of the discovered frequent itemsets.

For doing so, a minimum confidence has to be defined. The formal definition to calculate the rule confidence is given by the following equation:

$$Conf(X \longrightarrow Y) = \frac{count\ (X \cup Y)}{count\ (X)} \qquad (2)$$

The confidence of the rule $X \rightarrow Y$ is a measurement that determines how frequently items in Y appear in transactions that contain X. Different algorithms attempt to allow efficient discovery of frequent patterns and for strong ARs such as the famous *Apriori* algorithm [21] which will be used later in MFAR.

4   Methodology

MFAR consists of two main phases: online phase and offline phase. The next subsections describe in details the inputs, the outputs and the steps of each phase.

4.1   Offline Phase

The input of this phase is the image dataset which contains two modalities: the images and their associated text. First, the visual and the textual features are extracted to run the clustering algorithm independently over them. Then, the modified ARM algorithm will identify the relations among the clusters from each modality to construct the ARs (see figure 1.a).

For visual features extraction, we used a set of generic MPEG-7 descriptors [22]. The features are selected to balance the color and the edge properties of the images. After extracting the visual features, images of the dataset are represented separately as objects in multidimensional space models for each visual feature. For textual features, they were obtained by applying the standard Bag-of-Words technique which needs to perform several linguistic preprocessing steps (tokenization, removing stop words, and stemming). Then, each document is described by a vector of constituent terms that represents the frequency occurrence of each term in the document which construct the vector-space model.

The large quantity of images and the high dimensionality of the visual descriptors need for an efficient clustering (or indexing) algorithm. The high dimensional index technique called NOHIS (Non Overlapping Hierarchical Index Structure) [23] is used for the indexing process which generates the NOHIS-tree. Then, an adapted k-nearest neighbors search is used for retrieving. On the other hand, K-means algorithm will be used for the textual features.

To apply the ARM algorithm, we need first to determine the items set I and the transaction database T. In our case, the items set is the generated images clusters based on the text (denoted by Ct_i) and based on the visual features (denoted by Cc_j for color-based clusters and Ce_k for edge-based clusters) where i, j and k are the identifiers of the clusters in each modality. After quantifying the features space of each modality, we aim to associate the text clusters and the visual feature clusters.

Thus, we need to construct the transaction database T first to run the ARM algorithm over it.

Each transaction in T contains the similar clusters from different modalities. Similarity here means the overlapping degree between the clusters. If the cardinality of the common images set is not zero, the clusters combine at the same transaction. It is possible to represent that in the following example: If $| Ct_i \cap Cc_j | > 0$, then add $\{Ct_i, Cc_j\}$ to T. The hypothesis in constructing T is that similar clusters tends to be semantically related; therefore, they are combined at the same transaction. We are interested in the association between text clusters and visual feature clusters only. Each transaction contains a text cluster and at least one visual cluster. The following are examples of the obtained transactions: $\{Ct_0, Cc_{111}\}$, $\{Ct_0, Ce_{206}\}$, $\{Ct_0, Cc_{111}, Ce_{173}\}$.

Two different reasons let us adjust the formal definitions of support and confidence (definitions (1) and (2)). First, using the standard support/confidence definition for the semantic rules, which is calculated for the entire T, will affect the generated rules because their support is extremely low. Second, the calculation of support and confidence is restricted within the result set of the text clusters because we are testing the semantic relations between the text clusters and visual clusters. Thus, we define the support and the confidence of the rule $Ct_i \rightarrow Cv_j$ (where Cv represents the visual cluster) as follows:

$$Supp(Ct_i \rightarrow Cv_j) = \frac{count(Ct_i, Cv_j)}{count(Ct_i)} \tag{3}$$

$$Conf(Ct_i \rightarrow Cv_j) = \frac{count(Ct_i, Cv_j)}{max_k(count(Ct_i, Cv_k))} \tag{4}$$

Where $count(A)$ is the number of itemsets that contain A in T. Similarly in case there is more than one item at the right hand side of the rule is given by (5) and (6):

$$Supp(Ct_i \rightarrow \{ Cv_j | j=1,...,m\} = \frac{count(Ct_i, \{Cv_j | j=1,...,m\})}{count(Ct_i)} \tag{5}$$

$$Conf(Ct_i \rightarrow \{ Cv_j | j=1,...,m\}) = \frac{count(Ct_i, \{Cv_j | j=1,...,m\})}{max_k(count(Ct_i, Cv_k))} \tag{6}$$

We need to use a modified version of frequent itemsets mining algorithm based on *Apriori* algorithm with definitions (5) and (6) of support and confidence to discover all frequent patterns of the association between text clusters and visual feature clusters. The algorithm is in table 1. The algorithm do not start from 1-itemsets; that because we want to construct the relationships between text clusters and visual clusters; and in case starting from 1-itemsets, it is possible to build relations among visual clusters since they will be treated equally. The minimum support threshold should be given to run the algorithm.

Here, *apriori-gen* function is used to perform three main operations: (1) candidate generation; (2) candidate pruning; and (3) insuring that each candidate itemset should have one text cluster. The *subset* function is used to determine all the candidate itemsets in C_k that are contained in each transaction t. A transaction t is said to contain an itemset X if X is a subset of transaction t.

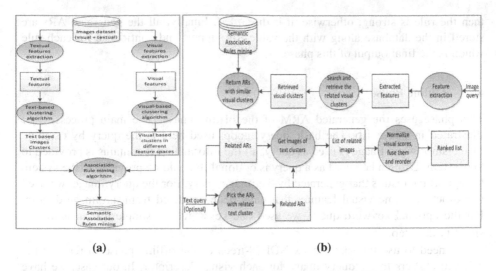

(a)
(b)

Fig. 1. The offline (a) and online phase (b) of MFAR

Table 1. Frequent itemsets mining algorithm based on Apriori

Input:
a)   The transaction database T
b)   *minsup* threshold
Output:
The list of frequently itemsets L
1) $L_2 = \{(Ct_i, Cv_j) \mid$ where $\mid Ct_i \cap Cv_j \mid > 0$ && $(Ct_i, Cv_j).$supp $\geq$ *minsup*$\}$; //Find all frequent 2-itemsets
2) for ($k = 3$; $L_{k-1} \neq \emptyset$; $k++$) do begin
3) $C_k =$ apriori-gen(L_{k-1}); // New candidates with k-itemset with only one text cluster in it and a
// combination of frequent sets from L_{k-1}
4)   for all transactions $t \in T$ do begin
5) $C_t =$ subset(C_k , t); // Identify all candidates that belong   to t
6)   for all candidates $c \in C_t$ do
7) $c.count++$;
8)   end
9) $L_k = \{ c \in C_k \mid c.supp \geq$ *minsup*$\}$
10) end
11) Return $\cup\ L_k$;

To generate strong ARs, the generated frequent itemsets L and the minimum confidence threshold value *minconf* should be used as input to the generating algorithm. The ARs in our case have one text cluster in the left hand side and one or multiple visual cluster(s) at the right hand side. There is no need to find all possible subsets of the large itemset L as in the original *Apriori* algorithm. For example, if $l = \{Ct_1, Cc_3, Ce_1\}$ is a frequent itemset, candidate rule is $Ct_1 \rightarrow \{Cc_3, Ce_1\}$. If the calculated confidence of the candidate rule using (6) is greater than or equal *minconf*, then the rule is strong; otherwise, it is discarded. Finally, all the generated ARs are stored in the database along with the values of support and confidence for each rule which is the final output of this phase.

4.2   Online Phase

This phase uses the generated ARM of the offline phase. The main processes are illustrated in figure 1.b. The basic query model used here is the query by example image since when image is used as query, all the information it contains is provided to the system. Using a keyword as a query is optional. It could be provided to the system to support the results that generated by the image query. For the query image, we need to extract the same visual features that have been extracted from the image dataset. For the optional keyword query, we used one keyword and simple text matching to simplify this step.

We need to use the same index NOHIS-trees of the offline phase to retrieve the relevant clusters to the query image for each visual descriptor. In our case, we have two different NOIHS-trees for two different feature spaces. For each feature, we calculated the top 500 nearest neighbors and returned their clusters. The search should be conducted on the trees in parallel. The output of this process is a list of visual clusters from different feature spaces.

Then, the next process "retrieve ARs with similar visual clusters" gets the list of the related visual clusters as input; and then it uses them to make a search in the ARM to find the rules that contain these clusters. If the keyword query was provided, the retrieved rules should be filtered to pick the rules which contain text clusters that have similar term to the text query. Then, the images' scores in those text clusters should be increased. The dashed arrow in figure 1.b indicates that it is an optional path.

For all the retrieved ARs, we need to get the images of the text-based clusters. For each image, the relevant score to the query image q should be calculated if the image is not from the top 500 images for each visual feature. Regarding score normalization, we used Zero-One linear method which maps the scores into the range of [0, 1] [24]. The normalized scores of different modalities should be fused using CombSum method [24]. Then, if there is a keyword query as input, the fused score of each image that correlated to term similar to the keyword query should be incremented by one. Finally, the fused list will be reordered based on the fused scores.

5   Experiment

5.1   Experimental Setup and Tools

MFAR has been evaluated using ImageCLEF 2011 Wikipedia collection. It consists of 50 topics and 237,434 Wikipedia images along with their user-provided annotations in three different languages [25]. Since some images in the dataset do not have English description and others do not have a description at all, only images with English description are considered. Thus, the used dataset is a subset of ImageCLEF 2011

Wikipedia which contains more than 54,500 images. Some example topics of the dataset along with their titles, the used text query, the number of image queries in the topic and the number of relevant images in the collection subset are given in table 2.

For visual features extraction, the two MPEG-7 descriptors: Color Structure Descriptor (CSD) and Edge Histogram Descriptor (EHD) are extracted from the dataset using the tool given in [26]. For textual features extraction and K-means clustering, Text-Garden software is used[1]. To cluster the extracted visual features, NOHIS algorithm library is provided by the author of the algorithm. The system prototype is developed in C#.NET Framework with simple GUI for experiment purpose only (see figure 2). Based on different experiments, we set *minsupp* and *minconf* to be 2% and 70% respectively.

MFAR was compared to our system without using ARs and to the online system MMRetrieval[2] [16]. Since MMRetrieval system supports different fusion methods, the well-known method CompSum with MinMax normalization is selected. We used the example images of all the dataset topics. For our system without ARs, the queries are only images. On the other hand, for MFAR and MMRetrieval, the query can be either image only or image with keyword. The text query is restricted to be one word.

Table 2. Information of some topics of the subset collection

Topic ID	Topic Title	Text query	No.# of query images	No# of relevant images
85	Beijing bird nest	Volkswagen	5	8
95	photo of real butterflies	Butterfly	5	37
107	sunflower close up	Sunflower	5	4
111	two euro coins	Euro	5	30
115	flying bird	Flying	5	46

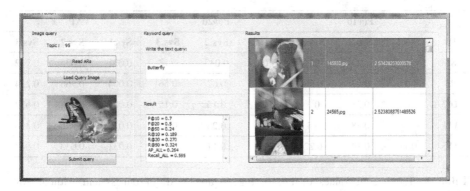

Fig. 2. Main GUI of MFAR

---

[1] Text-Garden – Text Mining Software Tools. http://www.textmining.net
[2] http://mmretrieval.nonrelevant.net

5.2   Experimental Results and Discussion

For evaluation, we used the Precision (P) at fixed rank (10 and 20), and the Mean Average Precision (MAP) [27]. The values of P@10, P@20 and Average Precision (AP) of five random categories (with different difficulty levels; and they are not the best results) are given in table 3. Each value in the table represents the average of the precisions for the five example images contained in the topic. In addition, table 4 shows the overall values of P@10, P@20 and MAP for all topics of the dataset. The results show that MFAR with composite query (image + keyword) performs better precision and MAP than the other two systems. Furthermore, the proposed system and MMRetrieval system have been evaluated with an image query only without using text; and the proposed system performs acceptable semantic results comparing to MMRetrieval system and provides better precision results than MMRetrieval. The precision values with image query mode in both systems are lesser than the systems with composite query.

We examined the retrieved ARs for different visual queries to study the relations between the image query and the rules. One example is an image from topic 107 with title "sunflower close up". Text cluster Ct_{645} is classified based on different words one of them is "sunflower". The retrieved ARs for the query in the two query modes: query by image only and the composite query contain rules that associate Ct_{645} text cluster to visual clusters consists of sunflower pictures. That means by using the visual features of the query image, it is possible to reach the text cluster which is semantically related.

In addition, we found that by using MFAR the search operation concentrate on the images subset that included in the retrieved ARs of the submitted query which increases the chance of retrieving a semantically related results.

Table 3. P@10, P@20 and AP of 5 different topics in: (1) Sys.1: our system without ARs (visual), (2) Sys.2: MMRetrival system (visual + text), and (3) Sys.3: MFAR (visual + text)

Topic ID	P@10			P@20			AP		
	Sys.1	Sys.2	Sys.3	Sys.1	Sys.2	Sys.3	Sys.1	Sys.2	Sys.3
85	0	0	0.2	0	0.013	0.13	0.001	0.035	0.282
95	0	0.72	0.66	0	0.62	0.56	0.004	0.366	0.234
107	0	0.28	0.3	0	0.15	0.15	0.004	0.468	0.658
111	0	0.38	0.4	0.01	0.23	0.47	0.018	0.236	0.350
115	0.12	0.14	0.22	0.07	0.11	0.18	0.031	0.033	0.047

Table 4. The overall values of P@10, P@20, and MAP of our system without ARs, MMRetrival system, and MFAR

Sys. without ARs			MMRetrieval			MFAR		
P@10	P@20	MAP	P@10	P@20	MAP	P@10	P@20	MAP
0.011	0.009	0.010	0.205	0.164	0.210	0.240	0.175	0.244

6   Conclusion and Future Work

In this proposed method, we used association rules mining algorithm in our image retrieval system to construct semantic relations between image clusters based on the visual features and the image clusters based on textual features for the same dataset. From information fusion perspective, we have used late fusion technique. The online phase uses the constructed ARs from the offline phase. Then, the retrieval process requires an example image query to start. The method gives the ability to retrieve images that are semantically related by using the extracted visual features of the query image and by exploring the related ARs from the constructed ARM. To support the results, it is possible to use a keyword query. The results show that the precision value of our proposed system is better than MMRetrieval system and the system without association rules.

The future work will involve using different clustering algorithm to improve the accuracy of the text clusters. The system with image query mode without keyword query needs for further improvements. Using pseudo-relevance feedback technique is one suggested solution. The correlated terms of the top retrieved ARs could be used to make feedback text query. Also, it is possible to generalize the proposed method to use it for image annotation system by associating the unannotated images with the semantically related text cluster.

References

1. Liu, Y., Zhanga, D., Lua, G., Ma, W.-Y.: A survey of content-based image retrieval with high-level semantics. Pattern Recognition 40(1), 262–282 (2007)
2. Datta, R., Joshi, D., Li, J., Wang, J.Z.: Image retrieval: Ideas, influences, and trends of the new age. ACM Computing Surveys (CSUR) 40(2), 1–60 (2008)
3. Wu, S., McClean, S.: Performance prediction of data fusion for information retrieval. Management Information Processing 42(4), 899–915 (2006)
4. Müller, H., Clough, P., Deselaers, T., Caputo, B.: ImageCLEF. The Springer International Series on Information Retrieval, vol. 32, pp. 95–114. Springer (2010)
5. Ferecatu, M., Sahbi, H.: TELECOM ParisTech at ImageClefphoto 2008: Bi–modal text and image retrieval with diversity enhancement. In: Working Notes of CLEF 2008, Aarhus, Denmark (2008)
6. Deselaers, T., Weyand, T., Ney, H.: Image retrieval and annotation using maximum entropy. In: Peters, C., Clough, P., Gey, F.C., Karlgren, J., Magnini, B., Oard, D.W., de Rijke, M., Stempfhuber, M. (eds.) CLEF 2006. LNCS, vol. 4730, pp. 725–734. Springer, Heidelberg (2007)
7. Gass, T., Weyand, T., Deselaers, T., Ney, H.: FIRE in ImageCLEF 2007: Support vector machines and logistic models to fuse image descriptors for photo retrieval. In: Peters, C., Jijkoun, V., Mandl, T., Müller, H., Oard, D.W., Peñas, A., Petras, V., Santos, D. (eds.) CLEF 2007. LNCS, vol. 5152, pp. 492–499. Springer, Heidelberg (2008)
8. Bellman, R.: Adaptive Control Process: A Guided Tour. Princeton University Press (1961)
9. Atrey, P.K., Hossain, M.A., Saddik, A.E., Kankanhall, M.S.: Multimodal fusion for multimedia analysis: A survey. Multimedia Syst. 16(3), 1432–1882 (2010)

10. Lau, C., Tjondronegoro, D., Zhang, J., Geva, S., Liu, Y.: Fusing visual and textual retrieval techniques to efectively search large collections of wikipedia images. International Journal of Business Intelligence and Data Mining, 345–357 (2007)
11. Frigui, H., Caudill, J., Ben Abdallah, A.: Fusion of multi-modal features for effiecient content-based image retrieval. In: IEEE World Congress on Computational Intelligence, pp. 1992–1998 (2008)
12. Bartolini, I., Ciaccia, P.: Scenique: a multimodal image retrieval interface. In: Proceedings of the Working Conference on Advanced Visual Interfaces, pp. 476–477. ACM, Italy (2008)
13. Zhou, X., Depeursinge, A., Müller, H.: Information fusion for combining visual and textual image retrieval. In: Proceedings of the 20th International Conference on Recognizing Patterns in Signals, Speech, Images, and Videos, pp. 1590–1593 (2010)
14. Tong, H., He, J.R., Li, M.J., Zhang, C.S., Ma, W.Y.: Graph-based multi-modality learning. In: Proceeding of the ACM Int. Conf. on Multimedia, pp. 862–871 (2005)
15. Escalante, H.J., Hernandez, C., Sucar, E., Montes, M.: Late fusion of heterogeneous methods for multimedia image retrieval. In: Proceeding of MIR, pp. 172–179. ACM, Vancouver (2008)
16. Zagoris, K., Arampatzis, A., Chatzichristofis, S.A.: www.MMRetrieval.net: a multimodal search engine. In: Proceedings of the Third International Conference on SImilarity Search and Applications, Turkey (2010)
17. Ah-Pine, J., Bressan, M., Clinchant, S., Csurka, G., Hoppenot, Y., Renders, J.: Crossing textual and visual content in different application scenarios. Multimedia Tools and Applications 42(1), 31–56 (2009)
18. Wei, S., Zhao, Y., Zhu, Z., Liu, N.: Multimodal Fusion for Video Search Reranking. IEEE Transactions on Knowledge and Data Engineering 22(8), 1191–1199 (2010)
19. He, R., Xiong, N., Yang, L., Park, J.: Using multi-modal semantic association rules to fuse keywords and visual features automatically for web image retrieval. In: International Conference on Information Fusion (2011)
20. Kouomou-Choupo, A., Berti-Equille, L., Morin, A.: Multimedia indexing and retrieval with features association rules mining. In: IEEE International Conference on Multimedia and Expo (ICME 2004), pp. 1299–1302 (2004)
21. Agrawal, R., Imielinski, T., Swami, A.: Mining association rules between sets of items in large databases. In: Proceedings of ACM SIGMOD, pp. 207–216 (1993)
22. Manjunath, B.S., Salembier, P., Sikora, T.: Introduction to MPEG-7: multimedia content description interface. Wiley (2002)
23. Taileb, M., Lamrous, S., Touati, S.: Non Overlapping Hierarchical Index Structure. International Journal of Computer Science 3(1), 29–35 (2008)
24. Wu, S.: Data Fusion in Information Retrieval. ALO, vol. 13. Springer, Heidelberg (2012)
25. Tsikrika, T., Popescu, A., Kludas, J.: Overview of the Wikipedia Image Retrieval Task at ImageCLEF 2011. In: Working Notes of CLEF 2011, Amsterdam, The Netherlands (2011)
26. Bastan, M., Cam, H., Gudukbay, U., Ulusoy, O.: BilVideo-7: An MPEG-7 Compatible Video Indexing and Retrieval System. IEEE MultiMedia 17(3), 62–73 (2010)
27. Müller, H., Clough, P., Deselaers, T., Caputo, B.: ImageCLEF. The Springer International Series on Information Retrieval, vol. 32, pp. 81–92. Springer (2010)

Graphical Querying of Model-Driven Spreadsheets*

Jácome Cunha[1,2], João Paulo Fernandes[1,3],
Rui Pereira[1], and João Saraiva[1]

[1] HASLab/INESC TEC & Universidade do Minho, Portugal
[2] CIICESI, ESTGF, Instituto Politécnico do Porto, Portugal
[3] RELEASE, Universidade da Beira Interior, Portugal
{jacome,jpaulo,ruipereira,jas}@di.uminho.pt

Abstract. This paper presents a graphical interface to query model-driven spreadsheets to simplify query construction for typical end-users with little to no knowledge of SQL. This was based on experience with previous work and empirical studies in querying systems. We briefly show our previous text based model-driven querying system. Afterwards, we detail our graphical model-driven querying interface, explaining each part of the interface and showing an example. To validate our work, we executed an empirical study, comparing our graphical querying approach to an alternative querying tool, which produced positive results.

Keywords: Model-driven engineering, graphical querying, spreadsheets.

1 Introduction

Spreadsheets are the most successful example of the end user programming approach to software development. Although invented to provide a simple, but powerful, graphical environment to express mathematical formulas, spreadsheet systems quickly evolved into powerful software environments able to manipulate complex and large amount of data. Indeed, spreadsheets are often used to perform operations usually associated to databases. Surprisingly enough, spreadsheet systems lack powerful techniques, researched and developed for decades, that make database systems so powerful to manipulate big data, namely the use of data normalization techniques [1] and the use of query languages to filter and transform data [2]. And even then, the construction of a textual query language is difficult for end-users.

The purpose of this paper is three-fold:

---

* This work is part funded by the ERDF - European Regional Development Fund through the COMPETE Programme (operational programme for competitiveness) and by National Funds through the FCT - Fundação para a Ciência e a Tecnologia (Portuguese Foundation for Science and Technology) within project FCOMP-01-0124-FEDER-022701. The first author was funded by FCT: SFRH/BPD/73358/2010.

S. Yamamoto (Ed.): HIMI 2014, Part I, LNCS 8521, pp. 419–430, 2014.

- Firstly, we introduce a single, but powerful, graphical model-driven query language: *Graphical-QuerySheet*. Like in databases, we use models to express the business logic of the data. As a consequence, we can express the query based on those models, rather than on large and complex data. We use well-known spreadsheet models, namely ClassSheets [3–5], where databases use the relational models. Our queries are then expressed on those models and not on the data, exactly as in databases. Querying data, using for example SQL [6], is not a simple task, even for professional programmers. To make querying data available to end users, we define a visual querying language. Moreover, we hid from end users the data (de)normalization tasks.
- Secondly, we present a complete graphical model-driven spreadsheet querying architecture and tool. We detail the graphical tool, and through an example, show how a user would build his/her query.
- Thirdly, we present an empirical study where we compare our graphical approach to spreadsheet querying with the language provided by Google on its spreadsheets. A group of end users was asked to perform a series of tasks using both query systems. We present the first results of such a study, showing that *Graphical-QuerySheet* increases productivity, is intuitive and human-friendly, and is easy to use for someone with little or no SQL knowledge.

This paper is organized as follows: Section 2 briefly presents Google's QUERY function, along with some of its disadvantages, and a textual model-driven querying system. Section 3 introduces our graphical model-driven spreadsheet query interface. Section 4 presents our empirical study. Finally, in Section 5 we conclude the paper, and mention some future work.

2   Querying Spreadsheets

Before presenting techniques to query spreadsheets, let us introduce a spreadsheet to be used as a running example throughout this paper.

Figure 1 shows part of a spreadsheet to store information about the budget of a company. In this spreadsheet, we have information about the Category of the budget used (such as Travel or Accommodation) and the Year. The relationship between these two entities gives us information on the Quantity, Cost, and the Total Costs, per year per category, defined by spreadsheet formulas.

Although spreadsheet systems do not provide mechanisms to query the data, the fact is that we often need to answer simple questions like:

> **Question.** *What was the total per year, ordered descendantly, from 2010 on wards?*

2.1   Google QUERY Function

Google provides a querying function, the Google QUERY function [7], which uses a SQL-like syntax [6], to perform a query over an array of values. An example would be the Google Docs spreadsheets, where the querying function is built in.

	A	B	C	D	E	F	G	H	I
1	Budget		Year			Year			Year
2			2005			2006			200
3	Category	Name	Qnty	Cost	Total	Qnty	Cost	Total	Qnty
4		Travel	2	525	1050	3	360	1080	
5		Accomodation	4	120	480	9	115	1035	
6		Meals	6	25	150	18	30	540	3

Fig. 1. Part of the spreadsheet data for a Budget example

	A	B	C	D	E
1	Year	Name	Qnty	Cost	Total
2	2005	Travel	2	525	1050
3	2005	Accomodation	4	120	480
4	2005	Meals	6	25	150
5	2006	Travel	3	360	1080
6	2006	Accomodation	9	115	1035
7	2006	Meals	18	30	540
8	2007	Travel	6	25	150
9	2007	Accomodation	3	360	1080
10	2007	Meals	9	115	1035

Fig. 2. Budget data (denormalized)

This function needs two arguments, consisting of a range as its first argument, to state the range of data cells to be queried (for example A1:Q13), and the actual query string.

So if we wanted to answer our previous question, we would have to write in a cell, the formula expressed as the pre-defined *query* function, as displayed in Listing 1.1, after denormalizing the data from Figure 1 to Figure 2:

Listing 1.1. Google QUERY function for our example Question

```
=query(A1:58; "SELECT A, sum(E) WHERE A >= 2010
              GROUP BY A ORDER BY sum(E) DESC")
```

While being a powerful query function, it still has its flaws. To run this function, the user needs to represent his spreadsheet information in a single table. This means that someone who has their spreadsheet information divided as entities with relations, would need to first denormalize the data (as shown in Figure 2).

Afterwards, the user would need to write the query string, and here comes the second flaw: instead of writing the query using column names/labels, one must use the column letters. As one would expect, this can get confusing, counterintuitive, and almost impossible to understand what the query is supposed to do, as shown in [8].

2.2   QuerySheet

We believe that querying spreadsheets should be simple and intuitive. This motivated us to design and implement a querying language simpler than Google's querying function, based on using some form of labels or descriptive tags to point to attributes and entities, as is in the database realm.

We turned to model-driven engineering [9, 10], a methodology in software development that uses and exploits domain models, or abstract representations of software. This has been successfully applied to spreadsheets, making model-driven spreadsheets [11, 12] and a model-driven spreadsheet environment (MDSheet) possible [13]. One of such spreadsheet models is ClassSheets [3, 4], a high-level and object-oriented formalism, using the notion of classes and attributes, to express business logic spreadsheet data. ClassSheets allow us to define the business logic of a spreadsheet in a concise and abstract manner, resulting in users being able to understand, evolve, and maintain complex spreadsheets.

To showcase ClassSheets, we present the ClassSheet model for our example spreadsheet from Figure 1. This ClassSheet model, named **Budget**, has a **Category** class (with a **Name** attribute) and a **Year** class (with a **Year** attribute) expanding vertically and horizontally, respectively. The joining of these gives us a **Quantity**, a **Cost**, and the **Total** of a **Category** in a given **Year**, each with its own default value. The corresponding spreadsheet instance conforms to the ClassSheet model as shown in Figure 3.

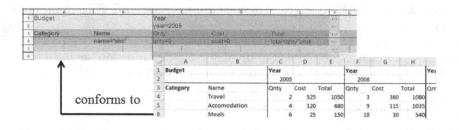

Fig. 3. ClassSheet model and conforming instance for the Budget example

Having ClassSheet models available, we designed a textual querying language to write the queries based on those models [14], allowing descriptive and human-friendly query construction, in contrast to Google's approach. Moreover, we implemented a query framework, called *QuerySheet* [15, 16], that automatically denormalizes the data (as shown in Figure 2), translates it to a Google QUERY, and executes it in Google's engine. Thus, answering the previous question would be as simple as looking at the ClassSheet and writing the query:

Listing 1.2. QuerySheet query for our example Question

```
SELECT Year, sum(Total) WHERE Year >= 2010
GROUP BY Year ORDER BY sum(Total)
```

3   Graphical Model-Driven Spreadsheet Query Language

In order to validate the model-driven query language, we have performed an empirical study with real spreadsheet users [8], and realized that we can simplify querying spreadsheets even further, especially for end-users.

Indeed, while the participants in our study who were experienced in SQL had no problems, all others expressed frustration with writing SQL queries, due to having to remember the syntax, forgetting a group by clause after an aggregation, or even simple typos. This in turn motivated us to design a way to abstract the users from the textual query language, to a simple point and click query construction interface, where we could once again take advantage of spreadsheet models, and our previous experience with *QuerySheet*. What we designed was a simple, interactive visual language for querying model-driven spreadsheets, called *Graphical-QuerySheet*.

3.1   *Graphical-QuerySheet*

To try to shorten, or even eventually eliminate, the knowledge of SQL needed to correctly construct queries in our original system, we began building a graphical interface for *QuerySheet*. The focus of this interface was to be as simple as possible, displaying all the information in our query language, but in a human-friendly way. The interface also had to be intuitive to use, both for an experienced SQL user, and an end-user. We also wanted the interface to reduce the amount of errors (at least in the query syntax and attributes' names), and let the user choose the attributes based on the spreadsheet's model.

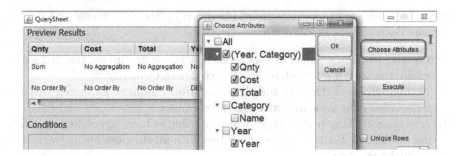

Fig. 4. Attribute selection in the graphical interface

What resulted was an interactive graphical query building interface named *Graphical-QuerySheet* integrated into the MDSheet framework, and launched by a simple button. This interface allows a less experienced user to use a series of drop-down boxes to select his/her filter conditions, attribute orders, aggregations, and other querying conditions, to easily construct the queries, eliminating any possible syntax errors. The actual attribute selection (or Select clause) is presented by a tree-list based on a ClassSheet model (as shown in Figure 4), where the user may choose (by checking the corresponding check-boxes) all the attributes, all from a specific class, or individual ones. These chosen attributes are then displayed in a *Preview Results* panel, each attribute in its own column, showing the user how the result is to be returned, and allowing the user to drag the columns left or right to organize how he or she desires.

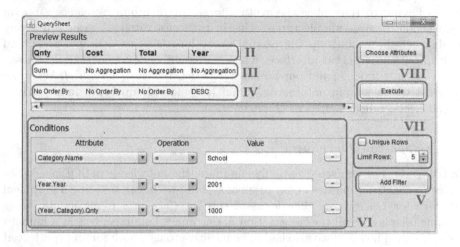

Fig. 5. *Graphical-QuerySheet* (The boxes and numbers do not belong to the interface and are only shown for identifying the various areas)

In Figure 5 we see the various areas, identified by the red[1] boxes and Roman numerals. Each area is as follows:

I   *Choose Attributes*. This button opens the Choose Attributes tree-list panel, where the user may check off which attributes to display.
II *Column Headers*. Display the chosen attribute names. Dragging this column, allows the user to rearrange the columns.
III *Aggregation*. This row displays which attributes have aggregations. Clicking on the cell displays a drop-down box with all the possible aggregations, or no aggregation.
IV *Order*. This row displays which attributes have an order clause. Clicking on the cell displays a drop-down box with the three possible options: ASC, DESC, or No Order By.
V   *Add Filter*. This button adds a new row in the Conditions panel, to allow the user to add a new condition (or Where clause).
VI *Conditions Panel*. Displays all the conditions in the query. Each row is made up of two combo-boxes (allowing the user to respectively choose which attributes and operations to be used per condition), a text box to

---

[1] We assume colors are visible through the digital version of this document.

state the value of the condition, and a remove button (displayed as a red minus sign) to remove the condition from the panel.

VII *Unique/Limit.* A check-box to choose to display unique rows, and a scroll panel to state how many rows to display in the results, respectively. If the scroll panel value is 0, there is no limit.

VIII *Execute.* This button automatically translates the visual language to our model-driven query language, and executes the query, displaying the results in the user's spreadsheet. Below this button is a progress bar to give the user visual feedback of the process.

The interface also displays tool-tips when hovering over the buttons, check boxes, etc, to help the user understand the various parts. Along with the helpful tool tips, if one were to hover their mouse over the selected attribute headers, the attribute's class name is displayed (as shown in Figure 6). This is useful for when an attribute has the same name as another, while also reducing the amount visual information presented to the user all at once (for example showing another row to display the class names).

Another useful addition is the automatic calculation of when a group by is needed. In other words, when an aggregation is detected with other selected attributes, the visual language automatically produces a grouping. This automatic calculation not only is practical in query construction, but also made it so one less query clause is needed to be presented in the graphical interface.

3.2 Building a Query in *Graphical-QuerySheet*

We will explain how one would construct the query from Listing 1.2 using *Graphical-QuerySheet*, as shown in Figure 6. The steps to construct this query are as follows:

1. Click on *Choose Attributes* and check *Year* and *Total*
2. Click on the *aggregation combo box* and choose *Sum*
3. Click on the *order by combo box* and choose *DESC*
4. Click on *Add filter*
5. Select the *Year.Year* attribute and *greater or equal to* operation using the combo boxes, and fill in *2010* in the *text box*
6. Click *Execute*

With this graphical interface guiding the user in his or her query construction, we are able to reduce a number of possible errors, and simplfy the user's experience. Using this interface, the user can have little to no SQL experience, and still perform queries.

3.3 Architecture

Since *Graphical-QuerySheet* builds upon *QuerySheet*, the only necessary extra work to build the former was to translate the visual query language that we introduce in this paper to our textual model-driven query language. The remaining steps of the process remain the same.

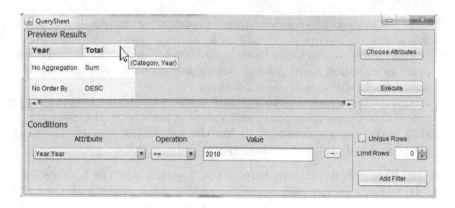

Fig. 6. *Graphical-QuerySheet*

When the user clicks on the Execute button, the visual language is translated, and the data is denormalized. Using our previous model-driven query techniques, we produce the appropriate Google QUERY function string, with the corresponding data, and send both to Google to be executed by its query engine.

The results are then passed through our model inference technique, generating a ClassSheet-driven spreadsheet, with the resulting model and instance. In fact, two new worksheets are added to the original spreadsheet: one containing the spreadsheet data that results from the query, and the other containing the ClassSheet model.

A complete illustration of the architecture that we have devised for *Graphical-QuerySheet* is shown in Figure 7. Indeed, we sketch how our tool produces the result of executing the query in Listing 1.2 on the spreadsheet of Figure 3.

An important aspect to note about our approach is that the result of executing a query is not only the data that it asks for, but also the ClassSheet model that such data conforms to, which is automatically inferred using a technique from our previous work [5]. This means that this result can be further queried in a model-driven fashion.

4   Empirical Study

In order to assess the use of *Graphical-QuerySheet* in practice, we planned and executed an empirical study with end-users. With this study, we wanted to obtain concrete feedback on our query system and to assess the productivity associated with its use.

The study was done one participant at a time, in a think-aloud session. By doing this, we were able to see each participant using our system and learn the difficulties they were having, and how to improve the system to overcome them.

We ran this study with seven students, ranging from Bachelor to PhD students. Before running the actual study, we prepared a tutorial to teach the

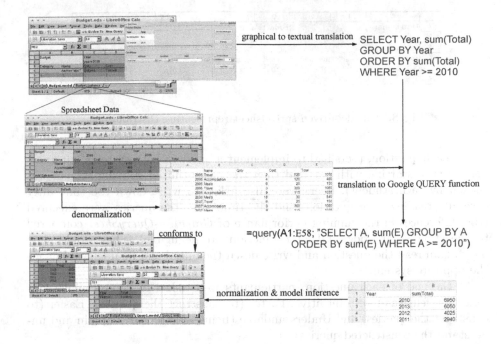

Fig. 7. The architecture of *Graphical-QuerySheet*

students how to use Google's QUERY function and the *Graphical-QuerySheet* system, with a series of exercises using both systems. When the students were comfortable with each system, the actual study was performed.

In the study, we used a real-life spreadsheet which we obtained, with permission, from a local food bank in our hometown of Braga. We thoroughly explained how the information was represented to the students, and how to properly interpret the spreadsheet information. This spreadsheet stored information regarding the distributions of basic products and other food bank institutions. This spreadsheet had information on 85 institutions and 14 different types of basic products, giving way to over 1190 lines of unique information.

We also denormalized the information for the students (to use with Google's QUERY function), and also prepared the spreadsheet model and conformed instance in the MDSheet environment. Since we can not show the actual spreadsheet data due to revealing private information, only the spreadsheet model is presented in Figure 8.

During the study, we asked participants to implement queries to answer the following four questions:

1. What is the total distributed for each product?
2. What is the total stock?
3. What are the names of each institution without repetitions?
4. Which were the products with more than 500 units distributed, and to which institution were they delivered to?

	A	B	C	D	E	F	G
1	Distribution			Product	name=""	...	
2					code=""	...	
3	Institution				stock=0	...	
4	code=""	name=""	lunch=0	dinner=0	distributed=0	...	
5	⋮	⋮	⋮	⋮		⋮	⋮
6						...	

Fig. 8. A model-driven spreadsheet representing Distributions

For each question, users had to implement a query in both systems, alternating between starting with one and then the other (initial starting system was chosen by each student). Users were also asked to write down the time after carefully reading each question, and the time after the queries were executed (the differences in the running performance of *Graphical-QuerySheet* compared to the standalone Google QUERY function are negligible). They would then once again read the question and write down the initial and final times, but for the opposite system.

At the end of each question, participants were asked to choose which system they felt was more: Intuitive, Faster (to construct the queries), Easier (to construct the queries) and Understandable (being able to fully explain and understand the constructed queries).

At the end of the study, participants answered which system they preferred and why, and what advantages/disadvantages existed between the systems.

4.1 Results

The results we obtained from our study were gathered and analyzed, and are presented in this section. In Figure 9, we analyze the differences in terms of performance between *Graphical-QuerySheet* and the Google QUERY function. The left side (Y-Axis) represents the average number of minutes the students took to answer the questions. The bottom side (X-Axis) represents the question the students answered. The green bars represent the Google QUERY function, and the blue bars represent the *Graphical-QuerySheet* system.

As we can see, users spent substantially less time to construct the queries using the *Graphical-QuerySheet* system, ranging from as much as approximately 65% to approximately 90%, averaging out to an overall of 80%. In the cases where

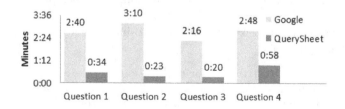

Fig. 9. A chart detailing the information gathered from the empirical evaluation

the queries or the results were incorrect, almost all (6 out of 7 errors) were with the Google QUERY function, varying between incorrect column letters chosen, bad query construction, and incorrect ranges.

Almost all, 104 out of 112 (4 points x 4 questions x 7 participants), chose our system in regards to the four previously mentioned points (Intuitive, Faster, Easier, and Understandable). The few cases where they preferred Google's approach, or neither, provided us with interesting information, allowing us to detect some of the drawbacks of this system.

The comments written by the students were also very positive. All preferred our *Graphical-QuerySheet* system over Google's QUERY function, finding the interface extremely intuitive and query construction facilitated. Some of the comments can be seen below:

- *Graphical-QuerySheet is very intuitive and quick to use, presenting an attracting interface.*
- *Graphical-QuerySheet allows me to complete my tasks much more quickly.*
- *It was easy to construct queries using labels instead of column letters, and ordering, grouping, and aggregations are much simpler with Graphical-QuerySheet.*
- *No need to know SQL, a normal user like myself can quickly and easily construct queries.*
- *I do not need to worry about using group by when I aggregate, Graphical-QuerySheet does it automatically for me.*

5 Conclusion

In this paper, we presented the design, implementation, and validation of a graphical query language interface for model-driven spreadsheets. The focus of our design for the graphical query interface was to provide a human-friendly, easy to use, interactive environment to quickly construct ClassSheet-driven queries, for users with different SQL skills.

We have implemented our graphical, model-driven query environment in a model-driven spreadsheet environment. The *Graphical-QuerySheet* was used in an empirical study where we were able to increase productivity by approximately 80%, while also meeting our goals of balancing simplicity with expressability.

Even with the good results and responses towards our graphical querying system, some interesting directions of future research were identified. Although the empirical results we have presented are interesting, they were the result of a study with a relatively small group participants. Thus, we plan to execute a second study, this time with more participants, and more end-users.

Acknowledgments. We would like to thank Professor José Creissac Campos for his helpful comments and insight regarding the graphical query interface.

References

1. Maier, D.: The Theory of Relational Databases. Computer Science Press (1983)
2. Hainaut, J.L.: The transformational approach to database engineering. [17], 95–144
3. Engels, G., Erwig, M.: ClassSheets: automatic generation of spreadsheet applications from object-oriented specifications. In: Proc. of the 20th IEEE/ACM Int. Conf. on Aut. Sof. Eng., pp. 124–133. ACM (2005)
4. Bals, J.C., Christ, F., Engels, G., Erwig, M.: Classsheets - model-based, object-oriented design of spreadsheet applications. In: TOOLS Europe Conference (TOOLS 2007), Zürich, Swiss, vol. 6, pp. 383–398 (October 2007); Journal of Object Technology
5. Cunha, J., Erwig, M., Saraiva, J.: Automatically inferring classsheet models from spreadsheets. In: IEEE Symp. on Visual Languages and Human-Centric Computing, pp. 93–100. IEEE CS (2010)
6. Melton, J.: Database language sql. In: Bernus, P., Mertins, K., Schmidt, G. (eds.) Handbook on Architectures of Information Systems. International Handbooks on Information Systems, pp. 103–128. Springer, Heidelberg (1998)
7. Google: Google query function (2013),
   https://developers.google.com/chart/interactive/docs/querylanguage
   (accessed on November 2013)
8. Cunha, J., Mendes, J., Fernandes, J.P., Pereira, R., Saraiva, J.: Design and implementation of queries for model-driven spreadsheets. In: Proceedings of the Domain-Specific Language Summer School 2013 (submitted 2014)
9. Schmidt, D.C.: Guest editor's introduction: Model-driven engineering. Computer 39(2), 25–31 (2006)
10. Bézivin, J.: Model driven engineering: An emerging technical space. [17], pp. 36–64
11. Ireson-Paine, J.: Model master: an object-oriented spreadsheet front-end. In: Computer-Aided Learning using Technology in Economies and Business Education (1997)
12. Abraham, R., Erwig, M., Kollmansberger, S., Seifert, E.: Visual specifications of correct spreadsheets. In: Proceedings of the 2005 IEEE Symposium on Visual Languages and Human-Centric Computing, VLHCC 2005, pp. 189–196. IEEE Computer Society, Washington, DC (2005)
13. Cunha, J., Fernandes, J.P., Mendes, J., Saraiva, J.: Mdsheet: A framework for model-driven spreadsheet engineering. In: ICSE, pp. 1395–1398 (2012)
14. Pereira, R.: Querying for model-driven spreadsheets. Master's thesis, University of Minho (2013)
15. Cunha, J., Fernandes, J.P., Mendes, J., Pereira, R., Saraiva, J.: Querying model-driven spreadsheets. [18], pp. 83–86
16. Belo, O., Cunha, J., Fernandes, J.P., Mendes, J., Pereira, R., Saraiva, J.: Querysheet: A bidirectional query environment for model-driven spreadsheets. [18], pp. 199–200
17. Lämmel, R., Saraiva, J., Visser, J. (eds.): GTTSE 2005. LNCS, vol. 4143. Springer, Heidelberg (2006)
18. Kelleher, C., Burnett, M.M., Sauer, S. (eds.): 2013 IEEE Symposium on Visual Languages and Human Centric Computing, San Jose, CA, USA, September 15-19 (2013); Kelleher, C., Burnett, M.M., Sauer, S. (eds.): VL/HCC. IEEE (2013)

Personalized Information Retrieval:
Application to Virtual Communities

Azza Harbaoui[1], Sahbi Sidhom[2], Malek Ghenima[1], and Henda Ben Ghezala[1]

[1] Laboratory RIADI-GDL, National School of Computer Sciences, University of Manouba
2010 la Manouba, Tunisia
{azza.harbaoui,malekghenima,hbg.hhbg}@gmail.com
[2] KIWI Research Team, LORIA, Lorraine University (Nancy), France
sahbi.sidhom@gmail.com

Abstract. Internet has become the largest library through the history of humanity. Having such a big library made the search process more complicated. In fact, traditional search engines answer users by sending back the same results to different users having expressed different information needs and different preferences. A significant part of difficulties [1],[4] is due to vocabulary problems (polysemy, synonymy...). Such problems trigger a strong need for personalizing the search results based on user preferences. The goal of personalized information [11] is to generate meaningful results to a collection of information users that may interest them using user's profile. This paper presents a personalized information retrieval approach based on user profile. User profile is built from the acquisition of explicit and implicit user data. The proposed approach also presents a semantic-based optimization method for user query. The system uses user profile to construct virtual communities. Moreover, it uses the user's navigation data to predict user's preferences in order to update virtual communities.

Keywords: personalized information retrieval, user modeling, user profile, virtual communities.

1   Introduction

With the large volume of information available on the web, browsing this content became a difficult task, especially to keyword-based search engines. User is more and more unsatisfied by web search results.15]

However, these search engines do not address vocabulary problems such as polysemy and synonymy. Polysemy is multiple meanings for a single word. For example, when a user searches for the word "Apple", the retrieved results may be related to "Apple fruit" or "Apple computer". Synonymy refers to the same meaning as another word in the same language. For example, when a user searches for the word "little", all results related to another word like "small" would be processed although the two words nearly have the same meaning.

S. Yamamoto (Ed.): HIMI 2014, Part I, LNCS 8521, pp. 431–438, 2014.

Personalized information retrieval can bring solution to the above problems by focusing on the most relevant results of a user query[14] that takes into account his/her preferences identified in his/her user profile. Existing personalization approaches try to determine users' preferences in order to assist them while searching for information. It is an emergent research field with the aim of facilitating the use of web content, and assisting the user to obtain the most relevant result.[18]

In this paper, a new approach (based on user modeling (multidimensional representation), for personalizing web search result is proposed.

In the proposed approach (figure 1), a user profile is built based on basic information (explicit, extracted from human user interface) and implicit through user feedback (history of sessions, printed documents ...etc.).Consequently, user profile is used to build virtual communities. In addition, and in order to keep up-to date user profile, we propose a semantic query enrichment technique based on user profile-related query, Wordnet Ontology and ODP ontology domain[9] (**O**pen **D**irectory **P**roject).

2   The Notion of User Profile

The term "user profile", appeared around the 80s, with interface agents, mainly because of the need to create custom applications adapted to user needs [5]. User profile is at the heart of personalized RI. Unlike context which covers contextual elements, profile is defined by contextual elements directly related to the user (his interests, preferences.). Several definitions [16] of profile have been discussed in the literature, of which we retain a few:

"All changes that characterize a user or group of users can be grouped under the term user profile "[2]

"User profile is a structure of heterogeneous information covering broad aspects such as users' cognitive, social and professional environment, this information is usually used in order to clarify their intentions during a search session"[3]

In summary, we can define RI profile as the set of all the dimensions that describe and/or infer their intentions and perception of relevance.

3   Modeling User Profile

Modeling the user is at the centre of the implementation of a personalized information search process. The goal of user modeling is to select the most relevant information that reflects users' interests[13]. This modeling consists of designating a structure in which we store information that describes essentially:

— User interests;
— Preferences;
— Context;

— Expected goal of the search;
— Individual traits;
— Experience

There are several definitions of user modelling in the literature [6][8]. We retain some below:

«A user model is a knowledge source in a natural-language-dialogue system which contains explicit assumptions on all aspects of the user that may be relevant for the dialogue behavior of the system"[17]

"User model is an explicit representation of the system of a particular user's characteristics that may be relevant for personalized interaction."[10]

"The process of gathering information about the users of computer systems [7]and of making this information available to systems which exploit it to adapt their behavior or the information they provide to the specific requirements of individual users has been termed as user modeling."

Several techniques were developed in the literature to model the user. They differ according to the approach of profile representation and construction [12]. We present in this section the data acquisition techniques and profiles construction techniques as proposed by several representation models: global, connectionist, semantic or multidimensional.

The objective of this research is to provide architecture of an information research system which should be:

— User-centred: by taking into account user's profile, preferences and interests in order to provide results, the most suitable to their needs.
— Interactive: through using a dialogue mechanism allowing a "natural" interaction with users during expression and refinement of their requests.

Therefore, we develop an approach that combines two processes:

An information search process and a user profiles building process in order to evaluate users' contribution (ratings, tags) in improving the information search process.

To this end, we set the following objectives:

— The definition of an approach that integrates to user profiles construction;
— The definition of a collaborative process: to determine the manner with which both processes (RI and profiles management) will complete each other;
— The definition of ontologies to build (domain ontology and profile ontology) to use for personalized search;
— The integration of the social aspect in constructing user's virtual communities.
— The study of the impact of the proposed approach on improving information search (in terms of evaluation metrics).

All these proposals are detailed in the next section which describes the holistic approach integrating the different objectives and contributions of this article.

4   Presentation of the Approach

This section describes the overall approach entitled "Personalized information search Approach based on influential networks". The approach we propose is a modular approach is composed of the following main modules:

Query Reformulation Module. This module will reformulate the query based on the initial user profile P_0. The query will be enriched with new concepts (new content added by user), users' ratings of the results generated from the RI classic process (bad, good, very good ...)

User Modeling Module. The construction of user profile will be based on certain criteria such as: explicit acquisition that will safeguard profile information and search motivation (user is motivated, less motivated ....), also an updating module (user-initiated update and an automatic update)

Navigation Data Acquisition Module. This module captures all user navigation data during search sessions namely: printed, saved, tagged documents and calculation of participation rate.

This module is powered by the already built user profile. It allows for grouping user profiles into similar profiles communities in order to classify new profiles in relevant communities. This classification could help new users by reasoning through similar search.

Once constructed, influential networks will be deduced from the communities in order to identify the most influential user profiles.

4.1   Formal Framework

User profile is represented under the following dimensions:

1. Interests;
2. Ontology domain ODP (Open Directory Project) is a widely used ontology. It represents the most complete web directory edited by humans and often used as a source of semantic knowledge)
3. Explicit and implicit feedback;
4. Virtual Community;
5. History: Past search and navigation data;
6. Personal data
7. User profile, noted Pu, includes:

$$Pu=\{D_p, D_{ci}, D_{cv}, D_N, F_{ei}\}$$

With:
$$Dp=\{I,Dd\}$$
$$Dci=\{Ci,q,d_{NI}\}$$

$Dcv=\{tp, tc, P_{cv}\}$
$D_N=\{\_l, \_s, \_i, \_tag\}$
$Fei=\{V_u, D_e, D_i\}$

Q	User query
P0	Use profile
PB	Preferences base
Tq	Set of a query terms
Si	Similarity between profile in vc
D	Document
Test	detector (of interest...)
DU	Usability of new documents
U	Usability threshold to launch an update.
Nbq, Nbd	Respectively number of queries and documents
Dp	Personal data
Dci	Interests data
Dcv	Virtual community data
DN	Navigation data
Fei	Explicit and implicit Feedback
I	Identity
Dd	Demographic data
dNI	Detector new interests
Ci	Concept
qi	Query during current session
tp	Participation rate
tc	Trust rate
αl	Reading time
Ai	Number of printed documents
As	Number of saved documents
αtag	Number of tagged documents
PRq	Set of profiles similar to one query

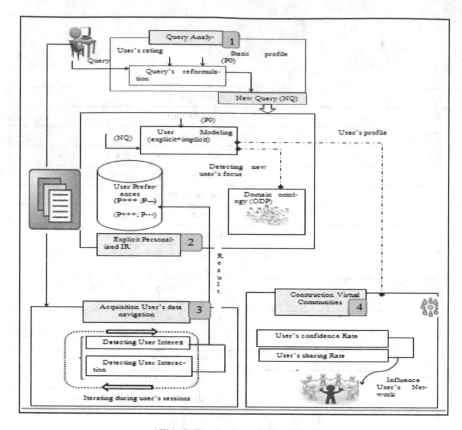

Fig. 1. The Proposed approach

4.2   Proposed Algorithms

We detail In this section the principle algorithms of the proposed approach

Algorithm 1: Algorithm for Building User Profile.

```
Entries: Qt = (w1, w2, w3 .... wn)
Outputs:
Pu = {Dp, Dci, DCV, DN, Fei
g
Start
If a user with an initialization session of a P0 profile
for each query submitted do
Save navigations or search history;
Calculate interest;
Infer or predict interest dimension;
Calculate I;
Inf-Interest (Dci, qi, Pu)
```

```
Pn
Case of an unregistered user in the System
Assign the user to a profile
For each query submitted do
Return to start
End
Return Pu
End
```

Algorithm 2: GetNewInterest Algorithm.

```
Entries:
Data: S: confidence level of new interest with the profiles database
BP: Base profile
qi: user query
Pi: Initial profile
Output: Result: Flag: flag value specifying the new interest CI
Start
Flag = 0
Score (qi) = GetSimilartity (qi, Pu)
Flag = 1
if Score (qi) <S then
Flag = 1
End
Return Flag
End
```

5   Conclusion

Although a considerable number of works focused on information retrieval, some important challenges for the research community still remain, the ultimate goal of personalization system being the satisfaction of the user. To reach this goal, the user has to be implied in the construction process in order to add the semantic value to the information retrieval. This paper proposed a personalized research information approach based on user modeling and the construction of virtual communities. The aim is to generate social relations from constructed community, which will allow us to infer influence user networks that relate to each other through their relationships and their sharing spirit. We plan to test the approach on real corpus of users of social networks.

References

1. Research, I.A., Zien, J., Meyer, J., Tomlin, J.: Web query characteristics and their implications on search engines. In: Zien, J., Meyer, J.O., Tomlin, J. (eds.) Proceedings of the 10th International WWW Conference, Hong Kong (2001)

2. Robertson, S.: The probability ranking principle in modern information retrieval. Journal of Documentation 33(4), 294–304 (1977)

3. Allan, J., et al.: Challenges in information retrieval and language modeling: report of a workshop held at the center for intelligent information retrieval. SIGIR. University of Massachusetts Amherst (September 2002)

4. Mianowska, B., Nguyen, N.T.: Tuning user profiles based on analyzing dynamic preference in document retrieval systems. Multimedia Tools and Applications (2012), http://dx.doi.org/10.1007/s11042-012-1145-6

5. Bouidghaghen, O., Tamine, L., Boughanem, M.: Personalizing mobile web search for location sensitive queris. In: Proceedings of the 2011 IEEE 12th International Conference on Mobile Data Management, Lulea, Sweden, vol. 01, pp. 110–118 (2011)

6. Ghosh, R., Dekhil, M.: Discovering user profiles. In: Proceedings of the 18th International Conference on World Wide Web, pp. 1233–1234. Polytechnic University in Madrid (2009)

7. Treur, J., Umair, M.: An agent model integrating an adaptive model for environmental dynamics. International Journal of Intelligent Information and Database Systems 5(1), 201–228 (2012)

8. Tanudjaja, J., Mui, L.: Persona: A contextualized and personalized web search. In: Proc. 35th Hawaii International Conference on System Sciences, Big Island, Hawaii, p. 53 (January 2002)

9. Trajkova, J., Gauch, S.: Improving ontology-based user pro_les. In: Proceedings of the 8th Conference of Recherche d'Information Assistée par Ordinateur, April 26-28, pp. 380–389. University of Avignon, Vaucluse (2004)

10. Wen, J., Lao, N., Ma, W.Y.: Probabilistic model for contextual retrieval. In: Proceedings of the 27th Annual International ACM SIGIR Conference on Research and Development in Information Retrieval, Shefeld, United Kingdom, pp. 57–63 (August 2004)

11. Tamine, L., Boughanem, M., Zemirli, W.N.: Exploiting multi-evidence from multiple user's interests to personalizing information retrieval. In: Badr, Y., Chbeir, R., Pichappan, P. (eds.) IEEE International Conference on Digital Information Management (ICDIM 2007), Lyon, France, pp. 7–12. IEEE Engineering Management Society (October 2007)

12. Micarelli, A., Gasparetti, F., Sciarrone, F., Gauch, S.: Personalized search on the World Wide Web. In: Brusilovsky, P., Kobsa, A., Nejdl, W. (eds.) Adaptive Web 2007. LNCS, vol. 4321, pp. 195–230. Springer, Heidelberg (2007)

13. Min, J., Jones, G.J.F.: Building user interest profiles from Wikipedia clusters. In: The Workshop on Enriching Information Retrieval (ENIR 2011) at Special Interest Group on Information Retrieval (SIGIR), Beijing, China (July 2011)

14. Lalmas, M., MacFarlane, A., Rüger, S.M., Tombros, A., Tsikrika, T., Yavlinsky, A. (eds.): ECIR 2006. LNCS, vol. 3936. Springer, Heidelberg (2006)

15. Maleszka, M., Mianowska, B., Nguyen, N.-T.: A heuristic method for collaborative recommendation using hierarchical user profiles. In: Nguyen, N.-T., Hoang, K., Jędrzejowicz, P. (eds.) ICCCI 2012, Part I. LNCS (LNAI), vol. 7653, pp. 11–20. Springer, Heidelberg (2012)

16. Stermsek, G., Strembeck, M., Neumann, G.: User profile refinement using explicit user interest modeling. In: GI-Jahrestagung Conference, pp. 289–293. Technical University in Berlin (2007)

17. Esparza, S.G., O'Mahony, M.P., Smyth, B.: Mining the real-time web: a novel approach to product recommendation. Knowledge-Based Systems 29, 3–11 (2012)

18. Formoso, V., Fernandez, D., Cacheda, F., Carneiro, V.: Using profile expansion techniques to alleviate the new user problem. Information Processing and Management (2012), http://dx.doi.org/10.1016/j.ipm.2012.07.005

Content Based Image Retrieval Using Quantitative Semantic Features

Anuja Khodaskar and Siddharth Ladhake

Sipnas' College of Engineering & Technology,
Amravati, Maharashtra, India
annujha_24@rediffmail.com,
sladhake@yahoo.com

Abstract. Retrieval of images based on low level visual features such as color, texture and shape have proven to have its own set of limitations under different conditions. In order to improve the effectiveness of content-based image retrieval systems, research direction has been shifted from designing sophisticated low-level feature extraction algorithms to reducing the 'semantic gap' between the visual features and the richness of human semantics. In this paper, the framework for Content-Based Image Retrieval system Fuzzy Logic approach is proposed to bridge the semantic gap between low level features and high-level semantic features with the aim to optimize the performance of CBIR systems.

Keywords: CBIR, Quantitative Semantic Features, Fuzzy Color Histogram.

1 Introduction

Content-Based Image Retrieval (CBIR) is an exciting and in-depth research area which has gained much interest over the past few years. There are two types of image retrieval methods exist: the text-based image retrieval and the content-based Image retrieval. In text-based image retrieval, query is based on keywords; and implementation of text-based image retrieval is easy. However, retrieving images based on text such as manual annotation of keywords, differences in perceptions is having many problems associated with. Due to this, it is necessary for CBIR, where images are retrieved based on automatically derived features, including color, shape, grain and the object's special relationship. Generally speaking, single feature cannot fully represent the content of an image. For example, one of the important features is color as it plays an important role in CBIR due to its robustness to complex background and independent of image size and orientation. However, using color alone is not sufficient to characterize an image because some images have the same color proportions but different spatial distributions. This results in CBIR scheme which combine multiple features in order to achieve better retrieval performance. However, most traditional multi-feature retrieval methods extract the features independently. Usually, they combine multiple features merely giving them different

S. Yamamoto (Ed.): HIMI 2014, Part I, LNCS 8521, pp. 439–448, 2014.

weights, which neglect the intrinsic relationship between two features. The CBIR technology has been used in several applications such as fingerprint identification, biodiversity information systems, digital libraries, crime prevention, medicine, historical research, among others. During the past decade, remarkable progress has been made in both theoretical research and system development. However, there remain many challenging research problems that continue to attract researchers from multiple disciplines. Not many techniques are available to deal with the semantic gap presented in images and their textual descriptions.

1.1   The Semantic Gap

The fundamental difference between content-based and text-based retrieval systems is that the human interaction is an indispensable part of the latter system. Humans tend to use high-level features (concepts), such as keywords, text descriptors, to interpret images and measure their similarity. While the features automatically extracted using computer vision techniques are mostly low-level features (color, texture, shape, spatial layout, etc). In general, there is no direct link between the high-level concepts and the low-level features. Though many sophisticated algorithms have been designed to describe color, shape, and texture features, these algorithms cannot adequately model image semantics and have many limitations when dealing with broad content image databases. Extensive experiments on CBIR systems show that low-level contents often fail to describe the high level semantic concepts in user's mind. Therefore, the performance of CBIR is still far from user's expectations. There are three levels of queries in CBIR.

Level 1: Retrieval by primitive features such as color, texture, shape or the spatial location of image elements. Typical query is query by example, 'find pictures like this'.

Level 2: Retrieval of objects of given type identified by derived features, with some degree of logical inference. For example, 'find a picture of a flower'.

Level 3: Retrieval by abstract attributes, involving a significant amount of high-level reasoning about the purpose of the objects or scenes depicted. This includes retrieval of named events, of pictures with emotional or religious significance, etc. Query example, 'find pictures of a joyful crowd'. Levels 2 and 3 together are referred to as semantic image retrieval, and the gap between Levels 1 and 2 as the semantic gap. More specifically, the discrepancy between the limited descriptive power of low-level image features and the richness of user semantics is referred to as the 'semantic gap'. Users in Level 1 retrieval are usually required to submit an example image or sketch as query. But what if the user does not have an example image at hand? Semantic image retrieval is more convenient for users as it supports query by keywords or by texture. Therefore, to support query by high-level concepts, a CBIR systems should provide full support in bridging the 'semantic gap' between numerical image features and the richness of human semantics [1].

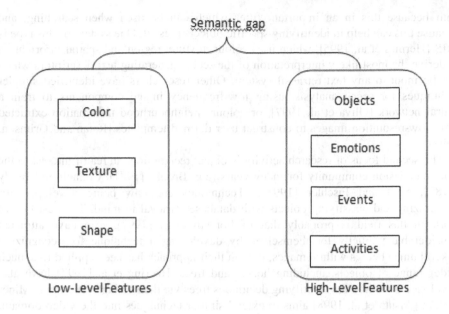

Fig. 1. Semantic Gap

1.2   High-Level Semantic-Based Image Retrieval

Low level image features can be related with the high level semantic features for reducing the 'semantic gap'. There are five categories of techniques to accomplish this (1) using object ontology to define high-level concepts, (2) using machine learning tools to associate low level features with query concepts, (3) introducing relevance feedback (RF) into retrieval loop for continuous learning of users' intention, (4) generating semantic template (ST) to support high-level image retrieval, (5) making use of both the visual content of images and the textual information obtained from the Web for WWW (the Web) image retrieval[1].

1.3   High-Level Quantitative Semantic Features

The vast majority of current CBIR techniques are designed for primitive-level retrieval. However, some researchers have attempted to bridge the gap between level 1 and level 2 retrieval. One early system aimed at tackling this problem was GRIM_DBMS [Rabbitti and Stanchev, 1989], designed to interpret and retrieve line drawings of objects within a narrow predefined domain, such as floor plans for domestic buildings. The system analyzed object drawings, labeling each with a set of possible interpretations and their probabilities. These were then used to derive likely interpretations of the scene within which they appeared. More recent research has tended to concentrate on one of two problems. The first is scene recognition. It can often be important to identify the overall type scene depicted by an image, both because this in an important filter which can be used when searching, and because this can help in identifying specific objects present. One system of this type is IRIS [Hermes et al, 1995], which uses colour, texture, region and spatial information to derive the most likely interpretation of the scene, generating text descriptors which can be input to any text retrieval system. Other researchers have identified simpler techniques for scene analysis, using low-frequency image components to train a neural network [Oliva et al, 1997], or colour neighbourhood information extracted from low-resolution images to construct user-defined templates [Ratan and Grimson, 1997].

The second focus of research activity is object recognition, an rea of interest to the computer vision community for many years (e.g. Brooks [1981], Connell and Brady [1987], Strat and Fischler [1991]). Techniques are now being developed for recognizing and classifying objects with database retrieval in mind. The best-known work in this field is probably that of Forsyth et al [1997], who have attracted considerable publicity for themselves by developing a technique for recognizing naked human beings within images, though their approach has been applied to a much wider range of objects, including horses and trees. Haering et al [1997] have also developed a method for identifying deciduous trees via their foliage. The ImageMiner system [Alsuth et al, 1998] aims to extend similar techniques into the video domain. All such techniques are based on the idea of developing a model of each class of object to be recognized, identifying image regions which might contain examples of the object, and building up evidence to confirm or rule out the object's presence. Evidence will typically include both features of the candidate region itself (colour, shape or texture) and contextual information such as its position and the type of background in the image.

In contrast to these fully-automatic methods is a family of techniques which allow systems to learn associations between semantic concepts and primitive features from user feedback. The earliest such system was Four Eyes from MIT [Minka, 1996]. This invites the user to annotate selected regions of an image, and then proceeds to apply similar semantic labels to areas with similar characteristics. The system is capable of improving its performance with further user feedback. Another approach is the concept of the semantic visual template introduced by S F Chang et al [1998]. Here, the user is asked to identify a possible range of color, texture, shape or motion parameters to express his or her query, which is then refined using relevance feedback techniques. When the user is satisfied, the query is given a semantic label (such as "sunset") and stored in a query database for later use. Over time, this query database becomes a kind of visual thesaurus, linking each semantic concept to the range of primitive image features most likely to retrieve relevant items.

2   Related Work

Ying Liu, Dengsheng Zhang, Guojun Lu, Wei-Ying Ma[1], carried out rigorous survey on content based image retrieval with high level semantics. They have provided comprehensive review on recent technical achievements in high level semantic based image retrieval. They have identified five major categories of the state-of-the-art techniques: (1) using object ontology to define high-level concepts; (2) using machine learning methods to associate low-level features with query concepts; (3) using relevance feedback to learn user's intention; (4) generating semantic template to support high level image retrieval; (5) fusing the evidences from HTML text and the visual content of images for www image retrieval.

Automatic objects spatial relationships semantic extraction and representation can bridge the Semantic gap in CBIR[2]. Based on low level feature extraction integrated with line detection techniques, all objects are identified. These objects are represented using Minimum Bound Region (MBR) with a reference coordinate. The reference coordinate is used to compute spatial relation among the objects. There are 8 spatial relationship concepts are determined : "Front", "Back", "Right" ,"Left", "Right-Front", "Left-Front", "Right-Back", "Left-Back" concept. The user query in text form is automatically translated to semantic meaning and representation.

Content based image retrieval using high level semantic features is proposed[3]. It is based on extraction of low level color features, shape features, and texture features and their conversion into high level semantic features using fuzzy production rules, derived with the help of image mining techniques.

A specialized approach using context-sensitive Bayesian network for semantic inference of segmented scenes is proposed by Yikun Lee and Timo R. Bretchneider [4]. They have discussed Semantic Sensitive Satellite Image Retrieval. The region's remote sensing related semantic concepts are inferred in a multistage process based on their spectral and textual characteristics as well as semantic of adjacent regions. The approach was implemented and compared with different strategy that utilizes the extracted features from the imagery directly to infer the semantics. The developed system achieved higher precision and recall rate using the same training data.

Patheja P.S. el at. [5] proposed an enhanced approach for content based image retrieval. new feedback based and content based image retrieval system. This new approach uses neural network based pattern learning to achieve effective classification and with neural network. Decision tree algorithm is used to make less complex mining of images.

3   Proposed Work

Existing CBIR systems which are based on low-level features have certain limitations, whereas CBIR system purely based on high-level semantic features (concepts) are difficult to implement. The proposed work is aimed at to design a framework for Content-Based Image Retrieval System to bridge the semantic gap between low level features and high-level semantic features. This can lead towards optimization of the performance of CBIR systems. In this paper, for bridging the semantic gap, we try to map high level semantics features (concepts) with the low level features such as color, texture, size etc. Let $I = \{$ I1, I2, I3,.............,In$\}$ be set of images (image database), $F = \{$ F1, F2,..........FN$\}$ be the low-level feature vector and $S = \{$S1, S2,........SM$\}$ be the set of high-level semantic features . Let us define a mapping f from F to S, i.e: F → S. Each feature vector Fi from the feature space is describing the image Ii from the image database.

3.1　Fuzzy Logic Approach

Values of low-level features are in crisp form, whereas high-level semantic features (concepts) take vague or imprecise values e.g. tall man, beautiful scene, unhappy crowd etc. These values can be represented well by using fuzzy logic. It is possible to form Fuzzy Inference System (FIS) to map crisp input values with vague output values. In this paper, the fuzzy inference system (CBIR.fis) is proposed. The proposed CBIR.fis is of 'Mamdani' type as shown in figure 2. The fis has three input variables : Color Feature, Texture Feature and Shape Features and one output variable : Semantic Features.

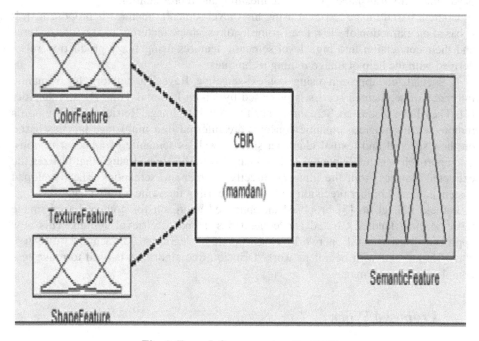

Fig. 2. Fuzzy Inference system for CBIR

3.1.1　Membership Functions for Input Variables
There are three input variables in CBIR.fis:

- Color Feature
- Texture Feature
- Shape Feature

Each of these variables are defined by using three membership functions. The membership functions for color features are : red, green and blue. as shown in figure 3.

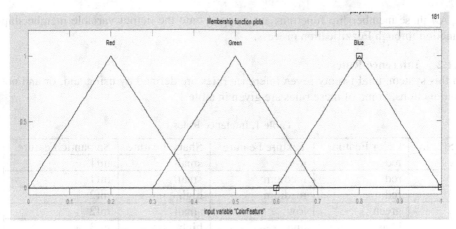

Fig. 3. Membership function for color features

Membership functions for texture features are: Low, Medium and High as shown in figure 4.

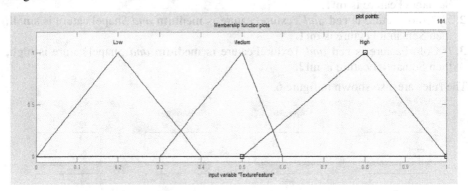

Fig. 4. Membership function for Texture features

The Shape feature variable has three membership functions: Small, medium and large as shown in figure 5.

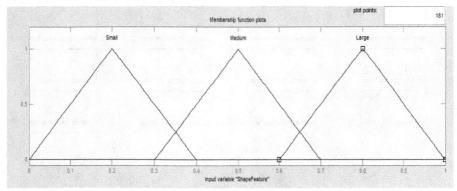

Fig. 5. Membership function for Shape features

All these membership functions are mapped onto the output variable membership function through Fuzzification process.

3.1.2   Inference Rules

In this system, total twenty seven inference rules are defined by using and, or and not conjunctions. Some of these rules are given in table 1.

Table 1. Inference Rules

Sr. No.	Color Feature	Texture Feature	Shape Feature	Semantic Feature
1	red	low	small	mf1
2	red	medium	small	mf1
3	red	medium	high	mf2
4	green	low	small	mf2
5	blue	high	high	mf3

Examples:

1. *If* ColorFeature is **red** *and* TextureFeature is **low** *and* ShapeFeature is **small,** then SemanticFeature is **mf1.**
2. *If* ColorFeature is **red** *and* TextureFeature is **medium** *and* ShapeFeature is **small,** then SemanticFeature is **mf1.**
3. *If* ColorFeature is **red** *and* TextureFeature is **medium** *and* ShapcFeature is **high,** then SemanticFeature is **mf2.**

The rules are also shown in figure 6.

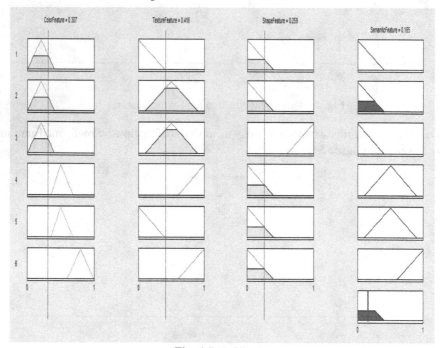

Fig. 6. Rule Viewer

4   Results

We have carried out experiments on some of the images form WANG and IRMA image databases. The performance of this system is evaluated on the basis of two parameters : *precision* and *recall*.

$$precision = \frac{\text{Number of images retrieved and relevant}}{\text{Total number of retrieved images}}$$

$$recall = \frac{\text{Number of images retrieved and relevant}}{\text{Total number of relevant images in the database}}$$

5   Conclusion

In this paper, we have discussed the fact that there is a semantic gap between low level image features and high level semantic features. The effectiveness of CBIR process can be increased if this gap would be bridged by some mean. We tried to propose a fuzzy logic approach to map two types of features. Experiments are conducted on few images from standard databases such as WANG and IRMA. The performance is evaluated on the basis of parameters such as precision and recall. However, it has been observed that, it requires rigorous work to achieve moreoptimum performance.

References

1. Liu, Y., Zhang, D.S., Lu, G., Ma, W.-Y.: A survey of content-based image retrieval with high-level semantics. Journal of Pattern Recognition Society, 282–287 (2007)
2. Wang, H.H., Mohamad, D., Ismail, N.A.: Semantic Gap in CBIR: Automatic Objects Spatial Relationships Semantic Extraction and Representation. International Journal of Image Processing (IJIP) 4(3), 192–204 (2010)
3. Tamane, S.: Content Based Image Retrieval using High Level Semantic Features. In: Proceedings of the 2nd National Conference INDIA-COM (2008)
4. Li, Y., Bretschneider, T.R.: Semantic-Sensitive Satellite Image Retrieval. IEEE Transactions on Geoscience and Remote Sensing 45(4), 853–860 (2007)
5. Patheja, P.S., Waoo Akhilesh, A., Prakash, M.J.: An Enhanced Approch for Content Based Image Retrieval. Research Journal of Recent Sciences 1(ISC-2011), 415–418 (2012)
6. Sethi, I.K., Coman, I.L.: Mining association rules between low-level image features and high-level concepts. In: Proceedings of the SPIE Data Mining and Knowledge Discovery, vol. III, pp. 279–290 (2001)
7. Chen, Y., Wang, J.Z., Krovetz, R.: An unsupervised learning approach to content-based image retrieval. In: IEEE Proceedings of the International Symposium on Signal Processing and its Applications, pp. 197–200 (July 2003)

8. Zhou, X.S., Huang, T.S.: CBIR: from low-level features to high level semantics. In: Proceedings of the SPIE, Image and Video Communication and Processing, San Jose, CA, vol. 3974, pp. 426–431 (January 2000)

9. Khokher, A., Talwar, R.: Content-Based Image Retrieval: State-of-the-Art and Challenges. International Journal of Advanced Engineering Sciences and Technologies 9(2), 207–211 (2011)

10. Dharani, T., Laurence Aroquiaraj, I.: Content Based Image Retrieval System Using Feature Classification with Modified KNN Algorithm. International Journal of Computer Trends and Technology (IJCTT) 4(7) (July 2013)

Types of Document Search Tasks and Users' Cognitive Information Seeking Strategies

Hee-Eun Lee[1] and Wan Chul Yoon[2]

[1] Department of Industrial and System Engineering, KAIST
291 Daehak-ro, Yuseong-gu, Daejeon, 305-701, Korea
[2] Department of Knowledge Service Engineering, KAIST
291 Daehak-ro, Yuseong-gu, Daejeon, 305-701, Korea
{lhe1008,wcyoon}@kaist.ac.kr

Abstract. For the researchers and learners, an unprecedented number of documents became available on the Internet and academic archives. Powerful search systems and sophisticated recommendation services are also available. Despite the IT assistance, finding the most useful information in daily knowledge works has become a cognitively demanding task more than ever due to the overwhelming number of documents. To improve the search systems with better human-computer cooperation, human information seeking strategies should be understood. This paper reports a study that identified the differences in the user search strategies with respect to two major search task types: open and purpose-driven exploring (OT) vs. closed and target-specified (CT) tasks. An observational experiment was conducted and the results were analyzed by mapping the user activities on a cognitive task-flow framework. The analysis comparing user activities in four search tasks revealed notable differences in their strategies to deal with the two task types. More frequent re-planning, especially goal reformulation, was observed for OT type tasks. The difference indicates that OT type tasks tended to trigger more knowledge-based behavior, while CT type tasks were performed relying more on rule-based behavior. These findings provide important insights for the design of search systems and user interfaces of knowledge-based systems.

Keywords: Information Search, Information Seeking Strategies, Task Types, Interaction Design, Decision Behavior.

1 Introduction

With the development of various smart-devices, such as smart-phones and tablets, information search activities have become daily tasks. With the rapidly increasing amount of content available in the Internet, people became more relying on the knowledge on the Web for learning, entertainment, research, shopping, and other daily activities. Search is in the center of the user activities interacting with the Web. Some researchers pointed out that the development of Web search systems has not sufficiently reflected the current situations of the increased Web usage and the growth of Web contents [3]. To overcome the limitations of the current systems, researchers have tried to develop various Web technologies including Semantic Web technologies

S. Yamamoto (Ed.): HIMI 2014, Part I, LNCS 8521, pp. 449–460, 2014.
© Springer International Publishing Switzerland 2014

and natural language search technologies [1, 9]. Despite the development of diverse innovative technologies, however, most Internet users still choose to stay with general Web search sites, such as Google, that are based on keyword search method. It might be noted that the most previous researches have focused on experimenting with Web search system design, not on investigating the users' Web search behaviors and epistemic user models. Some researchers have asserted that actual users' Web search tasks should be analyzed and applied in the process of Web system design to resolve the problem [4-5].

Web search is one of the keys to the Web's success [12]. In the academic circle, the research subjects of Web search are classified into three terms according to the targets of the search process, which are information retrieval (IR), information behavior (IB), and information seeking (IS) [4]. Regarding these classification, Järvelin [5] has described their differences in his paradigm model that IR focuses on the Web system, IB focuses on users' searching activities, while IS refers to the interaction between users and Web systems. Similarly, Xie has discussed the differences between IR and IS [13]. Based on his definition, IR is similar to information seeking (IS), but is more limited to the use of computer systems. In contrast, IS refers to purposive behavior including users' ways of using IR systems in order to pursue their information goals [13]. In this study, we considered Web search activities as the process of IS from the viewpoint of human decision making strategies.

Xie mentioned that research on information searching might be focused on different levels, which are tactics/moves, strategies, usage patterns, and models. His planned-situational interactive IR model assumes that the user would start from high-level goals or tasks to establish a plan to achieve them. The plan is then realized through information seeking strategies that comprises interactive intentions and retrieval tactics. After interaction with the IR interface, the user considers the resulting situation to decide whether the cycle should be continued according to the plan or disrupted to modify/replace the plan relying on his/her knowledge.

There have been some previous works regarding the effects of factors influencing information search strategies. Marchionini studied the different tendencies of search strategies in relation to open tasks and closed tasks. He designed an exploratory study for elementary school children to search an electronic encyclopedia on CD-ROM and found differences in information seeking strategies (ISS) according to tasks [7]. Navarro-Prieto conducted a study to determine the characteristics of ISS in accordance with the experience levels of searchers in given tasks. He classified the participants as experts and novices on specific search tasks. As a result, he could identify top-down and bottom-up strategies depending on the experience levels [6]. Some other researchers have been interested in differences in ISS according to age. Aideen studied the degree of searching capability and the difference in ISS pursuant to users' ages [10]. Similarly, Chin carried out a study on the effects of users' age that determine the types of ISS for medical diagnosis searching tasks [2]. The results of their works showed that older users tended to depend more on browsing strategies while younger users used more active exploring strategies.

Rasmussen's works [8, 11] in the field of cognitive engineering help understand how the ISS is formed and how the task types influence users' cognitive ISS. Rasmussen conducted research to understand human diagnostic strategies to locate failure points in machines. He carried out strategy analysis that identified four major types of fault-search strategies and represented them in information flow diagrams. In another study, based on cognitive task analysis for nuclear power plant operation, he established a framework that explains task-performing strategies, which was referred to as the decision ladder [8, 11]. For some tasks, the decision ladder can be fully traversed through the stages of acquisition of observable data, interpreting them to identify the current state, evaluating the state taking the system goal into account, determining necessary tasks, forming an appropriate plan, and finally to the implementation of the plan. However, depending on the characteristics of tasks and situations as well as human task knowledge, the process can partly be omitted using various shortcuts. The full decision making path tends to appear in *knowledge-based decision behavior,* while in *rule-based decision behavior* the high-level decision stages (e.g., goal consideration or task formation) are largely omitted due to accumulated experience.

Similarly, in the process of information seeking, it is reasonable to expect that task types together with the user's knowledge on the subject will shape the user's strategy. It is very important to find out the relationships between the task types and search strategies for developing effective search systems or devising suitable supporting features. With this motivation, we examined two types or modes, of information seeking tasks in this study; one is more open, exploring-like search and the other is more closed, tightly specified search. Those modes are expected to affect the degree of reliance on the knowledge-based or rule-based behavior in search.

We constructed an *IS task-flow framework*, a task-specific variation of Rasmussen's decision ladder, to analyze and explain the observed user activities and find evidences for the users' search strategies. The framework is in part similar to Xie's planned-situational interactive IR model, but it is designed to account for ad-hoc browsing tactics besides plan-initiated search actions. Using the framework, this study aims to identify users' actual searching strategies and find the effects of task types on the information-seeking strategies.

2   Hypotheses

While understanding human information seeking strategies is essential for designing better search systems and user interfaces, it may be pointless to establish a single model of human information seeking considering the diversity of task types that may shape the human strategies. There may be no universally optimal user interface design that facilitates all different types of search tasks.

We define two contrasting categories of search tasks to investigate the variation in human strategies. One is called OT (Open Task) type and indicates a search mode in which the searcher is relatively freer in pursuing target information. The search is more like exploration in knowledge space although the user has a solid information seeking purpose, not merely surfing or wondering. The task might be performed within a theme or a topic and have some criteria for usefulness of the finally acquired information. However, besides the purpose and quality to pursue, there may be little strict specification of target documents in terms of attributes or containing contents. An example of OT type task is "We need to prepare for a presentation on the topic of human memory. Get acquainted with the subjects and collect useful set of contents" Then, the user should find and choose relevant subtopics, theories, and cases that would be useful for the presentation. The user is free to select and organize information except that the information should effectively serve the given purpose.

The other search task type is CT (Closed Task) in which the user works with more narrowly specified attributes of the target to find. An example is "Regarding semantic web, what are its definition and important technical ingredients?" CT type search is undertaken when the user has to find some documents that contain specific contents.

In this study, we are mainly interested in information search under the purpose of learning. The classification of OT vs. CT is practically meaningful in learning situation. Both types of tasks are frequently experienced by students in searching learning materials on the Web and may lead to an important distinction in their strategic behavior during information seeking. OT type search typically appears in the early stage of learning new subjects or trying to grasp overall terrain of the domain knowledge of interest.

The criteria of performance may also differentiate between the two task types. In CT type search, fitness of the acquired information gets importance while in OT type the quality of information is emphasized. In CT type, more attention may be exercised to determine whether a particular document contains the information being looked for or falls in the range of target documents. In OT search, the user may be more engaged in evaluating various documents and accordingly adjusting the direction of search. These differences could closely be related with the distinction between knowledge-based and rule-based behavior.

We did not hypothesize on very detailed strategic elements that are expected to appear in the two types of tasks. The experiment was conducted largely as a primary observation to probe any patterns of activities that can separate a type of tasks from the other. Therefore, the hypotheses are defined at a rather high level, stating that

✧ There will be strategy differences between OT and CT type search tasks that can be found in terms of decision behaviors.
✧ The differences may be related with more generalizable distinction between knowledge-based behavior and rule-based behavior.

3   Experiment

To understand the effects of task types on information seeking strategies, an experiment was conducted with four searching task scenarios on a document search system. In the experiment, twenty participants carried out search tasks to achieve pre-specified goals and their actual searching actions were recorded and analyzed using the IS task-flow framework.

3.1   The System and Participants

The System. *CourseShare* search system (Figure 1) was developed at KAIST to support its students and educators to efficiently find the most suitable educational documents among overwhelmingly abundant materials available on the Web. The system is still in the experimental stage and growing in the number of indexed documents. We used about 1.1 million slide-type documents in this experiment. The search tasks were performed with the support of CourseShare's various search functions including keyword-based content search and attribute search with such slots as institute, author, and date, etc. The search system had a Web-based interface that was composed of main page, search list page, and detailed information page.

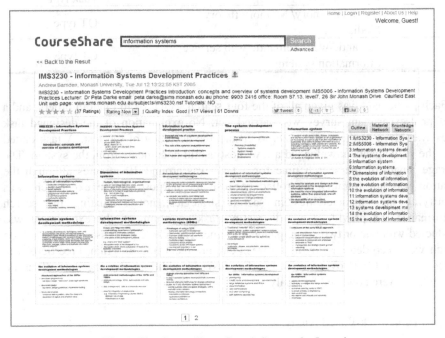

Fig. 1. The CourseShare Search System for Learning

Participants. Twenty students, 4 undergraduate and 16 graduate students (14 males and 6 females) participated in the experiment. The average age was 26 years with a standard deviation of 2.92. They were recruited from diverse majors to exclude particular training effects of a specific department. All participants were familiar with Web search tasks. Thirteen subjects answered that they usually performed Web search to find learning materials more than one time per day during their study. The other six students usually searched information on the Web for learning purpose two or three times a week. Only one student answered that he tended to search learning materials once in a week. However, all the subjects used CourseShare system for the first time in this experiment. Therefore, no previous learning of the given experimental system could influence the strategies and performance of the participants. Before the experiment session, participants were given simple five-minute training tasks, when the search system's characteristics and available features were instructed.

3.2   Tasks

Four task scenarios, two for each task type respectively, were devised with different themes or subjects. The themes of task scenarios and their task types are shown in Table 1.

Table 1. Task types and theme of task scenarios for the experiment

Task #	Theme of task	Task type
1	Human memory/ Memory theory	OT type
2	Media	
3	Semantic web/ Semantic web service	CT type
4	Information systems	

Each participant was given all of the four search scenarios in random orders, and a brief post-experiment survey was carried out. No explanation of the designed task types was given to the participants to ensure the accuracy of the test. A task ended after the participants downloaded a few most useful documents from the system. The average length of the search time for a task was around 10 minutes although the duration was not forcibly controlled because the purpose of the experiment was identifying the characteristics in search strategies, not evaluating the search performance. To provide a non-distracting task environment, the experiment was conducted with one or two participants at a time. The whole processes of information search were recorded employing a screen capture recording program, Free Screen to Video version 1.2 (Koyote software, Cyprus). In addition, the log data of users' search tasks were collected for analysis.

3.3   Framework-Based Analysis

The recorded video data and log data that were collected during the experiment were analyzed to investigate the users' information seeking activity and identify characteristic strategies employed by different groups and in different tasks. Data analysis was performed to identify the users' actions in terms of information seeking task flow. The results were later used for the evaluation of task categorization, which was to check the significance of the hypothesized task types as well as the fitness of the given tasks to the categories. Finally, strategy analysis vs. conducted to comprehend the information seeking process and find the effects of the two task types, or modes, on the information search behavior.

IS Task-Flow Framework. Human information-seeking activities can be represented as transitions in our *IS task-flow framework* that is shown in Figure 1. The whole search process was represented as a dynamic model aggregating eight search actions (i.e., the rectangles in figure 2), namely goal formulation, query formulation, search, system tool selection, browsing, selection and evaluation, utilization, and changing plan. Among them, four points of decision-making are of our special interest in association with information seeking strategies: query formulation (QF), browsing (BR), selection/evaluation (SE), and changing plan (CP). At the point of QF (query formulation), the decision is to choose a search keyword considering the search goal and the search history to the point. Next, at the point of BR (browsing), the user visually reviews the searched list to evaluate the results and find one or more interesting materials. SE (selection/evaluation) is a combination of a few processes: selecting an interesting document, opening the document, and evaluating whether the selected document is satisfactory or not. For example, if a user is not satisfied regarding the contents of a selected document, then she or he may click the back button and visit the list page (BR process) again to find other materials without changing the search plan. Otherwise, the user may move to the point of CP (changing plan) to re-plan the search. The re-planning may be changing the search direction and/or formulating another search keyword as they are expected to result in better searching.

All actions that the participants performed during the search task process were identified and put down on the corresponding transition flows (i.e., arrows) on the IS task-flow framework. The frequency of each transitional flow was accumulated. The relative frequencies of the transitions were calculated taking the total number of action steps as the denominator. Additionally, the number of search keywords and the performance time were checked in the data analysis.

4   Results

The statistical results of the experiment show that the task scenarios were properly devised to represent the two task types. Also significant differences are found in the information seeking process between the task types.

4.1   Task Performance

The search task activities of the 20 participants are summarized in Table 2. As seen in the results, OT types showed higher numbers of total actions during the search process than CT types. The total number of actions is the same as the sum of actions mapped onto the IS task-flow framework. OT type tasks also require more number of search keywords than CT types. In terms of the average task time for a search task, participants generally took longer time to perform OT types than CT types although the difference was not as big as the number of actions or keywords.

The results shown in Table 2 indicate that the influence of task type on the search process is notable on the whole. More numbers of action steps and keywords were needed for the OT type tasks as might well be expected. This result also confirmed that the categorization of OT vs. CT was meaningful and the four task scenarios appropriately represented the two types of tasks. More detailed analysis on how the task types affected the users' cognitive behavior in information seeking is called for. It is discussed in the next section.

Table 2. The results of task performance (twenty participants on four search tasks)

Task	Task type	Total number of action steps	Total number of search keywords	Average task time
1	OT type	1,027	99	11' 41'' 33
2		1,233	129	11' 40'' 39
3	CT type	736	66	9' 54'' 51
4		682	47	10' 57'' 30

4.2   Information Seeking Strategies

Using the IS task-flow framework, we analyzed the participants' search processes. Then we compared the effects of task types (OT types and CT types) on the strategies, by considering the recorded actions at the points of decision-making during the search process.

Re-planning Behavior. The results of description of the task-flow framework are shown in figure 2. As seen in the figure, differences are apparent between task types in the search process. For OT types, the results show that searchers change their search plans much more often during search tasks. Thus, for OT type tasks, search goals were more often reformulated and search keywords were also refreshed more times, whereas for CT types users tended to repeat the browsing process longer without changing the search plan. It is also noted that when changing search plan (CP), the relative rate of goal reformulation over mere change of queries is more than 8 times in OT, while the ratio stays within 3 times in CT type.

Decision Frequencies. It was mentioned that, in the task-flow framework, four points of decision-making are of our special interest since they may help identify information seeking strategies: query formulation (QF), browsing (BR), selection/evaluation (SE), and changing plan (CP). We performed qui-square tests between OT and CT types for the frequencies those decision points were visited during search. The results are summarized in table 3. At all four points of decision-making, significant differences are found between task types. Users show a tendency to perform query formulation (QF) and changing plan (CP) more in OT type search tasks than CT type. In contrast, browsing (BR) and selection/evaluation (SE was more often performed in CT type search than OT type.

Table 3. The analysis results of the effects of task types

Task types	QF	BR	SE	CP
OT vs. CT (Task 1,2 vs. Task 3,4)	Difference (p=0.046)	Difference (p=0.006)	Difference (0.030)	Difference (p<0.0001)
Comparison	OT >CT	OT<CT	OT<CT	OT>CT

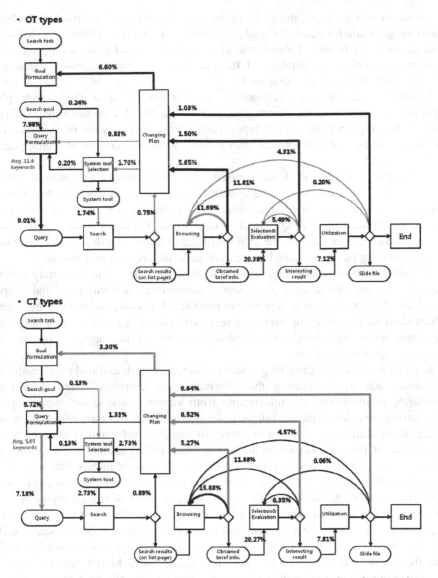

Fig. 3. The results of search tasks related to task types on the task-flow framework

5   Discussion

This paper reports a study to find and differentiate the user information seeking strategies in two different types of search tasks: open (i.e., more exploring) and closed (i.e., more target-finding) tasks. The study was done using an archive system, courseshare, which provided a vertical search engine and over one million academic slides. An observational study was conducted using four distinct settings of search missions. In two missions, the goals of the search were well-specified with clearly stated usage, while for others the goals were somewhat loosely defined, e.g. to collect a set of useful documents. To study the difference of user behavior, a superset model of search activities was established the observed transitions between elementary activities were recorded and compared.

Regarding the decision frequencies, participants changed the search plan, especially reformulating the search goal, more often in OT type tasks than CT type search. On the other hand, for CT types, participants' actions were more focused on the process of browsing and selecting/evaluating without alteration of search goal or search keywords.

The IS task-flow framework was devised tailoring Rasmussen's decision ladder for search tasks. The above mentioned differences provide good evidence that the OT type tasks require more knowledge-based decision making while CT tasks rely more on rule-based decision making. This has very strong implications in system design and interaction design because the characteristics of knowledge-based and rule-based decision-making behaviors have long been studied and are well understood.

The different search strategies in the two task types found in this study provide important insights for designing the search interaction, user interface, and support functions. Reformulating search plans and repetitive browsing/evaluating the searched information are two most important and very different subtasks. According to the task types, the more emphasized subtasks should intensively be supported by interface design or supporting features.

In an early stage of approaching a new subject, people should make rather abstract decisions such as interpreting the information in currently found documents, comparing or integrating the information from various sources, and evaluating the information considering the overall purpose of search. This in turn will suggest new directions of search or new set of keywords to use. New information acquired by the adjustment of plans or keywords are again evaluated to decide the direction was effective and should be continued or should be given up. It means that, to perform tasks at the level of knowledge-based behavior, much cognitive effort is required for users [8]. To help, the history of the search session, a list of related topics and key concepts, search by good examples, and an intelligent interface that supports the full cycles of such conceptual exploration may be very effective for OT type search tasks. Also knowledge-based reasoning depends on general background knowledge, rather than the search tactics, of the users. Therefore taking users' knowledge structure into account in interface or aiding, if at all possible, may also greatly help enhance human-system cooperation in OT type search.

For CT type tasks, users tend to perform the information search relying heavily on browsing with less frequent changes of search plans. Since the targets of search are well specified, the user concentrates on evaluating the fitness of found documents to the target. A rapid decision-making regarding the closeness of the documents to the set target is required. The search system could assist the user in such CT type tasks with more accurate recommendation features, filtering with easily adjustable and combinable criteria, deeper text mining functions, and some measures or guiding visualization that provides feedback on how the search is successfully approaching toward the target.

It should be noted that, while OT type tasks show similar characteristics with knowledge-based decision problems, it does not necessarily mean that OT implies that the user's training is low in the subject area. Neither does it mean the user can be trained to use CT type search instead of OT for the same problem. The knowledge-based vs. Rule-based dichotomy is about the decision behaviors and in many cases depending on the experience level of the user. OT-CT dichotomy is about the characteristics of the search task itself that tend to force one of the decision modes regardless of the human knowledge or training. In OT type tasks, the search decisions require more high-level or abstract knowledge, hence are more difficult for novices in the domain knowledge to handle.

Future work will be directed toward further clarification of the relationships between the user's background knowledge and the search tasks. As both the importance of search tasks and the possible technologies to assist knowledge search are increasing, studies on human information seeking strategies will become increasingly more valuable as the foundation of search system improvement.

Acknowledgement. This research was supported by Korea National Research Fund from 2011 to 2014.

References

1. Antoniou, G.: A semantic web primer. The MIT Press (2004)
2. Chin, J., Fu, W.T.: Interactive effects of age and interface differences on search strategies and performance. In: Proceedings of the SIGCHI Conference on Human Factors in Computing Systems, pp. 403–412. ACM (2010)
3. Hu, W.C., Chen, Y., Schmalz, M.S., Ritter, G.X.: An overview of world wide web search technologies. In: Proceedings of 5th World Multi Conference on Systems, Cybernetics, Informatics, SCI 2001, Orlando, Florida, pp. 22–25 (2001)
4. Ingwersen, P., Järvelin, K.: The turn: Integration of information seeking and retrieval in context, vol. 18. Springer (2005)
5. Järvelin, K., Ingwersen, P.: User-oriented and cognitive models of information retrieval. Understanding Information Retrieval Systems: Management, Types, and Standards 47 (2012)
6. Navarro-Prieto, R., Scaife, M., Rogers, Y.: Cognitive strategies in web searching. In: Proceedings of the 5th Conference on Human Factors & the Web, pp. 43–56 (1999)
7. Marchionini, G.: Information-seeking strategies of novices using a full-text electronic encyclopedia. Journal of the American Society for Information Science 40(1), 54–66 (1989)
8. Rasmussen, J.: Information Processing and Human-Machine Interaction. An Approach to Cognitive Engineering (1986)
9. Sánchez, D., Moreno, A.: Development of new techniques to improve web search. System 4(4), 2 (2005)

10. Stronge, A.J., Rogers, W.A., Fisk, A.D.: Web-based information search and retrieval: Effects of strategy use and age on search success. Human Factors: The Journal of the Human Factors and Ergonomics Society 48(3), 434–446 (2006)
11. Vicente, K.J.: Cognitive work analysis: Toward safe, productive, and healthy computer-based work. CRC Press (1999)
12. Wilson, M.L., Kules, B., Shneiderman, B.: From keyword search to exploration: Designing future search interfaces for the Web. Foundations and Trends in Web Science 2(1), 1–97 (2010)
13. Xie, I., Bates, M.: Information searching and search models. Understanding information retrieval systems, 31–46 (2012)

User Needs Search Using the Text Mining
- From Commodity Comparison, Understanding
the Difference of Users Awareness

Yukiko Takahashi and Yumi Asahi

3-5-1 Johoku Naka-ku Hamamatsu 432-8561 Japan
ne210026@gmail.com,
tyasahi@ipc.shizuoka.ac.jp

Abstract. In this paper, the authors establish that "To apply free description message options are good for product development." By using the technique of text mining, we show the awareness of the product user as an example a review site about cosmetic products.

We took up the major review site about cosmetics who can see the review of products freely. By using text mining, we show the awareness of users who are using products and how the images of product formed by elements and this analysis help the product development.

Keywords: text mining, frequently-appearing word, free writing.

1   Introduction

Recently, huge information has been accumulated by the development of the information technology in the Internet. Therefore, the enterprise can obtain the data that can be used for the business. As a result, the enterprise can obtain the data that can be used for the business. Written in the customer data, the questionnaire data, the complaint data, and the electronic bulletin board etc.

Especially, the number of users who used social sites such as "Mixi" and "Twitter" increased at last few years. Knowing the users opinion of the company's product and competitor's product is very important, because it help the development and improvement. It is very important to know competitor's product opinions. If we're making the request for the researching company, we have to spend a lot of money.

So, using text mining for review site is one of the effective measures. If the product is selling, you can get the users opinion about the product easily by using the review sites on the Internet. Review site, which anybody can access, is able to get the user's opinion of competitor's product

To use text mining for business, it will lead to discrimination from other companies. However, the text mining is a language of tongue twisters in Japanese as an actual current state compared with English, and the enterprises that positively analyze it is not so many. There might be information that cannot be obtained from

S. Yamamoto (Ed.): HIMI 2014, Part I, LNCS 8521, pp. 461–467, 2014.

information on useful choices for the product development and the improvement only to such a free description etc[3]. Not only having a questionnaire companies, but also by using Analyzed opinions on the Internet, It is possible to expand the range of product development strategy.

The purpose of this research is by using review sites about cosmetic we do text mining for 2 items, which supported by difference age and we analyze what elements make difference between ages. We derive a useful strategy for promotion from the result.

2   Target Sites for Analyzing and Items

2.1   Target Sites for Analyzing

In this research, we analyze the ranking data of free description opinion in cosmetic review sites @cosme. This site handled 21000 domestic and foreign brands and cosmetics information about the more than 200 thousand items. Reviews written by user's counts over 10.5million, Page view is 2,400 million per month, unique user is 7.7million. This shows users are interested in this site, so they visit (As of 2013.3).

2.2   Product to the Subject of Analysis

This research is doing text mining for the user's free description opinions on the manicure ranking (June, 2013). Analysis target is LE VERNIIS of CHANEL No.1 of the manicure ranking (June, 2013). These two items is not same age supporter. Under 20's support AT. Under 30's support LE VERNIIS.

Table 1. Analysis target (LE VERNIIS)

Ranking of @cosme	1
Interior content	13ml
Price	¥3,045(About $31)
Data collection period	2012/12/16〜 2013/6/15(half a year)
Number of Sentence	211
Number of character	75852

This research is looking for the elements which acclaimed elements by using text mining of review. We show about two items which target of analyze the information of price or how many reviews there is (Table1-2). The numbers of reviews of LE VERNIIS are 211. AT are 312. As we look the price, there are large differences of 2items. This shows that LE VERNIIS is brand name goods which came out from CHANEL, and AT is sold in 100shops. It is much related with review. The 100yen shop provides the products all price 100yen. It like ¢99Shop in USA. We should know user's awareness which the difference from the price.

Table 2. Analysis target (AT)

Ranking of @cosme	2
Interior content	10ml
Price	¥105(About $1)
Data collection period	2012/12/16～ 2013/6/15(half a year)
Number of Sentence	312
Number of character	72861

3   About Text Mining

3.1   Summary Introduction of Text Mining

Text-mining-Analysis is a technique that consists of two data mining "natural language processing" and "data mining". Text analysis had been used in automatic translation and automatic summarization of the document originally [2]. And discussions have been made in the field of language model research. Recently, a new phrase (term) "text mining" which means digging up the valuable information from large amounts of text data has been established. Text mining is a general term for technologies to obtain some findings by analyzing document data in large quantities.

3.2   Flow of Text Mining

Text mining is performed as following steps [1].

1. Morphological processing is divided into sentences written in natural language: morphological analysis
2. Dispose the unwanted words such as auxiliary verbs and particles for analysis or create a synonym: unification of synonyms, such as after an unnecessary processing
3. Process of analyzing the dependency relation with words: parsing
4. Analysis: analyze the frequency and number of occurrences, co-occurrence, clustering, and attributes

Is often carried out after the above one, working up to 4-2 is repeated while confirming the results. After step 1, repeat step 2 to 4 while affirming their results.

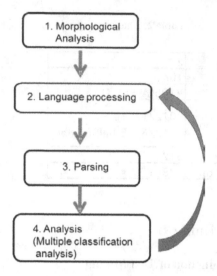

Fig. 1. Flow of text mining

3.3   Analysis Result (LE VERNIIS)

As we look at a result of analysis, frequently-appearing words in LE VERNIIS and AT are color and it is connected with many words. So, we can get to know the importance of color (chart2). We can draw a conclusion that the frequently-appearing words "color" is a strong reason for buying, and pink and beige are popular colors. Lame and Perl like luminescent things is connected with pink, so, we can expect this popularity is supported by young people. Other frequently-appearing words of LE VERNIIS, such as "Coloring" "Pink" "Piece" came at the top. The price in AT is at the top too. So, we checked out the co-occurrence relation and analyzed more. As we did co-occurrence, we got the result that LE VERNIIS is expensive and AT is cheap.

Starting from the left, table 3 the word of price back and belly, how many words in back and belly, how many words in back and total of back and belly, T level. No matter whether there is a co-occurrence relation or not, as judgment, it is intended that the value T in corpus linguistics statistically. T value, the statistical analysis is an index, which is used for example, when performing a test of the difference between the average values. This is corpus linguistics is widely used as an index to determine the presence or absence of co-occurrence relations. T value formula is the following. [10] Based on formula (1), the value of T is the result after certifying the difference of means.

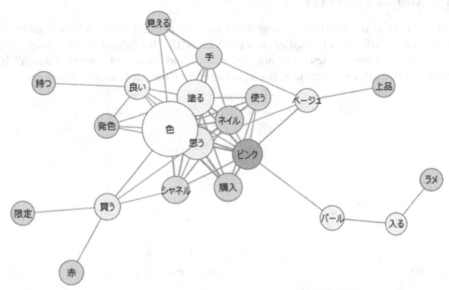

Fig. 2. Co-occurrence network of words (LE VERNIIS)

Value T = (measured value - mean) / Square root of actual measurement value (1)

"The square root of the measured value" in the denominator represents the approximate value of the standard deviation about the words co-occur with language center here.

In corpus linguistics it is considered as equal to or greater than 1.65, the co-occurrence of two terms is no coincidence. There is a co-occurrence relation if there is more than 1.65 T value based on corpus linguistics, this time you shall make any sense.

Also we can see that in LE VERNIIS, brand name CHANEL comes out many times. But we can't find the same situation in AT. Therefore, LE VERNIIS is trying to integrate the brand value of "Chanel". We connect these results to the product development, improvement and advertising slogan.

If we use the result of this analysis, we can promotion as CHANEL and except the increasing of repeater like expecting coloring, dry. And we can plan the new mini bottle which is cheap and reduced the amount of content. But when we check out frequently-appearing word, maker name is higher occurring frequently than name of article. So, we get to know the name of CHANEL has brand value. Now therefore, when we plan the new bottle promotion, it is not good to sell doing competition to keep the prices down. It's good to sell more expensive than competitor. And more it is good to sell by the price which teenagers can buy and a little more expensive than competitor.

3.4   Analysis Result (AT)

"Colors" is most frequently-appearing word as same as LE VERNIIS. But number of advent words difference is smaller than LE VERNIIS. But advent word is large. So, we can get to know reviews are not organized. And "word of mouth" "watch" is adverted. So, it affects the review. Brush is larger than nail. It is a special feature.

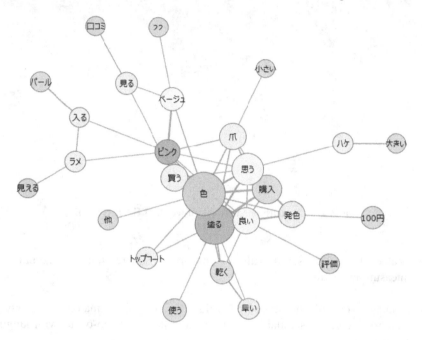

Fig. 3. Co-occurrence network of words (AT)

Table 3. The co- occurrence relation to the price(AT)

Rank	Word	Before	After	Span	T
1	low	1	4	5	2.144629
2	deserved	0	4	4	1.991654
3	and over	0	4	4	1.968704
4	think	0	3	3	1.70555

We did Co-occurrence analysis for the words "put on" "come off" "dry" "thick" "price". As a result, LE VERNIIS has almost positive opinions, But AT has negative opinions. There are positive and negative opinions. Positive opinions are "Easily put on" "Easy to use" "Easily to dry", negative opinion are "come off easy" "Easy to become irregularity". Furthermore result of the co-occurrence analysis for price, it became Table 3. The user recognizes that the price of this product is low. So, this product is easy to attract new users.

3.5   Analysis Summary of 2 Products

To summarize the analysis below, what the user feels for the two products are different. And furthermore we were able to visualize it. The quality of LE VERNIIS is good. And there is a brand value. However, since the price is expensive, purchase rate of young users is low. In contrast, AT does not broadcast TV commercial, but name recognition is up. This is because there is an effect of the review and cheap price. But there is room for improvement in quality. In this way, text mining would be helpful in the sales strategy of their products. And it is beneficial in corporate activities.

4   Future Outlook

This research analyzed the difference of user review comments not take the money to browse. Target prediction is essential to product planning. And knowing the opinion of the target's opinion will lead to good product development and improvement. There is definitely a demand for the text mining. But that analysis is difficult.

Then, the future task is to ensure that apply to business with less cost and less effort. Excellent open source software of the morphological analysis "Chasen" and "MeCab" is announced. In addition, it becomes a practicable level and has spread. We become necessary that while using them, we need to summarize user's opinion by using multivariate analysis. Making a text mining is one of the important thing for the company. And the text mining technology large amount of s benefits even in business activities. The text mining technology is expected to have on future research and application.

References

1. Hirohiko, A.: Introduction to questionnaire survey (2011)
2. Yumi, I., Takaaki, H., Isamu, W., Mitsuhiro, S.: Text mining- Case introduction. Japanese Society for Artificial Intelligence Magazine 16(2)
3. Tetsu, K., Seisyou, M., Masaaki, N., Tatsuo, O., Kenzi, Y.: Language and statistics of psychology. Iwanami Shoten Publisher (2003)
4. Barnbrook, G.: Language and computers. Edinburgh University Press (1996)

Supporting Collaboration

Understanding Pragmatic Aspects with Social Values in Web-Mediated Collaborative Systems

Rodrigo Bonacin[1], Julio Cesar Dos Reis[2], Heiko Hornung[3], Roberto Pereira[3], and M. Cecília C. Baranauskas[3]

[1] CTI Renato Archer and FACCAMP, Rod. Dom Pedro I, 143,6, 13069-901, Campinas, Brazil
[2] CRP Henri Tudor and University of Paris XI, L-4362, Esch-sur-Alzette, Luxembourg
[3] Institute of Computing – UNICAMP, Av. Albert Einstein, 1251, 13084-722, Campinas, Brazil

```
rodrigo.bonacin@cti.gov.br, julio.dosreis@tudor.lu,
heix@gmx.com, {rpereira,cecilia}@ic.unicamp.br
```

Abstract. Various aspects underlying collaborative discussions in web-mediated systems influence the interpretation of exchanged messages, which may prevent participants to better manage, retrieve and explore available content. In this article, we argue that pragmatics and social values play a key role in this scenario, influencing each other. We propose to articulate aspects of pragmatics and values, and conduct four empirical analyses in a real-world case study. We ground our analyses on concepts and methods of Organizational Semiotics. The paper presents an analysis of participants' interaction, a communication analysis based on a framework of illocutions, and a discussion on the shared social values. Our results indicate possible interdependencies between social values and categories of illocutions.

Keywords: Values, Intentions, Social Web, Pragmatic, Collaboration, Organizational Semiotics.

1 Introduction

Pragmatics plays a central role in problem solving processes and information sharing. According to Morris, Pragmatics is concerned with "the origin, uses and effects of signs within the behavior in which they occur" [1, p.13], considering aspects such as intentions, communication, conversations, negotiations, *etc*. Several areas study Pragmatics, including Human-Computer Interaction (HCI), Linguistics, Semiotics, Philosophy, and Sociology.

In a Web-based system, the participants' intentions influence the interpretation of content constructed in a collaborative problem solving process (*e.g.*, messages, discussions, documents) during information production and consumption. An interpretation might, among others, have an impact on the further problem solving process, as well as on information retrieval and the reuse of solutions in future problems. The design and construction of systems that take into account pragmatic aspects require a socio-technical and multidisciplinary view, and rely on research that

S. Yamamoto (Ed.): HIMI 2014, Part I, LNCS 8521, pp. 471–482, 2014.

still has many open issues. Although some existing design solutions enable users to express their intentions (*e.g.*, by marking messages with images that express intentions), few works explicitly investigate the impact of pragmatics in the Interaction Design (IxD) of Web applications — in particular for supporting collaborative problem solving.

We have studied the dynamic aspects of pragmatics in messages exchanged during collaborative problem solving processes within the special education domain [2, 3]. The conducted studies explored two scenarios: one in the *"Vila na Rede"*[1] Social Network System, which adopts a forum/"blog with comments" structure for questions and discussions, and the other within *"Yahoo! Answers"*[2], which adopts the structure of multiple answers to a single question. These studies served to identify "pragmatic patterns" of design [3], which represent recurring situations of use that might require a design of solutions to facilitate, promote, or avoid the manifestation of the pattern.

This article aims to extend and deepen the understanding of these aspects related to pragmatics and communication by incorporating the value concept in other empirical scenarios. According to Schwartz's Values Theory [7], values are desirable, abstract goals that vary in importance and serve as principles that guide peoples' lives. This theory understands values as beliefs tinged with emotions, as motivational constructs that transcend specific situations and actions, serving as standards or criteria to guide the selection of actions, policies, people, and events. As such, social values and pragmatics seem to be interdependent: the way how people express intentions and negotiate meanings depend on individual and group values and vice-versa. Although the literature has explicitly focused on values in technology design [4, 5, 9] as well as on Pragmatics in IxD [3, 10], the relation between values and pragmatics and their impact on the design of web-mediated social systems require further research.

In this article, we articulate the value perspective with pragmatic aspects using methods from Organizational Semiotics (OS) [1], Speech Act Theory, and Values Theory. To this end, we explore the framework of illocutions to analyze intentions [1] and the ten basic areas of culture. These ten areas are named Primary Message Systems (PMS) [6], and support the understanding of "culture as a form of communication". We furthermore investigate 28 key elements related to the PMS that represent critical aspects seen as values in systems aiming to promote social interaction [8].

Our case study investigates 27 topic discussions collaboratively conducted by inclusive education professionals in the TNR[3] system. We perform four distinct analyses: (1) a quanto-qualitative analysis of the social interactions; (2) a pragmatic and communication analysis inspired by [1]; (3) an analysis of values using the PMS; and (4) an analysis of the interdependency between social values and pragmatics.

We structure the remainder of this article as follows: Section 2 presents the background with the employed theories and methods; Section 3 presents a preliminary proposal to articulate pragmatics with social values; Section 4 describes our case study; Section 5 presents and discusses our findings; Section 6 concludes.

---

[1] http://www.vilanarede.org.br

[2] http://answers.yahoo.com

[3] TNR is a collaborative online system for promoting continuous learning and professional autonomy of education professionals: http://tnr.nied.unicamp.br

2   Concepts and Methodological Foundations

2.1   Organizational Semiotics and Pragmatics

We understand the pragmatics concept according to its definition in OS. Semiotics refers to the theory of signs. In particular, in Peircean Semiotics, "a sign is something [...] which denotes some fact or object [...] to some interpretant thought" (Peirce 1931-1935, vol. 1, par. 346), and which involves a signifier (or representamen), a signified (or object), and an interpretant. Liu [1] asserts that an organization refers to a social system in which people behave in an organized manner, and in which norms as well as people's individual or joint communication and interpretation of signs shape the organizational behavior. Hence, we understand the context of a Web-based collaborative system as an organization in which certain norms apply that define, for example, communication among participants or expected behaviors.

OS interprets the concept of Pragmatics as the relations between the intentional use of a sign and its effects on people in a social context, which is grounded on Morris' [1, p.13] understanding of pragmatics. In addition to Morris' syntactic, semantic, and pragmatic Semiotic layers (*i.e.,* structures, meanings and usage of signs), Stamper [11] has added additional three layers: physical, empiric, and social world. The *pragmatic layer* includes aspects such as: intentions, communications, conversations, negotiations, *etc.*; while the *social layer* includes aspects such as: beliefs, expectations, functions, commitments, contracts, law, culture, values *etc.* [1].

According to Liu [1], on the pragmatic level, human communication successfully happens when using a meaningful sign with an appropriate intention between the speaker and the listener. In pragmatic analysis, a communication act refers to the minimal unit of analysis. A communication act consists in a structure with three components: the speaker, the listeners (including the addressee), and the message. A message has two parts: the content and the function. The content manifests the meaning, while the function specifies the illocution, which reflects the intention of the speaker.

Liu [1] groups illocutions into three dimensions: *time* (*i.e.,* whether the effect is on the future or the present/past), *invention* (*i.e.,* if the illocution used in a communication act is inventive or instructive, it is called prescriptive, otherwise descriptive), and *mode* (*i.e.,* if it is related to expressing the personal modal state mood, such as feeling and judgment, then it is called affective, otherwise denotative). By using these dimensions, the illocutions are classified as: 1. *Proposal* (future, prescription and denotative), 2. *Inducement* (future, prescription and affective), 3. *Forecast* (future, description and denotative), 4. *Wish* (future, description and affective), 5. *Palinode* (present/past, prescription and denotative), 6. *Contrition* (present/past, prescription and affective), 7. *Assertion* (present/past, description and denotative), and 8. *Valuation* (present/past, description and affective). In this study, we employ the pragmatic analysis proposed by Liu to analyze pragmatic aspects in messages in a structured way.

2.2 Values and Culture

Friedman *et al.* [4] understand values as something that is important to an individual person or to a group of people. For Schwartz [7], values vary in meaning, importance and priority according to the culture under analysis and across time and space. Indeed, a value cannot be understood outside its cultural context since while a value indicates *what* is important for people, the culture explains *why*.

According to Hall (1959), culture relates to the very different ways of organizing life, thinking, and understanding basic assumptions about the family, the economic system, and even mankind; it refers to people's attitudes, material things, learned behavioral patterns, and values. The author understands culture as a form of communication and proposes ten basic areas ("Primary Message Systems") that represent the building blocks for mapping and analyzing culture. Hall suggests that cultures develop values according to these areas, explaining them as follows:

- *Interaction*: everything people do involves interaction with something/someone else: people, systems, objects, animals, *etc.* Interaction is at the centre of the universe of culture and everything grows from it;
- *Association*: all living things organize their life in some pattern of association. This area refers to the different ways that society and its components are organized and structured. Governmental and social structures may strongly vary according to the culture, not only in nature, form and function, but also in importance;
- *Learning*: refers to the one of the basic activities present since the beginning of life. Education and educational systems are strongly tied to emotion;
- *Play*: fun, emotion and pleasure relate to this area, which is linked to other areas: in learning it is considered a catalyst; in relationships a desirable characteristic, *etc.* If one controls the humor of a person, one is able to control almost everything else;
- *Defense/Protection*: cultures have different mechanisms of protection (*e.g.*, medicine, military strategy, religion) and defense is an activity of vital importance;
- *Exploitation*: relates to the use of materials to explore the world. Humans have made tools and artifacts for cooking, protecting, playing, learning, *etc.*
- *Temporality*: time relates to life in several ways: from cycles, periods and rhythms (*e.g.*, breath rate, heartbeat) to measures (*e.g.*, hours, days) and other aspects in society (*e.g.*, division according to age groups, mealtime). The ways people deal with time and the roles of time in society vary across cultures;
- *Territoriality*: refers to the possession, use and defense of space. There are physical (*e.g.*, country, house) as well as social (*e.g.*, social position, hierarchy) and personal spaces (*e.g.*, personal data, office desk). The understanding of space also may strongly vary according to the culture;
- *Classification*: refers to the differences in terms of form and function related to gender, also considering differences in socio-economic conditions, age, *etc*;
- *Subsistence*: ranges from people's food habits to the economy of a country. Professions, supply chains, deals, natural resources, are all aspects developed in this area; not only other areas but also geographical and climatic conditions may influence this area.

3   Articulating Values and Pragmatics in Communication

We must successfully cross all six semiotic layers to achieve successful communication [1, p. 35-36]. On the level of pragmatics, the communication partners need to understand the intentions of the speaker and listener, while on the social layer they need to consider the commitments and obligations created or discharged as the result of a conversation.

According to Stamper [12], norms stand for fields of force that govern how members think, behave, make judgments and perceive the world. Culture and values directly influence norms. People have different cultural systems that govern how they understand, value and react to material or speech acts. Considering Pragmatics, as understood by OS, values may act as norms that influence peoples' intentions, both when using signs and when interpreting them with respect to their effects on society. This means that when dealing with pragmatic aspects in collaborative problem solving we must consider the complex cultural context of people and their values. Considering OS and Values Theory, we rely on two assumptions:

1. *We can improve our understanding of the socio-pragmatics aspects of the communication when we consider the underlying value aspects related.*
   (a) Values may have influence on people's intentions (and other pragmatic aspects) and commitments (and other social aspects);
   (b) We can understand communication better if we understand "how this influence happens", *e.g.*, by correlating the values to illocutions and norms.
2. *We can improve our understanding of the values in a social system when we consider socio-pragmatic aspects of the interaction.*
   (a) The socio-pragmatics of the communication may influence on how users share and understand the social network's values;
   (b) We can understand the values better, if we understand "how this influence happens", *e.g.*, by correlating the illocutions and norms to values;

4   The Case Study and Methodology

This section presents how we conducted the study of the interdependencies of illocutions and values providing local evidences of these interdependencies regarding the studied scenarios.

We situate this case study in the context of computer-mediated continuous learning of Brazilian special education teachers, under the research project "Social Networks and Professional Autonomy". One of the project's main goals consists in creating a system for supporting collaborative case discussions. The project team adopts participatory methods and consists of researchers from the areas of Education and Computer Science, as well as of 28 Special Education Service (SES) teachers from all five geographic regions of Brazil.

Currently, the designed system has more than 500 registered SES teachers. We conducted our analyses on more than 1800 messages created by teachers between April and December of 2013, relative to the discussion of 27 topics in the system.

Each topic was introduced by an affirmation and a poll that prompted the teacher to decide whether the affirmation was true or false. Each poll had a separate comment section where teachers freely discussed the affirmation and related matters in a forum-like structure during a week. The affirmations were related to inclusive education and the different ways public schools in Brazil deal with children with special needs.

We conducted four distinct analyses.

1. *Analysis of interactions and messages.* We performed a quanto-qualitative analysis where we analyzed different aspects related to the social interaction. A set of key variables were collected directly from the database. Four analysts discussed the results to identify relevant aspects of communication. The key variables identified in the group discussion include: average size of messages and number of messages by topics and by participants, number of messages exchanged by participants. This analysis allowed us to observe general aspects regarding the messages and the participants under collaboration.

2. *Communication analysis.* We performed this analysis of communication inspired from the framework of illocutions [1]. Firstly, the theory and the analysis method were presented to a group of 14 analysts (3 professors, 2 postdoctoral researchers, 9 PhD/MSc students). The analysts' profiles included specialists in HCI, natural language processing, education, Semantic Web, e-Science and statistics. Since not all of the analysts were experienced in performing a pragmatic function analysis, ten topic discussions were analyzed by seven pairs of analysts in a face-to-face session after one of the authors presented an introduction to the pragmatic function analysis. The remaining 17 discussions were individually analyzed. We performed the analysis by using the following procedure: (1) the collaborative discussions were randomly distributed to the analysts; (2) the analysts read the texts systematically (word by word) aiming to identify the speech act units (*i.e.,* breaking messages in acts); (3) they annotated the text assigning continuous values from 0.0 to 1.0 for each dimension of Liu's [1] communication analysis; (4) we (the authors) performed an analysis of the frequency of the values assigned for each dimension and classified illocutions; (5) finally, we discussed the results and graphs, while aspects regarding the problem solving and discussion processes were observed by cross-referencing the cube/function analysis with the content.

3. *Analysis of values.* From the collaborative discussions, we analyzed the values shared by the participants. Four analysts read the exchanged messages after the communication analysis. They performed the value analysis to firstly identify common values of the social network present in various scenarios. One analyst produced general comments that were posteriorly discussed with the four analysts. Afterwards, the analysis focused on the most expressive aspects present on the scenarios. To this end, we selected two scenarios for a thorough study after a first analysis of the whole set of collaborative discussions. The used criteria for the selection relied on the aspects of the interesting elements with respect to values based on the used background, predominance of the value and influence on the discussion process.

4. *Analysis of interdependencies between values and pragmatics.* The analysts read the collaborative discussions again aiming to identify examples of communication acts with explicit references to the areas of culture. For each extracted example, we conducted a local and a contextual analysis of pragmatics. We aimed to observe interdependencies between the social values in the culture areas and the illocutions. The local analysis (denoted as ill_{loc}) presents the assigned values for the three dimensions of the framework of illocutions, considering only the communication act extracted. The contextual analysis shows the most frequent illocution category, considering all communication acts from the commentary (denoted as ill_{com}), where the extracted communication acts appear, and from the entire discussion (denoted as ill_{dis}).

5   Results and Discussion

The 27 topic discussions amounted to a total of 552 comments, 529 (95.8%) of which were analyzed (23 comments were duplicates). A discussion received an average of 20.44 (minimum: 7, maximum 36) comments and 33.3 votes (minimum: 15, maximum: 59). There was no correlation between the difficulty of answering a discussion's initial affirmation (measured in percentage of wrong answers) and the number of comments. Only a weak linear correlation existed between the comment number and the average discussion thread depth, but no correlation between difficulty and thread depth. During the last month of the analysis, the system had 539 registered users, 287 of whom accessed the topic discussions. On average, more than half of the registered users accessed the topic discussions at least once a month.

The average comment size was 79 words or 622 characters. Counting only the 85 users who effectively commented on topic discussions, each commenting user posted 6.5 comments on average. However, the distribution of comments per user followed a typical long-tailed distribution. The top-three users amount for approximately 25% of all comments, the top-ten for almost 50%, while more than half of the users who commented (45 out of 85 users) posted up to 3 comments. 54 of 85 commenting users posted or received at least one comment. The number of responses posted and received also followed a long-tailed distribution. Looking at single pairs of users, the relation between posted and received responses was relatively symmetric, with the exception of one user pair, where one user posted eight responses and the other zero. The analyses resulted in 1813 messages corresponding to 529 analyzed comments, *i.e.*, an average of 3.43 messages per comment, and an average message size of 156 characters or 24 words.

The dominating illocution types over all discussions and messages were assertion (51.7%) and valuation (29.8%), followed by proposal (8.2%), inducement (4.2%), and forecast (2.5%). Palinode, wish and contrition accounted for 3.5% of the analyzed messages. Some of the topic discussions showed a different distribution of illocution types, *e.g.*, discussion #1 with a high number of forecasts, wishes and inducements, or discussion #17 with a high number of forecasts and inducements.

5.1   Results of the Analysis of Social Values

At the home page of the TNR system, a *"Charter of Principles"* highlights and makes explicit the most important values shared by the network. The guiding principles of the TNR system include the "National Policy of Special Education in the Perspective of Inclusive Education" and the UN Convention on the Rights of Persons with Disabilities, as well as ethical principles concerning: accessibility, autonomy, collaboration, conversation, sharing and focus on the group. These values are shared by many participants and influence the network's activities, for example:

- In various discussions the participants emphasize these principles. Some conversations repeat a pattern, frequently when one participant posts/externalizes a "strong value" in the discussion, other participants answer with agreements;
- Some key participants took the responsibility to verify whether others follow the values. The discussions present some questions and inducements aiming to preserve the values and maintain some "homogeneity";
- Participants indirectly and subtly inquire on sensitive problems.

In the following, we present a brief characterization of two discussions.

Comments on two selected topic discussions.

Discussion #14: "The so called "inverse inclusion" (*i.e.,* including students without special needs in predominantly special classes) is a trick adopted by special schools to be characterized as inclusive schools."

- Initially, some participants shared a sequence of messages with agreements that the affirmation (#14) was true. This was influenced by shared values stating that "an inclusive education occurs in regular schools", instead of "special schools";
- After the initial sequence of agreements, users pondered on this in a further set of messages, arguing that the initial statement (#14) could not be generalized for all the "special schools". This sequence expose a chain of values about the "special schools", "what they want to achieve", "the schools intentions" and others. This sequence strongly deliberates that many participants admitted the possibility of the initial statement to be false according to the situation, as the following example of message: *"[...] By the time the institution had been able to break out of this process [inverse inclusion] and go for the full inclusion of students. For those who analyzed this [the adoption of inverse inclusion] from the outside it seemed to be a completely bad idea. For that institution, nevertheless, it worked as a transitory phase. However, this is not the reality of all the institutions [...] "*;
- In the same discussion, the entrance of a new participant strongly influenced the discussion. She made a global appreciation of the problem, and after doing this, she questioned some aspects in the discussion and shared an article about the History of Special Education in Brazil. Another participant appeared "vigilant", explicitly pointing out and demonstrating values present in the network, while at the same time explicitly presenting her intentions. Some examples of messages include:

(1) *"[...] Guys, please find attached an article that I found quite interesting on the History of Special Education. I hope that you read it and share your impressions here [...]"*; (2) *"[...] This text is directed specifically to a very specific audience, and we work with education in general, with specialized education support, we believe that we crossed this line [...]"*; (3) *"[...] I did not intended to align the ideas with the Special Education Polices, my intention was to disseminate a historical process that had not started in Brazil [...]"*; and (4) *"[...] In fact, the text you brought embraces concepts contrary to the Special Education Policy ..."*

Discussion #17: *"Adapted school curricula are recommended for including students with disabilities in regular classes of a primary school."*

- Various messages indicated that participants had not a shared understanding of the curriculum concept. Some participants perceived this aspects and explicitly mentioned this in some messages, *e.g.*: *"I agree with you that there are confused ideas [in the discussion] about: resources and curriculum adaptation. I think that it's better to stop now and think about these terms. Isn't it?"*, and *"... How about you post something about curriculum adaptation and creating/acquiring/producing AT [Assistive Technologies] for a specific audience?"*

- The lack of a common definition of the concept of curriculum reflected in messages about the key network values, *i.e.*, depending on how one understands this concept, one might interpret that some users were not respecting some of the key values on the "Charter of Principles". Conversely, if one assumes that participants shared the same values, one might assume that they do not share the same theoretical referential on school curricula, *e.g.*, *"... I observed that there are votes/opinions that agree with the affirmation [#17], however it is false! In an inclusive school, to adapt activities, separating them or assigning them only to students with disabilities is a discriminatory action [...]"*, and *"[...] But shouldn't the curriculum be open? If we do not adapt it, aren't we restricting the learning possibilities?"*

- The lack of definitions of the words "adapt" and "modify" (there is a linguistic subtlety regarding two verbs that were used by the participants: the Portuguese verbs *"adaptar"* (to adapt) and *"adequar"*; *"adequar"* can be translated to "to adapt", "to adjust", or "to modify") also resulted in misunderstanding and questions about the network values, *e.g.*, *"Should the activities be adapted or modified? And now?"*, and *"When we talk about curriculum we quickly think about adaptation, I (particularity) never liked the word adapt ..."*

5.2   Results of the Analysis of Interdependencies

Table 1 presents the areas of culture along with the values and examples. Note that some examples may fit into more than one area. Table 2 shows the detected interdependencies analyzed for each example presented in Table 1. Table 2 presents the illocution type of each example (ill$_{loc}$), as well as the predominant illocution types for the comment in the context of which the example occurred (ill$_{com}$) and for the discussion in the context of which the comment was posted (ill$_{dis}$).

Table 1. Areas of culture and extracted examples from the case study

	Area	Values	Extracted example/evidence
1	*Interaction*	Identity and Norms	*"...If I am wrong, please correct me, but we are here to show our ideas, beliefs and to enrich our curriculum..." (Norms)*
2	*Association*	Conversation, Groups, Relationship and Trust	*"...Let's think, talk and clarify our thoughts about these questions..." (Conversation and Groups)*
3	*Learning*	Meta-communication	*"...will have soon [...] a specific tool to this end, with which we will discuss our cases, elaborate our SES plans in a collaborative way..."*
4	*Play*	Aesthetics, Emotion and Affection	*"Hello! I liked a lot of the comments made by you...." (Emotion and Affection)*
5	*Protection*	Informed Consent, Reputation and Security	*"By reading this question I would like to use a text written in 2007 by Rita Bersch and others that cite..." (Reputation)*
6	*Exploration*	Accessibility, Object, Property (ownership) and Usability	*"This is a space for sharing! This space (the system) is yours enjoy it !!!" (Property)*
7	*Temporality*	Availability, Awareness and Presence	*"We are happy to have you here" (Awareness and Presence)*
8	*Territoriality*	Portability, Privacy, Scalability and Visibility	*"...Fill out your profiles and read those of your colleagues..." (Visibility)*
9	*Subsistence*	Autonomy, Collaboration, Reciprocity and Sharing	*"...Let's keep collaborating one with each other in order to deepen our knowledge about the SES in the inclusive perspective..." (Collaboration and Sharing)*
10	*Classification*	Adaptability	*"[For new users] Extend the TNR all over Brazil, contaminating the colleagues with this new way to constitute a strongly united group, full of enthusiasm for the changes caused by network communication..."*

Table 2. Analysis of interdependencies between areas of culture and the framework of illocutions based on the extracted examples of the case study

Area	local analysis (ill_{loc})				contextual analysis of comment (ill_{com})	contextual analysis of topic discussions (ill_{dis})
	T	**I**	**M**	**Category**	**Predominant Category**	**Predominant Category**
1	0	0	1	valuation	valuation	assertion
2	1	1	0	proposal	assertion	assertion
3	1	0	0	forecast	assertion	assertion
4	0	0	1	valuation	assertion	assertion
5	1	1	0	proposal	assertion	assertion
6	0	0	0	assertion	valuation	assertion
7	0	0	1	valuation	valuation/assertion	assertion
8	1	1	0	proposal	valuation	assertion
9	1	1	0	proposal	assertion	assertion
10	1	1	1	inducement	assertion	assertion

The examples presented in Tables 1 and 2 are not fully representative, but have been picked for illustrative purposes. For example, the contextual analysis of the whole discussion (ill_{dis}) showed a predominance of assertions. This contrasts with the incidence of just one assertion in the local analysis examples presented in Tables 1 and 2. Assertions and valuations are also frequent in ill_{com}. Consequently, we could not identify an explicit correlation of ill_{com} and ill_{dis} with ill_{loc}, nor any indication that the categories of ill_{loc} are consequences of a sequence of similar illocutions in ill_{com} or ill_{dis}.

Although the number of 1813 messages yielded significant results for the analysis of illocution types, it did not yield statistically significant results for each value in the different areas of culture. For example, no messages were found that could be associated with the value "scalability". On the other hand, the messages for the value "object" showed a distribution of illocution types that matched the distribution of all messages. Possible correlations between certain values and certain illocution types remain a question for future research. For example, there might be a relation between the value emotion and affect with illocution types containing mode "affective" (inducement, wish, contrition, valuation). We also need further research to answer whether or in which ways the analysis of values and illocution types in user generated content supports systems design. For instance, identity, norms, conversation, groups, relationship, and sharing are values that occurred frequently and that are regarded important by the research and design team. Reputation is a value regarded significant that occurred very infrequently. Does this mean that reputation is not important for users, or does it mean that this value manifests itself in other, less explicit ways?

As to our initial assumption, the interdependence of socio-pragmatic aspects and values, our analysis has provided various examples that show that considering values and illocution types together yields a better understanding than considering each one separately. For example, discussion #14 had a high percentage of messages about the values norms, conversation and groups, and a relatively low percentage of messages about the value object. It also had a balance between assertions and valuations, as well as a high percentage of affective illocution types. These pieces of information together indicate that, although its topic ("inverse inclusion") was relatively "unsuspicious", discussion #14 led to an engaged discussion in order to define some of the core values of the system. Another example is that of user 21 who posted a relatively high number of messages containing inducements and related to the values norms and groups. This can be interpreted as a user who took on the role to instigate others to discuss important values of the system.

6 Conclusion

Pragmatics and values play a central role for understanding and analyzing the human communication processes. The study of both concepts on collaborative systems may provide new alternatives for analyzing the social interactions and communication aspects. Nevertheless, the correlation between values and pragmatics and their impact on the design of web-mediated collaborative systems still remains uncertain.

This paper presented an exploratory study focused on the investigation of possible interdependencies between defined social values and categories of illocutions.

The achieved results pointed out promising opportunities for further explaining the communication in a structured way on collaborative systems. However, the study provides a limited view of the pragmatic and values aspects, and a deeper understanding of the interdependencies is required to concretely inform design. Our future work will propose a more detailed qualitative and quantitative investigation of these interdependencies, as well as expand the study on pragmatics and values, *e.g.* by analyzing the normative aspects.

References

1. Liu, K.: Semiotics in information systems engineering. Cambridge University Press (2000)
2. Bonacin, R., Hornung, H., Dos Reis, J.C., Pereira, R., Baranauskas, M.C.C.: Pragmatic Aspects of Collaborative Problem Solving: Towards a Framework for Conceptualizing Dynamic Knowledge. In: Cordeiro, J., Maciaszek, L.A., Filipe, J. (eds.) ICEIS 2012. LNBIP, vol. 141, pp. 410–426. Springer, Heidelberg (2013)
3. Hornung, H.H., Pereira, R., Baranauskas, M.C.C., Bonacin, R., Reis, J.C.: Identifying Pragmatic Patterns of Collaborative Problem Solving. In: Proceedings of IADIS International Conference WWW/Internet 2012, pp. 379–387 (2012)
4. Friedman, B., Kahn, P.H., Borning, A.: Value sensitive design and information systems. In: Human-Computer Interaction and Management Information Systems: Foundations, Armonk, pp. 348–372 (2006)
5. Knobel, C., Bowker, G.C.: Values in Design. Communications of the ACM 54(7), 26–28 (2011)
6. Hall, E.T.: The Silent Language. Anchoor Books (1959)
7. Schwartz, S.H.: Basic human values: Their content and structure across countries. In: Values and Behaviors in Organizations, Vozes, Rio de Janeiro. pp. 21–55 (2005)
8. Pereira, R., Baranauskas, M.C.C., da Silva, S.R.P.: Social Software and Educational Technology: Informal, Formal and Technical Values. Educational Technology & Society 16(1), 4–14 (2013)
9. Pereira, R., Buchdid, S.B., Miranda, L.C., Baranauskas, M.C.C.: Paying Attention to Values and Culture: An Artifact to Support the Evaluation of Interactive Systems. International Journal for Infonomics (IJI) 1, 792–801 (2013)
10. Hornung, H., Baranauskas, M.C.C.: Towards a Conceptual Framework for Interaction Design for the Pragmatic Web. In: Jacko, J.A. (ed.) Human-Computer Interaction, Part I, HCII 2011. LNCS, vol. 6761, pp. 72–81. Springer, Heidelberg (2011)
11. Stamper, R.K.: Information in Business and Administrative Systems. John Wiley & Sons (1973)
12. Stamper, R.K.: Information Systems as a Social Science: An Alternative to the FRISCO Formalism. In: Falkenberg, E.D., Lyytien, K., Verrijn-Stuart, A.A. (eds.) Information System Concepts: an Integrated Discipline Emerging, pp. 1–51. Kluwer Academic Publishers, USA (2000)

Development of Digital-Device-Based Cooperation Support System to Aid Communication between MCR Operators and Field Workers in Nuclear Power Plants (NPPs)

Seung Min Lee[1,*], Hyun Chul Lee[2], and Poong Hyun Seong[1]

[1] Department of Nuclear and Quantum Engineering, Korea Advanced Institute of Science
and Technology, 305-701, 291 Daehak-ro, Yuseong-gu, Daejeon, Republic of Korea
{jewellee,phseong}@kaist.ac.kr
[2] Division of I&C and Human Factors, Korea Atomic Energy Research Institute, 305-353,
989-111 Daedeok-daero, Yusong-gu, Daejeon, Republic of Korea
leehc@kaeri.re.kr

Abstract. Digital technologies have been applied in nuclear field to check task results, monitor events and accident, and transmit/receive data. The results of using these devices have proven that it provides high accuracy and convenience for workers to get obvious effects by reducing their work loads. In this work, as one step forward, the digital devices-based cooperation support system to aid communication between MCR operators and field workers in NPPs, Nuclear Cooperation Support and Mobile Documentation System (Nu-CoSMoD), is suggested. The suggested system is consist of the mobile based information storing system to supports field workers by providing various functions to make workers be more trustable for MCR operators, and the large screen based information sharing system to support meetings by sharing one medium to improve the efficiency of meetings. The usability was validated by interviewing field operators working in nuclear power plants and experts having experienced as an operator.

Keywords: Cooperation, communication, support system, nuclear power plants (NPPs).

1   Introduction

Since digital technologies were developed, they have been adopted as a way to reduce human errors and to improve human performance for nuclear power plants' (NPPs) main control room (MCR) operators and field workers. Digital technologies like PDA (Personal digital assistants), UMPC (Ultra mobile PC), smart phone, RFID (Radio frequency identification), and USN (Ubiquitous sensor network) have been applied to check task results, monitor events and accidents, and transmit/receive measured

---

* Corresponding author.

S. Yamamoto (Ed.): HIMI 2014, Part I, LNCS 8521, pp. 483–490, 2014.

values in nuclear fields. The results of using these devices have proven that it provides high accuracy and convenience for workers to get obvious effects by reducing their work loads. Thus, digital devices are strongly being considered to apply to wider fields with higher technological functions.

In this work, a cooperation support system to aid communication between MCR operators and field workers in NPPs, Nuclear Cooperation Support and Mobile Documentation system (Nu-CoSMoD), is suggested. MCR operators cannot monitor field workers who conduct their tasks at a real time. The records on paper procedure written by field workers are only given for MCR operators to check field workers task processes and task results. It is not easy for MCR operators to estimate field workers if they conduct their work correct, with enough time, at a right time, and without skipping necessary steps. Thus, for safety operation without any events induced by misunderstand and miscommunication between MCR operators and field workers, the NU-CoSMoD is necessary and it will be useful from the supporting cooperation point of view.

The suggested system, Nu-CoSMoD is consist of two sub systems, the mobile based information storing system and the large screen based information sharing system. To develop these sub systems, the requirements were identified by analyzing the results of using previous developments to make up their faults. The users who had utilize those developments for about three month were interviewed to draw their opinion.

Based on the requirements, the mobile based information storing system was developed to supports field workers by providing various functions to make workers be more trustable for MCR operators. And the large screen based information sharing system was developed to support meetings by sharing one medium to improve the efficiency of meetings.

The usability was validated by interviewing field operators working in nuclear power plants and experts having experienced as an operator.

2   Requirements for Cooperation Support Systems in Nuclear Fields

The digital device-based support systems have been developed to reduce the workload of operators and field workers especially like operating parameter management systems (OPMS) using the PDA, UMPC or smart phones.

Even though the systems have various positive effects as shown in Fig. 1, and related researches are still in progress, most of developments are under demonstration. Thus, it is necessary to analyze the results of utilization of existing developments to improve the applicability of newly developed systems. Through the analysis, the disincentive elements of using digital device-based developments were derived. Beside, by interviewing the users who utilized the developments for 2~3 months, shortcomings of the existing developments and recommendation for the new development were listed.

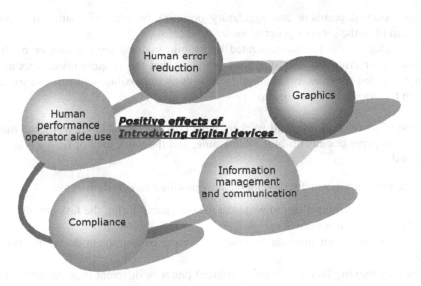

Fig. 1. Positive effects of introducing digital devices

- The disincentive elements of using digital device-based developments

— Field workers tend to avoid using mobile devices
   - o   Field workers concern the radioactive contamination, broken, loss (stolen) of devices. Because if there is any problem for their devices, then their individual equipment management scores are reduced
— Field workers are not accustomed to use new system because non user-friendly designed S/W and frequent error of S/W
— Field workers are usually utilize both a mobile based system and a paper document as a warning for S/W errors
— Field workers feel difficult to use mobile devices in tough environments like too dark, too hot, too much dust
— Mobile devices have limited power capacity, so field workers cannot utilized the mobile systems when they conduct long-time tasks if there is no power charging connection.
— The supervision department tends to distrust the electric document generated by mobile devices from the credibility point of view.
— Field workers utilize mobile systems and paper documents at the same time because mobile systems cannot cover all kind of tasks.
   - o   Work orders are conveyed by paper documents, and work procedures and the PJB (Pre-job Briefing) procedure are supported by mobile system. Thus, field worker should prepare the work order document to electric documentation after finishing their tasks.
— Frequent page moving in the mobile system is inconvenient compared to paper documents. Moving or opening different documents is much cumbersome.

— Supervision department and regulatory organization tend to distrust the mobile system from the security point of view
— When electric documents generated by mobile systems are missing or modified (deletion or erroneous modification), it means that the original documents are no more existed. Besides, re-creating documents is impossible, and it is not trustable even the document is re-created.

Because of above reasons, field workers must conduct the tasks by using the mobile system and paper documents at the same time, and the work load of field workers are increased.

• The recommendations for developing new mobile based system

— The easy writing functions to write the measurement during the tasks by using key pad or stylus pen is necessary.
— The easy correction function to write the correct measurement during the tasks is necessary.
— The easy moving function to refer different pages or different files during the tasks is necessary.
— The supervision departments have to acknowledge the mobile systems from the reliability and security point of view, and they also have to encourage using the mobile systems.
— The regulatory organizations have to acknowledge the mobile systems from the reliability and security point of view, so they have to concede the mobile documents identical to paper documents.
— Work order are covered by electric documents.
    ○ All tasks have to be covered by electric documents. Then field workers do not need to utilize paper document.
    ○ Approval for work order and checking also can be covered by electric documents.
— To effective use of mobile devices, LAN is necessary for data acquisition, uploading data, receiving or transmitting data and so on.
— Graphics like pictures, photos, and movies can be easily added compared to paper documentation.
— The auto calculation function during the tasks will be useful.
— The locking function after finishing the tasks will be useful.

Most of these analysis results, especially the function-related comments, were reflected to the new development. Detailed contents of the suggested system will be mentioned in following.

3   Development of Nuclear Cooperation Support and Mobile Document System (Nu-CoSMoD)

The suggested System, Nu-CoSMoD is consist of two sub systems; the mobile device based information storing system and the large screen based information sharing system. The structure of Nu-CoSMoD is shown in Fig. 2. They are connected through the data transmitter. The brief explanations about each sub system's development process and functions will be described.

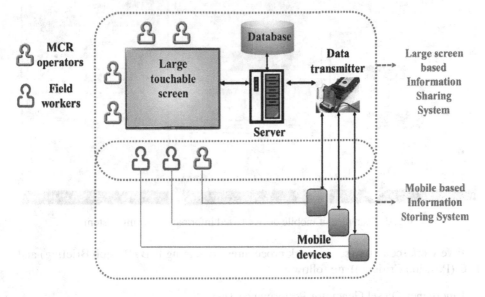

Fig. 2. The structure of Nu-CoSMoD

3.1 Mobile Device Based Information Storing System

To support cooperation between MCR operators and field workers means to provide accurate and detailed information about field workers' performance to MCR operators. But, it has limits for MCR operators to estimate field workers performance with records only on paper procedures written by field workers.

Thus, to support cooperation by recording high quality information about field workers performance by using mobile device with various on-board technical function, mobile information storing system is suggested.

Based on selected needs, five NPP`s work scenarios were chosen with some criteria:

(a) If the procedure contains as many needs as it can
(b) If the tasks of procedures can be supported by various functions of mobile devices
(c) If the tasks of selected procedures can represent most of the NPP`s work types
(d) Wireless function is not considered in this development

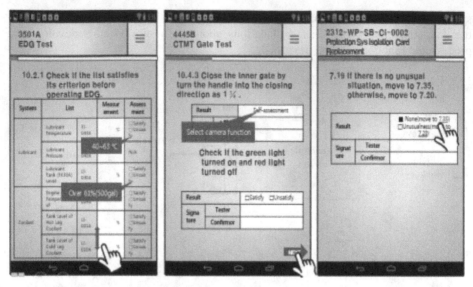

Fig. 3. Examples of mobile device based information storing system

Five work scenarios (seven work procedures containing PJB (Pre-job Briefing) and PJC (Post-job Critique)) are follows:

- Emergency Diesel Generator Performance Test
- Containment Gate Performance Test
- Protection System Isolation Card Replacement
- Remote Control System's Measurement Channel Performance Test
- Safety-related Valve Performance Test

Based on selected scenarios, the cooperation support system is configured, and examples of the screen composition is shown in Fig. 3. The left one, the EDG performance test screen shows the function of automated calculation and automated assessment. If workers fill the measurements in white boxes, then the rest assessment and calculations are automatically conducted. The middle one, the CTMT gate performance test screen shows that workers can apply the camera function for self-assessment. In the case of paper procedure, MCR operators have nothing to recognize the field workers performance. After the field workers who are tester and confirmer write on their signature, then the next button colored red is activated and field workers go to next steps. The right one, the protection system isolation card replacement case shows that field workers might skip some steps. In this case, the suggested mobile system can help to skip the steps and deactivated the skipped steps at the same time.

Besides, the suggested mobile system has various functions like providing pop-up, recognizing QR code, adding text memo, providing task progress bar, expending or reducing the size of screen, and the black box function recording all action that the field workers handle the device.

3.2   Large Screen Based Information Sharing System

Before and the field workers conduct their tasks with the suggested mobile devices, they and MCR operators have a meeting PJB to prepare the task and remind important points. After finishing field works, field workers and operators gather again and have a meeting PJC. During the meetings, meeting members discuss the tasks and the results of tasks, and write on signatures. A SRO (Senior Reactor Operator) sometimes provides an additional handout during PJB, and field workers sometimes spend long time to copy their work record to other document (if the tasks are conducted by many field workers or teams).

To support cooperation by improving the efficiency of meetings, the large screen based information sharing system is suggested. One large screen with size about 46 inch could be shared by all meeting members (usually less than ten persons). If all member stare the one same screen, then their concentration and understanding on meeting are improved. And as a digital device, using graphics like movies, photos, and pictures could also improve the meeting members understanding on tasks. It is connected to reduce human errors during field works.

Besides, additional handouts and memos could be offered with type of electric document to mobile devices. The work order and other hand out are supplied as electric documents. After work, field workers submit their report by transmitting electric files. So, the field workers do not need to prepare the paper document form and they can reduce their work load. There is no need to prepare and generate paper documents, the concerns about document storage could be also relieved.

To transmit and receive the data or electric files, a server of large screen and mobile devices are connected through a data transmitter. It reflects the circumstances that Korean utilities are too conservative to use wireless techniques.

The meeting support program(S/W) has another functions like moving and rotating screen, expending or reducing the size of screen, writing on text, digit, or signature using stylus pen, key-pad, or hands, providing pop-up, printing as electric file type or paper document type, and so on.

4   Conclusion

To support the cooperation between MCR operators and field workers in NPPs, the cooperation support and mobile documentation system Nu-CoSMoD is suggested in this work. To improve usability and applicability of the suggested system, the results of using existed digital device based support systems were analyzed. Through the analysis, the disincentive elements of using digital device-based developments and the recommendations for developing new mobile based system were derived.

Based on derived recommendations, two sub systems, the mobile device based information storing system and the large screen based information sharing system were suggested.

The usability of the suggested system was conducted by a survey with questionnaires. Field workers and operators, and nuclear-related person who had experiences as an operator, graduate students affiliated in nuclear engineering department used and tested the functions of the suggested system. Most of them needed period for adaptation, a couple of times trials, but after acclimatizing the system, users easily utilized it and showed the accurate and fast responses. The level of understand of meeting and tasks were highly estimated compared to paper procedure, and this effect is clearly appeared as the users have less experienced (graduate students and utility persons who has a little experience as an operator).

It is expected that the mobile based information storing system can reduce the field workers' work load and enhance the understanding of MCR operators about field operators work process by monitoring all work results and work processes stored in devices. And the large screen based information sharing system can enhance the level of understand, concentration and also help to share all members' ideas at the same time.

References

1. Han-Ul NPP Unit #2 procedure Emergency Diesel Generator Performance Test
2. Han-Ul NPP Unit #2 procedure Containment Gate Performance Test
3. Han-Ul NPP Unit #2 procedure Protection System Isolation Card Replacement
4. Han-Ul NPP Unit #2 procedure Remote Control System's Measurement Channel Performance Test
5. Han-Ul NPP Unit #2 procedure Safety-related Valve Performance Test
6. Han-Ul NPP Unit #2 procedure Pre-job Briefing
7. Han-Ul NPP Unit #2 procedure Post-job Critique
8. O'Hara, J.M., Higgins, J.C., Stubler, W.F.: Computer-Based Procedure Systems: Technical Basis and Human Factors Review Guidance. NUREG/CR-6634, BNL-NUREG-52564 (2000)
9. O'Hara, J.M., Brown, W.S., Lewis, P.M., Lersensky, J.J.: Human-System Interface Design Review Guidelines. NUREG-0700 (2002)

Collaborative Innovation Research on Co-working Platform Based on Lean Startup Model

Yin Li, Qinghua Guo, and Zhiyong Fu

Academy of Art and Design, Tsinghua University, Beijing, 100084, China
liyin1416@gmail.com, 342557604@qq.com, fuzhiyong@tsinghua.edu.cn

Abstract. In this paper, an infrastructure level and relevant characteristics of a target user focused on co-working platform is raised, exploring the spatial interactive prototypes that aim to build a co-working context and elements of related service system quickly. A web-based open source system integration solution is applied to test the co-working pattern and communication behavior of design teams, mean while, design process management features of cross-cultural remote collaborative platform is explored based on lean user experience design.

Keywords: Collaborative innovation, Co-working, lean Startup.

1 Research Background

With the ongoing increase of the innovative platforms in China, more and more innovating reams are in need of collaboration. Along with this related growing demand of innovating teams, many researches have put their focus on this issue. Furthermore, this demand leads to the teeming of the virtual design teams, and makes them more and more significant. The communication among team members thus becomes crucial during the cooperating process that driven by design. Last but not least, this situation has actually come up with a number of new requirements aiming at the collaborative working patterns and prototyping serving design.

2 Introduction

Through the research on collaborative innovation work demands of creative teams in different places under different conditions, a web-based open source system integration solution was created by a co-working team owned by service design lab of Tsinghua University, exploring the spatial interactive prototypes that aims at building a co-working context quickly, and elements of related service system. Different from existing systems, global laboratory exploration that based on Lean Startup model, more inclined to card the design processes as well as the idea of generating core concept. By inviting creative teams from different countries to run the tests to explore how the system could support collaborative innovation more effectively.

S. Yamamoto (Ed.): HIMI 2014, Part I, LNCS 8521, pp. 491–502, 2014.

3   Related Research

3.1   The Research Progress of Collaborative Innovation

The research on collaborative innovation in China takes enterprise as the medium relatively. Domestic scholars analyze the intension of collaborative innovation in the perspective of combining "innovation element collaboration" with "innovation subject collaboration". There is more literature about the intension of collaborative innovation abroad than it is in China, as the overseas studies began earlier. Abend·C. Joshua considers "innovative perception, process, people and organization" are core contents of collaborative management, collaborative subjects are no longer bound to enterprises but various organizations, and tools like brainstorming is an important mean to enhance productivity. Huber·George discusses issues between organizational learning and collaborative issue in depth, believes "innovation ability" can be increased by applying three patterns in organizational learning, and innovation pushes organizational learning level to a spiral through process practice. Brian Morris applied empirical study in innovative factors that exert significant impact to high-tech research and development through social networks, and further enrich the means to achieve collaborative innovation.

3.2   The Research Progress of CSCW

The research and practice in computer supported cooperative work and ubiquitous computing support the development of co-working field with theory, method, and technology. The rapid development of the internet facilitates not only promotes the study of CSCW itself, but also greatly promotes the development of online collaborative work applications, especially the development of cooperative learning systems in the Web environment. Such as the group visual learning system developed by Northwestern University: the goal of this program is to build an electronic community, which combines the teachers, students, scientists, and other museum education researchers to learn through interaction and cooperation among them; with the asking and solving problem approach to conduct learning activities, as well as establishing a bidirectional, shared virtual learning environment.

Such projects are mostly based on a single Web-based environment or a fixed space, but with less consideration in how to make it easier for a small team to build relevant service systems flexibly.

4   Explorations of Collaborative Working Platform Base Module

4.1   Target User

At the user research phase, leaders and team members interviewed by us are from 5 startup teams and 15 teams that participated in Makeathon held in Beijing. 20 interview videos and 24 effective questionnaires are obtained.

Table 1. Questionnaire

Questions	Options	Effective feedback
What kind of tool or service are your team using?	Knowledge sharing, read it later, version control, project management, time management, multi-user charts, cloud sync, network drives, file sharing, supplemented	73
How do your team discuss ideas or communicate?	E-mail, in the studio / conference room face to face, telephone / IM tool for discussion, using project collaboration tool	37
Have there been the following questions when using IM tools to communicate?	Dialogue is too long and useful information is submerged; too much discussion topic lack of purposeful; no voice recording tools; personal contact on the IM tools affect the progress of work.	32
Schedule tasks to others in the following ways:	Traditional means of communication; e-mail; IM communications tools; project collaboration tools.	52
When a task acquires several people to complete, you would encounter the following situations when handover tasks with others:	I will break down the task and assign the task to the right person; when handover task the details omissions; misunderstanding delays progress; no feedback after scheduled tasks; you can not know others' working progress.	66
The way you share information with team members:	Social networking, IM, Email, knowledge sharing, project management	71
How to preserve or organize the concept generated from discussion?	Notes; paper notebook; Evernote; sound recordings; photographs.	53
Do your team have following problems during discussion?	Do not understand each other's expertise during the discussion; the topics are too much to concentrate in thinking; unable to recall the details of the online conference discussion; some functions such as sketches exchanges cannot be achieved restrict to the online discussion tools and contexts.	48
The way to preserve the history versions:	Nomenclature, version snapshot, version control	30
When you have to modify a file with other people will you use following tools:	Use USB to copy the file to each other; network transmission; synchronization tools; Git / SVN share	45

The questionnaire investigates on knowledge sharing, communication approach, task management, knowledge management, document preservation and other aspects of the daily teams. According to the number of effective feedback from the chart above we can see that the team members are very concerned about problems such as how to share knowledge effectively, how to manage task, and how to comb and storage information from the process of discussion. How can collaborative work platform integrate existing features and tools quickly, flexibly and efficiently, and at the same time meet the need of collaboration of designers, engineers, and product managers? Therefore, the establishment of an effective coordination mechanism and service module is a necessary condition to achieve collaborative innovation (task).

4.2   The User Needs of Co-working

Based on video interviews and questionnaires, we collate the basic needs of typical user on collaborative work platform and. Most members of the innovative teams consist of students from different disciplines: design, management, and technology three typical users. At different stages of innovative teams, the number of the three typical users will be slightly different. It is very challenging to create collaborative work platform for task diversification, and multi-role participation. Though the three typical users have different disciplinary backgrounds, by planning the overall classification of the collaborative work platform, the basic needs of the collaboration platform can maintain the overall consistency.

Table 2. User Needs of Co-Working Platform

Availability	Collaborative	Persistency
Lower learning costs	Discussion with clear context	Reliable and stable
High efficiency usage	Information needs of symmetry	Improve mobile applications
	Easier to find data	More pleasant design

4.3   Base Module Features of Co-working Platform

By combing findings from user research and user needs induction, sorting out the three basic characteristics collaborative work platform base module should have.

Availability. Team members with various cultural backgrounds can communicate for the common goal of innovation on CSCW based collaborative work platform in different locations and time, even work together in the cloud storage supported network environment.

Collaborative. The platform must ensure the design environment and the context information between teams as well as team members is consistent. Due to personnel involved in the communication can be within the team, or also be derived from external members from other laboratories worldwide, the platform must be easy for teams to communicate efficiently by using variety of resources and information.

Persistency. Team managers and members in the process of the project can adjust the system modules quickly according to changes in mission requirements by increasing or decreasing the team staff, which requires the system with better scalability that enables dynamic integration of heterogeneous systems.

4.4   Basic Framework Structure of Co-working Platform

From the physical level to the virtual level, collaborative work platform system modules can be divided into four levels: physical space level, basic collaboration level, management level, and resource environment level.

1. Physical space layer mainly aims at the collaborative demand of different projects, and describes the scope of its structural and physical workspace requirements. Here are the rules: the size of the physical space, the regional function, shape, structure, materials, safety, environmental protection and many other attributes.
2. Basic collaboration level is after physical space level. Individual team members choose different collaboration tools accord with the project schedule based on individual and team needs. Tools of this level include physical and virtual collaborative toolkit, containing thought combing, instant messaging, data visualization, remote 3D printing etc.
3. The management level is the core level of the system module, a variety of creative collaboration ideas and vision are brought into it together for all the participants to involve in co-management, review, discuss and share jointly.
   New plan will be formed and unreasonable ideas will be eliminated through discussion and demonstration. This level includes project management, task management, schedule management, personnel management and other modules.
4. Environment level is a service level that sort out stakeholders for collaborative work platform in a multi-angle including individuals, teams, projects, etc. It provides teams with external resources recommendation, project process guidance, human resources management, project resource management and other services timely and efficiently.

5   Solutions

In order to verify the characteristics of collaborative work platform and the user needs, the basic collaboration and management level were chosen as the entry point for verification test, and project "Co-Matrix" was launched at the same time. "Co-Matrix" is a service module that helps start-up teams to improve working efficiency as well as optimize the design process experience. It mainly consists of hardware and remote communication systems of Matrix series in collaborative workspace, emphasizing the immediacy experience of working environment and controllability of the design process (Fig. 1 shows an example).

Fig. 1. Co-Matrix System Map

5.1   Design Method

Lean Startup thinking points out that the innovative team is not just creating valuable products, but to learn how to create sustainable growth business model, like Eric Ries describes in "The Lean Startup" as " validated learning." In project Co-Matrix, under the instruction of lean user experience design guidelines, various assumptions were implemented into prototypes during product iteration cycles. To verify whether the product truly hits the needs of users, and whether the user are willing to accept the functions provided as solutions to their needs.

5.2   Co-working Platform Back-end Implementation Methods

Use Web Socket communication protocol and WebRTC technology to build an HTML5-based multi-people involved cross-platform real-time collaborative system based on CSCW platform environment. Create collaborative server that provides a variety of collaborative services; using data management server to manage a comprehensive database and sharing module; provide users with various collaboration design tools, which can be dynamically added or subtracted through the application server. The Co-Working system structure is presented as follows   (Fig. 2 shows an example).

Fig. 2. Co-matrix System Structure

Based on the collaborative design theory described previously and take Node.JS as basic supporting technology, a data management server of Co-Matrix can be established, which achieves comprehensive management of the database, knowledge base, model base, and method base. By establishing collaboration servers, providing modular collaboration services, to enable collaborative design information integration, process integration and functional integration.

Collaborative design information integration includes: using HTML5 to achieve product structure information sharing management based on the sharing management information model. Collaborative design process integration includes: system management, mission planning and management, collaborative communication services, collaborative browsing service and other basic collaborative management services. Collaborative browsing service provides users with distance collaborative browsing that can view 3D models, 2D graphics and other text files. Under the support of comprehensive database, a knowledge management and integration systems is established, meanwhile the knowledge integration is achieved based on knowledge sharing and collaborative management model.

6   Testing and Evaluation

Eric Ries states minimum viable product (MVP) is the product that spends the least effort, the shortest development time to experience a complete 'development - Measurement - cognitive' loop in "The Lean Startup". Prototype testing was adopted as much as possible at the product concept exploration and design phases.

6.1   MVP Design and Testing (Phase One)

Prototype Design. The goal of the first phase of prototype test is to explore the basic collaboration level. Bringing team members in different locations to a same space to conduct creative communication jointly through video conferencing, remote whiteboard, sharing notes, and other toolkit. As the user operates the touch controller in the air the real-time trace of the controller can be presented on both screens, so that team members in different places can communicate or modify graphics in time in the audio and video state. The note-recording tool promotes the concept evolution within the team members by saving massive notes during the brainstorming process. It keeps the timeliness of brainstorming by recording the content of the notes in physical space and sending them to team members in the first place (Fig. 3 shows an example)

Fig. 3. Co-Matrix Prototype Design

Node.js was applied to build a server in this solution and it achieved remote video calls by using GetUserMedia API and RTCPeerConnection API provided by WebRTC; it also achieved functions like color recognition, canvas painting, and note snapping through the demo offered by tracking.js; and meanwhile it implement real-time communication between the clients by using socket.io to transmit critical data.

Prototyping. During Prototyping three groups of users were selected (2 user per group) for a 10-15 minutes unrestricted usage test in a simulated working context. Interviews with every group were conducted after the test and they also filled out questionnaires later on. User feedbacks from the interviews were organized and assessed. The questionnaire aims to score on the three interaction qualities: availability, collaborative, and persistency of the prototype, as presented in (Figure) in order to show the swiftness of MVP, score on a scale of 0 to 3.

The first group of tested users has computer science background. They think the performance of tested module reaches their expectations; the context of note snapping is very compelling to them; the context of the interactive pen is still up for debate.

The second group of tested users has design or computer science background. They have approval in terms of collaborative, and they also agree with the interaction context of note snapping. They have certain requirement on the interactive pen but they are not pleased by the test result.

Table 3. MVP (1) User Rating Table

Quality	Definition	User 1a	User 1b	User 2a	User 2b	User 3a	User 3b	Rating
Availability	Immediate, direct, fast, feedback	3	2	1	1	2	3	12
Collaborative	Unity, shared, adapted, inclusive, adjustable	2	3	3	2	3	3	16
Persistent	Open, free, natural, supportive	0	1	1	2	1	2	7

The third group of tested users has design background. They agree with the holistic context and they think the canvas painting and note snapping functions during the remote video communication meet their needs. During the test, they drew effective interaction prototypes onto the screen and also left useful discussion records via the tools provided. (The latency problem appeared in the video test was caused by the improper campus network settings.)

The current beta version can meet the remote collaboration needs of designers well through the analysis of interviews and questionnaires. To improve operating speed and functionality of the product functions for project managers and engineers would be the core demand of the next iteration. Adding user system and project management interface corresponds with the former system plan, which means to add management level onto the basic collaboration level.

Table 4. MVP (1) Function Improvement Table

Function optimization point	Product improvement points	Increased functionality
Draw smoothly	Responsive canvas, and stay the same context	User System
Part of screen recording	Miniaturize the interacting stick	Instant message
Color tracking algorithm's efficiency improvement	WIFI module using in transmission	Screen/Video/Audio recording
Audio processing to avoid noise	Users self register more color	Muilti-User video conference
Sharing Screen	Sharing drag event	Participate in conference without camera
Fluent and distinct video/audio signal	Video/Audio signal firewall traversal	Video room control privileges
iOS compatibility	Audio conference	

6.2   MVP Design and Testing (Phase Two)

For the lean user experience design, there has a similar "development - measurement - cognitive" loop, the "thinking - realize - test" loop. The involved feedback within the second loop not only includes external measurement data but also thoughts from designers. According to internal (self) and external (target object or demand side) feedbacks designers generate new cognitions to improve the plan. The plan will be validated and again new cognitions appeared which formed a cycle.

Management level was added after the first iteration of the functional prototype modules. The management level seeks to visualize data service information of the projects required to be displayed, so that the team managers and team members can learn about the project progress, time planning, resource allocation, personal health status and other information in real-time. By providing a unified data display format, it gives teams a design communication environment for integrated new product development.

Fig. 4. Smart City exhibition of Beijing International Design Week 2013

Content Display module provides team managers with an intuitive, efficient and operational service management operating system (Fig. 4 shows an example). Team managers can keep abreast of the current personal status, work progress, accomplished work, and relevant data of team members, also information of related expert consultants and energy consumption status of the entire team within the same project. In a cross-functional creative team, team members are from different regions with their own habits and work patterns, therefore the communication in a virtual environment requires consideration of the characteristics of different disciplines and cultural backgrounds. Content Display system aims to break the traditional work mode, making the whole project process transparent, mobilizing the team members' responsibility and enthusiasm to keep the entire project moving on properly.

The second prototype of Co-matrix attended the Smart City exhibition of Beijing International Design Week 2013. It withstood a lot of user testing during the exhibition and two successful remote online tests with the mobile lab of Delft University of technology and urban informatics lab of University of Queensland were carried out. And together with Seoul National University, Chiba University, and Parsons School of Design demonstrated accomplished projects in case study module. Through the real system test and user interviews during the exhibition the basic system module framework gave a lot of support to the basic needs of discussion within team members, as well as established a collaborative work context via the system tool module, which built a collaborative work experience.

6.3   Next Step

The goals of the third phase of the collaborative work platform will focus on the development of online develop toolkit of the collaboration level and the resources matching module of the environment level. The iteration of management level would be continued, as well as it of product optimization in terms of availability, collaborative, and consistency.

Table 5. The Analysis of Core Module of Competing Products

		BaseCamp	Asana	Teambition	Worktile	Tower	Matrix
Task	Inbox	O	O	O	O	O	O
	Quick Task		O			O	O
	RT Recording						O
	Sub Task		O	O	O		
Calendar	Calendar	O	O	O	O	O	O
	Cal. Service		O		O	O	
Discussion	Resource						O
	IM				O		O
	Camera						O
Rate	Function	3	3	4	5	4	3
	UI	4	5	5	3	4	4

Compared with competing products in the Internet field like BaseCamp, Asana, Teambition, Worktile, and Tower, removing basic task management, schedule management, document management functions, these products didn't make further development in discussion module and only Co-Matrix and Worktile have IM function. Co-Matrix builds a bridge across the gap between physical and virtual space in the context combining the discussion module usage with physical workspace. Otherwise, the resource matching and knowledge-sharing module is unique in the environment Level of Co-Matrix, which indicates the collaborative work platform not a collection of collaborative tools, but an aggregation of people, environment, and data. It's the future development direction of collaborative innovation platform.

7 Conclusion

This study is based on the agile experience design concepts and methods. First of all, using the co-working space model as the core, through the integrate research on usage scenarios formed by the offline contact points and the online information services, explores how creative teams perform effective teamwork in the creative phrase under typical development mode, also a diachronic analysis on creative concept development was performed. Through the rational use of existing mature information technology, integrating physical and virtual environment, combined with user research evaluation and user feedback data for rapid prototype iteration, building service prototypes and interaction solutions that are more easier for teams which have the nature of cross-time zone and cross-cultural to use. The final output of this study is a new solution in the aspect of service products and system prototypes, which consist of universal co-working service mode and effective online and offline communication channels for the global laboratory.

Acknowledgement. I wish to thank Jieyun Yang and Wenbo Yi for their hard work in this project. I also would like to thank Wei Liu and Prof. Marcus Foth for their support on remote testing, and Prof. Christopher Mustafa Kirwan for his instructions.

References

1. Joshua, A.C.: Innovation Management: The Missing Link in Productivity. Management Review 68(6), 25–30 (1979)
2. Chen, G.: Enterprise collaborative innovation research. Southwest Jiaotong University (2005)
3. Sun, C.-Q.: Yangtze River Pharmaceutical Industry Cluster Innovation Collaborative research. East China Normal University (2009)
4. Huber, G.: Synergies Between Organizational Learning and Creativity & Innovation. Creativity & Innovation Management 7(1), 3–9 (1998)
5. Morris, B.: High Technology Development: Applying a Social Network Paradigm. Journal of New Business Ideas & Trends 4(1), 45–59 (2006)

6. Wieimeier, G.F.L., Thoma, A., Senn, C.: Leveraging Synergies Between R&D and Key Account Management to Drive Value Creation. Research Technology Management 55(3), 15–22 (2012)
7. Liu, W., Pasman, G., Stappers, P.J., Taal-Fokker, J.: Supporting Generation Y Interactions: Challenges for Office Work. In: CSCW 2011, Hangzhou, China, March 19-23 (2011)
8. Goebbels, G., Laliot, V., Göbel, M.: Design and Evaluation of Team Work in Distributed Collaborative Virtual Environments. In: VRST 2003, Osaka, Japan, October 1-3 (2003)
9. Goebbels, G., Laliot, V., Göbel, M.: Co-Presence and Co-Working in distributed Collaborative Virtual Environments. AFRIGRAPH 2001, Capctown South Africa (2001)
10. Ropa, A., Ahlstrom, B.: A case study of a multimedia co-working task and the resulting interface design of a collaborative communication tool. In: CHI 1992 (1992)
11. Neale, D.C., Carroll, J.M.: Evaluating Computer-Supported Cooperative Work: Models and Frameworks. In: CSCW 2004, Chicageo, Illinnois, USA, November 6-10 (2004)
12. Fu, Z., Feng, X.: Virtual Environment Design Team Management Model. In: Tsinghua International Design Management Symposium (2009)
13. Li, Y., Fu, Z.: Explore campus-oriented startup team co-working model and service prototypes. In: IEEE Tsinghua International Design Management Symposium (2013)
14. Fu, Z.: The Design Theory and Research Framework for Public Service in Social Media Age, DMI, China (2011)
15. Moultrie, J., Nilsson, M., Dissel, M., Haner, U.-E., Janssen, S., Van der Lugt, R.: Innovation Spaces: Towards a Framework for Understanding the Role of the Physical Environment in Innovation (2007)
16. McCoy, J.M., Evans, G.W.: The Potential Role of the Physical Environment in Fostering Creativity. Creativity Research Journal Copyright 2002 by 2002 14(3 & 4), 409–426 (2002)
17. Pea, R.D.: The collaborative visualization project. Communications of the ACM 36(5) (May 1993)
18. Stickdorn, M., Schneider, J.: This is service design thinking. John Wiley & Sons, Inc.
19. Kolko, J.: Thoughts of Interaction Design. In: Management Complexity of Data, Information, Knowledge, Wisdom, ch. II, p. 46

A Learning Method for Product Analysis in Product Design

Learning Method of Product Analysis Utilizing Collaborative Learning and a List of Analysis Items

Haifu Lin[1], Hiroshi Kato[2], and Takeshi Toya[3]

[1] Ningbo Institute of Technology, Zhejiang University
Zero7284@gmail.com
[2] Center of ICT and Distance Education, The Open University of Japan
Hiroshi@kato.com
[3] Tokai University in Japan
ttoya@keyaki.cc.u-tokai.ac.jp

Abstract. Product design is an essential market research method for design planning. In this study, we propose a learning method for product analysis by combining collaborative learning and a list of analysis items by a learner who aims to become a professional designer. This proposal had the following features: (1) facilitation of multi-perspective analysis (even for beginners) based on a list of analysis items and (2) facilitation of objective analysis through the introduction of collaborative learning. In addition, we conducted two experiments to verify the effectiveness of the proposed method. As a result, the following learning effects were verified: (1) even a beginner can conduct a multi- perspective analysis and recognize improvement in analytical skills, (2) product analysis clarifies the direction for product improvement once the purpose of the product is understood, and (3) product analysis could be useful for discovering problems with the product.

Keywords: product design, product analysis, collaborative learning, list of analysis items.

1 Introduction

In recent years, the importance of user-centered design has been growing in the product design process. Therefore, the design plan stage, where a user's needs are grasped, has becomes vital. The design plan includes information gathering, product evaluation, and consideration of product image. In product evaluation, the acknowledgment, attributes, and operability of the product are evaluated (Wakayama University, 2000). According to our investigation concerning a company's design capability, it is obvious that the ability to analyze and evaluate a product is a design capability that professional designers expect (Lin, Kato, 2010). Current design styles can be understood by analyzing products. In addition, the features of a product can be

S. Yamamoto (Ed.): HIMI 2014, Part I, LNCS 8521, pp. 503–513, 2014.

obtained from the materials, fabrication technology, and other factors surrounding the product (Bruno, 2007). The technique and viewpoint of product analysis must change depending on the object of the analysis and its purpose. Therefore, the analysis quality also changes. An idea with business validity based on market needs is important for novice designers. Therefore, observation and analysis of the correct product are necessary. This research applies to product analysis in which the advantages and disadvantages of the product can be grasped, and through which the designer can understand a product from various perspectives.

Such product analyses use Yamaoka's 70 design items that support observation of the product (Yamaoka, 1998), and Bruno's analysis items that support product analysis (Bruno, 2007). The 70 design items that Yamaoka proposed are classified in 8 large categories according to the purpose of the observation. These analysis items are comprehensive, multilateral, and useful to a designer for practical purposes, but they are unpractical for the education of a beginner, because they are specialized and lengthy. On the other hand, Bruno suggests a list of 24 items, which are used as a checklist when the product is analyzed, and are characterized by a simple and easy to understand analysis viewpoint concerning the product. Bruno states that product analysis needs to consider both personal value and object value (Bruno, 2007); however, he does not suggest concrete ways to do this. A product analysis learning method that integrates collaborative learning and a list of analysis items will solve this problem (Lin, Kato, 2011).

In this study, we propose a product analysis learning method that integrates collaborative learning and a list of analysis items (hereafter referred to as the "PA learning method").

2   PA Learning Method

This proposal offers an easier method for beginners to not only analyze a product through various aspects such as the appearance, technology, functionality, and ergonomics of the design, but also obtain an objective value by comparing individual results with others viewpoints. This aims to understand the intention of the product in a systematic and straightforward manner.

List of analysis items: Bruno's 24-items list is classified into 7 large categories (name, molding, material, essence, cognition, and whistles).

Collaborative learning: Because the subjective value of the learner is reflected in each analysis item, the results of analysis are different for each learner. Therefore, in theory, the understood value of the product becomes objective by consolidating the results and discussing the analysis.

We performed the experiment to evaluate the learning effects of the learning method proposal (Lin, Kato, 2011). The subjects were 80 university students in a design course. The following learning effects were observed: (1) even a beginner-level learner could carry out the analysis and (2) the product analysis clarified the direction of product improvement after the purpose of the product was understood. Meanwhile, we discovered certain limitations in our proposed method. Learners were unable to understand how to effectively use the method because of a lack of sufficient explanation. Furthermore, the learners felt constrained because the direct use of the list of analysis items did not leave room for them to include their own ideas. Here, we studied the adequacy of the list of analysis items through a pilot experiment. In the pilot experiment, the learners analyzed the product through two methods, either with or without the list of analysis items. The cooperators were 4 university students in the design course.

As a result, two problems with the list of analysis items were discovered: (1) Learners thought that their own ideas were restricted when they consulted the list of analysis items in advance. Imagination and creativity are aspects emphasized in design education. For learners receiving such education, there is a consciousness that it is important to show their own ideas. Therefore, we can be assume that the checklist method felt restrictive. We thus improved the presentation method of the list of analysis items to respond to the imagination of the learners with the help of comments by learners. First, let learners think with their brains and give their own ideas as much as possible, and then let learners consult the list of analysis items when they cannot think of any more ideas. In this way, learners can think for themselves freely. Then, the viewpoints that he/she did not consider can be acquired from the list of analysis items. Furthermore, there awareness of problems and their imaginations deepen through discussion groups. (2) Students lost work hours because they could not initially understand the learning method, and the estimate of necessary hours was therefore wrong. Here, we took measures to explain the learning method and added content that had been lacking in the explanations of each stage before performing group learning. Furthermore, we responded by always announcing to the learners the working hours of each stage.

Table 1 shows the execution procedure of PA learning method.

First, procedure 0 was added before the conventional procedure 1, as there was no explanation about the learning method of this product analysis in the previous proposal. In this case, the explanation was added so that the learner could better understand the learning method before performing group learning. The contents were a training project outline, learning target, and learning implications. During each stage, the reasoning behind the subject and an explanation of the creation target were also added.

Procedure 1 explains the article name, unit price, and the function of the analysis object as advance preparation for analysis like before.

In procedure 2, participants elect a facilitator from the group. The role of the facilitator is to push the group's forward learning and summarize the results of the analysis as the MC for the group. Next, each group member assumes a specific user image and conducts product analysis as the user. The only improvement is adding an explanation about the technique of "user image" here.

The presentation method of the list of analysis items was improved in procedure 3. Conventionally, the list of analysis items was passed around, and learners analyzed a product by referring to it. In the improved procedure, time for learners to think freely was given before providing the list of analysis items. First, learners analyze the product from their own viewpoints. Next, the list of analysis items is distributed, and learners examine items that they had missed while referring to the list of analysis items.

Procedure 4 is improved by first illustrating with an example the reasons and standards of theme selection. Problems are preferentially solved based on the result of learners' analysis, and the solution direction for the contents is decided like before.

Procedure 5 remains the same as before. When a theme is chosen, solutions for the elected problem are examined and ideas are provided. When no theme is decided in procedure 4, a suitable theme for ideas is attached here.

Table 1. Execution procedures of PA learning method

Procedure	Items	Contents
(0)	Presentation of the learning method	Explain about training project outline, learning target, and learning implications.
		Explain the reasoning of the subject and the creation target during each stage.
(1)	Presentation of an analysis object	Explain the essential information about the analysis object.
(2)	Selection of facilitator	Explain about the setting method of user image.
		Select a facilitator from among the members.
		Learners design their own user image.
(3)	Selection of analytical items and analysis of product	Analyze the product from learners own viewpoints.
		Refer to the list of analysis items, and add necessary items.
		Consult the list of analysis items by the analysis object and select necessary items.
		All the members discuss and examine the merit and demerit of the product from the viewpoint of user roles.
		The facilitator concludes a result of the analysis on the paper.
(4)	Decision of solution direction	Explain about the setting method of the theme.
		Pick the problems that seem to be important and determine the direction of the solution, Set a development goal of adequacy in the contents. (one may go to step (5) when the development goal cannot be decided)
(5)	Issue selection and devising solutions	In case the development goal is determined in step (4): devise a solution according to the development goal.
		In case the development goal is not determined in step (4): devise a solution and set a reasonable goal last.

3   Evaluation Experiment

We performed an experiment to evaluate whether the problems were resolved. Our evaluation focused particularly on whether a free exchange of opinions occurred mutually within a group and whether the study method was acquired, without the learner feeling any restrictions. The review methodology involved performing a trial lesson using an enhanced method and considering the impact of these learning effects in order to compare the pre- and post-test results. The comparison of pre- and post-test results was conducted in terms of the abundance of ideas generated, their breadth, quality, and subjectivity evaluation aspects.

These results were then compared with those of group A (hereafter referred to as the "conventional groups") from the first experiment (Lin, Kato, 2011) in order to investigate the effect of improved learning methods (hereafter, the "improved groups"). In the first experiment, the experimental conditions determined four groups based on two factors: groups with or without the list of analysis items, and those using collaborative or non-collaborative learning. Group A used the conventional learning method: they were supplied with the list of analysis items and the learning was group-based.

The experimental methodology was as follows.

— Trial lesson: According to the above-mentioned improved learning method (Table 1), it experimented in lesson form. The course lasted 3.5 hours.
— Subject: The subjects were 16 students with an interest in product design in daily life. All participants were inexperienced with this type of learning method. In the lesson, they were divided into four groups comprising four students; by two groups replaced the analysis object of the pre-posttest and took counter balance.
— Implementing procedure: The implementation procedure involved the following five stages.

1. Explain the purpose of the experiment and let subjects write a cooperation agreement.
2. Distribute a specific product, two or three referential accessories, and associated standard documentation, analyze the object, and conduct a pre-test.
3. Use the lecture slides and teach the improved learning method to students, and then, let them implement the method in the group using the lecture slides.
4. Distribute a specific product, two or three referential accessories, and associated standard documentation, analyze the object, and conduct a post-test.
5. Let the students complete the questionnaire.

Firstly, in the pre-test, the homogeneity between groups and the validity of the comparison between the conventional and the improved methods were examined. The following aspects were consequently verified.

Effect on the Quantity and Quality of the Ideas. The pre-post-test comparison of the improved groups was conducted in terms of the number of analysis results and variations, and the content evaluation of the analyzed results.

Regarding the number of analysis results, each item pertaining to the adequacy or inadequacy of the product, which students filled out in the analysis sheets, was counted as a single unit. The analysis results were categorized, and categories with one or more items were assumed to be variations. The analysis results were evaluated in terms of the factors of "consent degree," "unique degree," and "importance." This evaluation was performed by college students who had not participated in this lesson;

these students evaluated the analysis results of one group in terms of each of the three factors in five steps. Inter-Rater Reliability was measured for thess evaluation results (Kuwabara, 1993) (Tsushima, 2010).

Effect of Improvement. The post-test comparison between the improved and conventional groups was performed in terms of the items of the number of analysis results and variations, and the content evaluation of the analyzed results using the two-sample t-test.

Post-test Questionnaire Comparison between the Improved and Conventional Groups. The analysis of the post-test questionnaire compared the improved and conventional groups, with the Mann-Whitney U test used to evaluate the improved effect of the subject factor in the improved groups.

4   Results

The verification of the homogeneity between groups for the improved methods for the product analysis revealed no significant difference. In the pre-test, the comparison between the improved and the conventional methods indicated no significant difference. Therefore, the two groups were not expected to show any differences regarding their product analysis capabilities, thus allowing the post-test of both groups to be analyzed.

4.1   Effect on the Quantity and Quality of the Ideas

As to the number of analysis results and variations, the pre- and post-test results were compared using each one-sample t-test. The results showed that post-test results were better than pre-test results in terms of the number of analysis results, with the difference being statistically significant ($t = 2.97$, $df = 15$, $p < 0.01$). Furthermore, the post-test results showed an improvement compared with the pre-test in terms of the number of variations, with the difference also being statistically significant ($t = 4.67$, $df = 15$, $p < 0.01$)(Table 2).

Table 2. The result of pre- and posttest-analysis of the improved groups. (( ) = standard variation, $**p < 0.01$, $*p < 0.05$).

		Improved group n = 16		t-test two-sided
		Pretest (SD)	Posttest (SD)	P-value
The number of analysis result**		10.12 (4.27)	13.56 (4.26)	$P < 0.01$
The number of variation of analysis result**		4.69 (1.62)	8.13 (2.75)	$P < 0.01$
Contents evaluation of analysis result	Content degree*	9.50 (3.92)	12.13 (4.03)	$P < 0.05$
	Unique degree**	0.88 (1.59)	2.50 (1.59)	$P < 0.01$
	Importance*	10.13 (4.27)	13.25 (4.34)	$P < 0.05$

The credibiity factors obtained an assay result of a = .81 (number of items = 8) of interrater reliability by ICC for the results that evaluated contents of analysis by 8 raters. According to the standard of the credibility factor of Landis (1977), it is assumed that there is almost perfect within the range of 0.81~ (Landis, 1977).

Table 3. The number of the contents evaluation of analysis result. (*Content degree, Importance: Intermediate $\geq$ 3.00, Unique degree: Intermediate $\leq$ 3.00).

	Content degree (Unit : item)		Unique degree (Unit : item)		Importance (Unit : item)	
	Pretest	Posttest	Pretest	Posttest	Pretest	Posttest
Improved group	**152**	**194**	**14**	**40**	**162**	**212**
Conventional group	182	212	30	52	182	216

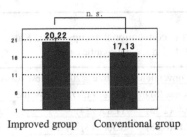

Fig. 1. The problem of the product could be found by analyzing the product

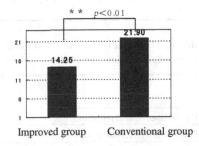

Fig. 2. It is useless to show the idea even if the product analysis was performed

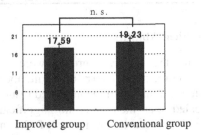

Fig. 3. An individual can analyze a product more objectively than in a group

For the content evaluations of the analyzed results (Table 3), the pre- and post-tests were compared using the one-sample t-test. The results revealed that the post-tests for the consent degree ($t = 2.13$, df = 15, $p < 0.05$), unique degree ($t = 3.15$, df = 15, $p < 0.01$), and importance ($t = 2.66$, df = 15, $p < 0.05$) were all improved as compared with the pre-test, with the difference being statistically significant.

Table 4. Pre-posttest comparison of the improved groups and the conventional groups. (( ) = standard variation, ** $p < 0.01$, * $p < 0.05$, † $p < 0.10$, n.s. = not significant).

		Improved group n = 16		Conventional group n = 20		t-test two-sided P-value
		Pretest(SD)	Posttest(SD)	Pretest(SD)	Posttest(SD)	
The number of analysis results		10.12(4.27)	13.56(4.26)	9.40(2.25)	11.85(3.54)	n.s.
The number of variation of analysis result *		4.69(1.62)	8.13(2.75)	4.15(0.88)	6.50(1.15)	$p < 0.05$
Contents evaluation of analysis result	Content degree	9.50(3.92)	12.13(4.03)	9.10(2.40)	10.60(3.47)	n.s.
	Unique degree	0.88(1.59)	2.50(1.59)	1.50(1.28)	2.60(2.48)	n.s.
	Importance †	10.13(4.27)	13.25(4.34)	9.10(2.22)	10.80(3.72)	$p < 0.10$

Table 5. The result of pre- and posttest-analysis of the conventional groups. (Lin, Kato, 2010) (( ) = standard variation, ** $p < 0.01$, * $p < 0.05$, † $p < 0.10$, n.s. = not significant).

		Conventional groups n = 20		t-test two-sided P-value
		Pretest (SD)	Posttest (SD)	
The number of analysis result **		9.40(2.25)	11.85(3.54)	$P < 0.01$
The number of variation of analysis result **		4.15(0.88)	6.50(1.15)	$P < 0.01$
Contents evaluation of analysis result	Content degree *	9.10(2.40)	10.60(3.47)	$P < 0.01$
	Unique degree **	1.50(1.28)	2.60(2.48)	$P < 0.10$
	Importance *	9.10(2.22)	10.80(3.72)	$P < 0.00$

4.2   Effect on Analytical Abilities

The post-test results for the improved groups were compared with those of the conventional groups using the t-test in term of the number of analysis results, number of variations, and content evaluation of the analyzed result.

The analysis revealed that there was no significant difference between the improved and conventional groups in terms of the number of analysis results (t = 1.32, df = 34, n.s.). In contrast, a statistically significant increase was observed in the improved groups compared with the conventional groups in terms of the number of variations (t = 2.21, df = 19.16, p < 0.05). In addition, the factor of importance in the post-test showed a significant improvement in the improved groups compared with the conventional groups(t = 1.82, df = 34, p < 0.10)(Table 4).

4.3   Subjective Factor Verification

The post-test questionnaire compared the results between the improved and conventional groups using the Mann-Whitney- U test. For the item "The problem of the product could be found by analyzing the product," the average score for the improved groups was 20.22, versus 17.13 in the conventional groups. On average, the improved groups showed a greater improvement, but it was not statistically significant ($U = 132.5$, $p = .386$, n.s.) (Fig. 1). Regarding the item "It is useless to show the idea even if the product analysis was performed," the average score for the improved groups was 14.25 compared with 21.90 in the conventional groups, thus showing better results for the improved groups ($U = 92$, $p = .030 < 0.01$)(Fig. 2). For the item "An individual can analyze a product more objectively than in a group," the average score for the improved groups was 17.59 versus 19.23 in the conventional groups. Although the improved groups had lower scores on average, the difference was not statistically significant ($U = 145.50$, $p = .848$, n.s.) (Fig. 3).

5   Discussion

5.1   Learning Effects

In the conventional learning method, the list of analysis items was shown to students before they were asked to complete the task. In the improved methods, the usage of this list was altered, and students' independence respected, as they were given the list after completing the test. Consequently, the interaction between students was strengthened.

Regarding the number of analysis results and variations, the comparison of the pre- and post-tests of the improved groups showed that they improved over time. This result was the same for the conventional groups (Table 5). From these results, we see that the improved methods had the same effect as the conventional methods in term of teaching analytical abilities. Moreover, even beginners were able to analyze a product from a multi-perspective.

In terms of the quality of the analyzed contents, the post-test results for the improved methods (consent degree, unique degree, and importance) were significantly improved compared with the pre-test. In the conventional groups, the post-test for the consent degree and importance were significantly improved compared with the pre-test, although the post-test for the unique degree did not (Table 5). From these results, it can be said that the improved learning method was more effective than the conventional learning method in terms of the uniqueness of product analysis.

Moreover, the improved groups performed significantly better than the conventional groups with regard to the number of variations and content evaluations (importance). It can therefore be said that the learning effect of the improved methods was greater than the conventional methods from the perspective of the analysis and quality of the analysis.

5.2   Subjective Factor Verification

For the item "The problem of the product could be found by analyzing the product," the improved groups showed an improvement from the average value, but the difference was not observed subjectively. Based on the questionnaire with the conventional methods (Lin, Kato, 2011), the results for the groups given the list of analysis items (average for group A was 3.45 and group C 3.40 (the conventional methods)) were significantly lower than those for groups without the list (average for group C was 3.60 and group D 3.80). The average for the improved groups was 3.63. These results cannot be directly compared with those of groups B and D, which did not have the list of analysis items. However, the average value, which reveals that the significant difference has been disappeared, indicates that the improved method has certain effect.

Regarding the item "It is useless to show the idea even if the product analysis was performed," the improved groups showed a significantly greater improvement compared with the conventional groups (U = 92, p = .030 < 0.01) (Fig.2). Therefore, it can be said that the student's feeling of being restrained by the list of analysis items was reduced by using the improved list of analysis items.

Concerning the item "An individual can analyze a product more objectively than in a group," the improved groups performed better than the average, but the difference was not significant. However, based on the questionnaire using the conventional methods (Lin, Kato, 2011), the results for the groups with collaborative learning (average for group A was 1.85 and group B 1.45 (the conventional methods)) were significantly higher than those for the non-collaborative groups (average for group C was 1.50 and group D 1.45). The average of the improved groups was 1.50. This result cannot be directly compared with non-collaborative learning Groups C and D. However, a constant trend was observed namely that collaborative learning allowed students to analyze a product more objectively because the disappeared significant different was seen from the average value comparison.

6   Conclusions

In this study, we proposed a learning method for product analysis by combining a collaborative learning approach with a list of analysis items.

Based on the experiments, the following learning effects were verified: (1) even a beginner can carry out an analysis from the multi-perspective and achieve improvement in analytical abilities, (2) product analysis clarifies the direction for product improvement after the purpose of the product is understood, and (3) product analysis could be useful for identifying problems with a product.

Although the learning method proposed in this study is targeted at learners who study design, novice designers employed by companies may also benefit from it. In that case, it is necessary for designer to understand the characteristic of an analysis object after a comprehensive analysis on the product, rather than from the perspective of the designer. Although a preliminary evaluation of the learning effect has not been carried out yet, we would like to one of the study tasks.

References

1. Yasushi, A.: The objective assessment to the value of the town. MACHINAMI Foundation 23(2), 10–13 (2004)
2. Munari, B., Yumi, K.: A Product is born from a Product, pp. 100–106. Misuzu Pablishing, Inc. (2007)
3. Wakayama University, Introduction to Design Information, Japanese Standards Association, pp.187–208 (2000)
4. Kuwabara, Y., Saito, T., Inagaki, Y.: Evaluation of Intra- and Inter-Ovserver Reliability. Kokyu To Junkan 41(3), 945–952 (1993)
5. Eiki, T.: Interclass Correlation Coefficient as a Reliability Indicatior, Hirosakii University (2010),
   http://www.hs.hirosaki-u.ac.jp/~pteiki/research/stat/icc.pdf
6. Landis, J.R., Koch, G.G.: The Measurement of Observer Agreement for Categorical Data. Biometrics 33(1), 159–174 (1977)
7. Haifu, L., Hiroshi, K.: Abilities Required for Product Designers and their Growth Process. Japanese Society for the Science of Design 57(2), 67–74 (2010)
8. Haifu, L., Hiroshi, K., Takeshi, T., Kazuhiro, N.: Product Analysis Learning Method: Collaborative Learning and List of Analysis Items. ED-MEDIA (2011)
9. Kikuchi, T., Yanagisawa, H., Aoki, N., Fukuzaki, A., Kostov, V., Konishi, F., Fukuda, S.: A Trial of Global Team-Based Product Design Education. Japanese Society for Information and Systems in Education 18(2), 210–217 (2001)
10. Toshiki, Y.: Use in product development process of human technology. Toshiba Review 53(7), 43–46 (1998)

Development of a Mobile Application for Crowdsourcing the Data Collection of Environmental Sounds

Minori Matsuyama[1], Ryuichi Nisimura[1], Hideki Kawahara[1], Junnosuke Yamada[2], and Toshio Irino[1]

[1] Wakayama University, 930 Sakaedani, Wakayama 640-8510 Japan
nisimura@sys.wakayama-u.ac.jp
[2] Nippon Telegraph and Telephone Corporation (NTT), Japan

Abstract. Our study introduces a mobile navigation system enabling a sound input interface. To realize high-performance environmental sound recognition system using Android devices, we organized a database of environmental sounds collected in our daily lives. Crowdsourcing is a useful approach for organizing a database based on collaborative works of people. We recruited trial users to test our system via a web-based crowdsourcing service provider in Japan. However, we found that improvement of the system is important for maintaining the motivation of users in order to continue the collection of sounds. We believe that the improved user interface (UI) design introduced to facilitate the annotation task. This paper describes an overview of our system, focusing on a method for utilizing the crowdsourcing approach using Android devices, and its UI design. We developed a touch panel UI for the annotation task by selecting an appropriate class of a sound source.

Keywords: environmental sound collection, user interface design, Android app, crowdsourcing.

1 Introduction

This paper introduces a mobile navigation system with a sound input interface that was developed on the basis of large-vocabulary automatic speech recognition. The system operates on Android[1] mobile devices. Figure 1 shows screenshots of our prototype system, which informs the user that there are problems in the wet area when it detects the sound of water flowing. The user can know that a patrol car is approaching when the siren is detected, as illustrated in the examples of the usage of the system depicted in Figure 2. The prototype system consists of an Android app and a web server program developed around the recognition engine.

To realize high-performance environmental sound recognition, we developed a database of environmental sounds collected from those encountered in our daily lives. A large amount of data is necessary because the recognition program

S. Yamamoto (Ed.): HIMI 2014, Part I, LNCS 8521, pp. 514–524, 2014.

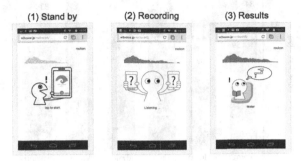

Fig. 1. Screenshots of our prototype system

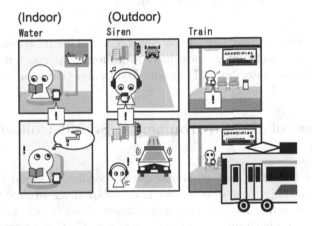

Fig. 2. Usage examples of the prototype system

utilizes a statistical pattern recognition algorithm. Our prototype system utilizes the Adaboost[2] algorithm and Hidden Markov Models (HMMs)[3] as the pattern-recognition method to identify the source of a sound. As shown in Figure 3, introduced from our previous experiments, it is necessary to improve accuracy in evaluating performances and classifying the six types of environmental sounds shown.

However,the sound data collected via Android devices in a real environment are limited. In the study reported in this paper, we succeeded in collecting sound data using a crowdsourcing approach[4]. Crowdsourcing is a practical method of employing human resources from the Internet. Further, crowdsourcing is a useful approach for developing a database on the basis of collaborative work that involves outsourcing tasks to a distributed group of people. We recruited trial users to test our system via the Rakuten research company[5], a web-based crowdsourcing service provider in Japan.

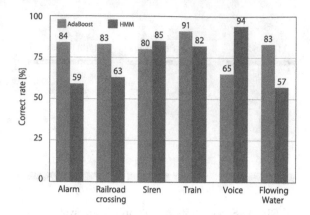

Fig. 3. Experimental results of classifying environmental sounds based on statistical pattern recognition algorithm (Our previous study)

This paper gives an overview of the environmental sound collection system, focusing on the method that utilizes the crowdsourcing approach using Android devices, and its user interface (UI) design. Data collection results are also discussed.

2   Overview of the Environmental Sound Collection System

Our system for collecting environmental sounds consists of cloud-based server-client programs. The client-side system is distributed as an Android app developed by us, which records sounds and uploads them to our web server. On the server-side, simple Common Gateway Interface (CGI)[6] programs are used to communicate with the client via HTTP[7]. The system gathers an acoustic signal for a duration of one minute, along with the GPS location information and the terminal settings with the Android OS version. Additionally, it is necessary to add metadata information, which indicates the sound-source type, to the uploaded data in order to develop a well-formed sound database. Because the system provides an annotation interface, the trial users could create the metadata information themselves.

We collected environmental sounds at the end of 2012. To collect the environmental sounds of the various regions, we first asked the Rakuten research company to prescreen trial users. We then sent the participants who registered with Rakuten research an email with the URL of the download site for our recording app. The trial users who received the email were then able to participate in the experiments by installing our app on their own Android devices. Each participant who recorded the sound and uploaded the data was given a Rakuten reward point.

Of 863 Android owners in Japan who we asked to record data, 428 sent us 841 datasets that we subsequently classified into the 92 classes shown in Figure 4.

airconditioning	cooking	jettowel	scooter	truck
airplane	cough	kettle	sea	train
alarm	crossing	lift	serverroom	TV
ambulance	crowd	lighter	shaver	vacuumcleaner
ATM	dehumidifier	mealtime	ship	vacuumtruck
baby	dog	motorcycle	sidewalk	voice
bar	doorbell	music	silent	warning
barber	drier	office	snoring	washingmachine
bicycle	dryingmachine	pachinko	snowplow	water
bird	electroniccalculator	party	stairs	waterfall
bousaimusen	elevator	patrolcar	station	WindowsOS
brass	escalator	PC	store	BAD_DATA
Buddhist altar bell	fan	piano	stove	UNKNOWN
bus	fireengine	powershovel	supermarket	
cafe	fireworks	printer	switch	
car	game	radio	telephone	
cat	gamecenter	railwaycrossing	temple	
chime	horn	rain	ticketmachine	
clippers	horse	river	toilet	
clock	hospital	runner	toy	

■ # >=10   ■ # >=20   ■ # >=30   ■ # >=40   ■ # >=50

■ # >=60   ■ # >=70   ■ # >=80

Fig. 4. Table of 92 classes defined by us, where the color of each cell indicates the number (#) of datasets collected

The overall recording time of the uploaded data was 10 hours five minutes. The classes were determined according to the type of the sound source (e.g., train, car, or bird).

Among the datasets obtained, we were not able to record the GPS position information for 253 because at the time those datasets were being uploaded, the data got corrupted as a result of network problems. In addition, because of problems associated with the accuracy of the GPS sensor of user's Android terminal, we confirmed that the GPS position information could not be acquired before the start of any recording.

3 UI Design for the Recording App on Android Mobile Devices

Crowdsourcing proved useful for easily developing the sound database. However,we discovered that improvements to the system were necessary to maintain the motivation of trial users in order for them to continue the sound collection activity. We believe that the enhanced UI introduced to facilitate the annotation task addressed this problem. Figure 5 shows our original UI for the annotation task; a text-input form is displayed for the user to input the sound source type. However, because some software keyboards on Android devices are too small, users often feel that it is too difficult to annotate the data.

Fig. 5. Original UI for the annotation task to decide on a sound source type via the software keyboard

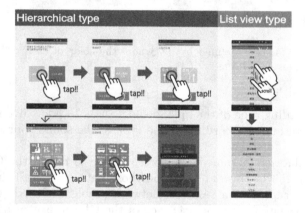

Fig. 6. Screenshots of new UI for selecting the appropriate sound-source class from the candidates

To overcome this problem, as demonstrated in Figure 6, we developed a new UI that enables users to simply select an appropriate sound source class from a list prepared in advance. In the new sound source annotation interface, we provided two types of UIs: a hierarchical type and a list view type. Table 1 compares the two types of UIs. When using the hierarchical type UI, the user can choose a class via touch panel operations by tracing a hierarchical tree of sound-source classes. We believe that the system can support step-by-step operations to choose the sound source, although the user does not know the entire class structure. In the list view, the candidate sound sources are arranged, and each user can select a sound source by scrolling the candidate list to the appropriate choice.

Table 1. Our basic design of the sound source annotation UI

Hierarchical type
Hierarchical tree view of the sound source classes structured in groups. The names of the groups with the higher level of abstraction are applied to ensure diversity of environmental sounds during recordings. To reduce the complexity of the operation, the depth of the hierarchy is limited to four levels.

List view type
A long list is presented without the candidates of the sound source class being separated. Users can select a sound source by scrolling the list displayed in alphabetical order. The abstracted groups are not directly introduced for sound-source class candidate selection.

Table 2. List of sound sources used in the annotation experiment

Large-number classes	Small-number classes
train, car, railway crossing, TV, voice, station, crossing, store, bird, rain.	cat, electronic calculator, piano, river, sea, ship, warning, lighter, stairs, telephone.

To evaluate our new UI, we developed a prototype application that runs on Android smartphones. Ten participants attempted to choose the appropriate class of a sound source after they listened to environmental sounds under the condition that the participants did not know the situations in which the sounds were recorded. The test samples for each participant were the 20 sounds listed in Table 2. Among them, 10 samples were extracted from the sound-source classes with a large number of sounds recorded, and 10 samples belonged to the classes that had only a small number of sounds recorded.

We counted the number of steps (the number of screen taps) and the elapsed time required to determine the class after listening to the audio signal. Tables 3 and 4 show the elapsed times and the number of steps, respectively.

From these results, it can be seen that the times required for decisions using the list view type are longer than those for the hierarchical type. We believe that the participants were able to imagine the source of the sounds by listening to the acoustic signals. When looking for a candidate from the list, the participants tended to carefully choose the class over time. On the other hand, in the hierarchical type UI, it is possible that the time required to browse classes was shorter because only a limited number of candidates was displayed on one screen.

Because in the list view type, a class can only be selected via the scroll operation, the number of steps is shown as approximately one. In the hierarchical type, the number of steps for the 10 classes with the highest number of samples is less than that for the small-number classes. For the 10 classes with the smallest number of samples, we observed that the participants could not identify the origin of the sound source while looking for a suitable class.

Table 3. Elapsed time [s] (Average)

	Large-number class	Small-number class
List view type	17.49	19.50
Hierarchical type	13.64	18.46

Table 4. Number of steps (Average)

	Large-number class	Small-number class
List view type	1.13	1.06
Hierarchical type	5.04	6.40

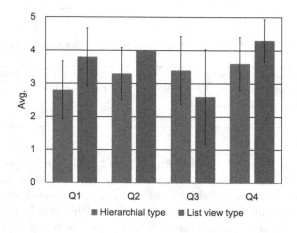

Fig. 7. Results of the five-grade evaluations of UI design

Next, we conducted five-grade evaluations in which we interviewed the participants. The following questions were posed to the participants:

Q1: Did you hesitate in selecting a class? (1: many times – 5: no)

Q2: Did the selected class match your image? (1: no match at all – 5: almost matched)

Q3: Were your operations affected by the visibility of the UI? (1: poor visibility, difficult – 5: good visibility, easy operation)

Q4: Could you operate using only the preliminary instructions? (1: very difficult – 5:very easy)

Q5: Which UI design did you prefer? ("Hierarchical type" or "List view type")

Evaluation results for Q1 to Q4 are shown in Figure 7. The bars display the averaged values from 10 participants, where the left bars are the results for the hierarchical type UI, and the right bars are for the list view type UI. Standard deviations are also indicated in the error bars.

In Q1 and Q2, the list view type UI received a high evaluation. Because the sound source classes presented in the hierarchical type are abstracted, the user may not be able to conceive of the lower layer classes. Using the list view type UI, however, the entire list of sound sources can be viewed. Therefore, the system did not give room to allow guessing so the participants hesitated to select one. We obtained high evaluations for the hierarchical type UI via Q3. The results demonstrate that the hierarchical type UI that reduces the amount of information simultaneously displayed on one screen is easy to see. We believe that the reason for the high evaluation of list view type in Q4 is the fact that the list view type UI has a familiar design that is similar to that of the smartphone apps the participants use on a daily basis.

In Q5, six participants chose the list view type UI, whereas four preferred the hierarchical type UI. Consequently, we concluded that there is no significant difference between both UIs in terms of convenience. In order to utilize the advantages of both types, we implemented an annotation UI that can be switched between both types of UIs.

4   Experimental Collection of Sounds in Real Environments

This section describes a small-scale environmental sound collection experiment performed preliminarily by using a modified application, which includes an annotation UI that can be switched between the list view type and the hierarchical type UIs. The experiment conducted asked that each participant select the sound source class without knowing the recording status of the environmental sound in Section 3. In addition to the information from the ear, visual information from the eye gives the impression of change in environmental sounds. In this study, we conducted trial tests of the improved application in the real world in order to investigate the affect of visual information. However, this experiment was small scale because it was only a preliminary investigation. Large-scale experiments with crowdsourcing will be conducted in the future.

The participants in the experiment were 11 students who are Android device users. The experiment was conducted over a period of three days, starting February 3, 2014. We asked the participants to record the environmental sounds they encountered in everyday life. However, we did not set a quota on the number of collections per individual. As a result, we were able to collect 79 environmental sound datasets.

In addition, we conducted interviews with the participants after this experiment. We asked the following questions in the interview:

Q1: Were your operations affected by the visibility of the UI? (1: poor visibility, difficult – 5: good visibility, easy operation)

Q2: Were you able to easily operate the app? (1: very difficult – 5: very easy)

Q3: Did you hesitate in selecting a class? (1: many times – 5: no)

Q4: Did the selected class match your image? (1: no match at all – 5: almost matched)

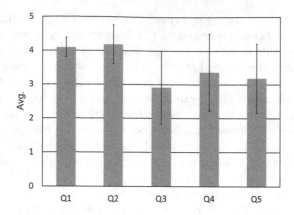

Fig. 8. Results of the five-grade evaluations in the environmental sound collection experiment

Q5: Do you think that the candidate sound sources displayed were appropriate?
(1: not appropriate – 5: appropriate)

The results obtained are depicted in Figure 8, where the evaluation values given from the 11 participants are averaged. We obtained evaluation values greater than four for the items visibility (Q1) and operability (Q2). The validity of the improved UI was also confirmed. The evaluation value for both Q3 and Q4 was approximately three. This is a result of a tendency that is different from the similar entry in Section 3. The cause of this difference lies in the fact that the participants were finding the target sound source that they would record as environmental sounds by themselves. Because the participants in Section 3 heard environmental sounds collected in advance, they could not have any material for determining the status of the peripheral as visual information. Therefore, the annotation task was actually one of guessing the sound source while viewing the candidates presented on the screen. In contrast, this sound collection experiment required that the participants have a concrete image of the sound source in order to perform the annotation task to determine the appropriate sound source class. We believe that if the sound source the participants expected could not be found on the screen, it became a worrying factor in determining the class.

In addition, we investigated the impression participants had of the collection tasks on the basis of a single representative word from each person. We presented the 14 words listed in Table 5 to express the impression (impression words) for them, and asked that they each select the word closest to the impression they felt. The set of impression words comprise seven positive words and seven negative words. Multiple answers for the impression words were allowed.

Figure 9 shows the number of times each impression word was selected. As can be seen in the figure, in many cases, participants had positive impressions associated with the use of our app. These results play an important role because keeping participants motivated is essential when crowdsourcing is used.

Table 5. 14 impression words in Japanese and English (translated)

Positive	楽しい (enjoyable)	心地よい (comfortable)	おもしろい (amusing)	めずらしい (unusual)
	新しい (novel)	賢い (smart)	さりげない (casual)	
Negative	うっとうしい (depressing)	難しい (difficult)	いいかげん (irresponsible)	なぞ (ambiguous)
	つらい (miserable)	恥ずかしい (ashamed)	めんどう (troublesome)	

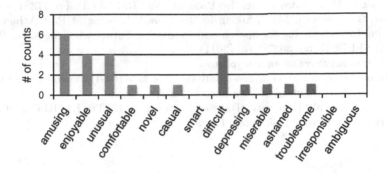

Fig. 9. Results for impression word evaluation in the environmental sound collection experiment

However, four participants had a "difficult" impression; therefore, further improvements to the system are necessary.

5   Conclusions and Future Work

This paper described an overview of our environmental collection system focusing on a method for utilizing the crowdsourcing approach using Android devices. We developed a touch panel UI for the annotation task by selecting an appropriate class of a sound source. The annotation system is composed of two types of UIs: a hierarchical type and a list view type.

We are planning to perform field tests of our improved sound collection system based on the crowdsourcing approach. We hope to involve many participants that are accustomed to working on advanced UIs to conduct the annotation work efficiently in our experiments. To realize this, we believe it is necessary to consider introducing shortcut and search functions to the sound source annotation UI.

Acknowledgments. This study was partially supported by the Ministry of Education, Science, Sports and Culture, Grant-in-Aid for Scientific Research (KAKENHI), Japan. We greatly appreciate the support provided by Mr. Takahiko Tsuda and Mr. Kyosuke Nakanishi (graduates of our laboratory).

References

1. http://www.android.com/
2. Freund, Y., Schapire, R.E.: A Decision-Theoretic Generalization of On-Line Learning and an Application to Boosting. Journal of Computer and System Sciences 55(1), 119–139 (1997)
3. Lee, A., et al.: Noise Robust Real World Spoken Dialogue System using GMM Based Rejection of Unintended Inputs. In: Proc. of INTERSPEECH, pp. 173–176 (2004)
4. Parent, G., Eskenazi, M.: Speaking to the Crowd: Looking at Past Achievements in Using Crowdsourcing for Speech and Predicting Future Challenges. In: Proc. of INTERSPEECH, pp. 3037–3040 (2011)
5. http://research.rakuten.co.jp/en/
6. Robinson, D., et al.: The Common Gateway Interface (CGI) Version 1.1. RFC 3875. IETF (Internet Engineering Task Force) (2004)
7. Fielding, R., et al.: Hypertext Transfer Protocol - - HTTP/1.1, RFC 2616. IETF (Internet Engineering Task Force) (1999)

MulDiRoH: An Evaluation of Facial Direction Expression in Teleconferencing on a Multi-view Display System

Shiro Ozawa, Satoshi Mieda, Munekazu Date,
Hideaki Takada, and Akira Kojima

NTT Media Intelligence Laboratories, NTT Corporation, Yokosuka, Kanagawa, Japan
ozawa.shiro@lab.ntt.co.jp

Abstract. We have developed a teleconference system called MulDiRoH (Multi-Directional Representation of Humans). It features the use of a QDA screen, one of the newest multi-view display techniques. A principal benefit of multi-view displays is they can show views of a remote participant from the direction in which the participant's face is pointing. This enables other participants to directly see the face of a remote participant who is actually looking away from them. However, all multi-view display systems share a common problem in that users who stand outside of the center area cannot observe geometrically correct images. To addressthis problem, we propose the use of the perspective transform method. We also evaluate the conveying of a person's facial direction by a communication game for multiple users.

Keywords: Teleconferencing, Multi-view Display, QDA Screen.

1 Introduction

Recent years have seen teleconference system displays that show people in remote places become increasingly important. In connection with such displays, multi-view viewing display systems that provide multiple images in different viewing regions are being developed and are expected to give rise to new systems. Such a system is our goal of our research; Fig. 1 shows an image of it. Since a multi-view display can show the field of view of remote participants from the direction their face is facing, it is especially useful as a display for showing multiple facial directions in a video conferencing system. This allows participants to look at a remote participant's face directly even though the participant is actually looking away from them.

In order to develop a video conferencing system using a multi-view display, Jones et al. proposed a system using a high-speed rotating mirror and a high-speed projector [1]. This system uses a computer vision technique to acquire a three-dimensional model of the remote user's face. In particular, it applies a pre-determined light pattern to the subject and a camera takes a picture to obtain the pattern. It then puts a texture on the obtained shape and produces an image of the subject. This system has been evaluated quite highly; however, there are some problems with it. First, arranging the

S. Yamamoto (Ed.): HIMI 2014, Part I, LNCS 8521, pp. 525–535, 2014.
© Springer International Publishing Switzerland 2014

Fig. 1. Concept image of our goal

mirror and projector may require considerable work. Second, conversations may be hindered by noise generated from the mirror. Third, using a mirror means it is quite possible the image resolution will decrease over time.

Feldmann et al. proposed a two-on-two-on-two system with a nine-aspect auto- stereoscopic display using a lenticular lens [2]. In this system, six participants sit around a table and each of them is allocated one auto-stereoscopic display from each remote participant. Since the participants' freedom of movement is restricted, however, they cannot get more than four of the nine auto-stereoscopic display views. A computer vision technique is used to acquire a three-dimensional model of the subject, which is then converted into a depth map for the auto-stereoscopic display. This is a good example of combining market products well to achieve teleconferencing. However, the six system users have little freedom of movement because of the restrictions on where they can sit. Another problem is the two-on-two-on-two limitation.

Many depth cameras such as Kinect [3] have been developed for teleconference systems, and are able to capture the human body as a three-dimensional model. With this technique, however, there is a domain where acquisition of form or depth is difficult theoretically. Therefore, more deterioration will be seen in the reconstructed image than for displayed images taken with common cameras. Moreover, a person's expression will be spoiled.

On the other hand, Otsuka et al. have proposed a system in which a camera is installed for every participant and takes a photograph of that participant, the background is removed so that only the person's image is extracted, and the image is displayed on a back projection type display [4]. A rotary motor is built into a projection screen and it is assumed that rotating the screen dynamically makes it possible to reinforce transfer of the facial direction of a photographic subject according to the direction acquired from the picture. Although image communication systems are currently used to express actual conversation situations, this system creates a new possibility of calling it reinforcing the expression of a person's facial direction by rotating a physical screen. In the system, no image processing other than background removal is added to the pictured person's image, but the displayed images have the image quality of a camera, and the images are not degraded by the rotation of the screen.

In an attempt to solve the problems of achieving sufficient image quality and communicating the facial directions of users, we have developed a system we call "MulDiRoH" (Multi-view Display system for Representation of Humans). It features a novel multi-view display we developed using a Quantized Diffusion Angle (QDA) screen [5].

In this paper we describe the system and our use of a communication game for multiple users to evaluate how well the system conveys a person's facial direction.

2   MulDiRoH

2.1   System Overview

The MulDiRoH system is basically classified as a rear projection display system and uses a QDA screen for the projection screen, three projectors, and three cameras for taking images of remote users. The QDA screen diffuses multiple, different images created by projectors at different directions to quantized diffusion angle regions, yielding multiple, different images in different viewing areas with no limit placed on the distance from the screen. Fig. 2 diagrams a MulDiRoH prototype system and Fig. 3 shows photographic views of the system.

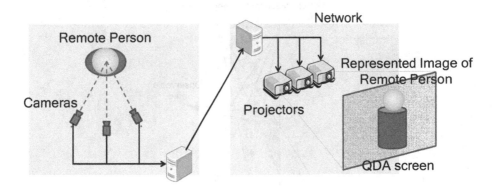

Fig. 2. Diagram of MulDiRoH

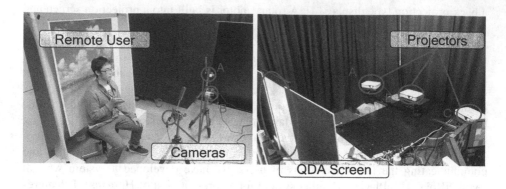

Fig. 3. Photographic Views of MulDiRoH

2.2   QDA Screen

A typical example of a multi-view display is a triple-view LCD using a liquid crystal TFT-panel and a parallax barrier as reported by Takaya [6]. With this method, however, increasing the number of viewing directions beyond four is quite difficult because of the attendant decrease in resolution and the requirement for high alignment accuracy in production. The method also has a very shallow viewing area because of the diamond shape of its individual viewing areas as shown by A, B, and C in Fig. 4. Outside of these diamond-shape areas, a mixture of individual images is likely to generate a cross-talk problem.

In an attempt to solve these problems, we have developed the MulDiRoH system featuring the use of a QDA screen. This screen diffuses the different multiple images created by projectors at different directions to quantized diffusion angle regions,

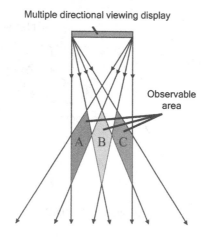

Fig. 4. Problem with diamond-shape areas [5]

which yields multiple (different) images in different viewing areas with no limit placed on the distance from the screen (Fig.5). This type of screen has three special features. First, the number of viewing areas can be increased by changing the lenticular lens parameters. Second, there is no need to install the projector within strict distance limits. This is because the screen's wide range of observable areas enables it to easily provide multi-view displays if the projector is set up within a range outside of that needed to quantize and radiate incident light. Third, its wide observable area enables images to be viewed further from given distances without restriction, though it is necessary for viewers to move somewhat away from the screen to see the images.

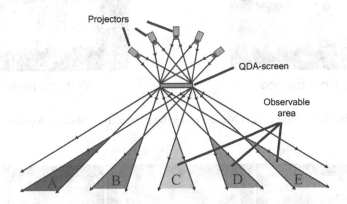

Fig. 5. QDA screen's observable areas [5]

2.3   Perspective Transform Method

All multi-view display systems share a common problem in that users who stand outside of the center area cannot observe geometrically correct images. Therefore, they cannot receive the correct facial direction of remote users. To solve this issue, we propose using the perspective transform method. Using this method, users can observe images of remote users that look as if the latter were standing right at the front of the display. Fig. 6 shows an example result obtained using the perspective transform method. The pictures displayed in a red lattice show the results for the right viewing area. The left side picture shows the original view and the right side one shows that obtained with our method. It can be seen that the pictures' horizontal sides are parallel and their displayed areas are rectangular.

Fig. 7 shows the results of representing a remote user from each of the three viewing areas. In each of the views the user's gaze is directed to the center viewing area. The results confirm that the system can accurately represent a remote user's facial direction. Since this enables the observer to feel that the remote user is looking directly at him/her, it allows the two persons to speak together in a natural manner.

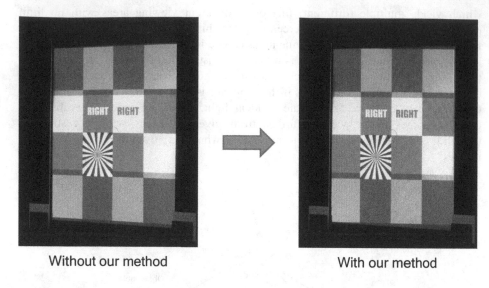

Without our method   With our method

Fig. 6. Example result obtained using the perspective transform method

Left area   Center area   Right area

Fig. 7. Views produced by MulDiRoH

3   Experiment

3.1   Design and Experimental Conditions

To evaluate the MulDiRoH system's effectiveness in expressing facial directions, we designed a communication game for users and asked them to play it. In this game, all players have to pay attention to the direction of other player's action while playing. The procedure for the game is illustrated in Fig. 8. A game set/session starts with four users standing in a circle facing each other. One of the users (the "start" player) points to another, who becomes the "first" player (STEP 1). That player then points to another, who becomes the "second" player (STEP 2). Then the two persons flanking the second player make a prearranged pose to end the set (STEP 3). All moves must be made at rapid-fire speed. If one of the players makes a mistake or stops the flow of the game, the set/session is over and the next set/session starts with the player at fault becoming the "start" player. The idea of the game is that all the users have to pay close attention to the pointing gestures of the others. A set/session ends when one of the following occurs:

1. The first player does not point to any second player.
2. A player other than the first player points to a second player.
3. One or both of the players flanking the second player do not make the pose.
4. A player other than the players flanking the second player makes the pose.
5. One of the players is too slow in making a pointing gesture or a pose.

Fig.9 shows the flow of the game. One cycle from STEP1 to STEP3 is defined as a "set," and a sequence of sets ending with a failure is defined as a "Session."

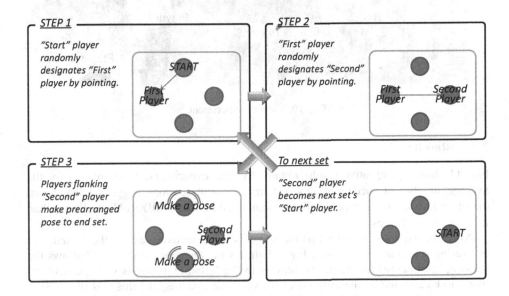

Fig. 8. Game procedure (example)

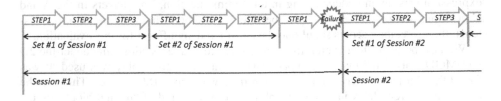

Fig. 9. Flow of the game

We conducted an experiment in which one of the users joined the game from a remote place by using MulDiRoH. Fig. 10 shows a view of users playing the game, with the remote user displayed on the screen. Four players at a time were given the task of playing the game for a three-minute period. They performed this task 12 times, six times using MulDiRoH and six times using a 2D display system for comparison. The remote player A was the "Start" player for each task. A total of 48 persons participated in the experiment.

The remote player "A" on the MulDiRoH

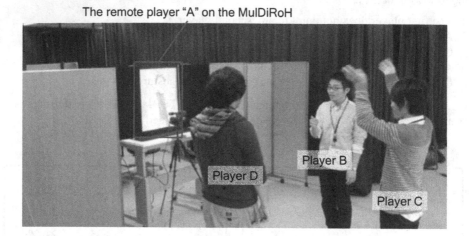

Fig. 10. View of experiment

3.2   Results

Fig. 11 shows quantitative results obtained in the experiment. T-test results for the average number of successful sets and unsuccessful sessions suggested that facial direction information is more easily communicated under MulDiRoH conditions than 2D display conditions.

After the experiment, we asked the subjects to subjectively assess the systems by answering questions about them. Fig. 12 shows the questions and Fig. 13 shows the mean opinion scores for them. The players in the B and D positions were particularly likely to be affected by the differences between the systems, and this was reflected in their scores: 3.9 for MulDiRoH and 2.5 for the 2D display system. This tends to demonstrate the superiority of the MulDiRoH system and it also suggest that the direction expression acts on an understanding in telecommunication. The players in the A and C positions were much less likely to be affected by the differences between the systems; therefore, their scores should not be considered significant for this evaluation.

We also performed an exploratory experiment to gauge reaction time under the 2D and MulDiRoH conditions as compared with that when no display was used. It was found that for the former case the reaction time was about 18% slower. This may be due to an inherent delay in using a display system or a kind of "mental block" on the part of subjects using such a system.

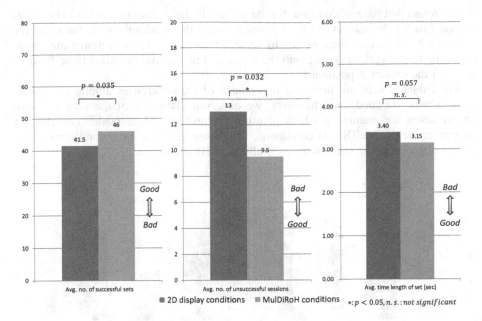

Fig. 11. Quantitative results of experiment

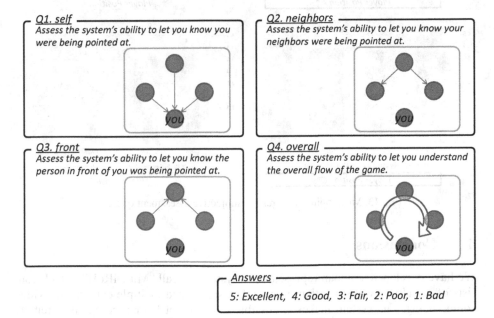

Fig. 12. Subjective assessment questions

We found that the reaction time for the subject in the B position tended to be slower than that for the subject in the D position. Since the conditions were the same for both, we had expected their results to be about the same. The difference may have been due to sunlight streaming into the room and producing an unfavorable field of view for the subject in position B.

The subjects were not informed in advance of the differences among the conditions. Under 2D conditions, however, we observed that some of the subjects were unsure about the manner in which pointing gestures should be made. This did not happen under the MulDiRoH conditions, which suggests that these conditions better enable directions to be transmitted naturally than 2D conditions.

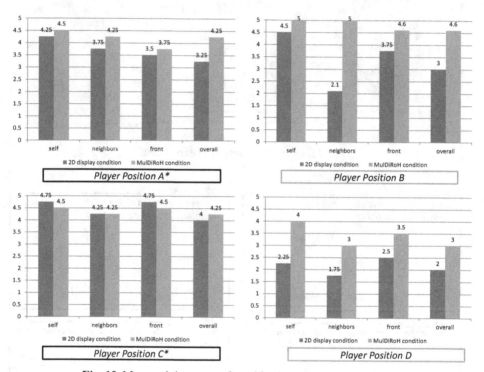

Fig. 13. Mean opinion scores for subjective assessment questions

4   Conclusions

We have developed a human representation system we call "MulDiRoH", which consists of a multi-view display that uses a QDA screen and multiple cameras for video conferencing. The system makes it possible to represent human beings in a remote space with a high degree of presence, because it provides multiple views of facial directions that enable observers to feel that remote users are looking directly at them.

In this paper, we reported an experiment using a communication game designed to evaluate the MulDiRoH system's effectiveness in expressing facial directions.

The results made it clear that giving directivity to images enables communication to progress more smoothly. They also suggested that the communication game progresses more naturally and smoothly under MulDiRoH conditions than the conditions of a 2D display system.

As a subject for future work, we plan to conduct an experiment in simultaneously providing multiple facial directions to a lot of people from persons in a remote place. We will evaluate the results and assess the impact they may have on computer supported cooperative work (CSCW) and on communications in general.

References

1. Jones, A., Lang, M., Fyffe, G., Yu, X., Busch, J., McDowall, I., Bolas, M., Debevec, P.: Achieving eye contact in a one-to-many 3D video teleconferencing system. ACM Trans. Graph. 28(3), Article 64 (2009)
2. Feldmann, I., Waizenegger, W., Atzpadin, N., Schreer, O.: Real-time depth estimation for immersive 3D videoconferencing. In: 3DTV-Conference: The True Vision - Capture, Transmission and Display of 3D Video (3DTV-CON), pp. 1–4, 7–9 (2010)
3. Microsoft Kinect, http://www.microsoft.com/en-us/kinectforwindows/
4. Otsuka, K., Mucha, S.K., Kumano, S., Mikami, D., Matsuda, M., Yamato, J.: A System for Reconstructing Multiparty Conversation Field based on Augmented Head Motion by Dynamic Projection. In: Proceedings of ACM Multimedia 2011, pp. 763–764 (2011)
5. Kawakami, T., Katagiri, B., Ishinabe, T., Uchida, T.: Multiple Directional Viewing Projection Display Based on the Incident-Angle-Independent Diffusion-Angle-Quantizing Technology. In: Proc. IDW 2010, pp. 1479–1482 (2010)
6. Takaya, T.: A Dual Directional Viewing LCD and A Triple Directional Viewing LCD. Sharp Technical Journal 96, 21–23 (2007)

Increasing Information Auditability
for Social Network Users

Alexandre Pinheiro[1], Claudia Cappelli[1], and Cristiano Maciel[2]

[1] Universidade Federal do Estado do Rio de Janeiro - UNIRIO, Rio de Janeiro, Brazil
{alexandre.pinheiro,claudia.cappelli}@uniriotec.br
[2] Universidade Federal de Mato Grosso - UFMT, Mato Grosso, Brazil
cmaciel@ufmt.br

Abstract. This paper sets out the challenge of how to provide information auditability to citizens regarding social networks. The aim is to discuss the issues concerning information published on social networks and specifically to describe how to verify the veracity of this information. It is based on the idea that it urgent improvement of interface requirements is necessary for this kind of software to provide users with ways to account for, validate, verify and control information. The paper reports the construction of a catalog of characteristics for information auditability in social networks. An exploratory study suggests mechanisms that can be used to implement these characteristics into this kind of software interface. The conclusion presents remarks on challenges and future studies.

Keywords: Auditability, Social Networks, Transparency, and Information Auditability.

1 Introduction

The concept of transparency was strengthened and began to be discussed internationally following initiatives in the public and private sectors. These sectors encourage the provision of information and seek for the participation of society in issues of common interest. To meet the demand for transparency, not only in the governmental area, but also in many areas where transparency is applicable, it is necessary for information systems that connect information senders and receivers to also apply transparency. Therefore, usability, accessibility and credibility of information have become some of the most essential requirements for information systems that aim to support transparency.

The participation of end users in content production on the Internet has impacted the relationship with information because it is no longer only the newspapers, television channels, radios and popular websites that provide mainstream information. . The way we/ interact with information has changed. The content generated by end users is not subjected to the same rules of traditional media. The collaborative and dynamic environment, full of interactions, does not allow us to evaluate information conventionally. The various users who interact with this environment can interpret

S. Yamamoto (Ed.): HIMI 2014, Part I, LNCS 8521, pp. 536–547, 2014.

information available in social networks differently. This information can be modified, lose context and change meaning during the interaction process. What happens when a curious user finds difficulties to use a social network interface and disseminates misinformation? What are the consequences of spreading this misinformation? As an example, we can mention Facebook®, which offers numerous features encouraging the sharing of information [1]. This range of features combined with people's excitement in various social network activities and usability problems can contribute to the spreading of information the content of which has not been evaluated by the user. Offering easy-to-use tools and clean interfaces is a requirement for a good user-system interaction design [2] and it allows the evaluation of information (auditability). Therefore, it contributes to the evolution of the social network and ensures the spreading of correct information.

Auditability is the ability to conduct a critical evaluation of information provided by users. To achieve this goal, information auditability in social network catalog is herein structured according to the settings of the NFR Framework [3]. The construction of this catalog is based on the Transparency Catalog developed by Cappelli [4]. The catalog for information auditability in social networks is composed of characteristics that contribute to achieving the concept of auditability in social networks. The operationalizations and mechanisms arise from the HCI area. They have been defined based on a literature review related to user experience in the use and interaction with web interfaces [2] [5], in the construction of quality systems [6] and in recommendations for best practices defined by international standards [7] [8] [9].

The purpose of this paper is to present this complete catalog to support the evaluation of information auditability in social networks. We hope to help users to distinguish reliable information from information without references, validity or source. Other social networks interested in offering their users the possibility of accessing and sharing reliable information can adopt the suggestions on auditability presented in this work.

2   The Challenge of Information Auditability in Social Networks

It is hard to ensure that conventional approaches to the concept of quality of information fit into a context characterized by interactivity, collaboration and constant symbolic exchanges mediated by the architecture of social networks in which the user starts to behave as an actor that not only uses, but also produces, remakes and qualifies the informational content [10]. When a user wants to upload a photo, the elements displayed by the system must be prepared for the action to be completed successfully. To publish a photo, some elements are required like a field to upload the image, the possibility of adding a heading, the possibility of identifying who is in the photo and other features. All those features are very common in social network software, but mechanisms to guarantee accountability, validity, verifiability, controllability and traceability are very rare. Auditing information in a social network seems to be a difficult job. Some examples, such as the paradox of information relevance from each user's point of view, the usage of colloquial language, information overload and user anxiety considering the dynamism of information [11] have been pointed out.

Social networks group a set of autonomous participants, linking ideas and resources around shared values and interests. Research on social networks evaluates behaviors or opinions of individuals according to the structures in which they are inserted. In these studies, the units of analysis are not the individual attributes like class, age, gender, but the set of relations that individuals establish through their interactions [12]. In social networks, users share the same space and are seeking to interact, share opinions, preferences and interests in various subjects. The diversity and large audience as well as the low segmentation make social networks spaces where each can publish without commitment to the truth. According to Lee [13], unverified and unclear information is daily broadcasted on the Internet. In his research he mentioned, as an example, a hoax that circulated during 2012 about the fact that former U.S. President Abraham Lincoln had registered a patent for Facebook in 1845. With an image of a supposed old newspaper and some elaborated history, in less than 2 days the link posted on Facebook containing the false news had already 16,000 Facebook "likes" and a lot of people believing that the prank was a real historical fact.

2.1   Related Work

Some related studies were visited. Most of them recognize the lack of information credibility in social networks as a big problem. Budak et al. [14] recognize the problem of the spread of misinformation in social networks and studied a way to decrease the number of people who believe in incorrect information. The research describes the use of prediction algorithms to verify the network nodes that can be affected by inaccurate information and then disseminate appropriate information to minimize the effects of misinformation for users connected by these nodes. His point is to deliver quality information before the user accesses some content without credibility, preventing the adoption and spreading of "bad information".

Vedder [15] analyzed misinformation through the Internet with an ethical and epistemological approach, highlighting the consequences of the use of unreliable information found on the web. An example used to show the misinformation problem is the adoption of pseudoscientific information by Internet users to determine a health care treatment. The decisions based on this kind of information can have consequences for the user's life. The survey also reports the use of inaccurate information for educational purposes that may harm the already established truths. The incorrect information may be dangerous to the receiver and is more dangerous when it reaches other people due the spreading capacity of the Internet. The suggested solutions to the problem of misinformation through the Internet are presented as strategies. The first strategy is based on the development of the user's ability to evaluate information. Training users to identify elements that can help to define the information's degree of credibility can implement this strategy. Another strategy mentioned is related to some factors such as disclosing the source of the published information and the existence of an institution with a recognized reputation which ratifies the information. The use of credibility-conferring systems can help to enforce these strategies so they can have a global reach.

Flanagin and Metzger [16] showed that people increasingly rely on Internet and web-based information although it is potentially inaccurate and biased. They asked 1,041 people whether they verified Internet information before using it. Overall, respondents reported they considered Internet information as credible as that obtained from television, radio, and magazines. Credibility among the types of information sought, such as news and entertainment, varied across media channels. Respondents said they rarely verified web-based information, which can be a great problem because most of these respondents all received information as being true.

In all these studies we can see the concern and need for information auditability circulating on the Internet mostly on social networks. Some have only cited the problem, others presented solutions but none of them defined mechanisms to effectively implement auditability in social networks. This paper seeks to systematize the implementation of these mechanisms.

3 A Catalog for Information Auditability in Social Networks

With the increase of transparency, social networks can be more auditable. Cappelli [4] defined the concept of transparency. This concept was modeled as a catalog with five degrees. All of them composed of a set of characteristics. The union of those characteristics contributes to transparency and represents the Transparency Catalog. The five degrees are: i) Accessibility (access to the information), ii) Usability (use of the information provided), iii) Informativeness (providing information with quality), iv) Understandability (understanding of the processes and information provided), and v) Auditability (ability to conduct a critical examination of the information provided). Each of these five sets of characteristics includes other characteristics, totaling 33 characteristics in all. Auditability is one of these degrees and is composed of accountability, controllability, verifiability, validity, and traceability.

In Software Engineering, catalogs have been used to store features of quality and elements for defining non-functional requirements. Catalogs represent a systematic way to decompose non-functional requirements and are a method to prioritize, operationalize and treat interdependencies between it [3]. Catalogs also gather operationalization, which is a set of practices to be followed in order to put certain characteristics in the desired context. Operationalizations become reality through the implementation of mechanisms.

The Transparency Catalog was created according to the SIG (Softgoal Interdependency Graph) notation. The SIG is a hierarchical structure, where characteristics and types are represented by clouds (softgoals). Softgoals are connected by links of interdependence, where a child softgoal contributes to the achievement of the parent softgoals. A SIG can also show the types of contribution among softgoals. These types of assistance may be BREAK (a negative contribution sufficient to prevent the top characteristic from being met), HURT (a partially negative contribution where the top characteristic is not met), UNKNOWN (it's unclear whether the contribution is negative or positive), HELP (partial positive contribution to meeting the top characteristic) and MAKE (a positive contribution sufficient for the top feature to be met).

3.1   Information Auditability in Social Networks Catalog construction

As previously stated, a catalog is composed of chacteristics, operationalizations and implementation mechanisms. Our approach to building the catalog of information auditability in social networks is based on Transparency and HCI areas. First, to identify the characteristics each of the 33 characteristics of the transparency catalog [4] was analyzed.

In the transparency catalog, the characteristic of *accountability* is defined as the ability to inform the reason for something. The importance of accountability to information auditability in social networks is related to the necessity of providing information about its operation, operation of their tools, guidance on how users should proceed in a situation (troubleshooting) and presentation of questions and answers. The environment of social networks should allow users to guide other users who have doubts about interaction and use of social networking as a whole. The characteristic of *controllability* is defined as the ability to control. We chose this characteristic due to its relationship with user control, what users are doing and the information they are accessing. We can make important inferences from analyzing actions, social presence, reputation and influencing the skills of a user. The *traceability* characteristic is defined as the ability to follow the development of an action or the construction of information. Traceability considers the changes and the justifications of the information transformation and it directly helps with the tasks related to audits once information is extremely changeable in a collaborative environment such as social networks. Tracking a page or a user that started spreading of a piece of information and analyzing the sources of this information are necessary resources to ensure auditable activities. Traceability can be an effective method for gathering data from users and can be used to support analysis of how users are using the system and what they are achieving [5]. Besides helping in transparency, the tracking of user information allows the analysis of their goals and actions. This kind of evaluation by users is a characteristic that web applications should implement to follow human-computer interaction international standards [7] [8] [9]. Another characteristic that contributes to auditability is *verifiability*. This characteristic is related to the necessary ability to legitimize something. The social network should allow the user to check whether information is legitimate. Some social networks such as Facebook have verified profiles that indicate that a user or a page is exactly what it is said to be. This kind of feature supports the legitimacy of identity. The characteristic of *validity* was also used in our approach because it is related to the ability of testing something by experiment or observation to determine if what is being done is correct. In the analysis of this characteristic, social networks should allow tests to validate the veracity of information. The result of these tests helps to ensure auditability.

In addition to the characteristics required for auditability already specified by the transparency catalog, there are other characteristics of this catalog that also contribute positively towards our goal of increasing information auditing in social networks. Among these characteristics there is adaptability. *Adaptability* is the capacity to change according to circumstances or needs. During the analysis we need to reorganize information in a different way from which it comes to us. The information will be adapted to satisfactorily suit different types of social network users. The ability to use something when it is needed is the definition of *availability*. To analyze information it is necessary to have access to it as well as the implementation mechanisms to validate it. In the case of social networks, availability is also a mainstay of the system itself, otherwise the lack of information would not be an incentive to attract users to use such a network. *Clarity* is an essential characteristic to check information. Some malicious pieces of information spread on social networks take advantage of the lack of clarity to trick users oblivious to the informational content but eager for information sharing. The dynamism of the interaction environment on social networks is another factor that makes the spreading of unclear information easy. The characteristic of *completeness* is related to the ability not to miss elements that the information could or should have. Comprehensive information allows better analysis by the users. The lack of correctness of information strengthens the need for tools that support the concept of auditability. The characteristic of *correctness* is related to the ability to provide information free of errors. *Composability* is the ability to construct information with different partitions. To audit information it is necessary to make inferences between existing data from the information and other gathered data. The characteristic of *dependability* is related to the unfolding of information. To evaluate information we need to know about the relationships of each part to the whole. When we share information, it should provide knowledge about all other parties involved in the process. Information with *extensibility* contributes substantially to auditability. In social networks information is often published without detail, which complicates its verification and validation. The characteristic of *decomposability* is related to the capability of partitioning something. During an audit we may need to split the information into smaller pieces and by doing this we can carefully evaluate each piece of information. The characteristic of *uniformity* is defined as the capacity to maintain a unique form. When information is uniformly provided it makes verification tasks easy and allows the user to make a relationship between how the information is presented and its content. The SIG of Information Auditability in Social Networks is represented in Figure1.

After identifying those characteristics, we applied the foundations and practices of HCI area to define operationalization and implementation mechanisms. The operationalization and implementation mechanisms have been defined based on a literature review related to user experience in the use and interaction with web interfaces [2] [5], in the construction of quality systems [6] and in recommendations for best practices defined by international standards [7] [8] [9].

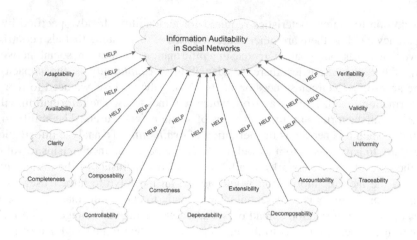

Fig. 1. Information Auditability in Social Networks Characteristics

For each characteristic identified to compose the information auditability in the social networks catalog, we identified elements to operationalize them and mechanisms to implement them in social networks. Table 1 shows some operationalization and implementation mechanisms defined for traceability.

An activity that contributes to misinformation in social networks is link sharing (URLs) together with unreliable stories, usually brought from outside the social network. These kinds of posts are spams, hoaxes and biased news that trick many users.

Table 1. Operationalization and implementation mechanisms of traceability

Traceability	
Operationalizations	Implementation Mechanisms
1)Identification of the origin, availability and security of the published URLs	• Check availability of the URL • Show the original URL • Emphasize Secure URLs (HTTPS)
2)Show Metadata from URL information	• Allow the URL information preview • Make hashtags from keywords defined in the metadata of the URL • Check page rank of the URL
3) Preprocessing the URL	• Apply web crawlers to analyze the construction and content of the website • Check if the website was developed according to web standards by reading its code.
4) Identification of nodes in the social network connected to the source of information	• Use reputation systems to validate user or page interaction with information.

An action to curb this type of activity begins with the availability of complete information about the spreaded URL, tracing its origin and allowing the user to make a comparative analysis with the post that contains the suspicious URL. In social networks, URLs must be accessible and the system needs to ensure this, maintaining its content up to date to enable the traceability of information and knowing the URL source. One way to do this is automating scripts such as web spiders, which test the links available in the environment. Another way can be through collaborative features using feedback from users on broken links or a links that represent a threat (e.g. a suspicious download). It is important that the user be able to refine the system by giving his opinion about the operation.

A common practice in social networks is the use of redirected or shortened links that do not allow viewing of the true URL. This makes it difficult to trace the origin of information and to analyze the URLs using this type of practice. A possible implementation is to show the original URL. Showing the full link also helps in users' direct memory retrieval. When the user knows the URL, he can make a mental association between the content of the website, where the URL leads to and the information containing or surrounded by the URL [5]. Another action that can be done is highlighting secure URLs to increase user safety because the link is already validated and authenticated. The choice of browsing through secure URLs should be displayed whenever a website presents this possibility.

By reading metadata from URLs published or recommended in social networks, the system can show information about the website before users access the link. Users will have the opportunity to evaluate the type of information they will encounter when accessing the link. When a website is built according to web standards there is concern on the part of the developer with the usability and the end users. Unreliable websites with dubious intentions and supporting spam, viruses, false information and all sort of unwanted content are normally developed without following web standards and do not show quality features. Another way to use the information found in metadata of websites is related to the use of the meta element called keywords. Meta elements are machine parsable and one of them is involves using keywords that define the content of the website. The characteristic of explicit indexing of keywords metadata can be associated with features of tagging. Tags represent terms related to information and thier use can help users to link information from different sources with the same content. With a variety of information related to the same content, the users can analyze how the information was constructed and check for characteristics that add value and credibility to it. We can also use indexing systems like Google's Page Rank that evaluate URLs according to the quantity and quality of links pointing to it. A website with a large number of links pointed at it has a positive contribution when we analyze its reliability. Although the analysis of metadata content helps with information evaluation, a website can still be manipulated to trick users and support misinformation. To make a deep evaluation of the content of a website we can submit the URLs posted on social networks to a crawler. Crawlers can visit webpages and trace the links on those pages. They will analyze each link traced and collect data about those websites. With the information gathered by the crawler, we can do a comparative analysis and check the information spread with the content of the website.

To improve the quality and to check credibility of information, social networks have a native characteristic, which is their collaborative capability. The collaboration capability allows network members to evaluate information. In the case of a positive consensus on the content, source and other aspects, individuals will have a reliability gain in the information trustability. To implement this feature as traceability operationalization some behaviors must be observed. Individuals can transform information in social networks and even original content can be turned into misinformation. Reputation systems can help to solve problems that happen when a large number of users interact with information, facilitating content creation and consumption. An example of reputation system that can be used in social networks relies on a chronological analysis of user contributions to information, increasing or decreasing reputation whenever new contributions are made [17].

3.2   Prototyping Implementation Mechanisms

This section shows some prototypes to demonstrate how the ideas proposed in this paper can be implemented. Imagine you access your news feed in a social network and someone places a piece of news. In general this post will contain a text and a link to the source of the news. Following the approach presented in this paper, by means of the mechanisms suggested in Table 1, the piece of news could have the format presented in Figure 2, where the numbers respectively represent: 1) The title of the URL retrieved from metadata of the website; 2) the title of the URL retrieved from metadata of the website; 3) A dialog box for user feedback about the link or any factor that could indicate problems with the information, such as broken or suspicious links; 4) Page Rank according to indexing and linking system; 5) Friends of the user who are interacting with the information and their reputation; 6) Tags automatically generated from the reading of the metadata keywords.

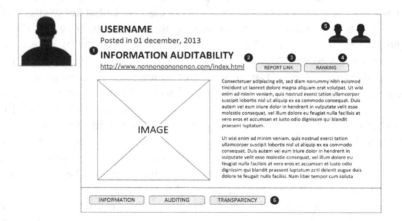

Fig. 2. An example of traceability mechanisms on a social network post

In another situation, imagine you are accessing a tag (Figure 2) about some content, for example auditability. When selecting a tag you can see your friends' list and all those who interacted with associated information based on social search. Your level of relationship and knowledge about their friends will help in the exchange and evaluation of information of some content. The amount of interactions with related information would be shown above your friend's picture as presented in Figure 3.

Misinformation and lack of security in navigation in social networks are normally associated with unknown, misunderstood or suspicious external links spread in the system. These kinds of URLs are accessed by users who don't know what the content of those links is. Figure 4 presents a feature that provides a preview based on pre-processing contents of external links that will help the users to evaluate if the website has the information it claims to have and if it is safe. Anxious users that access links and information without any concern are preferred targets of actions that reinforce the spreading of misinformation.

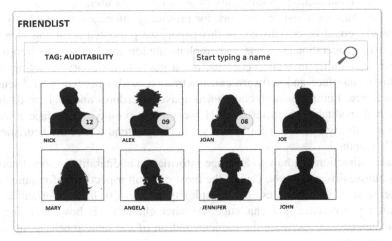

Fig. 3. An example of relation between your friends and information interaction

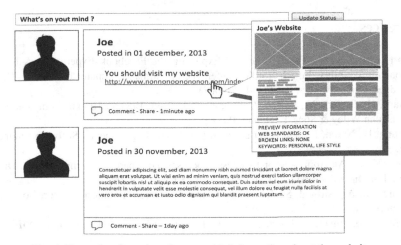

Fig. 4. Example of preview feature with information about the website

4   Conclusion

In this paper, we describe and demonstrate the construction of a catalog of characteristics for information auditability in social networks. The need for information auditability follows the current demands on transparency, especially in social networks, where everyone can post information.

The concept formalization seems to be an important step to achieve information auditability in social network. To formalize the information auditability in a social network concept, a set of characteristics, operationalization and implementation mechanisms were organized into a catalog from which design decisions could be taken.

The interface prototypes presented in this paper show that the catalog may lead to interfaces designed with more features that allow audit information. They also illustrate that the use of cited mechanisms is possible. The resulting interface has characteristics that should facilitate auditability by social network users.

The next challenges and future work for providing information auditability in social networks could be envisioned. In this paper, we presented a catalog identifying characteristics, operationalizations and implementation mechanisms to improve information auditability in social networks, but a guide is necessary to define how to apply this to interface and software construction. It is also necessary to discuss the target audience. Future research could encompass procedures and tools to design interfaces with auditable characteristics. However, the prototype interface must first undergo a usability inspection for which we initially intend to use the heuristic evaluation [18] method.

Research directions on how to leverage information auditability in social networks could comprise different ways. One of the most difficult aspects in information auditing is being sure about sources. The complexity and cost to have information about information provenience is a challenge. Another challenge is how to define some interface standards to facilitate the implementation of the same mechanisms making software auditable.

References

1. Hart, J., Ridley, C., Taher, F., et al.: Exploring the Facebook Experience: A New Approach to Usability. In: 5th Nordic Conference on Human-Computer Interaction: Building Bridges, Lund, Sweden, pp. 471–474 (2008)
2. Sharp, H., Rogers, Y., Preece, J.: Interaction Design: Beyond Human-Computer Interaction. John Wiley & Sons, England (2007)
3. Chung, L., Nixon, B., Yu, E., et al.: Non-functional Requirements. Software Engineering (2000)
4. Cappelli, C.: An Approach for Business Processes Transparency Using Aspects. Dissertation, Pontifícia Universidade Católica do Rio de Janeiro (2009)
5. Blandford, A., Attfield, S.: Interacting with information. Synthesis Lectures on Human-Centered Informatics 3, 1–99 (2010)
6. Software Enginnering. Product Quality, Part 1: Quality Model. NBR ISO/IEC 9126-1:2003, Brazil

7. Ergonomics of Human-system Interaction, Part 151: Guidance on World Wide Web User Interfaces. ISO 9241-151:2008(E), Switzerland
8. Ergonomics of Human-system Interaction, Part 210: Human-centered Design for Interactive Systems. ISO 9241-210:2010(E), Switzerland
9. Software engineering. Software Product Quality Requirements and Evaluation (SQuaRE). Guide to SQuaRE. ISO/IEC 25000:2005(E), Switzerland
10. Assis, J., Moura, M.: A Qualidade da Informação na Web: Uma Abordagem Semiótica. Revista Informação & Informação 16(3), 96–117 (2011)
11. Agarwal, N., Yiliyasi, Y.: Information Quality Challenges in Social Media. In: 15th International Conference on Information Quality, Arkansas, USA (2010)
12. Marteleto, R.: Análise de Redes Sociais – Aplicação nos estudos de transferência da informação. Programa de Pós-Graduação em Ciência da Informação UFRJ/ECO (2001)
13. Lee, N.: Misinformation and Disinformation. Facebook Nation, pp. 103–113. Springer, New York (2013)
14. Budak, C., Agrawal, D., El Abbadi, A.: Limiting the Spread of Misinformation in Social Networks. In: 20th International Conference on World Wide Web, Hyderabad, India (2011)
15. Vedder, A.: Misinformation through the Internet: Epistemology and Ethics. Ethics and the Internet, 125–132 (2001)
16. Flanagin, A.J., Metzger, M.J.: Perceptions of Internet Information Credibility. Journalism & Mass Communication, 515–540 (Quarterly September 2000)
17. De Alfaro, L., Kulshreshtha, A., Pye, I., et al.: Reputation Systems for Open Collaboration. Communications of the ACM, 81–87 (2011)
18. Nielsen, J.: 10 Usability Heuristics for User Interface Design (1995), http://www.nngroup.com/articles/ten-usability-heuristics/ (accessed November 10, 2013)

A Collaboration Support Tool for Multi-cultural Design Team Based on Extended ADT Model

Hidetsugu Suto[1], Patchanee Patitad[1], and Namgyu Kang[2]

[1] Muroran Institute of Technology, Muroran, Japan
[2] Future University Hakodate, Hakodate, Japan
info@sdlabo.net

Abstract. In design field, collaboration is a crucial key method which leads to widen conceptual design idea. Collaboration helps us to share our knowledge together and concert idea in a design process. We also can share diverse viewpoints among collaborations. In this paper, a collaboration support system which based on extended ADT model, TTS method ADT is proposed. ADT model is a representation model for conceptual design. It is used for grasping artifacts as a communication medium between designers and users. The process of observing, sharing and creating design plans are represented through the extended ADT model. During an observation process, three influential factors: physical factor, emotional factor and cultural factor are observed with diverse viewpoints. Each process is visualized and shared by using TTS method by using visual information such as idea sketch, note and photo. By using this tool, designers in a team can visualize their idea, share it with others, and create novel design plan which based on multi-cultural background. An example of design process with TTS method is given in order to show the efficiency of proposed method.

1 Introduction

A questionnaire survey is one of the most commonly used methods conducted by designers when they try to explore users' opinions and needs. However, it is difficult to investigate the users' potential needs which are not conscious clearly by the users with the questionnaire survey method. Observation is a useful method of a design process to understand users' various types of users' needs. Matsunami et al. [1] emphasized the importance of observation of users' requirements in their daily life. Regarding the importance of observation, Kelly of IDEO [2] has noted "Seeing and hearing with your own eyes and ears is a critical first step in improving or creating a breakthrough product." Kang et al. also have indicated that observation is one of the most powerful methods to find out users' potential needs. Consistent with these previous studies, there are many other studies that discussed roles and values of observations in a design process (especially User Centered Design (UCD) field). However, it has not been known the researches in which the ways to observe, share, and apply the information into the design plans are studied. It is difficult to make use of the collaboration if the results of

S. Yamamoto (Ed.): HIMI 2014, Part I, LNCS 8521, pp. 548–557, 2014.

observation could not share enough in a team. Thus, designers should consider not only relationship between designer side and user side, but also relationship in design team members for creating better design plan. For instance, Kang has produced several international design workshops and has found out that diverse viewpoint in observing process help to discover the users' various needs, which include potential needs [3]. In these workshops, each group consisted of participants who have a different nationality and major. Different nationality could lead to diverse viewpoints from their different experiments. Many new discoveries would be expected on the observation process through diverse viewpoints. Actually, many participants in the design workshops could not conduct an observation and share the observed information effectively. Some groups could obtain rich information from their observation but they could not share and apply the observed information adequately into their design plan. In this paper, a design process supporting method for sharing the observed information with group members and applying the information to create new idea is discussed.

2   Collaboration in Design Process

In designing process, the concept of diverse viewpoints is one of the most important factors which may contribute to create novel idea. Generally, human gains knowledge through experiences. Thus, a team in which each member has diverse experiences should have high possibility to create variable idea. According to James, different viewpoints in an observation are very important in a creative process [4]. Brown and Wyatt [5] have emphasized the importance of observations with multi- disciplinary team in design process. Kiyokawa et al. [6] have reported that personal characteristics influence process of knowledge activation in a creative work. Such diverse viewpoints in an observation process could find out unexpected users' needs. However, the personal viewpoint, which is formed through one's experiences, is hard to change suddenly. In order to expand conceptual idea, collaboration is an approachable key method for facilitating achievement. Collaboration is a process where two or more people work together with sharing their idea. Collaboration leads to widen possibility domain of design solution. Fig. 1 illustrates the basic idea.

In this figure, A, B and C indicate designers who have different backgrounds. Each circle indicates the sets of solutions as an innovation which can be reachable by a person. In this case, A, B, and C have different background, Such as different experiences, different knowledge and different skills respectively. Therefore, the expected outcomes of them are different with individuals, so the sets of reachable solutions are also different. This is a reason that the three circles do not overlap entirely with each other.

Assume the case in which A, B and C cooperate in a design process of C's context. The areas which indicated by white area means normal solution of C while gray color (A and B), mean additional knowledge, we call it prime solution for C. Collaboration helps the designers to share our knowledge together and concert idea in a design process. This situation may lead us to design new idea

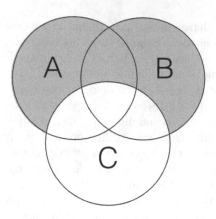

Fig. 1. Reachable solution areas of A, B and C

based on broaden concept domain. The above situation can be described as the following formula:

$$R = (A \cup B \cup C) \tag{1}$$
$$P = (A \cup B) - C \tag{2}$$

R means the set of whole reachable solutions under collaboration of A, B, and C, and P means the set of prime solutions for C. Collaboration manner in which the designers can reach many elements included in P is required for an effective design process.

3   Developing an Education Material

In this section, collaborative design based on the extended ADT model is conceptualized. Furthermore, a collaboration support tool based on the extended ADT model, TTS method, is proposed.

3.1   ADT Model

The Alethic/Deontic/Temporal (ADT) model is a represented model for a conceptual design [7]. It is used for representing an artifact which can be regarded as a communication medium between designers and users. Fig. 2 illustrates the framework of ADT model. This model consists of three layers; base layer, main layer, and top layer. The base layer represents causal relations which are caused from physical laws, mechanisms, and structures. This layer reflects the target user's environments. The top layer represents operational restrictions from designer's intentions. Instructions or warnings from the designers are described on this layer by using modal logic expressions. The main layer represents state transitions caused from operations. The possible operations for the users are

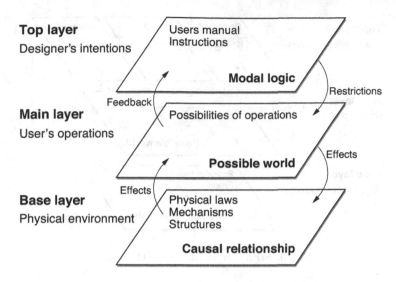

Fig. 2. Structure of ADT model

expressed on this layer. The interaction among the three layers illustrates interaction among designer, operator and environment. This model can be easily expanded to represent other kinds of systems by replacing the physical laws on the base layer with other ones [8].

3.2   Extended ADT Model

Generally, designers have own their own idea. The viewpoint of designers which have different background could be diversified. Therefore, the collaborative design which designers from various nationalities work together may expand possibility domain of design solution. This process let the designers cause awareness for prime solutions which are described in the previous section. To explain such situation, ADT model is extended for represents a concept of collaborative design as shows in Fig. 3.

On the base layer, restriction from environment is described. These restrictions are based on three factors: physical factor, emotional factor and cultural factor. The top layer represents designers' intentions which might be different depend on individual. The outcomes of their work are shown on the main layer. The circles on the main layer indicate the set of possible solution of each designer. As described in section 2, each circle does not overlap completely. With advantage of collaboration, the possibility of design domain is become broaden. Design works should convey designers' intention under restriction from environment. With the extended ADT model, we can understand the effects of collaboration in design process.

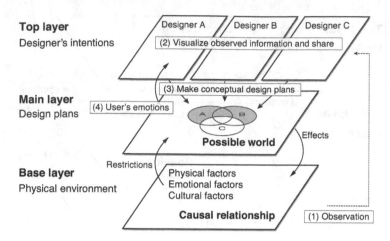

Fig. 3. Structure of extend ADT model

3.3 Collaboration Support Method Based on Extended ADT Model

Generally, conversation (language exchange) is a normal way to share own opinion and idea with others. Sharing with conversation is the handiest way because it does not need any tools. However, the conversation is likely be influenced by time series and is hard to conduct as a simultaneous work. Moreover, for multi-cultural design team, due to each member uses their own language, it is difficult to communicate and share information in the group immediately. Meanwhile, visualization is another promised way to share their opinions and ideas with others. By using the visualized information such as photo, sketch, and note are not affected by time series, is able to be conducted as a simultaneous work in the same time without a common language.

In addition, visualization as meta-recognition is very important in perceiving an idea in a design process [9]. Visualization as meta-recognition is a way to express own notion through the visualization such as idea sketch, note and photo. Beyond just expression tool, these idea-visualization tools are cognition tools as well. In addition, Takano et al. [10] proposed a tool for supporting conception by using the visualized languages of adjective, noun, and mimetic word in a group.

Thus, the authors have proposed a novel information sharing method for design process based on the extended ADT model to achieve information sharing in multi-cultural design team. This method is called TTS (Turning Thinking Sheet) method. The procedure of TTS method proceeds following schemata of the extended ADT model with drawing information on worksheets. Image of worksheet which is used in the method, turning thinking sheet (TTS), is shown in Fig. 4.

The TTS is used in process of observation, idea sharing and creating new design plans. Team members exhibit their own idea on TTS pages as visual information such as idea sketch, note and photo. TTS method is composed

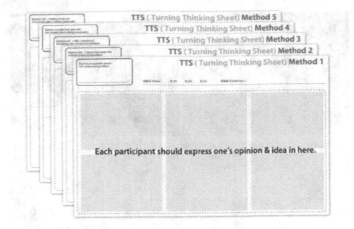

Fig. 4. Image of turning thinking sheet (TTS)

of the following four steps to make effective collaborative design with multi-cultural members:

Step 1 In the observation process, each member records the results of observation by using idea sketch, memo or photo on the first page of TTS.

Step 2 Members categorize observed data according to three factors (physical factor, emotional factor, and cultural factor) and record on the second page of TTS. Then, each member share own observed information via visualized information as meta-recognition approach.

Step 3 All members act in concert to sketch out conceptual design which fulfill the users' needs on the third page of TTS.

Step 4 On the forth page of TTS, members explain in which how users feel when users used their designed work. Every member has to show own opinion, experience, and idea on each TTS page and deliberate own TTS pages to all member in their team.

This process is corresponded to the scheme shown in Fig. 3.

4   Case Study

In this section, a design process with TTS method in a multi-cultural design workshop is shown as an example case. This workshop was held in Seoul, South Korea. Team members were students from Japan, China and Korea. The assignment given to the teams was "Eating in Korea." The TTS method was used in observation process, idea sharing process and designing process. Scenes of using TTSs in the workshop are shown in Fig. 5.

Fig. 5. Scenes of using TTSs in a multi-cultural design workshop

4.1   Observation

During the workshop, members instructed to observe cultures of South Korea. They found the following facts: (A) A tourist tries to taste different foods on one's journey; (B) Party with friends or family is always pleasant; (C) Koreans usually share a dish with others and they use chopsticks as utensil in their eating; (D) There are many side dishes in Korean food which, leads to a lot of space on a table are required and chopsticks set across plate of side dish are easy to fall into the table; (E) Sticking chopsticks into the food is considered as rude behavior in Korea.

4.2   Visualization for Sharing

The data from observation process were divided into three parts which are physical factor part, emotional factor part and cultural factor part. Consequently, each member shared own observed information with group member.

For the fact of (C) described in above section, a Japanese member pointed out that Japanese usually do not prefer to use their own chopsticks for share dishes. If the team consisted only Korean members, this idea should not come across because sharing foods with their own chopsticks is quit usual act for Korean. This fact was added on the TTS.

The shared information was generalized and reaaranged. The results of the sharing process are shown in Table 1.

Table 1. Observed information and the factor

Causal factors	Results of observation
Physical factors	(1) Many plates of side dishes need a lot of space on a table.
	(2) Chopsticks set across plate of side dish are easy to fall into the table.
Emotional factors	(3) A tourist tries to taste different foods on one's journey.
	(4) Party with friends or family is always pleasant.
	(5) Some people do not prefer to use own chopsticks for share dishes.
Cultual factors	(6) Koreans share the food with others.
	(7) Koreans use chopsticks in their eating.
	(8) There are many side dishes in Korean food.
	(9) Sticking chopsticks into the food is considered rude behavior in Korea.

4.3 Conceptual Design

After members shared their observed information within a design team, members considered all information together and drawn up design works which fulfills users' need. In this workshop, a team decided to develop an adjustable chopsticks for Korean food party. The rough drawing of the new chopsticks is shown in Fig 6.

The top of the chopsticks are made with magnets. The front parts of the magnets are attached to the right side of each plate. When users take some foods in the side dishes, users just change the top of chopsticks with the front part attached with the dishes. Then, take some side dishes to one's plate. After that, return the front part to the original position.

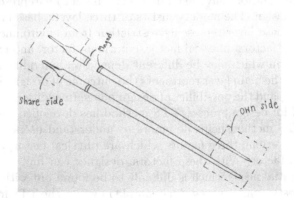

Fig. 6. Sketch of chopsticks for Korean food party

4.4 Considering Users' Emotion

The new chopsticks has been designed in order to help users to share side dishes on the table more convenient. The users can feel sanitary to share the food with others when using these new chopsticks. The new chopsticks are easy to used,

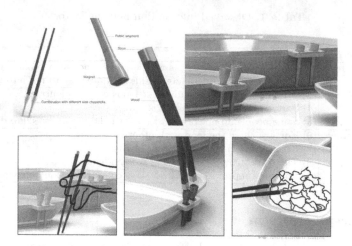

Fig. 7. Conceptual design of adjustable chopsticks

require just small space and do not obstruct the spoon of food. Moreover, with using these chopsticks, the table is become nice and tidy because we do not need to cross chopsticks on the plate of side dishes anymore. The conceptual design of adjustable chopsticks is shown in Fig. 7.

5   Conclusion

In this paper, the authors have extended ADT model for representing process of collaborative design. The model consists of three layers, base layer, top layer, main layer. The base layer represents restriction from environment which was divided into three factors: physical factor, emotional factor, and cultural factor. Designers' intention which may be different depend on individual is represented on the top layer. The main layer represents the outcome of design. The collaborative design can expand the possibility of design plans. In addition, a collaboration support method for design process, TTS method has developed based on extend ADT model. TTS method helps designers to understand users' situations and needs through observing three factors which are physical factor, emotional factor and cultural factor. With these factors, designer can find out users' needs including a potential needs which is difficult to be found out with the approach based on the questionnaire survey. An example in which the TTS method is used for collaboration among design team has been shown. The designers could find a unique design solution, in which multi cultural sense of values are reflected, with the proposed method.

Despite we can see the efficiency of the method, there are additional changes. The first, the format of sheets used in TTS method should be reconsidered. In the current study, a sheet used in each step has same format. Better format for collaboration should be developed. The second, designers have spent too times in first and second steps of TTS method. In order to easy to use, some procedures which took long times should be modified by using electronic technologies, such as digital camera and smart phone.

Acknowledgement. This work was supported by Grants-in-Aid for Scientific Research from the JPSP (No. 23611025 and No. 23653260).

References

[1] Matsunami, H.: Introduction of behavioral observations for business man, pp. 12–24. Kodansha Inc. (2011) (Japanese)
[2] Kelley, T., Littman, J.: The Art of Innovation. Currency books (2001)
[3] Kang, N.: Study on the Value of Sharing and Visualizing Observation Results through Multi-cultural Collaboration, Design Research Society (2012)
[4] James, W.Y.: Technique for Producing Ideas. McGraw-Hill Professional (2003)
[5] Brown, T., Wyatt, J.: Design Thinking for Social Innovation. Stanford Social Innovation Review Winter, 30–35 (2010)
[6] Kiyokawa, S., Washida, Y., Ueda, K., Peng, E.: Can Diverse Information Improve Idea Generation? Cognitive Study 17(3), 635–649 (2010)
[7] Suto, H., Kawakami, H., Katai, O.: A representational model for artifacts based on the modality of operations and states. Trans. of the Society of Instrument and Control Engineers, Series E 3(1), 40–48 (2004)
[8] Suto, H.: Media Biotope: Media Designing Analogous with Biotope. International Journal of Computer Information System and Industrial Management Applications, Series 3, 264–270 (2010)
[9] Suwa, M., Gero, J., Purcell, T.: Unexpected Discoveries and S-invention of Design Requirements. Important Vehicles for Design Process, Design studies, Series 2, 539–567 (2000)
[10] Takano, S., Sato, K., Matsuoka, Y.: Value Growth Design Model Towards an Embodiment of Timeaxis Design. Japan Design Society, Series 58, 68–69 (2011)

Design and Evaluation Methods
and Studies

A Study of the Factors Affecting Product Values and Preferences – Using Vacuum Cleaner as an Example

Wen-chih Chang and Hsiao-ying Tai

National Taiwan University of Science and Technology, Taipei, Taiwan
wchang@mail.ntust.edu.tw

Abstract. In an era of advanced technology and information, products change rapidly and manufacturing techniques continuously improve, thus, consumers have more options when purchasing goods and competition among brands becomes severe. In the market, there are various brands of vacuum cleaners. It is important for the products of different brands with similar functions to stand out in order to attract consumers. If they can have attractive appearance and provide consumers with visual differences, they will trigger consumers' purchase desire. This study treats vacuum cleaners as examples in order to determine the correlation between the actual prices of goods in the market and values and preferences of goods to the participants, as well as the relation between values and preferences according to questionnaire survey. Through in-depth interview, the participants suggested the factors of rising and falling ranks of values and preferences, in comparison to actual prices. Research findings will serve as reference for the development of product design. Several important conclusions are found as reference for the industry and designers.

Keywords: vacuum machine, perceived value, preference, rank difference.

1 Introduction

In an era of advanced technology and information, products change rapidly and manufacturing techniques continuously improve, thus, consumers have more options when purchasing goods and competition among brands becomes severe. In the market, there are various brands of vacuum cleaners. It is important for the products of different brands with similar functions to stand out in order to attract consumers. If they can have attractive appearance and provide consumers with visual differences, they will trigger consumers' purchase desire.

Yutani (1989) suggested that product purchase does not depend on the intrinsic value of goods, but is based on presentation value that shows the intrinsic value. "Intrinsic value" means the value of product life measure. In terms of material goods, it means product value. Intrinsic value can be classified into two parts: material value and function value. "Presentation value" is also called form value. Presentation value includes linguistic and non-linguistic presentation values. Linguistic presentation value includes value of nominal presentation (goods change value by names), value of descriptive presentation (linguistic description of goods, instruction of content, and

S. Yamamoto (Ed.): HIMI 2014, Part I, LNCS 8521, pp. 561–571, 2014.

description of expression). Non-linguistic presentation value means the value produced by elements controlled by vision, hearing, and touch. From the perspective of product design, it means the appearance of goods and modeling elements controlled by designers, which includes size value (units of vision, hearing, and touch), form value, and design value. Sasaki (1991) indicated that most of the value of artificial goods is between Use value and Esteem value. Baxter (1998) proposed that when consumers find products that are highly homogeneous and have similar functions, the value of the goods is the key factor of purchase. Value refers to perceived value, and perception is measured by the degree of value. Industrial designers transform non-linguistic presentation into modeling of products, while function is transformed into structure and interface. Consumers have evaluation of the presentation and form of the cognitive value of goods. An impression of "high-quality goods" or "cheap goods" means the value of product performance for individuals (Liang, 1992). Baxter (1998) suggested that visual modeling of goods is the most basic condition of attraction; in other words, to draw consumers' attention, appearance the products will be the key.

Most people suggest that in the market, regardless of product efficacy or brand, more expensive goods are attractive to consumers by their unique appearance. On the contrary, for cheaper goods, consumers usually have low cognition of appearance value. Hence, in order to explore reality, this study treats vacuum cleaners as examples in order to determine the correlation between the actual prices of goods in the market and values and preferences of goods to the participants, as well as the relation between values and preferences according to questionnaire survey. Through in-depth interview, the participants suggested the factors of rising and falling ranks of values and preferences, in comparison to actual prices. Research findings will serve as reference for the development of product design.

2   Research Method

The study includes two stages: questionnaire survey and in-depth interview.

2.1   Questionnaire Survey

Questionnaire survey steps include the collection of data related to vacuum cleaners, ranking of selling prices of products from top to bottom, screening of questionnaire samples, questionnaire design, and questionnaire survey.

Collection of Data Related to Vacuum Cleaners. First, the researcher collected the data of vacuum cleaners for 18 foreign and domestic brands sold in the market of Taiwan, including Canister, Stick, Upright, and Handy vacuum cleaners. Functions, power, sizes, and prices of goods were collected.

Screening of Questionnaire Samples. 5 samples were screened from each type of vacuum cleaner. The screening principle was that the main functions of products must be completely the same. Vacuum cleaners with similar functions, power, appearance, and size, were classified into high-price and low-price goods. In each category, the price difference between high-price and low-price goods should be at least NTD 5000. The selected samples were the products of 12 brands in the market, with a total of 20 tested samples. Pictures of samples include front view, perspective drawing, and actual pictures of goods for the participants to carefully observe the details of goods. In order to avoid the inference of brand factor in participant testing, LOGO pictures of samples were removed.

Ranking of Selling Prices of Goods from Top to Bottom. Ranking of suggested selling prices of samples was listed from the highest to the lowest, as shown in Table 1. Selling prices were based on suggested selling prices, as shown on the official websites of brands in 2011. When prices were not indicated on the websites, the researcher selected the lowest prices shown on two major online shopping malls in Taiwan.

Questionnaire Design. The questionnaire is divided into two parts. Part 1 is the participants' basic information, including gender, age, and educational level. Part 2 is the pictures and numbers of the tested samples. Prices of goods are not indicated. Pictures of tested samples include front view, perspective drawing, and actual pictures of goods, as shown in Table 2 for Canister vacuum cleaners. After careful observation, the participants are expected to develop ranking according to the values of the tested samples, as well as ranking of preferences regarding to the whole, forms, colors, and materials of the tested samples.

Questionnaire Survey. A questionnaire survey was conducted on 20 males and 20 females, aged 22-31. Their educational level was university and graduate school. Regarding occupation, they were mostly students and office workers. In the questionnaire survey, the researcher explained to the participants face-to-face and obtained 40 valid questionnaires.

2.2   In-Depth Interview

According to questionnaire survey results, the researcher found the samples with different rankings of product values and preferences from actual prices to conduct in-depth interviews and explore the difference factors. Through leading questions, the participants could specifically express their feelings about each sample, and the factors of rising or falling of preferences and values. Thus, the researcher could recognize consumers' preferences regarding form, color, and materials of vacuum cleaners. In the interview, the researcher explained the questions to the participants face-to-face. Each interview lasted for 120 minutes. Pictures of samples were magnified on A4 paper, with front view, perspective drawing, and actual pictures of goods for participants' careful observations.

The participants were selected from those in the first stage of the questionnaire survey, of which there were 10, including 5 males and 5 females, aged 23-26. Regarding educational level, two were graduated from universities and 8 were graduated from graduate schools or above. Regarding occupation, 4 were students and 6 were office workers, and 10 had design backgrounds.

Table 1. Ranking of actual prices of four types of vacuum cleaner

Stick Vacuum Cleaners				
S1	S2	S3	S4	S5
NT.8590	NT.3980	NT.3600	NT.2090	NT.1290
Canister vacuum cleaners				
C1	C2	C3	C4	C5
NT.32900	NT.23900	NT.9990	NT.5290	NT.4990
Handy vacuum cleaners				
H1	H2	H3	H4	H5
NT.9900	NT.2990	NT.2780	NT.2190	NT.1290
Upright vacuum cleaners				
U1	U2	U3	U4	U5
NT.21500	NT.11990	NT.9990	NT.4990	NT.3990

3   Results Analysis

3.1   Ranking of Actual Prices of Goods, Values, and Preferences

The statistics of the questionnaire survey on the participants' ranking of values and preferences for the four types of vacuum cleaners are as shown in Table 3. According to Table 3, the participants' ranking of product values is similar to the actual selling price, with the exception of C3, which shows that ranking of actual prices is third and value is the fifth. The ranking gap between values and actual prices is (-2). However,

Table 2. Pictures of tested samples for Canister vacuum cleaners

rise or fall of 2 in the ranking gap between preferences and actual prices is common, which demonstrates that preferences for more expensive products are not necessarily high.

3.2 Correlation between Values and Preferences of Products

Based on the results of the questionnaire survey and general rating, and regarding the correlation of participants' product values and preferences, by Pearson Product-Moment Correlation coefficient, correlation coefficient is ±1. When correlation coefficient is close to ±1, it means correlation is more significant, where (+) means positive correlation and (-) means negative correlation. According to the figures of correlation definitions of Product-Moment Correlation, when the correlation coefficient is 1, it means total correlation, 0.7-0.99 means high correlation, 0.4-0.69 means medium correlation, 0.1-0.39 means low correlation, and below 0.1 means extremely low correlation (Lee, 2008). The research shows a test result of a significance level of correlation coefficient by P. When P is lower than $\propto 0.05$, it means it reaches the significance level. Test results (see Table 4) demonstrate that most have medium positive correlation. Hence, the participants' preferences are influenced by products with value.

Table 3. Ranking of actual prices, values, and preferences, as well as a comparison of the difference

Canister vacuum cleaners					
code name	(C1)	(C2)	(C3)	(C4)	(C5)
Ranking of actual price (expensive-cheap)					
Ranking of value	(C2)	(C1)	(C4)	(C5)	(C3)
Difference of value ranking	-1	+1	-2	+1	+1
Ranking of preference	(C2)	(C4)	(C1)	(C3)	(C5)
Difference of preference ranking	-2	+1	-1	+2	0
Stick vacuum cleaners					
code name	(S1)	(S2)	(S3)	(S4)	(S5)
Ranking of actual price (expensive-cheap)					
Ranking of value	(S1)	(S2)	(S3)	(S4)	(S5)
Difference of value ranking	0	0	0	0	0
Ranking of preference	(S3)	(S1)	(S4)	(S2)	(S5)
Difference of preference ranking	-1	-2	+2	+1	0
Upright vacuum cleaners					
code name	(U1)	(U2)	(U3)	(U4)	(U5)
Ranking of actual price (expensive-cheap)					
Ranking of value	(U1)	(U2)	(U3)	(U4)	(U5)
Difference of value ranking	0	0	0	0	0
Ranking of preference	(U3)	(U1)	(U4)	(U2)	(U5)
Difference of preference ranking	-1	-2	+2	+1	0
Handy vacuum cleaners					
code name	(H1)	(H2)	(H3)	(H4)	(H5)
Ranking of actual price (expensive-cheap)					
Ranking of value	(H1)	(H2)	(H3)	(H4)	(H5)
Difference of value ranking	0	0	0	0	0
Ranking of preference	(H2)	(H4)	(H3)	(H1)	(H5)
Difference of preference ranking	-3	+1	0	+2	0

Table 4. Test results of correlation analysis of product values and preferences

Types of products	Pearson correlation coefficient (r)	Significance (two-tailed)	Correlation definitions
Canister vacuum cleaner	0.688	0.000**	Medium positive correlation
Stick vacuum cleaner	0.645	0.000**	Medium positive correlation
Upright vacuum cleaner	0.438	0.000**	Medium positive correlation
Handy vacuum cleaner	0.358	0.000**	Low positive correlation

**When significance level is 0.01 (two-tailed), correlation is significant.
* When significance level is 0.05 (two-tailed), correlation is significant.

3.3 Study on the Factors of Rising or Falling Ranks of Product Values and Preferences, in Comparison to Actual Prices

As show in Table 3, the rankings of preferences of many samples are different from the actual prices. For instance, in a canister vacuum cleaner, the ranking of C1 actual prices is first. However, values fall to the second and preferences fall to the third. The ranking of C2 actual prices is second, and values and preferences rise to the first. The ranking of C3 actual prices is the third. However, values fall to the fifth and preferences fall to the fourth. The ranking of C4 actual prices is fourth. Values rise to the third and preferences rise to the second. The ranking of C5 actual prices is fifth. However, values rise to the fourth, while preference is the same. Therefore, the researcher conducts in-depth interview on samples with different rankings of product values and preferences in order to determine the factors. For instance, why do the product values of the C1 vacuum cleaner fall to second, while preferences fall to third? According to results of in-depth interviews, form factors include the following: (1) because of transparent materials, goods are transparent inside and the appearance becomes too complicated; (2) modeling is round; (3) appearance is normal and not creative. Regarding colors: (1) the color is too normal (blue and white) and not attractive; (2) color is too bright; however, the vacuum cleaner should present a sense of stability; (3) the color is feminine; (4) color distribution is inappropriate. Blue part is in a large area and a transparent material, it looks cheap. Regarding materials: the percentage of transparent acrylic material is inappropriate, it is large, and made of plastic. Table 5, 6, 7 show the in-depth interview results of the four types of vacuum cleaners.

According to Table 5, regarding the factors of the rise of the ranking of product values and preferences, the forms should present the following: (1) modeling key words: simple, neat, streamlined, modernity, and consistent form; (2) sophisticated design of details; (3) different from normal vacuum cleaner form in the market and appearance is attractive; (4) vacuum cleaner is based on human factor design. For instance, it has comfortable handgrip, retractable cord or storage function; buttons are at convenient positions for users; (5) vacuum cleaners are commonly used by women.

Thus, feminine design will enhance preferences for goods. Regarding color (see Table 6): (1) key words of color: fashionable, technological, luxurious, soft, and comfortable; (2) decorated by bright color; (3) cold tone: it is more stable; (4) light color: volume of upright vacuum cleaner is larger than other types of vacuum cleaner. Hence, with light colors, users will feel it is easy to pull the vacuum cleaner while using. Handy vacuum cleaner is held by hand. With light colors, it looks less heavy for users. Regarding material (see Table 7): (1) various kinds of surface treatments: silvering, metal baking, and unique paints (such as leather paint, rubber paint, etc.), sandblasting treatment; (2) use of different materials: soft rubber material and colored acrylic.

Table 5. The factors of the rise and the fall in terms of form

Types of products	Ranking	Factor generalization	General generalization
Canister vacuum cleaner	Rise	· Simple and detailed · It is different from normal vacuum cleaner forms in the market and it is more special · Modernity	**Rise factors:** 1. Simple and neat 2. Modernity 3. It is different from normal vacuum cleaner forms 4. Streamlined 5. Human factor design 6. Consistent modeling 7. Sense of design (sophisticated design of details) 8. Feminine design **Fall factors:** 1. Normal, conservative and not special 2. Simple, without detail 3. Complicated modeling 4. Mechanical 5. Industrial 6. Heavy
	Fall	· Modeling is normal, conservative, and not creative · Form is too simple without details	
Stick vacuum cleaner	Rise	· Streamlined · Modernity · Human factor design · Consistent scale	
	Fall	· Overall modeling is inconsistent · Complicated lines of appearance	
Upright vacuum cleaner	Rise	· Simple and detailed · Feminine design	
	Fall	· Mechanical · Industrial · Heavy	
Handy vacuum cleaner	Rise	· Streamlined · Sense of design (sophisticated design of details) · Simple and neat	
	Fall	· Complicated modeling · Industrial	

Table 5 also shows that, regarding the falling factors of rankings for product values and preferences, forms are presented, as follows: (1) the following modeling key words should be avoided: too simple, without details, complicated modeling, and heavy; (2) it is similar to modeling of vacuum cleaners in the market, and it is not creative; (3) mechanical and industrial. Regarding color (see Table6): (1) the following key words of color should be avoided: old-fashioned and cheap, conservative and safe color (such as light blue), heavy color, and undefined color; (2) inappropriate color scale. Regarding materials (see Table 7): (1) single material or single surface treatment; (2) inappropriate percentage of material, such as over use of certain materials; (3) without special surface treatment or rough surface treatment.

Table 6. The factors of the rise and the fall in terms of color

Types of products	Ranking	Factor generalization	General generalization
Canister vacuum cleaner	Rise	·Fashionable (black and silver) ·Technological (black and silver) ·Metal color · Decoration of bright colors on products · Unique and new color (bright green) different from normal vacuum cleaner	1. Fashionable and technological 2. Metal color 3. Decoration of bright colors 4. Luxurious 5. Cold tone 6. Light color 7. Soft and comfortable
	Fall	·Old-fashioned and cheap looking (red and white)	**Fall factors:** 1. Old-fashioned and cheap
Stick vacuum cleaner	Rise	·Luxurious (metal color) ·Cold tone and more stable	2. Safe and conservative 3. The color cannot be defined and is not pure
	Fall	· Safe and conservative colors ·The color cannot be defined and is not pure	4. Color scale is inappropriate 5. Too heavy
Upright vacuum cleaner	Rise	·Light color	
	Fall	·Too many dark colors and it is heavy · Colors that are not suitable for household electric appliances (brown)	
Handy vacuum cleaner	Rise	· Soft and comfortable	

Table 7. The factors of the rise and the fall in terms of material

Types of products	Ranking	Factor generalization	General generalization
Canister vacuum cleaner	Rise	· Silvering material · Multi-level material · Sophisticated surface treatment (baking) · Decoration of little colored acrylic · Appropriate percentage of materials	**Rise factors:** 1. Silvering material 2. Sophisticated surface treatment · Metal baking · Rubber paint · Leather paint · Matted surface sandblasting · Flash finishing paint 3. Decoration of proper colored acrylic 4. Various material **Fall factors:** 1. Too much transparent acrylic 2. Without special surface treatment 3. Single material 4. Single surface treatment 5. Rough surface treatment 6. Total transparent acrylic
	Fall	· Too many transparent materials · Without special surface treatment · Single material and too plastic · Rough surface treatment · Inappropriate percentages of materials	
Stick vacuum cleaner	Rise	· White, bright and clean plastic	
Upright vacuum cleaner	Rise	· Various materials · Sophisticated surface baking	
Handy vacuum cleaner	Rise	· Sophisticated surface baking · Levels increased by different kinds of surface treatments (matted surface sandblasting)	

4   Conclusions

Conclusions are shown below as reference for the industry and designers.

1. Ranking of values is close to actual prices. In other words, more expensive goods have higher product values. Ranking of product preferences and actual prices is different. It means that more expensive products do not necessarily have higher ranking of preference.
2. There is medium positive correlation between value and preference.
3. Rising factors of value and preference in various forms: (1) the following modeling key words: simple, neat, streamlined, modernity, and unified form; (2) sophisticated design of details; (3) vacuum cleaner form different from those in the market,

and the appearance is attractive; (4) vacuum cleaner has human factor design, such as comfortable handgrip, retracting cord or storage function, buttons are at convenient positions for users; (5) vacuum cleaners are commonly used by women, thus, feminine design will enhance product preference. Regarding color: (1) the following key words of color: fashionable, technological, luxurious, soft, and comfortable; (2) decorated by bright colors; (3) cold tone: it is more stable; (4) light color: volume of upright vacuum cleaner is larger than other types of vacuum cleaners. With light color, users will feel it will be less difficult to pull the vacuum cleaner while using. Handy vacuum cleaners should be hand-held. With light color, it looks less heavy to users. Regarding material: (1) various kinds of surface treatments: silvering, metal baking, or unique paint (leather paint, rubber paint, etc.), sandblasting treatment; (2) Use of different materials: soft rubber material and colored acrylic.

4. Falling factors of value and preference in forms: (1) the following modeling key words should be avoided: too simple and without details, complicated modeling and heavy; (2) it is similar to the modeling of vacuum cleaners in the market, and is not creative; (3) mechanical and industrial. Regarding color: (1) the following key words of color should be avoided: old-fashioned and cheap, conservative and safe color (such as light blue), heavy color and undefined color; (2) inappropriate color percentage. Regarding material: (1) single material or single surface treatment; (2) inappropriate percentage of materials, such as over use of certain material; (3) without special surface treatment or rough surface treatment.

References

1. Baxter, M., Chang, C.C. (trans.): Product Design and Development, p. 67. Liuho Publishing, Taipei (1998)
2. Baxter, M., Chang, C.C. (trans.): Product Design and Development, p. 40. Liuho Publishing, Taipei (1998)
3. Sasaki, M.: Introduction of Design, p. 172. Yi Fong Tang Publisher, Taipei (1991)
4. Lee, C.J.: Guide of SPSS Applied Statistics, p. 198. New Wun Ching Developmental Publishing, Taipei (2008)
5. Yutani, J., Tung, C.T. (trans.): The Times of Consumers' Power, p. 45. Yuan-Liou Publishing, Taipei (1989)
6. Liang, C.J.: Multi-Stage Model of Consumers' Evaluation of Service Quality and Value-Banking Industry as Subject of Empirical Study. Master's thesis, Graduate Institute of Business Administration, National Taiwan University (1992)

The Influence of the Designer's Expertise on Emotional Responses

Hui Yueh Hsieh

Department of Visual Communication Design, Ming Chi University of Technology,
84 Gungjuan Rd., Taishan, New Taipei City, Taiwan
tsauk@mail.mcut.edu.tw

Abstract. This study examined whether people who had received design training responded differently to non-verbal risk communication materials. More specifically, it examined whether the level of expertise affected the emotions. The study measured emotional responses to visual stimuli in 324 Taiwanese participants (users, novice designers, intermediate designers and expert designers), using a Chinese translation of the abbreviated PAD Emotion Scales. Significant main effects of varying levels of expertise were found on all three dimensions of the PAD. Design expertise was inversely related to pleasure; the more design experience, the more unpleasant they rated the stimuli. Design expertise was positively related to arousal; the more design experience, the more arousing they perceived the stimuli. Design expertise was negatively related to dominance; the more design experience, the more 'submissive' they rated the stimuli.

Keywords: emotion, risk communication, design expertise.

1   Introduction

1.1   Differences between Designers and Users

Much of emotional design research revolves around the experiences and emotional responses of users. There are two fundamental incentives underlying efforts to study the effects of design on users' emotions. The first is that understanding the emotions of users can avoid provoking unexpected or undesired user responses, and the second is to create intended user responses [1]. These motivations also reflect ultimate questions –"Are the emotional responses of users differ to the emotional responses of designers?

Designers differ from other professionals in several ways. Lawson noted that many studies show that designers are highly perceptive and observant [2]. Eysenck [3] demonstrated that art and design students differed from non-art and design students in their personality, with art and design students scoring higher on Neuroticism and lower on Extraversion. Designers also differ from others in their problem-solving strategies [4]. Research also suggested that both novice and expert designers have an evident preference for intuitive ways of thinking and working [5]. In a study by

S. Yamamoto (Ed.): HIMI 2014, Part I, LNCS 8521, pp. 572–582, 2014.
© Springer International Publishing Switzerland 2014

Lawson and Spencer[6], which looked at the response of prospective users to a new university building, it emerged that the users' and the designers' perceptions were radically different.

1.2   Acquired Differences - Influences of Design Training

Psychology has a long history of studying visual art and music. Most studies have wrestled with this subject by exploring, personality, stimulus determinants, and training in art, and how these factors influence preference, evaluation and emotion. It seems worthwhile to explore some relevant studies in psychology of art/aesthetics.

Some studies have been conducted to understand whether training in art influences people's emotional responses to art [7, 8]. Some of such studies did not examine emotion directly, but instead they have been investigating how art experts and novices differed in their appraisals of what makes art interesting. They referred to these emotions as 'aesthetic emotions' [e.g. 8]. Although it is dubious whether these are emotions, these studies have provided some valuable evidences of the effect of art training. There are some established findings on expert-novice differences in preference for art: art experts have a preference for abstract [9] and complex-asymmetrical pictures [8, 10, 11], and they consider complex pictures more interesting and easier to understand [8]. Moreover, they tend to regard originality as an aesthetic quality more so than non-experts [9]. In the abstract art interpretation task, Blazhenkova and Kozhevnikov [12] found that visual artists (designers and painters) tended to see abstract art as abstract representations, but scientists and humanities/social science professionals tended to provide literal interpretations. Conversely, in the graph interpretation task, visual artists interpreted graphs literally (graphs-as-pictures), but scientists interpret graphs schematically.

In studies of creative artists, writers and architects, among others, some characteristics were found to be prevalent, including intuitiveness and emotional sensitivity [13]. There is evidence of oversensitivity being a common characteristic in creative people [14]. Creative people tend to have slightly higher basal levels of arousal than less creative people, while also being oversensitive to stimulation and physiologically overactive [15, see a review in 16]. Oversensitive people are prone to react strongly to stimuli such as light, noise, textures, air pollution and so on. When Martindale conducted electric shock tests on people, he found that the more creative ones evaluated the given shock as being more intense [16].

Opposed to speculative psychological aesthetics, scientific aesthetician Berlyne emphasized empirical validation [17]. He posited a set of properties which contribute to the impact of aesthetic stimuli, the so-called "collative properties". The collative variables comprise dimensions such as novel-familiar, expected-surprising, simple-complex, and ambiguous- clear. Specifically, for instance, novelty and surprise can increase one's arousal state [18, 19]. Demerath's knowledge-based affect theory proposed that when knowledge is strengthened the affective response is positive; whilst an increase in uncertainty produces a negative affect, such as fear and anxiety. The 'knowledge-based affect theory' occurs in response both to novel and familiar objects. When the certainty of the 'average' increases, the power of our predictions will increase and that will lead to a positive affect [20]. People tend to prefer highly prototypical stimuli—a phenomenon referred to as the 'beauty-in-averageness effect' [21]. Demerath deduced that people like novel stimuli not because they are unknown, but because they give the pleasure of gaining knowledge [20].

The mere-repeated-exposure theory posits that people tend to like objects that are more familiar to them. A considerable amount of research has demonstrated that repeated exposure to a stimulus generally induces an increased positive affect and preference for that stimulus, even under subliminal condition [22]. Studies have shown that familiarity affects emotional responses, and preference for music and pictures is influenced by the familiarity of the music and pictures [23].

1.3   The PAD Emotion Scales

The dimensional approaches of measuring emotions- the PAD Emotion Scales [24] were employed for this study. The PAD devised by Mehrabian and Russell is one of the most critically acclaimed emotional assessment instruments. Mehrabian and Russell [25] proposed a three-dimensional model of emotion, stating that all human emotions can be adequately described by three continuous, bipolar, and nearly orthogonal dimensions, pleasure (P), arousal (A) and dominance (D). One of the strengths of the PAD is that it permits calculation of the average emotional response of a group to any stimulus, and that it is designed to capture the entire domain of emotional experiences rather than to measure specific emotions.

The validity and reliability of the PAD is well established [26-28], and it has also been employed and gained recognition in various fields for assessing emotional responses, such as in consumer research [29, 30] and in design [31]. Evidence from a recent fMRI study demonstrated that a three-dimensional approach is a more robust emotional assessment method than the discrete approach. Morris and associates identified different functional regions of the brain that correspond to both the pleasure and the arousal dimensions of the PAD Emotion Scales, and found that there was a high correlation between the self–report PAD measurement and the fMRI data [32].

2   Method

2.1   Participants

A total of 324 Taiwanese participated in this study. The effective sample size was 289 (mean age 22.18, SD 6.08, range 18-63; 196 women: mean age 21.74, SD 5.30, range 18-45); 113 men: mean age 22.88, SD 7.10, range 18-63) after discarding invalid samples. Some data were eliminated from further analyses because of omitting items or a suspicion of careless responding, i.e. lack of variability and extremity bias [33]. Among the participants there were 180 from a visual communication design background and 109 from a non-design related background (such as engineering). Participants were disaggregated into four broad groups: users, novices, intermediates and experts. The distribution of the sample is presented in Table 1. The design students participating in the study were recruited from three universities in Taiwan.

Table 1. Distribution of sample participants by levels of design expertise

Group 1-4		Number	Percentage (%)	Mean age	SD	Age range
1	Users	109	37.7	22.38	6.55	18-60
2	Year 1	40	13.8			18-23
	Year 2	43	14.9	19.05	1.0	
3	Year 3	36	12.5			
	Year 4	11	3.8	23.26	10.11	19-45
	MA 1	28	9.7			
	MA 2	12	4.2			
4	Designers	10	3.5	36.70	6.55	28-63
	Total	289	100			

Note: Group 1: Users; Group 2: Novices; Group 3: Intermediate; Group 4: Experts

2.2 Materials

Stimuli. Fifteen visual stimuli were selected on the following criteria: (1) represented a range of content about various health risks; (2) represented different emotional values; (3) reduced linguistic demands from varying widely between stimuli.

PAD Scales. The Chinese-language PAD Emotion Scales[34] were used to assess participants' emotional responses (see Table 2).

Table 2. 12 items PAD Emotion Scales

Pleasure (P)	Arousal (A)	Dominance (D)
P1: Happy-Unhappy	A3: Frenzied-Sluggish	D1: Controlling-Controlled
P2: Pleased- Annoyed	A4: Jittery-Dull	D2: Dominant –Submissive
P3: Satisfied-Unsatisfied	A5: Wide awake-Sleepy	D3: Influential-Influenced
P5: Hopeful –Despairing	A6: Aroused- Unaroused	D6: In control-Cared for

2.3 Procedure

Participants were run in small groups in university classrooms in Taiwan. In a short introduction, the participants were briefed regarding the purpose and procedure of the study. Following completion of consent procedures, participants submitted basic demographic information including age, sex and education and were instructed to commence the task at their own pace. Using the 12-item Chinese version of the PAD Emotion Scales, participants viewed 15 visual stimuli and rated how each stimulus made them feel according to three dimensions of emotional response. They ticked one of seven spaces between two bipolar adjectives to show their evaluation. The experiment took an average of 30 to 50 minutes to complete.

3   Results

A series of ANOVAs were conducted to analyse the data. 2x4 (sex by expertise) ANOVAs with Fisher's least significant difference (LSD) post hoc tests were conducted to determine whether there were effects of levels of expertise and effects of sex between the participant groups to the ratings of pleasure, arousal, and dominance (PAD).

3.1   Effect of Sex by Expertise on the PAD

In order to determine whether differences between designers and users are associated with progressive design training, two (females, males) by four (users, novices, intermediates and experts) ANOVAs with LSD post hoc tests were conducted to assess the variation of the means between groups on the PAD. As shown in Table 3, the two-way ANOVA demonstrated significant main effect of sex on the dominance scale $[F(1, 281) =12.68, p<0.01]$ and significant main effects of varying levels of expertise on the pleasure scale $[F(3, 281) =2.65, p=0.05]$, the arousal scale $[F(3, 281) =5.43, p<0.01]$ and the dominance scale $[F(3, 281) =4.59, p<0.01]$. None of the ANOVAs yielded significant interactions between levels of expertise and sex.

Table 3. ANOVA summary for sex by expertise on the PAD

	Source	F
Pleasure	Females/Males	$F(1, 281) =0.14, p=0.71$
	Levels of Expertise	$F(3, 281) =2.65, p=0.05*$
	Females/Males x Levels of Expertise	$F(3, 281) =1.94, p=0.12$
Arousal	Females/Males	$F(1, 281) =0.97, p=0.33$
	Levels of Expertise	$F(3, 281) =5.43, p<0.01**$
	Females/Males x Levels of Expertise	$F(3, 281) =1.27, p=0.29$
Dominance	Females/Males	$F(1, 281) =12.68, p<0.01**$
	Levels of Expertise	$F(3, 281) =4.59, p<0.01**$
	Females/Males x Levels of Expertise	$F(3, 281) =1.31, p=0.27$

Note: ** indicates significance at $p < 0.01$; * indicates significance at $p < 0.05$

3.2   The Main Effect of Sex on the PAD

The two-way ANOVA revealed that the only significant difference between the females and the males was on the dominance scale. Table 4 shows mean score differences in each measure between groups. On the dominance scale, the mean score for the females was 3.56, compared to the males, whose mean score was 3.85. These scores indicate that the females perceived these stimuli as more dominant than the males.

Table 4. Mean scores for varying levels of expertise on PAD

	Females	Males	Users	Novices	Intermediates	Experts
Pleasure	4.72 (SD=0.51)	4.57 (SD=0.51)	4.57 (SD=0.56)	4.66 (SD=0.48)	4.76 (SD=0.46)	4.85 (SD= 0.44)
Arousal	3.22 (SD=0.42)	3.31 (SD=0.49)	3.35 (SD=0.47)	3.28 (SD=0.41)	3.14 (SD=0.45)	2.98 (SD= 0.26)
Dominance	3.56 (SD=0.57)	3.85 (SD=0.58)	3.76 (SD=0.49)	3.53 (SD=0.51)	3.64 (SD=0.68)	4.23 (SD= 0.85)

Note: 1=pleasure, 7= displeasure; arousal: 1 = arousal, 7 = non-arousal; 1=dominance, 7=submissiveness

3.3 Effect of Varying Levels of Expertise on the PAD

The pleasure-displeasure scale

The statistics in Table 4 show that there was a trend towards higher perceived displeasure with increasing experience in design (means for the four groups of expertise were 4.57, 4.66, 4.76 and 4.85, respectively). Design expertise was inversely related to pleasure; the more design experience, the more unpleasant they rated these stimuli (Figure 1). Post hoc LSD tests showed significant differences between the

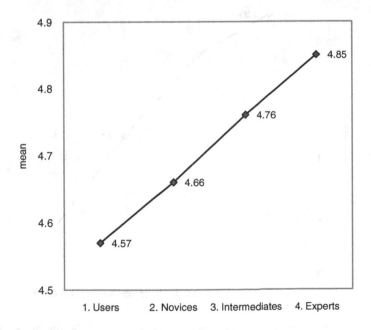

Fig. 1. Varying levels of expertise on pleasure (with lower scores indicating pleasure)

intermediate designers and the users on the pleasure rating (p=0.01).The result suggests that the intermediate designers perceived these stimuli of risks significantly as more unpleasant than the users. The finding of no significant difference between the expert designers and the users can possibly be attributed to the small sample size of expert designers.

The arousal/non-arousal scale

Table 4 shows that the mean arousal scores for each group were users: 3.35, novices: 3.28, intermediate designers: 3.14, expert designers: 2.98 (median score =4). These scores indicate that the expert designers perceived these stimuli as most arousing.

Post hoc LSD tests showed significant differences between the expert designers and the novices (p<0.05), and between the expert designers and the users (p=0.01), which indicate that the expert designers perceived these stimuli as significantly more "arousing" than the novices and the users. Significant differences were also found between the intermediate designers and the users (p<0.01) and between the intermediate designers and the novices (p<0.05), which indicate that the intermediate designers perceived these stimuli as more arousing than the novices and users. The differences were not significant between the intermediate designers and the expert designers and between the novices and the users. The results indicate that design expertise was positively related to arousal; the more design experience, the more arousing they rated these stimuli (Figure 2).

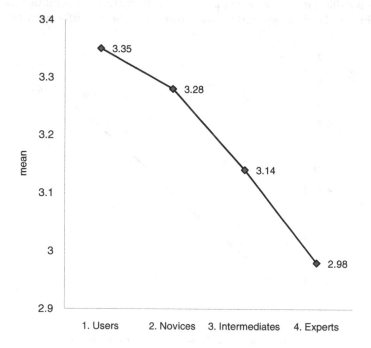

Fig. 2. Varying levels of expertise on arousal (with lower scores indicating higher arousal)

The dominance/ submissiveness scale

The descriptive statistics in Table 4 show that the mean dominance scores for each group were users: 3.76, novices: 3.53, intermediate designers: 3.64, expert designers: 4.23 (median score =4). These scores indicate that the expert designers perceived these stimuli as relatively more submissive.

Post hoc LSD tests showed significant differences between the expert designers and users ($p=0.01$), between the expert designers and the novices ($p<0.01$) and between the expert designers and the intermediate designers ($p<0.01$). These indicate that the expert designers perceived these stimuli as significantly more "submissive" than the users, the novices or the intermediate designers. Design expertise was negatively related to dominance; the more design experience, the more "submissive" they rated these stimuli (Figure 3). However, differences were not significant between the intermediate designers and the novices or between the intermediate designers and the users. Significant difference was also found between the novices and users ($p=0.01$), which indicates that the users perceived these stimuli as being more "submissive" than the novices.

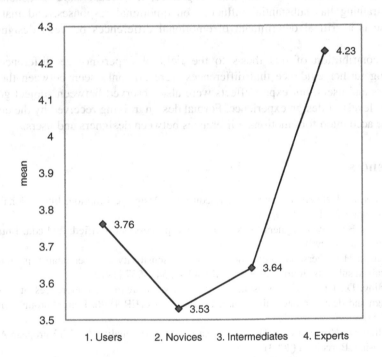

Fig. 3. Varying levels of expertise on dominance (with lower scores indicating higher 'dominance')

4   Discussion

This study examined the effect of the level of expertise to determine whether exposure to formal design training can explain emotional differences between designers and users, in which participants were disaggregated into four broad groups: users, novices, intermediates and experts.

The results showed there were differences among designers themselves. The differences between the designers and the users were associated with progressive levels of design training. This finding is in accordance with previous observations by Whitfield and Wiltshire (1982), who demonstrated that differences between designers and non-designers in the acquisition of aesthetic values are associated with exposure to formal design training gradationally.

Significant effects for the level of expertise were observed on all three dimensions of the PAD scales. In general, design expertise was inversely related to the pleasure and the dominance scale and positively related to the arousal scale. The more design experience participants had, the more "unpleasant", "submissive" and "arousing" they perceived the stimuli of health risks. Therefore, it is reasonable to conclude that design training has substantial influence on emotional responses, and that design expertise is a critical determinant of emotional differences between designers and users.

The contribution of this thesis to the field of expert-novice differences is in providing further evidence that differences were not only seen between the expert designers and users, but expert effects were also observed between subject groups at different levels of design experience. Formal design training received by the designers could be accounted for emotional differences between designers and users.

References

1. Desmet, P., Hekkert, P.: Special issue editorial: Design & Emotion. International Journal of Design 3(2), 1–6 (2009)
2. Lawson, B.: How designers think: The design process demystified, 2nd edn. Butterworth Architecture (1990)
3. Eysenck, H.J.: Personal preferences, aesthetic sensitivity and personality in trained and untrained subjects. Journal of Personality 40(4), 544–557 (1972)
4. Durling, D., Cross, N., Johnson, J.: Personality and learning preferences of students in design and design-related disciplines. In: Proc. IDATER 1996. Loughborough University (1996)
5. Durling, D.: Horse or cart? Designer creativity and personality. In: 5th European Academy of Design, Barcelona (2003)
6. Lawson, B., Spencer, C.P.: Architectural intention and user responses: the psychology building at Sheffield. Architects' Journal 167(18) (1978)
7. Cupchik, G.C., Gebotys, R.J.: Interest and pleasure as dimensions of aesthetic response. Empirical Studies of the Arts 8(1), 1–14 (1990)
8. Silvia, P.J.: Artistic training and interest in visual art: Applying the appraisal theory of aesthetic emotions. Empirical Studies of the Arts 24(2), 139–161 (2006)

9. Hekkert, P., van Wieringen, P.C.W.: Beauty in the eye of expert and nonexpert beholders: A study in the appraisal of art. The American Journal of Psychology 109(3), 389–407 (1996)

10. McWhinnie, H.J.: A review of selected aspects of empirical aesthetics III. Journal of Aesthetic Education 5(4), 115–126 (1971)

11. Barron, F.: Personality style and perceptual choice. Journal of Personality 20(4), 385–401 (1952)

12. Blazhenkova, O., Kozhevnikov, M.: Visual-object ability: A new dimension of non-verbal intelligence. Cognition 117(3), 276–301 (2010)

13. Lovecky, D.V.: Can you hear the flowers sing? Issues for gifted adults. Journal of Counseling and Development 64(9), 572–575 (1986)

14. Martindale, C., Anderson, K., Moore, K., West, A.N.: Creativity, oversensitivity, and rate of habituation. Personality and Individual Differences 20(4), 423–427 (1996)

15. Runco, M.A., Sakamoto, S.O.: Experimental studies of creativity. In: Sternberg, R.J. (ed.) Handbook of Creativity, pp. 62–92. Cambridge University Press, Cambridge (1999)

16. Martindale, C.: Biological bases of creativity. In: Sternberg, R.J. (ed.) Handbook of Creativity, pp. 137–152. Cambridge University Press (1999)

17. Berlyne, D.E.: Psychological aesthetics, speculative and scientific. Leonardo 10(1), 56–58 (1977)

18. Berlyne, D.E.: Curiosity and exploration. Science 153(3731), 25–33 (1966)

19. Cupchik, G.C., Berlyne, D.E.: The perception of collative properties in visual stimuli. Scandinavian Journal of Psychology 20(1), 93–104 (1979)

20. Demerath, L.: Knowledge-based affect: Cognitive origins of "good" and "bad". Sociometry 56(2), 136–147 (1993)

21. Winkielman, P.: Research article prototypes are attractive because they are easy on the mind. Psychological Science 17(9), 799–806 (2006)

22. Zajonc, R.B.: Mere exposure: A gateway to the subliminal. Current Directions in Psychological Science 10(6), 224–228 (2001)

23. Ali, S.O.: Music and emotion: the effects of lyrics and familiarity of emotional responses to music. Unpublished doctoral dissertation. College of Arts and Sciences of American University (2004)

24. http://www.kaaj.com/psych/scales/emotion.html (accessed May 2007)

25. Russell, J.A., Mehrabian, A.: Evidence for a three-factor theory of emotions. Journal of Research in Personality 11(3), 273–294 (1977)

26. Havlena, W.J., Holbrook, M.B.: The varieties of consumption experience: Comparing two typologies of emotion in consumer behavior. Journal of Consumer Research 13(3), 394–404 (1986)

27. Mehrabian, A.: Framework for a comprehensive description and measurement of emotional states, Genetic. Social and General Psychology Monographs 121(3), 339–361 (1995)

28. Brengman, M.: The impact of colour in the store environment - An environmental psychology approach. Universiteit Gent (2002)

29. Petermans, A., Van Cleempoel, K., Nuyts, E., Vanrie, J.: Measuring emotions in customer experiences in retail store environments. International Journal of Retail & Distribution Management, 2257–2265 (2009)

30. Spangenberg, E., Grohmann, B., Sprott, D.: It's beginning to smell (and sound) a lot like Christmas: the interactive effects of ambient scent and music in a retail setting. Journal of Business Research 58(11), 1583–1589 (2005)

31. Tsai, T., Chang, T., Chuang, M., Wang, D.: Exploration in emotion and visual information uncertainty of websites in culture relations. International Journal of Design 2(2), 55–66 (2008)
32. Morris, J.D., Klahr, N.J., Shen, F., Villegas, J., Wright, P., He, G., Liu, Y.: Mapping a multidimensional emotion in response to television commercials. Human Brain Mapping 30(3), 789–796 (2009)
33. Paulhus, D.L.: Measurement and control of response bias. In: Robinson, J.P., Shaver, P.R., Wrightsman, L.S. (eds.) Measures of Personality and Social Psychological Attitudes, pp. 17–59. Academic Press (1991)
34. Hsieh, H.Y.: Taiwanese Version of the PAD Emotion Scales. Kaohsiung (2011) (in Chinese)

Generative Product Design Inspired by Natural Information

Yinghsiu Huang[1] and Jian-You Li[2]

[1] Department of Industrial Design, National Kaohsiung Normal University, Taiwan
yinghsiu@nknu.edu.tw
[2] Department of Industrial Design, Ming Chi University of Technology, Taiwan
kensukai@gmail.com

Abstract. Today's computing capacity, however, has been far more than two decades ago, which only could convert 2D sketches to 3D models. Therefore, how to utilize the ability of generating 3D derivative model from natural inspirations for forming product shapes is the main problem of this research. In order to investigate the problem of this research, therefore, the objectives of the research can be divided into two stages: 1. to analyze principles from natural objects, components, or/and structures; 2. to simulate and create innovative shapes by applying computer 3D software, such as Rhino and Grasshopper, based on natural principles for developing new product designs. At the end of this study, with computer 3D derivative abilities and with the technologies of 3D-printing, the results of this paper will propose some generative product forms by simulating and inspiriting from natural creatures.

Keywords: Generative design, product design, 3D-Printing, natural creatures.

1   Introduction

In the 1970s, the invention of computer had changed human life, and also accelerated the various fields of study. In the field of design, computer-aided, -evaluated, and -manufactured design (CAD / CAE / CAM) are applied into the latter stages of design process. In these stages, the ideas from designs have been widely simulated, analyzed, and automated-manufactured by computers. However, with advances in computing speed, some research in the field of design are focusing on how could directly convert design sketches into 3D graphics software for modeling (van Dijk, 1995). Then, a lot of research studied on the computer-aided conceptual design (CACD) to help designers integrate the 2D cognition into the 3D cognitive feelings, such as: the Lipson & Shpitalni, 1996. By doing so, the generated 2D and 3D graphic by computer could represent design ideas using in the following design stages.

Nowadays, in the digital technology era, architectural design is facing not only just what we design, but also how we face the challenges of design. Zellner (1999) in "hybrid space" pointed out that "Buildings have been re-building through self-build

S. Yamamoto (Ed.): HIMI 2014, Part I, LNCS 8521, pp. 583–593, 2014.

system into a topology geometry research, which is a computing machine for recombining material goods to build-up an automatic and dynamic generative space."

As you can see, the impacts of digital technology on architecture design could not be imagined, such as Topological architecture, Dynamic architecture, Metamorphic architecture, Parametric architecture, Evolutionary architecture. The forming of new buildings based on these new digital technologies is changing the processes and structures of architecture design. These digital technologies also provide highly uncertain dynamic operations for design strategy, which could get rid of the fixed limitation of design ideas. Therefore, the unexpected, uncertain, and varied behavior of design process by utilizing digital technologies makes design process as a "finding of form" process.

However, the most imaginative and creative stage in the design process is the conceptive development stage in which designers analyzed design cases and formed a new design concept and shape by their imaginations. Today's computing capacity, however, has been far more than two decades ago, which only could convert 2D sketches to 3D models. Therefore, how to utilize the ability of generating 3D derivative model from natural inspirations for forming product shapes is the main problem of this research.

In order to investigate the problem of this research, therefore, the objectives of the research can be divided into two stages: 1. to analyze principles from natural objects, components, or/and structures; 2. to simulate and create innovative shapes by applying computer 3D software, such as Rhino and Grasshopper, based on natural principles for developing new product designs.

2   Related Works

2.1   Creative Computer Systems

Fisher (2000) explored symmetry of ignorance, social creativity, and meta-design to provide a conceptual framework for understanding creativity. By comparing multisystem support to the cooperation between several designers, cooperative design creativity can be inspired. Through these systems, users can process, share, and understand one other's works and learn from one another, thereby resolving the problem that computer computation systems based on cognitive science have been considered uncreative or even culpable for reducing people's creativity. These systems are so-called social creativity computer systems. In the metadesign environment, users are like designers, handling new conditions and limitations during a design and development process, and integrating and solving problems. The metadesign environment is a crucial source of social creativity.

Computer-aided design software based on parameter design achieves creativity objectives through parameter adjustment, construction process, and open source. Pro/Engineer and generative components have these functions and use intuitive and nonlinear methods to achieve divergent design and optimize their effects. When Rhinoceros 3D developed the Grasshopper plug-in, the number of logic operators increased and an object-oriented interface was used to write computer programs in combination with modeling instructions. Using elements in a series to compile computer programs allows parametric data flow and treatment to be easily handled and allows model construction processes to be presented. The use of Grasshopper is linked to Arduino and robot controlled entities, is beyond the original modeling purpose, and successfully leads other object-oriented programming languages to emulate Grasshopper (e.g., Nudebox).

In recent years, Grasshopper has rapidly developed and has been commonly and widely used in the digital construction sector. Particularly, free-form surfaces and digital construction have been embodied by using the parametric modeling tools. A computer can perform monotonous huge computation, and is therefore extremely helpful for the digital construction required for handling a huge amount of components with tiny changes. A computer can also perform rapid computation to present real-time changes, and therefore designers can repeatedly use dynamic and nonlinear design methods to present optimal forms and structures.

2.2   The Application of Digital Generative Forms

Observing, analyzing, utilizing, and learning from natural phenomena are critical for basic modeling training in traditional design education. From both macroscopic and microscopic perspectives, the aesthetic or functional importance of living creatures, nonliving things, and landscapes in nature are highly valuable in design. This is evolving into an independent subject, including design bionics and ergonomics, which are especially closely related to living creatures in nature. The causes of natural phenomena and patterns are complex but can mostly be explained in natural science or engineering. In the work by D'Arcy Thompson in 1917, the development or patterns of various living creatures were described using mathematical expressions. These results have recently been verified and applied using parametric programs and computer graphics (Fig. 1) (Thompson, 1917). However, design education still preferably focuses on the aesthetic characteristics of nature.

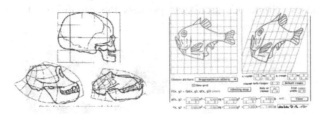

Fig. 1. The development or patterns of living creatures are verified using parametric programs and computer graphics

Design rules obtained from subjective observations but not from system measurement, generalization, and quantification can only be implemented by designers through manual operation and cannot be implemented with the help of digital auxiliary tools. Concurrently, students are limited by time and materials and therefore cannot adequately perform verifications and conduct tests. The reason is that traditional design education is aesthetics-oriented. Although numerous design departments belong to engineering schools, because of insufficient background knowledge regarding manufacturing engineering and technology, concepts of quantitative parameters and programming are not taught in depth for influencing design concepts (Fischer, 2001). In addition, no programming tool suitable for designers has been developed. Because people with design backgrounds are typically resistant to learning mathematics and programming languages, programming languages are still mainly used by professional program developers. From the 1970s to 2000, generative design theories such as shape grammar (Stiny and Gips, 1972), genetic algorithm (Frazer, 2000), parametric design, design rules, evolutionary design, and generative art (Soddu, 2006) had developed and become mature. Thus, rules, computations, and parameters were included in design concepts.

Fig. 2. Transformation of natural forms into products

Regarding architecture design in the digital age, we should not only consider what to design but also how to consider design challenges. The book "Hybrid Space" by Zellner (1999) indicates that architecture itself has become a study related to topology and geometry, a computational and recombined smart product, and an automatically generated and dynamic spatial form. To date, computational design has become an independent technology in architecture education and practice. Numerous architecture schools offer related courses. Architecture firms that are well known for their digital and curved styles have established computation technology departments and related technology databases. Numerous architects possess the capability of computational design.

Fig. 3. Forms constructed by architecture firms using computation technology and technology databases

Compared with the fields of architecture and arts, industrial design first acquired a history of digitization. In the processes of architectural and artistic digitization, computational design has not affected the generation and conceptualization of mainstream product design. As architecture in the past, the implementation of current industrial design methods is still limited by manufacturing technology and the black-box thinking of designers. Currently, only few designers can use computational design in combination with additive manufacturing (3D printing). The reasons are that design education does not teach related skills in core courses, numerous limitations regarding mold manufacturing exist, and free-form products generated through computational design cannot be massively produced using traditional molds, unlike curved architecture that can use special construction or precast methods to solve manufacturing problems. This is why additive manufacturing is considered the solution for manufacturing free-form surface products.

Fig. 4. Free-form surface product modeling

3   The Methodology and Steps

3.1   Investigations of Nature Forms

People often design by imitating and learning from the beauty of nature. People typically share common aesthetic experiences and convey aesthetic messages visually, psychologically, physically, emotionally, and socially. However, individual differences in physical and psychological aspects, developmental processes, and life experiences exist. Numerous factors affect the common aesthetic experience among people.

In the first part of this project, with basic forms and 3D generative design, students will be objectively taught how to identify objective patterns in nature that cause aesthetic experience through experience, observation, analysis, and generalization (i.e., the principles of aesthetic patterns) (Fig. 5) and to produce two- and three-dimensional designs. The principles of aesthetic patterns include repetition, gradient, rhythm, symmetry, contrast, radiation, specificity, balance, harmony, unity, and proportion. The elements and rules for the principles of various aesthetic patterns vary and their manifestations also vary. The principles of aesthetics can be analyzed by experiencing nature or artificial forms and aesthetic patterns can be presented in two-dimensional, linear, and massive structures using various materials such as watercolor, paper, wire, and cardboard. Students can gradually be trained to two- and three-dimensionally present an aesthetic concept.

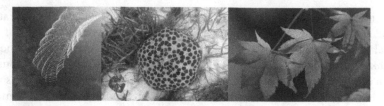

Fig. 5. Form analysis of nature

3.2   Basic Forms and Generative Design

For digital architecture and design computation, digital fabrication is the commonly used method, in which digital weaving and fabrication can be performed. Digital fabrication resembles the concept of quadrilateral continuity in graphic design. By digital fabrication, a simple rule for a tiny local portion is first defined and then basic elements perform generation and make judgments according to this rule. If this design rule is applied to a large curved surface, then a complex texture or structure will be formed. The complex texture or structure cannot be designed or constructed by people but can be done by a computer (which can perform large amounts of monotonous work). Digital fabrication and traditional product design differ in product characteristics. In Fig. 6, several products adopt the same concept. Considering another characteristic, these products were produced using 3D printing technology. These complex products cannot be produced using conventional open mold methods. Rapid prototyping additive manufacturing is a solution, and therefore, digital fabrication is massively coupled with 3D printing.

Fig. 6. Digital fabrication

4   Analysis and Results

Experimentation and analysis comprise two parts: (a) natural form analysis and development and (b) generative modeling. The first part was undertaken in a product modeling course. In the second part, three-dimensional models were constructed using the Rhinoceros 3D Grasshopper plug-in. The two parts are elaborated in the following sections.

4.1   The Analysis of Nature Form and Transformations

Natural form analysis and development were undertaken in a product modeling course. In this course, students first analyzed aesthetic patterns in nature. By analyzing the composition of aesthetic patterns, two-dimensional compositions were developed. Then, according to the two-dimensional compositions, three-dimensional structures were constructed using linear materials (e.g., wire). Finally, polyurethane (PU) was used to develop three-dimensional physical structures. Figure 8 shows a natural form analysis by a student. In Fig. 7, three elements are identified: (a) spiral line, (b) folding line, and (c) rolled surface.

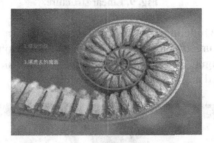

Fig. 7. Natural form analysis

Two-Dimensional Composition. In the exercise regarding developing two-dimensional compositions, based on the elements or composition derived from natural form analysis, natural forms were transformed into black-and-white two-dimensional compositions after numerous drafts were drawn, as shown in Fig. 8. The two-dimensional composition shown on the left side of Fig. 8 presents spiral lines with interwoven black and white stripes. On the right side of Fig. 8, the rotated surface of a different angle shows the gradual change of spiral lines from outside to inside.

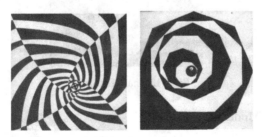

Fig. 8. 2D composition

Linear Structure. In the linear structure development exercise, students discussed with a teacher and chose the two-dimensional composition on the right side of Fig. 8 to develop a linear structure, as shown in Fig. 9. Ten octagons with gradual change from outside to inside were constructed using wire. As shown in Fig. 8, each line rotated to the right and then was radially arranged and fixed to the base to form a linear structure.

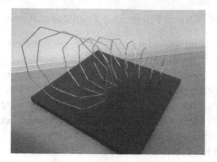

Fig. 9. Linear structure

Three-Dimensional Modeling. At the final stage, PU was used to develop a 3D physical structure. Figure 10 shows a similar three-dimensional form developed from the linear structure. Figure 11 shows the final three-dimensional form (30 × 30 × 30 cm), which was scraped and was sprayed with white paint.

Fig. 10. Development of a 3D form

Fig. 11. Final 3D form

4.2   Generative Modeling

In the second part, generative software, the Rhinoceros Grasshopper plug-in, was used to construct a three-dimensional form by analyzing the results obtained from the first stage. Before a three-dimensional form was constructed, the modeling power at the first stage must first be analyzed (Fig. 12). The basic cross-sectional shape of the form was first analyzed to form a path of three-dimensional modeling, and then each side length of the octagons was retracted to form the basic information for generative structure construction. Subsequently, the plug-in Genoform was used to produce a generative structure by changing parameters under the same framework. Finally, a 3D printer was used to print out various three-dimensional forms.

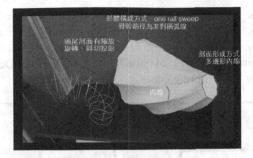

Fig. 12. Analysis of basic information for generative structures

Basic Polygon for Cross-Section. The first step of constructing a generative structure is to construct a cross-sectional polygon. The original form is an octagon. To produce variations, the number of cross-sectional sides can be changed from 5 to 15 (Fig.13, left). The arc caused by the retraction of the side length is formed by connecting the two endpoints of the side length and the displaced midpoint of the side length toward the center point of the polygon. The amount of displacement of the midpoint of the side length toward the center of the polygon can be changed.

Path Curve. Regarding path configuration, the two endpoints of the original side length and the displaced midpoint of the side length can form a curve (Fig. 13, right). The displacement of the midpoint of the side length is a variable. Concurrently, the vertical position of the midpoint can be set to be 20% to 70% to change the curvature of the path.

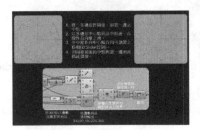

Fig. 13. Left: Basic polygon for cross-section; Right: Path with changeable curvature and midpoint displacement

New Cross-Section and a Rebuilt Form. In the previous step, a relatively long three-dimensional form was produced with the two ends of the cross-section perpendicular to the line connecting the two endpoints of the path, as shown on the left side of Fig. 14, left. In the third step, two planes were added to the positions at 20% and 80% of the path. The angle of the two planes is an adjustable variable. The two planes form a tangent to the three-dimensional structure, and thus the final generative three-dimensional form was produced.

Genoform. In this step, the Genoform, developed by Sivam Krish (2013), slider automatically uses the variable configured in Grasshopper to generate various generative structures (Fig. 14. right); for example, various polygons, various path curvatures, and various degrees of side length retraction. Designers can choose structures according to their preferences

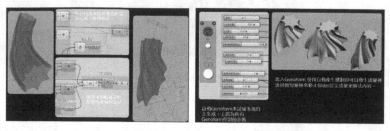

Fig. 14. Left: New cross-section and a rebuilt form; Right: Generative structures generated by the Genoform plug-in

3D Printing. Grasshopper and Genoform generate ideas about various three-dimensional forms, as shown on the left side of Fig. 18. In this study, six forms were selected, and they were printed out in physical form using a 3D printer, as shown on the right side of Fig. 15.

Fig. 15. Physical forms printed out using a 3D printer for generative structures

5   Conclusions

At the first stage of this study, students observed natural patterns and analyzed the principles of aesthetic patterns. Thus, students learned the basics of natural patterns. According to the information obtained from observation and analysis, students designed two-dimensional compositions and three-dimensional forms. At the second stage, the students used Grasshopper and Genoform to generate various physical models under the same modeling framework; therefore, students or designers were provided with various design ideas. In addition, the various forms generated by Genoform were similar to the drafts developed by students during the course. Thus, the Grasshopper and Genoform generative system constructed in this study can generate the ideas that may be developed by designers and therefore can serve as a reference for designers for developing ideas.

This study used computers not only to help design at the later stage of design when ideas are presented but also to provide students or designers with various design ideas during the process of developing product ideas. However, the generative system cannot replace a designer's ability to develop ideas. The generative system can use a computer's ability of rapid computation and randomization to produce ideas that designers may not have thought of. Therefore, the generative system can help designers evaluate their diverse design requirements.

In this study, various parametric values controlled by Genoform produced various forms; however, users possessed various emotional feelings toward the shapes of lines or curved surfaces. Therefore, in future research, Grasshopper and Genoform will be used to integrate forms that evoke emotions into generative design systems and to help designers or users generate product models that evoke emotions according to their individual emotional preferences. In addition, we will attempt to change existing traditional product design or industrial design. Regarding basic courses, we will attempt to change the structure of existing product design education and to use a computer to help design at the later design-presenting stage of design and to provide designers with creative design ideas during the process of developing product ideas. Furthermore, we will attempt to adopt concrete product design topics to help generate various forms.

References

1. Van Dijk, C.G.C.: New insights in computer-aided design. Design Studies 16(1), 62–80 (1995)
2. Lipson, H., Shpitalni, M.: Optimization-Based Reconstruction of a 3D object from a Single Freehand Line Drawing. Journal of Computer Aided Design 28(8), 651–663 (1996)
3. Zellner, P.: Hybrid Space: Generative Form and Digital Architecture. Rizzoli Publish (1999)
4. Fischer, T.: Teaching Generative Design. In: Conference of Generative Arts in 2001 (2001)
5. Thompson, D.W.: On Growth and Form (1917),
   http://en.wikipedia.org/wiki/File:Darcythompson.jpg
6. Stiny, G., Gips, J.: Shape grammars and the generative specification of painting and sculpture. In: Information Processing 1971, pp. 1460–1465 (1972)
7. Frazer, J.: Research on Application of genetic algorithms to computer aided product design: case studies on three approaches (2000)
8. Soddu, C.: Generative design. A swimmer in a nature sea frame (2006)
9. Krish, S. (2013), http://www.genoform.com

Application of a Requirement Analysis Template to Lectures in a Higher Education Institution

Koji Kimita, Yutaro Nemoto, and Yoshiki Shimomura

Dept. of System Design, Tokyo Metropolitan University, Tokyo, Japan
kimita@tmu.ac.jp,
nemoto-yutaro@ed.tmu.ac.jp,
yoshiki-shimomura@center.tmu.ac.jp

Abstract. Due to a declining population of 18-year-olds, higher education institutions are targeting new types of learners, such as adult learners who work full time while enrolled. To attract these new types of learners, higher education institutions need to provide education that takes account of the learners' requirements. To do so, this study evaluated education in higher education institutions from the viewpoint of learners. Specifically, we analyzed the requirements of learners using a requirement analysis template utilized in Service Engineering.

Keywords: Higher education, Customer requirement, Service Engineering.

1   Introduction

Recently, an aging society with a falling birth rate has caused the market to shrink. As a result, many service companies have been faced with seeking potential customers who were previously not their traditional targets. Higher education institutions have faced the same problem. Due to a declining population of 18-year-olds, higher education institutions are targeting new types of learners, such as adult learners who work in a full time job. However, higher education institutions do not necessarily provide education that satisfies the new types of learners. For example, they provide the same learning environment and tools to the new types of learners as they did to traditional students. To attract the new types of learners, higher education institutions need to provide education that takes account of the learners' requirements.

On the other hand, the authors of this paper conducted conceptual research on design services from the viewpoint of engineering. This series of research is called Service Engineering [1-3]. Its objective is to develop a fundamental understanding of services, as well as concrete engineering methodologies that can be used to design and evaluate services [1-3]. The value of a service is always perceived and determined by the customer: Providers can only offer value propositions [4]. Therefore, the design process proposed in Service Engineering includes procedures to understand a target customer and to extract his/her requirements. The functions and entities provided in the service are designed on the basis of these customer requirements.

S. Yamamoto (Ed.): HIMI 2014, Part I, LNCS 8521, pp. 594–601, 2014.

From the viewpoint of services, learners in higher education institutions can be regarded as customers. Therefore, the education in higher education institutions needs to be designed and evaluated from the viewpoint of learners. To do so, this study aimed to develop methodology for designing and evaluating the education from the viewpoint of learners. Specifically, we analyzed the requirements of learners using the requirement analysis template [3] proposed in Service Engineering.

2   Approach of This Study

2.1   Overview

To attract the new types of learners in higher education institutions, this study assumes that the education in higher education institutions can be regarded as a service. Based on this assumption, the objective of this study is to develop a methodology for designing and evaluating the education from the viewpoint of learners. As the first step of this study, in this paper, we focus on a lecture where the learners correspond to customers and the teachers correspond to providers. The requirement analysis template [3] proposed in Service Engineering is applied to the lecture to analyze the requirements of the learners that are used as target parameters in designing and evaluating the education.

Section 2.2 presents an overview of Service Engineering, and Section 2.3 introduces the requirement analysis template.

2.2   Service Engineering

Service Engineering is a new engineering discipline with the objective of providing a fundamental understanding of services, as well as concrete engineering methodologies to design and evaluate services. In Service Engineering, the service is defined as an activity between a service provider and a service receiver to change the state of the receiver [1-3]. Note that the term "service" is used in a broad sense. Thus, the design target includes not only intangible human activities but also tangible products.

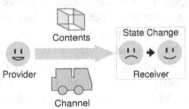

Fig. 1. Definition of a service [1-3]

According to the definition, a receiver is satisfied when his/her state changes to a new desirable state. Since the value of a service is determined by the receiver, service design should be based on the state change of the receiver. For design purposes, it is necessary to find a method to express the state changes of the receiver. The target receiver's state in service design is represented as a set of parameters called receiver state parameters (RSPs) [1-3]. RSPs are changed by "service contents" and "service channels," as shown in Fig. 1. Service contents are materials, energy, or information that directly changes the receiver's state. Service channels transfer, amplify, and control the service contents.

2.3   Requirement Analysis Template

The requirement analysis template was proposed to analyze the customer and to identify the requirements of a service [3]. This template enables designers to extract an exhaustive list of customer requirements and to provide objective evidence for the extraction of them.

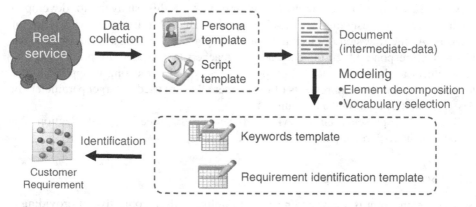

Fig. 2. Overview of the requirement analysis template [3]

As shown in Fig. 2, the requirement analysis template consists of four kinds of template: a persona template, a script template, a keywords template, and a requirement identification template. The first step in the requirement analysis is identifying the target customer. For the identification of the customer, a concept called persona [5] is adopted to describe a representative customer in the form of personal information. The concept of persona is frequently used in the practical design of software interfaces. The persona is a tool that generates a simplified description of a customer and works as a compass in the design process. Based on the persona, a service script is described in consideration of the customer's activities in the service. The service script is written in natural language. Thus, it enables designers to analyze scenes where the customer is satisfied and/or dissatisfied. From the script, designers identify "keywords" that can be considered important elements for the service. Specifically, the script is decomposed into keywords from the viewpoint of the service phases and 4W1H: what, what like, how, where, and when. Finally, each keyword is associated with required items/qualities and quality elements using a predefined template and vocabulary list. Here, the "required items" refer to what customers want to do, and the "required quality" is a linguistic expression of customer requirements related to the quality of the provided product/service. Namely, the required items/qualities indicate representations of "customer requirements" in the service. On the other hand, the quality elements are used as criteria for evaluating the quality. Ideally, the quality elements should be observable and controllable by designers.

3   Application

In this application, the requirement analysis template was applied to a lecture where students who correspond to learners conducted experiments of proportional integral derivative (PID) control. This lecture is geared toward students who major in mechanical engineering. The students learn the fundamental theory of (PID) control through modeling and control of a thermal system.

As the first step, a target student was identified by describing the persona shown in Fig. 3. The persona named "Koji Nemoto" is a 25-year-old Ph.D. student of mechanical engineering. As his personality, in this application, we described his behaviors and preferences.

Life style:
- Lives in Hachioji-shi, Tokyo
- Ph.D. student, majoring in mechanical engineering
- Spends weekdays at the laboratory
- Interested in design engineering

Basic information
- Name: Koji Nemoto
- Age: 25 years
- Gender: Male
- Residential status:
  Lives alone

Personality:
- He usually thinks a lot before he acts.
- He prefers lectures that contain active leaning rather than classroom lectures.
- His major is mechanical engineering, but he is NOT familiar with control engineering.
- He has learned a substantial amount of conceptual theory in his research. Therefore, it is easy for him to understand theories conceptually rather than mathematically.

Fig. 3. Persona template of the student in the lecture

Based on the persona, a service script was described in consideration of the student's activities in the lecture. Fig. 4 shows an example of the script that describes a scene where he received an introduction to the theory used in this experiment and worked on a PID control experiment. This script includes not only how he behaved in the experiment but also what he thought and/or felt. For example, he felt "it was still unclear how the modeling worked in this experiment..." in the introduction to the modeling (see the underlined part in Fig. 4).

Introduction to modeling

- The teacher moved on to the introduction to modeling, and he asked the students "What is modeling." I thought it was difficult to answer because the question was very abstract. I answered: "making a model, for example, a model plane, a model house, and so on". He agreed with my answer and added that a model is one way of transferring and sharing information about an object in an objective and logical manner. His explanation clarified my understanding of the concept of modeling. However, it was still unclear how the modeling worked in this experiment...

- After explaining the concept of modeling, the teacher introduced the modeling of the thermal system used in this experiment. I did not understand the equation that represents the thermal system and the relationship between the equation and devices used in the experiment. He asked us to develop the transfer function by using the Laplace transform. I learned the Laplace transform when I was an undergraduate student, but I did not have clear memory of it. Following his instruction, I somehow managed to develop the transfer function...

PID control experiment

- After the explanation of the theory of PID control, we began the experiment. In this experiment, we had to stabilize the temperature of water in an aquarium at 50 degrees Celsius using PID control. We measured the temperature of the water every minute. However, it was unclear how the PID control regulated the temperature. In addition, we calculated some parameters used in the PID control before the experiment. I did not understand how these parameters worked...

- Finally, the temperature of the water was stabilized at 50 degrees Celsius. Based on the temperature data, we evaluated quality of controlling from the viewpoints of readiness, stability, and stationarity. I found it difficult to understand the evaluation criteria using only the explanation in the textbook, but the supplemental explanation that the teacher provided with illustrations made me understand more clearly...

Fig. 4. Service scripts in the introduction of modeling and experiment of the PID control

From the script, we identified "keywords" that could be considered important elements for the lecture. As shown in Table 1, the script was decomposed into keywords from the viewpoint of the phases of the lecture and 4W1H. Instead of 4W1H, in this application, we adopted 3W1H: what, what like, how, and whom. For example, the action where the student measured the temperature of the water every minute was decomposed into: measure (action), temperature of the water (what), and every minute (what like).

Table 1. Keyword template in the introduction to modeling and the PID control experiment

Phases of service encounter	Action	What	What like	How	Whom
	Receive	Introduction to modeling		Oral presentation	
	Think	Abstract question about modeling	Difficult		
Introduction to modeling	Feel	How the modeling worked in this experiment	Unclear		
	Do not understand	Relationship between the equation and experiment devices			
	Think	Do not have a clear memory of the Laplace transform			
	Feel	How the PID control worked on the temperature	Unclear		
PID control experiment	Do not understand	How the calculated parameters worked			
	Feel	Understanding the evaluation criteria	Difficult	Textbook	

Table 2. Required items/qualities and quality elements in the PID control experiment

Keywords	Required items/qualities	Quality elements
Abstract question about modeling: difficult	- Receiving more concrete questions	- Concreteness of the question
How the modeling worked in this experiment: unclear	- Understanding of how the modeling works in this experiment	- Understanding of the role of the modeling in this experiment
Do not understand, the relationship between the equation and experiment devices	- Understanding the relationship between the equation and experiment devices	- Understanding of the relationship between the equation and the experiment devices
How the PID control worked on the temperature: unclear	- Understanding of how PID control works on the temperature	- Understanding of the role of the PID control
Do not understand, how the calculated parameters worked	- Understanding of how the calculated parameters worked	- Understanding of the role of the calculated parameters
Understanding of evaluation criteria: difficult	- Understanding of the evaluation criteria	- Understanding of the evaluation criteria

Finally, each keyword was associated with the required items/qualities and the quality elements, as shown in Table 2. For example, with regard to the keywords "How the modeling worked in this experiment" and "unclear," "understanding how the modeling worked in this experiment" was extracted as a required item/quality in the lecture. "Understanding of the role of the modeling in this experiment" was selected as a quality element that corresponds to an evaluation criterion for this required item/quality.

4   Discussion

To analyze the requirements of learners, in this application, a requirement analysis template was applied to a lecture where the students conducted a PID control experiment. The required items/qualities and quality elements were then extracted. For example, "understanding how the modeling worked in this experiment" was extracted as a required item/quality. To fulfill this requirement, the teacher could introduce the mechanism of the thermal system used in the experiment, and then model it step by step. This result is, therefore, useful for the teacher to improve his/her lecture from the viewpoint of the learners. In addition, the requirement analysis template was able to visualize the process for extracting the requirements of the learners. For example, the persona template can enable the teacher to understand the type of learners, such as his/her interests and research background; the service script can visualize contexts where students have certain requirements. The requirement template provides teachers with a greater understanding of students' requirements than traditional methods, such as questionnaires.

In this application, we focused only on a certain type of student and then described the persona of that student. However, in an actual lecture, there are several types of student. The requirements of learners vary depending on their types, and it is difficult to fulfill these requirements in the format of a traditional lecture. Therefore, a method needs to be developed to customize the lecture for each student type. In addition, collecting data to describe the service script of each persona would place a heavy workload on the teacher. Therefore, a learning management system needs to be developed to collect such data efficiently.

5   Conclusion

This study aimed to design and evaluate the education in higher education institutions from the viewpoint of learners. As the first step of this study, in the application, a requirement analysis template was applied to a lecture where the students conducted a PID control experiment. The results revealed that the requirement analysis template is useful for the teacher to understand students' requirements in more detail and to improve his/her lectures from the viewpoint of the learners.

Future work should include the development of a method to customize the lecture for each student type and a learning management system to collect the data for describing service scripts.

Acknowledgements. This research is supported by Service Science, Solutions and Foundation Integrated Research Program (S3FIRE), Research Institute of Science and Technology for Society (RISTEX), Japan Science and Technology Agency (JST).

References

1. Shimomura, Y., Hara, T., Arai, T.: A Service Evaluation Method Using Mathematical Methodologies. Annals of the CIRP 57(1), 437–440 (2008)
2. Shimomura, Y., Tomiyama, T.: Service Modeling for Service Engineering. In: Arai, E., Kimura, F., Goossenaerts, J., Shirase, K. (eds.) Knowledge and Skill Chains in Engineering and Manufacturing. IFIP, vol. 167, pp. 31–38. Springer, Boston (2005)
3. Shimomura, Y., Arai, T.: Service Engineering - Methods and Tools for Effective PSS Development. In: Sakao, T., Lindahl, M. (eds.) Introduction to Product/Service-System Design, ch. 6, pp. 113–135. Springer (2010)
4. Vargo, S.L., Lusch, R.F.: Evolving to a New Dominant Logic for Marketing. Journal of Marketing 68(1), 1–17 (2004)
5. Cooper, A.: The Inmates Are Running the Asylum. SAMS/Macmillan, Indianapolis, IA (1999)

User Experience Evaluation Framework
for Human-Centered Design

Hiroyuki Miki

Oki Electric Ind. Co., Ltd., R&D Center
1-16-8 Chuou, Warabi-shi, Saitama 335-8510, Japan
hmiki@cf.netyou.jp

Abstract. Recently, the word "User Experience (UX)" has been often used in usability-related areas such as web design and system design. Although it was defined in ISO 9241-210 and its importance has been growing, details of the notion and results of introduction of it have not been well clarified yet. In the previous paper, a UX evaluation framework based on ISO 9241-11 and ACSI (American Customer Satisfaction Index) was proposed. Following the previous paper, this paper proposes an integrated new evaluation framework of usability and UX, explains its usage, and discusses its application.

Keywords: User Experience, Usability, ISO 9241, ISO 13407, ISO/IEC 25010, Evaluation framework, American Customer Satisfaction Index.

1 Introduction

Usability is a notion, for example, that addresses a degree of how easy one can use products, systems, or services. As products, systems, or services become more complex and provide high-level functions to the user, designing and evaluating usability become more difficult. In addition, as business competitions go worldwide and become fiercer, conditions of successful products, systems, or services become more complex [4].

Norman considered this kind of changes and claimed that broader scope than usability should be considered [16]. He claimed that the user wants not only good usability but also high UX to be truly pleased with good products, systems, or services. To consider UX, one needs to consider user's good/ bad feelings and responses, namely results of relating products, systems, or services more than usability. It was the first time that UX was mentioned by a leading expert of usability.

Since international standards provide common bases for international businesses, it is quite reasonable that the word UX is introduced in them. However, details of the notion and results of the introduction of it have not been well clarified yet.

In the previous paper [15], a UX evaluation framework based on ISO 9241-11 [9] and ACSI (American Customer Satisfaction Index) [1] was proposed. Following the previous paper, this paper proposes an integrated new evaluation framework of usability and UX. After brief explanations of usability, UX, and Human-Centered Design

S. Yamamoto (Ed.): HIMI 2014, Part I, LNCS 8521, pp. 602–612, 2014.

in international standards in section two, the UX evaluation framework of the previous paper is explained in section three. Then the integrated evaluation framework of usability and UX is newly proposed in section four, followed by its example in section five, and discussions in section six.

2   Usability, UX, and Human-Centered Design in International Standards

2.1   Current Coverage of Usability and UX in International Standards

International Standards have the specific role to provide business organizations with technical standards. Currently, UX related standards are built mainly by the ergonomics committee (ISO/TC159/SC4) in ISO 9241 series and by the software quality committee (ISO/IEC JTC1/SC7/WG6) in ISO/IEC 25000 series.

ISO 9241-210 [8] defines Human-Centered Design as an iterative process of user research (understanding and specifying the context of use, and specifying the user requirements), design, and evaluation.

Current coverage of usability and UX by international standards is shown in Table 1. User research is covered for example by ISO/TR 16982 [11] which explains general methods for it and is applicable to both usability and UX.

Table 1. Design and evaluation covered by ISO

	Usability	User Experience
User research	Yes	
Design	Yes	Slightly yes
Evaluation	Yes	Slightly yes

On the other hand, coverage of usability and UX is different in design and evaluation. Firstly about usability, ISO 9241 series provide principles and guidelines as a design framework, and ISO 9241-11 provides an evaluation framework. ISO/IEC 25010 [10] also provides product quality model and quality in use model about usability. Product quality model can be used for both design and evaluation, and quality in use model can be used for evaluation. Quality in use model is almost same with ISO 9241-11 evaluation framework.

Secondly about UX, there has been no specific design framework in international standards so far. In addition, there have been claims that UX cannot be designed by leading experts. For example, Kim Goodwin says as follows.

"We can design every aspect of the environment to encourage an optimal experience, but since each person brings her own attitudes, behaviors, and perceptions to any situation, no designer can determine exactly what experience someone has." (pp.5 in [5])

Since there have still been disputes about this matter, creation of design framework of UX is premature.

Meanwhile, there are some descriptions related to evaluation of UX in international standards: definition of UX in ISO 9241-210 and similar descriptions to UX in sub-notions of satisfaction in ISO/IEC 25010. However, there has been no specific evaluation framework of UX yet in international standards. Since there were several evaluation frameworks of UX proposed by an ad-hoc work group [17], it is expected for international standard communities to create an evaluation framework of UX which goes along with related international standards.

2.2   Definitions of Usability and UX, and Evaluation Framework of Usability in International Standards

Before proposal of an evaluation framework of UX, differences between usability and UX are described.

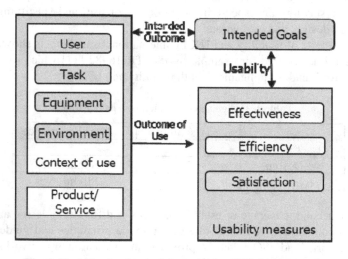

Fig. 1. Usability (evaluation) framework of ISO 9241-11

Fig.1 shows the usability evaluation framework of ISO 9241-11. There are three big boxes: Intended Goals, Context of Use, and Usability Measures. This figure shows that when a product or service is used by a user under the context of use and intended goals, usability is measured by effectiveness, efficiency, and satisfaction. By this figure, usability is described as it depends on a specific context of use, thus you cannot measure usability without determining a specific context of use. Definition of usability is specified as the following in ISO 9241-11.

- Definition of usability in ISO 9241-11:1998 [9]:
  Extent to which a product can be used by specified users to achieve specified goals with effectiveness, efficiency and satisfaction in a specified context of use.

In the meantime, there is no such evaluation framework of UX in international stand-ards. Only definition of UX is described as the following in ISO 9241-210.

- Definition of User Experience in ISO 9241-210:2010 [8]:
  Person's perceptions and responses resulting from the use and/or anticipated use of a product, system or service.

Definition of UX is very different from that of usability. Firstly, time span is different. While usability only deals with "during usage", UX deals with "before usage", "dur-ing usage", "after usage", and "over time" [17]. UX deals with a longer time span since subjective feelings are affected by many related things. Secondly, measures are different in subjective and objective measures. While effective and efficiency of usability are objective measures, UX is evaluated by subjective measures as with satisfaction of usability. These differences must be considered in a UX evaluation framework.

3   UX Evaluation Framework in the Previous Paper

Considering arguments of section 2, UX evaluation framework was proposed in the previous paper. After explaining ACSI (American Customer Satisfaction Index) framework [1] which is referenced in the framework, the proposed framework is ex-plained in section 3.2.

3.1   Inclusion of Concepts of American Customer Satisfaction Index (ACSI)

The American Customer Satisfaction Index (ACSI) (Fig.2) is the national cross-industry benchmark of customer satisfaction in the United States. Since 1994, ACSI is widely used to evaluate customer satisfaction across government systems and ser-vices, industries and their services, and so on. Based on ACSI, similar indices have been created in other countries as well, including ECSI (European Customer Satisfac-tion Index) and JCSI (Japanese Customer Satisfaction Index).

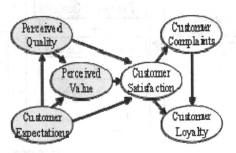

Fig. 2. American Customer Satisfaction Index (Arrows represent influence. This is created based on http://www.theacsi.org/index.php)

While core questions of ACSI are three questions on Customer Satisfaction ("overall satisfaction", "confirm/ disconfirm expectation", and "comparison with ideal"), standard model has about total 14 questions on 1-10 scale about six indices: customer expectation, perceived quality, perceived value, customer satisfaction, customer complaint, and customer loyalty. Six indices are ordered from left to right chronologically in Fig.2.

Starting from Customer Expectation, the index model shows causal relations of indices which are important to evaluate products and services in terms of customer satisfaction. While Customer Expectation evaluates the customer's anticipation of products and services before an actual usage, Perceived Quality and Perceived Value evaluate feelings during usage followed by Customer Complaints and Customer Royalty for the evaluation after usage.

From ACSI questionnaire, two kinds of results are obtained. One is score of each of six indices, which is used to compare different products and services. The other is weight of each arrow in Fig. 2, from which reason of high/ low score of each of six indices will be figured out.

Not surprisingly, since ACSI focuses on subjective evaluations of products and services, it does not include evaluations of design elements or objective measures.

3.2   UX Evaluation Framework in the Previous Paper

Fig.3 shows the result of the previous paper, namely an evaluation framework of UX based on ISO 9241-11 and ACSI. Three major components and relationship among

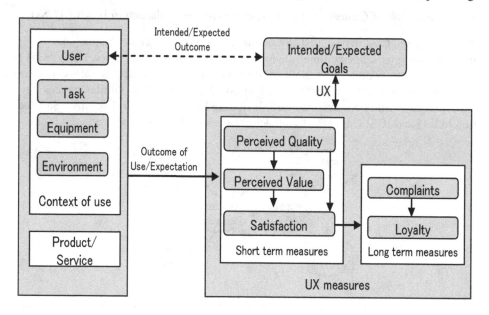

Fig. 3. UX evaluation framework based on ISO 9241-11 and ACSI of the previous paper

them are deployed from ISO 9241-11: Goals, Context of Use, and UX Measures. In the UX Measure component, components of ACSI are deployed. Along with ACSI, each component is supposed to be broken down into sub-indices (sub-questions).

Meanings of small components such as Goals, Perceived Quality, and Perceived Value are slightly changed from ISO 9241-11 and ACSI. First, Goals are specified as composed of Intended Goals of Fig. 1, and Expected Goals which correspond to Customer Expectation of ACSI.

Second, meaning of Perceived Quality is extended as composed of various qualities. Although Perceived Quality is calculated as a total score of desired and undesired degrees against needs in ACSI, since quality measures of UX other than satisfaction and long term measures vary a lot, appropriate measures should be selected for a system and a service.

Third, meaning of Perceived Value is changed as relative quality against input compared with the relative quality against price in ACSI. Examples of Perceived Value include relative pleasure against stress in game, relative relief against anxiety in public machine usage, and so on. Although usability international standards do not treat a value as a measure, it should be added to consider UX.

Long term measures, namely Complaints and Loyalty, are not changed from ACSI.

Advantages of the proposed framework are as the following. First, since ACSI has been widely applied to many products and services, the proposed framework are expected to be applied to many products and services as well. Second, since the proposed framework is based on ISO9241-11 framework (Fig.1), it will be easily integrated with it. In fact, the integration will be conducted in the next section.

4   Integrated Evaluation Framework of Usability and UX

Fig.4 shows the integrated framework based on the previous paper's framework (Fig.3) and the ISO 9241-11 framework (Fig.1). Large change of Fig.4 from Fig.1 is that Satisfaction of Fig.1 is replaced by UX Measures of Fig.3. While objective measures are still represented by Effectiveness and Efficiency, subjective measures are represented by UX Measures derived from ACSI. Fig.4 represents both objective measures and subjective measures of UX.

While objective measures are what designers want to measure, subjective measures of UX are supposed to represent as close user's subjective evaluations as possible. Basically, there is no direct connection between Effectiveness and Efficiency, and the subjective measures of UX. However, if measures of Effectiveness and Efficiency are well designed enough to represent user's subjective evaluation of Perceived Quality, Perceived Value, and possibly other measures of UX, the connection will be tighter. When considering UX, Effectiveness and Efficiency need to be reevaluated by Perceived Quality and Perceived Value toward satisfaction.

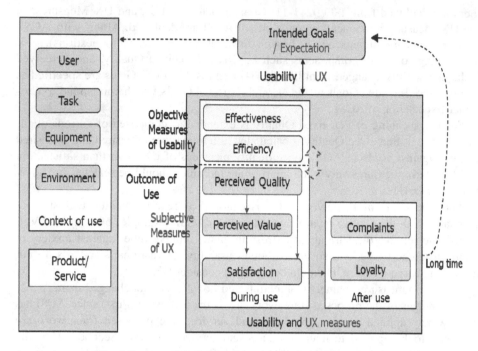

Fig. 4. Integrated evaluation framework of usability and UX

5   Example

Fig.5 shows an example of the right half of new framework, Fig.4. It is about a racing game. It does not show details of each element which is represented by a box, but illustrates causal relations of the framework.

Top part is about objective measures of usability consisting of Goal, Effectiveness, and Efficiency and bottom part is about subjective measures of UX consisting of ACSI indices. In this example, Goal is "getting to goal fast." When, as Expectation before usage, this person says "Since previous version of this game was fun, this new one should be fun," Expectation should be high. Although Effectiveness and Efficiency are high when this person plays this game, this person says "This version is a bit lazy than the previous version." Then result of Perceived Quality should be med. This result influences Perceived Value, and this person feels "Acquired fun level is just so-so compared with given complexity." Then evaluation result of Perceived Value should be also med. As a result, this person's Satisfaction should be most likely medium. After some time, considering results of Satisfaction, Complaint, and Loyalty, this person thinks to buy the next version as well as a result of med loyalty. These results will formulates this person's next Expectation as medium, so lower than the previous expectation.

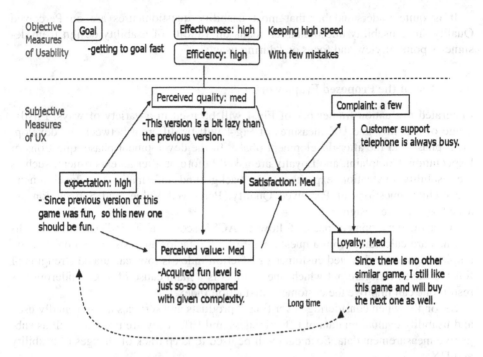

Fig. 5. Example of integrated evaluation framework of usability and UX

As you see in this example, when you consider UX, this level of causal analyses of subjective matters should be analyzed.

6   Discussion on the Proposed Framework

In this section, three points are discussed concerning the proposed integrated framework.

6.1   Comparison with Usability Questionnaires

As usability questionnaires, there are some well-known questionnaires such as QUIS [2], SUMI [11], PSSUQ [13], and SUS [1]. For example, SUS consists of 10 questions: disposition to use, complexity, easiness to use, support, functional integration, inconsistency, learnability, irritation, confidence to use, and volume to learn. Subjects are asked to answer each question with one of five responses that range from Strongly Agree to Strongly Disagree. These questions correspond to subjective measures of Fig.4. While irritation and confidence to use are about feelings and related to satisfaction, other questions are related to perceived quality and perceived value.

It is quite understandable that most usability questionnaires are on Perceived Quality since usability questionnaires focus on validity of usability design from designer's point of view and focus on "during usage".

6.2   Use of the Proposed Framework

Integrated evaluation framework of Fig.4 will be used in a variety of ways. Firstly, usage of usability and UX measures of Fig.4 will be different between the development phase and the after-development phase. In the development phase, questions of Expectation, Complaint, and Loyalty are asked before or after an experiment, such as the usability evaluation experiment, as background information of development. Meanwhile, questions of Perceived Quality, Perceived Value, and Satisfaction are asked to improve design.

After the development phase, following ACSI, scores of six indices and strengths of links are calculated from a questionnaire by the factor analysis and so on. For example, when the calculated customer satisfaction index is low, calculated strengths of links are used to figure out which line of links is a main cause of it. Considering this result, one can improve the customer satisfaction index.

Secondly, when considering "over time," products and services are repeatedly used and usability evaluation data of Effectiveness and Efficiency are taken as well as subjective measurement data. Such data will be used to keep track of changes of usability and UX.

Thirdly, when objective measures of usability, namely Effectiveness and Efficiency, are broken down into sub measures, Perceived Quality and Perceived Value will also be broken down into sub measures. In ACSI, it is often the case that Perceived Quality is broken down into sub measures in a specific domain like Fig.6 of government system since Perceived Quality has large impact on Satisfaction. Following ACSI, Perceived Quality of Fig.4 should be broken down when necessary.

Fig. 6. ACSI for government systems (This is created based on http://www. theacsi.org/acsi-model-for-most-government-agencies)

6.3   Core Three Questions on Satisfaction

In ACSI, although there are six measures in the standard model, core three questions of satisfaction measure, "overall satisfaction", "confirm/ disconfirm expectation", and "comparison with ideal", are most important to compare different products and services. By this reason, ACSI model can be consolidated into one measure, namely satisfaction with the three questions.

When using the three questions to evaluate satisfaction, degree of "overall satisfaction" will be clearer since "confirm/ disconfirm expectation" and "comparison with ideal" will contribute to adjusting degree of satisfaction to compare with other similar products or services. In this sense, when evaluating satisfaction for UX, the three questions are important in not only the consolidated version but also the non-consolidated version just like ACSI.

When subjective measures of UX are consolidated into one measure of satisfaction, the proposed framework is almost same with ISO 9241-11 usability framework. Difference is that satisfaction is asked by the three questions and comparisons with expectation and ideal are characteristic compared with ISO 9241-11. In such a case, however, it will be difficult to figure out reasons of low/ high customer satisfaction since strength of links cannot be calculated from a questionnaire. Hence, either consolidated version or non-consolidated version of subjective measures of UX should be selected properly in the proposed framework as well with ACSI by considering usage.

It is especially so when we consider internet questionnaire like Japanese Customer Satisfaction Index since large amount of questionnaire results will contribute to the calculation of link strengths of subjective measures of UX well.

7   Concluding Remarks

In the previous paper, a UX evaluation framework based on ISO 9241-11 and ACSI was proposed. Following the previous paper, this paper proposed an integrated new evaluation framework of usability and UX, explained its usage, and discussed its application.

Since UX is a complex notion [6, 13, 18, 19], the integrated new framework is expected to be applied to and examined against real applications. Results of this paper are also expected to be considered in the creation of UX related international standards.

References

1. ACSI: The American Customer Satisfaction Index, http://www.theacsi.org/the-american-customer-satisfaction-index
2. Brooke, J.: SUS: a "quick and dirty" usability scale. In: Jordan, P.W., et al. (eds.) Usability Evaluation in Industry, Taylor & Francis (1996)
3. Chin, J.P., et al.: Development of an instrument measuring user satisfaction of the human-computer interface. In: Proc. CHI 1988, pp. 213–218. ACM, New York (1988)

4. Christensen, C.M.: The Innovator's Dilemma: The revolutionary book that will change the way you do business. Harvard Business Review Press (1997)
5. Goodwin, K.: Designing for the digital age: how to create human-centered products and services. Wiley (2009)
6. Hartson, R., Pyla, P.S.: The UX Book: Process and Guidelines for Ensuring a Quality User Experience. Morgan Kaufmann (2012)
7. ISO 13407: Human-centred design processes for interactive systems. ISO (1999)
8. ISO 9241-210: Ergonomics of human-system interaction – Part 210: Human-centred design for interactive systems. ISO (2010)
9. ISO 9241-11: Ergonomic requirements for office work with visual display terminals (VDTs) – Part 11: Guidance on usability. ISO (1998)
10. ISO/IEC 25010: Systems and software engineering – Systems and software Quality Requirements and Evaluation (SQuaRE) – System and software quality models. ISO/IEC (2011)
11. ISO/TR 16982: Usability methods supporting human-centred design. ISO (2002)
12. Kirakowski, J., Corbett, M.: SUMI: The Software Usability Measurement Inventory. British J. of Educational Technology 24(3), 210–214 (1993)
13. Kurosu, M.: The conceptual model of Experience Engineering (XE). In: Kurosu, M. (ed.) HCII/HCI 2013, Part I. LNCS, vol. 8004, pp. 95–102. Springer, Heidelberg (2013)
14. Lewis, J.R.: Psychometric evaluation of the PSSUQ using data from five years of usability studies. Int. J. of Human–Computer Interaction 14, 463–488 (2002)
15. Miki, H.: Reconsidering the Notion of User Experience for Human-Centered Design. In: Yamamoto, S. (ed.) HCI 2013, Part I. LNCS, vol. 8016, pp. 329–337. Springer, Heidelberg (2013)
16. Norman, D.A.: Invisible Computer: Why good products can fail, the personal computer is so complex and information appliances are the solution. MIT, Cambridge (1998)
17. Roto, V., et al.: User Experience White Paper (2011), http://www.allaboutux.org/uxwhitepaper (electronic version)
18. Sauro, J., Lewis, J.R.: Quantifying the user experience. Morgan Kaufmann (2012)
19. Tullis, T., Albert, B.: Measuring the User Experience. Morgan Kaufmann (2008)

Proposal of Evaluation Support System of Nursing-Care Service Components

Takuichi Nishimura, Yasuhiro Miwa, Tomoka Nagao, Kentaro Watanabe,
Ken Fukuda, and Yoichi Motomura

Centre for Service Research, National Institute of Advance Industrial Science and Technology,
AIST Waterfront 3F, 2-3-26, Aomi, Koto-ku, Tokyo 135-0065, Japan
takuichi.nishimura@aist.go.jp

Abstract. We are trying to design employees' motivation and create technology
to realize sustainable improvement in nursing-care service field. Components in
nursing-care service such as how to care eating or how to help walking with a
robot should be evaluated in order to improve the action and raise the service
quality. But it is difficult to understand actions and results in the whole nursing-
care service field because employees do not have enough time to record them
and are not motivated to do so. Recording support mobile terminals cooperated
with various sensors embedded in the facilities and employees will support visualize situation in such collaborative and face-to-face service field. Moreover
motivation design for employees to record action and knowledge is crucial because human-sensor and human-computation ability is completely dependent on
their proactivity. In this paper we propose evaluation support methodology of
nursing-care service components with both direct effect and log-term effect of
the action by participatory interaction design, which we proposed previously.

Keywords: Nursing-care service, evaluation, service components, collaborative
system development.

1 Introduction

The national burden of long-term care insurance costs in Japan during FY 2009 rose
to 7.7 trillion yen, underscoring a continuously rising trend [1]. It is important to reduce this burden by improving healthcare service productivity and fostering a health-
conscious community.

The profitability of many care services is less than 5%. Moreover, healthcare
workers bear a large workload. Thus, improving productivity while maintaining the
quality of service is an urgent task. Nursing-care services comprise care facility services, visiting services, and assistive device services. This paper examines facility
services because they have more possibility to improve their teamwork. Many people
from different backgrounds and serving in different roles must collaborate to provide
nursing-care services for various residents and patients. For these reasons, service
processes vary widely depending on the workplace community characteristics related
to employees, patients, and the environment. Furthermore, it is difficult to collaborate

S. Yamamoto (Ed.): HIMI 2014, Part I, LNCS 8521, pp. 613–620, 2014.

effectively and gain patients' trust, both of which can greatly improve service productivity[12].

A business analysis of helpers in a care service facility was conducted with the co-operation of an assisted-living paid nursing home in the city of Osaka, Hirano Super Court (SC Hirano). The results, reported herein, indicate that 58% of the helpers' time was spent on work that was not directly related to nursing, and 30% of their time was spent recording and sharing information, especially computer work such as transcription and calculation. Such indirect work does not engender long-term care insurance points. Moreover, it is not directly related to the value of the care received. Therefore, research is being conducted to support the creation and visualization of work records.

To this end, attention is being devoted to the introduction of IT infrastructure to promote cooperation and alignment among employees. This should promote the development of a technological interface to facilitate an efficient workflow and limit the increase in data input work, which is not directly related to care.

This proposal encourages the active participation of employees in real-world environments to develop a system that can be expected to embed itself into the employees' natural workflow (Participatory Interaction Design). In addition, employees should be able to share knowledge in the workplace, using technology to record information whenever a task is completed (point-of-care recording). In the latter case, an input system that enables the ready sharing of necessary workplace-related knowledge should be realized, thereby creating a systematic information database that can be shared among workers.

The situation is similar in mutual-support communities, such as dance circles. Members want to improve their health condition, but some require more support from others instead of trying to change the situation proactively. The members have a varying ability to support the community, and have the potential to find a more adequate solution to activate their fellow members.

Participatory interaction design is important for this purpose, and so an activity methodology combined with technical systems should be investigated. Three steps towards participatory interaction design are proposed, and prototypes for the steps are proposed [12].

Components in nursing-care service such as how to care eating or how to help walking with a robot should be evaluated in order to improve the action and raise the service quality. But it is difficult to understand actions and results in the whole nursing-care service field because employees do not have enough time to record them and are not motivated to do so. Recording support mobile terminals cooperated with various sensors embedded in the facilities and employees will support visualize situation in such collaborative and face-to-face service field. Moreover motivation design for employees to record action and knowledge is crucial because human-sensor and human-computation ability is completely dependent on their proactivity. In this paper we propose evaluation support methodology of nursing-care service components with both direct effect and log-term effect of the action by participatory interaction design, which we proposed previously.

2   Evaluation Methodology of Service Components

In this paper we propose evaluation support methodology of nursing-care service components. The methodology is designed for employees to easily adopt it because the evaluation needs their endeavor and proactivity. We developed five stages as mentioned in Figure 1.

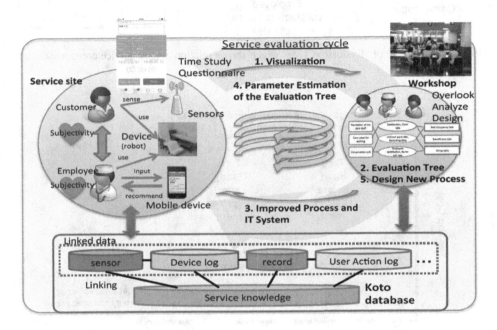

Fig. 1. Service evaluation cycle

1. Visualization
   Visualize status and activity in the service field as shown in Figure 3.
2. Evaluation Tree
   Create "Evaluation Tree" by workshop of employees and customers as shown in Figure 2.
3. Improved Process and IT system
   Apply Improved Process and   develop new IT System for further data collection and process improvement.
4. Parameter Estimation   of the Evaluation Tree
   Parameters are estimated by using data, which was collected in the service field.
5. Design new process by workshop
   As the results of the parameter estimation, if a certain service component is not effective, then it can be revised.

Fig. 2. An example of "Evaluation Tree" which shows relation among service components and KPIs

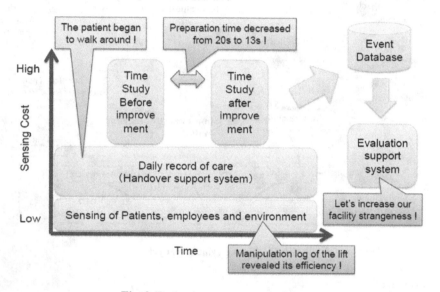

Fig. 3. Evaluation support methodology

"Evaluation Tree" is a tree which shows relationship among service components and KPIs(Key Performance Indexes) as shown in Figure 2. KPIs include sales, benefit, incident rate as well as employees' satisfaction, injury rate, separation rate or team work. Those evaluation trees are different and original because each nursing-care facilities have their own strategies and features. Therefore employees and customers should develop the tree by themselves.

But in order to develop appropriate evaluation tree, visualization of the employees' health condition, their vision, on site activities and customers satisfaction. Therefore as the first step, both direct effect observation of the action and indirect effect estimation of the action are important as shown in Figure 3.

- Direct effect observation: quality and time of each service component. This observation is achieved by time study, analyzing sensor data and questionnaires.
- Indirect effect observation: side effects after the service component. This observation is achieved by overlook action in workshop, analyzing handover messages and questionnaires.

Time study and questionnaire are usually burdensome and high cost but they are precise and quality is high. Handover support system and sensors are low cost and used in every day activities. Therefore the former methods are usually employed occasionally and enhance the data of the latter methods.

3   Support Tool Examples

We developed time study support tool with mobile device, which enable an observer to record direct effect such as an employee's action and quality quickly (Figure 4).

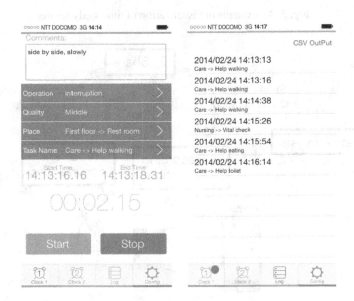

Fig. 4. Time study support tool for an observer to record category of task, place, quality and operation with some comments

The category definitions of tasks, places, quality and operation are easily introduced by table data beforehand and can be selected hierarchically on the spot. This application is available on Apple Co.'s iTunes store as a name of "QualityStudy free". The results of time study will reveal temporal and qualitative evaluation of the service components (Figure 5).

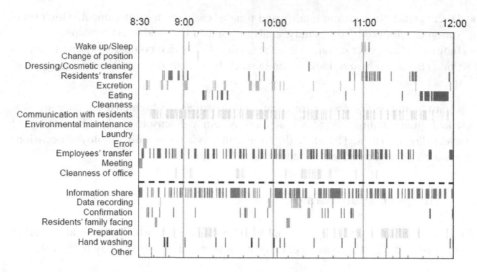

Fig. 5. An example of visualization of time study results

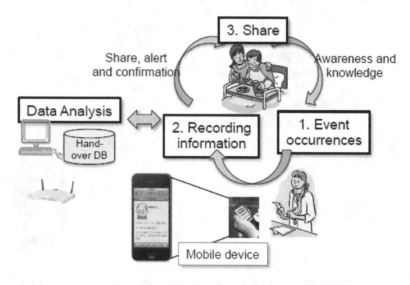

Fig. 6. Handover support system configurations

We will utilize our previous handover support system for recording indirect effect of the components. Employees usually use the system to share important events and actions for maintaining quality of service. Such daily system will help observes to find sub-effect of the components such as increase of patient's activity influenced by a walking support robot.

As Figure 6 shows, a user can use the server-side software via a wireless LAN by installing an application that has the function of capturing multimedia data such as pictures or sound. The following explains system features such as the related example function and search-term recommendations.

This handover support system has features shown in Figure 7. We suggested new workflow to the employees which enables quick input because, to change a patient's face sheet, the person and a category should be selected, which gives contextual information to the system to recommend appropriate candidates. Employees can easily change the face sheet while making handovers and can easily create a handover after changing the face sheet.

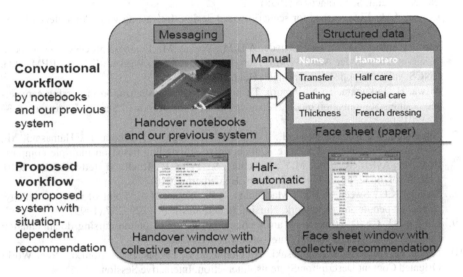

Fig. 7. Seamless between messaging and structured data

4   Conclusion

In this study, the authors proposed evaluation support methodology of nursing-care service components including five steps. And proposed visualization methodologies with both direct effect and log-term effect of the action by participatory interaction design, which we proposed previously. In future research, the authors will refine and validate each step by realizing evaluation support in actual service field.

Acknowledgments. This work was supported by JSPS KAKENHI Grant Number 24500676 and 25730190. This study was conducted as a (service engineering research and development) project to promote new market creation through the fusion of IT and business services commissioned by the Ministry of Economy, Trade, and Industry FY 2011. The authors thank the Wakoen Long-Term Care Health Facility, the paid

nursing home Super-court Hirano, and the Saga University Hospital for their cooperation in and support for this study. This work was partly supported by METI's "Robotic Care Equipment Development and Introduction Project" in 2013.

References

1. Ministry of Health, Labour and Welfare (MHLW) 2011, Survey Results of Nursing-Care
   Service Facilities and Companies in 2009 (in Japanese)
2. Pahl, G., Beitz, W.: Engineering Design – A Systematic Approach, 2nd edn. Springer,
   London (1996)
3. Beyer, H., Holtzblatt, K.: Contextual Design: Defining Customer-Centered Systems. Morgan Kaufmann, San Francisco (1998)
4. Carroll, J.M.: Five reasons for scenario-based design. Interacting with Computers 13, 43–
   60 (2000)
5. van der Aalst, W.M.P., ter Hofstede, A.H.M., Weske, M.: Business process management:
   A survey. In: van der Aalst, W.M.P., ter Hofstede, A.H.M., Weske, M. (eds.) BPM 2003.
   LNCS, vol. 2678, pp. 1–12. Springer, Heidelberg (2003)
6. Miwa, H., Fukuhara, T., Nishimura, T.: Service process visualization in nursing-care service using state transition model. Advances in the Human Side of Service Engineering, 3–
   12 (2012)
7. Nakamura, Y., Kobayakawa, M., Takami, C., Tsuruga, Y., Kubota, H., Hamasaki, M.,
   Nishimura, T., Sunaga, T.: Zuzie: Collaborative storytelling based on multiple compositions. In: Aylett, R., Lim, M.Y., Louchart, S., Petta, P., Riedl, M. (eds.) ICIDS 2010.
   LNCS, vol. 6432, pp. 117–122. Springer, Heidelberg (2010)
8. Dennis, K.E., Sweeney, P.M., Macdonald, L.P., Morse, N.A.: Point of care technology:
   impact on people and paperwork. Nursing Economics 11(4), 229–237 (1993)
9. Langowski, C.: The times they are a changing: effects of online nursing documentation
   systems. Qual. Manag. Health Care 14(2), 121–125 (2005)
10. Numa, K., Uematsu, D., Hamasaki, M., Ohmukai, I., Takeda, H.: ActionLog: Real World
    Oriented Content Description Systems. Interaction, Interactive Session (2005)
11. Hamasaki, M., Goto, M., Takeda, H.: Social Infobox: Collaborative Knowledge Construc-
    tion by Social Property Tagging. In: Proc. ACM 2011 Conference on Computer Supported
    Cooperative Work (CSCW 2011), pp. 641–644 (2011)
12. Nishimura, T., Fukuhara, T., Yamada, K.C., Hamasaki, M., Nakajima, M., Miwa, H.,
    Motomura, Y.: Teamwork Assist System Proposal for Nursing-care Services Realizing W
    orkplace Knowledge Sharing. In: The Fourth CIRP International Conference on Industrial
    Product- Service Systems, pp. 161–166 (2012)
13. Nishimura, T., Kobayakawa, M., Nakajima, M., Yamada, K.C., Fukuhara, T., Hamasaki,
    M., Miwa, H., Watanabe, K., Sakamoto, Y., Sunaga, T., Motomura, Y.: Participatory in-
    teraction design for the healthcare service field. In: Marcus, A. (ed.) DUXU 2013, Part II.
    LNCS, vol. 8013, pp. 435–441. Springer, Heidelberg (2013)

Selecting a Function
by How Characteristic Shapes Afford Users

Makoto Oka[1], Masafumi Tsubamoto[2], and Hirohiko Mori[1]

[1] Tokyo City University, 1-28-1 Tamadutumi, Setagaya, Tokyo, Japan
[2] YAHOO! Japan, 9-7-1 Akasaka, Minato, Tokyo, Japan
{moka,hmori}@tcu.ac.jp, mtsubamo@yahoo-corp.jp

Abstract. This study focused on shapes in accordance with the affordance theory. We would like to propose as a substitute for a mouse a new interface that enables humans to instinctively select functions. Instead of making the optimally shaped devices for each function of computers, the aim is to instinctively select functions with a minimum device. To this end, we verify what shape of devices would enable humans to imagine and select all the functions. The present study takes a close look at "how devices are held"; and we conduct experiments, focusing on musical instruments that are held in different manners.

Keywords: affordance theory, select function, menu.

1 Introduction

Humans select shapes that are suitable for specific functions. For example, how do humans use sticks? They sometimes write characters and pick up nuts with sticks, but do not use the latter as chairs. As such, constrained by the shape and size of things, humans subconsciously narrow down their functions. As time goes by, originally simple-shaped tools become fragmented depending on their respective functions, and keep evolving until they become the most appropriate shape.

On the other hand, taking a close look at computers, one may notice that they have evolved in the opposite direction of the reality. For example, one computer has multiple functions, such as "drawing pictures", "writing characters", and "calculating". These functions are expressed as icons and hierarchically structured menus, and manipulated with a mouse. Computers are distinct from the history of humans that have essentially conceived functions based on shapes. Humans cannot imagine the usage of mice that they directly touch.

The limitations that humans subconsciously have with respect to shapes are called the affordance theory [1]. Some alternative shapes to a mouse prepared with the use of affordances must enable humans to instinctively select and manipulate functions. Following the current hierarchical menu structure of computers, the phase of selecting the shape of such an alternative mouse would correspond to the first layer, and the phase of holding it in different ways would determine the second layer. Research on such "holding" interactions is underway.

S. Yamamoto (Ed.): HIMI 2014, Part I, LNCS 8521, pp. 621–628, 2014.

We call the "possibility of behavior constrained by the limitations that humans subconsciously have with respect to shapes and sizes" an affordance. To maximize the use of affordances, we would like to propose as a substitute for a mouse a new interface that enables humans to instinctively select functions. Instead of making the optimally shaped devices for each function of computers, the aim is to instinctively select functions with a minimum device. To this end, we verify what shape of devices would enable humans to imagine and select all the functions. The present study takes a close look at "how devices are held"; and we conduct experiments, focusing on musical instruments that are held in different manners. The study verifies whether users can identity a wider range of musical devices when they are given the opportunity to select and combine appropriately shaped devices for many musical instruments, compared to a case in which they are allowed to use a device of one single shape.

2   Related Work

Taylor proposed a function selecting method called "Grasp Recognition" [2]. Taylor made a device equipped with 72 touch sensors on its surface, displays on the front and back, and an acceleration sensor (Fig. 1). Those 72 touch sensors detected the points where fingers were touching the device. He examined how the subjects held the device in cases of a camera, a cell phone and a music player, as examples. He extracted data from 13 subjects, and analyzed the discrimination rates by machine learning. From the way they held the device, 70% of the discrimination rate was obtained for each of a camera, a cell-hone, and a music player. Taylor revealed that grasping could be one of the guidelines in selecting functions.

Fig. 1. Taylor's device (The Bar of Soap [2])

There have been studies of selecting the best functions by analyzing the grasping of a single shape of a device with multiple functions added. However, one single shape of a device limits the number of functions available to select from. We think that, thinking in the hierarchical menu, there would be too many functions in one hierarchy to select the functions by ways of grasping.

If we think about things that have evolved into the best shapes, it is difficult to think a knife to have evolved from a ball, or a glass to have evolved from a stick. If we trace things back to their origins, it is unthinkable that they all go back to one shape. Based in the affordance theory, it can be thought, by using a hierarchy of 'shape' before the hierarchy of 'grasping', we can increase number of functions. We think that combining objects of multiple shapes expands the range of functions and enables intuitive selections of functions.

3   Proposal

In this study, 'the possibilities of actions determined by the shapes and the mass of objects, which we humans may subconsciously have' are to be called 'affordance'. In order to maximize the use of the affordance in digital world, we would like to propose new interface that replaces a mouse, which allows you to select functions intuitively. Instead of using a different device of a different shape to match each function in the computer, we aim to develop a minimal shape of a device that allows you select functions intuitively. For that purpose, we examine what shape of device best enables you to imagine all the functions and select them. In this study, we focused on 'how to hold' musical instruments, which people might have diversified ways. For each kind of instrument, users (subjects) were to choose the shape of device or combine some devices of different shapes to best suit to the imagined instrument, and we examined whether the discrimination range widens compared to the case in which one single shape of device was used.

4   Overview of System

We thought that, if we can identify fingers that are touching the device, we could select more functions. 'Which finger, including palm, is touching where' is, we call it, 'finger touch information'; and we conducted function selecting by using the finger touch information. We limited the objects to only musical instruments, and we produced devices that are the supposed-to-be instruments, and glove type devices to obtain touch information. The devices measure the touch information, the tilt and the orientation of the devices.

When we hold something, there are two ways; one way is with fingers, and the other is with whole palm (Fig. 2). The difference is whether the palm is touching the object or not. If we can distinguish these two, then we would be able to judge the way he/she is holding the object.

When the shapes are similar, if we compare the ways of holding them, their postures may be different. In each device, by obtaining three axes of different angels against the ground, we can detect the differences.

Prior, we conducted a simple questionnaire to decide the shapes of the devices to be used in the study. Following the results of the questionnaire, we excluded complicated shapes, and selected five simple shapes of; elliptic column, cubic, circular corn, long and thick stick, and short and thin stick. Probably because sticks are versatile, these two types of sticks were selected, and we prepared both.

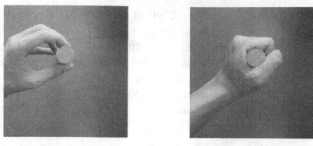

Fig. 2. How to hold (left: with fingers, right: with whole palm)

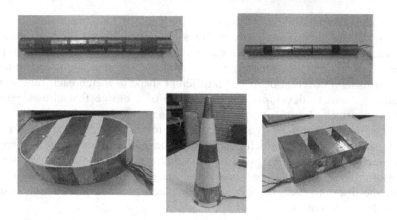

Fig. 3. Five objects (devices) for experimental system

We used two Arduinos to prepare the experimental system. The five devices we prepared were, as mentioned above, an elliptic column, a cubic, a circular corn, long and thick stick, and short and thin stick, and we also prepared gloves for both hands that can discern the fingers and the palm (Fig. 3).

5   Evaluation

We conducted discrimination experiment of the musical instruments as an example of function selection by devices. By discriminating instruments by the ways of holding the multiple shapes, we examined function selection when multiple shapes were used.

5.1   Musical Instrument (Function List)

The subject matters were string instruments, wind instruments and percussion instruments. Eleven instruments were studied. Eleven instruments of cylindrical shapes were; violin, guitar, cello, trumpet, saxophone, flute, piccolo, clarinet, recorder, ocarina and harmonica.

5.2   Evaluation Method

Experiment was conducted with 30 university students as subjects. As an example of single device function selection, we obtained data of the subjects' ways of holding the device imagining each instrument. Then, having the subjects choose a device best suited to each instrument from five devices of different shapes, we obtained data of the subjects' ways of holding device imagining each instrument.

Among those eleven different instruments, if the students (subjects) did not know certain instrument, or how to hold it, we excluded that data. We examined the discrimination rate by the finger touch information, the inclination of the device(s) and the selection and combination of the device(s). In order to validate the advantage of the multiple device function selection in comparison with the single device function selection, we used 'k-nearest neighbor algorithm' to conduct function selection. We used KStar of Weka 3.6 as k-nearest neighbor algorithm[1]. Afterwards, we conducted two-step classification; first by the shapes, using decision tree method; then by the ways of holding, and tried to validate the effectuality of the function selection by the shapes. We validated the data by 'cross validation', which enabled all data to be used as the classification data and the learning data.

6   Result

6.1   Selected Devices

When multiple shapes of devices are used, some instruments had divided tendencies of shape selections. In case of the violin, the selections of shapes were divided into two. One was elliptic column and the other was long stick.

In the case of the guitar, some subjects picked one device, the long stick; and others picked two devices, the long stick and the elliptic column, to express the instrument. The combination of the long stick and the elliptic column were thought to be more accurate for the shape of the guitar, but as it restricted the way of holding, more subjects picked the long stick only to express the instrument. For the cello, most of the subjects used two devices; the long stick and the short stick. Only one device was picked to express; the saxophone, the flute, the piccolo, the clarinet, the recorder, the ocarina and the harmonica. The long stick for the saxophone and the clarinet, the short stick for the flute, the piccolo and the recorder, the elliptic column for the ocarina, and the cuboid for the harmonica.

6.2   Result of One-Step Classification

With all the data obtained from the experiment, we conducted the instrument discrimination. We evaluated the function selection by using k-nearest neighbor algorithm, comparing the multiple shape device selection and the single shape device selection.

---

[1] http://www.cs.waikato.ac.nz/ml/weka/

In this study, we assumed that the long, thick stick is the most universal shape, and used it as the single shape device experiment.

We output the results of the single device discrimination to a table 1. Then, we studied the finger touch information, the inclinations of the devices, and the device selections and combinations in the feature quantity, and we output the results of the discriminations to the chart. Furthermore, in order to compare both cases, we indicated the conformance rate, the recall factor and the F-measure of each case in the chart.

The F-measure in the single shape device (the long/thick stick) was as low as 38.7. For the reasons of this low F-measure, the mix-up of the flute and the piccolo, and also mix-up of the sax, the clarinet and the recorder could be thought. The errors of recognitions of these instruments lead to the low F-measures. This corresponds to the fact that the subjects were remarking during the experiment, "we don't know the exact difference of each of these instruments". When the multiple shapes of devices were used, the F-measure was as high as 64.1. From these results, we can say that the function selection by using the multiple shapes of devices is more effectual than the function selection by simply ways of holding a single shape of a device.

As regard to the piccolo and the clarinet, the F-measure of each was as low as 25.0. It is possible that the subjects did not know the instruments enough. It was noted that, during the experiment, some subjects were holding the piccolo vertically, and holding the clarinet sideways. The data is thought to contain obvious errors of holding the instruments, causing miss-discriminations.

As some of the subjects obviously did not know how to hold some instruments, we, then, conducted a study and discriminations once again with the data of only those who answered 'they were sure of holding the instrument correctly' (subjects with high self-evaluations). The result of the learnt data of the subjects with the high self-evaluations was 69.3, and was much higher than the result of all data used for the discrimination.

Table 1. Result of One-step Classification

	Single shape			Five shapes		
	precision	recall	F-measure	precision	recall	F-measure
violin	0.571	0.640	0.604	0.824	0.519	0.636
guitar	0.615	0.615	0.615	0.828	0.857	0.842
cello	0.583	0.824	0.683	1.000	0.526	0.690
trumpet	0.323	0.385	0.351	0.654	0.630	0.642
sax	0.300	0.261	0.279	0.429	0.545	0.480
flute	0.500	0.391	0.439	0.500	0.667	0.571
piccolo	0.067	0.100	0.080	0.286	0.222	0.250
clarinet	0.000	0.000	0.000	0.217	0.294	0.250
recorder	0.294	0.370	0.328	0.633	0.679	0.655
ocarina	0.571	0.462	0.511	0.815	0.815	0.815
harmonica	0.176	0.120	0.143	0.800	0.769	0.784
total	0.387	0.396	0.387	0.670	0.634	0.641

Some of the subjects evaluated themselves high, although they had wrong ways of holding the instruments. We, then, excluded them, too, from the discrimination experiment. The discrimination rate was 71.5, in this case. However, as we have excluded some data, the number of samples turned out to be extremely low.

6.3   Result of Two-Step Classification

From the affordance theory, it can be said that we, humans, were controlled by the shapes of objects. With this in mind, we, first, conducted classification by the shapes, using the decision tree; and then we classified the output by the ways of holding them. The results of this two-step classification show table 2.

Table 2. Result of two-step classification

	One-step			Two-step		
	precision	recall	F-measure	precision	recall	F-measure
violin	0.824	0.519	0.636	0.900	1.000	0.947
guitar	0.828	0.857	0.842	0.947	1.000	0.973
cello	1.000	0.526	0.690	1.000	0.714	0.833
trumpet	0.564	0.630	0.642	0.714	0.714	0.714
sax	0.429	0.545	0.480			
flute	0.500	0.667	0.571	0.875	0.875	0.875
piccolo	0.286	0.222	0.250			
clarinet	0.217	0.294	0.250	0.833	0.833	0.833
recorder	0.633	0.679	0.655	1.000	0.960	0.980
ocarina	0.815	0.815	0.815	1.000	1.000	1.000
harmonica	0.800	0.769	0.784	1.000	1.000	1.000
total	0.670	0.634	0.641	0.919	0.900	0.906

The discrimination rate of the functions was 78.2 after this two-step classification, but the discrimination rates for the piccolo and the saxophone were too low to be classified correctly.

The instruments with low discrimination rates (the piccolo and the sax) were, when the decision tree was used, classified into the same group. The discrimination rates were low as the piccolo confused with the flute, and the saxophone confused with the clarinet. During the experiment, some subjects commented, "there is no suitable shape for the saxophone".

Having conducted the analysis with the piccolo and the saxophone excluded, we obtained F-measure of 90.6.

7   Discussion and Conclusion

In this study, we focused our attention on the function selection by the shapes based on the affordance theory. We experimented the function selection by the ways of holding multiple devices of different shapes. The functions were limited to the musical instruments of eleven representing instruments. When we compared the discrimination rates of the single device experiment and multiple device experiment, the latter showed higher discrimination rate of 64.1, higher by 26 points.

We, then, conducted classification, using the affordance theory, by shapes first, and then by the ways of holding. The result was, compared to the case we input the data in the classifier based in the shape and the ways of holding together, 78.2 of discrimination rate on the instruments, 7 points higher. As some instruments were similar in shapes and ways of holding, we limited the instruments to 9 different kinds, and re-evaluated the rate, which yielded an extremely high discrimination rate of 90.6 on the instruments.

This result revealed that the shapes are more important than the ways of holding, and the multiple shapes can lead to higher discrimination rate than the single shape, widening the range of functions available to select from.

8   Future Work

Most of the subjects in this study were inexperienced with musical instruments. It is possible that we could not obtain ideal training data. We think it is necessary, by limiting the subjects to those who are experienced with instruments, to obtain ideal training data and create a database. And, as the number of the subjects with experiences with musical instruments was small, the number of the samples and the data quantity was limited. In the future, we should increase the number of the samples.

In this study, we evaluated the selection of the musical instruments. In the future, we think it is also necessary to conduct an experiment and evaluations on more universal functions.

References

1. Gibson, J.J.: The Theory of Affordances: Perceiving, Acting, and Knowing. John Wiley & Sons Inc. (1977)
2. Taylor, B.: Grasp Recognition as a User Interface. In: CHI 2009 Proceedings of the 27th International Conference on Human Factors in Computing Systems, pp. 917–925 (2009)

Does ICT Promote the Private Provision
of Local Public Goods?

Yurika Shiozu[1], Koya Kimura[2], Katsuhiko Yonezaki[3], and Katsunori Shimohara[4]

[1] Faculty of Economics, Aichi University, Nagoya, Japan
yshiozu@vega.aichi-u.ac.jp
[2] Graduate School of Science and Engineering, Doshisha University, Kyoto
kimura2013@sil.doshisha.ac.jp
[3] Kyoto Institute Economic Research, Kyoto University, Kyoto
kyonezaki@hotmail.com
[4] Graduate School of Science and Engineering,
Doshisha University, Kyoto, Japan
kshimoha@mail.doshisha.ac.jp

Abstract. In this paper, we found three conditions to clarify the social network structure for local people solving local problems with social network analysis. One is that a core group exists in the community; the second is that the inside of the core group is an exclusive network; and the third is that a person who has high value of Betweenness centrality is next to the core group. And we showed that using ICT increases the density of the social network in our case.

Keywords: social network, centrality, local public goods.

1   Introduction

Many regions in Japan use ICT to supply local public transportation, and many of these services are based on an administration initiative. However, some people are now proposing that these systems should be private, which would not make services available to new residents. Local residents are in a better position to know the local requirements. Promoting the practical use of dormant resources in a region is one of the best ways to find a quick solution to a local problem. With conventional network analysis techniques, communication cannot be studied at informal places or through relationships, other than through a relative.

There were two research objectives for this paper. The first objective was to clarify the social network structure for local people solving local problems. The second objective was to verify whether or not using ICT increases the density of a network. We used social network analysis to reach conclusions for our objectives.

To attain our research objectives, we used an example of public transportation reservation. In the section taken up in this paper, an inhabitant per se gains a subsidy and inside with much section which works on an administration is conducting the actual proof trial run for alternative transportation operation, etc.

S. Yamamoto (Ed.): HIMI 2014, Part I, LNCS 8521, pp. 629–640, 2014.

2   Previous Studies

A social network refers to relationship of members of a society, such as an individual and a company, as well as local and other governments. The technique for clarifying these structures is called social network analysis.

From this point, in Section 2.1, we show the indicators for analyzing the whole network structure. In Section 2.2, we show the indicators for analyzing the internal network structure. Further, in Section 2.3, we describe previous research on using ICT and the strength of the social network.

2.1   Structure of Whole Network

In the social network analysis, the indicators for getting to know the fundamental structure of the whole network are diameter, density, and cluster coefficient. The time concerning transfer of information is so short that a diameter is small. It is expressed whether the relationship of density between each summit is dense. Cluster means the status where a certain person's mates are mates. Cluster can be denoted by a triangle. Cluster coefficient can be defined as the number of cluster formation of the practice occupied to the number which can be cluster achieved. Conversely, Cluster coefficient is set to 0 if one cluster is not achieved, either. Albert and Barabasi (2002) show the Cluster coefficient of the real networks are between 0.1 and 0.7.

If diameter is small, high-density, and Cluster coefficients take the value near 1, it is an exclusive network. If the diameter is large, low-density, and Cluster coefficients take the value near 0, it is open network.

There are three strengths of an exclusive network. One is that is easy to have a common purpose. The second is that it is easy to engender a sense of reliability, since members are mutual acquaintances. The third is that reciprocity is effective. A member cannot betray others easily, since they are acquaintances. That is, building loyalty is easy. On the other hand, since membership is fixed, it is hard to get new information and resources.

In an open network, since there are people connected with others outside the network, the advantage over an exclusive network is that it is possible to acquire new information and resources. However, since people in open networks do not have direct relationships, reaching agreement across the whole network is difficult. If we assume that the network is one decision-making entity, it is hard to show a path that carries the exchange of an idea.

There is disagreement over whether or not an exclusive network is better than an open network. Coleman (1988), advocating the superiority of exclusive networks, stated that few children ever dropped out of exclusive communities. In contrast, Burt (2001) showed that the more dominant structure in an adult society is when members have connections with other communities.

2.2   Internal Structure of the Network

It is important to capture not only the whole structure of the network but the internal structure as well. Several groups may exist on the inside of a network, especially if it is large. We call the indicator that divides a network into several groups a modularity. The group inside has dense relations if the value of the modularity is high. On the other hand, some groups can become alienated.

Newman (2004) was the first researcher to show modularity. Following that, various methods were proposed: Newman and Girvan (2004), Newman (2006), the CPM methods established by G. Palla et al. (2005), the local Newman methods shown by Clauset (2005), the L-shell methods proposed by Bagrow and Boltt (2005), and the procedure by Blondel et al. (2008), and so on.

There is also the sorting procedure that denotes the type of structure of the human relationships within the network. These indicators have been developed to clarify comparatively small network structures. One of these ideas is Centrality. Many indicators for measuring Centrality have been developed, for example, Degree centrality by Freeman (1979), Betweenness centrality by Brandes (2001), Closeness centrality by Sabidussi (1966), Eigenvector centrality by Bonacich (1987) and Page rank by L. Page et al. (1999).

These indicators are used in order to see the bull and bear of the relation that the person who becomes a reader exists in a network with everybody and a reader. If a certain specific person and other members have respectively powerful relation, a network is a structure of a top-down style. On the contrary, if two or more persons and everybody have relation like meshes of a net, a network has a horizontal structure. With a horizontal structure, a member tends to make mutual remark manifestation and suggestion.

Moreover, in order to measure network patency, we use Betweenness Centrality by Brandes (2001). Betweeness Centrality means whether there is any relation with the person of the inside and outside of a network through the person. As for the person who is influential in many fields, this value becomes high. If many high persons of Betweeness Centrality are contained in the network, calling in of information dispatch out of a network, and talented people and a resources will become possible.

Many techniques that analyze the whole network structure also examine validity using artificial data. Although the tools for analysis inside network structure have been applied to real data, validity changes with the candidate for analysis.

2.3 The Spontaneous Relationship between ICT and Local Residents

Whether or not ICT is stimulating spontaneous friendships among local residents awaits further research. According to the social trial runs by Hampton (2007) in the Boston suburbs, large differences were seen in the availability of electronic conference rooms and electronic bulletin board systems as well as the skills and life stage of individuals.

In this research, we supposed that participation in regional activity via ICT by the younger generation is being promoted. We also supposed that this usually results in changing the behavior of people who cannot easily participate in regional activities.

3   Analysis

We determined the research zone because of our research objectives. In section 3.1, we show the summary of this region. And we measured social networks using conventional techniques and by a social trial run that used ICT. Following section 3.2, we show the survey summary and the results.

3.1   Overview of the Subject Region

The region studied was Uji City, Makishima, in Kyoto, Japan. This city is near three larger cities. A "new town" undergoing a period of high economic growth is in Uji City, and the old and new residents are mixed in. Residents who were interested in city planning established a non-profit organization through which they plan and manage various local community activities.

In Japan, organizations with shared territorial bonding, like neighborhood associations, have traditionally organized local community activities. In Uji City, both the traditional neighborhood association and non-profit organizations complement each other when carrying out offering local community activities.

Public transportation stopped in three sections in Uji which will include Makishima area from April, 2013. For this reason, the travel difficulty person has arisen to each district. While in three areas, the inhabitant per se gained the subsidy and the Makishima area conducted the actual proof trial run for alternative transportation operation, etc. However, an actual proof trial run is not conducted in other two areas.

From our original survey in 2012, the use of cell phones and PCs in this district is shown below.

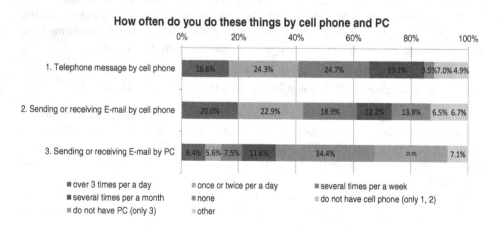

Fig. 1. Use of cell phones and the PCs in Makishima area

Our investigation showed that over 40% of the residents in Makishima are using cell phones for day-to-day telephone messages or e-mail. On the other hand, about 30% of the residents send e-mail by a PC (personal computer), even if this includes several times per person per month. From this, it can be determined that the cell phone is the ICT device used most often.

3.2   Social Network Analysis

The actual proof trial run of social network-analysis substitution transportation operation operated around the bus on demand, and the human performed the operation of the diagram installation. However, practical use of ICT became a future task from time and economic constraint. Then, ICT equipment with section inhabitants' high activity ratio will be chosen, and the procedure which can perform a clutch of demand will be developed jointly. We decided to conduct a social trial run using a smartphone as the ICT device based on the results of our investigation of the residents' trial outlined in the preceding paragraph. This is first time to test the system with inhabitants.

After receiving approval from the intramural Ethics Committee, we explained in advance how we intended to acquire personnel information to those cooperating with the trial run. We conducted the social trial run from November 11 to December 10, 2013.

Before the social trial run, we conducted a social network survey using conventional techniques with people who cooperated on 20 social trial runs from September 20 to October 5, 2013. The examination method used was the visit detention method. We designed a questionnaire using a name generator form. A name generator form differs from a normal questionnaire in several ways: first, the subject visualizes two or more people for a personal name relevant to questionnaire entries. Next, we ask

Table 1. Descriptive Statistics by name generator form

	Q1. Frequency by telephone				
	1st person	2nd person	3rd person	4th person	5th person
average	2.765	2.647	2.824	3.000	2.938
variance	1.239	0.934	1.087	0.588	1.309
N	17	17	17	17	17
	Q2. Frequency by SNS				
	1st person	2nd person	3rd person	4th person	5th person
average	3.000	2.500	3.286	3.429	3.333
variance	1.000	0.917	1.061	1.388	0.889
N	8	6	7	7	6
	Q3. Frequency of direct communication				
	1st person	2nd person	3rd person	4th person	5th person
average	2.650	2.500	2.684	2.944	2.706
variance	1.128	0.950	1.269	0.830	1.031
N	20	20	19	18	18

the relationship between the subject and those people. For this paper, the subject wrote down in the questionnaire five or fewer names of people whom he/she talks with about city planning. We asked them about those five people, including 1) the frequency that she/he talks by phone; 2) the frequency that she/he sends and receives e-mail; 3) the frequency that she/he talks through direct meetings, based on Likert's five-point scale. We also asked, using multiple choice, the place they were when they talked in a direct meeting. In addition, we asked the subjects to write down the name of the person whom she/he thinks is the leader for city planning activities. The ICT collection data used for this paper is obtained in this social trial run. The rate of collection was 100%.

Analysis of Social Network Structure by Name Generator Form. To grasp the fundamental structure of the whole network, we computed the diameter, cluster coefficients, and density. Most of the subjects are 60-70's, and they meet so often. Then, we analyze the data of the frequency of direct communications. The results are shown in Table 2. The whole network was not dense.

Table 2. Basic structure of the whole network

diameter	total number of clusters	average Cluster coefficient	density
5	87	0.117	0.063

To determine the inner structure of the network, we calculated modularity using the algorithm developed by Blondel et al. (2008). Our result: the modularity of the network in this research was set to 0.295. The number of groups was seven. In the central section of Fig. 2, we were able to find the group that most members belong to.

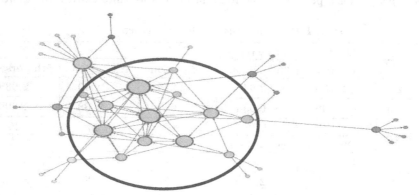

Fig. 2. Partition of the network by modularity

To understand the relationships inside the network, we used five indexes of centrality: 1) in degree centrality, 2) Betweenness centrality, 3) Eigenvector centrality, 4) Page rank, and 5) Closeness centrality. An assessment of these indicators is shown in Table 3.

Table 3. The results of each centrality assesement

Rank	In Degree Centrality		Betweenness Centrality		Eigenvector Centrality		Page Rank		Closeness Centrality	
	Value	name	value	name	value	name	value	name	value	name
1	13	T	95.0	Q	1.0	P	0.0895	P	2.818	F
2	11	P	71.4	E	0.93957	O	0.0879	T	2.75	G
3	9	Q	62.9	K	0.91685	T	0.0824	O	2.667	S
4	9	O	52.3	T	0.87113	K	0.0768	Q	2.571	D
5	8	K	42.7	M	0.83873	Q	0.0767	K	2.545	L
6	6	E	40.3	A	0.69547	M	0.0617	M	2.526	I
7	5	M	40.1	B	0.26340	B	0.0339	E	2.421	A
8	5	C	28.4	P	0.24437	E	0.0308	B	2.368	J
9	3	B	27.0	I	0.20171	I	0.0251	C	2.368	C
10	2	I	24.1	O	0.071688	C	0.0250	I	2.273	R
11	1	J	21.1	C	0.061688	A	0.0160	A	2.263	K
12	0	A	8.5	D	0.0468329	J	0.0146	D	2.211	B
13	0	D	3.3	J	0.0023015	D	0.0145	J	2.158	T
14	0	F	0.0	S	0.0	S	0.0102	N	2.158	P
15	0	G	0.0	R	0.0	R	0.0102	H	2.158	O
16	0	H	0.0	N	0.0	N	0.0102	R	2.105	M
17	0	L	0.0	H	0.0	H	0.0102	G	2.053	E
18	0	N	0.0	L	0.0	L	0.0102	S	2.05	H
19	0	R	0.0	F	0.0	F	0.0102	L	2.048	N
20	0	S	0.0	G	0.0	G	0.0102	F	1.0	Q

Compared with the results of asking the leader's name, the rank of each centrality of the leader usually was high, except 5) closeness centrality. Especially the person P who was supported overwhelming as the leader, ranked either first or second, were eigenvector centrality, page rank, and in degree centrality.

Fig. 3 shows the strength of their connections, when computed using Tarjan's algorithm (1972).

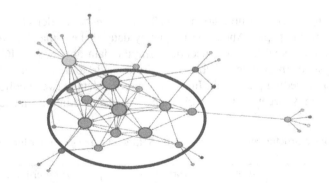

Fig. 3. Derivation of the core group

Although several members in Fig.2 were not included, most members had strong ties. In the network for this study, strong ties other than these were not detected. We defined this as the core group. The inside of the core group can be called an exclusive network.

When we observed a member of the core group using every index of centrality, they were located in a higher rank for all the indicators, except Closeness centrality. For degree centrality, eigenvector centrality, and page rank—indicators that evaluate relationships between members—the evaluator sees the entire network.

If we pay special attention to the directional movement of the arrows in the figure, when many arrows are aiming at a certain person, that person is said to be an authority. Conversely, someone who has many arrows going from them is said to be a hub. There was a person who was not only an authority but also a hub outside of the core group. After analyzing this network, we found several people with relationships to other groups that were next to the core groups.

After assessing the character of Betweenness centrality, which measures the degree of mediation with other networks or groups, we found that the core group could connect with other groups by having a relationship with the person whose Betweenness centrality has projected. That is, the whole network was an open network.

Analysis of Social Network Structure Using Social Experimental Data Based on ICT. The information was collected by ICT equipment using the smart phone. Table 4 shows the descriptive statistics of the transceiver registration of mail between social trial-run cooperators. During the survey time or an experimental period, since there is a person who did not transmit e-mail once, the number of samples used for the analysis is 13.

Table 4. Descriptive Statistics of e-mail sending/recieving with ICT

N	average	variance
13	2.362	0.364

It is verifying whether a utilization of ICT raising network density as for the second purpose of this paper. About the frequency data of the e-mail transmission and reception before a social trial-run inception, and the data obtained by ICT, the comparative analysis of the whole network structure is made to a beginning by the same technique as a preceding paragraph. In order to use the data between collection methods as a consistency target, ICT measuring data was changed into frequency data.

Table 5. Basic structure of whole network by SNS with name generator form and ICT

	diameter	total number of cluster	Average cluster coefficients	density
name generator form	3	6	0.145	0.005
data with ICT	3	186	0.707	0.276

From the table 5, the social trial run by ICT shows that the total number of clusters and the average cluster coefficients are increasing greatly. Moreover, density is also rising. These show that the exchange of mail between members increased and the share and the trade-off of the information on the whole network progressed by utilization of ICT in this network.

Subsequently, to know the structural change inside the network, each centeredness before and behind a social trial run is compared. The table 6 is a descriptive statistic of the data used for the analysis.

Table 6. Descriptive Statistics (N=13)

Centrality		average	standard deviation
Degree	Before	1.385	1.193
	After	8.154	5.829
Closeness centrality	Before	0.555	0.768
	After	1.211	0.874
Betweenness centrality	Before	0.000	0.000
	After	1.654	5.124
Page rank	Before	0.043	0.015
	After	0.042	0.011
Eigenvector centrality	Before	0.232	0.434
	After	0.519	0.088

We analyzed these centralities with the data by name generater form and ICT, using paired t-test. Table 7 shows the result.

Table 7. Results of paired t-test of each centrality with name generator form and ICT

	average	standard deviation	Confidence Interval		t-value	p-value
			lower	upper		
Degree	-6.769	6.274	-10.560	-2.978	-3.890	0.002
Closeness centrality	-0.655	1.064	-1.298	-0.012	-2.222	0.046
Betweenness centrality	-1.654	5.124	-4.750	1.442	-1.164	0.267
Page rank	0.001	0.019	-0.010	0.013	0.199	0.846
Eigenvector centrality	-0.287	0.475	-0.574	-0.000	-2.182	0.050

The slippage was observed in degree centeredness, proximity centeredness, and eigen-vector centeredness by 5% of the significance level from the result of the table 6. In this social trial run, since the e-mail and the telephone message to the person outside a network from the rule of a research-expenses use were forbidden, the transmutation was not looked at by mediation centeredness. However, the transmutation was looked at by the frequency of mail in the network, and the bull and bear of relation. The result especially with degree centrality significant also with the 1% plane was obtained.

A transmutation of degree centeredness is seen in Fig. 4. The left figure expresses social trial-run before, and the right figure expresses the time of a social trial run.

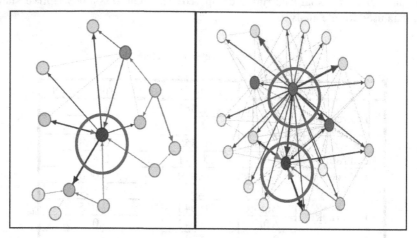

Fig. 4. Degree centrality before trial run and after

left side: before trial run   right side: trial run

Although the authority and the hub were only one place surrounded with a circle with the left figure, authorities and hubs are increasing in number to two places surrounded with a circle with the right figure. Furthermore, two authorities with degree centeredness (a figure round mark of the density) comparable as an authority and a hub are added.

In this social trial run, all members' contact address was beforehand registered into the leased equipment, and a short-term course of the transceiver procedure of e-mail was taken to the simultaneous. This led to utilizing ICT as a liaison policy with the information dispatch and the reader towards all members, or a secretariat.

4   Considerations and Remarks

We tried to find the features—from the structure of the whole network and the structure inside the network—of a social network that becomes successful when local community activity is led by residents.

We revealed three conditions for the local problem-solving network by residents from analysis using a traditional name generator form: One condition is that a core group exists in the community; the second is that the inside of the core group is an exclusive network; and the third is that a person who has high value of Betweenness centrality is next to the core group.

The above-mentioned conditions 1 share a local task, and it is shown that an existence of the group which carries out desire of the settlement is important. Moreover, when performing the business solution procedure, the conditions 2 suggest the significance of each one having detailed relation so that division of roles according to an aptitude may be made. As the conditions 3 showed, it turned out that a required resources can be raised also from an outside towards business solution in the member connected also with the external network existing.

Thus, a group with union strong against a community used as a core exists in a share of a local task, and a realization of the measure towards business solution, and it is important for the group that an outside has a point of contact.   The conventional shared-territorial-bonding structure is not necessarily filling them to the conditions 3, even if the conditions 1 and 2 are filling. Conversely, in a new structure, it is hard to fulfill the conditions 1.

Even if all the members are an old acquaintance's relations, it will be possible to raise the density of a communication using ICT. The aged are especially said to be hard to adapt themselves to ICT compared with a young man. However, from the result of this paper, gather at once, it is that simple usage is well-known to all the members, and the communization of the information became progressing   also among the aged.

The data-gathering by ICT can record conscientiously the exchange which simultaneous distribution of the mail which he was not conscious of, and an individual forget by a name generator form. Further, it became possible to measure relationships other than a relative relationship by handing a smartphone to many subjects simultaneously. But since personal information can be dealt with easily, careful remarks are required. There were many people who do not use the smart phone usually among these social trial-run cooperators, and they held the utilization school in advance. Then, the direction which noticed carrying out a simultaneous transmission at a threshold and convenience was also watched by the member. By the participant questionnaire after the termination of a trial run, because the comment that the use increased and the usage of e-mail were found, there was actually remark that he would like to use more. On the other hand, there was also a person who does not send e-mail at all. Since stopping a trial-run participation without a previous notice on the way had not barred, time may have stopped.

The social trial run did not necessarily target the whole region. From now on, by extending the number of candidates for our survey region, we would like to analyze the relationships between the core group and the whole community and to examine how to promote contiguity of new members using Betweenness centrality.

References

1. Albert, R., Barabási, A.-L.: Statistical mechanics of complex networks. Reviews of Modern Physics 74, 47–97 (2002)
2. Bagrow, J.P., Bollt, E.: A Local Method for Detecting Communities. Physical Review E 72 (2005)
3. Blondel, V., Guillaume, J.-L., Lambiotte, R., Lefebvre, E.: Fast unfolding of communities in large networks. J. Stat. Mech., 1000 (2008)

4. Bonacich, P.: Power and Centrality: A Family of Measures. AJS 92(5), 1170–1182 (1987)
5. Brandes, U.: A Faster Algorithm for Betweenness Centrality. Proc. of Journal of Mathematical Sociology 25, 163–177 (2001)
6. Burt, R.S.: Structural Holes versus Network Closure as Social Capital. In: Lin, N., Cook, K., Burt, R.S. (eds.) Social Capital: Theory and Research. Aldine de Gruyter, Hawthorn (2001)
7. Clauset, A.: Finding local community structure in networks. Physical Review E 72(2) (2005)
8. Coleman, J.S.: Social Capital in the Creation of Human Capital. American Journal of Sociology 94, S95–S121 (1988)
9. Freeman, L.: Centrality in Social Networks: Conceptual Clarification. Proc. of Social Networks 1(3), 215–239 (1979)
10. Hampton, K.N.: Neighborhoods in the Network Society. Information, Communication & Society 10(5), 714–748 (2007)
11. Newman, M.E.J.: Fast algorithm for detecting community structure in networks. Physical Review E 69, 66133 (2004)
12. Newman, M.E.J., Girvan, M.: Finding and evaluating community structure in networks. Phys. Rev. E 69, 026113 (2004)
13. Palla, G., Derényi, I., Farkas, I., Vicsek, T.: Uncovering the overlapping community structure of complex networks in nature and society. Nature 435, 814–818 (2005)
14. Sabidussi, G.: The centrality index of a graph. Proc. of Psychometrika 31(4), 581–603 (1966)
15. Tarjan, R.: Depth-First Search and Linear Graph Algorithms. SIAM Journal on Computing 1(2), 146 (1972)

Problems in Usability Improvement Activity by Software Engineers

Consideration through Verification Experiments for Human-Centered Design Process Support Environment

Yukiko Tanikawa[1], Hideyuki Suzuki[2], Hiroshi Kato[3], and Shin'ichi Fukuzumi[1]

[1] NEC Corporation, Kawasaki, Japan
y-tanikawa@cw.jp.nec.com, s-fukuzumi@aj.jp.nec.com
[2] Ibaraki University, Mito, Japan
hideyuki@suzuki-lab.net
[3] The Open University of Japan, Chiba, Japan
Hiroshi@kato.com

Abstract. We develop a support environment for software engineers that combine human centered design (HCD) policy with system development process to improve usability. We verified this support environment experimentally, and we observed that software engineers could not carry out works corresponding to "Analyze context of use", which is one of HCD activities and is usually done easily by usability engineers. Through this verification process, we found that there is some difficult task about HCD activities for software engineers to carry out.

Keywords: usability, software engineers, system development process, HCD activities, analyzing context of use.

1 Introduction

Usability importance in information systems has been increasing. By a rapid spread of a smart device, anyone has come to experience convenience of intuitive operation in everyday life. Thus, users demand usability severely to business systems namely information systems to use at work. Moreover, companies, government offices and local governments which introduce business systems focus on usability of a system from the standpoint of business challenge such as efficiency improvement and effect increase of work.

However, an approach to improve usability doesn't still infiltrate development frontline of information systems. E.Metzer [1] and T.Memmel [2] pointed out that it is caused by the gap between an information system development process and a usability improvement process.

There are two approaches that development frontline works on usability improvement. One approach is that software engineers who are system development specialist collaborate with usability experts who are usability improvement specialist in system

S. Yamamoto (Ed.): HIMI 2014, Part I, LNCS 8521, pp. 641–651, 2014.

development project [3]. The other approach is that software engineers work on usability improvement for themselves by using explicit knowledge which is formed through experiences and know-hows of usability experts [4]. In both approaches, it is necessary to bridge the gap between a system development process and a usability improvement process [1], [2], [5].

We have been researching a support method for software engineers to work on usability improvement for themselves. It is because the number of usability experts, especially in companies, is extremely small compared to that of software engineers and not many projects have sufficient budget to develop systems. We have integrated a usability improvement process into an existing system development process from a standpoint of E.Metzer [1]. Specifically we have developed the support environment for software engineers without expertise to improve usability of systems. In this environment, human-centred design for interactive systems (HCD) [6] is applied to the system development process and necessary activities are defined depending on each development phase [7] . In these activities, it is particularly important in upper process to clarify and describe customer needs related to usability such as "What managerial problems or business operational problems does a customer want to solve by improving usability?" and "What kind of usability does customer want?" It is because this activity is effective in improving usability, preventing rework of system development and improving customer satisfaction [8]. We, therefore, developed a method to support this activity that clarified and described customer needs concerning usability in upper process of system development [7].

We verified validity and usefulness of this support method. Usability experts tried activities from describing customer needs to specifying usability-related requirements at system planning and proposal phase in practical projects. Through this experiment, we found that customer needs described by using the method and those described by the usability experts themselves were confirmed to be almost the same. From this, validity of the method was verified. We also found that man-hour to these activities, such as preparation for hearings with a customer, was reduced in trial using the method. Additionally, the participants of this experiment pointed out that the method made them possible to extract evidence-based requirements and to improve quality of their activities. From this, usefulness of this method was also verified [7].

After this verification, we conducted experiments to verify whether software engineers were able to apply this support method. In this paper, results of the verification experiments are described. Problems in usability improvement activities by software engineers also found through analysis of the results and work process in the experiments are considered.

2   Support Method to Describe Customer Needs

Goals to achieve concerning usability should be drafted based on customer needs drawn out. They should be revised through close examination with customers, and finally should be arrived mutual agreement with the customers. It is important to do these activities properly in upper process of system development, in order to develop a system with high usability [8].

The method we developed supports activities which should be done for drafting customer goals concerning usability. Customers in this paper mean stakeholders who might be affected by use of a system, and they include system users, system operations management organization, and managers, etc. The activities are "specifying users and their tasks" and "describing characteristics of users and their tasks", corresponding to "Understanding and specifying the context of use" of HCD [6]. "Describing customer needs and specifying usability-related requirements" corresponding to "Specify the user requirements" of HCD [6] is also included in the activities. Features of the method are outlined as follows.

2.1 Activity Definition and Its Procedure Design for Clarifying Customer Needs

Procedure to derive usability-related customer needs from system user characteristics and task characteristics and to associate the needs with requirements is devised.

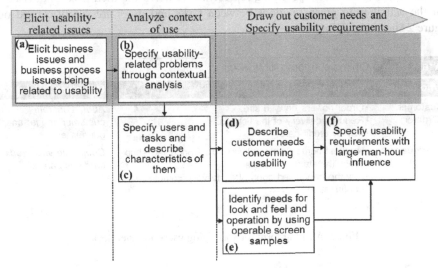

Fig. 1. Activities to specify customer needs concerning usability

Concrete activities and procedure are depicted in figure.1. (c) Each user's characteristics and the characteristics of each task are described specifying the main tasks and the representative users whom a system supports. Based on these characteristics, (d) customer needs concerning usability are described, and (f) usability requirements for achieving the needs are specified. Moreover operable screen samples are provided to draw out customer needs that are hard to communicate by verbal, such as look and feel of a system and the operation. As for them, some kinds are prepared according to the characteristics of users and tasks. Procedure for (e) identifying customer needs by using these operable screen samples [9] and (e) associating the needs with usability requirements is devised.

On the other hand, exploring a little deeply customer demand concerning usability might be necessary according to customer's awareness of issues, characteristics of tasks whom a system supports, and system scale, etc. Procedures (a) and (b) for supporting such cases are devised in our method.

2.2   Expressly Specifying Main Tasks and Representative Users

In activities for specifying usability-related customer needs, it is fundamental to grasp relations between tasks and users whom a system supports. System scale grows as technology progresses and range of tasks has extended. This makes data and functions of a system complex and diverse, and also makes system users diverse. As a result, relation between users and tasks become complex, as data exchanged and functions to use are different in each user for instance. However, activities to grasp relations between tasks and users whom a system supports are rarely done in a system development process expressly.

Thus, a filling form for specifying representative users and their tasks is devised so that the activities to grasp relations between tasks and users are surely carried out. Figure 2 shows the filling form.

A task	Online shopping for flowers	
Who (users)	**What (work)**	**Questions**
Customer (Orderer)	• Order flowers on web site. • Request delivery of the flowers. • Pay by credit card.	*About concrete customer image; age, gender, etc.*
Headquarters	• Request home flower delivery to a franchised shop • Track the status of orders • Pay the franchised shop after delivery completion confirmation	*Cooperate with credit card companies?*
...	....	

Fig. 2. A filling form for specifying users and their tasks

2.3   Confirmation Items about User Characteristics and Task Characteristics

Confirmation items are devised to describe characteristics of each user and task that a system supports. Indispensable information for improving system usability in addition to necessary information for grasping system development conditions are organized based on HCD [6], and are listed as these items. They are for instance items to confirm age group of users, their proficiency in tasks, and frequency of task execution. These items can be easily specified by software engineers without expertise concerning usability improvement.

2.4   Association Rules between Usability-Related Requirements and User and Task Characteristics

(d) Customer needs concerning usability and (f) usability requirements for achieving the needs in figure.1 are listed as items based on usability improvement guideline for in-house [4], which was developed by systematizing principles of usability and know-hows of usability experts. Specifically, customer needs concerning usability are divided into categories such as basic input operation and data display method, and are defined as items. Usability requirements are defined as items according to a customer needs item. Besides, among these requirement items, those which have significant influence on man-hour especially in lower process of system development are selected.

Moreover, customer needs concerning usability and usability requirements are identified according to a user characteristic item or a task characteristic item. Association rules between needs, requirement and characteristic are created based on this. Figure 3 is a concrete example of the association rule.

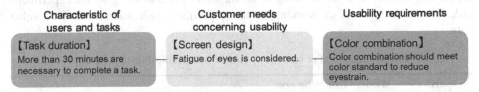

Characteristic of users and tasks	Customer needs concerning usability	Usability requirements
【Task duration】 More than 30 minutes are necessary to complete a task.	【Screen design】 Fatigue of eyes is considered.	【Color combination】 Color combination should meet color standard to reduce eyestrain.

Fig. 3. An example of the association rule to derive usability-related requirements

The support method makes it possible to derive usability-related customer needs from system user characteristics and task characteristics and to associate the needs with requirements. By using this method, system engineers without expertise are possible to describe customer needs and specify requirements.

3   Verification Experiment of Support Method

We conducted experiments to verify whether software engineers were able to apply this support method and to derive usability-related requirements. Software engineers who were research participants were required to try a series of defined activities necessary for specifying requirements using this method and their trial process was observed.

The activities are "specifying users and their tasks" and "describing characteristics of users and their tasks", corresponding to "Understanding and specifying the context of use" of HCD [6]. "Describing customer needs and specifying usability-related requirements" corresponding to "Specify the user requirements" of HCD [6] is also included in the activities.

The support method provided a filling form for "specifying users and their tasks" and confirmation items for "describing characteristics of users and their tasks".

Association rules between usability-related needs, requirement and characteristic were also provided for "describing user needs and specifying user requirements".

Six software engineers cooperated in the verification experiments as research participants. They tried the activities for a system in charge now or in the past.

3.1   Verification Experiment 1

The purpose of this experiment was to examine whether a software engineer was able to specify usability-related requirements using the support method.

Methods. A participant was a software engineer who had seven years working experience in system development. The participant was required to try the activities using the support environment that the method was incorporated into.

A usability expert who knew this method well sat next to the participant as an experiment supporter and advanced a whole experiment. The expert explained the experiment task and procedure, and answered questions from the participant. The participant was asked to use thinking aloud methods while working on the experiment task. The entire process of working on the experiment task was recorded as video data.

Table 1. A fragment of interaction protocols in verification experiment 1

Expert:	*What is troubling you?*
Participant:	*I'm thinking about system users. Staff members use the system, and as an industry characteristic, many contract workers and part-timers also use the system. Additionally, tasks to use the system are quite different in each section. So, I thought that user groups might be decided by both such an employee attribute and a section. And I'm wondering how I can specify users. User groups seem to increase terribly if I specify users as staff member users of department A, part-timer users of department A, etc.*
Expert:	*You gave examples such as staff member users of department A, part-timer users of department A. Is there a difference between them?*
Participant:	*Hmm, I don't know in detail. I cannot explain explicitly, but needs for the system should be different. Then, it might be good in this approach.*
Expert:	*Do you mean that you don't know criteria to divide user groups?*
Participant:	*I don't know criteria.*

Results. The participant was observed having a hard time in "specifying users and their tasks". Table 1 shows a fragment of interaction protocols when the participant was troubled with work.

In the next "describing characteristics of users and their tasks", the participant smoothly selected most items to specify characteristics. However, she was observed hesitating over which items to choose about a part of characteristics. Table 2 shows a fragment of protocols when the participant was hesitating.

On the other hand, in "describing customer needs and specifying usability-related requirements", we observed the participant checking requirement items without hesitation. These items were what the method derived automatically from selected characteristic items by using the association rules between usability-related needs, requirement and characteristic.

Table 2. A fragment of protocols in verification experiment 1

Participant:	*How long does a user take to complete this task once? Hmm, how should I do? Let me think. Tasks to use the system are various in each section, and time necessary to complete depends on tasks. A certain task takes a couple of minutes and another task takes more than 30 minutes. So, I cannot specify necessary time and don't select any item.*

Discussion. The participant specified just one task for the entire system at the beginning of activities in the experiment. However, she repeatedly mentioned that tasks to use the system are different in each section, as illustrated in table 1 and table 2. This suggests that task specification is inappropriate. In other word, she set a range of one task too big. It is considered that it is caused by inadequacy of the range setting for one task that she (the participant) was troubled with specifying users and selecting items to specify characteristics. Besides we consider that the participant only ambiguously realizes tasks and users are related.

While the participant relatively smoothly worked on "describing characteristics of users and their tasks" and "describing customer needs and specifying usability-related requirements", she was troubled with "specifying users and their tasks". We consider the reason as follows. The participant could not understand what she should do in the experiment task because she was not familiar with directions for the experiment task and could not obtain information to promote understanding of directions such as analysis examples. Namely we speculate that this problem is caused by difference in notations, languages, and operation constraints between software engineers and usability experts [10], [11].

3.2   Verification Experiment 2

Based on the results and discussion of experiment 1, directions for the activities defined in the method were improved to suit notations, languages and operation constraints that the participant was familiar with. Methods and standard procedure manuals that software engineers used in everyday work were referred, in this improvement. The purpose of the experiment 2 was to verify whether a software engineer came able to specify users and tasks smoothly and appropriately by this improvement.

Methods. Participants were four software engineers. Three of them were leaders of system development teams who had around ten years working experience. Other one participant had three year experience in system development.

They were required to try "specifying users and their tasks" and "describing characteristics of users and their tasks". They were offered remade filling forms with paper, whose directions for the experiment task were supplemented and modified. They were required to fill in the forms by handwriting. Handwriting was adopted to make participants fill in users and tasks of systems in charge as they usually grasped, without newly elaborating for the experiment.

A usability expert who knew this method well explained the experiment task and procedure to participants, and observed them working on the experiment task. The expert briefly interviewed participants after they completed the experiment task.

Tasks	Apply for a visit
	Apply for an entrance certificate
	Manage facilities

Who (users)	What (work)
Staff members	• Apply for a visit
Staff members	• Apply for an admission • Apply for extension of entrance period • Apply for acceptance of visitors
Managers	• Approve application
Facilities managers	• Approve application • Manage facilities
• • •	• • • •
Card issue center	• Issue an entrance certificate

Fig. 4. An example of results in verification experiment 2

Results. It was only one person in four participants that appropriately specified users and tasks. This participant was a leader of a system development team. In the results of this participant, relation between tasks and users were clear and work flow in each task was also clear. Moreover it was added to the form that a user who took charge of a certain work and a user who took charge of another work were the same person, without any direction. This was that the participant defined a user in the physical viewpoint.

On the other hand, in the results of other three participants, two or more tasks were specified. Figure 4 shows an example of results in experiment 2. Work corresponding to different tasks was associated with one user together. Thus, relation between tasks and users were uncertain and work flow in each task was difficult to see. Users they specified were department names and position titles. Besides, one of these three participants filled in almost the same content to a task and work.

The expert observing these experiments reported that all participants filled in the form while referring documents of system development projects. In addition, a fragment of interaction protocols in table 3 were reported.

Table 3. A fragment of interaction protocols in verification experiment 2

Expert:	*About the new tasks, can you fill in a form in the same way?*
Participant:	*Maybe I can't.*
Expert:	*How do you think that you can do it?*
Participant:	*First, I will think of one task, then think of its work flow. If I do it in such a way, I think that I can do it.*

Discussion. We found that participants don't come able to specify users and tasks smoothly and appropriately by the improvement. It is considered that there is possibility participants regarded users as not the person who took charge of a specific part of work flow in a task but the person who had a specific access right in a system, based on the users they specified in the results of experiment. We consider that there is also a possibility participants picked up information from system development documents without thinking though they couldn't find descriptions suitable for the purpose of the experiment task from the documents, based on the observation result that they filled in the form while referring to the documents. Moreover we found that procedure for specifying users next to tasks may interrupt thinking of participants who think about work flow necessary for a task achievement next to a task, from a fragment of interaction protocols shown in table 3. From the above, we speculate that a problem is caused by difference in the meaning of "users" and in procedure between software engineers and usability experts.

3.3 Verification Experiment 3

Based on the results and discussion of experiment 2, procedure for the activities defined in the method was revised. The revised procedure has two phases. First phase is describing work flow necessary to achieve a task after specifying tasks, and defining roles taking charge of a specific work in the work flow. Second phase is specifying a user by bringing roles together by the viewpoint that one physical person takes charge of. In addition, an example that a context of use of a certain system was analyzed and the form was filled in was made.

The purpose of the experiment 3 was the same as the experiment 2, which was to verify whether a software engineer came able to specify users and tasks smoothly and appropriately by this revision.

Methods. A participant was a software engineer who had six years working experience in system development. The participant was required to try "specifying users and their tasks" and "describing characteristics of users and their tasks". He was offered remade filling forms whose procedure for the experiment task was revised, and he was also offered the example. The filling forms were divided into plural sheets with the procedure revision. Thus the participant was required to fill in the forms electrically on a computer. This was because the convenience of participants was considered.

A usability expert who knew this method well explained the experiment task and procedure to participants, and observed them working on the experiment task. The expert briefly interviewed participants after they completed the experiment task.

Results. The participant smoothly and appropriately described work flow necessary to achieve tasks after specifying tasks, and defined roles taking charge of a specific work in the work flow. However, he was not able to specify a user at all by bringing roles together by the viewpoint that one physical person takes charge of.

The participant talked in an interview that he was unable to specify tasks and to describe work flow if an example was not offered because he didn't understand the appropriate range setting for one task. Moreover he talked that he could not understand the meaning of the experiment task about "specifying a user by bringing roles together by the viewpoint that one physical person takes charge of". And he added that an example offered made him confused further. He came to understand the relationship between roles and users and the meaning of the experiment task from the explanation of the expert.

Discussion. We found that a participant still have trouble with specifying users and tasks by the revision. About specifying tasks, it is considered that a participant isn't familiar with concept of the range setting for one task and this causes a problem, based on talk of the participant. About specifying users, we consider that a participant doesn't recognize a user as a physical person and this causes a problem, based on the results of experiment and talk of the participant. And it is suggested that specifying users is especially difficult for software engineers.

4   Conclusions

Through analysis of these verification experiments process and results, we found that software engineers cannot appropriately carry out "identifying each relevant user and task in a use scene of a system", which is the base work for clarifying and describing customer needs concerning usability and is usually done without difficulty by usability experts. That is it is suspected that software engineers may develop systems without appropriately recognizing the users and their purposes of system use. Moreover, it was suggested that it was caused by concepts which were difficult for software engineers to understand because the engineers were not conscious of them, in addition to differences in notations, languages, and operation constraints between software engineers and usability experts [10], [11]. The range setting for one task and a user as a physical person are examples of such concepts. These are considered problems in usability improvement activity by software engineers.

Based on these considerations, we would investigate difference in thinking and approach to grasp a target system between software engineers and usability experts and also would seek clues to solve those problems we found.

References

1. Metzker, E., Offergeld, M.: An Interdisciplinary Approach for Successfully Integrating Human-Centered Design Methods into Development Processes Practiced by Industrial Software Development Organizations. In: Nigay, L., Little, M.R. (eds.) EHCI 2001. LNCS, vol. 2254, pp. 19–33. Springer, Heidelberg (2001)
2. Memmel, T., Gundelsweiler, F., Reiterer, H.: Agile human-centered software engineering. In: Proceedings of the 21st British HCI Group Annual Conference on People and Computers: HCI..But Not as We Know It, vol. 1, pp. 167–175 (2007)
3. Göransson, B., Gulliksen, J., Boivie, I.: The usability design process–integrating user-centered systems design in the software development process. Software Process: Improvement and Practice 8(2), 111–131 (2003)
4. Hiramatsu, T., Fukuzumi, S.: Applying Human-Centered Design Process to System Director Enterprise Development Methodology. NEC Technical Journal 3(2), 12–16 (2008)
5. Nebe, K., Paelke, V.: Usability-Engineering- Requirements as a Basis for the Integration with Software Engineering. In: Jacko, J.A. (ed.) HCI International 2009, Part I. LNCS, vol. 5610, pp. 652–659. Springer, Heidelberg (2009)
6. IS9241-210: Human-centred design for interactive systems (2010)
7. Tanikawa, Y., et al.: Proposal of human-centered design process support environment for system design and development. In: 4th International Conference on Applied Human Factors and Ergonomics, pp. 7825–7834 (2012)
8. Seffah, A., Gulliksen, J., Desmarais, M.C. (eds.): Human-Centered Software Engineering-Integrating Usability in the Software Development Lifecycle, vol. 8. Springer (2005)
9. Okubo, R., et al.: UX Embodying and Systematizing Method to improve user experience in system development-applying to planning and proposal phase. In: 4th International Conference Applied on Human Factors and Ergonomics, pp. 7815–7824 (2012)
10. Ferre, X.: Integration of Usability Techniques into the Software Development Process. In: Bridging the Gaps Between Software Engineering and Human-Computer Interaction, p. 28 (2003)
11. Seffah, A., Metzker, E.: The obstacles and myths of usability and software engineering. Communications of the ACM 47(12), 71–76 (2004)

Requirements Engineering Using Mockups and Prototyping Tools: Developing a Healthcare Web-Application

Leonor Teixeira[1,3], Vasco Saavedra[1],
Carlos Ferreira[1,3], João Simões[4], and Beatriz Sousa Santos[2,3]

[1] Department of Economics, Management and Industrial Engineering,
University of Aveiro, Portugal
[2] Department of Electronics, Telecommunications and Informatics,
University of Aveiro, Portugal
[3] Institute of Electronics and Telematics Engineering of Aveiro (IEETA), Portugal
[4] Truphone, Lisbon, Portugal
{lteixeira,vsaavedra,carlosf,bss}@ua.pt, jpasimoes@gmail.com

Abstract. Healthcare web-application development teams involve non-computer experts working (clinicians) on the requirements specification that is later processed by software engineers/analysts (conceptual model) and coded by software programmers (software project). The management of this process, which involves different levels of abstraction and professionals with different backgrounds, is often complex. As such, mediators and facilitator's mechanisms for the requirements-gathering process and information transfer are needed. The main purpose of this work is to minimize the problems associated with this complex process, supporting the requirements engineering process of a healthcare web-application in a rapid prototyping model. The results proved that a rapid and functional prototyping model can improve the effectiveness of the requirement elicitation of any software development.

Keywords: healthcare web-application, software, requirement engineering, requirement elicitation, mockups, prototyping.

1 Introduction

The success of any software depends on how well it fulfills the needs of its users and of its environment. Software requirement comprises these needs and Requirements Engineering (RE) is the process by which the requirements are determined, being a fundamental part of the development process of any software. The first stage of the RE process, commonly known as requirement elicitation, is recognized as one of the most critical activities of the entire development lifecycle, since it is the stage where the main stakeholders are identified and involved in order to specify, analyze, and define the software goal and respective software requirements. It is a negotiation process during which intense capturing, combination and dissemination of knowledge

S. Yamamoto (Ed.): HIMI 2014, Part I, LNCS 8521, pp. 652–663, 2014.

occurs, and different stakeholders exchange information about the context, and the tasks that will be supported by the software under development [1]. However, the involvement of stakeholders is not always an easy process, and the degree of their involvement depends on several factors, such as: (i) newness of the project; (ii) degree of complexity of the system; (iii) techniques and methods used by the analyst to promote the elicitation and validation the requirements, and; (iv) the geographical dispersion of potential users, which can difficult the joint meetings usually required to identify and validate the requirements.

Particularly in the health domain, the low rate of technology acceptance and the percentage of software projects that have failed in this area continue to be a phenomenon that has placed challenges to researchers that work in this knowledge area. The literature indicates that non-acceptance of a particular technology is frequently associated with the non-involvement of potential users in the development process, and a great part of the failed projects are due to the lack of systematic considerations of human aspects throughout the design process [2, 3]. Regardless of application domain of the software/Information System (IS), the involvement of the users, although important at all stages of the project, requires a special attention in the early stages of the process and should be mediated with a set of techniques and methods appropriate to the context and type of problem.

Accordingly, there are different methods and techniques that are used by system analysts to manage the RE process, such as UML models, task analysis, and prototyping. Within the scope of prototyping, there are a variety of technological solutions that allow the creation of mockups, being Lumzy[1] one of them. With tools like Lumzy, it is very easy to create mockups, share and send them to the stakeholders involved in design process in real-time, putting the emphasis on collaboration and interactivity, and promoting the clarification and validation of the software requirements, when the support team is geographically distributed.

The aim of this work is to present our perspective on the requirements engineering process of a health information system, as well as the lessons learned from our experience with the development of a distributed web-application to support the Portuguese National Registry of Hemophilia and other Congenital Coagulopathies (NRH&CC), using Lumzy as the prototyping tool. To present this subject, this paper is structured in four sections. In section 2, an overview of the related work in the requirements engineering and prototyping is presented. Section 3 presents our case study concerning the RE in a process of a health information system development using a prototyping model. Finally, in section 4, the main conclusions of the paper are presented.

2   About Requirements Engineering and Prototyping

In the software/Information System (IS) development context, a requirement is a property that a system must exhibit in order to meet the system's motivation need. A

---

[1] http://www.lumzy.com/

software requirement is a property which must be exhibited by the software developed to solve a particular problem within one specific context. Requirements Engineering (RE) is a science that studies, analyzes and documents the requirements, and is presented in the literature as a knowledge area of Software Engineering that specifies, analyzes, and defines the product goal and functionalities of the final solution [4, 5]. RE can be described as series of stages including elicitation, analysis, specification, validation, and management of the software requirements. During the first stage of the RE process, which is referred to as the requirement elicitation phase, systems requirements are discovered, discussed and agreed by the stakeholders. This stage is defined by Pohl [6] as a core RE activity aiming to determine relevant requirements sources, to identify functional and non-functional requirements from these sources and to discover new requirements. RE activities are vital in ensuring successful projects and shortcomings in requirements elicitation can have a negative impact on the overall development process and consequently can lead to higher costs for the involved organizations [7]. Furthermore, the task of requirements elicitation is highly collaborative and involves many stakeholders, including the users who interact with system and usually represent the domain experts.

According to Sommerville [8], the process of requirements engineering is difficult for several reasons, emphasizing the fact that: (i) in many cases the users/clients[2] are not completely sure about their real needs, and often don't know what they want from the system, except in general terms; (ii) users/clients express requirements in their own language and with implicit knowledge of their work, and requirements engineers without experience in the user domain must understand these requirements; (iii) different stakeholders have different requirements, which they may express in different ways.

To help the process of requirements engineering and minimize the difficulties inherent to this process, the literature presents a set of tools and methods to assist the organization of the requirements, consistency checking, preparation of the specification, and formalization and validation of these requirements.

Usually, requirements are obtained and documented in a natural language (list of textual requirements) after they are modeled using a formal requirements representation (e.g. UML models, task analysis) or figures (e.g. mockups) in order to validate the requirements. While techniques like interviews, questionnaires, user observation, workshops, brainstorming, card sorting, and think aloud are used to obtain the software requirements, UML/Use-cases, task analysis methods and prototyping are examples of tools to model these requirements, providing mechanisms to assist a possible validation. However, few of these tools and methods provide any valuable help for obtaining, representing and validating the requirements by potential users who are geographically distributed and have no availability to attend to team meetings.

A number of studies have considered prototyping as an excellent vehicle for requirements discovery and validation [9, 10], since the prototype model can help elicit the requirement from the changing and complex environment, decomposing high-level requirements into details. Prototyping is a popular requirements elicitation

---

[2] Non-technical stakeholders involved in requirements identification.

technique because it enables users to develop a real sense about final systems that have not yet been implemented [10]. Through the use of prototypes, users can identify the true requirements that may otherwise be impossible to identify, by visualizing the software systems to be built, being especially useful when there is a great deal of uncertainty about the requirements [11].

In the RE context, prototypes can serve different purposes, and may be classified as low-fidelity prototypes and high-fidelity prototypes [12]. The low-fidelity prototypes are those that do not resemble the final product, being widely used in the exploratory phase or in the early stages of system development. Usually this type of prototypes is simple, easy to produce and therefore involves low costs of production. The high-fidelity prototypes are closer to the final product and usually use the same techniques and materials in its development. This type of prototype has a much higher associated cost in comparison with the former type. Regarding the implementation, it is possible to classify the techniques of prototyping in two methods: throwaway or evolutionary prototyping. The former is the development of a prototype which aims to increase the quality of the requirements document and is generally based on the most complex requirements. This type of prototype is discarded after fulfilling its purpose. Examples of this type of prototype are the paper prototype and the wizard-of-Oz prototype [13]. The wizard-of-Oz prototype is often used in situations with complex functionalities or situations needing to test new ideas, simulating system responses according to user actions. Evolutionary prototypes, on the other hand, are developed as a portion of the actual system and focused on the requirements that have already been well understood and new requirements are incrementally added, as the development proceeds in an iterative manner.

To meet the needs in the context of RE, and taking into account the cost/benefit relationship of this process, low-fidelity prototypes of the throwaway type are the most used to obtain early feedback in uncertainty environments, being discarded after finalizing its purpose. In order to assist the RE process through this type of prototype, there are a variety of tools (desktop or online applications), that allow to draw mockups and create wireframes, such as Balsamiq, Visio Professional, OmniGraffle, Prototype Composer, ConceptDrawPro, SmartDraw, Pencil Project, MockFlow, fluidIA, Pidoco, or Lumzy. These tools include libraries with graphical elements, which enable managing and publishing information elements, as well as incorporating new graphical components [13]. A prototype generated by such tools have the same advantages as a paper prototype, having a low cost, easiness of construction and use, and providing an interface that allows the user to perceive that is using a disposable prototype. Additionally it inherits some useful features of the wizard-of-Oz prototypes, and even of the evolutionary prototypes, to the extent that it's possible to include interactivity, with actions responding to user events. With this type of tools, clients can design their own interface as they would like to use it, simply dragging components into the canvas. Some of these tools also have the particularity to be accessible online, thus not requiring any additional software installations by the user.

With Lumzy, the tool used in our case study, is very simple to create mockups, share and send them in real-time to the stakeholders involved in the design process. Lumzy is a web-based wireframing tool for rapid user-interface prototyping, emphasizing collaboration and interactivity, as well as promoting the clarification and validation of the software requirements without the presence of stakeholders in the same geographical space. Lumzy represents a powerful simulation software that enables users to rapidly build functionalities without writing code, offering both technical and non-technical users to experience, test, collaborate and validate the simulated program, also providing reports with annotations.

This paper reports a case where a rapid prototyping was adopted to elicit and validate the system requirements at a healthcare level and Lumzy was the tool used to mediate and manage the RE process.

3   Practical Application: Requirements Engineering Process in a Health Information System (IS) Using Lumzy Prototyping

This work aims to present the requirements elicitation process of a health information system (Health-IS) development, as well as the lessons learned from this experience. The Health-IS involved is a distributed web-application to support a National Registry of Hemophilia and other Congenital Coagulopathies (NRH&CC) in Portugal, and prototyping was the main technique used in the requirements elicitation.

3.1   Motivation and Overview of the Project (Health-IS)

The present project is a joint initiative between the hemophilia healthcare professionals, represented by the Portuguese Association of Congenital Coagulopathies (PACC) and a group of researchers from the University of Aveiro (UA) responsible for analyzing, developing and implementing the technological solution.

The lack of a NRH&CC in Portugal, associated with the difficulty that clinicians of this area faced in order to manage this specific patient information, motivated a group of physicians to search for a technological solution that allowed to facilitate and optimize the information management process. Thus, the need arose to develop a project that led to the creation of the NRH&CC in Portugal, and the PACC members constituted themselves as the main clients/users of this project, using their experience as a basis for the requirements definition process. The University of Aveiro (UA) was designated to develop the project, having the responsibility to conceptualize, encode and implement the technological solution (named *hemo@record*). Given the complexity of the project, which involved a broad range of demographic, social and clinical data, and the geographic dispersion of the users/clients responsible for defining the requirements (associated with the limited availability), the process of Requirements Engineering emerged as the main challenge of project.

3.2   Requirements Engineering Process Using a Prototype

The process of developing an application with the described features is always complex, as in addition to the development team members having very diverse backgrounds, they are geographically dispersed. In order to perform the process of requirements engineering of this project, we chose to use a mediator and facilitator method for obtaining and managing the requirements, specifically the throwaway prototyping method, which consisted of a development lifecycle model by which a prototype is created for demonstration and requirements elicitation. The sequence of the steps followed using this technique is described below and depicted in Figure 1.

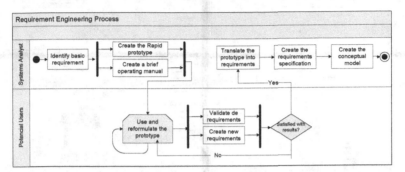

Fig. 1. Phases of the requirement engineering process

First Step (Start-up Meeting). The process started with a meeting attended by the members of PACC (users and clients of the project) and the members of the team responsible for the development, having been defined the objectives as well as the high-level requirements to include. This meeting produced a first draft of the Requirements Specification Document (RSD) in a text format, with some very high-level requirements.

Second Step (1st Version of Prototype Building). Given the high level requirements defined in phase 1, complemented with the results of a previous study of the authors [14] and based on the analysis of the national reporting systems already implemented in other countries, the systems analyst drafted the first version of the prototype (designated *prototype-hemo@record*), using the Lumzy prototyping tool. This version of the prototype included a set of requirements not yet validated by the stakeholders. The purpose for this inclusion was to stimulate the curiosity of the stakeholders, forcing them to validate and possibly to add missing requirements and/or delete irrelevant requirements. As can be seen in Figure 2, this version structured the information through a side menu, which according to the selection of the user allowed to access several interfaces for data entry or present the information displayed in different formats, descriptive text and graphics representations.

It should be noted that Lumzy, despite its easiness of use, can still cause some resistance from users without computational background if not properly contextualized and introduced in the environmental analysis. In order to eliminate this barrier, we prepared a small manual of instructions, which was sent to each participating stakeholder, with the access codes to use the *prototype-hemo@record* application. Eight invitations were sent to eight clinicians and future users of the technological solution.

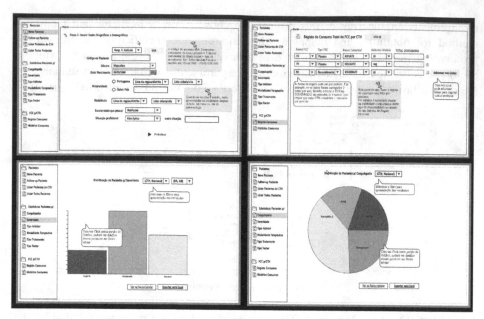

Fig. 2. First version of the *prototype-hemo@record*: same examples of mockups (in Portuguese)

Third Step (1st Prototype Validation and Reformulation). After sending the invitations with the access credentials and instructions, the clients/users were encouraged to use and test the prototype, being able to change, remove or add new features. This phase took place over three months, involving an iterative and incremental process of evaluation and redesign of the prototype. As the prototype was modified, the analyst gathered the main features and the necessary data for defining the conceptual model and, at the same time, was able to understand the main difficulties of the users. During this phase, the analyst also had an important role in the maintenance of the prototype, ensuring the organization of the elements (icons) that were placed by the users on the interface, and, in some situations, converting the requirements inserted by the users in the annotation format, in actual functionalities of the prototype. Based on this prototype version, the functional requirements were identified. In terms of nonfunctional requirements, the analyst became aware of difficulties in using the prototype by some users, more specifically on the usage of the navigation system. The information did not appear to be easily found by users, causing them to replicate on certain pages, the information already presented on others. The identification of these difficulties prompted the need to rethink the organization of the information and the navigation mechanism, thus resulting in a new version of the *prototype-hemo@record*.

Fourth Step (2nd Version of Prototype Building). This version included all the requirements already identified in the previous version, and a completely restructured layout and navigation mechanism (Figure 3). At this stage, and taking into account all the requirements previously identified, the analyst, in collaboration with the

developers of the system, proposed a new navigation mechanism, specifically oriented to processes. Each information process would be presented in the first interface
(Figure 3 – Interface A), with the sub-processes being presented in the subsequent
interfaces. Thus, all the information not relevant to the process involved would be
hidden.

After this restructuring, a new version of the prototype was submitted to be evaluated by the same group of eight users, in order to validate the functional requirements
in the new layout, while at the same time, testing some non-functional requirements.
The access to the previous version was maintained, to allow to perform direct comparisons with the new version, thus allowing the users to indicate the version they
found more intuitive and easier to use in the scope of the tasks they needed to
perform.

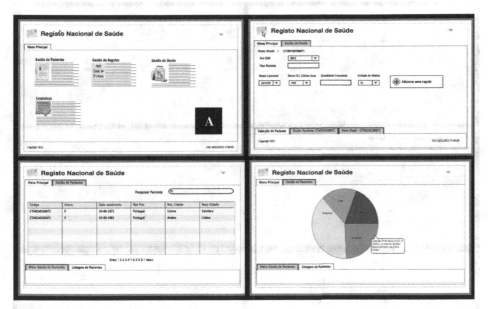

Fig. 3. Second version of the *Prototype-hemo@record*: same examples of the mockups (in
Portuguese)

Fifth Step (2nd Prototype Validation and Reformulation). This version was iterat-
ed until the users were satisfied with the system and lasted about two weeks. Although this version does not add new functionalities, it allowed to analyze each of
them with greater detail, since the tasks where unfolded to their most atomic elements. Moreover, this release was determinant in the selection of the type of system
to implement (modular design), as the aspects related to the non-functional requirements, and more specifically the structure, organization and navigation, were
assessed. Thus, a modular design was the selected approach, with each module responsible for implementing a single information process (workflow).

3.3   Results: Using Mockups and Prototyping to Identify System Requirements

After completing the process of requirements elicitation, performed iteratively and incrementally around the five phases previously presented, the analyst converted all the functional requirements identified in a formal representation, in order to facilitate the communication with the system programmers. For this representation, the UML notation was used, specifically the use-case diagrams to represent the actors and inter-actions of these with the application, and the class diagram to represent the conceptual model of the application domain.

Left Side: Examples of Mockups representations resulting from 2nd Prototype

Right Side: Example of User Interfaces representa-tions resulting from the final application

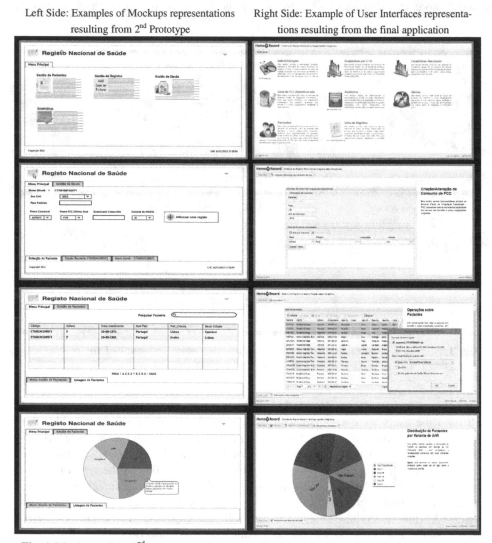

Fig. 4. Mockups of the 2nd prototype and corresponding user-interfaces from the final application

Additionally, and as mentioned before, this process of requirements elicitation has also had a strong influence on the identification of some non-functional requirements, having the 2nd prototype a pivotal role in this issue. As such, 2nd prototype was thoroughly analyzed by programmers in order to develop the interface technology solution according to the mockups validated by users abreast of the functionalities identified in the use-case diagrams, and data model in a class diagram.

In a nutshell, Table 1 summarizes the main activities of the present RE process, the stakeholders involved in each activity, as well as the main inputs and outputs.

Table 1. Main activities, inputs and outputs of the RE

Activities	Start-up meeting	1st Prototype	2nd Prototype
Stakeholders	– Programmers – Systems analyst – Users /Clients	– Systems analyst – Users /Clients	– Programmers – Systems analyst – Users /Clients
Times / Period of evaluation	– One meeting	– About three months	– About two weeks
Inputs	– An idea and a requirement	– Outputs of the start-up meeting; – results of a previous study of the authors [14] – Results of an analysis of the national reporting systems already implemented in other countries	– Outputs of prototype 1 – Experience of the programmers
Outputs (main results)	– Objectives of the system – Some very high-level requirements	– High-level functional requirements – Some low-level requirements	– Low-level requirements – Non-functional requirements

4   Conclusions

It is an established fact that shortcomings in requirements elicitation can lead to inadequate implementations, thus leading to higher costs in the development of any software [15]. Particularly in the phase of requirements elicitation (one of the main critical stages of RE), the participation and collaboration of the stakeholders are crucial activities in the survey process and requirements elicitation. Beyond being a complex process, it can still become even more difficult if the stakeholders involved are geographically dispersed.

In reality, and particularly in the areas further away from engineering and computer science, the largest part of the requirements is in the implicit knowledge and experience of potential users, being difficult to extract this knowledge without an active and collaborative involvement of those potential users (clients/users). Accordingly, techniques that promote the requirements elicitation, and at the same time assist in converting the implicit knowledge (user experience) into explicit knowledge (documented knowledge) should be used.

In this article, and working in the domain of a complex health problem, the authors proposed a method for eliciting requirements based on participation, collaboration and negotiation of requirements by the different stakeholders of the project, supported by the method of prototyping. This method promotes an approach of stepwise refinement of requirements, starting with general ideas until the low-level requirements are achieved. Since this is a prototype, this method was also essential in the identification of some non-functional requirements that complemented the definition of the functional requirements.

This process involved a group of 10 members (8 of them physicians and future users), who started by defining the general objectives in a face-to-face meeting. After this meeting, the analyst designed the first version of the solution using Lumzy, having thereafter sent individual invitations to other participants with a small user manual. Each participant had access to the Web platform (using a login and password), and was able to define new requirements, modify existing and eliminate non-relevant ones by defining the interface required for each requirement. At the same time the participants used and modified the interface according to their needs, the analyst was notified of changes and collected the requirements. Several versions of the prototyping solution were achieved during this process, and the requirements were collected from a very broad and geographically distributed community of physicians, without the need to promote other joint meetings. In addition to the gathering of requirements, the platform allowed to drill-down into each requirement in terms of more elementary tasks, allowing the definition of the data model with full accuracy by the analyst.

It should be noted that in this study the rate of participation in the definition and validation of the requirements through this platform exceeded our expectations and the results were very satisfactory. Based on the experience obtained with this case, it is possible to conclude that prototyping tools like Lumzy are very appropriate to use in the process of requirements gathering, when the system involved is complex, and dynamic in terms of its definition, and the stakeholders of the project are in dispersed locations.

The results of the case study were promising, as they showed that for the example at hand, the method of requirements elicitation by prototyping can be crucial to the success of the software development project.

Acknowledgments. This work is funded by National Funds through FCT - Foundation for Science and Technology, in the context of the project PEst-OE/EEI/UI0127/2014. We would also like to acknowledge the valuable contribution of the clinical professionals of Portuguese Association of Congenital Coagulopathies (PACC) for all the help in the requirements analysis.

References

1. Laporti, V., Borges, M.R.S., Braganholo, V.: Athena: A collaborative approach to requirements elicitation. Computers in Industry 60(6), 367–380 (2009)
2. Teixeira, L., Ferreira, C., Santos, B.S.: User-centered requirements engineering in health information systems: A study in the hemophilia field. Computer Methods and Programs in Biomedicine 106(3), 160–174 (2012)

3. Teixeira, L., Ferreira, C., Santos, B.S.: Using Task Analysis to Improve the Requirements Elicitation in Health Information System. In: 29th Annual International Conference of the IEEE Engineering in Medicine and Biology Society, EMBS (2007)
4. IEEE Recommended Practice for Software Requirements Specifications. IEEE Std 830-1998, pp. 1–40 (1998)
5. Abran, A., et al.: SWEBOK - Guide to the Software Engineering Body of Knowledge. IEEE Computer Society, California (2004)
6. Pohl, K.: Requirements Engineering: Fundamentals, Principles, and Techniques. Springer, Heidelberg (2010)
7. Meth, H., Brhel, M., Maedche, A.: The state of the art in automated requirements elicitation. Information and Software Technology 55(10), 1695–1709 (2010)
8. Sommerville, I.: Software Engineering, 8th edn. Addison-Wesley, Harlow (2007)
9. Zhang, X., et al.: Applying evolutionary prototyping model for eliciting system requirement of meat traceability at agribusiness level. Food Control 21(11), 1556–1562 (2010)
10. Fu, J., Bastani, F.B., Yen, I.-L.: Model-Driven Prototyping Based Requirements Elicitation. In: Martell, C. (ed.) Monterey Workshop 2007. LNCS, vol. 5320, pp. 43–61. Springer, Heidelberg (2008)
11. Davis, A.M.: Operational prototyping: a new development approach. IEEE Software 9(5), 70–78 (1992)
12. Rudd, J., Stern, K., Isensee, S.: Low vs. high-fidelity prototyping debate. Interactions 3(1), 76–85 (1996)
13. Arnowitz, J., Arent, M., Berger, N.: Effective Prototyping for Software Makers, p. 624. Morgan Kaufmann Publishers Inc. (2006)
14. Teixeira, L., Ferreira, C., Santos, B.S., Savedra, V.: Web-enabled registry of inherited bleeding disorders in Portugal: conditions and perception of the patients. Haemophilia 18(1), 56–62 (2012)
15. Teixeira, L., Ferreira, C., Santos, B.S., Martins, N.: Modeling a Web-based Information System for managing clinical information in hemophilia care. In: Conference Proceedings: Annual International Conference of the IEEE Engineering in Medicine and Biology Society, vol. 1, pp. 2610–2613. IEEE Engineering in Medicine and Biology Society (2006)

Suggestion of Operation Method of the Interest Shift Model of the Twitter User

Yusuke Ueda and Yumi Asahi

Shizuoka University

Abstract. Being interested in Twitter is modeled. The model is called a concern shift model. The concern shift model is constructed based on the linear differential equation model and the Kermack-Mckendrick model. This model has the feature in which it is interested. It analyzes it for the case to be interested by using the concern shift model on Twitter and CGM (Consumer Genelated Media). The tendency to analyze by the analysis is quantitatively shown. In doing the comparison between a proposal of the marketing technique and existing analysis service from the feature and the analysis result of the model, The model's view in the future is shown.

1 Introduction

Twitter is SNS site to contribute the short sentence within 140 characters. The user reach 13,920,000 people, it is the second scale next to Facebook in Japan. It is said that 14% of the amount of tweet that is frequently used in Japan and exchanged all over the world is Japanese [8]. The business use was also active, and in the realities of the use of social media of the enterprise in 2011, Twitter was 58% and 1st place [5]. It keeps taking the user communications as a use case with Twitter and the construction coming of an excellent relation. The satisfaction is given to the user and the case where the brand image royalty is improved rises [8]. The enterprise wants to contribute tweet and to learn the size and the directionality of user's interest from these cases. The real experience and the true opinion become important sources because a commodity, a frank opinion of service, and the evaluation are written as a user, and it reflects it. In a word, the element that bears sales and people's interests becomes it , saying that "Very good word of mouth is generated, and it is diffused". First of all, it is necessary to contribute tweet to give birth by word of mouth good, and to diffuse it. It is necessary to know timing to which the size and tweet of people interested in the matter that it wants you to tweet it are contributed.

The index that measures the size of the interest is assumed to be a number of tweet including the word that shows the object case. It is possible that tweet is not contributed and the user who has a potential interest that has the interest exists. Therefore, it is called the user who has the interest including them. The strength is not considered and only the interest existence pays attention to the size of the interest. When announcing of the new item and service and putting it

S. Yamamoto (Ed.): HIMI 2014, Part I, LNCS 8521, pp. 664–677, 2014.

on the market, a definite moment in a big event etc. are the most comprehensible at time that tweet is contributed. These events can be paraphrased as the boom. In the present study, it pays attention to the transition of the tweet number including the word of the object case at the boom, and making the size of the interest and the timing of the contribution visible is tried.

The differential equation model has been widely treated from the previous work to the transition of the state and the spread of information. The model whom Nakagiri and others [7] are proposing analyzes two or more cases, is done the comparison with real data, and shows the consumer's state transition in the boom quantitatively. Ueda and others [1] and Shirai and others [3] are analyzing the spread of the boom and information by using Kermack-Mckendrick model. Therefore, the present study tries whether to function in the information medium formed by the exchange of one user a person such as Twitter by using these models as an existing model. The model to make them adjust to Twitter user's interest is constructed.

The purpose of the present study constructs Twitter user's interest shift model, The case with the boom is analyzed, the transition of user's interest is read, and the factor to rouse the contribution of tweet is derived, and it proposes the marketing technique that uses Twitter.

2   Existing Model

2.1   Model of Liner Differential Equation

Standard Model. The standard type of model of linear differential equation that Nakagiri and others produced is called standard model.

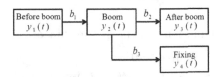

Fig. 1. Standard model

Fig. 1 shows the shift of the state of interest. Those states are shown below.
Before boom : The state that don't purchase products because of the boom
Boom : The state that purchase products because of the boom
After boom : The state that don't purchase because of tired of products
Fixing : The state that continue purchasing the product regardless of a boom
The authors postulates the total of the population of consumers always keeps constant value N.

$$y_1(t) + y_2(t) + y_3(t) + y_4(t) = N \tag{2.1}$$

Indicate the differential equation means shift of consumer.

$$\acute{y}_1(t) = -b_1 y_1(t) \tag{2.2}$$
$$\acute{y}_2(t) = b_1 y_1(t) - (b_2 + b_3) y_2(t) \tag{2.3}$$
$$\acute{y}_3(t) = b_2 y_2(t) \tag{2.4}$$
$$\acute{y}_4(t) = b_3 y_2(t) \tag{2.5}$$

(2.2)~(2.5) mean changing number of consumer in unit time. $b_1 \sim b_3$ mean rate of consumer that shift next state.
About initial condition,

$$y_1(0) = (1 - k)N \tag{2.6}$$
$$y_2(0) = 0 \tag{2.7}$$
$$y_3(0) = 0 \tag{2.8}$$
$$y_4(0) = kN \ (t \le T) \tag{2.9}$$

It is said that I always take constant values until a boom begins. T is the time when a beginning boom, $k(\ge 0)$ points at the rate of consumers who have already become the Fixing. When present initial conditions (2.6) to (2.9), The number of consumers who are in each state obtaind by differential equation (2.2) to (2.5).

Sudden Model. Sudden model is the model what expended Standard model. It is suitable for an example to attract the interest of people rapidly. Show this in Fig. 2.

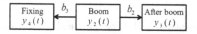

Fig. 2. Sudden model

Indicate differential equation to express the shift of consumer.

$$\acute{y}_1(t) = 0 \tag{2.10}$$
$$\acute{y}_2(t) = -(b_2 + b_3) y_2(t) \tag{2.11}$$
$$\acute{y}_3(t) = b_2 y_3(t) \tag{2.12}$$
$$\acute{y}_4(t) = b_3 y_2(t) \tag{2.13}$$

It takes the value that b_1 has a very big ($b_1 \to \infty$) to become the (2.10), therefore the consumers before the boom shift to the boom instantly In addition, the number of consumers who are in each state in T becomes (2.14) to (2.17) at the boom start time.

$$y_1(T) = 0 \tag{2.14}$$
$$y_2(T) = (1 - k)N \tag{2.15}$$
$$y_3(T) = 0 \tag{2.16}$$
$$y_4(T) = kN \tag{2.17}$$

When present initial conditions (2.10)~(2.13), The number of consumers who are in each state obtaind by differential equation (2.14) ~ (2.17).

2.2   Kermack-Mckendrick Model

Sir Model. Kermack-Mckendrick model expresses the shift of a population infected with an epidemic. In previous reserch, simulation of the social boom and the spread of the information. Thus, the authors can expect an estimate, the prediction of the shift of the interest of the user. This section shows SIR model [1] from Kermack-Mckendrick model.

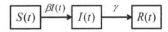

Fig. 3. SIR model

From Fig. 3, replace symptoms of individual with the state of user's inrterest in Twitter

S(t) : The number of users without the interest in object

I(t) : The number of users that the interest become obvious in object

R(t) : The number of users whom the interest in object was settled down

That user's interest become obvious mean the contribution of a tweet. After all, $S(t)$ points the user who contributes a tweet. In this reserch, the content of a tweet doesn't matter. The total of a user belonging to each state is N.

$$S(t) + I(t) + R(t) = N \tag{2.18}$$

The state shift of a user is (2.19) to (2.21).

$$\frac{dS(t)}{dt} = -\beta S(t)I(t) \tag{2.19}$$

$$\frac{dI(t)}{dt} = \beta S(t)I(t) - \gamma I(t) \tag{2.20}$$

$$\frac{dR(t)}{dt} = \gamma I(t) \tag{2.21}$$

$S(t)I(t)$ in (2.19) to (2.20) points at the number of times that a user who is interested comes into contact with an uninterested user. Express it in other words with "The user who did not yet show interest in an object is followed" and "Read tweet about object". The parameter β, γ is as follows.

β : The transmission of a interest

γ : The rate that interest drops

Seir Model. SEIR model is the model who added state E of the user who had a potential interest in SIR model. Potential interest is added to the process that

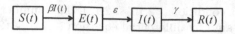

Fig. 4. SEIR model

a user is interested, Thus, this model can expect expression by a realistic shift of a interest.

Added state E points that there is the interest, but does not contribute the tweet.

$E(t)$: The number of users having the interest in object potentially

By this model, estimate the potential interest of an invisible user. The total of each state becomes (2.22) from Fig. 4 and (2.18).

$$S(t) + E(t) + I(t) + R(t) = N \tag{2.22}$$

The state shift of a user is (2.23) to (2.26).

$$\frac{dS(t)}{dt} = -\beta S(t)I(t) \tag{2.23}$$

$$\frac{dE(t)}{dt} = \beta S(t)I(t) - \epsilon E(t) \tag{2.24}$$

$$\frac{dI(t)}{dt} = \epsilon E(t) - \gamma I(t) \tag{2.25}$$

$$\frac{dR(t)}{dt} = \gamma I(t) \tag{2.26}$$

Parameter ϵ is the rate that the potential interest of the user become obvious. It shows that a contribution of tweet affects other users.

3   Interest Shift Model

3.1   Summary

The authors build the model who expressed the shift of the interest of the Twitter user based on an existing model.

The SEIR model considers potential interest. However, this model is made so that potential interest always shift a interest becoming obvious. The existing model is not suitable for a change of the interest of real people including Twitter user. The user whom read among users of Twitter and CGM exist 33% in Twitter as of September, 2011 [4]. As explained above, the authors suggest the interest shift model that expressed a change of the interest of the Twitter use.

Show below each state of the Figkanshin.

Indifference : The state without the interest in object

Interest(1) : The state that the interest become obvious in object

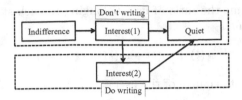

Fig. 5. Interesr shift model

Interest(2) : The state having the interest in object potentially
Quiet : The state whom the interest in object was settled down
It allowed a user of Interest(1) to diverge in Interest(2) and Quiet in the interest
shift model. The interest shift model has two superiority and novelty.

1. Reflection of the action of the social media user whom worked as including Twitter
2. Visualize potential interest by considering a user receiving information generated in Twitter

In consideration of a user only for reading, the authors realize the change that is almost real social media and raise the precision of the analysis. In expressing the change of the user with the potential interest again, the authors catch the domain that was invisible with the tendency of the example until now. Make use for marketing and a trendy prediction.

The interest shift model builds two of "the linear model that assumed a linear differential equation model the basis" and "the non-linear model that assumed a Kermack-Mckendrick the basis".

3.2   Linear Interest Shift Model

The authors make three assumption on building the linear interest shift model.

1. The number of contributed tweet is the size of an appearing user's interest.
2. The contribution of tweet is suddener than the consumption activity in the existing model.
3. The change of the number of tweet before the boom does not consider it.

The linear interest shift model built by the above becomes Fig. 6.

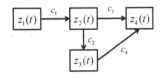

Fig. 6. Linear interest shift model

The authors assume the ratio of user belonging to each state $z_1(t) \sim z_4(t)$ in parameter of the time t

$$z_1(t) + z_2(t) + z_3(t) + z_4(t) = 1 \tag{3.1}$$

Expression of the state change of the user

$$\dot{z}_1(t) = -c_1 z_1(t) \tag{3.2}$$
$$\dot{z}_2(t) = c_1 z_1(t) - (c_2 + c_3) z_2(t) \tag{3.3}$$
$$\dot{z}_3(t) = c_2 z_2(t) - c_4 z_3(t) \tag{3.4}$$
$$\dot{z}_4(t) = c_3 z_2(t) + c_4 z_3(t) \tag{3.5}$$

Parameter to be given $c_1 \sim c_4$
c_1 : Percentage of the users who begin to get interested
c_2 : Percentage of the users who occur surfaced interest
c_3 : Percentage of the users who settle down before surfaced interest
c_4 : Percentage of the users who cool down gradually after surfaced interest
The value that is in each state at the time of the boom

$$z_1(T) = (1 - l - m) \tag{3.6}$$
$$z_2(T) = l \tag{3.7}$$
$$z_3(T) = m \tag{3.8}$$
$$z_4(T) = 0 \tag{3.9}$$

l is ratio of user of "Interest(1)", and m is ratio of user of "Interest(2)".
Give differential equation (3.2) $\sim$(3.5) condition (3.6)$\sim$ (3.9), and the solution of the differential equation is found.

3.3   Non-linear Interest Shift Model

The authors show the model what let SEIR model adapt to the interest shift model.

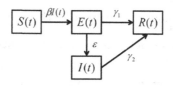

Fig. 7. Non-Linear interest shift model

By Fig. 7, the grand total that is in each state equals expression (2.22). The state change of the user becomes (3.10) to (3.13).

$$\frac{dS(t)}{dt} = -\beta S(t)I(t) \tag{3.10}$$

$$\frac{dE(t)}{dt} = \beta S(t)I(t) - (\epsilon + \gamma_1)E(t) \tag{3.11}$$

$$\frac{dI(t)}{dt} = \epsilon E(t) - \gamma_2 I(t) \tag{3.12}$$

$$\frac{dR(t)}{dt} = \gamma_1 E(t) + \gamma_2 I(t) \tag{3.13}$$

γ_1 and γ_2 point at recovery rate. the rate that γ_1 calms without interest being appeared, γ_2 is the same as γ in Fig. 4. Each parameter sets it as follows. The authors apply β for average of the number of the followers. γ, γ_1 and γ_2 are found from the reciprocal number of the mean infection period. It is the average of the period when interest lasts during the mean infection period, the authors estimates it from a change of the number of tweet. ϵ is found from the reciprocal number of the period awaiting mean infection. It is the average during the period to take before potential interest is appeared during the period awaiting infection. This period is elected optionally by a change of the number of tweet, adopt the most suitable value.

Next is given as an advantage of the non-linear interest shift model. It does not need to set the outbreak time of the boom. The authors can analyze it without dividing an object into two after the boom before a boom. Correspondence is possible for the phenomenon that is complicated because it is a non-linear model.

4   Analysis by Linear Interest Shift Model

4.1   Analysis Method

Whether Nakagiri and others linear differential equation model and linear interest shift model correspond to the boom on Twitter is analyzed. The domination of the linear interest shift model is shown from the comparison of the analysis results. Moreover, the case is analyzed and the tendency to the case is requested.

The data of the analysis used and acquired real-time, high index site TOPSY[6] around Twitter. This is called and real data is called. The object of the analysis greatly interests the user, and elects the case where the aspect of the boom is shown. It is provided the place word after the ranking of the Google retrieval rise retrieval word the first half of 2012 (The word ranking in 2012) and the nuclear power plant. The word ranking is July, 2011 to September, 2012 in 2012 in nuclear power plant September, 2010 to May, 2012 for the acquisition period of data. High-ranking word of word ranking is "sutema, siri, annular eclipse, annular eclipse of the sun, hikarie, sky tree, and comp-gatya" in 2012. The one that the user had been greatly interested in the tweet number of word rankings [2] calls the boom from showing expanding rapidly and getting depressed within a short term and is all right.

Comparison of the Model. The domination of the model is judged from the comparison of fitting in the application about real data and estimation. The analysis object is assumed to be "Nuclear power plant". It is clarified that the linear interest shift model is a model the goodness of the application fitting in by both models is compared that is appropriate for Twitter. The index of the application fitting in used for the comparison is assumed to be coefficients of determination R^2 to which an eye measurement and real data of the graph are derived by the regression analysis of which the explanatory variable the objective variable, and is estimation.

Analysis of the Example. The analysis of the case clarifies interesting in each case by using the linear interest shift model. The tweet number is presumed according to the interest shift model. The validity of the state transition of user's interest is judged by the value of R_2 and measuring the graph with eye. The tendency is considered from the content of the background and tweet that surrounds the value and the case with the set parameter about the transition of the interest and the classification and the factor are derived.

4.2   Analysis Result

Real data and standard, broken break out $Tw \times y3$ indicate estimation to *data* recorded in the graph. The backgrounds of the nuclear power plant that is the investigation object are a chain of accidents of the first nuclear power plant in Fukushima generated along with a East Japan great earthquake. The analysis results of the tweet number by an existing model become Fig. 8.

Fig. 8. Estimated result by existing model (Nuclear power plant)

Estimation cannot catch up with the transition of real data, and can be said that it is incompatible in a standard model. The explanation attaches from 0.007 the value of R^2 to it. The result by a model broken because of one side shows an intimate transition to real data from taking of the eye measurement of the graph and the value of R^2 0.605 compared with a standard model and it is understood that accuracy has improved. However, even the phenomenon of the decreasing tweet number's rising again was not able to be reproduced.

The estimated results of the tweet number by the interest shift model are shown in Fig. 9.

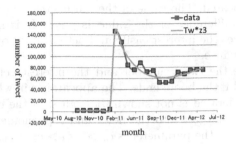

Fig. 9. Result by interest shift model (Nuclear power plant) $R^2 = 0.895$

Showing in Fig. 8 was able to show an impossible part. It can explain the accuracy according to the eye measurement of the graph and the size of the value of R^2 Among three models used for the comparison from Fig. 8 and Fig. 9, the accuracy of the presumption of the interest shift model is the most excellent. Therefore, it can be said that the interest shift model is a model that is appropriate for Twitter.

It was possible to classify it from the transition of the state of the interest of the user who had obtained it from the analysis of the tweet number as shown in table 1.

Table 1. Location of case

Case	Target Example (Coefficients of determination)
CONTINNUATION	genpatsu(0.896), sutema(0.877), hikarie(0.919)
THE SECOND BOOM	siri(0.718), sky-tree(0.884)
ONE-SHOT	kinkan-nissyoku(0.908), kinkan-syoku(0.780), comp-gacha(0.920)

The value of R^2 of each case can be said that it is overall excellent, and there validity in the state transition of the interest with 0.7 to 0.9. The tendency is considered from the analysis result of the case where it belongs to the classified each case.

Continuance is a case to keep keeping the interest of a constant amount after the boom is generated. A constant amount indicates the interest of a high level is kept compared with before the boom is generated. The value of the parameter is $c_4 > c_1 > c_2 \geq c_3$. Big bias are not, and can be said the case with an active change of the interest to the size of the value. The user to whom the interest is actualized has the tendency to make quietly at the early stage while the period when do the latency of the interest is long.

The second boom is a case to show an exponential increase again when it has settled down the transition of the tweet number. The transition of the interest shows the aspect that looks like continuance against the tweet number in which a sudden change is repeated. The value of the parameter is $c_4 >> c_1 > c_2 >> c_3$. ">>" indicates the difference of the value is great. It is gotten tired of the interest that actualizes the interest easily and actualizes at once compared with in the case of continuance.

It is a case where the tweet number and the interest get depressed similar before it is generated if the boom ends. The appearance in which it is interested after the boom is generated is not shown. It is guessed the case forgotten as it is as a word that doesn't get into the news and a phenomenon that has been concluded. The value of the parameter is $c_4 >> c_3 > c_2 > c_1$. The rate that the interest to which the ratio with the interest begin is actualized small unlike in the case of current is made quiet is very large. Therefore, the loss boom ends the interest one after another as for the user who had the interest when the boom is generated. It gets depressed so that user's interest may respond to the tweet number, too and it makes it quietly.

5   Analysis by Non-linear Interest Shift Model

5.1   Analysis Method

The analysis process is done in order of the analysis by the extraction and the model who acquires of data and analyzes it.

The method of acquiring data makes the script using Twitter Streaming API by Python and acquires data. Neither the key word nor the user are squeezed from the public time line and data is acquired at random. It acquires it concurrently including the content of tweet at the account name and the contribution time. The time zone on July 4th to July 21st is made 8:00-24:00 for the period in 2013 that is the House of Councilors election campaign period of 2013.

GNU R and morphological analysis engine MeCab are used at the extraction to be analyzed. The transition of each word is derived by dividing the content of tweet acquired by using the morphological analysis into a significant, minimum word, and showing the occurrence rate of each word from the frequency analysis. As a result, the object case is extracted. It squeezes it to the noun that indicates the name of the event when the object case is extracted.

Odesolve Package is introduced into GNU R, the nonlinear interest shift model is mounted, and the object case requested from the frequency analysis is presumed. The number of users that has the interest actualized by using the account name acquired with tweet of the object case is requested. The tendency to the case is led from the transition of user's interest as well as the analysis of the case and the precision of analysis of the model is confirmed.

5.2   Analysis Result

As for the acquired data, the contributor's of tweet 200161.3 matter, each day average became the average a day tweet number with 188818 person and user's people of number 54.4 of average followers. The acquired data extracts the event that the aspect of the boom is shown from data because it cannot use it for the analysis as it is by the diversity of the contribution number and the content.

The frequent occurrence word by the morphological analysis and the frequency analysis became the result of the word's without the meaning in the unit like the sign and the particle, etc. that composed the numerical value, URL, and the emoticon occupying the high rank. The word that was able to be caught here as an event was only "Election. "

It presumes according to the SIR model and the SEIR model who is an existing model intended for the election.

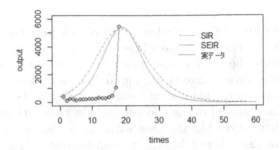

Fig. 10. Transition of the user interested in election by SIR model and SEIR model

Fig. 10 As for the transition of real data, an abrupt increase is shown as well as the object case that has been analyzed up to now, and not very different is understood even if taking the place from the number of months the unit of time of days the shown transition. A lot of users are having the interest actualized on the boundary of the 21st that it is an election year final day and is the ballot counting day. The estimation before the boom and the unbridgeable gulf of real data became large results. It will not be possible to correspond to a sudden change of the value. Estimation by the SEIR model is approached the transition of the event of the reality to consider the user who has a potential interest from approaching to real data and leads to the precision enhancement compared with the estimation of the SIR model.

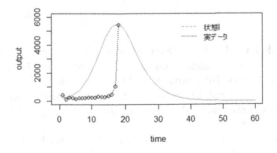

Fig. 11. Transition of the user who did tweet of election by nonlinear interest shift model

It presumes continuously according to the nonlinear interest shift model.

The estimated result became a result just like the SIR model and the SEIR model of figure from Fig. 11.

6   Conclusion

Two operation techniques of the interest shift model rise. First, proposal of marketing technique that uses factor to rouse contribution of tweet. Second, comparison with existing Twitter analysis service that bases novelty and domination of model.

Marketing Technique. Three tendencies to obtain from the analysis of the case are classified into two. The case where user's interest continues is Continuance and The second boom. The case where user's interest doesn't continue is One-shot. The factor divided into two is big and small of two parameter c_1 and c_3. The factor to decide the bigness and smallness of c_1 and c_3 can be guessed according to the background of the content and the case with tweet as follows. It derived to various topics like the case with the nuclear power plant around the case, and in the case where it belongs to continuance and the 2nd boom that became $c_1 > c_3$ the tweet number and it was interested. The topic did not derive after generating the boom and the case with single-engined that became $c_1 < c_3$ was made quiet. It becomes a factor that this rouses the contribution of tweet. It proposes the marketing technique by using the factor.

Comparison with Existing Twitter Analysis Service. The part that should be paid attention is up to to limit the object of the analysis from existing analysis service only to the user who contributed tweet. 1/3 or more of the Twitter user is a user only of inspection like being in the meaning that the interest shift model constructs, and the size cannot be disregarded. The improvement of accuracy by which user's reaction and needs are read becomes possible by taking their interests into consideration by the quantification of a potential interest that is the novelty of the interest shift model.

References

1. Hiroshi, U., Youhei, O., Itsuki, K., Syu, S., Taku, Y., Katsuhide, W.: Mathematical principle of propagation phenomenon in society. In: MODELing Seminar: Spread Team of Remark Theory, Information, and Culture (2006)
2. GoogleJapanBlog. Retrieval key word ranking that became topic in the first half of 2012, http://googlejapan.blogspot.jp/2012/06/google-2012.html, final indorsement: 2013/9/18
3. Takashi, S., Takeshi, S., Fujio, T., Kosuke, S., Kazuhiro, K., Itsuki, N., Masasuki, N., Satoshi, K.: Estimation of False Rumor Diffusion Model and Estimation of Prevention Model of False Rumor Diffusion on Twitter. In: The 26th Annual Conference of the Japanese Society for Artificial Intelligence (2012)

4. Ministry of Internal Affairs and Communications. White paper on telecommunications in Heisei 23, `http://www.soumu.go.jp/johotsusintokei/whitepaper/ja/h23/html/nc232330.html`, final indorsement: 2013/9/18
5. Chen, Y.: One consideration about an effect of Collective Intelligence and the company use of social media, pp. 241–266. Osaka Sangyo University
6. TOPSY, `http://topsy.com/`, final indorsement: 2012/9/30
7. Yuko, N., Osamu, K.: On a Differential Equation Moel of Booms. Transactions of the Operations Research, 83–105 (2004)
8. Yoshio, H.: A Study on the business and take advantage of social media, pp. 155–179. Osaka Sangyo University. (2012)

The Historical Evolution Research of Information Interaction Design

Yangshuo Zheng

Academy of Art & Design, Tsinghua University, Beijing, China
zhengyangshuo@163.com

Abstract. This paper focuses on three parts: first, based on interdisciplinary, summary and expand the information interaction design concept and connotation system, clearer information interaction design system and constitute essential characteristics; Second, original build the information interaction design system thinking model in four dimensions "environment -- human --technology--objects", launched research on social environment context, psychological needs of information users, Information technology research, information interaction design products; Third, combined and summarized information interaction design thinking model in existence and characteristics way of various forms of society, from the perspective of society evolution form the essence analysis of information interaction design, explored the transformation process of correspondence between information interaction design and the development of society patterns.

Keywords: information Interaction Design, Historical evolution, Information society.

1   Background

With the continuous progress of science and technology, information and explosive expansion of knowledge has become the core of today's social life. In the mid-20th century, the outbreak of a third world scientific and technological revolution, that the information technology revolution. Its Essence and core is the development of the information science and technology, including information related to human understanding of information understanding, information creation and dissemination of information, covering a very wide range. IT revolution involving either from the scope and scale of scientific thought or innovation disciplines are much higher than the previous agricultural revolution and the industrial revolution. Can be easily found that, we are experiencing the information technology revolution in human history to bring the greatest period of change. This information technological revolution is not only to showcase the vision of a new world, and to construct a new scientific way of thinking, that is-information thinking.

With the number of worldwide microcomputer persistent rapid increase in the increasing popularity of the Internet and wireless communications to Information

S. Yamamoto (Ed.): HIMI 2014, Part I, LNCS 8521, pp. 678–689, 2014.

Technology, information technology revolution makes people's life has changed dramatically, and it brought to mankind is not only science great progress on the technical level, but also to enhance the whole level of information society, has been fully reflected in the mode of production, lifestyle, fashion and other sensible perspective. The rapid development of information technology has become a huge impetus to the economic development of the society, information technology revolution and human life has been closely together. Basis of the information technology revolution is the great development of computer and network technology, and huge information can now be digitalized. digitalized information promote the rapid development of the information technology revolution, and triggered a series of changes. Massachusetts Institute of Technology professor and director of the Media Lab, Negroponte was in his monograph " Being Digital, " which said that the development of information technology will change the way humans learn, work, entertainment, namely, information technology change the human way of life. "Digitized so that the information can instantly reach the other side of the world, so that people experience a sense of closeness to the world of space, so as to promote the progress of human civilization. " Negroponte in 1995 for the development of information science and technology have made academic thesis has become a reality today. Human learning, work, entertainment or even the whole way of life have undergone tremendous changes in the way we perceive the world also undergone tremendous changes, which almost are closely related to the information technology revolution.

Today, a wide range of information is not only ubiquitous in life, and has become an important part of the social operation. IT revolution has made the depth and breadth of information dissemination has been greatly improved, each user access to information and means of transmission of information has become increasingly rich, convenient and quick. Digitalized information allows us to use a simple binary code "0" and "1 " to achieve the sound, text, pictures, video and other types of data coding and decoding ; all kinds of information processing, storage and transmission are achieve standardization and high speed processing mode of the network, which greatly enhances the ability of human information processing and transmission of information. IT innovation has spawned countless new digital information products, the Internet has developed into a variety of applications that can accommodate advanced information platform. With the further development of the information technology revolution, the future of the lifestyle, information transmission mode, the user emotional demand will continue a series of new development and change.

2   Significance: A Systematic Theoretical Research Thoughts

Information interaction design is cross-disciplinary integration research direction of design disciplines and humanities, information engineering disciplines, and etc. Information interaction design based on In information science, organizational behavior, interdisciplinary research biomechanics, kinematics, physiology, automatic control theory makes the user experience as the core, with the digitization of information collection analysis and statistical techniques as a reference, finally to expand the experimental studies on the information product interacts with the environment, explore human-machine sensors, interactive, human-computer interaction and other information interactive mode works. The development of information interaction design has an important-looking and leading role for the survival and development of design discipline. With the continuous development, the design theoretical study also presents new features, it is no longer confined to the words of pure theory, but increasingly focuses on practical applications for design guidance and reflection. Information Interaction Design is one of the most typical representative, it embodies the direction of today's latest development and application of design.

This article will try to build the research framework for information interaction design, using the theory and methods of multidisciplinary scientific and comprehensive study is a great research potential and challenging. From the social history and cultural heritage point of view, reconstruct the cognitive knowledge of information interaction design, exploring various forms of information interaction design on specific applications through the whole development of society; construct "environment - human - technology - objects "systems thinking, comprehensive and systematic analysis of the various constituent elements and parse" environment - human - technology - objects "relationship between the various elements of the system, and ultimately restore the essence of design behavior:" Not only is a creative activity, but also for humanity creating a more rational, more healthy lifestyle production and to build a sustainable and harmonious society. "

3   About Information Interaction Design

3.1   Basis of Information Interaction Design

The establishment and development of information interaction design is based on the "information technology". UNESCO makes definition of Information Technology: " Used in information processing and processing of science, technology and engineering training methods and management skills; The above methods and techniques of application; Computer and its interaction with people, machine; Corresponding social, economic, culture and almost various kinds of things. "Researchers Don Schultz and Philip Kitchen define IT (information technology) as " can make human knowledge, data and experience on a global scale organizations or between individuals a simple, fast transfer of equipment, technology and performance integrated. It is a way to include a variety of new electronic data storage, transmission, distribution and analysis constituted, not only contains various forms of common tools, further including the most sophisticated forms of mathematical analysis and calculation methods." Although there is no very clear uniform definition of IT, but their essence is a way to extend and expand the means and methods of human information functions.IT revolution is rapidly changing information media and its environment, IT becomes technical support almost all media composition, technical standards and development orientation, become the most popular medium of information interaction on new meaning.

On the perspective of design disciplines, in the computer, Internet and other information tools has been more deeply universal applied today, research width and depth of information interaction design research has been greatly expanded. Information interaction design primarily study the way of human society and the transmission of information and get responding information, ultimately to establish contacts with the outside world. Since it adequately reflects the tendency of service design for users, therefore, information interaction design should be part of an important branch of "Information Science and social studies" field.

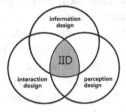

Fig. 1. Concept of information interaction design

3.2   Concept of Information Interaction Design

Research subject of this paper, "Information interaction design" is actually a systematic cognitive design fields, composed of the three design direction: information design, interaction design, perception design. As early as 1999, Shedroff published papers pointed out that should the information design and interaction design considerations together, treat it as a unified field of design theory. Seedorf argued that the information interaction design is integrated consisting of "information design", "interaction design" and "perception design", Shedroff call it "Information Interaction Design". Information Interaction Design should be designed to standardize and facilitate information-oriented mode of human interactions with the theoretical prototype, the focus should be to build more rational human information interaction and corresponding conduct under the information society background. As can be seen, Information Interaction Design reflects the design trends in information society with its own attributes in accurate way, which can be the most cutting-edge contemporary design direction is inevitable.

Information Interaction design is about the artifact objects research, the main contents include a new generation of natural harmony of man-machine dialogue mode, the language of communication design, product design principles, information services, software application mode, no interface design technology, HCI design Principles and etc. As a design discipline has a strong social application, Information Interaction design can real-time reflect the information technology development and application trends, thus facilitate communication between user and the outside world in an innovative way. Information interaction design itself is in a continuous integration and rapid development process in order to adapt the changing environment. Information interaction design emphasis on expanding and extending from the " non-material " perspective, through information communication, information interaction, information applications and information services. It should be emphasized that information interaction design is not a new design concept in an absolute sense, but as a integrated result of the development of history, advances in technology, human improvement of consciousness thinking.

In the "Information Interaction Design" concept system framework, "information design" is not a substitute for graphic design or visual communication design tool, but to provide a framework for interactive information, organization and forms the main concern of the data. " Interaction design " is a symbol of "creating and telling stories ", focusing on how to use reasonable skill and application, creating a pleasant user experience, which through across the field of art and information technology. "perception design " is a harbinger of future trends and directions of IT development. Perception design studies information possibilities, determine how can the information interaction and information application create reasonable way, as how deep and wide of the information dissemination. Therefore, "Information Interaction Design" have a systematic, research -based holistic basis: Information Design focuses on the level of information to convey, Interaction design focuses on interactive technology to achieve the design goal, perception design focuses on the user's emotional and demand levels ; these three directions composed a systematic theoretical design system.

3.3   System Model of Information Interaction Design

On the basis of the Information Interaction Design concept, I created a "environment-human - technology - objects" system model of Information Interaction design. "environment", "human" constitute the external environment of information interaction design activity; "technology", "objects" constitute the internal environment, including the development and application of information technology, the concept of settings and details of products. On the one hand you can understand the "environment", "human", to grasp the macro direction of information interaction design; On the other hand, through the organization and expression of the "technology", "objects", to grasp the micro realization of information interaction design approach. External and internal environment can be seen as a parallel relationship, integration and balance between them is the key of information interaction design.

In short, the existence and development of information interaction design, is the relationship between its environment, human, technology, and objects; either from the perspective of user-oriented design, but also from the information activity with its environmental point of view are true.

Relationship between information interaction design and **environment**, mainly refers to the relationship with the social environment. Phenomenological theory thought that the environment is not an abstract place, but by the specific things that the composition as a whole. Information interaction activities require different environments as a basis, in order to facilitate information interaction activities generate. We can say that environmental factors determine human behavior, determines the attributes of the information interaction design. Information interaction design activities and environmental linkages, provided its hold in the environment of the significance of a particular role. Through this research perspective, information interaction design activity embodies the value of user functionality in the social environment, which provide the information for the application, but also reflects the cultural values in the process of social development. In the system model, environmental products (dominant presence), user (intellectual existence) and culture (invisible presence) nicely connects together.

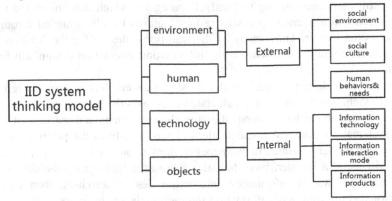

Fig. 2. IID design system thinking model

Relationship between Information interaction design and **human**, mainly refers to users of user-oriented design. In a sense, Information interaction design is based on users' creative process, and its purpose is to help users solve problems, improving the user experience, and then realize the target audience emotional resonance. From this perspective, this relationship includes applications of sensory experiences (how to use visual, auditory, tactile, olfactory, gustatory perception meet user needs), the user's mental model and user behavior. Information interaction design From the "Design for others" to "Collaborative others for Design" is the most unusual place with other design, to some extents, users can determine even the direction of design.   future users will be involved in the design, become collaborators, eventually decision-makers. Therefore, from the study of "usability", "ease of user" extends to how to play to users' "initiative", "creative", will be key to the future development of Information interaction design.

Relationship between information interaction design and **technology**, mainly refers to the relationship between design activities and information technology. The traditional design perspective, often makes "technology" and "objects" as a whole, which leads to neglecting the real technology. IT does not seem only simple tools, information technology for the design often have a decisive significance and effect. Kevin Kelly even claimed that "technology is the seventh existence of life. Technology is an extension of life, rather than something separate and life beyond." In fact, every technology innovation will make technical elements improved, bring new opportunities and new changes and diversity final design mode.IT will be a key factor in promoting the progress of information interaction design, makes predicting the future development trend of information interaction design possible.

Relationship between information interaction design and **objects**, mainly refers to the intrinsic relationship between the specific interaction information to convert the design process and results, and its essence is an internal agreement of contact. The development of information technology has given the diversity of forms of objects (material and non-material), but from the perspective of artificial fact is concerned, the matter is still mentioned belong to "artifact" category, which determines the type of objects. Information interaction design reflect features mostly achieved through the "objects" as the carrier. Thus, many of the traditional design for the "objects" rule, characteristics, cognitive attributes in the information interaction design still have in common.

In the previous design research study, most design emphasize form design while ignoring the inherent design factors associated even with the history, culture and other factors discussed in the background, showing the limitations and the lack of a more overall systematic theoretical research ideas. Therefore, from the perspective of the design system model presented in this paper to think about the information interaction design, will make a broader, more holistic, more accurately grasp the development context and the law of information interaction design activities, then carry out exploration and innovation of information interaction design in future.

4   Historical Evolution Research of Information Interaction Design

Human society is constantly moving forward, information interaction design also will continue to move forward. We can say that the development of human society to move forward with information interactive design is synchronized at every stage of historic evolution, social development are accompanied by great changes in information interactive design.

4.1   Primitive and Agricultural Society

Ever since mankind went out of the forest, tribal clan is relying gregarious subsistence hunting and gathering together, this is because in primitive society the harsh natural environment, human needs through collaborative social way to live together to overcome individual weaknesses. Dissemination of information and the development of human society is synchronized. We can say that gregarious subsistence model is the foundation of human information dissemination, burrowing cultural history is the earliest history information dissemination.

From a macro broad view of design history development, the human birth, the technology birth, and then culture birth, therefore it can be said that design birth. In Primitive society, human clearly understood that struggling with nature, the ability of human beings is very limited. In agricultural society, agricultural and animal husbandry means the relationship between humans and the natural world level had been leaped, on behalf of human life from relying on natural adaptation sources, change and transformation for the use of natural productivity, production level has been largely increased. The production relationship in agricultural society is a relatively expanded reproduction mode, the technological level compared to the later industrial society is still low, still reflects a strong natural features.

From the information interaction design perspective, in primitive society, orality to the original human society has far-reaching significance, it essentially is a major social activity of people, thus forming a culture of orality. Before oral communication, human only through body movements and simple facial expressions, vaguely describe their desired information expressed. Oral communication is the major source of social information interactively to improve the human understanding, and improve the ability to adapt and transform nature, to enhance the human emotion, memory and thinking level. In agricultural society, the invention of papermaking and printing made human extending the visual ability, and promoted the development of social productive forces, gradually formed a society of printing culture, represented the arrival of the substance for the information age. A number of people work specializes in the dissemination of information, knowledge, ideas and a wide range of information start quickly and spread widely in the crowd, a symbol of an epoch-making power of the human society development. Papermaking and printing enhances the understanding of the human experience and the ability to grasp the whole world.   Although it is impossible to make information generated input and output in interaction synchronization peer, but has liberated the dissemination of information to the inherent limitations of space -based printing information interactively, it can save both time and information transmitted across space constraints, given the abundance of information may be copied.

In the period of primitive society and agricultural society, the development of information interaction mode from facing the information interactively gradually evolved into the form of written text-based separation behavior, the evolution of information interaction mode allows the sender and receiver of information is no longer necessary limitations at the same time and place to complete information interactions. Although the information interaction mode in primitive and agricultural society is relatively simple, and has a strong regional characteristics; but for the human spirit to enjoy the social life and cultural transmission, provides the necessary conditions for the material basis for the development of world science and culture has played a huge role. Following the text, the subsequent development of information interaction mode also continue the trend to extend the message sender and receiver separated and play spatial characteristics, in the existence of a more diversified approach.

4.2   Industrial Society

For society under the great influence of the industrial revolution, all kinds of people start quickly production of creation, production, human greatly improved understanding of the material world and transform ability. The industrialization of the social development has made remarkable achievement, makes the human can fully enjoy the energy resources and material resources, all kinds of machine effectively expanded the human body, promote the development of social productivity. And the great change of information technology in the industrial society has also promoted the information interaction mode forward.

In industrial society, human interaction in the past information uncertainty, geographic limitations, low efficiency has been improved to a large extent, the value and importance of information dissemination have increasingly been revealed. Telephone, telegraph, radio and television, etc. These great invention are enough to load the history of human civilization, finally shorten the distance between people, speed up the society develop pace, improving the people's information communication efficiency. Telephone represents the ability to extend the range of human hearing, radio and television represents the human auditory and visual ability diversify; variety of new information technologies continue to invent and popularize of carrier applications, interactive way to help the development of information interaction mode. Electronic equipment as an information interactive medium has become the mainstream of society, which has a very distinct and accurate, efficient features, information interactive activity has basically no longer limited by traditional factors of time, space and so on. Quality and efficiency of information dissemination during the industrial society has made great progress in the emotional level and technical level have a great impact on information users, and its breadth and depth compared to agricultural society has been a huge improvement.

Overall, the information interaction mode in industrial society, although expression in the form of information and user information dissemination process perceived need at the technical level has been greatly improved, but for the individual in terms of information interactive, comprehensive grasp of the overall demand for information has not been fully met. For the system concept of information interaction design, in industrial society period, the completion of information design were ahead of interaction design and perception of design. unidirectional dissemination of information were still the vast majority, the process of information dissemination in time and space were spatially separated, there has primary and secondary in the order, and existed a certain degree of time cost. Mainly in the lack of feedback and loop of information dissemination, ignored the psychological complexity of information user, inadequate grasp the relationship between the whole and the constituent elements of information dissemination.

4.3   Information Society

Information society is the social forms of rapid development of information technology and widely used as main indicator. In information society, information have been rapidly accumulating, transmitting, storaging, the value of information has been fully played, creating wealth for human society and to some extent, improve the people's living environment. Information Society represents a new transformation of human civilization.

Information society means new information economy generated, based on a universal application of computer and Internet, reducing the time and space for the entire production process society. Information interactive content of the information society through the spread of bits in the form of raw data, eventually revert to the form of information via communication networks; bits can be produced anywhere and at any time. Compared to traditional interaction mode like newspapers, radio, television and other, Internet highlights the more rapid, convenient and efficient features and is suitable for two-way and multi-directional information interaction. Information Society integrates of a variety of information interaction forms, eventually gave rise to pleasant user experience. "We media" as the representative of the new information interaction product, brings personalized information and high-speed information transmission speed and extremely timely, bring people high-quality information services and information experience.

Information technology have driven the cost of production of information products decreased, product replacement cycles are getting shorter. Since the development of information technology for internal information -driven, relevance of information interactive products will be the main concern of information interaction design goal. In essence, the biggest change from industrial society to information society is reflected in the economic structure of society, from production economy to service economy, which human is the most important. Firstly, the features of user needs began quietly changing, design in the pursuit of product features, while increasing emphasis on diverse forms of cultural diversity. Secondly, the design objects began to shift to information services, information technology is the changing basis; For more information on the service requirements of personalized attention can customize content and interactive user experience, a new design and new content service system may arise.   Furthermore, the design content is designed from a single or a single series to a system design. in information society, the content has been designed from the object itself, turning on the functional design objects, people, society, culture various elements of the system the overall relationship between system design.

In summary, information society create a new context environment for information interaction design, both the authenticity of the existence of the real world, and the virtuality of the online world. Information interaction design is essentially an act of creation, through induction and integration of the relevant elements of whole system, guide the user to build more innovative reasonable information interaction activity.

Table 1. Comparison of IID between different societies

	Primitive and Agricultural society	Industrial society	Information society
Core elements	Natural objects	Objects and energy	Information and knowledge
Technological revolution	Agricultural revolution	Industrial revolution	Information revolution
Symbolic Inventions	Bronzes and iron	steam engine	Computer and Internet
Economy Features	Acquisition of natural resources	Production of material resources	Information services based on knowledge
culture	Regional	Globalization	Diversity
Human needs	Survival needs	Possession of material requirements	Spiritual pleasure needs
Information Interaction Characteristics	Closed	One orientation and open	Interaction and open

4.4   Evolution of Information Interaction Design

In any form of society, there exists communication needs for people anywhere, which determines the general society have the necessity of information interaction activities. Evolution of information interaction design is a process of evolution, the development speed and completeness of information dissemination in a social environment, in a sense marks a level of civilized society.

In primitive and agriculture society, since the text had appeared, in the true sense of mankind from the beginning of information dissemination, papermaking and printing makes the emergence of information communication began to popularity. Limited to the historical period, information dissemination only had slow speed, the content is also relatively simple, can only be passed with relatively simple text and symbol message information.

In industrial society, dissemination mode of information had turning to mechanization and electronic communication type, information contents can be audio, video, images and other forms of integrated information. The invention of telegraph, telephone, radio, television means that the speed of information dissemination is close to the speed of light, which greatly accelerated the pace of development of human society. Information can be spread short distances, spread further expand the scope to further, eventually improved information transmission efficiency.

In information society, The information interaction mode are very diverse, both through traditional mass media (such as face to face, phone calls, letters) to expand information interaction activities, but also relies on new information technologies (such as Email, Facebook, instant messaging, Internet phone) Internet applications. The two sides continue to exchange information dissemination and reception of information through internet-based information media and supplement the information at any time and modify each other's feedback. Compared to the traditional way of information interaction, Internet-based information interactively contain a certain time cost, compared to face impression formed more slowly, but eventually can achieved with the same exchange effect like face to face. The existence of the Internet as information interaction activities, create an unprecedented space, network anonymity, motivate people new information applications, either from the expansion of the quantity or quality of people 's information interactions. From whatever perspective depth, breadth and interactive view of the extent, the information society are far better than in the past any form of society.

5   Conclusion

With the evolution of society history, information interaction design showed more penetration and influence on the development of society. Information interaction design not only meet the needs and desires of human life, but also increasingly coordinate with the objective nature and the human instinct, continuously enhance the quantity and quality of information interaction activities. Computers and Internet as a symbolic product of today's information technology, goes beyond the mere meaning of information tools; with its help, the relationship between humans and information society becomes more closely as human contact and social media. Compared with traditional designs, information interaction design can be seen as the extension of traditional design, but the essence is still the high level human thinking of how to achieve a more rational way of human living.

Maximum theoretical contribution of this paper is that from the perspective of the social development, did a number of in-depth research of information interaction design, combines and summarizes the evolution essence of information interaction design, linked it with the modern concept and traditional scientific knowledge system, clearly presented the development of information interaction design in theoretical way. This article highlighted that information interaction design not only exists in information society, but in the era of the information society becomes more clear to the past.

In short, the research of information interaction design and its "environment - -human - - technology- -objects" design system thinking model, not only a macro thinking based on historical forms of social development characteristics, but also a design theory research innovation of information interaction design. By combing and summarizing the development of information interaction design evolution, the paper also shows the future direction of information interaction design development, information interaction design will become the most representative design branch of future development. I wish this study will bring more enlightenment for contemporary design research and the development of social sciences.

References

1. Liu, G.: Design Methodology, vol. 3. Higher Education Press, Beijing (2011)
2. LU Xiaohua:core of the media operations,
   http://news.xinhuanet.com/newmedia/2005-01/07/content_2427865.htm
3. Shedroff, N.: Information Interaction Design. In: Jacobsen, R. (ed.) A Unified Field Theory of Design in Information Design, pp. 267–292. The MIT Press, Massachusetts (1999)
4. Zhang, L.: Semiotic approach to product design, vol. 126. China Building Industry Press, Beijing (2011)
5. Kelly, K.: What technology wants. Preamble. CITIC Publishing House, Beijing (2011)

Author Index